The Definitive Book of

HUMAN DESIGN
The Science of Differentiation

A Message from Ra Uru Hu
For the Readers of this Book

To Those Who Would Live Life as Themselves:

Human Design offers a mechanical understanding of the nature of being. With understanding comes a genuine revolution, the realignment of a life and the awakening of awareness. Human Design offers a methodology uniquely tailored to your design that liberates you from 'not-self' conditioning. It is called Strategy & Authority and it is the catalyst of transformation.

Most important to recognize is that this is knowledge to be experimented with. There is a 'way' but it can only be your way. Allow this work to guide and inform you and then, if it is correct for you, enter into the most extraordinary journey of your life.

Ra Uru Hu
Ibiza, Spain
March 1, 2011

THE DEFINITIVE BOOK OF

HUMAN DESIGN

THE SCIENCE OF DIFFERENTIATION

LYNDA BUNNELL
DIRECTOR OF THE INTERNATIONAL HUMAN DESIGN SCHOOL
AUTHORIZED BY AND IN COOPERATION WITH
RA URU HU
FOUNDER OF THE HUMAN DESIGN SYSTEM

Library of Congress Control Number: 2011963112
ISBN-978-0-615-55214-9

HDC Publishing
7040 Avenida Encinas, #104-380, Carlsbad, CA 92011
Email: hdcpublishing@gmail.com
www.ihdschool.com

Printed in China
Authorized by and in Cooperation with Ra Uru Hu
Cover and Illustrations by Maurizio Cattaneo, Human Design Concepts
BodyGraph images created from Jovian Archive's © Maia Mechanics Imaging Software
Book Design and Layout: Beth Black and Lynda Bunnell
Editorial Advisor: Ra Uru Hu
Editors: Beth Black and Lynda Bunnell
Contributing Editor and Advisor: Donna Garlinghouse
Previous books written by this Author include
The Living Your Design Student and Teacher Manuals

Fifth edition published April 2020
Fifth printing, April 2020

For information about special discounts for bulk purchases,
or inquiries about Human Design presentations, workshops, or events,
please contact HDC Publishing at hdcpublishing@gmail.com

DEDICATION

This book is dedicated to Ra Uru Hu,
the founder and messenger of
The Human Design System,
to our grandchildren,
and to all future generations.

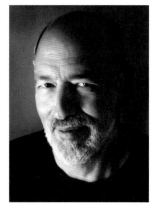

RA URU HU

HUMAN DESIGN FOUNDER, MESSENGER & TEACHER OF THE HUMAN DESIGN SYSTEM

Ra Uru Hu, born Robert Allan Krakower, was the fourth child of a cultured, upper middle class family from Montreal, Canada. He was surrounded by the arts and learned to express himself through music as a composer and performer, an avocation he pursued until his death. He completed a Bachelor of Arts Degree at Sir George Williams University, but his career path led him into the business world as an advertising executive, magazine publisher and media producer.

One morning in 1983, he simply walked away from his family and fast-paced life as an entrepreneur – from life as he knew it – and 'disappeared.' Several months later he found himself on the beautiful and temperate island of Ibiza, in the Mediterranean Sea off the eastern coast of Spain. This 'Eden', as he liked to call it, is where his 'real' life as Ra Uru Hu had its beginnings.

On the evening of January 3, 1987, he encountered the 'Voice.' It was a terrifying experience. The Voice said, "Are you ready to work?" And for eight days and eight nights he worked, transcribing in detail what is now known as The Human Design System. Ra speaks of the encounter as a wake-up call, an education which showed him how blind and ignorant his assumptions were about the nature of being, the cosmos and the way things work.

Ra considered himself the messenger of The Human Design System, now his legacy, and dedicated his life since the encounter to disseminating the Science of Differentiation around the world. He lived and worked in Ibiza where he enjoyed teaching, playing music, gardening and spending time with his wife, three children and his grandson.

As Ra has said many times, "Don't believe a thing I tell you, try it for yourself." There are now thousands of people across the world who have worked with The Human Design System, and found that it does indeed accurately reveal the mechanics of the way life works.

Ra passed away in his home on March 12, 2011 at 5:40 AM, less than a month from his 63rd birthday.

LYNDA BUNNELL

HUMAN DESIGN TEACHER AND DIRECTOR
OF THE INTERNATIONAL HUMAN DESIGN SCHOOL

Lynda Bunnell is the Director of the International Human Design School. Working closely with Ra Uru Hu since 1999, she was one of the first to begin teaching and training Human Design Analysts and Teachers world-wide, including the first class of analysts under the new educational program re-structured by Ra in 2003. In 2005, she and Ra were among the first to teach Human Design on-line creating a virtual space where students from all over the world could meet and study together. In 2006 at his request, she re-introduced the Living Your Design Guide training program. Lynda has pioneered many of the training methods and modalities used in the on-line training programs today, and is the author of the Student and Teacher Editions of the Living Your Design books.

Ra asked her to become the Dean of the International Human Design School in 2006, and in June of 2010 turned the school over to her completely, entrusting her with his educational programs as well as maintaining the global standards for education within The Human Design System. Lynda is a fervent pioneer in moving Human Design out into the world, and works full time to support and expand the community of students and professionals throughout the world, dedicating herself to preserving The Human Design System as taught by Ra.

"For the 12 years that I worked with Ra, I had the profound good fortune to be in effect his private student as we corresponded almost daily about the details of The Human Design System knowledge, and his vision for it. He taught me how important it is to maintain the authenticity of the knowledge he was given, and he confided to me his dreams, wishes, and overall vision for The Human Design System. In the process, he transformed my life and the way I view the world around me. And he instilled in me the tools I need to continue to bring this knowledge to all who can use it, and for this I am eternally grateful."

Lynda's background includes thirty plus years as a successful businesswoman, and a passion for spiritual and metaphysical studies. She was raised and still resides in Southern California, and is the mother of two and grandmother of four.

THE IMPACT OF THE HUMAN DESIGN SYSTEM
AROUND THE WORLD ...

"It is with great pleasure that I can finally say, 'Here it is.' This book is for all of those seeking a comprehensive and authoritative description of The Human Design System and its formula. This volume sets out the step-by-step progression of the work from foundation knowledge to the finest nuance of who we are, and how we may encounter our lives as ourselves. To my knowledge, it is the only published work that has enjoyed the active collaboration of the founder and first student of the system, Ra Uru Hu. I cannot recommend it more highly."
    – J.R. Richmond, Sedona, AZ, USA, Chairman and current Registrar of the IHDS

"I have been using The Human Design System both for myself, and as a resource with my students, for the last several years. As a teacher and counselor of inner-personal development this system has become one of my most accurate and reliable tools. Once understood it can give the user personal insight into issues we all face daily. You can find new comfort in your experiences by knowing your design. You learn how to just 'be' in life while still doing. Lynda has taken The Human Design System which is multidimensional, and found a way to simplify it into a meaningful easy to follow book. This is THE system, developed by Ra Uru Hu, that takes us all into, and supports us as individuals, in the future."
    – Dr. Barbra Dillenger, Del Mar, CA, USA, MscD, Transpersonal Development, Founder of Metanoia Services

"Since meeting my design, my level of honesty and trust in my authority to make decisions has increased in proportion to my level of self love. Honesty is self love. And for me that has come through multiple baptisms of fire. It has been very uncomfortable at times, yet is the only true path I've found to the freedom and responsibility and 'no choice' of being my real self. The Human Design system is like the Wiki-leaks for the true self. It tells the whole truth. No nuance of myself can escape."
    – Becky Markley, Seattle, WA, USA

"Human Design, what has it done for my life? That is so simple and complex to explain. Simple because it just allowed me to really know who I am without all the conditioning and my mental distortion of who I thought I was! Human Design is such a complete system that it is like a never-ending story of discovering who I am. I say this several times and this is my inner truth: Human Design is the best thing that has ever happened to my life."
    – Idalina Fernandes, Porto, Portugal

"Human Design readings have blessed me with profound insights about lifelong tendencies. They have given me so many gifts, especially an awareness of the optimal approach for making my decisions and charting my course. I would invite anyone who is truly dedicated to personal awakening to open themselves to the powerful gifts of Human Design."
    – Dr. Roger Teel, Senior Minister, Mile Hi Church, Lakewood, CO, USA

"While working on this project I was once again struck by the beauty, scope and magnitude of The Human Design System, but it is the simple, practical and effective methods for reclaiming oneself, exquisitely tailor-made for each individual human being, which ended my seeking and brought me home."
    – Donna Garlinghouse, Alexandria, MN, USA

"Human Design has been a very personal and intimate journey for me for more than a decade. Understanding and then living my uniqueness has brought acceptance and grace into my life. Not only do I live life as myself, but I also accept my family, friends and others as themselves. That is quite a gift."
    – Cathy Kinnaird, Vancouver, WA, USA

THE IMPACT OF THE HUMAN DESIGN SYSTEM
AROUND THE WORLD ...

"Human Design has given me a unique yet systemized perspective of myself, others in my life and in the world. It has provided awareness, and understanding on many different levels. I particularly like it when I can determine why something is happening and have one of those 'ah ha' moments. I have found it to be a valuable tool for change. No matter how people choose to work with it – from just using a few basic guidelines to diving in and becoming a serious student – Human Design is a useful and fascinating method of self discovery."
  – *Martha Morow, Vista, CA, USA*

"Through the years I have worked with many different modalities and many gifted teachers, and I have learned from all of them. What has helped me in terms of Human Design is a sense of my individuality. Let me give a few examples: When I learned that I am a "social/hermit" I realized how important my private time is to me. When I get up in the morning and make a pot of coffee, the next half hour is spent in reading quietly without interruptions. That means that I am not available to anyone but myself and the book I am reading. It took a while for my wife to get used to this but she does now respect it. When we looked at our combined charts my wife and I learned that talking together in a public setting, such as a restaurant, helps us to be more effective in our communication. It gives a whole new meaning to dining out. What a great system."
  – *Michael MaKay, Del Mar, CA, USA*

"Finding Human Design has had an immense impact on my life. Through it, I discovered ways I was fighting my true nature. By experimenting with and embracing my unique design, I stopped comparing myself to others and let go of the need to 'better' myself in order to fit in. It brought a new sense of honoring and accepting the differences of other people as well. Sharing this information has been truly rewarding. When faces light up and smiles emerge, it lets me know a recognition of one's true, authentic self has been seen, perhaps for the very first time."
  – *Erica Teel, Lakewood, CO, USA*

"I have enjoyed learning more about Human Design. It has helped me become more aware of my personal makeup, and understand more about the way I have been conditioned versus the way I really am. The awareness alone has helped me in understanding how I can approach day-to-day experiences from my internal authentic self versus from my head. I am also having readings done on my children. I think it is important to learn more about who they really are. I am hoping it will enhance our communication. Taking the knowledge and practicing what I have learned, it's really fun."
  – *Kathy Kinley, Carlsbad, CA, USA*

"I know it wasn't luck that led me to discover the Human Design System back in 2004, though I do feel lucky. It offers a richness of life that's physically satisfying, mentally stimulating, and spiritually fulfilling. Now having validated that personally, I share it with my Professional Coaching clients and Human Design students in a way that brings real change to their life. Human Design is a highly evolved system, beyond what I was exposed to growing up (and perhaps you too). Yet to me its power is in its practical application to everyday life, despite the limited mental conclusions and past conditioning we might have developed. It transcends my desire to blend in and play it safe. It lets me rise up, shine, and witness my light, and bring that out in others."
  – *Carol Zimmerman, Los Gatos, CA, USA*

"Thank you Ra, thank you Lynda, thank you Human Design for giving me 'my' life back."
  – *Bethi Black, Ashland, OR, USA*

TABLE OF CONTENTS

ONE - THE FOUNDATIONS OF A REVOLUTIONARY NEW PERSPECTIVE

TWO - THE NINE CENTERS

THREE - AUTHORITY

FOUR - THE FOUR TYPES AND STRATEGIES

TABLE OF CONTENTS

FIVE - THE FIVE DEFINITIONS

SIX - CIRCUITS, CHANNELS AND GATES

SEVEN - THE 12 PROFILES

TABLE OF CONTENTS

EIGHT - THE GLOBAL INCARNATION CROSS INDEX

NINE - SAMPLE CHART OVERVIEWS

TEN - HEXAGRAM LINE DESCRIPTIONS

ELEVEN - OTHER RESOURCES

As this book was nearing completion,
Ra Uru Hu wrote
the following Foreword for its readers:

With The Human Design System's rising popularity, there are unauthorized books emerging. There are very few students of mine that I have encouraged and authorized to write books on the knowledge. It is a pleasure for me to have a work of this quality and depth made available to the public and written by one of the leading educators in Human Design. I have watched Lynda's process for many years, as student, analyst, teacher and ultimately Director of the International Human Design School. She has made and continues to make a major contribution to the continued integrity of the knowledge and its growth in the world.

Ra Uru Hu
Ibiza, Spain
February 8, 2011

PREFACE
BY LYNDA BUNNELL

Imagine for a moment how different your life might have been for you and your parents if a User's Guide had accompanied your birth. Imagine what it would have been like as a child to have been encouraged to connect with the part deep inside you that always knew what was correct or not correct for you; a place you could have trusted to say "yes" or "no" to whatever you met in this life. Imagine for a moment how wonderful it would have been to know how incredibly unique you were born to be, how unlike any other person alive, and to celebrate that uniqueness by loving yourself without comparison. And imagine how wonderful it would be today to have your uniqueness celebrated and encouraged by your family and friends. This is the possibility that The Human Design System holds for you and future generations.

Though Human Design wasn't here when most of us were born, it can touch and transform a life at any age. My own personal experience with this remarkable system began when I was in my early forties. As a successful and well-established businesswoman in Southern California in the 1990's, I thought I had achieved everything anyone needed to be happy – yet I knew I wasn't happy. There was a disconnect between what my mind thought and my own inner truth. No amount of exploration through other systems of self-discovery had succeeded in making that connection or filling the void I sensed within.

A new chapter of my journey began in 1998 while vacationing in southern Spain. My traveling companion, a spiritual seeker like myself, had brought some cassette tapes with her describing a whole new system for personal transformation. We listened as we roamed the hillsides in our car. Little did I suspect that this man's amazing encounter while on a tiny island in the Mediterranean – only a few miles away from us at that time – would turn my life upside down and inside out. The man's name was Ra Uru Hu and the system was Human Design.

It took a bit of convincing by my friend, but once I received a Human Design reading I was hooked. I discovered that Human Design was what I had been seeking. I left my career behind without a backward glance and immersed myself in reading and listening to everything I could find about the knowledge. I participated in private readings and took extensive classes with Ra in Europe and America for days and weeks at a time. It was an incredible, life-reorienting experience of step by step, decision by decision, dismantling my firmly held misconceptions about myself and life.

As I surrendered to my inner wisdom, life took me in unexpected directions to satisfying destinations I could not have dreamed of for myself. There were moments of deep and difficult inner transformations as well. Human Design had not only shown me why my early successes in life had left me feeling empty, it set me on a unique path that has brought me to this moment, fulfilled, challenged and satisfied by my work – part of which is writing this book. This science is precious to humankind. I've watched Human Design grow over the years, and I am still as passionate about it as I was when I first encountered this amazing body of knowledge. As it has grown in popularity, and as materials began to be published by others around the world, Ra asked me to compile a definitive and comprehensive book in collaboration with him, that would represent and accurately record the knowledge.

As we were getting ready to go to press with this book, Ra died suddenly at his home in Ibiza, Spain. He has been my teacher, mentor and friend since 1999, and I will forever miss his larger than life presence. He lived what he taught, and used his own life experiences to validate the knowledge. Little did I know while working toward this book release that the meaning of it for me would expand into a tribute honoring this man and his contribution to humanity.

Over the years, Human Design has proven itself to me and never let me down. It is incredibly accurate and deeply transformative. There are now thousands who have found their own truth by stepping onto the path of awakening through Human Design.

Once you, too, begin to grasp your uniqueness, and to understand that you were not meant to be like anyone else, you will experience the exhilarating freedom of living the person you were born to be. It is never too late for you to start living into the fullest expression of yourself.

Welcome to the journey,

Lynda Bunnell
Director, International Human Design School
Carlsbad, California 2011

RA URU HU
5/1 MANIFESTOR

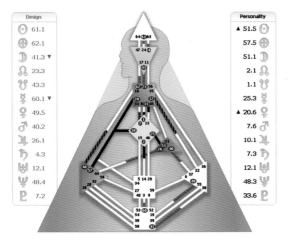

LYNDA BUNNELL
4/1 MANIFESTING GENERATOR

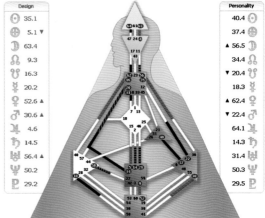

ACKNOWLEDGEMENTS

First I have to thank Ra Uru Hu. We spent a great deal of time collaborating on various projects over the years, and I thank my lucky stars that the fates and my own trajectory put me in alignment with this rare, brilliant and unusual man. He brought real, lasting and meaningful mutation to my life and the lives of tens of thousands. I predict his legacy will continue on far into the distant future and touch many generations. We had the love of Human Design in common and I am satisfied that I expressed my gratitude to him time and time again over the years. He was a good man, he never wanted to be followed as a Guru, and his students knew how much he loved his family and his life. It's a rare event indeed that a person comes into the world to be the clarion planting the seed of a body of knowledge such as this. "It never hurts to be grateful," he said to me during one of my talks with him – and grateful I am. I am also deeply grateful to Ra's family, his wife Ambuja, daughter Sarah, son-in-law Mau, sons Loki and Jiva, and grandson Kian, for providing him with a loving family and support system which allowed him to do his work. Human Design could not have happened without them.

This book has been a labor of love and has taken a monumental effort to bring it into existence. I have to pay a special tribute to Donna Garlinghouse as contributing editor and advisor on this project. Donna worked with me step-by-step for the past few years as this book took shape. She has a 'left-mind' and I have a 'right-mind' which made for an excellent collaborative effort. Donna is a force of nature and a gift to us all. She helped me to see things clearly during some difficult times. She is an amazing woman and we are all blessed to have her as part of our community.

A heartfelt thank you goes to Bethi Black. Her contributions as advisor, editor, and in book design and layout, were priceless. Although we have worked together on other projects, little did I know that when I called her the summer of 2010 to ask her to help me with the school that we would end up working on *this* project together. In looking back I see how it was so perfectly and divinely orchestrated. Bethi literally moved into my house so we could eat, breath, sleep, and work this book into existence during the final home stretch. On many levels, it would have been impossible to get through this past year without her.

And thank you to Becky Markley, contributing editor for the Living Your Design manuals, for your sharp eye for detail and help with feedback and editing; Cathy Kinnaird and Carol Zimmerman, for your inspiration, love and support; Genoa Bliven, for understanding the importance of preserving and honoring Ra's work and legacy; and both Mary Ann Winiger and Randy Richmond, treasures in our community, for providing objective guidance for us all.

Sarah Krakower and Maurizio Cattaneo, with Human Design Concepts, provided a brilliant book cover and amazing graphics. Ra used to say, "Human Design is a visual medium, a visual road map to understanding our true nature," and Mau clearly knows and embraces this in his core as we see with the beautiful illustrations in this book. Sarah and Mau make a great team, and it is very apropos that their love and energy are part of this book.

There are many people in the community who have contributed in more ways than I can name as friends, contributors and associates. They include the entire International Human Design School Faculty and the National Human Design Organization Directors: Lynette Hagins, Bethi Black, Deborah Bergman, Genoa Bliven, Alokanand Diaz, Carol Freedman, Cathy Kinnaird, Josette Lamotte, Becky Markley, Dr. Andrea Reikl-Wolf, J.R. Richmond, Peter Schober, Dharmen and Leela Swann-Herbert, Carol Zimmerman, Richard Beaumont, Nicholas Caposiena, Maurizio Cattaneo, Viviana Farran, Unnur Inga Jensen, Sarah Krakower, Spyraggelos Marketos, Inaki Moraza, Meris Oliveira, Virginia Page, Joyce and Alex Huang, and Koji Ueda. We all have something in common – we want what is best for the perseverance and growth of The Human Design System.

Thank you to my sister Kathy Kinley, daughter Alisa Hawkins, and son-in-law Matt Hawkins, for their love, support and encouragement – and patience as my life was consumed by this project as I approached the finish line; and to my grandchildren, Sara, Sabrina, Kingston and Landon. Spending our magical times together fed my soul and was my much-needed reprieve. I want to also acknowledge my son Rod Lopez. And thank you to Jerry and Ida Bunnell for bringing me into this world; John and Shirley Barry for taking me under your loving wings many years ago; Michael and Barbra MaKay for your encouragement and inspiration; Martha Morrow and Kate McCavitt, supportive, dear and loving friends; and my Projector friend Judy Thompson, for persisting and asking me, three times, if I wanted to have a Human Design reading. A special thank you to my lifelong friend and daily confidant Dona King. She has been right there beside me the whole way through this project asking every day, "Are you going to work on the book today?" I wonder what she will ask me now that it is done!

Although there are too many to name, this book owes its greatest debt to the students, analysts and teachers of The Human Design System – these are the true heros and pioneers. As we each live our lives according to our true nature, we change the world for the better one person at a time. Human Design could not have progressed to where it is today without all of you doing your great work in the Human Design community. I know that I have been touched in some way by all of you. We stand on the shoulders of those who have gone before us, and we uplift and support those that are joining us in this incredible movement of The Human Design System out into the world. Ra handed us the baton the day he passed from this earth, and now it's up to us to continue what he started.

"THE HUMAN DESIGN SYSTEM IS NOT A BELIEF SYSTEM. IT DOES NOT REQUIRE THAT YOU BELIEVE IN ANYTHING. IT IS NEITHER STORIES NOR PHILOSOPHY. IT IS A CONCRETE MAP TO THE NATURE OF BEING, A MAPPING OF YOUR GENETIC CODE. THIS ABILITY TO BE ABLE TO DETAIL THE MECHANICS OF OUR NATURE IN SUCH DEPTH IS OBVIOUSLY PROFOUND BECAUSE IT REVEALS OUR COMPLETE NATURE IN ALL ITS SUBTLETIES. HUMAN DESIGN OPENS THE DOOR TO THE POTENTIAL OF SELF-LOVE, A LOVE OF LIFE AND THE LOVE OF OTHERS THROUGH UNDERSTANDING." – RA URU HU

INTRODUCTION
THE HUMAN DESIGN SYSTEM

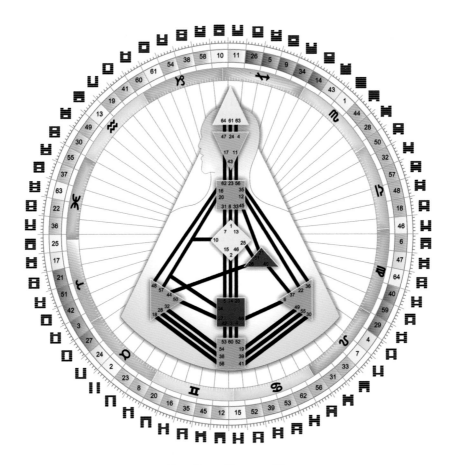

THE RAVE MANDALA™
TRADEMARK OF JOVIAN ARCHIVE CORPORATION
AND THE HUMAN DESIGN SYSTEM

**BY COMING TO MEET THIS BODY OF KNOWLEDGE YOU ARE
EMBARKING ON AN ADVENTURE; A JOURNEY OF DISCOVERY
TOWARD FULLY EMBODYING WHAT IT MEANS TO 'BE YOU'**

INTRODUCTION

THE LIFE TRANSFORMING EXPERIMENT OF
LIVING AS YOURSELF AND CLAIMING YOUR UNIQUENESS

The Human Design System is the Science of Differentiation. It shows each of us that we have a unique design and a specific purpose to fulfill while on Earth. Endless possibilities for individual uniqueness lie within our genetic matrix. There are millions of variations of human beings, yet each of us has a specific and unique Human Design configuration with a clear Strategy that effortlessly aligns us to our uniqueness. Human Design does not ask you to believe anything. It invites you to participate in a potentially life-transforming living experiment, and provides you with the practical tools and information needed to live life as yourself. Without this individualized – and individualizing – living experiment, Human Design is just a complex system of fascinating information to entertain the mind.

In looking at thousands of charts, one thing stands out – no two are exactly alike. Even if someone had a chart very much like yours they would not be you. But how do we determine our unique design?

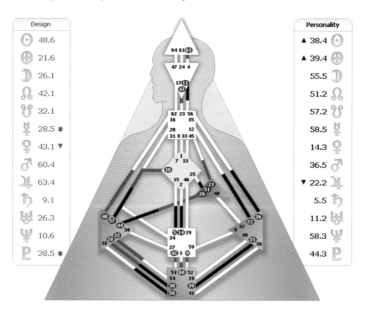

A Human Design Chart or BodyGraph is a precise map and user guide that gives you access to how we are genetically designed to engage with the world, and how our unique inner guidance system operates. Never before have we been able to see all of the parts of ourselves so clearly. The conscious and unconscious parts of ourselves, the aspects of us that no one can take away from us, as well as the aspects that we have been taught or conditioned to believe are us, but are not.

As Ra Uru Hu has often said, "What you can rely on you've never relied on in your life. What you can't trust you've been trying to trust all your life. What you've been trusting has never been you. What you've been ignoring has always been you. Try to trust what's really you and see what happens." Each of us is meant to be different from everyone else. Now we can see and get in touch with those differences. We are here to live our lives and express our truths in our own unique ways. Understanding this can lift a great weight from our shoulders. How often have we compared ourselves to someone else? How often as children were we compared to someone else by a parent, teacher or peer? Comparing ourselves to others creates an impression deep inside of us that it is not okay to be who we are. When we add that to the conditioning of our early years, we find ourselves trying to change or adapt how we act to suit others, which further distances us from the person we were born to be. When we begin to understand and accept our own uniqueness, something inside of us opens up and relaxes. The layers and layers of conditioning slowly fall away, and the person we were meant to be, our inner essence, begins to emerge.

The First Step is Obtaining Your Human Design Chart

You will want to have the charts of your family and friends in front of you as you continue through this book. You can obtain free charts in English here:

The International Human Design School   www.ihdschool.com

A complete list of authorized Human Design Organizations, in other languages, is provided in Section Eleven of this book. You can download a free version of the official and authorized Maia Mechanics Imaging software to run charts for yourself at: www.jovianarchive.com.

What Your Chart Reveals

- Your chart shows your specific genetic design: affirming who you really are, how to be yourself, and how to navigate successfully through a constantly changing world.
- It provides you with the tools you need to live an aware and awake life – a simple Strategy you can trust that reliably connects you to your personal Authority in order to make moment-to-moment decisions that are correct for you so that your unique life purpose can unfold naturally.
- Your Strategy will help you eliminate resistance (frustration, anger, disappointment, bitterness) and fear in order to live in a relaxed, unique, creative and evolutionary/revolutionary way.
- Your chart maps out your relationship dynamics to help you understand how the attractions, resonances and conflicts between you and others play out.
- It gives you guidance on how to align yourself with people who enhance your vitality, support your life purpose, and share your true path.
- Understanding the charts of others illustrates the truly unique and individual natures of those close to you, like family and friends, and how best to respect and interact with them.
- Most importantly, a chart shows us how to create the best environment for children so that they are empowered to be their unique selves, and to learn and develop as individuated human beings.

WHO YOU ARE – THE FOUR HUMAN DESIGN TYPES

Your chart gives you your Type, Strategy, and Authority (body-centered intelligence) tools to show you the way you are designed to navigate through life and interact with the world. While there are millions of variations of designs, there are just four Types of human beings. Each of us is one of these Types, and your Type stays the same throughout your entire life. Here is a very brief explanation of the Four Types. (The Types are covered in depth in Section Four.)

GENERATORS, THE BUILDERS, represent about 70 percent of the population. Their Strategy is to engage with life by waiting for things to come to them so that they can respond. When they initiate rather than wait to respond, they usually end up feeling frustrated. Generators are the life-force of the planet and are designed to know themselves by observing what they respond to. Through responding they experience satisfaction in their life and work. Their work is their gift to the world.

PROJECTORS, THE GUIDES, are approximately 20 percent of the population. Their Strategy for engaging with life is to wait for their specific qualities to be recognized and invited into things. It is through an invitation that they experience recognition and success in their lives. If they initiate rather than wait, they experience resistance and rejection and can end up becoming bitter. The Projector's gift to the world is to understand and be a guide for others.

MANIFESTORS, THE INITIATORS, compose about 9 percent of the population. Their Strategy is to inform others of their decisions before they take action in order to eliminate resistance. When Manifestors cannot manifest in peace, they experience anger. Manifestors are designed to have a powerful impact and be initiating mechanisms for the other Types. Initiating is their gift to the world.

REFLECTORS, THE DISCERNERS, represent approximately 1 percent of the population. Their Strategy is to wait through a full cycle of the Moon before making major decisions. Reflectors delight in life's surprises. When they initiate and don't use their Strategy, they end up disappointed with life. Reflectors are designed to be the judges of humanity, to reflect back the injustices humanity inflicts on itself. Their ability to clearly discern the 'this and that' of the world is their gift.

THE EXPERIMENT OF LIVING YOUR STRATEGY AND AUTHORITY

The heart and soul of The Human Design System lies in the potential awakening that is available to you through the actual living of your unique design. Strategy and Authority, which will be explained in detail later in this book, are the doorways to living as yourself, affirming who you really are, and understanding and letting go of what you are not.

In the past we navigated life with our minds as the ultimate decision maker. Our minds are not equipped to do this for us any longer. The mind's real genius is for collecting information and experiences, measuring this against that, and contemplating unique perceptions and reflections that can be shared with others. It can only do this, however, when it is not making decisions for us. The mind is now at its best as a passenger – here to watch the movie and to view the scenes of life as an involved observer.

What actually moves us through life on our unique path is the superior consciousness or intelligence of our body, the form we inhabit. The Human Design System is the revelation of how our form works, and how it becomes the guiding source of our personal Authority. We are each designed with a unique way to make decisions with our body consciousness, and every decision is critical as each one moves us along life on a particular trajectory. One wrong decision can set our life on a course that can have serious consequences. Mental decision-making is rarely more than a 50/50 guess, and the mind is not a trustworthy personal guidance system. To survive on this planet, we each need to know how to access our own Authority. It is the decisions that come from deep within that either put us back on or keep us on the correct path for our life, empowering us to live life authentically from our personal truth.

The Human Design System's tools for awakening are like no others. Once you are familiar with your unique design and learn how to use your Strategy and Authority effectively, you can immediately begin to experiment with and discover for yourself how they transform your life. By living as you are designed to live, as yourself, your mind starts to play a much different and more appropriate role as an objective observer and resource, freeing you to experience what it is to be an awake and aware passenger. Your mind participates in your process of self-discovery but does not interfere with your day-to-day decisions. Human Design gives you the tools and points the way, but it's up to you to use them.

"IF YOU LIVE BY YOUR PERSONAL STRATEGY AND AUTHORITY THERE IS NOTHING TO DO - THE DOING HAPPENS AND 'YOU' ARE NOT INTERFERING." – RA URU HU

THE AUTHENTIC SELF

Throughout the book we will compare the authentic (or true self) to the not-self. When we talk about the authentic self or true self we mean our pure and natural behavioral nature designed to emerge without resistance into the world. Another term used for this is our purpose, our reason for being here – being the person we were born to be. The not-self is conditioned programming masking our authentic self. As we become aware of our not-self through our Strategy and Authority, we slowly become aware of our authentic self always present, but concealed just behind it. Self-hatred also has its source in the not-self; we simply hate our failure to fulfill the layers and layers of expectations that we have taken on or placed on ourselves. When we know and accept – and live – from a comfortable place of authenticity, we will naturally come to love ourselves.

As you journey further into your personal experiment to know yourself, you will witness every possible variation of your not-self conditioning and the resistance it creates. The more clearly you see that, the more clearly you will see your true self. Knowing yourself is the path to loving yourself. The Human Design System shows you how.

Human Design focuses on the health, stability and direction of our life contained within our bodies. Once the form (body) is functioning optimally, the light of our psyche (Personality) or soul shines through all we think, say and do with an empowering clarity and gentle ease. This is authenticity, living as we were designed to live.

THE DECONDITIONING PROCESS

Deconditioning, as it is called in The Human Design System, is a process of letting go of what we are not. It is a slow process because it is a deep process. When we re-claim our Authority, changing how we make decisions and navigate through life, we actually change the way our cells function within our body. Life moves in seven-year cycles, as it takes approximately seven years for all the cells in our body to be renewed. The moment we begin to align with our own nature, the moment we allow our body to live its life without resistance, we begin this deep process of deconditioning. Seven years later we emerge closer to the person we were born to be. It is not easy to start as an adult, but as we have heard over and over – it is NEVER too late to begin.

As far back as ancient China, thinkers and philosophers espoused the idea of not-doing as a way of doing. There is a pleasant ease that comes from living your life surrendered to your inner guidance system. Being awake and aware of yourself, living authentically and in harmony with your design, is so much more interesting than living asleep and lost in the expectations of the conditioning of the homogenized world. Learning to make decisions from deep within yourself, so that you and others can fully benefit from you being you rather than a carbon copy of someone else, is worth the effort, the time and the patience that it takes to get there. To know your self IS to love yourself. Deconditioning will be discussed throughout this book.

SIGNPOSTS OF RESISTANCE

Once we begin living our life authentically through our Type, Strategy and Authority, we can begin to pay attention to whether we experience ease or resistance along the way. When we have acted from decisions made by our thinking minds, rather than our Strategy and Authority, we experience resistance. Continually making decisions from our mind means we are living a life that isn't ours; and the accumulated stress from such actions jeopardizes our physical, mental and emotional well-being. The not-self themes of Anger (Manifestor), Frustration (Generator), Bitterness (Projector), and Disappointment (Reflector) are signposts of resistance that alert us that we have veered off course by failing to follow our Strategy and ignoring our Authority. In other words, it is our not-self actions and decisions that are resisted, not our authentic selves! If taken personally, we experience resistance as rejection or suppression of our true self by others. On the other hand, when we become conscious and aware of what resistance is telling us through these signposts, it affords us an opportunity to take a step back and reassess our approach/action/words. When we become ill or dis-eased or accident prone, we know that continued outside resistance has manifested on the inside. As our authenticity is lived out, our purpose in life is freed to accomplish its essential mission and brings us our full true-self measure of satisfaction, success, peace or surprise. (This topic is explored more thoroughly in Section Four.)

THE BOTTOM LINE – AWAKENING

Human Design is a new kind of awakening. It is a process of coming to awareness that aligns our mind and body with their appropriate roles. It requires making an ally of the mind through understanding the mechanics of our design while simultaneously living our lives according to our

Strategy and Authority. Once we understand the nature of the true self and the not-self, and are making life decisions from our personal Authority, we can release our attachment to the mind and its control over our lives, and free its incredible gifts to be of service to others. In doing so, we become aware and awake passengers, and our minds become objective observers of our life. Each individual's singular path to awakening begins with a growing awareness of our sophisticated body's heightened intelligence, and a deep trust in this intelligence to be our compass through life. We cannot, dare not, release our mind's hold until we know we can trust ourselves implicitly. By fully trusting our own ability to navigate life, we become more accepting of ourselves, and able to genuinely love ourselves – and others. This, in Human Design, is the point of personal transformation – seeing through the illusion, and moving through life awake and aware.

How to use this Book

Even though The Human Design System is a deep and complex body of knowledge, it is accessible for everyone. This book is designed to take you through this knowledge step by step, one layer building on the next. Each of these sections is presented in a specific order, introducing and explaining terms that you will need as we progress. Initially it will be helpful for you to proceed section by section. Once you have become familiar with the various levels of information and how they inter-relate, you can then use this book as a reference guide.

1. The Foundations of a Revolutionary New Perspective, Human Design from the Beginning

An overview and introduction to the basic concepts and origins of The Human Design System. This will lay the groundwork for your personal experiment into the foundation of you.

2. The 9 Centers, The Flow of Energy

Understanding the Centers is bedrock Human Design information. In order to unlock your Type, Strategy, Authority and ultimately your true self, you must understand how the centers operate.

3. Authority, Our Unique Authentic Truth

Decisions are key to navigating through life and living our truth and purpose. Using our personal Authority for our decisions is self-empowering. Understanding how to make decisions as yourself keeps you aligned with your correct life path.

4. The Four Types and Strategies, Living Our Design

An exploration of the nuances of the Four Types and each type's Strategy in detail. Understanding how we correctly move through life allows us to relax and surrender to our unique life purpose.

5. The Five Definitions, Energy Dynamics

Understanding the pathways through which our energy flows reveals how we process information and how we best interact with others.

6. Circuits, Channels and Gates, The Circuit Board of the Life Force

We are a mix of Tribal, Collective and Individual life forces, ways that we are designed to meet the world, as we support, share with, empower and mutate each other.

7. The 12 Profiles, The Costume of our Purpose

Profiles help us to understand our roles, the ways we express our unique character on the stage of life. When we live out our profile, we meet our life purpose.

8. The Global Incarnation Cross Index, Our True Purpose

A introduction to our unique life purpose, achieved and expressed as a result of authentic living.

9. Sample Chart Overviews, Human Design in Practice

Sample chart overviews for each of the types that will provide you with a superficial example of keynoting, and the synthesis that takes place when an analyst works with your chart. The basis of an in-depth reading, by a professionally trained analyst, is the weaving of your genetic information with practical tools for living your unique life.

10. Hexagram Line Descriptions, A Deeper Exploration

A resource for a more advanced exploration of the Human Design System. The Hexagram Line Descriptions provide a deeper look into the line level characteristics of your chart, as well as a wonderful meditation on what it is to be you.

11. Other Resources, Glossary, Keynotes and More

While this book is filled with profound and practical information, it cannot replace a personalized reading by a thoroughly trained IHDS Certified Human Design Analyst, which itself can be a life-transforming experience. You will find a list of IHDS Certified Analysts at www.ihdschool.com, or by contacting an authorized Human Design National Organization listed in Section 11.

Reading this book is excellent preparation for a personalized foundation reading, and provides you with a solid platform for experimentation with your own design and future study. There are other areas to explore in The Human Design System also listed in Section 11. If you are interested in learning more, please visit www.jovianarchive.com and www.ihdschool.com. We have a worldwide network of National Organizations, and excellent Analysts and Teachers ready to support and guide you in the exploration of this knowledge.

"MOST PEOPLE WANT A QUICK FIX OR QUICK ANSWERS TO THEIR PROBLEMS. THIS IS PROFOUND KNOWLEDGE AND IT REQUIRES AWARENESS, EXPERIMENTATION, SELF-REFLECTION AND TIME. THE HUMAN DESIGN SYSTEM GIVES YOU THE KEYS BUT IT'S UP TO YOU TO USE THE TOOLS IT PROVIDES. THIS IS THE USER MANUAL FOR YOUR LIFE BUT YOU HAVE TO JUMP IN, TURN THE KEY, AND DISCOVER FOR YOURSELF. THE MAGIC IS IN THE EXPERIENCE." – LYNDA BUNNELL

WOULD YOU LIKE TO TAKE THIS JOURNEY?
PLEASE CONSIDER YOURSELF INVITED ...

"TO BE AWAKE IS REALLY MUNDANE. IT'S WHAT WE'RE SUPPOSED TO BE. IT'S NOT SOME HIGH EXALTED STATE THAT WE HAVE TO SUFFER TO GET TO. THAT'S NONSENSE. WE JUST HAVEN'T HAD THE EDUCATION UNTIL NOW. IT'S EASY TO BE AWAKE. LIVE OUT YOUR TYPE, STRATEGY AND AUTHORITY FOR SEVEN YEARS AND YOU'LL BE AWAKE AS BUDDHA." – RA URU HU

SECTION ONE

THE FOUNDATIONS OF
A REVOLUTIONARY NEW PERSPECTIVE

HUMAN DESIGN FROM THE BEGINNING

SECTION ONE

THE FOUNDATIONS OF A REVOLUTIONARY NEW PERSPECTIVE

HUMAN DESIGN FROM THE BEGINNING

Two incidents occurred in the first months of 1987 while Ra Uru Hu was living on Ibiza, a tiny Mediterranean island off the coast of Spain. The first was his encounter with the Voice. In "Encounter," a video recording of his reflections on the event, he talks candidly about the shocking experience which began late in the day of January 3, 1987. For eight straight days and nights a Voice, as he called it, penetrated him; it revealed scientific information regarding the origins and workings of the universe and gave him the formula for The Human Design System. He emerged from this mystical experience with a new name, a different perspective on life, and a deeper understanding of the mechanics of the universe. Several years of formulating and experimenting with the information followed the encounter. From 1987 to 2011, Ra dedicated his life to moving this empowering body of knowledge, in practical ways, out into the world.

The second incident was an extraordinary cosmic event that was seen with the naked eye from a mountaintop observatory in Chile. It was a supernova or the death of a star, initiating a vast explosion of incredible intensity. With its dying breath, that star bombarded our planet with subatomic information, and for 14 minutes everybody on Earth received three times as many neutrinos as normal. The impact or imprint of that event on human consciousness continues to unfold within and around us to this day.

The Human Design System, the Science of Differentiation, is a new system of self-knowledge that differs fundamentally from anything else that exists in the world because it is the only one designed to directly address the transformation of 9-centered human beings. According to the Voice, 1781 marked a major evolutionary shift which forever impacted humanity's direction, momentum and innate capacity for self-awareness. It was the shift from the mind-directed and other-directed 7-centered human being to our more sophisticated, inner-directed 9-centered transitional forms. All of us alive today inhabit 9-centered forms.

The Human Design System synthesizes aspects of two types of science: The ancient observational systems of Astrology, the Chinese I'Ching, the Hindu-Brahmin Chakras and The Tree of Life from the Zohar/Kabbalist tradition; and the contemporary disciplines of Quantum Mechanics, Astronomy, Genetics and Biochemistry. As a logical, empirical and practical system, Human Design does not ask you to believe anything. It merely offers you the opportunity to explore and experiment with the mechanics of your nature, and your evolving consciousness, in order to find out for yourself exactly what works for you.

PART ONE
THE HUMAN DESIGN SYSTEM

SYNTHESIZES ANCIENT AND MODERN SCIENCE

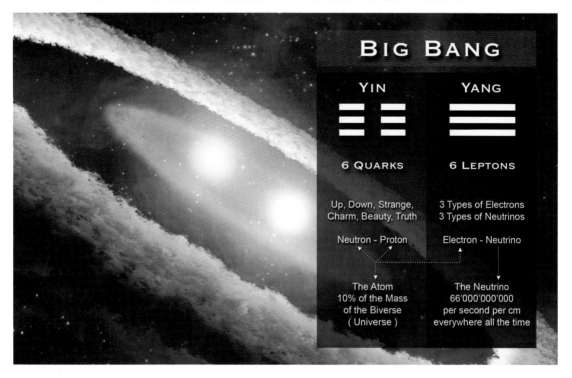

Astrophysicists have established that our universe began 13.7 billion years ago following an astronomical event they called the Big Bang. The most extraordinary thing to ponder about this event is that before the Big Bang everything that had mass existed in one single particle that was smaller than an atom. Something ignited this speck and the resulting 'explosion' caused the universe to begin to expand. As it expanded, and continues to expand at an ever-increasing rate, everything that existed separated into two groups creating a basic duality: quarks and leptons, or a yin family and a yang family.

As the illustration shows, the yin family is fundamentally material (has mass) and is made up of six quarks. Quarks are the smallest known building blocks of matter, and are usually found in combinations. Scientists gave them the names "up, down, strange, charm, beauty and truth." Two of these six quarks, namely up and down, gather together into two groups (up, up, down; and down, down, up) and form what are called the proton and the neutron of the atom. Protons carry a positive electric charge while neutrons are electrically neutral elementary particles. On the other side of the duality is the yang family, which is considered to be pure energy or light. This family is called leptons (leptos is a Greek word meaning thin or small). There are six leptons as well: three different types of electrons and three different types of neutrinos. Electrons are negatively charged particles. When an electron, a proton, and a neutron come together they form the atom.

Scientists say if we add everything together that we know is atomic, which is to say has mass – the stars, all the galaxies and super clusters, and everything else including us – we will discover their sum represents less than one-tenth of the whole universe. The rest, or the space in between everything, is made up of such things as dark matter and dark energy. That brings us to the enigmatic neutrino.

THE NEUTRINO – THE FIRST PREDICTION FULFILLED

During Ra's experience he learned that neutrinos were capable of leaving an imprint, which meant that neutrinos were particles carrying mass. This had not been proven by science yet. At first scientists thought these subatomic particles (neutrinos) streaming through space were pure energy like the photon, but since they travel 1 to 2 percent slower than the speed of light, they could not be pure energy. This first prediction was scientifically proven 11 years later. By 1998, scientists had proven that the largest of these unusual and barely detectable particles bear an infinitesimal amount of mass: about one-millionth the weight of one proton. Having mass allows neutrinos to carry information, yet they are small enough to pass through any atomic barrier without resistance.

These tiny cosmic messengers are referred to as the breath of stars, the exhaled energy of stellar fusion, and there are more of them than anything else in the universe. Three trillion neutrinos, and the material information they carry, pass through every square inch of our planet – and us – every second. Our Sun, which is the closest star to Earth, produces about 70 percent of all the neutrinos that travel through our solar system. The remaining 30 percent are emitted by other stars in our Milky Way Galaxy, and a small percentage are from the planet Jupiter.

Neutrinos could be regarded as the modern equivalent of what the ancients called chi or prana. These extraordinary particles are penetrating us with bits of information all the time, which means we live and move through a vast, continuous and inescapable information field.

CRYSTALS OF CONSCIOUSNESS

The incredibly detailed scientific information received from the Voice about the nature of the cosmos placed the Big Bang, acknowledged by physicists as the accepted beginning of the expansion of the known universe, into a larger context. The Voice described the Big Bang as merely the conception of our universe, not its birth. That means our entire universe is one single living entity, a fetus not yet born, still expanding and moving toward its moment of birth.

In the beginning, said the Voice, there was a yin egg, a cosmic egg containing all of the (atomic) material of the universe. This egg's structure is best described as crystalline. While not a crystal per se, the term helps us visualize it. There was also a yang seed that contained another crystal-like structure. When the yin egg and the yang seed came together at the Big Bang, there was a shattering and an infinite number of crystalline aspects spread throughout the expanding universe, each aspect bearing a "consciousness" of its original yin/yang orientation. Everything that we can imagine and all forms of life on this planet – even inanimate objects – are endowed with these Crystals of Consciousness. We will explain in Part Two of this Section how the crystals get imbedded into the body.

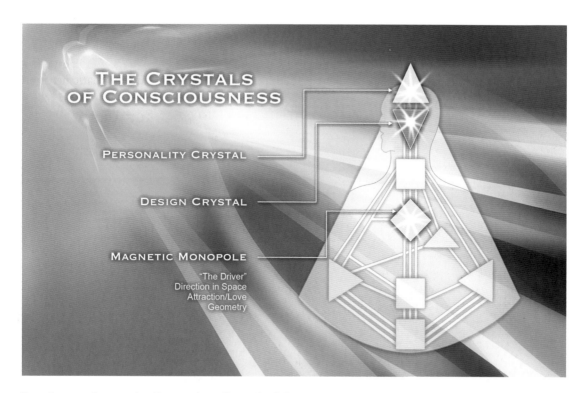

In a human being, the Personality Crystal of Consciousness, an aspect of the original yang seed, sits above your head (just above the scalp) in the Head Center at the top of the BodyGraph. This Personality Crystal manifests what you identify with as your Self, or who you think you are, and is called the passenger or passenger consciousness. The Design Crystal of Consciousness, an aspect of the original yin egg, is seated in the Ajna Center (between the eyebrows) and manifests the biogenetics of your body, or the physicality of the form. It is referred to as the vehicle or form consciousness. The relationship between these two crystals is likened to a backseat passenger (Personality) who rides in a vehicle (Design) operated and navigated by a third party - the driver.

THE MAGNETIC MONOPOLE – THE SECOND PREDICTION FULFILLED

The driver of the vehicle, the Magnetic Monopole, is the third key component described by the Voice. On September 4, 2009, the Voices' second prediction was substantiated when the scientific community announced that it had observed the existence of magnetic monopoles. Briefly, monopoles are particles that carry a single magnetic attraction, either a north or a south pole. They had eluded detection since the search for them began in the early 1920's.

According to the Voice, our Magnetic Monopole is located in the sternum area known as the G Center, and has two different functions. First, it holds us (and everything) together in the "illusion" of our separateness. As a monopole or a magnet that only attracts, it holds the Personality Crystal and the Design Crystal together in a relationship, much like a marriage holds two people together in a mystical union. The second function of the Magnetic Monopole is to connect us to our movement in time through space, guiding us along our path or our geometry in life – what we call destiny. This connection can be likened to the way the arm of a streetcar hooks up to an electrically powered grid. All life forms are endowed with a Magnetic Monopole.

THREE COMPONENTS OF THE NAVIGATION SYSTEM

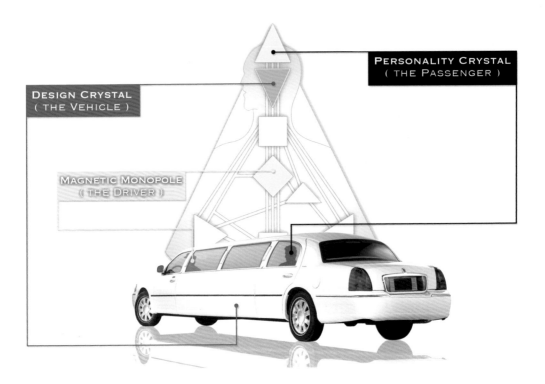

Returning to the analogy of vehicle, passenger and driver, imagine a limousine with a driver behind the wheel who knows exactly how to operate the vehicle, where to go and how to get there. The vehicle represents the Design Crystal and the driver is the Magnetic Monopole. The Personality Crystal, or who we think we are, is neither the vehicle nor the driver. The Personality Crystal has no idea where to go or how to get there; it is simply the passenger. A passenger is meant to be quiet and relaxed, and to watch the scenery go by instead of fighting with the driver for control of the steering wheel. The Human Design System's tools for living make the passenger comfortable in the back seat of the vehicle so it can sit back and enjoy the ride.

THE TRANSITION FROM 7-CENTERED TO 9-CENTERED BEINGS

With the discovery of the planet Uranus by Herschel in 1781, we moved into the Uranian Era when human beings with highly evolved 9-centered forms began replacing the 7-centered, mind-oriented Homo sapiens. By the late 1800's the process was complete, making all of us alive today 9-centered beings, or "Homo sapiens in transitus," a term coined by Ra Uru Hu to distinguish 9-centered beings (an interregnum species) from Homo sapiens and the new, more highly evolved forms coming in 2027.

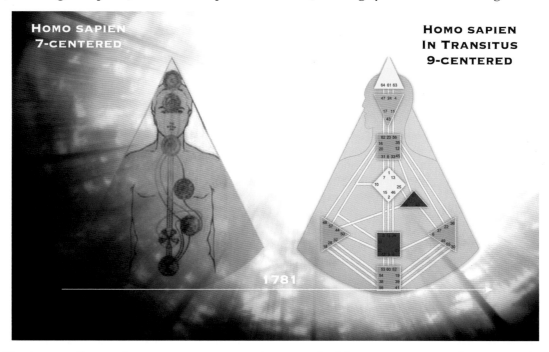

HOMO SAPIEN 7-CENTERED

HOMO SAPIEN IN TRANSITUS 9-CENTERED

1781

This historically significant moment in our evolution marked the movement away from our need to focus on survival through the mental awareness or mental intelligence of the strategic mind. Our newer 9-centered forms, freed from addressing those basic fears for survival, are once again attuning to the flow of the natural order. Subtle yet marked genetic changes are still taking place within our physiology, which support complex neurological advances within the Solar Plexus Center, in preparation for its emergence as the center of spirit awareness in 2027. (The Solar Plexus Center is discussed fully in Section Two.)

For the purposes of this book, understanding Homo sapiens' lengthy evolutionary journey, compared to our barely 230 year presence on this planet as Homo sapiens in transitus, gives us a perspective on the pervasive impact that living in these transitory times as an interregnum species has on us. It affects how we make decisions, relate to one another, break away from the controlling modes of the past, and attain our full potential as conscious, awake and aware beings. Briefly, anthropologists speculate that 5-centered Neanderthal hominids, who relied on instinctive splenic intelligence and their keen senses to survive, were animistic and deeply connected to and influenced by the forces of or 'gods' of nature. They lived as small family groups in harmony with the solar/lunar cycles of the natural order, and appear to have been peaceful and non-aggressive.

As the Cro-Magnon mutation took place over thousands of years, the stage was set for the evolution of modern man, for 7-centered Homo sapiens, our precursors. Their progress was greatly enhanced beginning 85,000 years ago when the larynx mutated, increasing space in the cranium for neurological advances in the neocortex and visual cortex which further delineated the characteristic raised foreheads and binocular vision common to our species. Existential, instinctual and instantaneous Splenic awareness was soon overshadowed by mental awareness, which found expression through the voice.

This metamorphosis continued to distinguish humans from the rest of the mammalian kingdom. Being able to make and systematize a variety of repeatable sounds led to language. The unique ability to communicate and share intelligence opened the way for cooperation, specialization, and eventually, organization into villages. All of these evolving traits ensured new levels of personal and group mastery as part of Homo sapiens' thriving existence.

With Cro-Magnon man, the emphasis shifted from survival of the form and living attuned to the natural flow, to focusing on and revering the powers of the strategic mind that dominated the natural flow. This is how Homo sapiens made it to the top of the food chain. Shrewd and inventive strategic thinking replaced fears for survival with strategies formulated to control the environment, and eventually the people in it. As a species, Homo sapiens were conditioned to look to forces beyond themselves for authority, such as gods, priests and kings, to guide, rescue and support them, as well as to justify their often aggressive conquests.

By 1781, the remarkable, strategic mind had succeeded in taking the 7-centered form to its zenith of human potential. Enter 9-centered Homo sapiens in transitus. The 7-centered Homo sapiens had a shorter life expectancy marked by the Saturnian cycle. Our new 9-centered forms or bodies have an 84-year life expectancy marked by the Uranian cycle. We need to live longer in order to process and integrate increasing amounts of information, and to develop technologies that will be needed in the future. Driven by the genetic imperative to reproduce, 7-centered beings found communion through sexuality. The 9-centered being is here to find communion through awareness. The ways we communicate, and the shape our relating/relationships will take in the future, are an intrinsic part of the transition to living completely as 9-centered beings.

By 1987, as the entire planet was flooded with the potential for heightened awareness, the stage was already set, and the tension elevated between our body's consciousness and our mind's domination. The moment was ripe for The Human Design System and its effective and practical way of addressing this dilemma. The bottom line is that our now highly evolved 9-centered forms, our vehicles, are designed to guide us through life decision by decision. We no longer need to look to an outer authority through our mind for direction. This is a huge blow to the strategic mind in its determination to retain its former control of our decision-making process. Through Type, Strategy and Authority, The Human Design System bridges the evolutionary progression from the mental outer authority of the 7-centered being to the revolutionary, aurically connected, personal authority of the 9-centered form.

PART TWO
THE RAVE MANDALA

A SYNTHESIS OF FOUR ANCIENT ESOTERIC SYSTEMS WITH MODERN SCIENCE

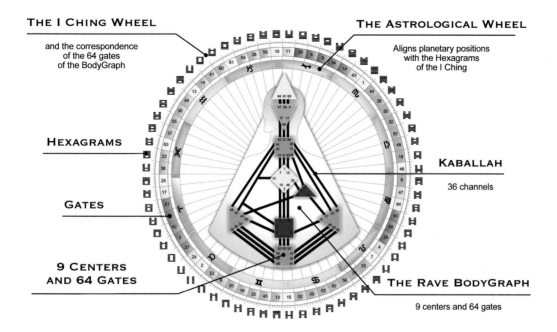

THE I CHING WHEEL

and the correspondence
of the 64 gates
of the BodyGraph

THE ASTROLOGICAL WHEEL

Aligns planetary positions
with the Hexagrams
of the I Ching

HEXAGRAMS

KABALLAH

36 channels

GATES

9 CENTERS
AND 64 GATES

THE RAVE BODYGRAPH

9 centers and 64 gates

The beautiful Mandala above is an amazing synthesis. At its center is the 64-gate matrix of a human being, the Rave BodyGraph, the single most important feature within The Human Design System. The synthesis is comprised of four ancient esoteric systems or early sciences, four distinct ways of understanding the rhythm and flow of life, the cosmos, and humanity's essential place within it. Western Astrology and the Chinese I'Ching form the outer rings of the Mandala, while the Hindu Brahmin Chakra system and the Zohar or Kabbalist Tree of life form the foundation for the BodyGraph centered within. Altogether they form the basis of a new, multi-faceted and deeply complex system, providing us with a comprehensive means of understanding the mystery of life and the mechanics of the universe, The Human Design System.

Each of the four ancient systems, plus the role neutrinos and the Magnetic Monopole play in bringing the Mandala to life, will be discussed individually to demonstrate their relationship to each other and their function within the synthesis. The synergy of this whole makes it much greater than the sum of its many parts.

"HUMAN DESIGN IS A MIRROR OF OUR AGE OF GLOBALIZATION AND SYNTHESIS. THERE LURKS REAL DANGER IN CLINGING TO RELATIVE ABSOLUTES AS THIS IS THE FORCE THAT CONTINUES TO CONDITION US AWAY FROM ACCEPTING OUR ONENESS. HUMAN DESIGN IS NOT ABOUT SEEING OR ACCEPTING THAT THERE IS ONE SPECIFIC WAY. THE WAY IS ALL WAYS. SYNTHESIS EMBRACES ALL OF THE COLLECTED WISDOM OF THESE CULTURES AND THEIR SYSTEMS AND IT DOES NOT DISMISS OR LESSEN THE VALUE OF THE KNOWLEDGE AND WISDOM DERIVED FROM THESE EARLIER SYSTEMS. IT BRINGS THEM ALL TOGETHER INTO THEIR GLOBAL BODY, INTO THEIR PROPER PLACE WHERE THEIR CONTRIBUTIONS CAN BE PROPERLY RECOGNIZED AND HONORED. EACH CULTURE IN ITS EVOLUTION HAS EXPLORED AND DISCOVERED ASPECTS OF THE TRUTH. THE SYNTHESIS OF THESE DIVERSE ASPECTS CREATES A COMPLETE BODY OF KNOWLEDGE AND, AS DEMONSTRATED BY THE LAW OF MATHEMATICS, THE WHOLE IS GREATER THAN THE SUM OF ITS PARTS." – RA URU HU

ASTROLOGY – THE INNER RING OF THE MANDALA

The inner ring of the Mandala represents Astrology's contribution to the synthesis. This 360-degree circle, with its 12 signs of the Western Zodiac (Aries, Taurus, Gemini, etc.), is the way early human beings represented the universe, and tracked the movement of heavenly bodies in the night sky. The Human Design System uses the Mandala to calculate and record two precise moments in time and space within the synthesis. The first, based on the exact time of your birth,

is recorded as the Personality data. The second, which is 88 degrees of solar arc or 3 months prior to your birth, is recorded as the Design data. The use of two calculations distinguishes The Human Design System from traditional astrology. (The calculation of data is discussed in more detail in Part Three of this section.)

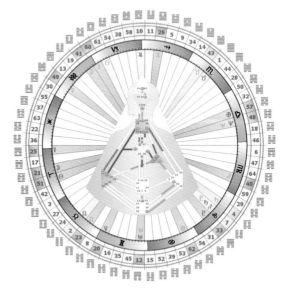

We are *surrounded* by an enormous star field which generates the neutrino stream that is constantly penetrating and informing the objects it passes through. A kind of communication occurs during the encounter when the neutrino's infinitesimal mass interacts with or rubs against the object on its way through. For example, when the neutrino stream goes through Mars it communicates with Mars and an exchange takes place. After being filtered by Mars, the stream passes

through humans and there is another exchange. It's as if a black car and a white car bang into each other, and there is now a little black paint on the white car and a little white paint on the black car. Each car is altered by the encounter just as we are altered by this neutrino interaction. In this way, each planet contributes its essence to the way we are imprinted with the neutrino stream. Even though we all exist in the same neutrino program, the unique way we manifest that program is determined by the precise moment of our birth and the two calculations discussed above.

THE I'CHING
THE OUTER RING OF THE MANDALA

"THE INFORMATION CONTAINED IN THE HUMAN DESIGN MANDALA IS EXTRAORDINARY AND ITS SYMMETRIES ARE BEAUTIFUL. THE HEXAGRAMS AROUND THE WHEEL HAVE AN ASSOCIATION DIRECTLY ALIGNED WITH OUR GENETIC CODE, THE CODON. THE WAY IN WHICH THE AMINO ACID CODON INFRASTRUCTURE OF A HUMAN BEING OPERATES IS THROUGH SPECIFIC IMPRINTS. IF YOU GO DOWN INTO THE NUCLEUS WITHIN THE CONSTRUCT OF THE CELL ITSELF, DOWN INTO ITS DNA, YOU FIND THAT EVERYTHING IS THERE, ALL THE FUNDAMENTAL COMPONENTS OF A HUMAN BEING. THIS IS TRUE WHETHER IT'S A BLOOD CELL OR A MUSCLE CELL." – RA URU HU

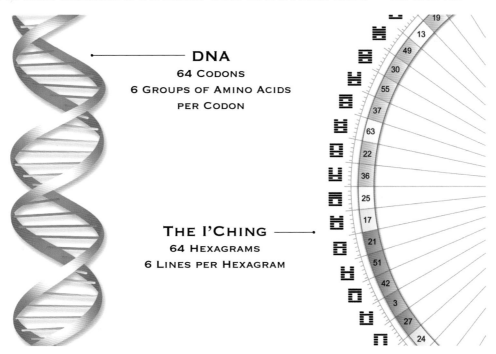

DNA
64 CODONS
6 GROUPS OF AMINO ACIDS
PER CODON

THE I'CHING
64 HEXAGRAMS
6 LINES PER HEXAGRAM

The ancient Chinese I'Ching or Book of Changes, one of the first books ever written, reads like a dictionary of archetypal wisdom on the seasons of life. What makes the I'Ching so extraordinary in this synthesis, however, is not its philosophical or ethical text, but rather the amazing mathematical structure of its 64 hexagrams. Specifically, the 64 numbered sections you see in the outer ring of the Mandala represent the 64 hexagrams of the I'Ching. Each of these Hexagrams, pictured around the outside of the wheel, is made up of a particular combination of six broken (yin) or solid (yang) lines. There are 64 hexagrams, each composed of 6 lines, which makes a total of 384 line markers around this outer ring. Each Line contains a 'bit' of information specific to its particular position in the hexagram.

In the 1950's biologists Watson and Crick cracked the genetic code, and it was later observed that DNA codons and the hexagrams of the I'Ching share identical binary structures. Our genetic code consists of four chemical bases arranged in groups of threes, which is similar in organization to the lower and upper trigrams of the hexagrams of the I'Ching. Each of the chemical groupings relates to an amino acid and forms what is known as a codon. There are 64 codons in our genetic code, just as there are 64 hexagrams in the I'Ching. The 64 hexagrams around the outer wheel, translated into the BodyGraph as Gates, can be used in Human Design to thematically understand or interpret our genetic imprint, and provide very specific detail about the characteristics that make up each and every one of us.

THE RELATIONSHIP BETWEEN HEXAGRAMS (GATES) AND DEGREES

Generally speaking, the inner ring of the Mandala is used for calculation, and the outer for interpretation. This illustration shows that every hexagram, with its corresponding gate, has a specific place and measurement of arc in the outer ring. In order to determine its place, we need to understand

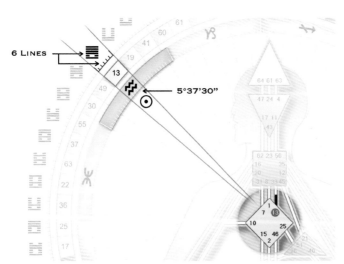

again that the 64 hexagrams (each with six lines) have a total of 384 lines, while each of the 12 houses of the zodiac encompasses 30 degrees, for a total 360 degrees.

When the 384 line demarcations, visible around the outer ring, are measured by or aligned with the 360 degrees of the inner ring, we can see that each hexagram covers a space/time of 5 degrees, 37 minutes and 30 seconds of arc. This arc is an imprinting field, a place in space; when a planet passes through it, information is exchanged via the neutrino stream.

When we are born, we are imprinted with the qualities of a specific hexagram for each specific planet (or Node of the Moon) in the chart. The information carried by the neutrino stream at that precise moment imprints us in this specific way for the rest of our life. The moment is captured and instantaneously recorded in our BodyGraph as our definition, our blueprint.

In the illustration above we have an example of the calculation used. When we know the position of the planet's location in the inner astrological ring, we can see its correspondence to the hexagram in the outer ring. The example above has the Sun positioned in the zodiacal constellation of Aquarius, which aligns it with a corresponding division in the I'Ching wheel in the 13th hexagram. This information is then transferred into the BodyGraph. We will explore the BodyGraph in more detail later in this section.

THE HINDU BRAHMIN CHAKRA SYSTEM
THE NINE CENTERS

The Hindu Brahmin Chakra System is the third component of the synthesis, bringing us to the nine centers. One major difference between the traditional chakra system and the nine centers of the BodyGraph illustrated below is simply that there are seven chakras and nine centers. This difference reflects the cosmic shift that occurred in 1781 signaling an evolutionary progression within our species from 7-centered beings to 9-centered beings.

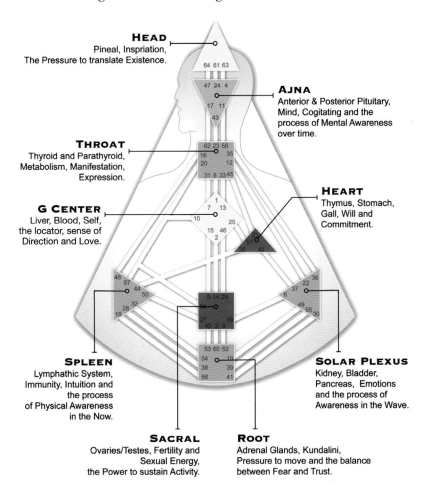

HEAD
Pineal, Inspriation,
The Pressure to translate Existence.

AJNA
Anterior & Posterior Pituitary,
Mind, Cogitating and the
process of Mental Awareness
over time.

THROAT
Thyroid and Parathyroid,
Metabolism, Manifestation,
Expression.

HEART
Thymus, Stomach,
Gall, Will and
Commitment.

G CENTER
Liver, Blood, Self,
the locator, sense of
Direction and Love.

SPLEEN
Lymphathic System,
Immunity, Intuition and
the process
of Physical Awareness
in the Now.

SOLAR PLEXUS
Kidney, Bladder,
Pancreas, Emotions
and the process of
Awareness in the Wave.

SACRAL
Ovaries/Testes, Fertility and
Sexual Energy,
the Power to sustain Activity.

ROOT
Adrenal Glands, Kundalini,
Pressure to move and the balance
between Fear and Trust.

This process involved a complex internal reorganization of the form, not simply an addition of two more energy centers. Each of the nine centers is an energy hub with its own distinct biological correlations. (The Centers are discussed in depth in Section Two.)

THE KABBALAH - THE TREE OF LIFE
THE 36 CHANNELS AND 64 GATES

The Tree of Life from the Zohar/Kabbalistic tradition is the fourth component of the synthesis. It makes its contribution as the pathways energetically connecting the centers through the gates. These pathways, called channels, create a living circuitry that unifies the BodyGraph and directs the flow of energy within it (illustration below on left). At either end of each channel, where the channel opens into a center, you will see a number indicating a particular gate (illustration below on right). The 64 gates correlate to the 64 hexagrams of the outer ring of the Mandala, allowing us to transfer the information from the hexagrams directly into the BodyGraph.

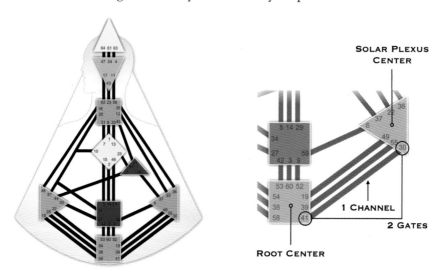

Single gates are the way energy enters and exits a center; they are open to meeting the energy at the other end of the pathway. It takes definition in both gates at opposite ends of the pathway to complete or define a channel. As individuals we can have both gates defined ourselves, and thus define the channel, or we can have only one gate defined and meet others who complete the channel for us.

As an example, when a person has a gate at one end of a channel they are attracted to a person who has the gate at the other end of the channel. Their coming together completes or energetically connects them through the newly completed channel. This third dynamic in their lives is experienced as an electromagnetic connection. It feels like a spark of attraction. This is one of the many ways in which we are designed to meet and interact with other people in our life. Basically, the channels connect the energies of two different centers thus generating something new described as a quantum. Each channel has its own characteristics and keynote, but remains a flexible or dynamic quantum of the energy of the 2 gates, 12 lines and 2 centers it brings together. Defined or colored-in channels become a dominant feature in a person's life and we call this definition your "life force." This is discussed in more detail in Part Three of this section, as well as in full detail in Section Six.

PART THREE
THE HUMAN DESIGN BODYGRAPH

THE MAP TO NAVIGATE BY

"WHAT MAKES HUMAN DESIGN SO EXTRAORDINARY IS THE BODYGRAPH. THE BODYGRAPH HAS NEVER EXISTED BEFORE. YES, OBVIOUSLY, THERE HAVE BEEN GRAPHIC ILLUSTRATIONS OF BODIES AND SYSTEMS, BUT THERE HAS NEVER BEEN ANYTHING LIKE THE BODYGRAPH IN THE CENTER OF THE MANDALA. THE BODYGRAPH IS UNIQUE. FIRST OF ALL, IT IS BASED ON AN ENTIRELY NEW NUMERICAL CONFIGURATION. THIS IS NOT A 7-CENTER CHAKRA SYSTEM. THIS IS A 9-CENTERED BEING. THE WAY IN WHICH THE INFORMATION IS DRAWN TOGETHER HAS DERIVATIVES IN OTHER SYSTEMS. THE BODYGRAPH IS THE REAL SYNTHETIC FIELD." – RA URU HU

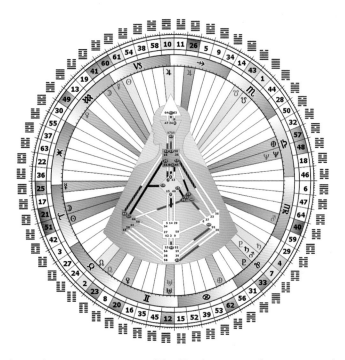

Conception marks the moment when a Design Crystal, along with its embedded Magnetic Monopole, enters the ovum through the process of fertilization. As the Design Crystal begins receiving the streaming neutrino information, it separates from the Magnetic Monopole and initiates the building of the fetus. The fetus will continue to develop until the end of the second trimester of pregnancy when the neocortex, the special brain faculty unique to humans, is fully formed. At this point, the Magnetic Monopole sends out a signal which brings the Personality Crystal, also called the soul or psyche, into the body. The moment of birth, which occurs approximately three months later, marks the moment the Personality Crystal receives its indelible imprint from the neutrino stream. The Birth time is the moment the baby has left the womb and is separate from its mother's body, outside the mother's body, and not the time when the umbilical cord is cut. Human Design illustrates our uniqueness in precise detail, and it is very important, therefore, to begin analysis with accurate birth data, especially birth time. If you are unsure about your birth time, please check with the organization that records births in your country/state of birth. If you have no way of acquiring an accurate birth time you can hire an astrologer who specializes in what is called "chart rectification." The astrologer will take you through a process to determine your birth time as precisely as possible.

THE BODYGRAPH

Two calculations are needed to generate a BodyGraph. We begin with the date, place and exact time of each person's birth to establish the Personality or natal calculation. When the birth data is entered into Maia Mechanics Imaging software, the program automatically calculates a second set of data, the pre-natal or Design calculation.

The natal or Personality calculation (in black column below) is based on the moment of birth, and the pre-natal or Design calculation (in red column below) is based on a time approximately 88 days (or precisely 88 degrees of the sun) prior to the actual birth. On your own chart you will

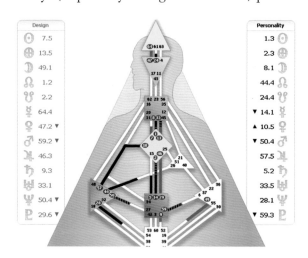

see that you have both a Design birth date and a Personality birth date. Since both calculations are based on the moment of your birth, it does not matter whether you were a full-term baby, premature or delivered by caesarian section.

The two sets of calculations are recorded on your chart as the Design column (in red) and the Personality column (in black). The gate numbers indicate which hexagrams have been activated, and the symbols indicate which planet was in the neutrino stream of that hexagram. The gate numbers are also recorded in the centers within the BodyGraph. In the charts on the opposite page that separate the Design from the Personality, you can see where the Design gates and Personality gates are located; in

YOUR HUMAN DESIGN CHART INCLUDES YOUR BODYGRAPH AND PLANETARY DATA

the third chart you see how they appear when combined in the BodyGraph. The locations of the gates in the BodyGraph do not change; they are always in the same place for everyone. What does change is *which* specific gates are activated by the planets at the moment of each calculation.

THE SIGNIFICANCE OF THE RED AND BLACK

The Personality and Design can be viewed as separate charts. The red and black sets of information are both part of your design, but represent aspects that are accessed differently by you. The Personality information in black is what you have conscious access to; you know these things about yourself and you can work with this information. This is who you think you are, the 'you' with whom you identify. Having this conscious access is like sitting on a hill overlooking a highway. You can see the road, the traffic on the road, the direction they are going, and you can wave at the people as they go by. In other words, you are a fully participating observer. The Design information in red is one of the most important advances introduced by The Human Design System. It shows you the nature of your unconscious, what is going on below your level of consciousness. It also represents your genetic inheritance, or your bloodline, as a theme from your mother and father and grandparents. You cannot consciously access the information in red. It is like looking at a tunnel. You have no idea what is going on inside the tunnel because you can't see the objects or which way they are moving. There is nothing you can do but wait and see what emerges. In other words, what comes out of your mouth can be as much of a surprise to you as it is to others! Even though with age, experience and the proper reflection you learn to know the unconscious part of yourself, it is important to remember that you can never control it. Gates and/or channels colored in with red and black stripes on a chart indicate that there are multiple planetary activations in that gate or channel in both your Personality and Design. Those activations function both consciously and unconsciously in your experience of life.

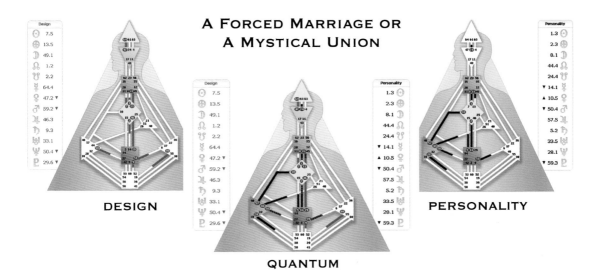

A FORCED MARRIAGE OR A MYSTICAL UNION

DESIGN

PERSONALITY

QUANTUM

The juxtaposition of your Personality and Design on either side of a BodyGraph, as in the illustration above, can be revealing. The Personality is who you think you are; the Design is how you are genetically programmed to move through time in space. These two completely different aspects merge into the BodyGraph and are held together by the Magnetic Monopole as an integrated field, a mystical union. It can also be likened to a forced marriage because the two aren't naturally compatible. The Personality thinks it's in charge of the life while, in fact, it's the Design and the Magnetic Monopole that actually are. Most of the conflicts that arise, and the resistance you meet in life, stem from the Personality trying to manage your life rather than assuming it's proper role which is to sit in the back seat and enjoy the ride.

The Personality is not aware of the Design's existence, which is why consciously knowing how to access your form's intelligence through your Strategy and Authority is so important, and a major focus of this book. When the Personality passenger is surrendered to its Strategy and Authority, the Personality and Design can live in harmony, in union, as they individually perform their intended roles. This is when you find your path, and when the foundation for all love emerges – the love of self. Without self-love inside, there is no love for others. With self-love inside, you will know who is right for you on the outside.

DEFINITION IN A BODYGRAPH

As the activated gates from both the Design and Personality columns are added (colored in) on the BodyGraph, channels are formed and centers are defined. Specifically, when the two gates at both ends of a channel are activated by a planet, they form a defined channel and are colored in on the Bodygraph. When a channel is defined, the centers at either end are defined or colored in as well. This is called definition in a chart. Definition creates what is called our life-force.

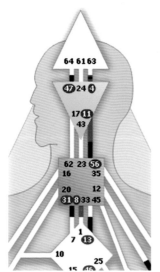

For example, definition is created in this chart when Gates 11 and 56 define the Channel of Curiosity (11-56), which in turn defines the Ajna and Throat Centers. Your total definition (the colored-in channels and centers of your chart) shows you what is consistent throughout your life, what is reliably you. Definition is always there, every second of every minute of every hour of every day of every week of every year until the end of your life. It establishes the characteristics of your life force in precise detail. Definition establishes your Type, Strategy and Authority and shows you where you can find your reliable 'yes' or 'no' when making decisions.

Definition is the core of our being, a potential that we grow into as we fully inhabit our 9-centered vehicles by living authentically. This is the self we know deep inside, and the unique (life force) frequency we project aurically into the world from birth. Our BodyGraph confirms this, and The Human Design System encourages us to live it.

Definition tells our story. The Science of Differentiation's complex and revolutionary perspectives required the creation of a new language to communicate that story. Ra called it keynoting. Keynotes form a living, symbolic language, the language of Human Design. They are a means by which a great deal of information is referenced or compressed into a single word or phrase. Almost every aspect of the system has its own keynote associated with it. Like a mantra, keynotes invoke or awaken or connect us with our body's chemistry and our own unique frequency. Learning and using the language of keynotes is like thinking within the body's hormonal messaging system; it allows us to connect energetically with others.

By stringing the keynotes of one's definition and open centers together, professional analysts create a word picture or story line of a person's character and purpose. Once the keynotes are delivered, the story penetrates the person beyond the level of the mind. As an example, in the illustration above, the Ajna Center is connected to the Throat Center via Channel 11-56. This definition tells us that this person will want to speak his mind and say what he is thinking. Channel 11-56 is called the Channel of Curiosity, a design of a searcher or a seeker. The 11th gate is the Gate of Ideas, and the 56th gate is the Gate of Stimulation. It is his ideas that he wants to share. With this definition, he helps make every dinner party he attends a success because he is willing to talk to anybody who will listen. He enjoys keeping everybody stimulated or engaged in his stories.

Although he has a lot of ideas, and often says he plans to do something with them, he rarely does. His ideas do not materialize. Knowing this about himself, but not understanding it, is a source of deep frustration for him. There is, however, a reason why he has this dilemma; his definition stops at the Throat Center, the center of communication. If the Throat Center were connected to one of the body's four motors or energy resources (Heart, Solar Plexus, Sacral and Root Centers, which are discussed in more detail in Section Two) then this person could turn communication into action. He could act on his ideas. In truth, this person is not meant to do anything himself with his ideas. Instead, he is to share them, and perhaps one day to verbally stimulate someone else into bringing his ideas into reality. Following his Strategy of waiting until he is asked or invited to share his ideas will increase his chances of success.

DEFINED AND UNDEFINED FORM A BINARY:
NATURE AND NURTURE – OUR SENDERS AND OUR RECEIVERS

"WHEN YOU ARE LOOKING AT DIFFERENT ACTIVATIONS IN A CHART, YOU ARE LOOKING AT THE UNIQUE IMPRINT OF A PERSON. WE HAVE RECEPTORS TO EVERYTHING. EVERYTHING THAT IS WHITE IN THE DESIGN IS A RECEPTOR. THE IMPRINT IS WHAT MAKES YOU DIFFERENT; IT ISN'T WHAT MAKES YOU THE SAME. WHAT MAKES US THE SAME IS THE WHOLE MAP IN ITS ENTIRETY; WHAT MAKES US DIFFERENT IS OUR INDIVIDUAL IMPRINT. THIS IS THE SCIENCE OF DIFFERENTIATION AND HUMAN DESIGN TEACHES US ABOUT OUR UNIQUENESS, WHAT IT IS TO BE UNIQUELY OURSELVES WITHIN THE TOTALITY." – RA URU HU

Definition is a fixed and dependable part of us that is to be embraced, expressed and lived. It is consistent throughout our lifetime and therefore reliable. Definition establishes the parameters for who we are becoming, the potential we grow into over our lifetime. That which is not defined in our chart remains white (undefined). These parts are neither empty nor broken. They are a valuable and fully functioning part of us, but because they operate inconsistently they are simply not a reliable basis for decision-making. Our openness is our living classroom and the ultimate source of the wisdom that we share with others. It is our openness that also determines which challenges or fears we will face, and what we are here to learn and to discover about ourselves and the world.

Taken together, the defined and undefined portions of our chart form an interactive binary between what is fixed and what is flexible in our design. This is where nature, or who we are by definition, and nurture meet. People are inclined to think that definition is superior to lack of definition. This is not true. It is simply a duality, like day and night.

Our definition is like a transmitter, a message or defining frequency that is sent out into the world through our aura. What we send out conditions others. Conversely, our undefined centers, gates and channels are like receivers. Through our openness we experience, reflect (mirror) and magnify the energies we take in from others. For good or bad, it is through our receivers that we are nurtured by and learn from our environment. Our openness is also where we are the most vulnerable to conditioning. Most people have a mixture of defined and undefined centers in their design. Rare exceptions do occur where a person will have all the centers in their chart either defined or open. We will explore the defined and undefined centers thoroughly in Section Two.

THE SUN, MOON, NODES AND PLANETS IN THE BODYGRAPH

You might call the Sun, Moon, Nodes and planets the local programming agents of our solar system. The locations of these celestial bodies at the time of our birth determines the way they influence or 'flavor' how we experience our definition. Over the eons, each has taken on specific mythological and thematic characteristics.

Without the BodyGraph, there is no possible analysis. The database within the BodyGraph is made up of a total of 26 activations, 13 each from the Design and the Personality positions. According to the "Voice" no other objects in the heavens, other than the ones listed, can activate gates. This is not to say that an object, such as Titan, the great Moon of Saturn that is larger than Mercury, does not have an effect. It filters the neutrino stream, and like everything else adds its quality, but it does not activate a gate.

Kiron (Chiron), the comet fragment that was discovered in the late 1970's, also does not activate or 'open a gate.' If the thematic presumptions are correct, however, and this object is associated with healing/wounding, then seeing where it is in the BodyGraph can provide an insight. The same is true for the astrological ascendant, midheaven, Arabian points, etc., which do not activate gates either.

Below is a list of the celestial bodies used in Human Design. In addition to flavoring how we experience our life, they also act as our teachers.

	TEACHER	WHAT THEY EXPRESS AND TEACH
☉	Sun	Personality Expression/Life Force
⊕	Earth	Grounding/Balance
☽	Moon	Driving Force
☊	North Node	Future Direction/Environment
☋	South Node	Past Direction/Environment
☿	Mercury	Communication/Thinking
♀	Venus	Values/Sociology
♂	Mars	Immaturity/Energy Dynamics
♃	Jupiter	Law/Protection
♄	Saturn	Discipline/The Judge/Restraint
♅	Uranus	Unusualness/Chaos and Order/Science
♆	Neptune	Illusion/Art/Spirituality
♇	Pluto	Truth/Transformation/Psychology

The following pages explain the Sun, Moon, Nodes and Planets and their themes, or keynotes. They also provide a short description of how they are used in The Human Design System.

⊙ **Sun – Life Force.** The Sun in our chart represents our core energy, our primary yang force. It is our 'self' as well as what we 'do' and represents the theme of our incarnation. The Sun represents the archetype of the Father. (70 percent of the neutrinos that condition us are from the Sun). Our Personality Sun is how we express our 'light' in the world. Our Design Sun represents genetic themes we have inherited from our Father.

⊕ **Earth – Grounding and Balance.** The Earth represents where we concretize or bring into form, and how we ground and balance the Sun's energy within our forms, our bodies. The Sun and Earth always operate together and are located opposite each other in the Mandala. The Earth provides the primary yin balance, the archetype of the Mother. We find conscious balance when we are able to integrate the Personality correctly in our life, and we find our stability (or unconscious balance) when we come to grips with the world of form. The Earth is the backbone of our stability.

☽ **Moon – Driving Force.** The Moon represents what moves us, the driving force in our design. The pull of the Moon is a force that is powerful, always there, and always willing to embody the message of our Sun's energy. The input comes from the Sun, but the direction or force or drive is represented by the Moon. The Moon is the archetype of the eldest daughter, and makes possible the task of the Earth (Mother) to drive and move the form, thus ensuring evolution. The Moon is also the reflected light that others see in our inner nature brought to the surface and placed on display.

☊ **North Node of the Moon – Future Direction and Environment.** Although not planets, the Nodes of the Moon are equally powerful. On the Personality side the Nodes are not who you are, but instead frame what your Personality thinks about the world and itself. On the Design side the Nodes frame your relationship to the environment and the people in it. The North Node is the mature stage of experiencing life and shifts from the South Node at our Uranus Opposition (38-43 years). Movement into the North Node signals a process of letting go of what no longer serves us, and retaining what does.

☋ **South Node of the Moon – Past Direction and Environment.** The South Node represents our developmental stage of experiencing life, our immaturity, until we arrive at our Uranus Opposition. In our 9-centered Uranian bodies, our transition from the South Node to the North Node symbolizes mid-life and our entry into adulthood. The Nodes represent the stage on which our lives are played out, how we perceive the world around us, and the environments that we will experience throughout our lives that will support us in living out our unique destiny.

☿ **Mercury – Communication and Thinking.** Mercury, the archetype of the eldest son, represents the expansion of human consciousness, as well as the need within us to communicate. Mercury is closest to the Sun and thus metaphorically has its ear. Mercury programs the Personality Crystal from the time it enters the body until birth. Where your Personality Mercury is defined gives you insight into what you need to communicate in this life. Your Design Mercury also has something to communicate, but we often do not know why we are telling something to someone when it expresses through our unconscious form.

♀   **Venus – Values.** Venus establishes our values, and represents our morals and the natural laws for how we deal with each other and the world around us. Venus is the archetype of the youngest daughter, and also represents love and beauty. For you personally, Venus is the right and the wrong, and your moral questions and issues. If you do not act with moral clarity, and if those around you do not act with moral clarity, Venus can be harsh in her retribution. The values that are established in Venus become laws in Jupiter, and any retribution takes place through Saturn.

♂   **Mars – Immature Energy.** Mars is the archetype of the youngest son, energetically immature and free of responsibility. Passive until it gets rolling, and then a force to be reckoned with. Once ignited, Mars' capacity to build momentum can result in mindless outbursts where even the most basic inhibitions can be overwhelmed. Mars in your chart represents an extraordinary energy that when refined over time can settle into a powerful and mature wisdom about the correct use of energy. Mars plays a significant role in our personal transformation.

♃   **Jupiter – Law and Protection.** Other than the sun, no object exerts greater influence over us. Jupiter is the logos for the universe and defines our outer development in 11+ year cycles, as well as our relationship to the other and the whole. We are each imprinted with a very focused theme of what is correct for us, our law as written by Jupiter. If you live by that law you can gain great good fortune as Jupiter is very generous at times, but your ability to benefit from the generosity comes from deep obedience to your own law.

♄   **Saturn – Discipline (The Judge).** Saturn is the place in your chart where you must deal with the consequences of your actions. A very ancient yin force, it represents the judge, and the places in your life where you will pay for any incorrectness when not following your own laws and morals. Saturn is a profound signpost that allows you, over time, to see the progress in your process. Saturn is an expectant task-master without praise. If Saturn is leaving you alone, this is a signpost that you are living correctly; however, if you break your own rules, values and laws, Saturn will punish you.

♅   **Uranus – Unusualness, Chaos and Order.** Where Uranus shows up in your design is where you express your unusualness. The evolutionary mutative undercurrent of Uranus allowed us to transform our understanding of the Maia and extend our life span to the current 84 years. Uranus also introduced us to the tripartite life process of subjective youth, objective mid-life, and transcendent older age.

♆   **Neptune – Illusion and Spirituality.** A great teacher who demands total acceptance. Neptune in any gate veils its potential. This veiling can deeply disturb the not-self as it is not possible to see through the veil, and we lose the ability to see any limitations, which can lead to abuse. Surrender to Neptune, leave it alone, and you allow the potential magic to emerge from behind the veil. You also learn a great deal about the nature of surrender.

♇   **Pluto – Truth and Transformation.** Pluto brings the forces of the subconscious to the surface; it represents rebirth. Pluto is the 'truth teller', bringing truths that are hidden to the surface for you to look at directly and squarely in the eye – truth brings transformation. Wherever you see Pluto in your chart, this is your Truth. Pluto's deepest lesson is to find the light within the darkness. The mystery of Pluto, the mystery of you, takes a lifetime to explore.

THE NEUTRINO TRANSIT FIELD

We are all constantly subjected to conditioning forces, either through the chemistry of those around us, or by the planetary transits from the greater cosmic environment in which we live. In The Human Design System, the definition is the "student," the undefined centers are the "school" and the transiting planets are the "teachers." The transiting planets inform and affect us directly through their capacity to filter the neutrino stream.

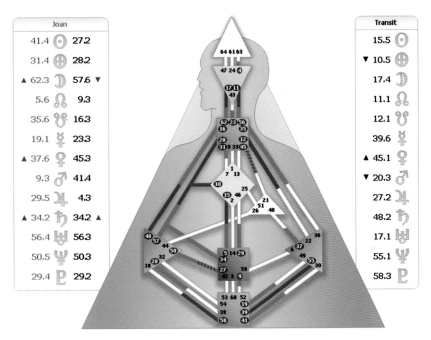

JOAN'S ENCOUNTER WITH A DAILY TRANSIT

Only the Personality/black calculation is used to create a transit connection chart. Both the red and black sides of this design are represented by the green activations in the BodyGraph above. The neutrino planetary transit field is shown in blue. We can see where the transit field brings new activations to Joan for this moment in time, which is how it influences or informs her as it passes through her. By staying true to her Strategy and Authority, she can stay grounded in her own design, and avoid being distracted from her course, or by the people around her who have also been effected by the transit.

A CONNECTION CHART GRAPHICALLY ILLUSTRATES
THE INTERPLAY BETWEEN TWO PEOPLE

We are also impacted and conditioned by those around us, especially those close to us. The three charts on the right demonstrate how a connection chart is created. John's definition is represented in blue and Mary's in green. Together they create a quantum field that is greater than either one of them alone. New channels are defined and open centers are filled in. A great deal can be learned from the connection chart about how these two people interact with each other, how they unknowingly influence each other's actions and decisions, and what they project as a couple.

The topic of Connections is vast and requires a more thorough exploration than can be provided in this book. To understand a Connection chart thoroughly, one needs to consider many things including: Type, Strategy, Authority, profile, definition, gates, lines, and centers; and it is recommended that a Human Design Analyst be consulted. The following general information describes four ways people connect with each other energetically:

ELECTRO-MAGNETIC: This is where each partner defines one gate, or one half of a channel, in their BodyGraph. Together they define the whole channel, establishing a vital flow of energy between the two centers at either end of that channel. This connection represents the basic attraction-repulsion dynamic in relationships.

DOMINANCE: Here one partner's entire channel (for example, channel 7-31) is defined while the other person's is completely open or undefined. With this configuration in place between them, the person with no definition can only experience their partner through acceptance and surrender to their partner's definition, which is fixed and consistent.

COMPROMISE: In this case one partner defines the whole channel and the other defines only a single gate in the channel. The partner that only has one gate of the channel activated is always compromised by the partner with the complete channel.

COMPANIONSHIP: With this connection both partners have the same channel or gate defined in their Bodygraph. This commonality carries the greatest potential for friendship, for comfortably sharing the experience of life and living with each other.

The synthesis of many systems reflected in your Human Design chart provides you with an extraordinary new view of your life, and an understanding of the genetic continuity that flows between the seemingly separate aspects of your design. The combined interplay between your definition (the true self) and your openness (the not-self) form the foundation for understanding the ways you will live out your design. Awareness of both who you are designed to be, and where you are open to taking in the outside world, allows you to have the fullest experience of life, and to authentically live out your unique purpose as a part of a greater totality.

CREATING A CONNECTION CHART

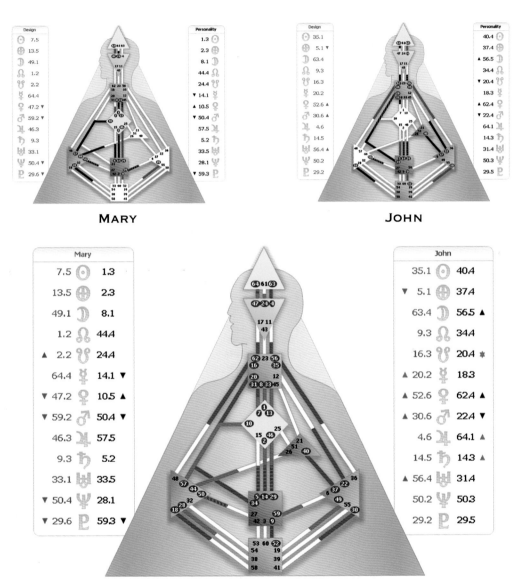

MARY

JOHN

COMBINED CHARTS

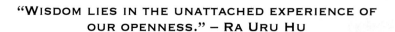

"WISDOM LIES IN THE UNATTACHED EXPERIENCE OF OUR OPENNESS." – RA URU HU

Section Two
The Nine Centers
The Flow of Energy

SECTION TWO

THE NINE CENTERS

THE FLOW OF ENERGY

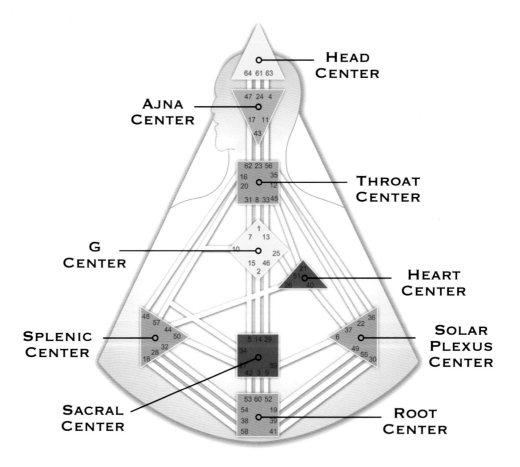

The nine centers are energy hubs that transform or transmute the life force as it flows through the BodyGraph. The overview on the opposite page will introduce you to each of the nine centers by name, its distinguishing function(s), and its location within the BodyGraph.

Please note that the Root and the Solar Plexus Centers each appear in two categories. Each of the nine centers will be covered in more detail later in this section.

ONE MANIFESTATION CENTER: "All roads lead to Rome." The Throat Center establishes the context for our discussion of the nine centers. Its extraordinary and unique function is similar to that of a town square. All energy is being moved through the other eight centers toward the Throat, where it is given a 'voice' as a means to physically manifest and/or verbally communicate our human intelligence. The Throat Center is how we express precisely what it means to be a differentiated human being at the top of the food chain.

TWO PRESSURE CENTERS: The Head and Root Centers are two pressure sources that move the energy toward the three awareness centers. They are the pressures to 'know' and to 'do,' to think and to stay alive. The Head asks the question which moves the energy on to the Ajna to conceptualize the answer. Root pressure provides the adrenalized drive to survive, the momentum for moving life forward. This fuel is a potent energy which is further refined by the Splenic, Solar Plexus and Sacral Centers on its way to the Throat where it will be communicated or acted upon.

THREE AWARENESS CENTERS: The Splenic, Ajna, and Solar Plexus Centers are three potential areas of self-consciousness and self-awareness. Each focuses and interprets our life experiences energetically as body, mind or spirit awareness. (The other six centers function at a mechanical level.) Upon reaching the Throat, the energy becomes an expression of our conscious intelligence: either as Splenic intelligence (survival awareness) or as mental intelligence (cognitive awareness) or as emotional/spirit intelligence (relational/social awareness).

FOUR MOTOR (ENERGY) CENTERS: The Root, Solar Plexus, Sacral and Heart Centers are motors; specific frequencies that provide us with the energy resources needed to manifest our life. The Root provides us with momentum to keep going. The emotional wave of the Solar Plexus provides us with the impetus of desire for more experience, for intimacy in relationships, and for spirit awareness. In the Sacral we have the creative life force, the generative energy to support the continuation of the species. The Heart is the motor energy behind the "I, me, mine," the source of our willpower. It insures our survival on the material plain through communal hierarchies.

ONE IDENTITY CENTER: The G Center is home to the Magnetic Monopole. Strategically located in the BodyGraph as the center of the Mandala, it establishes our identity as a direction through time in space called our geometry. This is where our own unique energy flow or definition connects to the flow of all life – or how we are wired to the Universe. The Magnetic Monopole pulls our life toward us. We might say the universe lives life through us.

DEFINED AND UNDEFINED CENTERS

It is common in most people's BodyGraph to have some of the centers defined or colored in and some open or white. The centers that are defined are considered fixed, meaning they project a reliable and consistent energy through the aura that is unique and recognizable. The white centers are not broken, they are not empty, and they don't need mending. They are places where we are most vulnerable to influences from outside of ourselves, which makes them valuable learning centers. As students of life, the open centers become for us the greatest source of our education and our maturing wisdom. Since most of us are made up of a combination of defined and undefined centers, it is important to accept that one is not better than the other. The process of living into ourselves is one of recognizing where we are available to take in conditioning from others, how conditioning affects us, and how to put it in its proper context. What we call wisdom is achieving a working understanding that allows us to interact with the world around us, the school of life, without losing our center or our direction.

UNDEFINED CENTER CONDITIONING AND
THE NOT-SELF MIND

When we transitioned from 7-centered to 9-centeredness in 1781, the strategic (decision-making) role of the mind shifted from directing our lives to becoming a source of wisdom and outer authority for others. The mind still insists on doing what it has done for thousands of years – it does not grasp

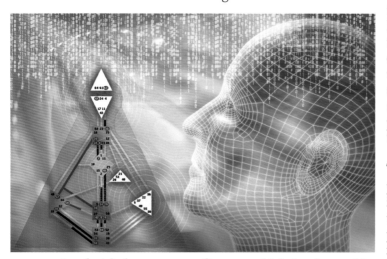

the fact that its job description has changed, which creates tension between our form and our mind, as well as between the true self and the not-self. Our incredible minds are not capable of being the personal Authority of our new 9-centered form.

The Personality Crystal (or passenger consciousness) is invited into the fetus during the last three months of pregnancy after our body is fully formed. The passenger gets acquainted with the neocortex of its new vehicle, but has nothing directly to do with creating any part of the form or body. Without something specific to do, the passenger decides to take on the job of back-seat driver, without a license. From its lofty position in the Head Center, it thinks it is best equipped to run the show, your life.

There are two significant details, however, that the passenger mind isn't aware of. The first is that you already have a driver, your Magnetic Monopole. The second is that your vehicle has recently evolved to a level of sophistication and consciousness that far exceeds the mind. That is to say, the mind reached its zenith in the 7-centered being, having guided humanity to an unprecedented level of consciousness and scientific achievement. However, after 1781, our forms took an evolutionary leap, and our bodies now have nine functioning centers with a built-in connection to a trustworthy, individualized compass.

We each have our own GPS, and it is hard-wired to the universe. Our mind can no longer compete successfully in decision-making with this new 9-centered form or body that it is joined to, but does not understand. Undeterred by these facts, the mind continues doing what it has always done – it tries to direct your life. This does not make our mind an enemy to be overcome, repressed, or ignored, but rather a creative force that is here to be reckoned with and befriended. Our mind's designated role, for which it is perfectly suited, is to think and to dream, to inspire and to formulate, and to make sense out of life. The mind is an amazing gift when freed from decision-making, and used in service to humanity. The mind is meant to be a tool for us, and a potential teacher for others. What stops that from happening is our ignorance about the mechanics of how we are designed to operate. By making our mind an ally, and liberating it from the task of decision-making so that it can settle comfortably into its role as a self-reflected conscious observer, we allow our mind to reveal its true treasures and make its rightful contribution.

From birth, we are continuously in the auric fields of our mother, father, siblings, relatives and others. Our undefined or open channels, gates, and centers are constantly being defined or energetically filled in by the definition of others. Over time, we are subtly but deeply influenced by their energy fields – as well as by their growing expectations of us. This is what The Human Design System describes as conditioning. Although we never lose touch with who we really are, by the time we have reached seven years of age, several layers of familial and societal conditioning have been piled over our true selves.

Conditioning cannot be circumvented or escaped, nor is it inherently a bad thing. It is simply unavoidable. Planetary transits, people, and all life forms, including insects, birds, animals and plants, connect to us and can influence our thought patterns, our behavior and our decisions, especially if we are not grounded in our design through our Strategy and Authority. Throughout our life, the natural curiosity of our open centers attracts us to people with definition in those centers. Absorbing their frequencies, however, puts pressure on our openness and triggers our mind into thinking about all we are missing.

The open spaces in our chart are referred to as the source of our not-self simply because they are energetically inconsistent and unreliable. It is when we begin to confuse what we experience through our openness (that which is not us) with our defined self or true self (that which is consistent within us) that we run into problems. The Human Design System carefully scrutinizes where we are open to the impact of conditioning and distinguishes it from our definition. It shows us that, by following our Strategy and Authority, we are thoroughly and uniquely equipped to face and resolve the dilemmas arising from our not-self constructs.

Our undefined centers are open to stimulation, and are literally designed to draw us into life. When we use our mind to make decisions, however, our open centers become part of what is called our not-self mind. Since that which is reliable and consistent about us is not really interesting to our busy mind, what is open or undefined becomes a source of deep attraction. It is what we long for, what we feel drawn to experience, and what we think we have to have or want to be. Unfortunately, the seduction of this attraction can lead us away from our core nature, which is why we do not often live out our own unique potential. The problem is that when we try to be what we are not designed to be, everything gets distorted; we become lost, caught up in chasing after what constantly eludes us in our life. Basing decisions on ever-changing and illusive desires – on what is not consistently us – is like trying to build a house on shifting sand. Eventually, a false assumption begins to grow that this IS our life. The result is a sense of fatigue and failure, along with frustration, bitterness, anger, and disappointment with life.

In the early years of your life, your passenger-mind thought its decisions were protecting you and your vehicle from being overcome, or hurt, by the experiences coming through your open and vulnerable places. Your mind got caught up in your body's innate fears for its physical, mental and emotional well-being; its need for security, love and support. Those fears were amplified many times in your open centers, so your mind developed a hyper-vigilance to your environment. It used how others responded or reacted to you to keep you compromising your true self, always comparing yourself to other's expectations and needs of you. It drove you to conform in order to fit in, and to make life comfortable for you and for those around you. And it worked – for a while. There were even rewarding trade-offs, but in the end you paid a price.

Each decision we make in life either keeps us on our path or takes us on a confusing and sometimes painful detour; either moves us closer to or further away from our true nature and purpose. Correct decisions made from our personal Authority, from that which is defined in us that we can trust, align us with our destiny, and place us in relationships, locations and jobs that are correct for us. Decisions made by our mind, and based on conditioning from our undefined centers, cause us to veer from our course. When this happens we find ourselves confronted by situations we are not equipped to deal with, making commitments that drain our energy and inhibit the use of our true talents.

Society places a huge emphasis on the mind, or mental awareness, and on making things happen. The conditioning pressure on us isn't going to go away anytime soon. Since we usually have more undefined spaces than definition in our chart, the vast complexity and amplification of our openness by the not-self mind easily exerts inordinate power over our lives. It is extremely difficult for our definition to stand up to the pressure coming through such openness, especially when half of our definition lies below our level of consciousness. Fortunately, our Strategy and Authority simply by-pass the illusory net of the mind's persuasions and allow the driver to drive. This is called surrender, the state of awareness we seek.

NOT-SELF OPEN CENTER QUESTIONS

The open centers in our BodyGraph reveal key vulnerable soft spots, and how our mind has used them to create its own decision-making strategy in an attempt to keep us from further confusion and pain. Over time, the mind's protective strategies become unhealthy habitual behaviors or unconscious habits that carry over into adulthood. Once you can see where the ineffective habits come from, and that they come from a space that is not you in the first place, it is much easier to let them go. As we begin to see just how easy it is to become lost in our openness and then identified with it, we also begin to see the undefined centers as the rich sources of exploration they are supposed to be. Through them come our most unexpected encounters, greatest discoveries and deepest insights, all joining together to become wisdom over time. With the knowledge that The Human Design System gives us about ourselves, we can begin to appreciate and enjoy our openness in a new way. Wisdom lies in the unattached experience of our openness. Every one of the undefined centers, channels and gates in our chart holds the potential for such wisdom.

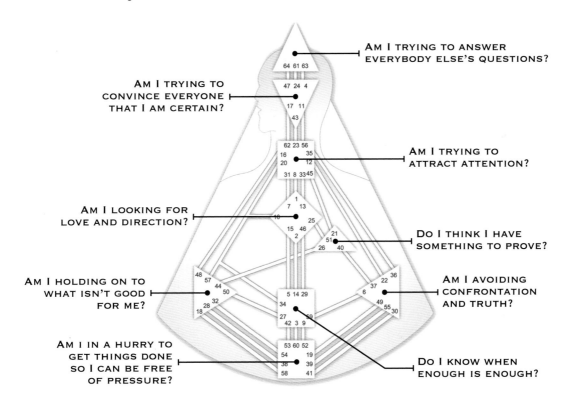

The illustration above lists the not-self mantras for each of the open centers. They are questions that we can ask ourselves to determine if we are operating from our true self or our not-self. We will explore each of these centers and their not-self constructs in more depth, however, taking time now to ask yourself the questions which apply to your open centers can be a most illuminating exercise, and an effective way to discover how subtle yet pervasive not-self conditioning can be.

THE NOT-SELF KEYNOTED IN A BODYGRAPH

Precise analysis of our BodyGraph allows us to literally map how we have been conditioned to think throughout our life, providing us with amazing details and insights into the workings of our mind. What we discover is a very strong and powerful link between our mind, early painful experiences

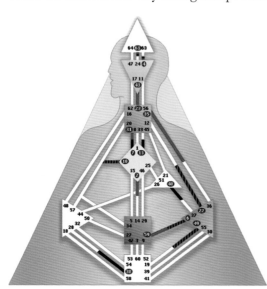

and our undefined centers. The chart example to the left has been keynoted to illustrate where this person has been most vulnerable to conditioning throughout her life. Beginning with the undefined Splenic Center, which is about security, she has been conditioned to hold onto things such as jobs, relationships, places and attitudes in order to feel safe. The undefined Spleen is concerned about survival; its easily aroused fears can cause one to stay in jobs and relationships long after they have ceased being healthy. Through the undefined Heart Center, she is conditioned to prove her worth – that she is good enough, sexy enough, loyal enough, pretty enough, smart enough and so on. She is prone to making promises that she does not have the willpower to keep, but tries (and fails) to keep them to prove how valuable she is, ultimately resulting in low self-worth. The undefined Head Center is a mind that is occupied with thinking thoughts that don't matter. Her mind is busily engaged in trying to resolve people's unanswered questions. With an undefined Root Center she feels pressure to hurry through things, and to get things done so she can move on to the next and get rid of the pressure.

The keynotes of her undefined centers create a picture of what her mind has been focused on, and basing her decisions on, most of her life. When we synthesize all this information into a sentence, we have a person afraid of losing her relationship or job security so she works very hard to get things done quickly, trying to resolve everyone's questions in order to prove how valuable she is.

If it is your path to move toward transformation and awareness, you will slowly but surely stop giving authority to your mind and surrender to the Authority of your form. You will let go of the mind's idea of what you should and shouldn't do, and what you think your life is supposed to be like. Though surrender is not a natural state for the mind, the mind can learn to surrender to your Strategy and Authority and assume its true position as an aware passenger and observer, having the ride of its life in a vehicle that knows exactly where to take it.

"RA URU HU IS NOT WHO I AM. RA IS SOMEBODY I WATCH. I'M NOT ATOMIC. I'M MADE OF DARK MATTER. THAT'S WHAT IS WATCHING. IT'S WATCHING THROUGH THE PRISM OF THE ATOMIC MEDIUM BECAUSE WITHOUT IT THE I AM IS FOREVER SILENT. THE PASSENGER THAT I AM THAT ISN'T ATOMIC CAN BE FREE IN LIFE INSTEAD OF DEATH. THAT'S THE POINT." – RA URU HU

DEFINED, UNDEFINED AND COMPLETELY OPEN CENTERS

The way our activated gates are configured within a center determines how the center operates, how it is experienced within us, and how it interacts with the environment and people around us.

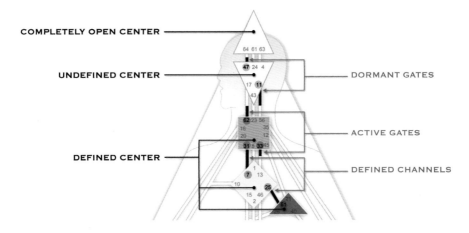

DEFINED CENTER: In the illustration above, when two gates at both ends of a channel come together they form a definition. Gates 7 and 31 form the Channel of The Alpha, defining the G and the Throat Centers, and Gates 51 and 25 form the Channel of Initiation, defining the Heart and G Centers. A defined center is a hub of consistent and reliable energy within us. Single gate activations in a defined center (Gates 33 and 62 in the example) are 'hanging gates' that dependably contribute their theme to the overall definition. Altogether, definition is the energy frequency of our differentiated self which is communicated to others through our presence.

UNDEFINED CENTER: The undefined or white centers are places of vulnerability where we are open to opportunities for learning, and to the influence of conditioning forces around us. An undefined center in a chart has one or more dormant gates. They can be unconscious (red) or conscious (black) aspects of our design. Dormant gates are alone in the channel; they hang out, waiting to be sparked by an electromagnetic connection, the gate at the other end of the channel. The dormant gate filters or directs the incoming energy toward the undefined center(s), making us more aware of its presence within us.

COMPLETELY OPEN CENTER: Though it shares many characteristics with the undefined center, the phenomenon of a completely open center is quite different. Without the presence of a dormant gate there is no familiar and consistent theme or feeling to hold on to which connects us to our self. Such openness can leave us confused, vulnerable to conditioning, and exposed to the amplification of information pouring through that center's energy field. Fortunately, the converse is also true. With no dormant gates in place to filter or prejudice incoming energy, we are open to the center's full potential for experiential learning which becomes a source of wisdom as we mature.

On the pages that follow we will explore each center's characteristics, how its energy plays out in your life, and its true self and not-self themes. Please refer to your Human Design Chart and follow along to discover the story of you.

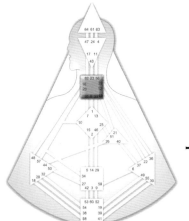

THROAT CENTER

COMMUNICATION AND MANIFESTATION
METAMORPHOSIS AND TRANSFORMATION THROUGH INTERACTION WITH THE WORLD

BIOLOGICAL CORRELATION

Biologically, the Throat Center is associated with the thyroid and the parathyroid glands. These are endocrine glands which are responsible for metamorphosis and transformation. The thyroid system oversees metabolic processes: how we assimilate our food, whether we digest it quickly or not, how we burn energy, whether we are fast or slow, whether we are big or small, skinny or fat. Resistance experienced from premature, unwelcome words and actions, or from speaking when we should be silent, can manifest in our physiology by compromising the health and well-being of our vocal chords and thyroid function.

MANIFESTATION AS COMMUNICATION AND/OR ACTION

Key physiological changes in the location and structure of the larynx, with a concurrent development of the neocortex, have shaped the evolution of our species for the past 85,000 years, resulting in our capacity to express a self-reflected consciousness. These changes made it possible to fully manifest what it means to be human, both through verbal communication and as deliberate action. Whether defined in our BodyGraph or not, the Throat Center plays a central role in how we express our self as well as how we manifest our life vocationally. Even though its function is purely mechanical and unaware, the Throat Center remains a major focus within the BodyGraph.

If we think of the BodyGraph as the map of a town, the Throat Center would be the town square. As the central and most complex of the nine centers, all energy flowing through the BodyGraph is under tremendous pressure to get to the Throat to be communicated or acted upon. The phrase, "All roads lead to Rome," sums it up quite nicely. The energy flowing through the BodyGraph is metabolized and transformed within the body itself through the related biological processes of this center.

The Throat Center's *primary function* is manifestation through communication, expressing who we are, what we are thinking, feeling, creating or learning, what we know or want to contribute, and what we have seen or heard and can say to empower others. With its manifesting potential and 11 gates or voices, the Throat naturally attracts a lot of attention that is designed to set the stage for manifestation. We are not designed to be alone or isolated from each other. Our ability to communicate effectively ensures the quality of our relationships, and therefore, our survival. Language and communication are not about telling others what to do. They are about how to manifest or make ourselves known to others in unique ways so they can respond to or interact with what we are saying and doing. Through communicating before acting, we can see beforehand what is viable and what isn't.

Our own voice comes from specific gate activations or channel definition in our BodyGraph. Any center in our design connected to our Throat Center has a direct outlet through that channel, and this is where our own consistent and reliable voice (and/or action) comes from. It is so important that our words and actions count, for they are our truth. What an invaluable gift it is to be able to trust our Authority for guidance, and our Strategy for the correct timing to manifest it.

With so much pressure on the Throat Center to speak and to do, many people are prone to act or to say things either too soon or too late. By knowing our voice(s) and what we are here to express or to do – as well as which gates are open to amplification – we can relax and wait for the proper moment to engage others in ways that are correct and fulfilling for us. The Golden Rule of the Throat Center is "Follow your Strategy and Authority and the timing will always be perfect." This way our words and actions will be received with their full impact, without resistance and confusion or distortion.

The Throat Center's *secondary function* is manifestation as action. Manifestation is possible when a motor is connected to the Throat. Those with this kind of definition are true doers who can set things in motion, and bring to completion what they envision. Of note: Manifesting Generators (defined from the Sacral motor to the Throat) are the exception as they follow a Generator Strategy of waiting to respond, not initiating. These distinctions are further elaborated upon in Section Four on Types.

Society, as well as the not-self, places tremendous demands on us to become something, to make a contribution with our life, such as choosing a job or vocation. The ability to grow into who we are designed to be, however, is totally dependent on uncovering our authentic self – and living it.

The Throat Center's strategic position in the BodyGraph, and its metamorphic function in the body, make it a natural place for directing and effecting transformative, mutative change at all levels of living. The specific frequencies or gates activated in the Throat Center on our chart indicate just how the changes needed to further our transformation and evolve humanity will be expressed and moved along through us.

The gates of the Throat Center are listed on the next page.

Gates of the Throat Center

Gate 62 - The Preponderance of the Small The Gate of Detail	I think or not Communicating the detail and facts
Gate 23 - Splitting Apart The Gate of Assimilation	I know or not Communicating individual insights
Gate 56 - The Wanderer The Gate of Stimulation	I believe or not The stimulating storyteller
Gate 16 - Enthusiasm The Gate of Skills	I experiment/identify or not To skillfully master something
Gate 20 - Contemplation The Gate of the Now	I am now or not Instantaneous clarity/action
Gate 31 - Influence The Gate of Influence	I lead or not The influential elected leader
Gate 8 - Holding Together The Gate of Contribution	I can make a contribution or not Unique self expression
Gate 33 - Retreat The Gate of Privacy	I remember or not Sharing lessons of the past
Gate 35 - Progress The Gate of Change	I experience/feel or not Progress through experience
Gate 12 - Standstill The Gate of Caution	I know I can try or not Socially cautious
Gate 45 - Gathering Together The Gate of the Gatherer	I have or not The king/queen leading through education

The Defined Throat Center — 72% of the population

Although we assume when we speak that we are expressing the thoughts of our mind, what we communicate is actually determined by the 11 themes of the gates in the Throat Center. The Throat is the energy hub for 'messages' coming from all parts of the BodyGraph; it transmutes and directs how that information manifests in the world as communication and action.

Potentially, the Throat can express or act directly from six different centers: the Ajna, Solar Plexus, Heart, G, Sacral and Spleen. The healthy Throat Center speaks from its reliable source of definition. For example, a Throat connected to the Heart Center speaks from the 'I' as in "I want that, I have that, I will do that." If the Throat is connected to the Ajna, one speaks what the mind is thinking and conceptualizing. If the Throat is connected to the Solar Plexus, one speaks or acts on emotions or feelings. If the Throat is connected to the Spleen, one speaks spontaneously from an intuitive knowing in the moment. If the Throat is directly connected to the Sacral, one speaks and acts on the responsive sounds of the Sacral. If the Throat is connected to the G center, one speaks from personal identity and direction, from the higher self. Therefore, the mark of a defined Throat is the consistent but limited way it reliably expresses itself.

Those with a Throat Center defined to a motor can always 'do' or manifest, but it does not mean they always should! Having a Throat Center connected to a motor can fuel the urge to be impulsive, to succumb to the tendency to talk too much or do too much, and to give energy away to every impulse. When they confidently and comfortably rely on their Strategy and Authority, and know where their voice comes from and when to use it, people with defined Throat Centers can manifest their truth with ease, honesty and clarity.

THE UNDEFINED THROAT CENTER – 28% OF THE POPULATION

The not-self theme of the undefined Throat Center is "Trying to attract attention." People with undefined Throat Centers are afraid they won't be noticed, so their not-self mind jumps at the chance to think up ways to attract attention. They can easily succumb to an amplified pressure to talk, to act, to make an impression, to interrupt or to be the life of the party. They don't realize that the open Throat naturally attracts attention, and if they wait, invitations to speak will come to them. In this way, they will receive the proper attention, at the most opportune time, with no need to waste precious energy doing or saying something to move the process along – as long as their Authority agrees that they do have something to say that needs to be said. By reducing the urgent pressure they feel to speak, they reduce stress on their vocal chords.

If the amplified pressure to speak that they experience in their undefined Throat Center has been conditioned by someone else's Throat definition, what they say will be unpredictable and probably poorly received by others. Over time, they can become fearful of opening their mouths. Feeling out of control and unable to communicate effectively can be most disturbing in our highly verbal culture. This is remedied by those with open Throat Centers gaining confidence in their Strategy and Authority to guide their conversations, and learning to understand the way(s) this center functions at a mechanical level in their design.

When around others with a defined Throat Center, they may feel uncomfortable and end up doing most of the talking just to relieve the extra pressure. They also spend a lot of mental energy figuring out what they are going to say next, only to be surprised and perhaps uncomfortable when they say something completely unexpected. The dilemma is that they cannot plan what they say with any consistency.

The healthiest approach for open Throats is to stop trying to control what they say; they are designed to speak spontaneously and to enjoy the different voices or forms of expression that come through them. They understand that they do not need to 'do' anything to attract attention. Though they feel the pressure to speak when they are with others, they are relaxed and comfortable with their natural state of silence. They know that if they wait, the invitation and proper timing to participate will present itself. Their wisdom is recognizing who is speaking and acting from their truth – or not.

If not comfortably oriented by their Strategy and Authority, they can become preoccupied with the questions, "How can I attract attention?" or "What am I going to become in life?" Trying to figure these out mentally only leads to poorly timed decisions and abortive actions, putting pressure on their thyroid glands.

THE COMPLETELY OPEN THROAT CENTER

A completely open Throat is most rare as the Throat Center has 11 potential activations. People with this open configuration have no idea what to say, or what action to take. For example, children with an undefined Throat Center may take longer to learn to talk, and should be encouraged to speak at their own pace. When the not-self in either children or adults dictates how and when to attract attention, talk and act, they will find themselves speaking with a voice 'borrowed' or conditioned by someone else. The result is saying the wrong thing at the wrong time, or being ignored altogether. The resistance they meet builds over time, affecting both their self-confidence and their thyroid function.

Once they are comfortable with the flexibility and unpredictability of their speaking, and confident in their Authority's guidance, the considerable wisdom potential of this center emerges. Among other things, they will know who articulates well and who is speaking with authenticity from their own journey.

NOT-SELF TALK OF THE UNDEFINED THROAT CENTER

The not-self mind is the spokesperson for the undefined centers, and tells us what we should say or do. Noticing this talk is essential to deconditioning. Here are some examples of what the not-self mental dialog could sound like with an undefined Throat Center: Where should I go so that I can get the attention I want? Is anyone noticing me? If I say this then I will be noticed. If I initiate this conversation then I will get the attention I deserve. I better say something because this silence is making me uncomfortable. What should I manifest? I better manifest something. What or who will I become in life?

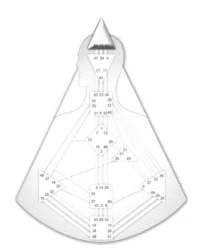

HEAD CENTER

Mental Pressure
Inspiration
Questions, Doubts
and Confusion

Biological Correlation

Biologically, the Head Center is associated with our pineal gland which regulates the flow of information between the gray areas of the brain and the neocortex, or between the Head and the Ajna Centers. More than 90 percent of mental processes take place deep within the gray areas of the brain, below our level of conscious awareness, and everything that is processed by our brain is filtered through accumulated past experience. This creates a pressure that manifests as questions seeking answers, or the need to know the 'whys' of life. It fuels or drives our thinking and conceptualizing, and how we process the consciousness field.

Mental Pressure and Inspiration

As above – so below. At the top of the BodyGraph is the Head Center with its mental pressure, understood as inspiration. At the bottom is the Root Center with its adrenalized pressure, understood as stress. The Head Center functions as the pressure to comprehend, to think, and to make sense of things in the world. It's pressure moves our thoughts toward conceptualization in the Ajna Center by pushing our questions toward formulas and opinions, our pondering toward clarification and insight, and our confusion toward realization and ideas – and then on to the Throat Center where they are transformed into language. Human Design refers to this pressure as inspiration, the ways we have of taking in information from the cosmic field of consciousness.

The inspiration of the Head Center is not a motorized energy that leads to action, but rather a pressure that drives our mental activity. It stimulates our imagination, our unique mode of thinking (Head) and conceptualizing (Ajna), and initiates our everyday, mundane thoughts as well as our most lofty and probing questions about the mysteries of existence. Quite simply, this is the pressure to ask questions, and expect answers, that we experience throughout our day.

Our Head Center pressures or directs mental activity to the Ajna along three channels that represent three time frames. It formulates questions focused on securing our future (Gate 63); it takes in and processes what is new and worth pondering in the moment (Gate 61); and it begins sorting through the sometimes confusing muddle of past experience to find its meaning (Gate 64). This routing is crucial to setting the three sources of inspiration in motion, and decoding them so that they arrive at the Throat with their maximum potential to impact and communicate still intact. This questioning curiosity of the intellect, the mind's extraordinary gift to penetrate the unknowable, to make sense of life and to be an inspiration for others, is here to be enjoyed as a source of never-ending wonder.

Each decision that liberates our mind from running our life, releases and refocuses the mind's tremendous creativity so it can make its essential contribution to the understanding, the evolution, and the quality of life on the planet. Unfortunately, when the not-self usurps the role of our personal Authority, the Head Center begins a stream of meaningless questions and thoughts about things that truly do not matter. This can become an incessant pressure to know that fills us with doubt and confusion, driving us further away from ourselves. If the pressure builds without release, it can result in severe headaches like migraines. Another consequence of letting our not-self distract the Head Center from its proper role is that we keep our mind from reaching its potential in our life as the true source of wisdom that it actually can be. It is from the Head Center that we learn about the nature of inspiration, how to experience the pressure without losing sight of the wonder, and how to recognize what/who is truly inspiring or not.

THE GATES OF THE HEAD CENTER

There are only three gates in the Head Center. The nature of the pressure and the theme of each gate establish its parameters and mode of inspiration. Pressure from the Head Center moves inspiration toward the Ajna for conceptualization and then on to the Throat to be communicated. The pressures described below nag at us until we let them go or find a way to resolve them.

Gate 64 - Before Completion The Gate of Confusion	Abstract pressure to make sense of the past, and to resolve the chaos and confusion
Gate 61 - Inner Truth The Gate of Mystery	Mutative pressure to know something new, to understand the mysteries, to know the unknowable
Gate 63 - After Completion The Gate of Doubt	Logical pressure to make sense of the pattern through doubt; looking for the logic or a new pattern

THE DEFINED HEAD CENTER - 30% OF THE POPULATION

Definition between the Head and Ajna Centers creates a consistent mental pressure to ask and to answer the question, and to grasp and to understand things, including consciousness itself. Dealing with the persistent pressure of inspiration is often difficult and can heighten mental anxiety, as inspiration is always about what has not yet been grasped; it merely frames the question. Those with defined Head Centers have a fixed way of thinking. The themes of their particular gates and channels become the subject or source of inspiration available to others. When they are part of a group, their auras put people with undefined Head Centers under pressure to think. Only 30 percent of the world's population has a defined Head Center, but they are capable of inspiring (or pressuring) the remaining 70 percent who do not.

The Head and Ajna Centers are not connected to one of the four motors, therefore, there is no energy for them to bring their thoughts and ideas directly into manifestation. Struggling to do so only leads to frustration, anger, bitterness or disappointment. By waiting for the opportune moment to motivate people with their stimulating questions and possibilities, such as people who can put the ideas to work, those with a defined Head and Ajna eliminate the resistance they meet when they impose their ideas on a world not yet prepared to act on them. That is to say, relying on their Strategy to determine the timing and receptivity of their audience will save them valuable energy, reduce anxiety, and increase their self-confidence. It is natural for those with defined Head and Ajna Centers to feel under continual pressure to resolve their thought process, to understand their own inspiration, and answer their own questions. If, however, they succumb to impatience with this persistently unresolved state, and turn the mental pressure inward on themselves, they can experience deep anxiety, self-doubt and depression. If they attempt to relieve the pressure by turning it outward into action, the result is usually a hasty, incorrect decision, and a missed opportunity to be a true inspiration. The challenge is to accept the mental pressure without trying to act on it or escape it. Confusion, doubt, and clarity are natural processes that have their own inner timing and resolution. Under the guidance of one's Authority, they become qualities which stimulate thought-provoking questions, and a wide array of answers capable of uplifting, inspiring and empowering others.

THE UNDEFINED HEAD CENTER - 70% OF THE POPULATION

Those with an undefined Head Center have no consistent way of deliberating mental information. If normal inspiration becomes an amplified pressure to think about things that don't matter, they can get lost in their own mental monologue. Meaningless not-self thoughts and questions will ultimately steer them away from correct decision-making processes. As anxiety increases, they may seek to assuage it by looking for someone or something inspiring to focus on. Undefined Head Centers tend to either avoid intellectual pursuits, or throw themselves into one mystery after another. They are easily caught up with trying to make decisions and solve problems that are not even their own, becoming lost or overwhelmed by doubt and confusion which actually belongs to someone else. Pressure to resolve other people's questions as soon as possible weighs them down, making it difficult to empty all the 'stuff' out of their heads so they can relax, which puts even more pressure on their minds to try and figure things out, to answer their unending questions. Since they can't solve their problems with the same not-self mind that created them, the key to emerging out of this swirl of confusion and doubt is to bypass the mentally busy undefined Head Center by relying on their Authority to guide them. The secret to maintaining mental health is to refuse to act out of mental pressure by remaining a detached observer of their thoughts, and letting their Authority direct them to appropriate ways of using their minds.

The real potential of the undefined Head Center is to wonder and explore the mystery of life, human consciousness, and the intellectual possibilities of an infinite range of subjects. It can discern which inspiration is worthy of contemplation and how much of the mental field is simply a distraction – who is inspiring and who is confusing. People with open Head Centers can use the information that they take in from others to become great reflectors of what other's are thinking, and help discern the value of these thoughts for humanity. They are open to new insights, and love to be filled with inspiration and ideas from all directions. They enjoy the pressure to know more without becoming identified with or overwhelmed by it. When experiencing confusion or doubt, they let go of the compulsive need to resolve it because they know it will pass. Ultimately, they can be open to the beauty and depth of the unknown, and enjoy both the question and the confusion while trusting that things will become clear, or not; whichever is correct for them.

THE COMPLETELY OPEN HEAD CENTER

Those without gate activations in the Head Center have no innate way of recognizing when one thing is more inspiring or interesting than any other. There is no consistent means of connecting mental pressure to the rest of their design, or to naturally ease them into a familiar way of thinking about things or entering into dialogue with another person. They don't know what to focus on, especially in this overwhelming age of information. They simply don't know what to think about, what matters or doesn't matter, or why, and often fear thinking about anything at all. Such anxiety can lead to disconnecting from their intellect and avoiding conversations that are intellectually stimulating. Or, they can become easily distracted by the pressure to think up answers, or give away their Authority by relying on others to tell them what is interesting, inspiring or important. In order to enjoy their healthy and boundless capacity for wisdom, and to understand the pressure behind the question and discern what is inspiring, completely open Head Centers need to allow the often amplified mental pressure they experience to pass through without identifying with any part of it. As they become comfortable with themselves over time, they become sensitive to the nuances of the Head Center and its true gifts, and can gauge who uses their minds effectively, and who does not. They may even be sensitive enough to ascertain what others are thinking. In this way, deep explorations into all that their mind can inspire will fill them with wonder.

NOT-SELF TALK OF THE UNDEFINED HEAD CENTER

The not-self mind is the spokesperson for the undefined centers, and tells us what we should say or do. Noticing this not-self talk is essential to deconditioning. Here are some examples of what the not-self mental monolog could sound like with an undefined Head Center: I need to find something inspiring. Maybe if I go there I'll find something inspiring. I need to find an answer to my questions. Where can I go to find the answers? Who has the answers? I've got to understand this and/or make sense of this. Where can I go or whom can I talk to in order to find the answers? Is this supposed to be interesting? What should I be thinking about?

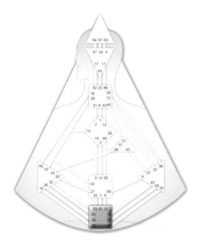

ROOT CENTER

PHYSICAL ADRENALIZED PRESSURE TO SUSTAIN MOMENTUM FOR LIVING, STRESS

BIOLOGICAL CORRELATION

Biologically, the Root Center is associated with the adrenal system and the production of stress hormones. Stress, as understood in the context of this center, is merely a fuel. It energizes certain biochemical processes deep within us that are designed to help us master the situations we meet in life, and sustain our momentum to progress and evolve. Stress cannot be avoided, nor can we fight against this vital fuel without paying the consequences. If we do not understand the mechanics of this pressure on our body, we can easily push ourselves too hard. If we turn this pressure inward, we can become depressed and suffer deeply. One by-product of maintaining a healthy balance between too much and too little stress is a sense of vitality that spills over as joy for living.

ADRENAL PRESSURE (FUEL) AND MOTOR ENERGY

Both the Head and Root Centers are sources of pressure, or fuel, which drive energy towards the Throat for communication or manifestation. This similarity gives these two centers a deep and inherent connection to each other. While the Head Center brings mental pressure in the form of doubt, confusion, and inspiration, the Root Center brings the pressure and fuel to evolve, to adapt to the world, and to get us through our most difficult challenges. It provides us with our purest and most powerful energy and momentum to keep life moving forward.

Unlike the Head Center, however, the Root Center is unique in that it is both a pressure center and a motor. Nine different life processes are fueled by energy that originates in the Root Center. They ultimately make their way to the Throat Center, but only after this powerful fuel that moves them along is processed or tempered by passing through the centers around it: the Sacral, Spleen, or Solar Plexus. The Root's pressurized or adrenalized energy is far too strong to be directly connected to and manifested by the Throat Center.

GATES OF THE ROOT CENTER

Gate 58 - The Joyous The Gate of Vitality	Pressure to correct and perfect, to make things better
Gate 38 - Opposition The Gate of the Fighter	Pressure to find or struggle for purpose in life
Gate 54 - The Marryng Maiden The Gate of Drive	Pressure to achieve, to rise up, to transform
Gate 53 - Development The Gate of Beginnings	Pressure to begin, to start new things
Gate 60 - Limitation The Gate of Acceptance	Pressure to mutate, to transcend limitation
Gate 52 - Keeping Still (Mountain) The Gate of Inaction	Pressure to focus your energy, to concentrate
Gate 19 - Approach The Gate of Wanting	Pressure to be sensitive to basic needs
Gate 39 - Obstruction The Gate of the Provocation	Pressure to find the passion and spirit in life, Pressure to emote
Gate 41 - Decrease The Gate of Contraction	Pressure to feel, the desire for a new experience

Root pressure literally gets the body moving, and is an essential ingredient of manifestation in our lives. How we direct the stress, which by itself is neither good nor bad, is determined by our own unique Root Center configuration (the specific gates that are defined or undefined).

THE DEFINED ROOT CENTER – 60% OF THE POPULATION

A defined Root Center has a fixed and particular way of dealing with stress, and the pressure to move ahead in the world. The Root can be defined to three different centers: the Sacral, Spleen, and Solar Plexus.

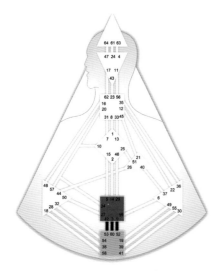

The three connections or channels between the Root Center and the Sacral Center (in the illustration to the left) are called Format Energies. They dictate whether the way we operate in the world is logical and focused, cyclical and developmental, or unpredictable and mutative. Those with the logical format energy (the Channel of Concentration 52-9) live life in a step-by-step logical, detailed and organized way; those with the abstract format energy (the Channel of Maturation 53-42) live life in multiple experiential cycles with distinct beginnings, middles and ends; and those with the individual format energy (the Channel of Mutation 60-3) live life with on and off power bursts of mutating energy. These Format Energies powerfully permeate the entire design of those who have them, and have a significant influence on people that come in contact with them.

In order to stay healthy and thrive in the material world, those who have the Root Center defined to the Splenic Center are able to rely on their fixed way of dealing with the pressure to survive, move up, and correct what isn't working. In this way, the Root fuels existential awareness and survival consciousness, including the joy of being alive in a body.

One who has the Root Center defined to the Solar Plexus Center will have a fixed way of dealing with emotional stress, with what is new and desirable, and with personal and social relationships. This is pressure fueling emotional awareness or emotional/relational intelligence.

It is possible for people with defined Root Centers to also succumb to not-self stress. If the powerful pressure they feel all the time is not properly guided by their Strategy and Authority, they can become obsessive. They go about their life initiating, and thus meet resistance in the form of the wrong kind of stress which is detrimental to their health. Their tendency is to project this pressure or stress onto others in the form of unreasonable expectations.

Once they are comfortable with their own consistent internal pressure, they can be alert to times when people with an undefined Root Center are allowing unhealthy levels of magnified Root pressure to drive them. As long as they begin something out of their Strategy and Authority, and a place of stillness and joy, then no matter how challenging or stress-filled their endeavors, they will remain grounded in their Root Center's sustaining energy.

THE UNDEFINED ROOT CENTER – 40% OF THE POPULATION

The undefined Root Center absorbs stress from its environment. People with an undefined Root are subject to pressures from those with a defined Root. Because the amplified pressure is uncomfortable, they are always trying to get rid of it, yet as soon as they do another pressure takes its place. They rush around and accomplish the work of three people, trying to resolve pressure that cannot be resolved. It's an endless, unsustainable cycle that eventually results in burn out.

Undefined Roots take in and amplify the adrenalized Root Center stress in the world, but are not equipped to sustain that level of momentum for long. Over time, this kind of conditioning can become hyperactivity, uncontrollable restlessness and an inability to focus. Children often pay the biggest price. When the amplification of energy from others through their open Root Center is misunderstood as misbehavior or uncooperativeness or mental deficiency, they are usually punished, humiliated, or referred to therapists. Think about all the children with open Root Centers who have been given drugs to calm them down. Understanding the overall mechanics of a child's design makes it possible to explore new ways of working with these energy dynamics, without damaging our children.

Most people operate without awareness and allow outside pressures to drive them. When adults or children with undefined Root Centers begin to understand that the pressure they feel is not their own, they can find ways to avoid being overwhelmed by it. Basically, there are two things they can do when experiencing stress. One is to step away and avoid it while taking deep breaths to release some of the pent-up pressure, and the other is to take advantage of the adrenalized energy. For example, an on-stage performer with an undefined Root Center can be empowered by the adrenaline rush from an enthusiastic audience. The opposite reaction to a huge shot of external adrenaline is paralyzing fear or stage fright. Living off the adrenalized pressure can become a habit, or an addiction, leaving one vulnerable to all sorts of health issues and accidents.

When operating correctly, undefined Root Centers wait for their Authority to guide their decisions. They do not judge themselves to be lazy or incompetent if they fail to work quickly, or simply refuse to. They can distinguish between healthy and unhealthy environmental pressure and are not addicted to either – they simply recognize them for what they are. They know when to use the pressure correctly to increase their productivity, and when not to. They give themselves the time needed to actually enjoy completing a task once it has been properly committed to.

The wisdom to be gained from the undefined Root Center comes when they no longer identify with or are lost to the habits of their conditioning. At that point they are able to observe how stress functions, and to discern how to use it properly. They know when it is healthy to take advantage of the adrenalized pressure and when to avoid it. The key is to recognize what pressure belongs to them and what does not.

THE COMPLETELY OPEN ROOT CENTER

Those with completely open Root Centers can experience the full range of its pressure, from the deep stillness of focused concentration to intense hyperactivity, but they don't understand it. When they are not paying attention to their Authority, they tend to operate unconsciously, allowing amplified adrenal pressure and incorrect mental decisions to push them through life. They automatically answer the phone, say yes, speed up, become accident prone, and hurry through things so they can be free of the pressure, all the while believing this is the way to live. Because they neither understand nor recognize the pressure, or the fact that it is amplified and not their own, they don't know how to use it productively. Their system cannot sustain that level of amplified pressure or momentum for long and will eventually collapse in on itself. Examples would be extreme cases of stage fright, or panic attacks where they cannot move forward at all in the moment, or move on with their life. They can lose their joy of being alive.

Nature is a place of peace for them, a respite and peaceful buffer zone from the stressors of the demanding, fast-paced world we live in. Once they have let the pressure that is not their own pass through them, and their system is quieted, they can re-connect with a comfortable and livable level of pressure within themselves. By using their Strategy and Authority, they maintain a healthy and productive balance between the pressure that moves life forward, and the pressure to be still. Peace, patience and balance are then possible, along with the wisdom to clearly see and evaluate the nature and effects of this fundamental yet often overwhelming stress on individuals and humanity.

NOT-SELF TALK OF THE UNDEFINED ROOT CENTER

The not-self mind is the spokesperson for the undefined centers, and tells us what we should say or do. Noticing this talk is essential to deconditioning. Here are some examples of what the not-self mental monolog could sound like with an undefined Root Center: What am I going to do to make my life better? Where is my purpose? I have to achieve something in my life. I better hurry up and get this done. I have to start something new now. How can I get past this limitation? What am I going to focus on? I need something to focus on. I need to be needed. Who needs me? Where can I go to be needed? Where is my passion? What am I passionate about? I feel like a new experience. I have to hurry up and initiate a new experience. I don't want to waste any time. I have to get this done.

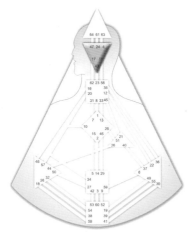

AJNA CENTER

MENTAL CONSCIOUSNESS
CONCEPTUALIZING,
INTERPRETING
ANSWERS AS OPINIONS,
CONCEPTS, AND THEORIES

BIOLOGICAL CORRELATION

Three biological functions are associated with the Ajna Center: the neocortex, the visual cortex and the pituitary glands. The tiny anterior and posterior pituitary glands, located at the base of the brain, act as our body's maintenance headquarters. They send hormonal messages to the thyroid glands with instructions that keep us alive, on track and functioning optimally. These master glands of the endocrine system are intimately connected to all parts of our body, and it is not surprising that for eons we have lived a mind-dominated life. Although the pituitaries still oversee our entire system, the body's overall level of conscious awareness has evolved, and the role of the mind has shifted.

MENTAL AWARENESS, THE MIND AND DECISION MAKING

Of the nine centers in our BodyGraph, three are Awareness Centers: the Spleen (Body Consciousness), with its body and survival intelligence, the Ajna (Mind Consciousness), with its mental intelligence, and the Solar Plexus (Spirit Consciousness), with its emotional intelligence and emerging spirit awareness. It is through these awareness centers that we become conscious of our experience of being alive, and in relationship with others. The other six centers are purely mechanical, operating below our conscious level of awareness.

The Head and Ajna Centers function together as the mind. The Ajna Center is a processing hub, transforming the pressure of inspiration from the Head Center, into useful information for review, research, and communication. The Ajna is merely an interpreter; like the Head, it cannot manifest. The Ajna, flanked by the Head and Throat Centers, is the only awareness center in the BodyGraph locked away from motor energy. The other two awareness centers do have access to motors; they can act out of their awareness. The Splenic Center is next to the Sacral and Root Centers, and the Solar Plexus, a motor itself, is next to the Root, Sacral, and Heart Centers. Mental awareness, which was the second awareness to evolve (Splenic awareness was the first), dominates the way we perceive our world today.

Our perceptions are derived from two major processes: one is visual and one is acoustic. The visual, associated with development of the visual cortex, is concerned with what has been and what might be. The acoustic is associated with pure inspiration and the pressure to know now.

The awareness frequency of the Ajna Center is different from that of the Splenic Center. Splenic awareness is existential, spontaneous, in the moment. The frequency of our mental process operates over all time. A decision made mentally has a long shelf life and can be mulled over until death! This means that any decision we make based on what is coming out of our openness will be lived over and over for the rest of our life. We will remain stuck in its illusory web. For example, if you make a decision from your not-self mind and it doesn't work, your mind will automatically suggest that you try another option. If that doesn't work, it will say you should have used yet another option. None of these options are correct for you, and none of them will work, ever. You have simply become trapped in a web of ineffectual suggestions and dead ends. Recognizing that the mind has no authority in your life is the only way to extricate yourself from confusion and disappointment, and from making incorrect mental decisions.

The mind measures or processes information in a dualistic 'this or that' manner – a valuable asset for simultaneously weighing two or more sides of any concept. The Ajna can look at the positives and the negatives of a decision, and construct two arguments that are opposite to each other. One argument says the option is bad 'because,' while the other says it's good 'because.' This is all the mind can do, however; it argues back and forth. It can neither judge nor know which is best. It simply determines how many sides of any issue there are to consider.

Imagine that you have had a misunderstanding with someone and you want to straighten it out. You want to talk to the person about it and get it off your chest. You can use your mind's analytical gifts to come up with lists on both sides of the argument, but don't call the person yet! Let your Strategy and Authority guide you as to when you are to speak and what you are to say, otherwise, you will replay that conversation over and over again. "Did I do the right thing? What if I had done it this way or said it that way?" Pain and regret, rather than resolution, are the consequences of poorly-timed reactions, simply because the dualistic mind cannot let go of the other side of any issue. We cannot know our own truth from this place of mental rationalization and comparison. Our truth must come from our personal Authority.

Awareness is the end result of successfully dealing with fear, and each awareness center has its own forms of fear to confront. The fear experienced by the Ajna Center is expressed as mental anxiety fed by the fear of not knowing something, or the fear of being misunderstood. Both fears are healthy when they drive us to better understand our ideas and communicate them clearly. When communication fails, however, the anxiety comes to the surface. How we deal with the anxiety will either lead to our mastery and awareness, or to a further heightening of the anxiety. Whether our Ajna is defined or undefined, we all carry these fears. They are magnified in the undefined Ajna.

The value of awareness, or mental intelligence, does not come from being in control, but rather from our ability to share and empower others with our unique perspective, at the right time and in the right place. We are here to encounter each other; to articulate our experience of being human; to enrich, educate, and store history for future generations; and to contemplate and explore life's possibilities.

Each gate in the Ajna Center carries a form of mental anxiety that alerts us to the possibility that we are succumbing to external expectations which thwart our awareness, and put our mental health in jeopardy.

GATES OF THE AJNA CENTER

Gate 47 - Oppression **The Gate of Realization** *Fear of Futility*	Making sense of the confusion. Mental anxiety that life is oppressive and futile, that you cannot make sense of the confusion.
Gate 24 - The Return **The Gate of Rationalization** *Fear of Ignorance*	Knowing the answer in a pulse. Mental anxiety that you will never know the answer, that inspiration will never come, or that you won't be able to explain your knowing.
Gate 4 - Youthful Folly **The Gate of Formulization** *Fear of Chaos*	Formulating a logical answer. Mental anxiety that you will never find order in your life and that you will always be in chaos, the need to find and give answers.
Gate 11 - Peace **The Gate of Ideas** *Fear of Darkness*	Having new ideas to share. Mental anxiety about not having a new stimulating idea to think about or learn, anxiety about sharing and manifesting your ideas.
Gate 43 - Breakthrough **The Gate of Insight** *Fear of Rejection*	Having unique perspectives. Mental anxiety that your ideas are too weird and will be rejected, the need to make sense to others.
Gate 17 - Following **The Gate of Opinion** *Fear of Challenge*	Having opinions based on the facts. Fear that your opinions will be challenged so you don't share them, the need to have the details to back up the opinions.

THE DEFINED AJNA CENTER – 47% OF THE POPULATION

Those with defined Ajna Centers conceptualize the same way most of the time, resulting in consistent, specific, and trustworthy mental functions. Their mental preferences and predispositions are determined by their gates/channels, and they are not easily influenced by another's presence. They can conceptualize, inspire and pressure others to think. Their minds are used for processing data, creativity, and as an outer authority for others. In these ways, they condition the mental field and people in their aura.

Defined centers are always 'on,' and those with defined Ajna Centers are always thinking, always processing. They may find it difficult to meditate because they can't stop or control their mental activity. On the other hand, they enjoy their mental stimulation. The Ajna can be defined to either the Head or the Throat Center. If their definition is between the Ajna and Throat, they can always speak their mind according to their Strategy and Authority. Either definition can create a head-strong tendency to make decisions from the mind, which often leads to feeling inadequate or hypocritical if one can't follow through on what was said. When people with defined Ajna's become over-reliant on their minds, they tend to waste a lot of energy obsessing about an uncompleted action or decision that is too late to do anything about.

THE UNDEFINED AJNA CENTER — 53% OF THE POPULATION

If the Ajna Center is undefined in a chart, the Head Center will also be undefined. Gate activations in either undefined center provide themes for the ways our mental activity connects us to people with whom we interact.

Open Head and Ajna centers can have an open and flexible mind. This is a sign of the mental intelligence indicative of thinkers or intellectuals like Freud, Jung, Einstein or Madame Curie. Once a person's mind is set free from conditioning, it is open to a full range of intellectual stimulation and creativity. Innate and learned wisdom about the intricate workings of the mind can come to the surface. When they do not hold onto concepts, ideas or opinions as their own personal truth, or become overly identified with any one of them, these open minds are able to deeply contemplate and discover the world through their intellectual gifts.

Those with undefined Ajnas are able to discern which concepts have value, and to recognize who is capable of providing an answer to the question(s) under consideration. They have the capacity to sift through the myriad of possibilities and gather what matters. They often pick up thoughts and ideas before someone in the group speaks them aloud.

As a child, they might grow up feeling that their ideas, which seem to come from nowhere or everywhere, are irrelevant or wrong. Fear and conditioning lead them to believe they need to be certain about their ideas in order to appear intelligent. Fearful of looking stupid, they pretend to be certain about things that don't matter. As this can become a habit over time, they may do it without even knowing it.

Imagine a child with an undefined Ajna Center being taught by someone with a defined Ajna Center. A parent, for example, putting pressure on a child to think logically when the child is designed to think abstractly. The child feels pressure to think in one particular way, and when he or she cannot do this consistently, begins to feel inadequate. Such children will grow up feeling something is wrong with them, and through conditioning will compensate by pretending to be certain about things in order to feel accepted and acceptable.

Once they realize and have accepted that their mind operates in an inconsistent way, however, and that they can never really be certain about anything, their mind becomes a playground. It reverts to its correct role as a classroom, a delightful source of entertainment, and a treasure trove of wisdom for others.

THE COMPLETELY OPEN AJNA CENTER

Those with a completely open Ajna Center and a completely open Head Center can have difficulty knowing what to think or how to interpret or conceptualize what they do think, which is so important in terms of fitting in to our mind-oriented culture. With no gate activations, or guiding channel through which to organize their thoughts, they have nothing fixed and reliable to depend on. This can leave them with a sense of helplessness, anxiety and even futility about the benefits of thinking at all. If their not-self takes advantage of this situation by strengthening its arguments for running their life, it will lead to the abdication of their personal authority.

Those with a completely open Ajna Center can derive great pleasure in contemplating a wide variety of theories, concepts and insights – without becoming attached to any of them, or to any particular way of thinking about them. They learn to recognize a good thought or concept which, when stimulated by a proper invitation, may be able to move to the next level. One of their most practical contributions is helping us see through the ways the not-self and not-self mind seduce us away from our true path and purpose.

NOT-SELF TALK OF THE UNDEFINED AJNA CENTER

The not-self mind is the spokesperson for the undefined centers, and tells us what we should say or do. Noticing this talk is essential to deconditioning. Here are some examples of what the not-self mental monolog could sound like with an undefined Ajna Center: I better figure this out; we have to figure this out. What should I do with my life? I've got to figure out what to do with my life. Where is my next move? I am certain that _____ (fill in the blank). I have to figure out life because it feels futile. I have to 'know' the answer. I have to put order to my life to get rid of the chaos. I have to make this new idea a reality in my life. I better not share this because people are going to think I'm weird or strange. I'm not going to share my opinion because I don't want to be challenged. I have to be ready for the challenge. What am I going to say?

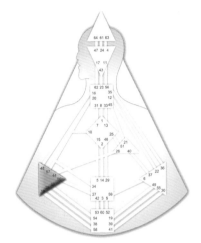

SPLENIC CENTER

BODY CONSCIOUSNESS
FULL EXISTENTIAL LIVING,
SPONTANEITY,
HEALTH AND WELL-BEING,
VALUES,
IMMUNE SYSTEM

BIOLOGICAL CORRELATION

The Splenic Center is associated with our lymphatic system, the spleen and T-cells. The cells of the lymphatic system act like little ears, noses, and tongues all over the body. Ever alert, they are constantly listening, tasting, and smelling to make sure everything in our environment is healthy and in balance. If something isn't, they warn us. This is the hub of our immune system. When T-cells (splenic soldiers which make up about one fifth of our body's cells) are called into action, they attack and destroy anything that invades the body. Their job is to protect us from disease.

Children with undefined Splenic Centers are probably the first to come home with any illness out there, like the flu, a cold, measles or mumps. It is their body's way of slowly building up a natural immunity to common diseases. The key to maintaining the health of these children is to allow them to heal completely after they are sick. Give them a few more days off from school to regain their full vigor. Teach them how to take care of themselves in order to strengthen their potential well-being. As adults, they will be sensitive to their health and to how they feel, learning about what food and health remedies work for them and what to avoid. Typically, they need gentler health remedies than those with a defined Splenic Center.

Those with a defined Splenic Center tend to take their health for granted, and benefit from regular checkups to make sure their hard-working Spleen isn't concealing potential problems. When they do succumb to illness, they usually require a lengthy recuperation time. It is imperative that they heal completely before returning to a full, active schedule.

AWARENESS AS FEAR FOR OUR SURVIVAL

This amazing center, with its primal fears for our survival and well-being, is also a source of our light-heartedness and laughter, our spontaneity and daring. Its existential awareness, its awareness in the now moment, keeps us moving safely forward, while deep inside it steadily cleanses built-up toxins and the adverse effects of negative vibrations and memories from our system. (In review: of the nine centers in the BodyGraph, only three are described as awareness centers – the Splenic, Ajna and Solar Plexus. Awareness is what allows us to be conscious of our experience of life. The other six centers function on a purely mechanical basis.)

Awareness has evolved over millions of years, and each of the three awareness centers represents a different phase in that evolutionary process. The Splenic Center is the oldest. Its survival-driven primary awareness connects us with all life forms – plants, reptiles, birds, insects, and our closest relatives, mammals (see designs below). As the oldest awareness center, and the center most common to all life, its essential function has always been to keep the form alive – literally keeping it from becoming someone's or something's lunch.

The work of this center is instantaneous, instinctual alertness for anything that threatens our well-being, including negative emotional vibrations. Fear is its mode of operating as fear for survival generates alertness. Over time, these primal fears evolved into a form of intelligence, a type of body awareness or body consciousness focused on what is needed to survive, adapt, and thrive in the mundane world. This intelligence remains alert and on guard within us to this day.

Of the three awareness centers, the Ajna (unique to human beings) is twice as strong as the Splenic, and the Solar Plexus (not yet fully evolved as an awareness center) is twice as strong as the Ajna. The fact that the Splenic Center, with its responsibility for life-and-death, is the weakest of the three indicates how fragile life is. The not-self voices of both the Ajna and the Solar Plexus Centers can easily override the quiet little alerts coming from our Splenic awareness.

DESIGN OF PLANTS

DESIGN OF INSECTS

DESIGN OF MAMMALS

DESIGN OF FISH, BIRDS, REPTILES

For a complete listing of the Designs of Forms, please see Section Eleven.

All awareness begins with fear, and each of the three awareness centers has its own fear frequency. Each gate in the Spleen represents a primary fear for survival. The Splenic system's awareness is an aspect of our intelligence that is created each time we face and survive a fear-filled challenge to our existence, our confidence, and our well-being.

GATES OF THE SPLENIC CENTER

Gate 48 - The Well **The Gate of Depth** *Fear of Inadequacy*	Awareness of a potential solution, or not. Fear that you don't have enough depth or are seeking depth to resolve the fear.
Gate 57 - The Gentle **The Gate of Intuitive Clarity** *Fear of the Future*	Awareness to hear truth in the now, or not. Fear of what the future will bring so you hold back.
Gate 44 - Coming to Meet **The Gate of Alertness** *Fear of the Past*	Awareness through smell for the talents and potentials of others, or not. Fear that the past baggage will catch up with you.
Gate 50 - The Cauldron **The Gate of Values** *Fear of Responsibility*	Awareness to be responsible for the preservation of others, or not. Fear of taking on responsibility or taking on too much responsibility due to fear.
Gate 32 - Duration **The Gate of Continuity** *Fear of Failure*	Awareness of what can be transformed, or not. Fear of failure holds you back from doing what you want to do.
Gate 28 - Preponderance of the Great **The Gate of the Game Player** *Fear of Death/Purpose*	Awareness to struggle for purpose, or not, not taking risks out of fear. Fear that life has no purpose unless you take risks.
Gate 18 - Work on what has been Spoilt **The Gate of Correction** *Fear of Authority*	Awareness of the pattern that needs to be corrected, or not. Fear of being judged by others and/or too much self judgment.

THE DEFINED SPLENIC CENTER – 55% OF THE POPULATION

The Splenic Center is responsible for our surviving and thriving with a sense of well-being in the world. It manages our instinct, intuition and taste which are processes for discerning what is or isn't healthy for our survival. Its non-verbal recognition operates in the present moment, in the 'now.' This vital, spontaneous information is what we call intuition, gut instinct or a hunch; it allows us to make trustworthy spontaneous judgments/decisions. Moment-to-moment awareness, however, means that the Spleen never repeats its first alarm. If we do not pay close attention to those little alerts immediately, we will miss their warning which is always rooted in what is needed for survival right now.

Those with a defined Spleen Center as their Authority must listen to their intuition, do what it tells them to do, and not let their not-self or anyone else's mind distract them from following their own instincts, which are trustworthy and produce reliable results. They then remain alert and protected, feel good, and can enjoy the benefits of a strong immune system. They can project a state of well being that is envied by those with undefined Splenic Centers who do not consistently feel good. Living fully in the present moment with a care-free but prudent abandon is the by-product of a deep attunement with existence. It requires an ever-growing dependence on their vehicle's awareness, their body's intelligence, to guide them and protect them throughout their life, second by second by second.

The mind is not an authority, even though its loud, reasoned thinking can easily overwhelm the Spleen's subtle messaging system. When a person receives a sudden warning, there is no time and no way to figure out why the Splenic Center sent the message. Existential awareness cannot be rationalized; it must simply be trusted. Understanding the fuller perspective of an experience can only happen by looking back after the fact. And what is not correct for a person one moment, may be correct 30 minutes or a day later. For the Spleen, the present moment is all that matters, all it is aware of.

After years of letting the mind override the intuitive knowing and awareness of the Splenic Center, people can end up completely out of touch with their instincts, put their life at risk, and suffer unnecessary ill-health and unhappiness. They 'think' they dare not follow their body's intuitive intelligence, yet it can be disastrous for them not to.

UNDEFINED SPLENIC CENTER – 45% OF THE POPULATION

Seven primal fears reside in the Splenic Center, and when the center is undefined, these fears are easily magnified. Those with undefined Spleens need to face each of their fears, one by one, in order to become fearless in a healthy way. This is how they develop awareness, and honor and learn from their fear rather than suppress it or pretend it's not there. Confronting and handling the fear makes them stronger and less frightened each time the fear returns. The result is a sense of well-being. If they are unable to do this, however, the conditioned not-self may become overwhelmed by the fears.

Those who are born with an undefined Splenic Center enter the world with a fundamental fear that they are not equipped to survive here on Earth. They are also open and sensitive to the lack of well-being in the world and interpret this personally. When people in their environment with defined Spleens condition them, they feel better and safer. They grow up unconsciously seeking and clinging to people with defined Spleens for the security and sense of well-being it seems to provide – regardless of what else comes with it. They typically end up holding on to what is not good for them, and this can lead to all sorts of unhealthy dependencies, especially in familial relationships, such as children with an undefined Spleen who have a Splenically defined parent. Even if the parent is abusive, these children will do everything they can to hold on to the parent simply to access the conditioning 'feel good' frequency of the defined Splenic Center. They will be terrified if sent to their room alone, and often feel rejected, abandoned and fearful that they cannot survive. This causes them to cling to the security of the parent even more, eventually creating an unhealthy dependency. Because of this early conditioning, the not-self minds of these children will convince them to hold on to what is not good for them as they mature.

At the adult level, those with an undefined Spleen who are in a relationship with a defined Spleen that is no longer healthy for them, will say things like: "It will be better tomorrow" or "Maybe the therapy will work" or "What about the children?" This is the dilemma for many battered women who go back to abusive spouses. The deep fears of survival, the attraction to be with a defined Spleen, can blind them to who is good for them and who isn't, or to when to hold on to a relationship and when to let go.

When an undefined Spleen is temporarily defined by a defined Spleen or passing transit connection, it can experience a deceptive sense of security. The mantra for someone with an undefined Splenic Center is 'never make a spontaneous decision.' Being spontaneous, except in potentially harmful or threatening situations, poses a risk to the undefined Spleen because it cannot trust the ever-changing impulse of the moment. The not-self of the undefined Spleen is attracted to spontaneity in an effort to feel good and make the fear disappear, but it usually comes with a high price.

When undefined Spleens are in the aura of a defined Spleen, they are naturally under pressure to be spontaneous. In most cases they are unaware this is happening, but what they end up doing is living the life of the person pressuring them. It is not their life, however, and it may not be safe for them. If they follow their Strategy and the guidance of their Authority, they avoid the temptation to be impulsive. Impulsive decisions made in the moment from a conditioned undefined Splenic Center may cause them to let go of beneficial things as well. "Oh, I don't need that (or them) anymore." Once the conditioning is broken, however, they realize they made a mistake and let go of something that really was good for them. Sudden decisions made without relying on one's consistent Authority can have long-term consequences.

People with a healthy orientation to their undefined Spleen can discern the difference between what is their own need to attend to, in terms of some aspect of their health, and what is a lack of well-being coming from the environment. When they are with unhealthy or deeply unhappy people and find themselves feeling ill, they understand that they are probably absorbing the other person's ill health or unhealthy vibrations. They can sense when someone or something is not good for them. They can be tuned into their instinctual and intuitive awareness, yet know this is not the authority for their decisions. They pay close attention to their health and nurture their body's resilience. They understand how important it is to face their fears, and how to deal with the fear of survival. They develop the wisdom to know how intuition works, who has it and who does not. Ultimately they can become highly intuitive themselves. Their undefined Spleen is never a reliable resource for making decisions, however, because it is very vulnerable to the conditioning in their environment. By entering into new relationships through their Strategy and Authority, they get the correct Splenic conditioning in their lives.

The wisdom that comes over time through the undefined Splenic Center allows many professional healers to bring great benefit to their patients. When they step into their client's aura, there is a spontaneous recognition, a sense of whether the person is healthy or ill, and what might be out of balance. Such intuitive empathy emerges as the undefined Spleen learns to distinguish between what it is filtering through from others, and what energies are its own. Intuitive awareness or wisdom about someone else is available to the undefined Spleen only when it does not identify with what the other person is experiencing.

COMPLETELY OPEN SPLENIC CENTER

There is a healthy and natural level of fear in all of us. When children or adults with a completely open Splenic Center lose contact with the fears that keep them alive and healthy, they can become insecure and fearful of everything. They do not know what to be afraid of, and can also become fearless to the point that they do foolish, risky and unhealthy things.

The same wisdom of the undefined Spleen, described above, is enhanced by their complete openness to the full range of instinctual and intuitive intelligence vibrating through this center. This awareness includes the ways laws, values, and our entrepreneurial endeavors nurture, protect and ensure the survival of our offspring, thus promoting the growth of a healthy society.

NOT-SELF TALK OF THE UNDEFINED SPLENIC CENTER

The not-self mind is the spokesperson for the undefined centers, and tells us what we should say or do. Noticing this talk is essential to deconditioning. Here are some examples of what the not-self mental monolog could sound like with an undefined Splenic Center: Let's not do that because it makes me insecure or because I'm afraid or I feel fearful every time I think about doing it. Let's not say that because it might upset that person. I'm afraid that I will feel inadequate if I do that. I'm not going to do that because I might fail. I'm afraid of doing that because I'm afraid of what the outcome will be or what the future will bring, or I'm afraid of the responsibility or the criticism. I can't do that because I might lose my connection with that person. They might leave.

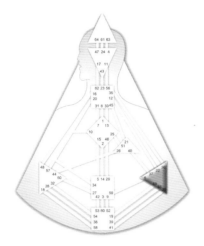

SOLAR PLEXUS CENTER

SPIRIT CONSCIOUSNESS
EMOTIONAL AND SOCIAL AWARENESS,
PASSION AND DESIRE,
ABUNDANCE OF SPIRIT,
FEELINGS, MOODS, SENSITIVITY

BIOLOGICAL CORRELATION

The Solar Plexus Center is associated with the lungs, kidneys, pancreas, prostate gland, and the nervous system. Its themes are feelings, emotions and sensitivity, and its function is to allow us to gain a sense of emotional clarity and well-being. When a person's emotions run unconstrained over time, the physical well-being of several major organ systems is directly affected. Water retention and weight gain are common examples of the consequences of unresolved emotional stressors.

The Solar Plexus provides the potent energy driving the cyclic nature of human experience; its desire frequency is continually moving us toward encounters with pleasure and its opposite, pain. It is the center of revolution, poetry, romance, compassion, spirituality and religion. We seek to prolong its highs to stay connected to spirit, and we do everything in our power to avoid its lows, our unfilled expectations and sense of separation. With half of humanity acting impulsively from these emotional ups and downs, and the other half avoiding dealing with emotions altogether, we find ourselves living in an emotionally distorted world.

These distortions permeate every aspect of life on this planet. No other center in our time has a deeper impact on humanity, individually or globally, than the Solar Plexus Center. Comprehending the mechanics and chemistry of this center can release years of painful emotional patterns, re-establish physical health, open the way for renewed pleasure with living, and engender a wholesome compassion toward ourselves and others.

EMOTIONAL AWARENESS AND FUTURE SPIRIT CONSCIOUSNESS

Each of the three awareness centers has a unique frequency. The Splenic Center governs the immune system and operates in the now, spontaneously and existentially. The Ajna Center governs mental awareness and operates over all time. The Solar Plexus Center, which is both a motor and an awareness center, governs emotions and operates on a biochemical, oscillating wave over time.

The Solar Plexus began a mutative process several thousand years ago, sometime between the birth of Buddha and the birth of Jesus, moving us toward a new kind of awareness referred to as spirit awareness. The process will be culminated when it is cosmically supported beginning in 2027. Spirit consciousness is the opposite of differentiation; it is about oneness, and experiencing ourselves as a single entity. Such consciousness results when the emotional waves between two or more beings are in resonance. As a highly differentiated, interregnum species, we cannot even imagine how it will feel to share such consciousness so deeply with others. This developing awareness lies beneath the surface of our present emotional system.

As 9-centered beings we are just beginning to explore, and to discover experientially, the breadth and depth and comprehensive implications of this Solar Plexus mutation that we are all a part of. What we do know is that when we bypass the mind's conditioning, and live our differentiation and our own truth by understanding, accepting, and loving who we are, we free spirit consciousness to mature on the planet, and to move the mutation toward its future fulfillment.

THE FREQUENCIES OF THE EMOTIONAL WAVE

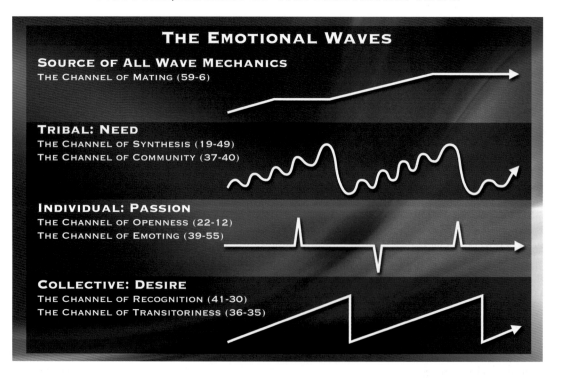

The defined Solar Plexus Center releases a wave pattern that takes us from one end of the emotional spectrum to the other. It is a chemistry that we experience as feelings, needs and desires. Each cyclical wave goes from hope to pain, expectation to disappointment, joy to despair – and back again. To create emotional stability in our lives and throughout the world, we must understand, accept, and eventually transcend this wave pattern, none of which is achieved by mind control. The key to transcending the emotional system, and the potential waves it sends into the environment, is 'waiting.' As we wait through the ups and downs, our understanding is deepened, the wave begins to level out, and clarity eventually arrives. Understanding this continual wave movement, and waiting for clarity, can stop one who is emotionally defined from sending out reactive, premature, chaotic or harmful emotions into the environment.

THE SOURCE OF ALL WAVE MECHANICS (Channel 59-6) operates out of the 6th Gate as this is where the emotional wave is created, and then reaches across to meet the fertile sacral power of the 59th Gate. It is here that need, passion and desire are created in order to break down barriers, and penetrate and bond us together in the dance of intimacy. This emotional wave feels very stable and takes another person to bring it to the surface.

The three emotional waves are categorized by their frequency. A person may experience a singular frequency, or a combination, depending on the definition.

THE TRIBAL WAVE (Channels 19-49 and 37-40) operates through physical touch and sensitivity to needs. This wave ratchets up until it explodes and then resets itself to start the process all over again. Let's take an example of a man whose wife is doing something that bothers him. He doesn't tell her how he feels about it so it continues for weeks. Each time she does it, his emotional wave ratchets up a notch until one day it explodes. The wife had no warning, didn't see it coming and is taken by surprise. The emotional outburst could be hard on her, but once he releases his built-up emotions, he is back to normal; all is fine. When both partners understand the mechanics of this Tribal wave – how to anticipate the explosion, how to sort out the real issues, and how differently the outburst affects each of them – they will reach new levels of comfort and understanding in their relationship. For instance, a gradual build-up of emotional tension, mixed with a desire for intimacy, can be quietly and effectively released by a sensitively-placed hand on the shoulder at the end of a long, hard day. No words are necessary for the Tribe; its all in the touch.

THE INDIVIDUAL WAVE (Channels 39-55 and 22-12) operates through the expression of moodiness, emotions, melancholy or passion (but only when in the mood). It moves along on an even keel most of the time, with smaller, shorter, up and down spikes. Knowing when to be alone and when to be social makes all the difference, and those with this wave might feel melancholic for a short time until they are moved to a new place along their wave and their mood shifts. Emotional tension in their relationships arising from the low end of their wave is eased by knowing when to take time to be alone with their creative muse.

THE ABSTRACT WAVE (Channels 36-35 and 41-30) operates through desire and feeling, and moves from peaks to valleys. Based on expectation, this wave crashes when the desire or expectation is not met. The trick to transcending this wave is to enter into something just for the experience, without placing any expectations on the outcome. For example, a woman imagines herself in love after a few dates. She fantasizes about how great the man is and how wonderful their future will be, only to discover he does not live up to her expectations or share her feelings. Repeated spikes and crashes like these can be tough to handle, and may become personally destabilizing over time if she has no awareness of the mechanics of the emotional wave.

What is most important to understand about the emotional wave is that it is simply an inescapable chemical process that keeps the wave constantly in motion. No explanations accompany its shifts and swings. Unfortunately, without this awareness, those who are emotionally defined attempt to rationalize their emotions, and to explain or make up a reason why they are up or down on their wave. When they feel sad, their friends want to know why and what they can do to make them happy. It can become more important to them to put the blame somewhere, rather than to embrace and accept the depth and beauty of the chemistry itself. Blaming something or someone for what is pure emotional chemistry can be a source of great confusion when all they need to know is that, as the wave moves to another place they will feel different. There is no need for a reason for where they are now on the wave, or where they will be tomorrow. They are simply always moving with it.

Generally speaking, whether we are emotionally defined, or undefined and taking in the conditioning waves of others, we have to be careful not to identify with the wave or its movement as if it were us. Remain the objective observer; we are not the wave but we are being taken to our depths by it. Both the highs and lows of the wave can be beautiful when we don't let either of them disturb our inner tranquility, the tranquility of knowing what is 'normal' for us. Society perpetuates the notion that we should be happy all the time. Because of this, most emotionally defined people live their lives fighting against the down side of their wave, convinced that something is wrong with them. True liberation comes when they learn to observe, accept and embrace the full gamut and gifts of their wave.

AWARENESS AND NERVOUSNESS

The fears that accompany the Solar Plexus Center's present state of emerging awareness are experienced as nervousness based on emotional uncertainty. One never knows for certain how to feel about something or someone, or what feeling to base a decision on. Because of the social/relational nature of the Solar Plexus, with its broad movement from hope to pain, this nervousness can be powerful and pervasive. As people are moved forward along the wave, nervousness is either amplified or disappears; is there or not there. Emotional uncertainty can distort the way we view things, making mountains out of molehills.

The vague or haunting nervousness that arises from living with uncertainty is a form of fear that needs to be confronted in order to be overcome. When those with a defined Solar Plexus Center go through their wave, accessing the depth of their truth and waiting for clarity, they are able to either confirm or dispel the uncertainties and suspicions underlying their nervousness. By properly identifying and effectively confronting their uncertainty, they can move beyond their emotional fears (nervousness), and transcends them over time. In this way, fears become emotional intelligence.

Each awareness center engenders a particular form of fear. In the Solar Plexus, fear manifests as nervousness about engaging others, as the constantly moving biochemical wave leaves it emotionally uncertain. Each gate description on the opposite page reveals how fear as nervous uncertainty is experienced.

GATES OF THE SOLAR PLEXUS CENTER

TRIBAL WAVE - NEED

Gate 37 - The Family The Gate of Friendship *Fear of Tradition*	Generates the bargain based on the principles of the Tribe. Nervousness about possibly having to take on traditional roles in life.
Gate 6 - Conflict The Gate of Friction *Fear of Intimacy*	A kind of diaphragm that generates a wave by either opening or closing to intimacy. Nervousness about revealing who you really are.
Gate 49 - Revolution The Gate of Principles *Fear of Nature*	A wave that either accepts or rejects principles based on the needs of the tribe. Nervousness about rejection, unpredictability and consequences.

INDIVIDUAL WAVE - PASSION

Gate 22 - Grace The Gate of Openness *Fear of Silence*	Open to listening - when in the mood. Uncertain that any one will listen to you or that there is anything worthwhile to listen to.
Gate 55 - Abundance The Gate of Spirit *Fear of Emptiness*	A melancholy that is personal. Nervousness arising from not knowing what to be passionate about.

COLLECTIVE WAVE - DESIRE

Gate 36 - The Darkening of the Light The Gate of Crisis *Fear of Inadequacy*	Driven by the hunger to have the challenge of a new experience. Nervousness about one's sexual/emotional adequacy.
Gate 30 - The Clinging Fire The Gate of Feelings *Fear of the Fates*	Produces a very powerful wave fueled by desire to feel deeply. Nervousness about what might or might not happen.

THE DEFINED SOLAR PLEXUS CENTER – 53% OF THE POPULATION

THERE IS NO TRUTH IN THE 'NOW.' TRUTH REVEALS ITSELF OVER TIME.

For those with a defined Solar Plexus Center, this is their place of personal Authority, and it operates as awareness over time. They are designed to wait through the ups and downs of the emotional wave before making decisions. It is not easy for them to be patient. The Solar Plexus is an immature emotional center driven by a motor, and it houses a lot of energy. Their task is to learn how to patiently harness the potential benefits of this energy as they flow with it. Their tendency is to jump in when they are high on their wave and jump out when they are low. In both circumstances, they are emotionally impulsive rather than emotionally clear. Clarity is only available after waiting out the emotional wave. At a minimum, those with a defined Solar Plexus Center need to sleep on things before making an important decision.

When the Solar Plexus is defined, the feelings these people have about 'this' or 'that' become an authoritative guide. These feelings are indicators of what is correct for them or not. "Does it feel good to do that? How do you feel about it?" These are important questions they need to be asked. It is essential for them to take time to fully experience their range of feelings without being rushed. Emotional clarity is reached when there is no longer an emotional charge attached to the decision. Making decisions from still waters is easier said than done. When people are excited they tend to jump, only to regret it after they reach emotional clarity. Patiently waiting for clarity will protect the defined Solar Plexus Center from making spontaneous decisions that may result in poor choices.

As people move through their wave, it helps to understand that the emotional cycle is a dynamic, chemical process, and that hope and pain are not end points of awareness. Awareness comes as clarity at the end of the emotional wave's cycle. Knowing what is correct takes time, and there are no short cuts. In addition, emotional clarity is not a certainty. The Splenic Center gives an absolute answer in the moment, while the constantly moving Solar Plexus wave samples the present moment as one of many points along the way. In the end, there is no guarantee that 100 percent emotional clarity is possible because the wave keeps moving. There will come a time, however, when emotional calmness is reached and a deeper truth is recognized about the decision to be made.

Solar Plexus energy is juicy, seductive, and powerful, which gives those with emotional Authority an advantage if they wait out their wave. It is kind of like playing hard to get. The longer others wait, the more they will want the Solar Plexus' warmth and energy. In a business negotiation, waiting until they are clear rather than consummating a quick deal, gives them the upper hand. If the other backs out before the defined Solar Plexus reaches clarity, the deal probably wasn't correct for them to begin with.

There is a complex interaction between those who are emotionally defined and those who are open. Those with definition are responsible for the emotional environment as a whole because they color it with their waves. They impact others merely by how they feel inside, by the pure mechanics of their chemistry and how it is transmitted through their aura. When those with definition feel good or bad, those with undefined emotional centers will feel VERY good or VERY bad as they amplify the frequency. In other words, the undefined center reflects back to those with defined centers just how they are feeling, or where they are in their emotional process. It's interesting to note that people with emotional definition, being so familiar with it, don't always notice their emotionality, whereas those who are undefined are conditioned to think that they are the moody, emotional ones instead.

The attraction between an undefined and a defined Solar Plexus is both common and strong among couples. Despite the warmth and strong attraction of this center, those with a defined Solar Plexus need to take their time when entering into a new relationship. It's only over time that they will know if someone is right for them or not. When they learn to know someone through their wave, they will know them deeply. They will see how their emotions impact the other person, how that person handles the highs and lows of their emotional wave. Manipulative and passive-aggressive behaviors can surface in relationships between defined and undefined emotional systems, and it takes time for these patterns to reveal themselves. Long courtships are not only advisable – they are essential to the success of the relationship.

The advantage of having emotional definition is the depth that can be cultivated on any topic. As one moves through the wave, its many perspectives can bring great insight. For example, a photographer who wants to understand the nature of a flower. The Splenically-oriented photographer would take one picture capturing an exquisite moment, but for those with a defined Solar Plexus, one picture would never be enough. They would take a series of pictures all day long, changing the light, the perspective, the camera. They would know how the flower looks in the morning and how it looks when the sun sets. They would know its fragrance, how it feels to the touch, and how it looks bending in the wind. When the emotional system is given the time it needs to unfold, it becomes an intelligence with deep sensitivity that grasps things at the ever-changing emotional level, the level of spirit.

When those with a defined Solar Plexus Center do not wait out their wave, they tend to be impulsive, jumping in and out of experiences and decisions on the high or low end of their emotional wave, thereby creating chaos and confusion. They put others in their environment under pressure to make immediate emotional decisions with them. When they are upset, they blow up rather than wait for a moment of calm from which to act or speak, only to regret later what they said or did. They do not recognize the importance of being alone when down in their wave.

Waiting through their wave allows emotionally healthy people to be in touch with how they are feeling as they move along their wave. Without being impulsive or spontaneous, they take their time and ride out their emotions until they feel a sense of clarity before making a decision. They understand how their emotions affect others and do not place pressure on them by being pushy. They know how to take advantage of the seductive side of their emotional definition by using their need "to wait" to reach carefully considered agreements that satisfy the desires of all involved.

THE UNDEFINED SOLAR PLEXUS CENTER – 47% OF THE POPULATION

The undefined Solar Plexus Center absorbs and amplifies the emotions present in its environment. This center carries an especially deep conditioning potential, and can be particularly vulnerable to the needs, moods, and feelings of other people. It is critical for the health and well-being of the emotionally undefined to know when the emotions they are feeling and expressing are not entirely theirs, and that they can release them and protect themselves by not identifying with them. Otherwise, they bounce up and down on the emotional waves of others, knowing their emotions are out of control but interpreting that as something wrong within themselves. They repeatedly make emotional decisions which leave them regretful and plagued by shame or blame, a burden the undefined Solar Plexus is not genetically designed to handle.

Open centers are like open windows. The Solar Plexus is designed to take in and sample the emotional field, but only for informational purposes. It is not healthy to identify with or personalize that field, or it becomes theirs, and they do not have a reliable built-in way to deal with it. They lose their transparency, their ability to merely reflect an emotion back to its owner.

Those with an undefined Solar Plexus may feel as though they have been emotionally out of control all their lives. When emotionally confronted, they may experience sensations that include fear, terror, shock, and anger. They may bounce from happiness to depression, personalizing emotions and feelings as if they were their own when, in fact, they are simply taking in, amplifying, and distorting the emotions of those around them. They may suffer from being punished and rejected by others who perceive them as emotionally unstable. They often feel something is wrong with them. They are generally so sensitive to the emotional climate that they have personalized emotionally charged events over the years, hanging on to and taking the blame for what does not belong to them.

Children who are open emotionally take in and personalize their family's emotional ups and downs, amplifying and often 'acting out' their confusion. Thinking that they are personally responsible for making the waves, they decide at an early age that it is better to lie about or hide the truth of themselves deep inside rather than suffer a parent's emotional outburst. When the situation is reversed, and the parent is open emotionally and the child defined, the parent can lose control and become over-reactive while amplifying the emotions of the child. Understanding these dynamics can help us raise healthy, stable, independent children – and enjoy parenting.

Confrontation makes emotionally undefined people nervous. As they mature, they develop not-self strategies to avoid emotional backlash by steering clear of confronting others for fear of rocking the boat or upsetting someone. They develop a persona that says, "I won't upset you if you won't upset me." They attempt to sidestep any potential confrontation that might follow if they dare to express their own truth or needs. Though those with open Solar Plexus Centers will never enjoy dealing with emotional confrontation, their Strategy and Authority will guide them to confrontations which are correct for them to face.

It is often just the thought of confrontation that keeps those with an open Solar Plexus frozen in terror. The actual confrontation may be much easier than imagined when they stand in their own Authority, and the results may end up being the best thing that could happen because it is correct. If confrontations are always avoided, life is lived on a superficial level. It helps to remember that on the other side of pain is pleasure, and on the other side of fear is the freedom to be ourselves. Confrontation when handled correctly, when we simply speak our own truth rather than blaming someone else, is a catalyst for healthy transformation.

Access to the full spectrum of this center's great pleasures, such as sexual energy, food, passion, excitement, romance and music, is available to those with defined or undefined Solar Plexus Centers. For emotions to be a beautiful experience for the undefined center, however, they cannot identify with them. Awareness of the emotional wave allows them to let go of patterns and emotions that never belonged to them, which in itself can bring tremendous relief. When they understand why emotions have been so difficult, they can begin to properly realign their lives to their own personal Authority. They are able to discern who is or is not emotionally healthy for them, and when it is appropriate to confront others with their truth or needs, or to walk away. They discern which emotional fears are theirs to deal with and which are not, and do not make emotional decisions. They realize the emotions they take in and feel in an amplified state are from others, and do not attach to them.

A healthy undefined Solar Plexus Center is a barometer of the emotional health of others; it can be a good objective observer of the emotional climate. Its wisdom takes the form of discerning who is making progress toward emotional health, stability and spirit awareness. On its own, it can remain emotionally cool, and allows those with undefined Solar Plexus' to rely on their Strategy. When they suddenly feel uncomfortable emotionally, they know they can leave the room, and the conditioning auras of others, until the coolness returns. It is a good practice for them to enjoy some time alone every day in order to release the emotional conditioning they have taken in.

COMPLETELY OPEN SOLAR PLEXUS CENTER

Although many characteristics of the undefined Solar Plexus Center also apply, the completely open Solar Plexus differs in that it does not have any way of filtering or connecting to incoming potent, emotional energy. Those with a completely open center can be confused by what they are feeling, and don't know how to interpret it. They don't know what to desire, when to be sensitive or passionate, or how to recognize and deal with people's needs or moods. They often feel something is wrong with them emotionally. The potential wisdom is to know and understand the emotional waves in their purest state without anything coloring or prejudicing them.

NOT-SELF TALK OF THE UNDEFINED SOLAR PLEXUS CENTER

The not-self mind is the spokesperson for the undefined centers, and tells us what we should say or do. Noticing this talk is essential to deconditioning. Here are some examples of what the not-self mental monolog could sound like with an undefined Solar Plexus Center: I don't want to go there because I don't want to deal with the confrontation. Let's go here because there won't be any confrontation to deal with. Let's not say that because it might upset that person. Let's say it like this to soften the potential confrontation. Let's be really nice and smile a lot so they like me. There is no point in going there because I might be disappointed or be rejected. It's not worth it. I'm afraid it won't work out so why bother. I'm afraid to tell her the truth because I don't want to hurt her feelings.

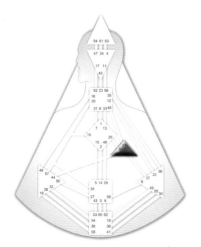

HEART CENTER

WILLPOWER
EGO AND
THE MATERIAL WORLD

BIOLOGICAL CORRELATION

The small size and unobtrusive position of the Heart Center in the BodyGraph is deceiving, as it has a significant physiological impact on our life. Its four gates are associated with the stomach (Gate 40), the thymus gland (Gate 26), the heart (Gate 21) and the gall bladder (Gate 51). Those who are unaware of how this center operates are more vulnerable to diseases of the heart and digestive system. And when the heart stops, everything stops!

WILLPOWER AND SELF ESTEEM

The Heart Center is a powerful motor that drives willpower and ego power, enormously influential forces in the world. The bedrock of society is rooted in the will – the will to survive in community and thrive on the material plane. The Heart Center has a direct connection to the Throat Center, and therefore speaks and acts for the tribe. From the beginning, it has been the Tribe that provided the support system that ensured the survival of the family, community and nations. It established the foundations for our communal and entrepreneurial ways of life. Community organization created a safe, interdependent environment, that made it possible for people to specialize, take their unique skills to great heights, and progress as groups or as individuals. Our great civilizations could not have been built without the Tribe's supportive, hierarchical structures held in place by the four gates of the Heart Center.

These gates determine the different ways members of the Tribe connect to one another in order to successfully live out what is called the material way. These gates are about making our daily bread, bonding and living in harmony with others, bringing children into the world, and creating infrastructures like societies, cultures and religions, to nurture and support what we create.

At the present time the Tribe is undergoing stressful, structural change that challenges its entrepreneurial and communal foundation; changes which call into question the authority and stability of our most fundamental traditions and institutions. The fear engendered by these changes magnifies the pressure on those with open Heart Centers to prove their worth in order to survive the uncertainty. Issues of self-esteem and self-worth surface and affect every level of our life, from relationships, to our work, to what we believe, to giving ourselves permission to play and enjoy this incredible life we have been given.

The bottom line is that self esteem is a place from which we move into the world with confidence as a valued and contributing member of society – and receive material and personal support in return. Without this firm belief and trust in ourselves and our own value, we lose our will to meet the challenges of life. Unless the ego is affirmed in its healthy state, and reassured of its value by our self or others, it shuts down and self-esteem becomes self-loathing. Self-hatred exacts a terrible price from humanity.

In this context, it becomes clear why so many heart and digestive problems are related to the ways in which the not-self compensates for poor self-esteem. The tendency toward over-achievement, making promises or bargains that we don't have the will power to keep, and laboring beyond what our heart muscle is able to support in order to prove our worth, are all symptoms of trying to prove our worthiness. Understanding the mind's role in determining how we ultimately value our self, or not, can eliminate a great deal of unnecessary pain and suffering in our life.

GATES OF THE HEART CENTER

Gate 21 - Biting Through The Gate of the Hunter/Huntress	To be in control To control the circumstances
Gate 40 - Deliverance The Gate of Aloneness	To deliver The will to provide
Gate 26 - The Taming Power of the Great The Gate of Egoist	To be the best The salesperson/marketer
Gate 51 - The Arousing The Gate of Shock	To be competitive To be first at something

THE DEFINED HEART CENTER – 37% OF THE POPULATION

If you have a defined Heart Center, you like to be in control of your own life and your resources. That includes what you wear, when and where you work, and which demands on your time you will respond to. You also recognize your own value, although at times you may tend to inflate it.

It is healthy for those with a defined Heart Center to exercise their willpower, to make and keep promises with regularity. With consistent access to their willpower, they have no problem making and keeping their promises or resolutions. It is important that they do what they say they are going to do. Since this is how others develop a level of trust in them, they should only make promises they can and will keep. In this way, they strengthen their natural sense of self-esteem.

They enjoy working, though they prefer to be in a position where they can be their own boss. In this way they can follow their natural internal mechanism which tells them when to work and when it is time to rest. They enjoy successfully delivering the goods, and being willful and competitive comes naturally to them. When they listen carefully to their inner guidance, they will know when their great ego strength can best be brought to bear on a situation, and still maintain a balance between work and rest.

Those with a defined Heart Center should not allow anyone to deny them an honest and clear expression of their ego and will power. Their assertive 'I, me, mine' statements strengthen the heart, whereas suppressing their natural ego energy can be detrimental to their health. They are proving themselves all of the time, which is both important and correct for them, and they will do it naturally as long as they follow their Strategy and Authority. They willingly commit their willpower to provide for the family and the community when it is right for them to do so. Even though they enjoy their work, they like to be appreciated and rewarded for their contribution.

With a defined Heart Center, it is easy to get carried away and come across as too forceful. When not guided by their Strategy and personal Authority, they can place unrealistic expectations on those with an undefined Heart Center to be competitive and willful as well. They can attempt to pump others up, or push them to perform beyond their capacity, which eventually leads to unnecessary pain and misunderstanding. Eventually, these behaviors will meet with resistance, indicating that it is time to step back and regain a healthy inner balance of power.

THE UNDEFINED HEART CENTER — 63% OF THE POPULATION

People with undefined Heart Centers are not designed to be willful and competitive, yet they often feel driven by a need to find the courage to exercise their will. "Why can't I get what they have?" they ask. "Why can't I be as fast or as good as they are? I should be able to compete with them." While they want to exercise willpower, and to make and keep promises, they do not understand that they have no consistent energy to support either one.

We live in a world that sends a constant stream of messages that we should/could/can be better, prettier, richer, faster, and more successful if only we would do this or that. This propaganda puts tremendous pressure on us to make more, do more and be more. People with an undefined Heart Center get trapped in a vicious cycle. If they fail to live up to expectations, or to fulfill their commitments and promises, they make further promises to make up for their sense of self-deficiency, only to fail again. Each time they fail, they feel worse and their self-esteem spirals down further.

Over-achieving is one way the undefined Heart Center compensates for its seeming lack of will, for a sense that it doesn't have what it takes. When a person undervalues themselves to begin with, they will attempt to accomplish more than anybody else in order to prove how valuable they are. They 'will' themselves into impossible situations, trying to do something they can't possibly complete.

An undefined Heart Center is susceptible to amplification by a defined Heart Center's will power, and can deceive itself into thinking it suddenly has the will to make and keep a commitment. This 'borrowed' willpower evaporates, however, as soon as the person with Heart Center definition leaves. This is frequently the case during motivational workshops, where one supposedly leaves with enough direction and enthusiasm to follow through and accomplish the goal, only to watch the good intentions and the will power fade away when on one's own again.

The challenge for those with an undefined Heart Center is that they generally do not consider themselves worthy and will accept less of everything, including love, money and happiness, because they assume they do not deserve it. If they rely on their minds, rather than Strategy and Authority, they will be proving themselves forever. The more the mind gets into the game of trying to prove value or worthiness, the more one is going to fail, and the cycle of self-deprecation will continue to repeat itself. The solution is to relieve the mind of its assumed authority and return the authority to where it belongs.

The mantra for an undefined Heart Center is: never make a promise to yourself or others. The open Heart has NOTHING to prove to anyone, under any circumstance, ever. It is such a gift not to have to prove one's worth. Imagine 63 percent of all people at peace with themselves, knowing that they will be guided to commitments which are correct for them by their personal Authority, not by a need to appear worthy.

With this realization comes wisdom and awareness. A person without Heart Center definition can take in the vibration of other egos, becoming wise about who has a healthy sense of self-esteem and who does not. They recognize who can or cannot deliver on a commitment. They learn that they do not have to compete with anyone, and they do not let anyone convince them to do or to commit to anything merely to demonstrate their worth.

THE COMPLETELY OPEN HEART CENTER

People with completely open Heart Centers do not naturally have a good, solid grasp of what worthiness is, how to measure it, or what one needs to do to achieve it. When not living within their realm of personal Authority, they are prone to wavering between feeling an exaggerated sense of importance and of having no worth at all. With fragile or inconsistent self-esteem, and a nagging sense of inadequacy, they are particularly vulnerable to being manipulated and controlled by people who promise to convey worthiness on them by association, or by believing this or that propaganda.

When it comes to wisdom about the trustworthiness of one's word, and the use of money and personal power on the material plane, however, these are people to look to. Their wisdom is released by accepting that they have nothing to prove, and that they can rely on their Strategy and Authority to provide for their needs.

NOT-SELF TALK OF THE UNDEFINED HEART CENTER

The not-self mind is the spokesperson for the undefined centers, and tells us what we should say or do. Noticing this talk is essential to deconditioning. Here are some examples of what the not-self mental monologue could sound like with an undefined Heart Center: I better do this because if I don't, I won't be worthy. I have to be in control. I have to be brave. I have to pump myself up so I feel worthy and good about myself, and then others will see my value. I have to be loyal so that others will see how valuable I am, and so that I can prove to myself how valuable I am. If I just tell it like this and make this promise, then they will see how wonderful I am. If I show them how trustworthy I am then they will like me. They think I can do this so I better prove to them that I can. If I am in control then I can prove my worth. I'm not a good wife, lover, friend unless I prove it.

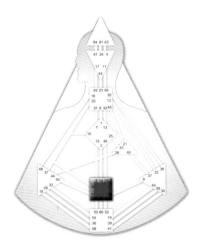

SACRAL CENTER

POWER OF FERTILITY
VITAL ENERGY,
RESPONDABILITY,
AVAILABILITY,
SEXUALITY

BIOLOGICAL CORRELATION

The Sacral Center corresponds to the ovaries in a woman and the testes in a man. All life on the planet is fostered by the creative life-force energy generated in this center. It empowers our survival by replicating life and by providing the impulse to nurture and care for our young. Sexuality, work, fertility, vitality, movement, and persistence are its major themes.

As the body's prime motor, the Sacral has enormous power that works in both a generative and a degenerative way. If we do not understand how to properly engage and support the mechanics of the Sacral, it will atrophy and degenerate prematurely, leaving one frustrated and unhealthy. This motor's built-in work/rest cycle requires that it exhausts its supply of available energy each day in order to sleep well. While it rests, it recharges its batteries. If it is forced to do what it hasn't responded to, its generative capacity quickly becomes degenerative and burnout results. The Sacral Center's generating capacity peaks around age 18 in men, and between ages 33-34 in women.

WORK, REPRODUCTION, SEXUALITY AND PERSEVERANCE

Anyone with a defined Sacral Center is a Generator by Type. The Sacral generates the creative life force, and has the power to guide and sustain life. Its receptive frequency is designed to respond to what it meets in a protective, healthy, honest, creative and persevering manner. This center distinguishes itself from the other centers in three significant ways: its complexity (second only to the Throat Center); its capacity to generate the life force; and its ability to communicate its moment-to-moment availability through its own responsive guttural sounds. Those sacral sounds emerge out of a trustworthy inner guidance system that existed long before the capacity for speech evolved. With almost 70 percent of the world's population capable of being guided by defined Sacral Centers, there is a huge but as yet untapped potential among humanity for awakening and awareness.

The receptive Sacral Center is designed to respond to life, to what is being asked of it, by making expressive noises and sounds. These primal sounds, which do not originate in our Throat Center, but vibrate from our midsection (like a diaphragm opening or closing), let us know if we have the energy for something, or not. These sounds tell us if we like what we see or hear, or are asked to do, or not. Everyone who honors the nature of their Sacral, and the guidance of its sounds, is in touch with their own power.

The sounds can vary person to person, culture to culture, but they are simple and easily recognized. A 'yes' might be an open ended sound like ah-HUH (with the accent on the last syllable), while a closed UHN-un (emphasis on the first syllable) means 'no'. If the answer to a question is hmmmm (or I don't know), then perhaps the timing is not right or the question needs to be re-phrased. People with defined Sacral's do not, and cannot, really know what is correct for them unless they hear their Sacral's response. Reconnecting with and learning to trust their sounds once again are the first steps toward living true to themselves, and establishing the potential for personal transformation. Generator children make these sounds naturally until they are conditioned to answer with words; they will make little ah-huh or uhn-un noises when asked yes or no questions. Parents who encourage such responses when they ask questions, and who honor their child's inner guidance, nurture self-confidence.

The Sacral Defined to the Throat

The manifesting energy of Throat-to-motor connections with the Heart, Solar Plexus, and Root Centers pushes outward or moves toward something or someone, and is described as an initiating energy. The specific, enveloping energy that the Sacral motor emits naturally draws life and people into its embrace so it can respond to them, and is described as responsive. This is why Generators meet with resistance when they try to initiate. They are attempting to reverse the Sacral's natural energy flow.

When the Sacral motor is defined to the Throat Center, however, through Channel 34-20 for example, we have an anomaly where the Sacral's generative power is converted into a potential for manifestation. The defined Sacral then has the potential to move immediately from response to action. People with a Sacral-Throat connection, called Manifesting Generators, often experience their responses as actual physical movement toward or away from something or someone, rather than simply as Sacral sounds. Manifesting Generators are discussed in more detail in Section 3.

The nine gates of the Sacral Center describe the availability of the life force, and reveal the many processes the Sacral Center supports, or not. The gates of the Sacral Center are described in the table on the next page.

GATES OF THE SACRAL CENTER

Gate 34 - The Power of the Great The Gate of Power	Pure power to empower
Gate 5 - Waiting The Gate of Fixed Patterns	The energy to set and repeat patterns and rituals in order to ensure a consistent flow
Gate 14 - Possession in Great Measure The Gate of Power Skills	Releases energy (money, resources) to empower direction in life
Gate 29 - The Abysmal The Gate of Perserverance	Commits to an experience completely for true discovery potential
Gate 59 - Dispersion The Gate of Sexuality	The sexual energy to bond with a mate
Gate 9 - The Taming Power of the Small The Gate of Energy for Detail	Concentrated energy to establish a pattern
Gate 3 - Difficulty at the Beginning The Gate of Ordering	Brings order to the mutative pulse frequency
Gate 42 - Increase The Gate of Growth	Closes a cycle and brings things to an end
Gate 27 - Nourishment The Gate of Caring	Nourishes and protects for survival

THE DEFINED SACRAL CENTER – 66% OF THE POPULATION

Those who enter the world with a defined Sacral Center are the custodians of an enormous source of power. Every day their Sacral motor generates a certain amount of energy that feels like a constant buzz humming away within them. This is a genuine vitality which can be experienced as restlessness, an inability to sit still, or a need to burn energy by being active. Nothing is more important for them than to find personal expression and deep satisfaction by using their daily supply of energy for work or activities they love to do.

The Sacral is very powerful in response. When asked a yes or no question, its immediate response reveals whether the energy requested is currently available to itself and others, or not. If a response is affirmative, or moves toward something, the Sacral's full power is behind the decision. If the response is unenthusiastic, or the energy feels like it is pulling back, the activity cannot be sustained without overextending the Sacral's generative energy.

For example, when somebody asks, "Do you want to learn how to play tennis?" and you hear the Sacral say "uhn un," that is the truth. And this truth must be honored because it is the only way defined Sacrals will know if they have the energy for what they are being asked to do. In practical terms, what they heard was their Sacral voice telling them that the energy is not available at this time. Each negative Sacral response sets a clear and healthy boundary that protects them from potential harm, embarrassment or from merely overextending their energy. They cannot stick with commitments they have not entered correctly through response. Sacral energy is simply not available to support decisions made with your mind. This is why it is essential to know how to respond, and how to correctly engage this energy in productive and fulfilling ways. If Generators allow a mental decision to usurp their Sacral's immediate response, they will most likely meet resistance, experience exhaustion, frustration and unhappiness, or quit.

Not completing what they have started has earned Generators a reputation for being quitters. Avoiding this scenario begins with understanding that the nature of the Sacral's frequency is to persevere in order to master a skill or achieve competency. This energy is set in motion and sustained by response, by correctly committing their energy to begin with. Unlike manifestation, which occurs through the Throat Center, Sacral energy reaches plateaus and must have the power to persist through those 'stuck' points until a sudden breakthrough (initiation) propels one to the next level of mastery. Without Sacral energy, these recurring plateaus can become insurmountable obstacles, sources of frustration, fatigue and the temptation to quit. The only way that those with a defined Sacral can make sure that their persevering Sacral energy is firmly behind them from the beginning is through an affirmative response.

The mantra and Strategy, therefore, for the defined Sacral Center is 'do not initiate.' Never take the first step or move toward something without being asked so it can respond. The moment one initiates, the connection to the sacral source of the power to persevere is broken. The secret is to wait, and keep the Sacral available so that it can respond to exactly what is right for each of us individually. Listening to the primal sounds of the Sacral responses tells one if there is energy available. Knowing that there is reliable energy to fulfill a commitment, and finding satisfaction in doing it, builds a Generator's confidence in making decisions that are correct, and builds trust in sacral sounds.

Others can feel the powerful and available resources of a defined Sacral Center, and they will want to take advantage of this energy. Letting the mind talk the Sacral into doing something that is not right for it will simply lead to frustration and a society of laborers working at something they do not love. We must honor the Sacral's limitations by honoring its guidance through the sounds it makes.

Perhaps the hardest thing for people with Sacral definition to accept is that their trustworthy response is a mechanical process, and neither rational nor aware. Responses are not judgments of right or wrong, and they do not come with the rational or articulated vocabulary to explain them. Response is so pure that it bypasses awareness altogether. Generators often describe it as life making a decision through them, and that's exactly what happens. It doesn't matter what they 'think' their life should look like, as the life force knows what is correct for them, and what they have energy for. This is their truth. Their patient and expectant waiting allows the universe to bring life to them, while their responses attune them to the ebb and flow of the unique path and pupose they are here to live.

The Undefined Sacral Center — 34% of the population

The undefined Sacral Center is always vulnerable to the intense conditioning field (or buzz) created by the majority of human beings on the planet with defined Sacrals. It is extremely sensitive to the energy levels in people and places, and is capable of magnifying those energies. Those with undefined Sacral's are subject to elevated levels of energy pumping through bodies that are not equipped to handle it. They often run on this 'borrowed' energy and over-extend themselves, leading to breakdown and exhaustion. Not designed to live in response, they can never rely on their own sounds to guide their decisions, or to tell them when enough is enough.

Without a defined Sacral Center, the Manifestor, Projector and Reflector Types are particularly subject to energy excesses. They are not born knowing when enough is enough, or how to establish healthy boundaries for themselves. With their undefined Sacral filled to overflowing by other people's energy, they are always busy with work and family and never know when to quit. They take on too much and feel like slaves, but don't really know what to do about it. When they recognize they are tired, they override this and push on through, jeopardizing their health. They don't know when (or understand how) to pull away from the Sacral energy around them and realign with their own personal Authority.

It is difficult for them to know when it is correct to enter a situation or relationship versus when to wait, or how long to stay or when to get out. They are constantly taking in other people's Sacral fuel, so it is wise to make sure that the fuel is the right kind for their vehicle. Understanding how they connect to the people around them is the key to maintaining their vitality and a healthy open Sacral, and this can only be achieved by experimenting with their Strategy and Authority.

The Sacral Center is about the availability, or not, of pure, generative, life-force energy, particularly sexual energy. The undefined Sacral has no consistent boundaries, and with a potential for deep conditioning in this area, can be anywhere from mildly curious to obsessed with sex. Each sexual experience will be unique because the undefined Sacral is being conditioned either positively or negatively by its partner. This information is especially important for teenagers as they mature. The potential wisdom of this undefined center is to learn about healthy sex and safe boundaries, and to be able to discern when enough is enough. This includes learning to rely on their Strategy and Authority to enter relationships correctly in the first place.

Consistent levels of generative and persevering energy are not available to people with an undefined Sacral; the energy is there and then it's not there. If they understand and respect this, they will take time to rest when rest is needed. They should not ignore their energy levels. Failure to properly manage their energy can lead to serious sleep problems, resulting in insufficient, non-rejuvenating rest. Just as they amplify the defined Sacral's energy, they can also magnify its fatigue, erroneously thinking it is their own. The healthy bedtime practice for undefined Sacral's is to go to bed early, before they are tired, to ease into sleep. They need this quiet time alone to release the Sacral energy buzz they have taken in during the day.

Most people with undefined Sacrals, when truly honest, admit they don't really want to work. They would love to relax and let others do the hard work. When we observe those with undefined Sacrals, however, this usually is not what we experience because the Sacral is one of the most easily and deeply conditioned centers. The sheer number of defined Sacrals, and size of the overall Generator field on the planet, easily overwhelms undefined Sacrals.

When at peace with their undefined Sacral, however, the three open-Sacral Types are relaxed, have healthy boundaries, and through their Authority know when enough is enough. They work in spurts, taking plenty of time for rest. They respect their inconsistent energy flow. They enjoy taking in the life-force energy of others without responding to it or identifying with it. They balance their work with rest, and become wise about the ways the creative, powerful and responsive energy of the Sacral operates, and can be best utilized by those who are generating it.

THE COMPLETELY OPEN SACRAL CENTER

The completely open Sacral does not know what to use its energy for. It finds its own energy scattered all over the place, drawn to this thing or that thing. There is no longer a question of knowing when enough is enough; it merely waits for exhaustion from inappropriate and excessive activity to overwhelm it so it can stop.

Many have been drawn through this openness into a fascination with who we are and why we exist. People with completely open Sacral's like Krishnamurti, Osho and Ra Uru Hu have given us deep insights into the nature of being. The wisdom available here is that one can truly measure the life force – can become wise about what energy is really for – and can then express or describe the many qualities this unique energy makes available to humanity.

NOT-SELF TALK OF THE UNDEFINED SACRAL CENTER

The not-self mind is the spokesperson for the undefined centers, and tells us what we should say or do. Noticing this talk is essential to deconditioning. Here are some examples of what the not-self mental monolog could sound like with an undefined Sacral Center: Let's keep working. We really need to get this done. We need to say yes to that otherwise we might miss out on something. I can keep going. Let me just get a cup of coffee. We can do that too. Not a problem. We're not tired yet. I don't want to take a nap or lay down – there's too much to do. Let's take care of that for them. I have to do it myself. Let's go find a mate. Who can we take care of? Life is juicy – who wants to say no. Yes, we are doing all the work but then someone has to do it. I don't think it's enough yet. Boundaries? What boundaries?

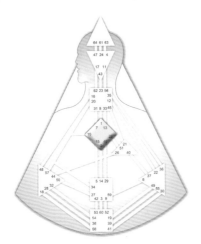

G CENTER

LOVE, IDENTITY AND DIRECTION

(SEAT OF) THE MAGNETIC MONOPOLE, HIGHER SELF

BIOLOGICAL CORRELATION

Biologically, the G Center is associated with the liver and the blood. Liver function determines the health of our blood, and blood carries nutrients and oxygen to every organ and cell in the body. Once liver cells are damaged, they cannot be replaced. We know that alcohol destroys the liver and robs a person of their identity. The spiritual nature of this center has its roots in Indo-European traditions which held that reincarnation took place through the liver. This coincides with The Human Design System's understanding of the role of the Magnetic Monopole in our incarnating process. It draws us into a body and leaves when that body dies.

LOVE, IDENTITY AND DIRECTION

LOVE: The G Center is the most extraordinary center in the BodyGraph. Its essential and mystical component, the Magnetic Monopole, is a magnet with a single pole. (Everything else in Human Design exists as a binary.) This single pole only attracts, and what it attracts is love and beauty. Take a moment to look at your own Mandala. Notice the spokes of your definition radiating from the outer wheels inward toward the yellow diamond at the center of the BodyGraph. The G Center's strategic position illuminates its importance in the Mandala and in our life. It illustrates how the cosmic/planetary influences revolve around this center, while the Magnetic Monopole within it draws toward us what is specifically ours (by definition) to experience over the course of our lifetime. We are designed to live that love which is attracted to us, beginning with loving ourselves.

Prior to our incarnation, the Magnetic Monopole and the Design Crystal fit together perfectly. As the baby's body forms during pregnancy, the Design Crystal moves into the Ajna Center and the Magnetic Monopole takes up residence in the G Center, creating what is described as the illusion of separateness. Their separation creates a sort of longing between them that we experience as a life-long search for love. And love, in one form or another, is what life is all about. This feeling of separation is what drives us to look outside ourselves for love, trying to get a sense of where we are going and who we are in relation to others. We are trying to become worthy of the illusive love we seek. The mind takes advantage of this seeking and, through our open centers, exaggerates both our longing and our desire to know ourselves. The joke is that everything has been right here within us all along; we do not have to look outside ourselves to discover who we are, or where to go to find love. The G Center holds love. Love is the force that permeates and binds the universe, pulling everything toward a state of oneness again. Surrendering to the direction of our form is how we are designed to experience the fullness of that love.

"WE ARE NOT HERE TO BE LOVED, BUT TO BE LOVE." – RA URU HU

IDENTITY: The Magnetic Monopole is responsible for several aspects of our experience of life, from before birth to after death. One aspect is creating our identity during life by holding the Personality and Design Crystals in quantum in our BodyGraph. This unique and individual blueprint separates or differentiates us from everyone else. Even if we don't have a conscious or enduring sense of our self, we can know, and literally see in the BodyGraph, that it is there.

DIRECTION: Another aspect is the internal pull exerted by the Magnetic Monopole which holds us in our place within the totality, and keeps us on our path. It is like having our own inner GPS, and this pull allows our unique role in life to naturally play out. Without it we would have no sense of differentiation; we would feel at one with the totality rather than being individuated. There would also be nothing to hold us together, along with everything else in the universe, in our perceived separateness. It is the Magnetic Monopole that differentiates or separates us, and its mysterious and mystical attracting force is called love. Our Personality and Design Crystals are held together like two people in a forced marriage. Once we accept their specific roles, and resolve our own internal conflict between these two sides of our being, we can attain a state of self-acceptance, and self-love. Only then are we capable of receiving and giving the love we enter life yearning for.

The Magnetic Monopole knows where we are, where we are going and how to get us there. It attracts all the people, places, and events that we are here to encounter to us, determining the way life itself is attracted to and authentically lived through us. We call this movement in time through space our trajectory, or direction. We are moved along this trajectory one correct decision at a time. It is futile to go looking for anything since living correctly will bring to us the life and the love that is perfect for us. We have a driver to get us there, and all we have to do is sit back, and through our Strategy and Authority, let the Magnetic Monopole guide our vehicle.

"SINCE THE BEGINNING EVERYTHING HAS BEEN MOVING UNI-DIRECTIONALLY IN SPACE. EVERYTHING THAT EXISTS, IN ANY SHAPE, STATE OR FORM, IS PART OF THIS MOVEMENT. ACCORDING TO ONE OF THE GREAT LAWS OF SCIENCE, "NO TWO OBJECTS CAN OCCUPY THE SAME PLACE AT THE SAME TIME," EVERYTHING THAT IS MOVING, AND EVERYTHING IS MOVING, HAS A UNIQUE GEOMETRY. OUR LIVES ARE ABOUT GEOMETRY. THE ANCIENTS REFER TO THIS AS DESTINY. THIS WORD HOWEVER OFTEN IMPLIES PREDETERMINATION. THE DIFFERENCE BETWEEN DESTINY AND GEOMETRY CAN BE BEST SEEN IN THE WAY THE TWO EXPLAIN DEATH. DESTINY OR PREDETERMINATION SAYS THE "TIME" OF DEATH IS FIXED, WRITTEN. GEOMETRY SAYS ONLY THAT THE "DIRECTION" TOWARDS DEATH IS FIXED. – RA URU HU

INCARNATION CROSSES OF THE VESSEL OF LOVE AND THE SPHINX

When placed within the Mandala, the eight gates of the diamond-shaped G Center form a symmetrical configuration that brings the 12 signs of the Zodiac from the inner wheel into a conversation with the eight gates of the G Center in the outer wheel. The Mandala illustrates the way the Magnetic Monopole, through its core of love inside us, draws our life to us from the macrocosm of the universe that surrounds and informs us.

Two pivotal Incarnation Crosses are represented in this configuration. The first is the Cross of the Vessel of Love. Its four gates represent the love of humanity (Gate 15), the love of self (Gate 10), universal love, the ability to love existence without discrimination (Gate 25), and the love of the body (Gate 46). The Magnetic Monopole regulates the mechanics of these transpersonal forms of love as well as their integral opposites, forms of hate. Without the longing the Magnetic Monopole creates in its separation

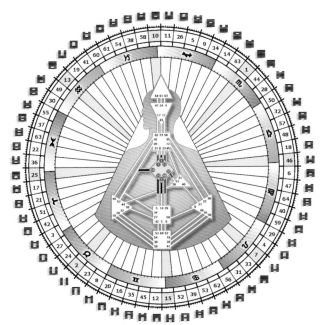

from the Design Crystal, or without the tension between the Design (red) and Personality (black) that it holds in quantum as our identity, there would be no place to experience the push/pull of a love/hate binary. We live in a duality, and one cannot exist without the other. What we seek is balance and harmony between them. The Cross of the Sphinx, which represents direction, is the second. With separation and differentiation comes the need for a reference point from which to take our bearings, a point of comparison. If there were no differentiation of the self, there would be no direction and no need for us to have one. If all is one, there is nowhere to go. Three of the four gates of the Cross of the Sphinx operate like perspectives that points us toward the past, the present, or the future. The fourth gate is the driver (Gate 2). The driver can look at its place in the now (Gate 1), it can look back (Gate 13), or it can look ahead (Gate 7). These same four gates are also called role gates, and our role in life is lived out according to the correctness of our geometry, our direction.

The complex and fascinating mathematics, beauty, and symmetry of these two crosses are explored in greater detail in advanced courses of study, but of note here is how the Cross of the Vessel of Love encompasses the full cycle of life. Its four gates mark the beginning of each of the four seasons. The vernal (spring) equinox takes place when the sun enters the 25th gate. The summer solstice is celebrated when the sun enters the 15th gate. The autumnal equinox occurs when the sun enters the 46th gate, and the winter solstice, the shortest day of the year, begins when the sun enters the 10th gate.

GATES OF THE G CENTER

GATES OF DIRECTION

Gate 1 - The Creative The Gate of Self-Expression	Our place in the now The capacity for creativity
Gate 13 - The Fellowship of Man The Gate of The Listener	Direction or directing by looking back Hearing other people's secrets
Gate 7 - The Army The Gate of the Role of the Self in Interaction	Direction or directing by looking forward Leading by influence
Gate 2 - The Receptive The Gate of the Direction of the Self	Direction or vision The director or the driver

GATES OF LOVE

Gate 15 - Modesty The Gate of Extremes	Love of Humanity, embracing different rhythms and extremes of behavior
Gate 10 - Treading The Gate of the Behavior of the Self	Love of the Self The love of being oneself
Gate 25 - Innocence The Gate of the Spirit of the Self	Universal love, retaining innocence despite circumstances
Gate 46 - Pushing Upward The Gate of Determination of the Self	Love of the body Determination to follow through

THE DEFINED G CENTER – 57% OF THE POPULATION

Those with a defined G Center have a fixed and reliable self-identity, a sense of being loved and loveable. Secure in their love for themselves, they can love others without becoming dependent on them. They have a sense of their own correct direction or mission in life, and are naturals at pointing out new directions – and possibly new loves – for others. With a deep sense of connectedness to their center, they have the capacity to comfort people who are concerned about the direction humanity is heading in, by helping them understand the nature of our evolution as a species.

A common dilemma for them, especially if not relying on their Authority, is expecting everyone to go wherever they are going, even though they don't always know where life will take them or how they will get there. This can be divisive if they try to direct or lead others without waiting to be asked or invited; if they forget that not everyone is designed to go the same way they are going. What they don't understand is that they cannot change or control their own direction, so if another person isn't comfortable with it or able to follow along, both parties need to be free to follow their own path. Although their G Center is defined, succumbing to expectations imposed on them or conditioned by others, while rejecting their own direction and thereby denying themselves love, can lead them to experience such a sense of loss in their life that they give up on themselves altogether.

THE UNDEFINED G CENTER – 43% OF THE POPULATION

People with undefined G Centers have no fixed identity. This is not a handicap, and there is absolutely nothing wrong with them. What is difficult for them to comprehend is living without knowing who they are, or having a consistent and reliable sense of identity. No one truly knows the parameters of their open personality – and neither do they! They blend in or adapt to the people they interact with, and they can fit in anywhere or nowhere. One way or the other, they are always subject to the auric influences (definition) of the people in their environment. They are here to be initiated into the many ways there are of 'being.' Over time, a comfortable sort of identity emerges for them when they are in stable relationships that are correct and supportive of them.

They are most vulnerable to begin with in relationships, because opposites still attract. A person with definition is naturally attracted to a person with an open center, and vice versa. Those with open G Centers gain security from a sense of 'borrowed' identity and direction, and those with a defined G Center see themselves reflected back and think, "They are just like me." If open G's are aligned with their own design, they will recognize that what the other person sees is merely a reflection, and the defined G's will recognize that their partner is NOT just like them. If the relationship continues while ignorant of the differences, the defined partner will impose themselves, their identity and their direction, without realizing what is happening.

People with an undefined G are not without direction. They do have an internal direction finder that is always working, but not in the same way as a defined G Center. Undefined G Centers will be directed here or taken there, and can be conditioned to go most anywhere by others. It is part of their path. This sampling of directions is the way they determine which one is correct for them. They also collect places that are right for them that they can return to, such as the right places to eat, shop, work, and play.

The mantra for the undefined G Center is: if you are in the wrong place, you are with the wrong people/person. The undefined G is specially equipped to sense when the environment they are in isn't correct for them. If someone takes them to a restaurant, home, store or office that doesn't feel right, they will automatically transfer that feeling of unease to the person who took them there, to the people they meet there, or to proposals or commitments suggested while there.

As an example, you might take a woman with an open/undefined G to a restaurant in order to introduce her to a potential business partner, but if the restaurant is the wrong place for her, the connection can't work. Try changing restaurants. When you find the one that is right for her, then the viability of the connection can be accurately assessed. This is how undefined G Centers discover others on their trajectory. It's all about place. When those with an undefined G are in the right place, the direction of their life is correct, and the people they meet will be correct. They will thrive as their undefined center amplifies and reflects the correct energy of people around them, as if where they are is what they are. In other words, the wrong house, job or relationship can be the cause of great unhappiness.

The beauty of having this center open is that people around the Open G often become their willing allies, full of suggestions and eager to help. New directions and new loves are brought to them all the time. Friends show them where everything is, and take them to the correct people, places and jobs. The undefined G Center's not-self question is, "Am I still trying to find direction and love?" When aligned with their vehicles, they do not have to find anything themselves. In fact, they cannot find it for themselves. It doesn't work that way for them.

Let's say you need a new place to live. You would begin by calling your friends and realtors with a description of exactly what you are looking for. Then you sit back and wait to see what they show you. By visiting each place they have found for you, you will get a sense of which one is correct for you. Once you find that place, you do not owe the people anything other than their fee and an expression of gratitude for showing it to you. They were merely being of service to you which is their proper role in your life. The same strategy applies to love. The moment you stop chasing after love, it comes to you. Understanding and accepting that you are designed to wait for others to initiate you to your direction and place can be profoundly liberating. People with an undefined G Center need their independence, and need to have people around them who support their freedom to explore the expansiveness of their lives. If they find themselves in a relationship that is not correct, they will feel trapped and begin looking for a way out!

Making sure that a child with an undefined G Center feels comfortable in their bedroom or special playroom can mean the difference between simply existing and thriving in their formative years. If there is anything about a place that is uncomfortable or unpleasant, change it whenever possible. The same applies to school. If school does not feel like a good place, the child will not thrive or learn. Even moving the student to a different seat can make a difference.

A powerful and cogent motivation underlying the thinking of undefined G's is, "Which direction will take me to love?" Almost every decision the mind makes through its dialogue with the not-self is filtered by this question, "Is this where I will find love?" The not-self can become obsessed with where they are headed, and when they are going to find love. It prods them to search for identity by trying to understand who they are. They can become preoccupied with earning titles and adding letters behind their name so they can say, "I am a doctor or professor or lawyer." They initiate over and over again only to meet resistance. Not knowing who they are leads them to believe something is wrong with them, and this sends them searching for the illusive self. Life without a fixed sense of direction can feel disorienting. And place seems to be a mystery because it's not about what our mind thinks it is. When people with an undefined G try to understand themselves with their minds, they miss both love and correct direction. Strategy and Authority are always the solution for this.

When at peace with themselves, undefined G's do not need to anticipate their next move, or when love will come again. They are comfortable waiting for something or someone in the environment to initiate them. They realize that it is not up to them and trust that they will be shown the way. They do not become attached to the people who take them to the correct place or love; they simply thank them and move on. This frees them to be comfortable with all types of people, and discerning about who is living life authentically.

Instead of feeling lost, people with undefined G Centers can enjoy what is being shown to them; they can enjoy the people and places they encounter, and are free to take advantage of the guidance given by others. They can tell us what love and direction are because they take in all the possibilities of love, and experience all the different directions. Though they can never see their destination, they know each next step will be revealed if they live as themselves. Ultimately, there are no better guides in life than those with undefined G Centers. By letting go of their need for identity and love, they can step into anyone's shoes and offer loving, correct guidance. They are here to become wise about the ways identity is expressed through a person's behavior. Many great actors of stage and screen have undefined G's with no strong fixed identity of their own. By taking the role (identity) they are to act deeply into themselves, they can reflect it back as a convincing and compelling portrayal of that character.

THE COMPLETELY OPEN G CENTER

A completely open G Center leaves one without clear identifiable personality parameters and an inherent sense of direction. If not grounded in their personal Authority, completely open G's feel afloat and unsure of themselves, turning to others to identify and direct them, and to affirm their lovability. This leaves them vulnerable to manipulation, and open to the conditioning dictates of others. Once they give their authority over to another person, authority figure, or institution, they can no longer live out their true potential.

Over time, as they become comfortable with the openness of their design, they do discover their way or direction, and a sense of their unique being. Like those with undefined G's, their broad experience and comprehension of the nature of being, self love, and the way we are designed to move through life, is wisdom we can all benefit from.

NOT-SELF TALK OF THE UNDEFINED G CENTER

The not-self mind is the spokesperson for the undefined centers, and tells us what we should say or do. Noticing this talk is essential to deconditioning. Here are some examples of what the not-self mental monolog could sound like with an undefined G Center: Who am I? Where should I go to find out who I am? Who can show me? Who am I going to love? Who is going to love me? How do I find them? Where can I find them? What am I going to do with my life? Where should I go to figure out what to do with my life? Is it there? Is it here? Where is it? Do I feel lost? Let's go here because we might find something that will show me who I am or what to do with my life. Let's have a relationship with this person because I will get a sense of who I am.

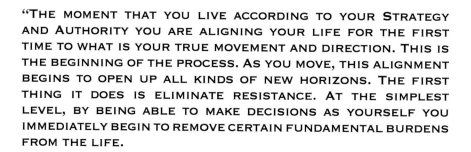

"The moment that you live according to your Strategy and Authority you are aligning your life for the first time to what is your true movement and direction. This is the beginning of the process. As you move, this alignment begins to open up all kinds of new horizons. The first thing it does is eliminate resistance. At the simplest level, by being able to make decisions as yourself you immediately begin to remove certain fundamental burdens from the life.

You begin to see that you can trust a decision-making process within you. You begin to be comfortable with your own authority, something that human beings have been robbed of from the time they came into the world. We are dominated by the authorities of others. And you can see in this struggle that if you depend on your mind to help you it is going to be overwhelmed by the openness." — Ra Uru Hu

SECTION THREE
AUTHORITY
OUR UNIQUE AUTHENTIC TRUTH

SECTION THREE

AUTHORITY

OUR UNIQUE AUTHENTIC TRUTH

In Section Two of this book, you were introduced to the myriad ways your strong and gifted mind tries to be the authority for your life, convinced that it knows what's best for you. Your mind will use and think anything in order to maintain its semblance of control, which makes it part of the dilemma that we face as highly differentiated beings. You can make an ally of your mind, however, by defining and honoring your Authority, and deepening your understanding of your Type's Strategy. Practiced together, these tools free the mind to observe the life of the Form as a relaxed, reflective passenger able to enjoy its ride and fill its role as an Outer Authority for others.

The Human Design System teaches human beings how to live by their own authority; how to make decisions that are individually correct. Although we are all conditioned to seek approval and authority outside ourselves, and to make decisions from the mind, we do have a trustworthy personal Authority that we can actually rely on to make choices. When we intentionally practice our Strategy and Authority, we align with our unique geometry; subsequently, our genetic makeup, our reason for incarnating and our uniqueness are all expressed through us as our true self. Things just naturally fall into place, such as where we live, our job and our relationships.

There are several centers in the BodyGraph that can be defined as a personal Authority, and each represents a different way or mode of making decisions. The hierarchy of modes is listed below and elaborated upon in the pages following. Once the mind has been freed from decision-making, it can take its rightful place in our life as a valued and valuable witness of our life, and Outer Authority for others.

THE HIERARCHY OF AUTHORITY

- Solar Plexus (Emotional Authority)
- Sacral (Sacral Authority)
- Spleen (Splenic Authority)
- Heart (Ego Authority)
- G (Self Authority)
- Environment (No Inner Authority)
- Moon (Lunar Cycle)

Your personal Authority is listed on your Human Design chart. Each type of Authority is described in the summaries that follow.

SOLAR PLEXUS AUTHORITY

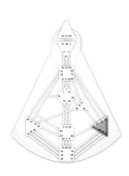

When the Solar Plexus Center is defined, it takes precedence over all other authority centers in a chart. In Section Two we discovered that the Solar Plexus operates through an emotional wave, and that waiting for clarity is the key to living in harmony. Fifty percent of the people on the planet have a defined Solar Plexus and are designed to wait out their emotional wave before making a decision. Their motto is 'there is no truth in the now.' Truth reveals itself in its fullness over time, and emerges eventually as a sense of clarity. Patience is the key component in waiting out the emotional wave before making a decision. As there is no truth in the moment, spontaneous decisions are untrustworthy and not-self based decisions. Time is the key with this Authority; the more time the better. Time puts distance between the moment a decision is called for and the decision itself. As you wait you will gain clarity, although total clarity or total certainty is rare. The goal is to become as clear as possible.

It's best to avoid making decisions from the emotionally charged high or low points along your wave, as this sends chaos into the world and usually results in regret. Depth is not accessible to you in the immediacy of the present moment. Though it's difficult to contain the impulse to react immediately, its best to wait for calm waters before you make your decision. Remember, your truth (clarity) comes to you over time. As you surrender to the depths of your uncertainty you can move beyond the 'for or against' reaction of the moment. You can use this built-in waiting period for discernment, and to avoid making spontaneous mistakes. The Solar Plexus is a potent motor and a source of warm, seductive energy that others desire access to. Waiting for clarity can often be used to your advantage. If you ask others to wait while you take time to properly consider their offer, they may find you or your abilities even more essential and attractive to them, assuming what they are offering is correct for both of you. By experimenting, you will learn and understand this form of decision-making, and discover for yourself just how powerful it can be to wait.

SACRAL AUTHORITY

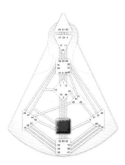

When the Sacral Center is defined without the Solar Plexus Center, we have Sacral Authority, the domain of the Generator. Usually the Sacral voice or familiar ah-huh (yes) or uhn-un (no) is immediately heard or felt when Generators are asked to commit their energy to an activity or relationship. If there is any hesitation, such as hmmmm, the answer is, "I don't know right now – ask me again later or ask me in a different way." Sacral Authority shows Generators, through response, what is correct for them, what their boundaries are, and what they currently have energy to support and engage with. As compared to the Solar Plexus Center which shows its truth over time, this is truth in present time. The Sacral Center only functions in the present moment; it can't predict the future. Its responses tell you whose energy or requests are correct for you, and if your energy is available to give to others or a task. When you hear your Sacral give the go-ahead, you know you will have the energy resources to persevere until you bring the task or relationship to completion, or until you don't have the energy for it any longer. Sacral response is a reliable, honest and trustworthy guide to reducing resistance and maximizing satisfaction.

After many years of conditioning, however, you may find that you need to re-connect with your Sacral response. One good way is to find people who can ask your Sacral 'yes' or 'no' questions. When you are asked, let your sacral response flow immediately. It may take a little time to get comfortable with your Sacral answering, but the more you do it, the clearer your response will become. This is a wonderful way to reawaken and re-strengthen your response, and successfully re-engage this always-ready-to-respond inner guidance system.

SPLENIC AUTHORITY

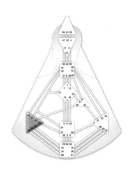

When the defined Splenic Center stands alone without Sacral or Solar Plexus definition, one has Splenic Authority. This can be felt as an instantaneous resonance or recognition with something or someone, and an inner knowing as to whether it is healthy for you, or not. Our highly evolved survival intelligence alerts us to which environments, direction, opportunities and people are safe and advantageous for us to engage with, and which ones aren't.

This type of authority requires a deep level of attention to many subtle physiological sensations, and an ability to act if necessary and correct, no matter what the consequences. The Splenic voice speaks softly and does not repeat itself. Staying in the present and tuned into what your body is telling you is critical to your survival. This is a purely existential authority designed to keep you safe. Do not allow your mind, or the emotional needs, wants and pressures of others, to cause you to second guess or override your Splenic Center's messages.

The Splenic Center is constantly and spontaneously communicating with you about your moment-to-moment well-being, so there is great wisdom available in listening to its alerts. Those with Splenic Authority don't have time to go deep, and to ponder the broader ramifications of their decisions over time. Decisions must be made in the moment. Wait, and the moment and information are gone.

The Splenic Center is not aware of the future, so 10 minutes or an hour or a day later, what was correct for you may change, and your activity along with it. You will 'know' instinctively when something is correct and safe for you in the now moment, and when it is not. To reacquaint yourself with and honor your Spleen's guidance requires experimentation, and a deep trust in the inherent wisdom of your vehicle to take you safely where, how and with whom you need to go.

HEART CENTER (EGO) MANIFESTED AUTHORITY

Ego Manifested Authority is driven by the Heart Center's motor to manifest. Manifested Authority is about articulation. Your Authority is expressed through the Throat Center verbally, and it is important for you to listen to what you 'say' in order to know your truth, rather than what your mind is telling you. Your informing as a Manifestor needs to be verbalized in the moment, as it is not what you think you should say, but rather what you do say when you are not trying to control it. The not-self is always trying to control what we say and, in effect, whatever you blurt out in the moment (bypassing the mind) is your truth. If you try to script what you say in any manner you have lost your connection to your Authority. You are designed to have impact, and it is important for you to trust what you say without the mind overriding it. Surrendering to the truth of your voice is key for you; this is where your impact comes from. With so many open centers competing for your attention, you cannot trust your not-self mind to speak for you. Your voice initiates and runs your life. Your voice leads and you follow. Trust in your voice.

HEART CENTER (EGO) PROJECTED AUTHORITY

For those with Ego Projected Authority, the Heart connects to the G Center through the Channel of Initiation (Channel 25-51). This is a rare form of Projector, and Strategy and Authority are essential to these beings as the only thing they can trust is waiting for the invitation. With a very powerful G Center of identity surrounded by several undefined centers, it is easy for you to get lost in all of this openness. Following your Projector Strategy of waiting to be recognized and invited is the key as there is no motor connected to the Throat Center. You need people in your life to come to you and invite you. Projector leadership is a powerful force in other people's lives, and is here to guide us. You have an enormous capacity to be a transformative force when invited. If lost in the not-self openness, however, you will not find the success that is available to a Projector in life. When making a decision, be selfish and ask, "What do I want? What is in it for me?" The Heart Center is a motor, and you will either have the will (energy) to do something or you won't. While you are waiting to be recognized, it is also important that you use the time to prepare by learning about a system(s) that will help you guide others.

In either form of Ego Authority, or even if not the Authority, a defined Heart Center stays healthy by making and keeping promises, and proving that it has the will to complete what it appropriately committed to doing. To avoid taxing the physical heart, one must be correct when entering into situations that require a commitment of energy over a prolonged period of time.

In addition, the defined Heart must have a balance between work and rest. In effect, the Heart Center works so that it can also have the time to play. Maintaining this balance is essential energetically as well as physically.

SELF-PROJECTED AUTHORITY

Self-Projected Authority originates out of the G Center and connects to the Throat Center through one of four channels. The key with this Authority is to listen to what you say. Whatever you need to know is in what you say, and you have a G Center, a very powerful voice of identity, that speaks for you in reaction to an invitation. Your truth is always expressed through the core of your identity. If there is no truth for you, there is no success for you. When you are invited, listen to what you say. Don't try and figure out mentally what you are going to say; simply listen to and trust your own voice at that moment.

There are no motors present in this type of Authority, and you can become totally lost in the conditioning through your open centers. It can be easy for you to ignore your own voice in the moment, and thus not fulfill what it is to be uniquely you. You are designed to be guided in your decisions by what makes you feel like you, and brings 'you' enjoyment and pleasure. Ask yourself, "Will this make me happy? Will this give me self expression? Am I heading in the right direction for me?" Discussing your impending decisions with others in order to hear yourself, to sense what level of self-satisfaction your decision might bring, is very helpful. To avoid making a decision from your mind, focus on listening to what you are saying without thinking about it. People with a defined G Center often provide direction for others, but only hear their own direction by listening to what they themselves are saying in the moment.

ENVIRONMENT (MENTAL PROJECTORS)

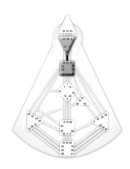

A Mental Projector can have the Ajna Center connected to the Head Center, or the Ajna Center connected to the Throat Center, or the Head, Ajna and Throat Centers all connected to each other. To have no center of inner personal Authority is rare and unique. When there are no centers defined below the Throat Center, we have a design that receives guidance from sensory information about the environment through its open centers. If the environment feels wrong, the people you are with, or ideas exchanged and bargains made there, will not be right either. The first question to ask is, "Is this environment correct for me?" The caution here is to be aware of the strength of your mind and it's tendency to intervene in decision-making. When making a decision about what the correct environment is for you, it is healthy and beneficial to physically visit the environments in question, and notice and recognize within your body how they 'feel' to you.

Though it is good for you to have a group of trusted advisers to turn to, its best *not* to discuss a decision in order to get opinions or advice. Your advisers are best used as sounding boards in order for you to hear *your* own ruminations about the decision.

LUNAR AUTHORITY (REFLECTORS)

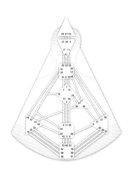

When there are no centers defined in a chart, we have a Reflector whose personal Authority is established by the way their design connects to the lunar cycle. A reliable and repeatable pattern is created as the Moon transits each of the 64 gates around the Mandala every 28 days for as long they live. Before making an important decision, Reflectors need to spend at least one lunar cycle contemplating and discussing the issue. If they understand their Strategy and rely on their lunar Authority, they can achieve clarity in their decision-making process and enjoy being constantly surprised and delighted by life. If they do not honor their lunar cycle, they may suffer disappointment and dis-ease. A key for Reflectors is to slow down and not let the world rush them.

It is important for Reflectors to pay attention to the environment, as they mirror it. The core of the Reflector is their undefined G Center, and being in the correct place with the correct people is imperative to their well-being. If the environment does not feel good to them, or is unhealthy, they won't feel well, or will be ill-at-ease. Conversely, if the environment feels good, they feel good. Reflectors must also have trustworthy advisers or confidantes with whom to discuss any situation and potential decision during this cycle. By hearing themselves talk over time, Reflectors will one day simply arrive at an inner knowing, a deep inner sense of which decision is correct for them. Please see Reflectors in Section Four for more information.

THE LIBERATED MIND AS AN OUTER AUTHORITY

Following our Strategy connects us to our own personal Authority. When we are operating as our unique authentic self, our undefined centers become places of great wisdom. Rather than conditioning us in a distorted way, these undefined centers inform us clearly and accurately about what is going on in the world around us. Once we are on track and aligned with our correct geometry, the mind can begin revealing its own potential as an extraordinary outer Authority for others. It can express our intelligence, commune with others to share our unique experiences and perceptions, and inspire them with what we have learned. The mind is here to think, question, interpret, teach, inspire, remember, organize, name and process data. These are ways we share the gifts of our mind with those who are here to receive them, and respond to them from their own Authority.

The more we free the mind from making decisions by practicing our Strategy and Authority, the more valuable our outer Authority becomes to others. Once aligned with our true nature, we are in tune with our own life force energy and our true purpose in life. Something of unique value then naturally emerges from the mind, something others have been waiting to hear. And our liberated mind regains the potential to ultimately express our unique reason for incarnating.

**"SEE THE BODY AS THE SOLUTION,
NOT AS THE PROBLEM." – RA URU HU**

Section Four
The Four Types and Strategies
Living Our Design

SECTION FOUR

THE FOUR TYPES AND STRATEGIES

LIVING OUR DESIGN

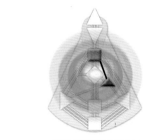

MANIFESTOR

GENERATOR

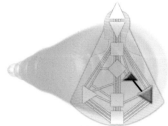

PROJECTOR

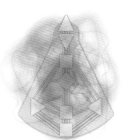

REFLECTOR

The shift that heralded the appearance of Homo sapiens in transitus beginning in 1781, also precipitated the division of humanity into four distinct Types: Manifestors, Generators, Projectors and Reflectors. Type embodies the essence of The Human Design System, and is the basis for its most practical, empowering and transformative information – Strategy and Authority. In The Human Design System, Type concerns the body, our genetics, and our aura; it has nothing to do with psychological or personality typing. Each Type defines a particular mode of operating energetically as a prime auric frequency that is as distinguishable as our blood type. Our practical use of Type is based on an understanding of the subtle and unconscious dynamics of human interaction through the aura. What we communicate through our aura is determined by our body's genetic makeup, which we see defined in our BodyGraph. Definition determines Type, and Type is expressed through our aura.

The four Types are grouped according to their ability to consistently generate or initiate energy, or not. There are two 'energy' types (Manifestor and Generator) and two 'non-energy' types (Projector and Reflector). Non-energy types do not have constant access to their own generating and manifesting capacity, and their energy and stamina for work is not reliably available to them. Following their Strategy maximizes their available energy potential.

OUR AURIC PRESENCE IN THE WORLD

"AURAS ARE A FULL EXPRESSION OF THE BEING, AND A CONTROLLING AGENT OF THE WAY THE FORM IS GOING TO WORK. AURAS ARE THE WAY WE CONNECT TO AND ARE EXPERIENCED BY THE OTHER." – RA URU HU

There is an electromagnetic energy field surrounding and extending outward from every living thing. In the case of human beings, that field extends about two arm lengths in every direction from the body. Auric connectivity is a powerful and non-verbal form of communication that cannot be ignored. If we understand and honor the key differences between Types at this auric level, we create the potential to interact and communicate successfully and amicably with one another on all levels. The provocative nature of our aura does the talking for us: Generator auras provoke others to ask them so they can respond; Projector auras provoke recognition and the invitation; Manifestor auras challenge or initiate; and Reflector auras provoke others to look to them for their reflection/assessment. Each Type can relax into their Strategy with confidence when they understand and allow their aura to do the work for them.

In order to evolve and fulfill our purpose as highly social beings, we must be able to communicate or commune with others. To express our uniqueness with compassion, appreciating and respecting the uniqueness of others, is the consequence of coming to deeply know and love ourselves. Mastering this level of auric communication between Types begins with following one's Strategy.

STRATEGY REFLECTS EACH TYPE'S UNIQUE AURIC MODE

When we talk about an individual's Strategy by Type in Human Design, we are referring to a way of being in the world without resistance; a method that aligns us with our unique geometry in the overall flow of the totality, and supports the process of becoming our authentic self. Strategy is not a philosophy; it is based on the way our vehicle is genetically designed to operate on all levels. Strategy accesses the unique ways energy is designed to flow through each person's BodyGraph, and ultimately determines the way our health, sexuality, relationships, and life purpose play out.

All chart analysis begins at the level of Type. Each Type has a simple, understandable Strategy for efficiently and successfully interacting aurically with the other Types. The Human Design Mandala and BodyGraph provide the specific cosmic backdrop and blueprint, respectively, for determining this Strategy. Once you begin living your Type's Strategy, you will experience its rewards as your Type's signature: as peace (Manifestor), satisfaction (Generator), success (Projector), or as surprise (Reflector). You will discover something inside of you that was hidden by overlays of conditioning. You will get in touch with the part of you that always knew what was correct or not correct for you; that place inside that you can trust to say yes or no to whatever you meet in this life. Strategy breaks through the habit of comparing yourself to others, and opens the way for you to discover your uniqueness so you can simply enjoy being who you are. Strategy frees your inner essence to thrive so your purpose can naturally unfold. Living life according to your Strategy launches your individual experiment. You can test your Strategy yourself and find out if it works for you. Let your own Strategy and Authority begin to replace the blind faith that most of us place in any and all authorities outside of ourselves.

THE MANIFESTOR

CLOSED AND REPELLING AURA

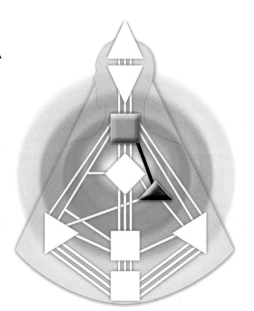

NOT-SELF THEME: **ANGER**

STRATEGY: **TO INFORM**

SIGNATURE: **PEACE**

THE MANIFESTOR TYPE

Two things in particular distinguish a Manifestor's design from the other Types. First, it conspicuously lacks Sacral definition, which immediately places Manifestors in a global minority. Second, there is either a direct or indirect connection between the Throat Center and one or more of the three remaining motors in the BodyGraph: the Heart, Solar Plexus and Root Centers.

Manifestors are somewhat rare, comprising less than 10 percent of the world's population.

OVERVIEW

The saga of humankind unfolded as it did because Manifestors didn't have to wait for the 'gods' or for forces outside themselves to move them into action. Manifestors' exceptional ability to bring into being or make manifest what they envision, in combination with the protection of their closed and repelling aura, often placed them in positions of rulership such as a warrior king or high priest. As the only pure doers among the Types, Manifestors conquered and defended kingdoms, and secured and maintained their power and authority by establishing the laws. Our remaining religious and secular hierarchies are a result of the Manifestor's attempt to retain control and to avoid being challenged.

The traditional ruler's role that Manifestors held for centuries ended around 1781, however, when humans transitioned from the 7-centered to the 9-centered form. Today's Manifestors, still the instruments of the yang/yang principle (primal force), are now living in a yin/yin (receptive) Generator-dominated environment. Instead of dreaming empires into being or determining the course of civilizations, they are now looking for a way to integrate their inherent independence, and unique essential power to impact, into a society that has stripped away their freedom to act.

In today's world the Manifestor's incredible gifts are their ability to act independently, to initiate action, and to impact others. When perceived as threatening or unpredictable, however, these same qualities can make the other three Types uncomfortable, and often lead to overt attempts to control the Manifestor. Manifestors are at ease with solitude, and find a nourishing peace in manifesting what they want for themselves. This is their natural way and they don't require outside assistance. They can't understand why others would even care about what they do, much less want to resist or control them, but try to control they do – from parents on up. An early and unpleasant history of conditioning experiences, mixed with resistance, pushes the Manifestor toward its not-self theme of anger. This anger will be expressed in one of two ways: as anger/rage and rebelliousness, or as passivity and accommodation. Both expressions repress the power of Manifestors and keep them from realizing their worth, which is why Strategy is so important. By informing, and thus relaxing the resistance met from others, Manifestors find what they seek most in life – the peace to do what they want, when they want to do it.

Manifestors are not particularly interested in themselves, nor do they need to rely on other people to ask them or invite them in order to act on their Authority. They are self-contained, independent agents. They tend to see others as rather alien, behind the times, and stuck or unable to move themselves out of predicaments. With their ability to glimpse the future, Manifestors often feel as if they are waiting for everyone else to catch up.

The questions Manifestors ask are, "Will I be answered? Will someone be enlivened by my impact, or respond to my initiating question?" This underlying pressure to impact, to make things happen, is key to fulfilling their purpose. Manifestors are most comfortable when left alone to do as they please, yet the other three Types are waiting for the Manifestor to initiate them, or a new process, so each can contribute their essential part. Manifestors often look to the other Types to provide the specific energy needed to complete what they themselves dream. In a perfect world, Manifestors get things started; Projectors guide the process; Generators provide the energy to realize or complete it; and Reflectors tell them how well it is going.

MANIFESTOR STRATEGY: TO INFORM

Manifestors have a long-standing reputation of posing a threat to order and stability. Their independence and closed, repelling aura, which literally pushes their energy outward, is often experienced (and misinterpreted) by others as the Manifestor's need to take control or be in charge of the situation. People often feel ignored or run over by 'out-of-control' Manifestors and tend, therefore, to fear them. Conversely, Manifestors grow up conditioned by the fear of being controlled, and rebel by doing the opposite of what is healthy for them. The Manifestor's repelling aura causes other auras to contract, putting people in a defensive or protective mode. Which is to say that most interpersonal confusion or misunderstanding between Types is set up energetically, far below one's level of consciousness, before verbal communication is even initiated.

The Manifestor's simple strategy – to inform – breaks through this highly charged auric interaction, and effectively opens the way to clear, productive and peaceful communication. Informing is the only way Manifestors find the freedom from resistance that they need in order to manifest. Technically, Manifestors need to inform after they have made a decision but before they act on it, or at least as they are acting on it. Additionally, when they decide not to do something any longer, they must inform about that too.

Though informing is far from pleasant and natural for a Manifestor, life is so much easier when they learn to do it, and do it well. It is only by informing that they remove resistance from their path, and put others at ease aurically, without being either passive or aggressive. As a child, informing takes the form of learning politeness and asking permission. From an early age, however, Manifestors often choose not to ask permission or inform, either because it is too much bother, or because they think that by keeping what they are going to do a secret they can avoid being rejected and controlled.

Informing becomes an acceptable, practical part of the decision-making process when Manifestors understand and embrace the impact they have on others. Manifestors do not need people in the same way the other Types do, and are generally not concerned about how others perceive them. They are generally genuinely surprised to learn that they have an impact at all. Becoming aware of the many ways their impending decision will affect others is the first step to bridging relations, and releasing their full initiating power. As Manifestors learn to inform before they act, to prepare people for how they might be affected by their actions, they will begin to feel a new kind of support and receptivity from others. When resistance is no longer an issue, anger subsides and peace prevails. And Manifestors also feel honored and respected when others include and inform them.

To put informing and impact into perspective, let's say a Manifestor goes to work and mid-morning suddenly begins to see a way out of what had begun to feel like a dead-end job. In a flurry of excitement, and with her vision leading her, she packs up her office, places a brief letter of resignation in the boss's mail box, says goodbye, wishes everyone well and walks out. Everyone else then experiences what feels like chaos because they were not properly informed or prepared for the action of the Manifestor. The boss is left without help, the Manifestor's fellow employees wonder what they did to offend, and the Manifestor's family is concerned about the security of their future. The impact of the Manifestor's unanticipated action will most likely meet with some form of resistance from those whose lives were affected by its abruptness.

The Manifestor had a plan of action, and did not need anyone else's advice or input to make it happen. Remembering to inform all of those who would be impacted by the decision, however, would not only have reduced resistance, but also may have garnered the support needed to achieve the new vision in peace. Informing paves the way for manifesting; it is the only solution for the Manifestor.

This strategy seems both logical and simple, and yet, most Manifestors think of themselves as alone in the world, and informing is the last thing that naturally comes to mind. When they take the time to write down the names of all the people their future decision might affect, they will usually see that they are not isolated and their decisions do have impact. When Manifestors are aware of how they impact, the logic of informing becomes apparent, and this knowledge alone can transform them. In the end, informing is about showing respect for the other. When Manifestors don't inform, others feel disrespected and ignored, whereas, informing dispels fear and builds trust which in turn dissolves the need for control on either side.

THE IMPORTANCE OF AUTHORITY

In truth, as compared with the other Types for whom Strategy is a mechanical part of their design, Manifestors have their Strategy artificially imposed on them as a means of eliminating or alleviating resistance. Honoring their own Authority, therefore, becomes even more significant in their lives. To attain the full expression of their cognitive potential, and to have the proper impact, they must act out of their inner truth, and not from the mind. If they make up something to do using their mind, just to release the pressure to get things moving, they will meet with resistance.

MANIFESTORS WITH EMOTIONAL AUTHORITY

As true initiators, the timing of Manifestor's actions are of utmost importance to them, especially Manifestors with a defined Solar Plexus Center. Neither their truth nor their moment of clarity can be accessed in an instant. Emotionally defined Manifestors who don't wait out their emotional wave are more reactive or impulsive; consequently, they meet with more resistance and tend to get into trouble. By honoring and accepting the chemistry of their emotional wave, they can use their waiting time beneficially to determine who will be impacted by their decision. Time brings clarity. By the time they get to the end of their wave, and have reviewed the list of those most impacted, they may decide to not even take action. Emotional authority requires that Manifestors nurture patience in themselves, which can result in a win/win position for everyone.

There is a big difference between actions directed by the mind, and manifesting coming from a place of inner clarity. If Manifestors feel an exaggerated urgency to act or implement their idea, that impulse is usually not coming from their Authority, but rather from the amplified conditioning of an open center expressing through their mind. Sometimes waiting can feel like an excruciating punishment to emotionally defined Manifestors, but it keeps them from acting too quickly and suffering unwelcome and avoidable consequences.

If Manifestors wait through the movement of their wave, they will notice one of two things. Either the feeling of wanting to act has subsided, meaning it was not meant to be, or they still feel they want to make that decision or take that action, and they will when the time feels right. There is no longer a sense of urgency or pressure connected to the decision. Everything can happen naturally when they observe their wave, and inform as they prepare to act. This is the only way emotional Manifestors can reach their goal of living as themselves in peace.

MANIFESTORS WITH SPLENIC AUTHORITY

Unlike the emotionally defined Manifestor's need to be patient and wait for clarity, the action and initiating of the Manifestor with Splenic authority flows out instinctively and naturally in the moment. Such spontaneity, although freeing, creates the dilemma of having to inform when one has only an inkling of the impact that the immediate decision or action might have. It takes a firm intention on the part of the Manifestor to live closely attuned to Splenic Authority, and still effectively inform. For example, if a Manifestor takes that first step into a restaurant with friends and his body stops him, he has no choice but to pay attention to it. Though it is obviously not healthy for him to enter, his Splenic alert did not come with an explanation. All he can do is honestly inform his companions of what action is correct for him right now, and be aware of how his sudden decision impacts everyone's plans.

MANIFESTORS IN RELATIONSHIPS

Despite the fact that they are perfectly capable of great love and devotion for their families, it's not easy for independent loners like Manifestors to be in relationships. Their closed auras do not naturally embrace or take in others. Neither are they penetrable, which means others cannot easily get to know a Manifestor well. This is particularly difficult for a mother or lover because it can create confusing barriers to intimacy. Understanding how Strategy opens the way to clearer auric interaction between Types allows for genuine compassion, and helps to ameliorate any pain associated with misunderstanding the differences.

Additionally, whether male or female, Manifestors have to do the initiating to be correct. For example, if a Manifestor likes somebody, it is proper for them to make the first move instead of hoping they'll be noticed and approached. They need to take the initiative, to pursue the person and let them know what they feel, and what they want or envision. It's a risky business and makes them acutely vulnerable to rejection. Being a Manifestor, though, is about breaking free from the safe routines of tradition. The fears this freedom raises in the Manifestor must be faced and overcome in order to move forward. Just because they are loners doesn't mean Manifestors don't truly desire, or can't have, warmth and companionship and long-term associations.

A peaceful relationship for the Manifestor is based on practicing politeness and informing. They cannot walk out of the house without telling their partner where they are going as this will only create resistance upon their return. "Where have you been?" the partner will ask. "What did you do? Why didn't you tell me?" To avoid the interrogation, all the Manifestor needs to do is inform. "I'm going to the store and I'll be right back." The partner of a Manifestor often perceives the Manifestor's independence as a silent but effective 'do not disturb' sign – which isn't true. Manifestors feel respected when others also keep them informed. Reciprocal informing dissolves much of the resistance, eliminates the anger, and enhances mutual respect between partners in a relationship. You can't tell Manifestors what to do, or ask them like you would a Generator, or invite them like a Projector. If you inform them, however, "We are out of coffee," their Authority will guide them to act on it, if it is appropriate and correct for them to do so.

MANIFESTOR CHILDREN

Perhaps Manifestor children are misunderstood because they are now so rare. Their strong, repelling auras are felt the moment they come into the world, putting their parents immediately on the alert. Even as children, though, they need to be respected and treated as Manifestors, and given a healthy amount of freedom of movement. It is essential to teach them their Strategy early on, for when they are polite and ask permission, they will more often than not be allowed to do what they want to, except when safety is an issue for them or anyone else impacted. Putting excessive controls on Manifestor children forces them to rebel or become passive.

MANIFESTORS AND THE EFFECTS
OF LIVING FROM THE NOT-SELF

Manifestors living and making mental decisions or decisions from their not-self meet a lot of resistance, and may see themselves as victims of control and punishment. They do not experience their inherent power, but instead feel restricted and powerless. These are deep sources for most Manifestors' anger, which may become depression or despair if turned inward on themselves. "Life is so unfair!" To avoid being controlled or rejected, not-self Manifestors tend to relinquish their power, pretending they are not powerful. They behave like Generators by waiting rather than initiating, responding to what others want from them. They become impulsive workaholics but end up accomplishing little. Their timing is completely off as they aggressively initiate but refuse to inform, generally crashing through things and creating all sorts of resistance in their lives. In these ways, powerlessness replaces their authentic power. The overall result is exhaustion and ineffectiveness.

What they forget is that they are still Manifestors, and for anything of value to happen in a Manifestor's life, it is the Manifestor who has to initiate it – including reconnecting to their own life, to their own Authority. They are here to have an impact!

When Manifestors enter their experiment of following their Strategy to inform, and relying on their Authority for decisions, they will have to confront the following fears in order to succeed:

- Fear of upsetting someone
- Fear of informing because it might cause confrontation
- Fear of informing because someone will try to control them
- Fear of informing because they might meet resistance or rejection
- Fear of one's own anger

HEALTHY SLEEP HABITS FOR MANIFESTORS

It is best for Manifestors, with their open Sacral Center, to go to bed before they feel totally exhausted. By lying down or relaxing as much as an hour before they would like to be asleep, they give their bodies a chance to unwind. Additionally, their auras have time to release energies that do not belong to them, thus preparing them for a peaceful, refreshing night's rest.

SIGNATURE GOAL: PEACE

What Manifestors desire more than anything else is peace; a place of no resistance. Breaking away from living a not-self life is what opens the way to that peace. This means dreaming and pursuing their visions, doing what they want to do and are here to do, out of a deep sense of calmness and inner stillness. When they find themselves in this state of peace, they know they are aligned to their Authority by their Strategy of informing, and are empowered to manifest and have their unique and essential impact on the world.

FAMOUS MANIFESTORS

Adolf Hitler, Johannes Kepler, Helmut Kohl, Elisabeth Kubler-Ross, Krishnamurti, Hermann Hesse, Jack Nicholson, Bruce Springsteen, Mao Tse-tung, Jesse Jackson, Maya Angelou, Art Garfunkel, Tracey Ullman, Martha Stewart, Tommy Smothers, George Carlin, Ra Uru Hu, Robert De Niro, Bob Newhart, Jennifer Aniston, Susan Sarandon, Tim Robbins, George W. Bush.

THE GENERATOR

OPEN AND ENVELOPING AURA

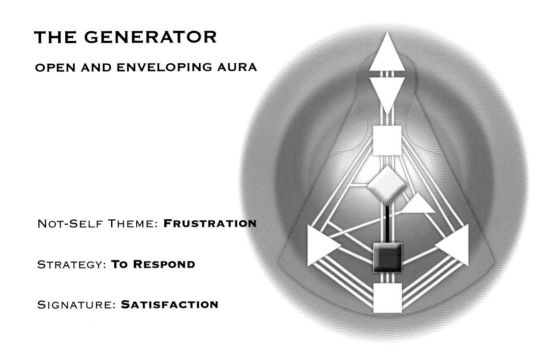

NOT-SELF THEME: **FRUSTRATION**

STRATEGY: **TO RESPOND**

SIGNATURE: **SATISFACTION**

THE GENERATOR TYPE

A defined Sacral Center is indicative of the Generator Type and is of central importance to their well-being. This center both cradles and generates the pattern of life on the planet. When the Sacral Center is defined in a chart, the person is either a pure Generator or a Manifesting Generator. What distinguishes them is that the pure Generator has a defined Sacral but no direct connection or definition between any one of the four motors and the Throat Center, while the Manifesting Generator has a defined Sacral plus a motor-to-Throat connection. The Manifesting Generator is not a separate Type, but rather a variation of the Generator Type. It's a subtle distinction that lies in their auric frequency. Manifesting Generators are Generators by Type, and are designed to follow the Generator Strategy to respond.

As approximately 70 percent of all people are Sacrally defined, the Generator's creative life-force energy dominates the global frequency of the planet. Pure Generators comprise approximately 37 percent of humanity, and Manifesting Generators about 33 percent.

OVERVIEW

Throughout human history, the creative energy and stamina of Generators made them a valuable and desirable commodity. At the same time, ignorance of their own potential made them easy prey for those who could take advantage of their gifts. Generators have always been deeply envious of the ability of Manifestor's to manifest what they envision. Unable to mimic or compete with Manifestors without meeting resistance and failure, they grudgingly surrendered to the Manifestor who ultimately enslaved or controlled them to erect huge empires. Generators became forced laborers, the great builders of our civilizations.

They retain the role of builder to this day, although they now have the tools at their disposal to live this role awake and aware, free of oppression, and with full knowledge of their incredible Sacral potential. They can know exactly what they are here to do, and love doing it – in cooperative and mutually beneficial ways with the other three Types. This new phase of understanding and appreciating their place in the whole is slowly evolving. It will be a reality when Generators relax into responding, when Manifestors initiate, when Projectors guide and when Reflectors reflect the level of satisfaction and authenticity in the world.

All Generators are born to work and to love the work they do, completely exhausting their measure of creative Sacral energy every day. Their Sacral motor doesn't give up until what it has committed to is accomplished. This is what brings deep satisfaction with life and a restful, regenerating night's sleep. The other three Types are looking outward – the Manifestor is focused on impacting, the Projector on knowing about how other Types use their energy resources, and the Reflector on understanding the environment. Generators, however, are focused on knowing themselves and understanding their own process. Generators find their life through their work, through how they respond to using their daily supply of energy. The right work actually transforms their life and slows the degenerative process of their bodies.

Generators are designed to respond with their Sacral Center either through sounds, as a vibration that rises to their throat from their midsection (pure Generators), or as actual movement toward engaging in the activity (more common to Manifesting Generators). Responses are based on the availability of their Sacral energy to do what they have been asked. Once pure Generators respond and are engaged in an activity, they go through a step-by-step process which thoroughly covers each stage of its development. They have no motor connected to the Throat Center, and will hit plateaus of energy along the way. At each of these stuck points, they need to be initiated again by new input, insight, or further instructions so they can respond. In order to avoid the temptation to quit when they reach these moments of transition, their Sacral must be committed to the process from the beginning. The gift of pure Generators is their ability to perfect or master a task or project or skill.

In contrast, Manifesting Generators have a motor connected to the Throat, which enables them to move quickly from response to manifestation. This allows them to see which steps are essential and which steps can be skipped, resulting in the gift of efficiency. This same efficiency creates a dilemma for them, however, which is a tendency to be so impatient and move through a task so fast that they miss steps. They often have to go back and complete those steps which creates frustration. This frustration can be avoided, and efficiency increased, by slowing down enough to pay more attention to their responses as the process unfolds. Manifesting Generators are more prone to impatience and aggression than pure Generators. Because of the motor connection to their Throat Center, they tend to bypass their sacral sounds. It often takes the Manifesting Generator more practice and patience to re-establish a connection to and trust in their Sacral.

GENERATOR STRATEGY: TO RESPOND

"LIKE THE PRIESTESSES OF DELPHI, YOU HAVE TO ASK GENERATORS; OTHERWISE YOU GET NOTHING." – RA URU HU

All Generators have embracing auras that transmit the creative/creating life force of their Sacral Center, and establish an energy field of 'availability' around them. In order to access their enormous wealth of energy and power, one must ask for it so the Generator's Sacral Center can respond. Generators must wait until something comes toward them, so that their Sacral can either fully embrace it or remain closed to it. A Sacral 'ah-huh' carries enough energy to complete the task or honor the request, while an 'uhn-uh' is a 'no' and warns against committing to it.

This kind of clear, objective, honest, moment-to-moment mechanical response connects Generators directly to their own truth, revealing who they are, and what they love and value. Emanating through their aura, the persevering power of their creative life force draws others to them like a magnet, while their Sacral response sets clear personal boundaries. For Generators, life is renewed with each response because each decision moves them along their path toward the perfection of their unique potential.

Generators often misinterpret or equate 'waiting to respond' with 'doing nothing.' It is impossible for them to do nothing because they are constantly busy generating. If they are doing the work they love, or if they retreat from a dog's growl, or smile when a bird sings, or hum along with a tune, or enter a conversation when asked, they are living in response. Generators are designed to wait, trusting that life will come to them. They simply respond from the moment they get out of bed in the morning until they fall back into bed at night. A revolution of Generators living completely through response could change the frequency on the planet from frustration to satisfaction. This is why the Generator's mystical path and contribution to humanity is to wake up their Sacral, and to live surrendered to its subjective truth.

It is helpful for the other three Types to understand that once a Generator has committed to a task or a direction, they cannot quickly change gears. To a Manifestor, the Generator feels slow and ponderous, and a Projector offering guidance may feel like the Generator is not listening. Only by being asked again, so they can respond, are Generators able to disconnect from where they are in the moment, and reconnect to something different. When asked so they can respond, there is a clearer, more straightforward, and productive exchange between Types. Learning to ask Generators good 'yes or no' questions makes all the difference.

Half of the battle for Generators is accepting the fact that they cannot manifest their ideas for their own life. They need to give up any pictures that their minds have about what their life 'should look like.' Desires and fantasies, usually based on comparisons coming through their open centers, push them into actions intended to force those dreams into reality. Such initiating merely meets with resistance, however, not satisfaction. Frustration is the guidepost that reminds Generators to return to their own one-of-a-kind responsive life.

The following narrative about a Generator and a Manifestor illustrates the difference between responding and initiating. You will recognize their Strategy by the roles they play. The setting is a dusty western town, and sitting in front of his office is the sheriff. The townspeople are in an uproar because they have heard that a gunslinger is on his way to town. Everyone tries to get the sheriff to move, to do something to protect them. The sheriff just sits and waits. The gunslinger arrives in town, dismounts, walks into the middle of the street and informs the sheriff of his intentions. The sheriff responds and steps away from his office and into the street to face him. The gunslinger draws his gun and the sheriff, empowered by waiting, shoots him dead. The moral of the story is that Generators who wait until they are fully empowered and perfectly clear in their response will find their actions are well-timed and right on target.

GENERATORS WITH EMOTIONAL AUTHORITY

Emotional Authority adds another dimension to the waiting game for Generators. Their warm, passionate energy has enormous value to others, which gives their waiting a subtle element of seduction, and allows Generators to shape the outcome of an offer on their own terms. No one has the right to gain immediate access to their energy. They become their own worst enemy if they succumb to impatience by hurrying the process, initiating, accepting less than they should have, or jumping into a commitment prematurely. A few handy phrases that give them time to wait out their wave while leaving doors open to their availability are, "It is a good offer, but I would like to sleep on it. It is a lot to consider; may I have some time to think about it?" A non-emotionally defined person might take this as a rejection of the proposal, but if it is correct for both parties, their auras will pull them back together even stronger for having gone through the process properly.

Emotional definition need not be a frustrating detour to living. For Generators, following their emotional wave reveals new perspectives on a decision or situation at each point along the way. Very often the first response is correct, but waiting for clarity allows them to make sure that there is time to uncover all the important things that would otherwise be missed. And sometimes the 'yes' ends up being a 'no' once they have time to see all the information and details that only waiting reveals. Staying with the wave as it cycles, and not rushing into decisions, adds depth to one's life. In order to appreciate this process as it unfolds, however, all involved must be patient.

GENERATORS IN RELATIONSHIPS

To the casual observer, two Generators making a decision in relationship can appear both awkward and hilarious. She might express an idea or possibility and ask him for his response. Since the idea came from her head as an initiating thought, he then has to ask her if it is something she really wants to do also, so she can hear her response. If her sacral says 'uhn-uh', they start all over again, either by refining the original idea or testing a new one. This is the way Generators determine what will ultimately bring the pleasure and satisfaction they seek with each other, in both business and interpersonal relationships. If Generators begin a relationship correctly, they will end it correctly, and leave without blame or guilt. If they don't enter it correctly, they can't leave it correctly, and they may carry a wound inside that can take seven years to resolve. This wound can negatively condition all future relationships. The secret to success is for Generators to begin and build relationships as themselves, through response.

GENERATOR CHILDREN

When Generator children answer with their Sacral voice of ah huh or uhn-uh, they are often told this is not polite. They are forced to stop making sounds and to speak with words and sentences instead. When this happens, the doorway to their Sacral truth closes, and they are cut off from developing genuine self-esteem and self-love. Parents must learn to respect and encourage the Sacral sounds of their children. Generator children are designed to be busy and active until their Sacral energy is used up, and they fall into bed exhausted. Forcing them to take naps before they are tired will meet resistance and frustration on both sides. Aware and understanding parents can develop sensitivity to the energy and inner rhythms of their Generator child.

RECOGNIZING NOT-SELF GENERATOR BEHAVIORS

Generators living as Manifestors are easily recognized by their frustrated, unfulfilled state of being. From childhood on, Generators have been told to "go out there and make it happen." When Generators initiate, however, the energy gets stuck and can't move forward. To compensate, the mind pushes them on ahead or becomes attached to the outcomes they think they want. Instead of finding satisfaction, they can't even finish what they start. They end up exhausting their energy with no satisfaction, their work has no meaning, and their relationships don't measure up or bring them pleasure – life doesn't work for them. This scenario is also why they are great quitters, and yet, the last thing that occurs to them is to wait to respond.

Many Generators have been conditioned since birth to suppress or deny their primal sounds, and instead rely on the mind's open center not-self commentaries to guide them. Generators have become comfortable living their unfulfilling not-self lives, which makes it difficult for them to now revive or reconnect to their Sacral response. They are fearful of the possibility that they may not be able to hear their response, as well as fearful of the change response might bring. They have no real idea what life lived as their true self may be like. After years of practicing vegetarianism, for instance, they might hear their Sacral respond ah huh to a steak!

Generators need to know that there is a time for everything if they wait, and that they can respond to anything as long as it is coming toward them. For example, their minds can't determine what they want to eat. They need to be asked or to hear what is on the menu so they can respond. This is especially important for beginners. Asking themselves questions, talking to themselves in the mirror or responding to questions they have written down, is not the same as responding to something coming toward them from the outside. These shortcuts will not bring Generators to their inner truth. To be effective, another person is needed to ask the clarifying questions.

The underlying question for a Generator is "Will I be Asked?" Or, "If I wait to be asked, will anything ever happen?" Understanding the beauty of their open and enveloping aura, which is designed to draw the question from others, allows them to watch and wait – and relax into living.

As Generators begin to honor their strategy they will have to deal with mental fears such as:

- Fear that no one will ask them or that they will have nothing to respond to.
- Fear of the unknown.
- Fear that nothing will happen in their life or that their survival will be in jeopardy.
- Fear of losing control over their life.
- Fear of failure.

HEALTHY SLEEP HABITS FOR GENERATORS

For Generators, true rest will not come until they have finished generating and burned off that day's supply of energy. When they do fall into bed exhausted, they will sleep better and feel fresh and new in the morning. Manifesting Generators should get into bed before they are exhausted however, and work, read or watch television until they are finished generating. They need to allow their energy to calm down, and yet still continue to move them to a point of exhaustion.

SIGNATURE GOAL: SATISFACTION

What Generators seek most in life is satisfaction. Their minds will never figure out what brings them that kind of deep satisfaction, yet response brings it with ease. There is nothing more rewarding for Generators than to feel a sense of satisfaction in their work, and in their relationships.

FAMOUS GENERATORS

Pure Generators: Dalai Lama, Albert Einstein, Carl Gustav Jung, Mozart, Madame Curie, Luciano Pavarotti, Dustin Hoffman, Greta Garbo, Madonna, Elvis Presley, Walt Disney, Anthony Perkins, Dolly Parton, Mel Gibson, Meryl Streep, Eddie Murphy, Robin Williams, Celine Dion, Garrison Keillor, Ram Dass, Kreskin, Johnny Carson, Oprah Winfrey, Ellen DeGeneres, Paul Simon, Truman Capote.

Manifesting Generators: Mother Teresa, Vincent van Gogh, Friedrich Nietzsche, Alois Alzheimer, Marie Antoinette, Mata Hari, Kate Winslet, Bruce Lee, Charlie Chaplin, Bill Cosby, Barry Manilow, Donald Trump, Tom Hanks, Elton John, Billy Joel, Liza Minelli, Angelina Jolie, Nicole Kidman, Arlo Guthrie, Sidney Poitier, Gwyneth Paltrow, Lily Tomlin, John Denver.

THE PROJECTOR

FOCUSED AND ABSORBING AURA

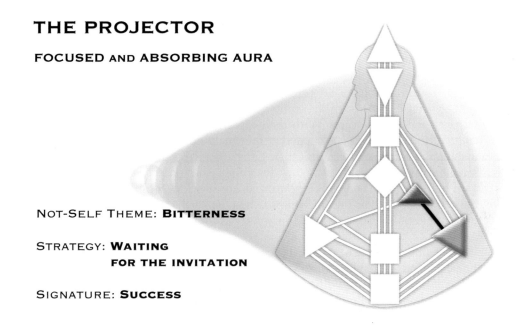

NOT-SELF THEME: **BITTERNESS**

STRATEGY: **WAITING FOR THE INVITATION**

SIGNATURE: **SUCCESS**

THE PROJECTOR TYPE

Two things stand out in a Projector's BodyGraph. The first is an undefined Sacral Center, and the second is that there is no motor connection with the Throat Center, meaning Projectors have no built-in potential for generating or manifesting. Because they possess no consistent, reliable means of manifesting or generating energy, Projectors are classified with Reflectors as a non-energy type. These two Types use their experiential wisdom about energy to increase the understanding and productivity of the energy types (Generators and Manifestors). Projector's charts can be configured with as few as two and as many as eight defined centers. They make up approximately 21 percent of the population.

OVERVIEW

Projectors represent a new energy archetype on the planet that emerged after 1781. Until the advent of The Human Design System, Projectors had no direct means by which to fully comprehend either their unique auric field, or the particular role they are here to play as one of the four Types. Up until the last century, Manifestors and Generators dominated positions of leadership and authority around the world. In the future, however, it is the Projector who will begin to move into positions of greater power, taking leadership itself in a new direction. This will happen when the energy types recognize and empower the Projector's natural potential by inviting the Projector to guide them. As Manifestors are freed to initiate processes, and Generators begin to realign with their own natural power as creative builders, Projectors will emerge as the administrators of the new order.

The Projector's focused, probing aura, and complex way of interacting with people at deeper energetic levels, sets them apart from the other three Types. With their natural brilliance and openness to taking on the expectations and energies of others, they have managed to effectively imitate both Manifestors and Generators, losing themselves in the process. How Projectors reclaim that self, along with their significant and rightful place in the whole, begins with a comprehensive look at the complex nature of their unique configuration.

Projectors have a general openness to life, combined with a penetrating aura that absorbs and energetically tastes the energy of others. With their capacity to see the big picture, recognize the talents and gifts of others, and bring people together, they make exceptional advisors, administrators, networkers and natural mediators. Projectors can be gifted organizers, and masters at understanding how to maximize energy and resources as they see things that others often miss. Just because Projectors can see how a person's energy is best utilized, however, doesn't mean they can tell others what to do. A specific part of their role and purpose here on earth is to guide others by knowing how to ask the right questions. Projectors have a natural gift for diplomacy that is wise to nurture.

Projectors are rising naturally to the top of the Type hierarchy, however, they still have a long way to go, and a great deal depends on having awake and aware Manifestor and Generator energy to work with. Projectors are more interested in other people's designs than they are in their own, and they normally seek out systems that help them to understand individuals, groups and the ways people work together more efficiently and effectively.

Recognition is the Projector's key to understanding the way their Strategy connects them to their Authority and the world. In some ways, recognition is to Projectors what responding is to Generators. Their powers of strategic recognition provide them with their boundaries, which they maintain by being selective when accepting invitations. Both the Projector's ability to recognize what is available to them from others, and the need for their own unique gifts to be properly recognized by others, are part of the specific way their auras are designed to connect. The Projector aura is an I-am-open-to-an-invitation field that draws people in and out of their lives by provoking invitations from them. Recognition, accompanied by a formal invitation, is the way the other Types honor and empower Projectors.

As with Generators, waiting is a quality of the Projector's Strategy, however the clarity of their answer is not as immediately accessible as a Sacral response. To further analyze these subtle differences, we have divided Projectors into three basic categories based on the chart configurations illustrated on the following page.

THE THREE CATEGORIES OF PROJECTORS

MENTAL PROJECTORS

Mental Projectors are defined by any combination of defined Head, Ajna, and Throat Centers, but have no definition below the Throat Center. They have an open design and a deep reliance on their mind. They tap into their environment and read its transient energies through all of their undefined Centers. Mental Projectors are the archetype of outer Authority, which is to say one who provides valued information and guidance for others. It is difficult for them to accept the fact that their strong and agile minds cannot be their personal Authority. For Mental Projectors to reach clarity in decision-making, it is helpful to bounce things off others so they can hear it themselves. Their surroundings can have a definite influence on their decision-making process, so it is also important that they get a sense of how the environment is affecting them. With so much of their design open and vulnerable to conditioning, understanding how others impact them can prove an invaluable tool. Through studying other people's designs, Mental Projectors begin to understand the similarities and differences in their own process. As they become awake and aware, their own strategy begins to work for them.

ENERGY PROJECTORS

Energy Projectors have one or more motors, except the Sacral Center, defined in their design. They need to pay close attention to the guidance of their Authority, being extra vigilant for invitations from people who want access to their energy just to fill a vacant position or get a job done. Even though these Projectors are under pressure to discharge built-up energy from the motors defined, it is essential they expend it either by doing something they enjoy, or by doing what they have been recognized for and properly invited to do. This extra energy creates two temptations for Projectors. The first is initiating an action just to release the pressure. The second is unwittingly committing to an activity whereby they become a laborer, rather than the one who can see how to direct a process towards greater efficiency and success.

CLASSIC PROJECTORS

The Classic Projector's definition lies below the Throat Center but never includes a defined motor center. Without motor definition in their design, they can test or taste the fuel from the motors of others, and discern which people are correct for them and which are not. This gives them the potential to be more objective and more selective about the invitations they accept. For example, Projectors take in, experience and magnify the creative life force energy of a defined Sacral Center. This can be exhilarating, but can also make them prone to any toxic or detrimental frequencies attached to that energy. It's like ingesting a poison which then smothers or destroys their vitality, and compromises their physical or mental health. Since all Projector decisions connect them to energies which either empower or enslave them, becoming conscious of the purity of the fuel emanating from people they accept into their lives is critical to their overall well-being.

ALL PROJECTORS

The dilemma for all Projectors is waiting for the invitation. They want to be, and must be, recognized and invited in order to fulfill their purpose as administrators and guides. Personal success for Projectors is dependent on having energetically healthy people around them who acknowledge their Projector skills and offer them their energy resources to work with.

When not-self Projectors, eager for recognition of any kind, try to meet the expectations of others and thus are recognized instead for who they are 'not', they can get confused and attach themselves to anyone, even someone who is detrimental to them. Healthy Projectors are those who avoid this trap by recognizing themselves, and understanding their own limitations. When they are no longer dependent on external sources for affirmation of any kind, the true Projector gift of recognition is returned to its rightful and properly functioning place in their Strategy.

The most basic but essential function of recognition for Projectors relates to choosing people to be in their inner circle, people who will keep them aligned with their own path and purpose. Because Projectors are designed to penetrate other's centers so deeply, and because they cannot fulfill their purpose without access to the energy and resources of other people, Projectors need to know who is right for them; who recognizes or sees them for who they truly are.

This applies to the ways they connect to the wider community as well. For example, if you are a skilled classical guitarist, you wouldn't book a concert to entertain a crowd expecting to dance to rock n' roll, unless your personal gifts include converting the casual listener to classical guitar music and you have been invited to do just that. Without the invitation, you would be wasting your precious Projector gifts and leave the place without recognition, embittered by the experience. No amount of money could buy or replace what you would lose.

Nothing boosts the mood of Projectors like being recognized, or drops them faster into a state of bitterness when they are not. When Projectors try to get others to see them, they are perceived as needy and demanding. Other Types feel this 'need' for recognition and resist it. By initiating and inviting themselves, Projectors are giving their inherent power to the other person, which places them at a huge disadvantage. This often happens in family relationships where they have not been seen as themselves from the beginning. Taking their power back is difficult at first; it involves shifting their focus, standing securely grounded in awareness of their own gifts, and waiting until their own auric message is clearly received. This allows the people around them to recognize and invite their real gifts into the relationship, and changes the basis for the relationship as a whole.

PROJECTOR STRATEGY: RECOGNITION,
TO WAIT FOR THE INVITATION

Projectors are designed to be seen. They are always being noticed, but one must question what is really getting the attention. Are they being recognized for their true gifts or not? When Projectors are truly recognized, they feel it in their core and there is no doubt. The Projector Strategy and decision-making process is to wait for the recognition, and then the invitation. Recognition and invitations come from silence. When Projectors grasp that waiting quietly is a quality of readiness, they can watch their strong aura pull people and recognition to them. Once they have been recognized and invited correctly, their gifts and skills are empowered as they are filled up by a transient energy that is theirs to choreograph. The energy they connect with and commit to managing sort of flows through them. It is not theirs, but they get to utilize its potential to benefit others for as long as that invitation lasts.

Waiting for the invitation has specific qualities to it that are subtly different from the waiting Strategy of Generators, who wait for their life to be directed from moment to moment through response. Projectors are waiting for what is best described as a more formal, long-term invitation. They are waiting for 'investors' to recognize, request and empower their special skills – in exchange for ample compensation! That invitation offers the Projector access to the investor's initiating and generating energy resources. This is what the Projector lives for, how their genius is empowered, and how they will experience the success they are here to achieve in their lifetime. The relationship between the Generator and Projector is both essential and interdependent, as neither has the power to fulfill their purpose without the other.

Investor invitations generally, but not exclusively, apply to the four major decisions one makes in life: the invitation to love, to a career, to bond with others, and to a place to live. Once an invitation is received and accepted, Projectors can use all the skills at their disposal, within the parameters set by the invitation, for as long as the investor remains open and receptive and willing to play their part. This can be for a few weeks, a few months, a few years, or for the rest of their life. When entering into any of these major long-term commitments, Projectors need to be intentional and deliberate in following their Strategy and Authority.

The next essential step for Projectors is being selective. Just because they finally received an invitation doesn't automatically make it right for them. Their Authority will guide them to the right energy exchange for them. Each Projector's decision-making process is unique, and the best way to determine what a correct invitation looks like is to measure the level of resistance they meet when they act on one. Over time, and with increased self awareness, the Projector's proficiency at recognizing correct invitations improves, and the process itself is refined. When Projectors are recognized and invited, they suddenly have access to the reliable energy of others, which in turn releases their own Projector gifts and outer authority. Patience and careful observation are once again key factors.

All invitations come with an expiration date. If the invitation has lost its energy or excitement, it is possible that the invitation has been withdrawn, or perhaps the job is complete but no one has noticed. The Projector may feel that things just aren't working anymore, such as money, interest, support, or adequate time are no longer available. At this point, it is helpful to discuss the situation with the investor in order to clarify the status of the invitation. Once aligned in their own power, Projectors can let their auras do the talking. Their silent waiting is the most effective way to elicit correct invitations from others. Gradually, the people and invitations that were not based on recognition will slowly fall away. If Projectors trust in the silent magic of their chemistry, there is no need to do the inviting themselves; opportunities will come to them.

When Projectors understand the sanctity of their aura, they will nurture and protect it. This begins with creating an essentially aura-free space in their home they can retreat to in order to properly relax and release the auric energies they have absorbed during the day. Sleeping alone is also important for a Projector because 70 percent of the population is generating Sacral motor energy. In order to enter a deep, restful sleep, Projectors must first take time to diffuse the extra energy they have taken in. Achieving a healthy balance between activity and rest in their life begins with learning to sense when enough is enough, when to let go of the residual auric energy of others, and when to be alone.

PROJECTORS WITH EMOTIONAL AUTHORITY

Projectors have been waiting so long for invitations that even those with emotional definition have a tendency to jump at the first opportunity. Unfortunately, what appears to be a great invitation when they are up in their wave can turn into a horrible commitment when they are down in their wave. We are all conditioned to be polite and answer spontaneously when someone invites us to accept a job, or attend an event. It's also easy for emotional Projectors to get hooked into someone else's energy field, which adds to the confusion. They need to wait, discuss it, wait, and discuss it yet again. By waiting for clarity they may, in fact, receive an even more delicious invitation. The strategy for emotional Projectors is simply to request a day or two to think it over. If they're still not clear by then, they should unashamedly ask for more time and/or clarification of the details. Part of the experiment for them is to observe how and if their auric field draws the other person back again to renew the invitation while they themselves are waiting for clarity.

PROJECTORS IN RELATIONSHIPS

For a relationship to work, Projectors must be recognized, formally invited into it, and given an essential role in its unfolding. Projectors who are neither appreciated nor recognized are stuck in a dependent and weak position, which leaves them feeling bitter. Life and relationships lose their sweetness. The best advice, as with all types, is to enter relationships correctly from the beginning.

PROJECTOR CHILDREN

It is particularly important to the extremely sensitive Projector child that parents be intentional about their own energy mechanics. Part of parental support includes recognizing ways the child manages or interacts with healthy energies early on. Teaching Projector children to recognize themselves, to know when they are recognized by others, and to recognize what a correct invitation feels like, places them on the track to success. This is all the encouragement they need to practice their Strategy and Authority, and to appreciate their uniqueness as a Projector.

Parents who invite and recognize their Projector children give them a chance to develop, express and feel the power of being who they truly are. Children who are taught to recognize and wait for the correct receptive audience grow up to be successful, well-adjusted adults who can express their gifts with clarity and integrity in the world.

Emotional Projector children must also be invited, but without any pressure being placed on them to make a decision in the moment. This gives them a chance to get in touch with their emotional wave. When they are in a community that recognizes them, they will grow and thrive. If they are put under pressure to accept invitations or make decisions before they have a chance to process and know what is right for them, they can easily end up confused, bitter and unsuccessful.

PROJECTOR RECOGNITION AND THE NOT-SELF

When Projector's hear about their Type, there is an immediate resonance with the keyword 'invitation.' They suddenly realize that they have been the ones doing the inviting! In their restlessness and insecurity, they treated others the way they themselves were meant to be treated, which naturally met with resistance. After a lifetime of feeling unrecognized and uninvited, Projectors become deeply pessimistic about people showing a genuine interest in them.

When Projectors feel starved for energy, they will compromise and settle for an invitation to the wrong energy exchange. Accurate recognition and a proper invitation is what sets a Projector' gifts in motion and increases their value to others. For example, when someone says to an emotionally defined Projector, "I love the way you process your decisions through your feelings," they know the person sees them. This gives the Projector access to clean energy and, potentially, a receptive ear for their insightful guidance and advice.

Once a proper invitation is completed or withdrawn, the Projector's job is complete. Because the energy they were committed to managing is no longer available to them, however, their not-self may panic and interfere with their letting go and moving on. Their not-self has no confidence in Strategy or their Projector auric invitation field, which can lead to them holding onto people, not knowing when enough is enough, trying to prove themselves, accepting a wrong invitation to begin with, or being fearful of not being invited again.

It is through understanding others that Projectors arrive at a clear understanding of themselves. If their agenda for reaching out to people comes with the expectation that they will get attention or recognition, however, they will meet with resistance. Like all types, they need to be aware of their underlying agenda and hidden expectations.

Projectors have a very strong intellect. They like to study and take in information. Because of this, they tend to have a deeply conditioned mind that tries to control their lives and circumstances through the not-self strategies of their open centers. They tend to feel they will not get the life they really want, so they compromise in their relationships and jobs by settling for what they think they can get. Settling is a huge problem for the Projector, especially when there are bills to pay.

HEALTHY SLEEP HABITS FOR PROJECTORS

It is best for Projectors, with their open Sacral Center, to go to bed before they feel totally exhausted. By lying down or relaxing as much as an hour before they would like to be asleep, they give their bodies a chance to unwind, and their auras time to release energies that do not belong to them, thus preparing them for a peaceful, refreshing night's rest.

SIGNATURE GOAL: SUCCESS

Success dispels bitterness and maximizes the Projector's sense of well-being. Recognizing the uniqueness and potential in others, and guiding them by asking the right questions without a personal agenda, is the Projector gift. The right questions ultimately open the door to satori, transforming and awakening someone to their own unique truth. Success also means getting to a place within where being a non-energy type is no longer an issue. Waiting for a respectful, formal invitation, accompanied by the appropriate rewards and energy resources, is the Projector's Strategy for the big decisions in life, thus reducing the likelihood of overexertion or mental and physical breakdown. By moving from success to success, the Projector learns how to use their limited energy wisely.

FAMOUS PROJECTORS

Nelson Mandela, John F. Kennedy, Queen Elizabeth II, Fidel Castro, Josef Stalin, Karl Marx, Osho (Baghwan Shree Rajneesh), Mick Jagger, Barbra Streisand, Marilyn Monroe, Woody Allen, Steven Spielberg, Princess Diana, Thomas Gottschalk, Berthold Brecht, Ralph Nader, k.d. lang, Kirstie Alley, Whoopi Goldberg, George Clooney, Jon Bon Jovi, Demi Moore, Denzel Washington, Goldie Hawn, Ron Howard, Melissa Etheridge, Katharine Hepburn, Josh Groban, Diane Keaton, Ringo Starr, Candice Bergen, Shirley Maclaine and Barack Obama.

THE REFLECTOR

SAMPLING AURA

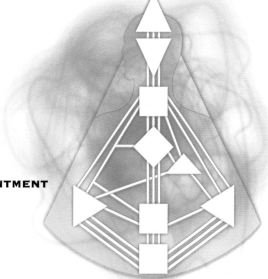

NOT-SELF THEME: **DISAPPOINTMENT**

STRATEGY: **WAITING
A LUNAR CYCLE**

SIGNATURE: **SURPRISE**

THE REFLECTOR TYPE

Reflector BodyGraphs are easy to identify because all nine centers remain white. Instead of a fixed definition, Reflectors have gate activations. These gates form a channel when connected to a harmonic gate courtesy of other people's auras, or transiting celestial bodies. The unusual way Reflectors process and experience energy, quite different from that of the other Types, means that Reflectors live by a different set of rules. They are truly extraordinary in many ways, and make up approximately 1 percent of the population.

OVERVIEW

Reflectors stand alone. They are totally unique in their perspective, quietly unobtrusive in their auric presence, and extraordinary in their role. They are born with a special attunement to the cosmic environment, and to the impact of the neutrino field on human beings. Like a canary in a coal mine, they sample, reflect and judge the quality of the environment on any given day. Reflectors can be so attuned to the transit program that they can also measure other's attunement to it. They sense who is living authentically, or who has been conditioned by the transit field and become a victim of it. The more people allow their lives to be conditioned by the transits, the farther away they are from fulfilling their unique potential. Reflectors can tell who is ready to become their own authority. They sense or feel the physical, psychic or emotional health of an environment, community or group, and they are here to judge what is working correctly or not. As people become awake and aware, Reflectors are there, ready to objectively share or reflect what they have sampled. This process is how the Reflector moves to the center and becomes 'visible.'

Reflectors are here to enliven and lift up the energy of others. In a rather extraordinary way, Reflectors can amplify and reflect or mirror other people's energy back to them. It is a unique aptitude which facilitates an experience of heightened awareness in terms of what they see in the other, yet in a non-judgemental way. The unimposing, non-intrusive nature of their auric presence also makes Reflectors particularly effective facilitators of the group process. All of this remains only a potential for Reflectors, however, until they are able to operate as themselves, rather than an amplified version of the homogenized world around them.

Many of the characteristics that differentiate Reflectors today resonate from a time when our earliest human ancestors lived in harmony with the cosmos, in flow with nature, and in community with each other. Over the eons, their ways of surviving within the natural flow were systemically replaced by the aggressive, strategic ways of evolving mental awareness. Once mental superiority was in place, hierarchies arose based on dominance, and unimposing, gentle Reflectors were not among them.

A new natural hierarchy is beginning to emerge, however, in which Reflectors will play an exquisite role as they stand for ultimate justice. With their quiet, unobtrusive aura, they will fill their rightful place at the center of the Type hierarchy by reflecting back into the world the not-self injustices they see humanity perpetuating on itself. They are here to prod humanity toward a cooperative, just, peaceful and equitable global community in preparation for those born after 2027 with spirit awareness. For Reflectors to move into this position and fulfill this role, the three other Types must be authentic, aware and open to the Reflector's assessment or judgment.

Manifestors, Generators and Projectors are solar Types, meaning their purpose 'shines' through them. As the only lunar Type, the Reflector is designed to operate as a lunar reflection of the sun's programming. They reflect the planetary program's neutrino imprinting process. Like the moon, the Reflector's 'glow' is subtle, yet wields substantial influence, especially when it is detected by others.

The chemistry of Reflectors' nine undefined centers can sample as well as magnify the frequencies of everything and everyone in their environment, giving them the potential to taste or sense what is really happening in a way no other Type can. The unique potential of their openness is to reflect everything around them with perfect equanimity, which makes their openness an exceptional window to wisdom. Even with all nine centers open, however, Reflectors are not more vulnerable to conditioning than the other Types. Reflectors are, in fact, the most resilient of the four Types, protected by an aura that is described as resistant and sampling. This unusual aura allows them to appraise or read transient auras without taking in the frequencies too deeply. It is a gift that specially equips them to discern if and when a person is ready to step out and express their uniqueness, rather than remain absorbed in the homogenized world of the not-self.

When Reflectors know their design clearly, and avoid yielding to the pressures of society to conform, their auras will protect them from identifying with anything that they take in through their openness. They can become wise about the process, and simply remain wide open to what is passing through them. Detecting a blip, or something that is unusual or out of line around them, is an aspect of their gift. With their potential to easily connect to a celestial body in an ongoing and profound way, particularly the Moon, they can have a mystical life that most of us cannot know. In many respects, they are our key to understanding and participating in global consciousness, as their extraordinary openness is continually filtering the consciousness field. They are actually here to sample and be one with the totality.

Reflectors are not necessarily interested in studying themselves. They are not overly interested in their impact on others either. Every day is different for a Reflector, so the questions uppermost in their mind are, "Who am I today?" and "Will I be surprised, included or invisible?" If they live as themselves, theirs is truly a carefree and joy-filled nature designed to live in the wonder of the moment. The real magic of Reflectors is expressed best in the newness, freshness and surprise that they experience every day, and their sense that there is always something more, always something else. Unfortunately, most Reflectors live a homogenized life, trying to be something they are not simply because they haven't been understood or encouraged to embrace their difference. Too often, finding the world unreceptive, cold and disappointing, they give in to expectations just to survive. When they begin to appreciate their uniqueness and practice detachment from (or not identifying with) what they are mirroring, they will be less apt to become lost, confused and caught up in the turmoil around them. They will accept their place in the center rather than be left feeling invisible, and on the outside looking in.

PLACE IS KEY TO THE REFLECTOR'S HAPPINESS

Unique to Reflectors is their need to find their place in the heart of the community, or the center of the group, so they can freely sample and reflect auric information from those around them. It is their rightful place, and where they need to be to fulfill their purpose. They are here to be accepting of others, to reflect the truth, and to teach the rest of us that most often what we judge as good or bad in the world is just a revelation of our diversity. To do this, Reflectors must move freely in their environment or amongst the participants in a gathering, and also must also be free to leave when they realize that their reflections will not be solicited. They operate by a different set of rules then the other Types. Reflectors truly march to a different drummer, and to know that is to honor and respect their place and purpose. Finding the right environment within the right community to call home, and how they go about that, is one of the most important decisions Reflectors face. With their undefined G Center it's helpful for them to know that people with defined G Centers are here to initiate them; to introduce them to new people and places. Once Reflectors have been introduced, it is their job to be discerning. When someone introduces them to a new place or person they then come to love, Reflectors should avoid a not-self tendency to become dependent or attached to the person who took them there.

If Reflectors remain in an unhealthy environment for any length of time, they may take on that energy and get sick themselves, or be drained of their vitality. It's essential for Reflectors to have a dedicated, creative space of their own; a place where they can take time alone to shake off the conditioning they are exposed to on a daily basis. If they don't, they can easily become dependent on the energies of those around them, which is a good reason to select with care the people they allow into their inner circle of friends and family.

REFLECTOR STRATEGY: WAITING THROUGH THE 28 DAY LUNAR CYCLE

Reflectors have no fixed definition in their chart and no dependable source of personal Authority. There is no reliable source of yes or no inside them to guide them in making major decisions in their life. The Reflector's Strategy is to connect to the lunar cycle, the Moon's approximately 28-day cycle around the Mandala, which encompasses all 64 gates in the wheel. This reliable and repeating pattern provides Reflectors with a sense of consistency comparable to, but not the same as, having a fixed definition.

Reflectors need to be initiated for the big decisions in life. Their lunar cycle (decision-making process) begins when an important offer has been made or an invitation extended to them by others. They cannot initiate themselves. As they progress toward clarity through their lunar cycle, their Reflector perceptions will change. During this time, they will want to talk with others, not to seek advice but to articulate their own thoughts and hear their own potential truth. The quality of their associations and the way their aura filters the world around them over time refines their decision. They need to be encouraged to take their time, and not allow themselves to be pressured or rushed. They will know suddenly, deep inside, if the offer was right for them or not. If they have completed their lunar cycle however, and they are still not clear, it is advisable to wait for clarity to arrive, keeping in mind it may take more than one cycle.

Although this lunar basis for decision-making is unique to Reflectors, all Types can benefit from understanding the Moon's repeating but transitory influence on their lives. Following the way the lunar cycle connects to your own chart is a fascinating process. (Examples of mapping a complete lunar cycle and a transit connection chart are included at the end of this section.)

REFLECTOR RELATIONSHIPS

The extreme openness of Reflectors can put them at the mercy of their partner's definition, making it easy for an element of narcissism to enter the relationship. Reflectors mirror and magnify their partner's definition back to them so what the other person may see, and may unwittingly fall in love with, is their own reflection, not the Reflector. People who don't like themselves often fall in love with themselves through somebody else; this process of self discovery is facilitated by the Reflector's openness. Without understanding, personal authenticity and clear boundaries on the part of both partners, Reflectors' deep-seated fears of remaining invisible, of not being seen for who they really are, may well be realized.

When Reflectors are constantly rushed into decisions, or are not secure in their decision-making process, they run the risk of becoming dependent on those who have a reliable personal Authority. They then allow their partners to make decisions for them, to determine their mode of sexual expression, their eating and sleeping habits, their occupation, where to live and their place in the family. Reflectors can be at the mercy of the people around them. If they allow themselves to be dominated by not-self oriented people, they will amplify that distortion in their energy field and feel deeply disappointed by their own experience of life. There are no moment-to-moment rules for a Reflector to follow, only the authority of waiting out the lunar cycle so they can be clear when making a decision. Such a process is foreign to the other Types, and when not understood it can bring discord into the relationship and suffering to the Reflector. Reflectors that allow themselves to be rushed and pressured are likely to have health problems later in life.

For the Reflector, a relationship is of greatest value when it is fertile and productive. Most Reflectors love having children around them, as they bring an innocent and consistent connection to the Reflector's design. They enjoy relating with and 'reflecting' people who share their awe and wonder for life. It is often difficult for Reflectors to cut the apron strings when it comes time to let their children go.

REFLECTOR CHILDREN

When parents learn the lunar pattern of Reflector children, they can encourage them to grow according to their personal rhythm. It's very important not to rush a Reflector child, but rather to allow them to develop at their own pace. Over time, the children will learn to be patient and comfortable with waiting through their lunar cycle before making any major decisions. It is important that parents help these children find a supportive learning environment with teachers who will let them develop naturally. Reflector children need to be actively involved in a learning community, but not in the usual expectation-laden way. As free spirits who operate by a different set of rules, they will absorb and process information differently. Remember that Reflector children take in and reflect back exactly what is going on in the family and the classroom. A thriving and healthy Reflector child or a sick and sad Reflector child says a lot about the state of the environment. Reflector children, like Reflector adults, need their own space so they can withdraw and be alone when they need to be away from others. With patient practice, parents can teach their child to protect themselves from taking in or acting on the pain of others, even though they will feel it.

THE REFLECTOR QUESTION AND
THE CONSEQUENCES OF NOT-SELF BEHAVIORS

The Reflector's deepest fear is invisibility, of not being included in a participatory way. To assuage that fear, even though conditioning does not 'stick' to their aura, they may give in to the typical not-self behaviors simply to gain attention. When Reflectors do not understand their auras, and natural attunement to the rhythms of the cosmos, they can become confused and overcome by the motorized energy and expectations of the dominant solar Types. They experience disappointment with others, and are dejected by the resistance they meet in trying to initiate or manifest. Instead of being the hub of a community, Reflectors end up feeling left out. They endure, or are overcome by, constant identification with other people's fears, emotions, stress, and anxiety. The key for Reflectors is to stay neutral, to avoid identifying with other people's pain, and to remain the sampling observer. As Reflectors become comfortable with the lack of fixedness in their design, flowing with the lunar cycle and testing the auras of those around them, they will reflect the truth rather than the pain of others. Instead of being distracted by their openness, they can develop the potential for great wisdom and focus on, "Who am I right now? Who am I today?"

The fears Reflectors deal with when they begin to live as themselves are:

- Who am I right now? Can I be myself?
- Will I remain invisible, or will somebody see me for my differences and include me and my reflections?
- Am I able to move freely within my environment so I can find my place?
- Without a fixed identity, how can I keep from taking on the anxiety, fears, nervousness and ill-health of the not-self world around me?

HEALTHY SLEEP HABITS FOR REFLECTORS

It is best for Reflectors, with their open Sacral Center, to go to bed before they feel totally exhausted. By lying down or relaxing as much as an hour before they would like to be asleep, they give their bodies a chance to unwind, and their auras time to release energies that do not belong to them, thus preparing them for a peaceful, refreshing night's rest.

SIGNATURE GOAL: SURPRISE

The not-self theme for a Reflector is disappointment at the homogenized world with its distorted not-self interactions and relationships. Reflectors live for moments when they can sample difference, and experience awe and wonder. By remaining unattached and unidentified with energies in a wise way, their sampling auras are rewarded by surprises. Surprise for a Reflector can mean being included as a participant and no longer merely an observer. Reflectors are enlivened or empowered when initiated, asked or invited to mirror the difference they see, or to share what they see is needed.

Since they notice who is operating correctly according to Type, they are here to be a signpost for those ready to break the pattern of the illusion and become their unique, authentic Self. This is a Reflector's special contribution. To awaken someone to the possibility and promise of experiencing their life as themselves is a great source of surprise and delight for the Reflector.

FAMOUS REFLECTORS

Rosalyn Carter (wife of Jimmy Carter), Eduard Mörike (a German poet), Thorwald Dethlefsen (a German psychologist and author of esoteric literature), Ammachi (the Hugging Saint), Scott Hamilton (Olympic gold medal skater), Dick Smothers, Fyodor Dostoyevsky, Sandra Bullock, Richard Burton, H.G. Wells, Yul Bryner, James Frey (A Million Little Pieces).

MAPPING A LUNAR CYCLE

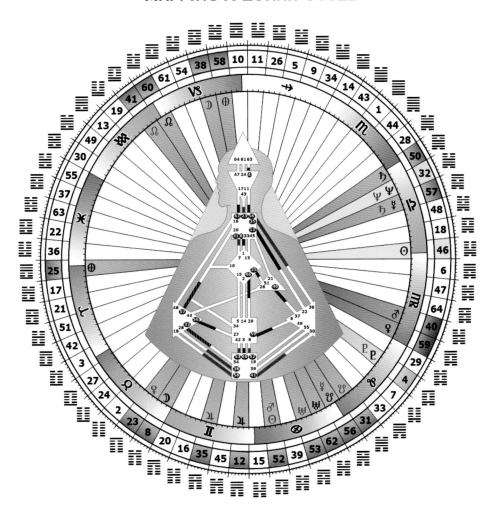

REFLECTOR MANDALA AND BODYGRAPH

The Reflector BodyGraph in the Mandala above has many gate activations, or dormant, hanging gates. Each one is a receptor seeking its harmonic gate at the other end of the channel. As the Moon moves counter-clockwise through the 64 gates of the I'Ching (approximately every 28 days), transiting planets will form harmonic connections to the Reflector's hanging gates, thus creating temporary definitions. Although each definition created may last only half a day, over time it becomes part of a consistent monthly pattern that provides a reliable framework for the Reflector's decision-making process. (See the graph that follows.) This lunar cycle's pattern is the Reflector's personal way of reflecting the Moon's frequency on Earth, and supports and defines the Reflector's innate sense of self. A Reflector's identity is not revealed on a moment-to-moment basis, but through the rhythm and flow of the full lunar cycle.

FOLLOWING A LUNAR CYCLE THROUGH THE GATES

As the lunar cycle brings definition to the Reflector's chart on the previous page, he will sample the energy frequencies and definition of a Projector, Manifestor and Generator, in addition to that of a Reflector. Each time that the moon moves into a new gate, there is the potential for definition. The moon takes approximately 28 days to go around the earth, however, it takes about 30 days to go from full moon to the next full moon.

Having temporary definition doesn't mean Reflectors become Generators, Manifestors or Projectors, but they can sample those particular energies. No one every changes Type. Each Reflector's lunar cycle is unique, and will be the same every 28 days.

DATE	TIME	PLANET	GATE	CHANNEL	ENERGY
6/16/2011	22:42:11	Moon	38	None	Reflector
6/17/2011	08:44:11	Moon	54	Root - Splenic	Projector
6/17/2011	18:52:30	Moon	61	None	Reflector
6/18/2011	05:07:24	Moon	60	None	Reflector
6/18/2011	15:29:05	Moon	41	None	Reflector
6/19/2011	01:57:40	Moon	19	None	Reflector
6/19/2011	12:33:10	Moon	13	None	Reflector
6/19/2011	23:15:31	Moon	49	None	Reflector
6/20/2011	10:04:30	Moon	30	Solar Plexus - Root	Projector
6/20/2011	20:59:50	Moon	55	None	Reflector
6/21/2011	08:01:03	Moon	37	Heart – Solar Plexus	Projector
6/21/2011	19:07:37	Moon	63	None	Reflector
6/22/2011	06:18:53	Moon	22	Throat – Solar Plexus	Manifestor
6/22/2011	17:34:04	Moon	36	Throat – Solar Plexus	Manifestor
6/23/2011	04:52:19	Moon	25	None	Reflector
6/23/2011	16:12:43	Moon	17	Ajna - Throat	Projector
6/24/2011	03:34:18	Moon	21	None	Reflector
6/24/2011	14:56:05	Moon	51	Heart - G	Projector
6/25/2011	02:17:04	Moon	42	Sacral - Root	Generator
6/25/2011	13:36:18	Moon	3	Sacral - Root	Generator
6/26/2011	00:52:54	Moon	27	Sacral - Splenic	Generator
6/26/2011	12:06:01	Moon	24	None	Reflector
6/26/2011	23:14:54	Moon	2	None	Reflector
6/27/2011	10:18:56	Moon	23	None	Reflector
6/27/2011	21:17:35	Moon	8	None	Reflector
6/28/2011	08:10:25	Moon	20	Throat - Splenic	Projector
6/28/2011	18:57:09	Moon	16	None	Reflector

DATE	TIME	PLANET	GATE	CHANNEL	ENERGY
6/29/2011	05:37:35	Moon	35	None	Reflector
6/29/2011	16:11:39	Moon	45	None	Reflector
6/30/2011	02:39:20	Moon	12	None	Reflector
6/30/2011	13:00:46	Moon	15	None	Reflector
6/30/2011	23:16:07	Moon	52	None	Reflector
7/01/2011	09:25:37	Moon	39	None	Reflector
7/01/2011	19:29:34	Moon	53	None	Reflector
7/02/2011	05:28:20	Moon	62	None	Reflector
7/02/2011	15:22:15	Moon	56	None	Reflector
7/03/2011	01:11:46	Moon	31	None	Reflector
7/03/2011	10:57:16	Moon	33	None	Reflector
7/03/2011	20:39:13	Moon	7	Throat – G	Projector
7/04/2011	06:18:02	Moon	4	None	Reflector
7/04/2011	15:54:09	Moon	29	Sacral – G	Generator
7/05/2011	01:27:59	Moon	59	None	Reflector
7/05/2011	10:59:58	Moon	40	None	Reflector
7/05/2011	20:30:29	Moon	64	None	Reflector
7/06/2011	05:59:55	Moon	47	None	Reflector
7/06/2011	15:28:37	Moon	6	Sacral – Solar Plexus	Generator
7/07/2011	00:56:55	Moon	46	None	Reflector
7/07/2011	10:25:08	Moon	18	Splenic – Root	Projector
7/07/2011	19:53:35	Moon	48	None	Reflector
7/08/2011	05:22:30	Moon	57	None	Reflector
7/08/2011	14:52:11	Moon	32	None	Reflector
7/09/2011	00:22:50	Moon	50	None	Reflector
7/09/2011	09:54:42	Moon	28	Splenic – Root	Projector
7/09/2011	19:27:59	Moon	44	None	Reflector
7/10/2011	05:02:55	Moon	1	Throat – G	Projector
7/10/2011	14:39:42	Moon	43	Ajna – Throat	Projector
7/11/2011	00:18:32	Moon	14	None	Reflector
7/11/2011	09:59:38	Moon	34	Sacral – Splenic	Generator
7/11/2011	19:43:14	Moon	9	Sacral – Root	Generator
7/12/2011	05:29:34	Moon	5	None	Reflector
7/12/2011	15:18:52	Moon	26	None	Reflector
7/13/2011	01:11:23	Moon	11	Ajna – Throat	Projector
7/13/2011	11:07:23	Moon	10	G – Splenic	Projector
7/13/2011	21:07:09	Moon	58	None	Reflector

SAMPLING THE FULL TRANSIT FIELD

In addition to the lunar cycle, Reflectors also sample the transit field, experiencing the planetary flavors of the day. The way the transit field connects to their charts provides an ever-changing source of personal discovery, and always carries the potential for surprise.

SAMPLE TRANSIT FOR THE DAY

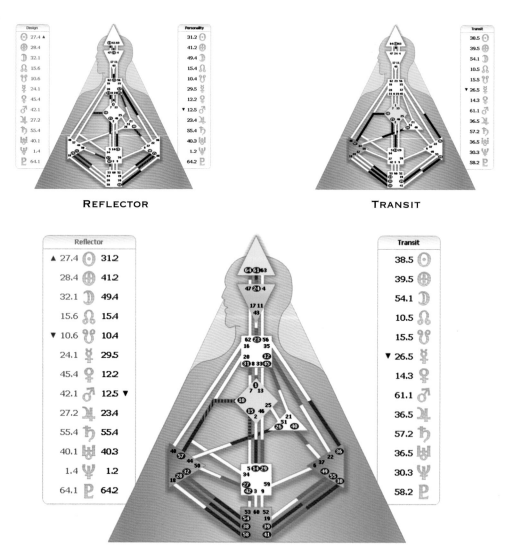

REFLECTOR   TRANSIT

THE IMPERSONAL NEUTRINO CONDITIONING FIELD - IMPACTING HUMANITY

On the page to the left are three illustrations showing a Reflector chart, a transit chart (the impersonal neutrino conditioning field of the Program) and a chart connecting the two. The paragraphs below describe how the connection might be interpreted.

The beauty of waiting: On this particular day the Reflector is going to be under tremendous pressure to act (Root Center) spontaneously (Splenic Center) on emotional desires (Channel 41-30) which have arisen unexpectedly (Cross of the Unexpected). This hunger (Solar Plexus Center) for new experience (Gate 36) has the potential to be spontanously expressed (Splenic Center) as crisis (Gate 36), potentially sending this Reflector into a new not-self direction of trying to perfect his form (Channel 57-10).

In addition, he is under tremendous mental pressure (Head and Ajna Centers) to try and make sense of life's mysteries (Channel 61-24), and if the Reflector succumbs to the mental and physical pressure to take action (Head and Root Center) in the moment (Splenic Center) he can be left feeling moody and depressed (Channel 39-55). In addition, he can struggle for the wrong purpose (Channel 38-28), experience the wrong spontaneous transformation (Channel 54-32) or enter into the wrong experience (41-30).

To use this transit correctly, the Reflector should wait and observe all of the sensations he is experiencing to see what is happening in the larger collective environment. By observing, he will discover if it is personally correct to engage this energy, or if the pressure will simply dissipate with the movement through his lunar cycle. By continually observing his own experiences, patterns will emerge which can eventually be creatively expressed as the wisdom of his outer authority.

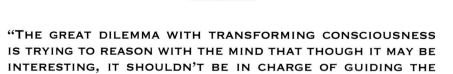

"THE GREAT DILEMMA WITH TRANSFORMING CONSCIOUSNESS IS TRYING TO REASON WITH THE MIND THAT THOUGH IT MAY BE INTERESTING, IT SHOULDN'T BE IN CHARGE OF GUIDING THE LIFE. THIS IS AN ENORMOUS CHALLENGE." – RA URU HU

SECTION FIVE
THE FIVE DEFINITIONS
ENERGY DYNAMICS

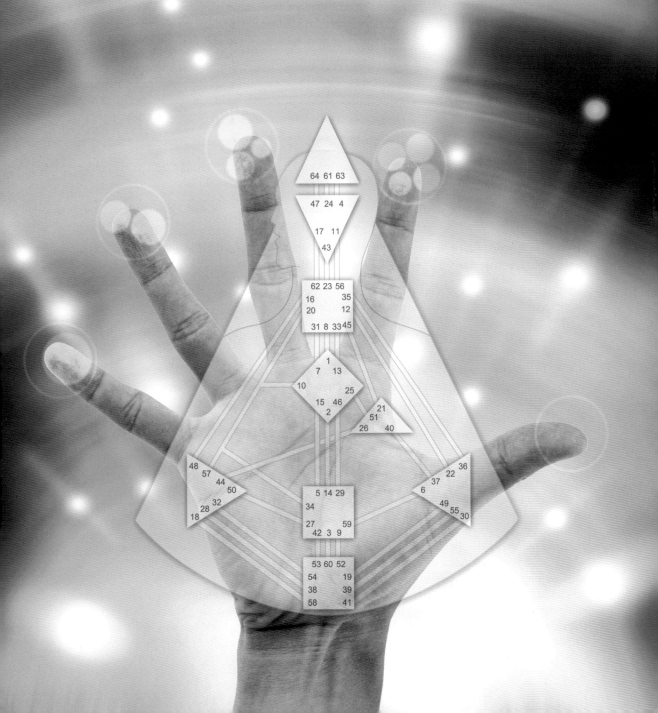

SECTION FIVE

THE FIVE DEFINITIONS

ENERGY DYNAMICS

As we continue to explore the different ways in which we are subject to conditioning, we come to the five ways our definition can be configured in our BodyGraph (listed below). Each represents specific ways we are set up to take in conditioning. Remember, when we are surrendered to our Form's intelligence by following our Strategy and Authority, we bypass all conditioning elements except as sources of information and potential wisdom. The five ways in which definition is expressed and experienced are:

- **NO DEFINITION** – a Reflector with no centers defined (approximately 1 percent of the population).

- **SINGLE DEFINITION** – all defined channels and defined centers in the design are connected in one continuous flow (approximately 41 percent of the population).

- **SIMPLE-SPLIT DEFINITION** – two separate areas of definition that are not connected to each other (approximately 46 percent of the population).

- **TRIPLE-SPLIT DEFINITION** – three separate areas of definition that are not connected to each other (approximately 11 percent of the population).

- **QUADRUPLE-SPLIT DEFINITION** – four separate areas of definition that are not connected to each other (approximately 1 percent of the population).

SPLITS AND HOW WE EXPERIENCE THEM

A split in a design means all defined channels and centers are not continuously connected within the BodyGraph; a gate or channel remains open between two, three or four areas of definition. When you have a split in your design, the quality and characteristics of the 'missing' gate or channel that would bridge the split is a motivating factor in your life. You will pursue the qualities of the missing gate or channel as though it represents something that is incomplete or wrong with your life, or as if this is a part of you that needs to be completed or repaired.

These open gates or channels create not-self behaviors as a motivating force, and cause you to initiate in order to fulfill what is perceived as missing. Remember that the missing gate/channel is not you, but it does represent certain people you will meet over and over again, who have the missing gate or channel, because you are drawn to the specific energy they carry within them. The attraction of that 'missing piece' is literally magnetic. By following your Strategy and Authority, you will meet those who bridge your split naturally and correctly. In fact, there is nothing at all you need to do about this missing piece. If you have multiple single-gate bridges that connect your split, each of them impacts you in this way. Unfortunately, most people as not-self pursue their missing pieces because they misinterpret the missing gate or channel as something incomplete within them. If you take a look at the description (in Section Six) of the missing gate or channel that bridges your split, you will notice important themes in your life that you most likely have been pursuing in order to feel complete.

EXAMPLE OF DEFINITION
(SIMPLE-SPLIT)

When we have a design with a simple split, for instance, the single gate or gates that bridge the split become the primary conditioning forces in the life. In this illustration, the defined Ajna and Throat Centers are split off from the defined Splenic, G, Sacral, Root and Solar Plexus Centers

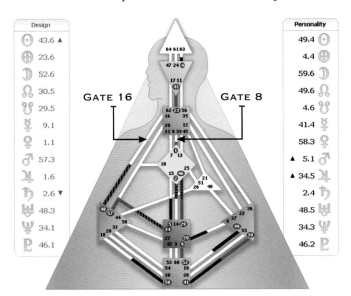

with Gate 16, 8 or 20 needed to bridge the split. Let's concentrate on Gate 16 for this example. This person has Gate 48, but Gate 16 at the other end of the channel is missing. Throat Center Gate 16, therefore, becomes a bridge or theme this person seeks. This means she will naturally meet lots of people with Gate 16 because Gate 48 is always looking for its 'harmonic gate.' Every gate has a harmonic partner located at the other end of the channel, and the two gates coming together literally spark each other to create life force energy as a quantum of the two gates.

Gate 48 is the Gate of Depth; Gate 16 is the Gate of Skills. For this person's depth to express itself through the Throat Center, she needs Gate 16. She may never feel she is skillful enough, and will go out into the world looking for ways to develop her skills. In fact, she is designed to meet people with Gate 16 who can skillfully express *her* depth while they work with her.

Gate 8, The Gate of Contribution, is also a bridge (missing gate), and this can drive her to think she has to make a contribution. In reality, it is her not-self that is trying to fill the mis-perceived void. She wants to literally become that missing piece, and ends up making mental decisions to attempt to do just that. With a Split Definition, one will generally feel a lack of wholeness until the split is bridged through a relationship with another person. For good or bad, this dynamic is the basis for many relationships.

In a wide split, which means it takes an entire channel or multiple gates to bridge the different areas of definition, one will experience the split as being the other person's problem, or from a not-self perspective, the other person is the cause of the problem. This can engender blame and victimhood that are not true. On the other hand, there is a potential for wisdom in a wide split if one uses it as an opportunity to become an unattached, objective observer of others, and does not get locked into the blame game. Once you stop pursuing and identifying with the bridge in your split, you begin to realize how important the people are who actually do bridge it. There have been many successful partnerships formed by two individuals bridging an important aspect in each other's design such as John Lennon (Gate 48) and Paul McCartney (Gate 16). Seeing how splits operate in a healthy way helps us to understand one of the ways we are designed to be together in relationship. In this respect, saying "you complete me" is both profound and true. We will only have healthy and effective relationships, however, when they are entered into correctly through Strategy and Authority.

There is a hierachy to conditioning that depends on the type of split definition. The conditioned not-self mind will focus on the open gates, channels or centers to formulate its decision-making strategy, based upon the specific definition. For a Simple-Split Definition, the bridging gate(s) that connect the two definitions is the most powerful conditioning element in your design, followed by the centers. If you are a Triple-Split, undefined centers are the most powerful conditioning elements in your design, and then the bridging gates/channels. For a Quadruple-Split, the bridging gates are again the most powerful conditioning elements, and then the undefined center.

Initiating when inappropriate, lack of patience, impulsive action or premature speech are the biggest problems for splits when they don't take time to follow their Strategy and Authority. Those with Split Definitions require more time to fully take in, process and digest information, simply because the separate pieces of their definition are not connected. Until the separate definitions are connected, all Split Definitions may feel uncomfortable, or incomplete, and unable to make clear decisions. They must take their time, be patient, and wait for a sense of wholeness to happen. Seeking wholeness with a specific partner by initiating, rather than waiting, is a not-self activity. If you have a split, you are designed to have others naturally bridge your split(s) as you move through your life day by day. Let your Strategy and Authority do the work for you.

This digestion and assimilation process is aided by spending time in public places where you will be provided with neutral bridging gates by others. The best way to bridge a split, when making a difficult or important decision, is to make use of a public place where you can still be alone, such as a bookstore, coffee shop or walking in a shopping mall. These public melting pots of designs will help provide neutral auras, and neutral conditioning, to assist you in the assimilation process. The bridging available from a public place provides you with new perspectives as you ponder the decision, whereas constantly being with friends or partners when making a decision limits you to the ways their designs consistently connect to and condition yours.

Strategy and Authority will protect you from the potential traps set up by your splits, and you will become more peaceful and less anxious about getting your splits resolved. Take your walk in the world. Relax, surrender, and live from within your own personal integrity through Strategy and Authority, and the bridging will take care of itself. The most important things to remember if you have a split definition of any kind are to give yourself time to process information, and to trust in your design to bring you what you need.

Let's look at a few examples on the following pages.

SINGLE DEFINITION #1

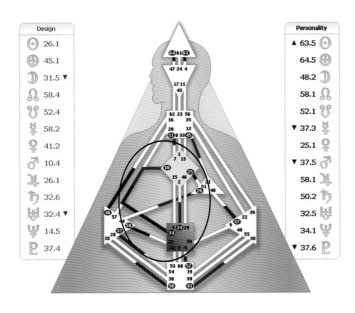

Elizabeth Barrett Browning is the first example of a chart with Single Definition. Compare this chart with Cosima Wagner's chart below.

Single Definition describes a chart where the energy flows continuously through defined channels and centers without a break, connecting all defined centers in the chart. It can be a single channel like Elizabeth's or more than one channel like the next example. Single Definition people are at some level self-contained because their definition forms a single, continuous, constant, ever-present and reliable energy. These designs can have a very singular focus, and don't have the same need to reflect on different aspects of themselves that the splits do. Single Definition designs do not need others to assist them in the assimilation of information, or to feel a sense of wholeness. They digest information rapidly, unless of course they are emotionally defined.

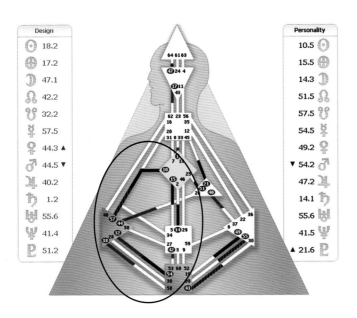

SINGLE DEFINITION #2

In Cosima Wagner's chart we see a Single Definition that has multiple centers defined (three) which are continuously connected by the two defined channels in her design. These two channels link the Root, Spleen and G Centers together for one continuous flow of energy. Her information assimilation process is very quick.

SIMPLE-SPLIT DEFINITION

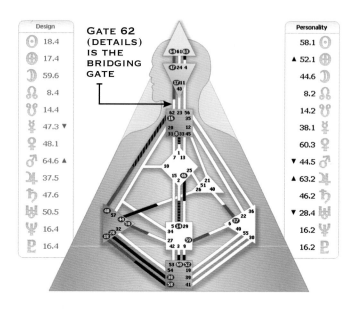

Henry Miller's chart is an example of a Simple-Split Definition bridged by a single gate.

Simple-Split Definition describes two defined areas that do not connect to each other, where the energy flow is broken and not continuous. Because of this split in Henry's energy flow, in order to feel complete, he always sought a bridge (the missing gate) to link the separate energetic definitions between his mind and his Throat. One single gate bridges this split, Throat Center Gate 62, the Gate of the Preponderance of the Small (Detail). Gate 62 bridged his mental process to his intuitive knowing, and was a very significant gate in his life. His life was focused on the details; researching the details and meeting others who could supply the detail. And Henry was indeed very focused on writing down the details in the books he authored.

WIDE-SPLIT DEFINITION

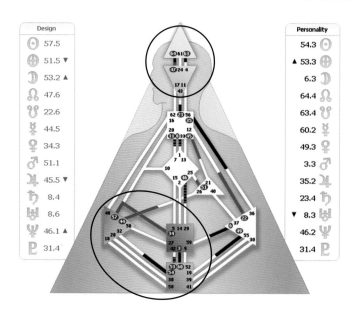

Comparing Stephen Hawkings' Wide-Split Definition with Henry Miller's Simple Split, we see a Wide-Split Definition bridged by multiple gates or a channel through the Throat Center. The bridge for this split is through Gate 20 plus Gate 43. Stephen would experience his incompleteness, or sense that something is missing, as "the other person's problem" rather than his own. He can and does use the wide split as a source of potential wisdom, observing and studying the world (or universe) quite objectively.

TRIPLE-SPLIT DEFINITION

Like Timothy Leary (shown here), Triple-Split Definitions have three separate areas of definition in their design that are not connected to each other. These individuals need several bridges to connect all of their defined channels. The main conditioning elements for them are their undefined centers. In Timothy's design, the undefined Heart and Solar Plexus Centers are the main conditioning elements. The gates that bridge the splits are also conditioning elements, but are not as powerful as the undefined centers. Triple-Splits are subject to impatience and often act prematurely. They can be seen as

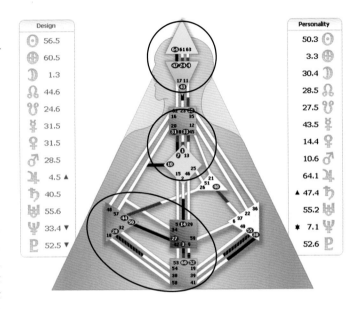

driven, ambitious and assertive. It is healthy for those who have Triple or Quadruple-Splits to interact with a number of different people (many different auras) each day. If they are continually conditioned by one person, they can feel trapped.

QUADRUPLE-SPLIT DEFINITION

Dr. Phil McGraw is a Quadruple-Split Definition with four separate areas of definition in his design that are not connected to each other. These designs have either eight or all nine centers in the BodyGraph defined. The main conditioning elements will again be the undefined gates or channels that are needed to bridge the splits. Quadruple-Splits may appear slow in developing because it is difficult for them to be flexible, or make decisions quickly. Forcing themselves to comply with others' expectations is destructive to all levels of their being. They need to take their time in their information assimilation process.

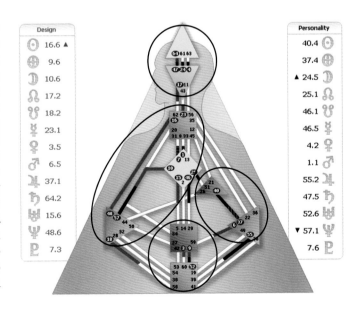

"THE MOMENT THERE IS THIS POSSIBILITY FOR A QUANTUM, A WHOLE THAT IS GREATER THAN THE SUM OF ITS PARTS, THEN THE WHOLE TRANSCENDS ITS PARTS, AND BECOMES THE PHENOMENON OF WHAT IS CALLED THE LIFE FORCE." – RA URU HU

SECTION SIX
CIRCUITS, CHANNELS & GATES
THE CIRCUIT BOARD OF THE LIFE FORCE

SECTION SIX

CIRCUITS, CHANNELS AND GATES

THE CIRCUIT BOARD OF THE LIFE FORCE

Circuitry explores the way energy circulates through the channels within the BodyGraph. When the circuits are diagrammed as illustrated, the BodyGraph resembles a circuit board. Understanding circuitry opens the door to understanding the flow of the life force, and reveals the way all life forms are differentiated yet designed to connect to each other. Circuits are composed of channels. A channel is composed of two gates and connects two centers. The gates in a chart are entry and exit points for the flow of energy to and from the centers. Centers are the hubs that transform and transmute the frequency. The flow or circulation of energy through a channel is like a spark of

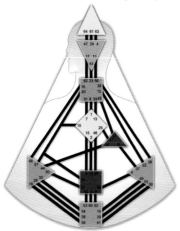

life that establishes communication between two centers. This basic form of communication is called a "life force" because it carries the potential for growth and evolution within the form.

This resulting life force definition is projected and communicated through our auras, and influences or conditions those close to us. Definition in our chart both defines our gifts and determines our limitations for the duration of our life. Each person's or each form's life force is unique and distinguishable from all others. Definition represents our reason for incarnating, and it must be expressed through us authentically without the not-self distortion of conditioning. There are 36 channels and 64 gates within the Rave BodyGraph. Circuitry ties them together and gives the bodygraph a solid infrastructure. This infrastructure is composed of the Integration Channel and three main circuit groups that map the distinctly different yet interconnecting routes or ways energy flows between centers.

Circuitry creates a general framework for interpreting the chart of a complex human being. Each channel, with its two gates, adds its theme to that framework.

THE INTEGRATION CHANNEL AND THE THREE CIRCUIT GROUPS

In Section Two we learned that pressure from the Head and Root Centers moves energy through the BodyGraph toward the Throat Center for expression. As energy flows along the BodyGraph's pathways, channels and their gates are bundled together forming six basic circuits, plus four additional channels that are known together as the Integration Channel. The six basic circuits form three main circuit groups, the Individual Circuit Group, the Collective Circuit Group and the Tribal Circuit Group. The Integration Channel is a distinct and unified field of energy. When viewed through the context of circuitry, the definition in a chart shows the ways our fundamental nature, values and principles connect to, interact with and impact others. It is often here, in the realm of circuits and channels, that the source of resistance and conflict between people is revealed, along with their conditioning. The keynotes, therefore, are of great significance in providing important insight into understanding the unique frequency, or combination of frequencies, of one's auric projection.

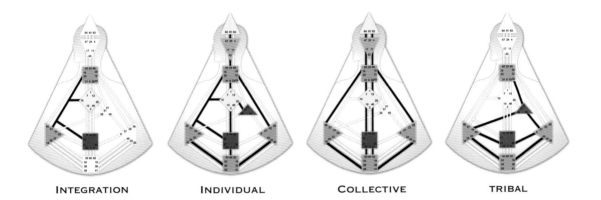

| INTEGRATION | INDIVIDUAL | COLLECTIVE | TRIBAL |

On the following pages, you will find a complete description of the 36 channels and 64 gates. Below please find an index that will help you locate your channels and gates by page number. In the Gate descriptions, RAC is Right Angle Cross, JC is Juxtaposition Cross, and LAC is Left Angle Cross. For more information on the Incarnation Crosses please see Section Eight. Additionally, the Hexagram Line names are listed with each gate. For more information on the Hexagram Lines, please see Section 10.

INDEX OF CHANNELS/GATES

THE INTEGRATION CHANNEL
SUPER KEYNOTE: SELF-EMPOWERMENT

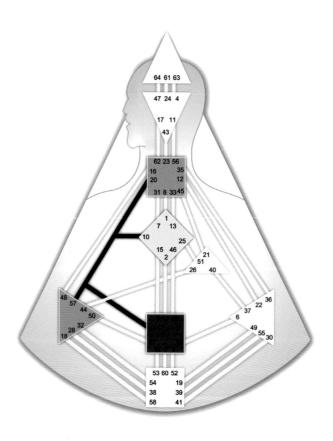

CHANNELS:

34 – 57	POWER *An archetype*	57 – 10	PERFECTED FORM *Survival*
34 – 20	CHARISMA *Where awareness must become deed*	10 – 20	AWAKENING *Commitment to higher principles*

The Integration Channel stands on its own alongside the three main circuit groups in the infrastructure of the BodyGraph; it defines the most fundamental and complex organization of channels in circuitry. This group of four channels, which forms a backbone-like structure in the BodyGraph, serves as the key defense mechanism of the form. Integration is the core component of the individuation process, the process of distinguishing ourself from others. Without it, we could not have differentiated from our primate ancestors. The Integration Channel fuels the evolutionary process of humanity person by person, and contains the full, active expression of the life force of the form.

With a super keynote of 'self-empowerment,' the Integration Channel is focused entirely on self-preservation and empowering the individual nature, expression, knowing, direction/identity and behavior of the self. Fulfilling their self-absorbed drive to survive as a unique and differentiated Individual is essential to ensuring the survival of all three circuit groups: Individual, Collective and Tribal.

The natural primal reflexes built into Integration assure us that we can trust the life that lies within us when it is empowered by response (Gate 34), guided by intuition (Gate 57), directed by the correct behavior (Gate 10) and manifested in the now (Gate 20). When expressed as a unit, using Integration's keynotes by channel, it says, "I love myself and I empower myself by listening to my intuition in the now." Or, "Through response I am intuitively equipped with the right behavior to survive any circumstance in the now." Those with definition in the Integration Channel are concerned with self-empowerment, and express themselves with a notable self-sufficiency and self-assuredness that neither looks to nor easily accepts direction from others. They should be allowed and encouraged to be self-sufficient.

The Channels and Gates of the Integration Channel are discussed on the following pages.

THE CHANNEL OF POWER: 34 - 57
A Design of an Archetype
Integration Channel   Channel Type: Generated

The Channel of Power links the Splenic center to the Sacral Center through the Gate of Intuitive Insight (57) and the Gate of Power (34). Channel 34-57 is the archetype of what it is to be an individuated human being. Its energy empowers our intuitive capacity to survive through response, keeping us alive by alerting us to danger.

Background: In the Channel of Power, the generative life force of the Sacral empowers the existential awareness (survival intelligence) of the Spleen, keeping us alert, attuned to our bodies and constantly on guard for anything that might constitute a threat in our immediate environment. Gate 34 has great power to engage in and sustain activity. Gate 57 operates on an inner sound/vibration level, constantly penetrating and screening its environment. When the two gates are combined within the channel, an archetype emerges based in ancient mammalian memory with a fight or flight instinct to survive. Without this defensive intuitive intelligence empowered to act spontaneously, we would not and could not have individuated or evolved as a species. It is through the 57th Gate that the entire awareness process began its flowering within humanity. Intuition is rooted in Splenic awareness, and arises instantaneously, free of the time constraints of mental and emotional awareness. In other words, it is never what we *think* is good for us that will protect us, but rather how we intuitively respond to the diverse vibrations of places or the people around us in the moment.

Personal: In order to react clearly and quickly, or make those split second decisions needed to literally save your life such as jumping out of the way of a speeding car, you must be consistently grounded in and connected to your body consciousness. This often means being highly selective regarding the verbal input of others, and always listening with your right ear to hear what they are really saying. Following your Generator Strategy frees up your blend of Splenic intuition and Sacral power, allowing it to bring you safely through each moment of your life. Determined to keep you independent, alive, acoustically alert and physically fit, this is an amazing capacity that you can learn to trust completely. Finely honed to your individual survival, it does not take into account the needs and wants of anyone other than you. The great and enduring power undergirding this channel of the "archetype" is the experience of yourself as an aware and unique being. Once self-empowered, you become an inspiring example of what it means to enjoy being a vitally alive, differentiated human being, pure and unconditioned, living moment by moment in response. If you find yourself prone to melancholy, embrace your moods without trying to fix them or figure them out.

Interpersonal: People with the Channel of Power have the potential to perfect their powers of survival through intuitively-based response. They do not generally take kindly to anything or anyone that dares to disturb their realm of well-being, and can become defensive, if necessary, in order to maintain it. Having evolved beyond the eat-or-be-eaten level of existence, they now rely on their alertness to sustain a healthy vitality that allows them to survive long enough to experience and appreciate the gifts of our species' growing powers of awareness.

GATE 34: THE POWER OF THE GREAT - THE GATE OF POWER
– Power is only great when its display or use serves the common good –
Center: Sacral   Quarter: Mutation   Theme: Purpose fulfilled through Transformation
RAC of the Sleeping Phoenix – JC of Power – LAC of Duality

Gate 34 is a potent and impressive source of energy that empowers us toward individuation, displaying and celebrating our uniqueness in the world. Two qualities distinguish this gate from the other eight in the Sacral: its asexuality and the unavailability of its power to others. If connected to Gate 10 in your G Center, your energy will be focused on social behaviors or roles that support your strong convictions. If connected to Gate 20 in your Throat, your power will be resolved to act on your own behalf, to turn your thoughts into deeds, and to express your ability to manifest and thrive. If connected to Gate 57 in your Spleen, your intuition will empower your ability to hear what you need to survive perfectly in each moment. Without the Spleen's direct intuitive guidance, this relentless power to act may become an unhealthy, meddlesome and misdirected energy, and you may feel lost in your own momentum, expending energy that serves no one. Though admired, and even sought after, your energy is simply not available to others. It must remain pure in its power, and always accessible to you as you seek to be independent and unique, to act on your convictions, and to triumph, which means to survive as yourself.

Line 6 - Common Sense	Line 3 - Machismo
Line 5 - Annihilation	Line 2 - Momentum
Line 4 - Triumph	Line 1 - The Bully

GATE 57: THE GENTLE - THE GATE OF INTUITIVE INSIGHT
– The extraordinary power of clarity –
Center: Spleen   Quarter: Duality   Theme: Purpose fulfilled through Bonding
RAC of Penetration – JC of Intuition – LAC of the Clarion

With its clarity of intuitive insight, Gate 57 has the capacity to penetrate to one's core in the now. You have a deep inner attunement to sound that is constantly alert to the vibrations coming from your physical, emotional and psychic environments. Moment by moment your intuition registers a sense of what is safe, healthy and good for you, and what is not. Gate 57 is the gate of the right ear. If you want to hear what someone is really saying to you, listen with your intuitively attuned right ear. You must be alert and focused in the now to hear the messages from your Spleen, or the information you are getting for survival may be ignored. You may sometimes appear deaf to others, or be accused of selectively hearing what they have to say, but your intuition is your only guide in determining what the perfect behavior is that will insure your well-being. The only way you will alleviate your fears for the future is to pay close attention to your instinctual hunches, to that little voice that only speaks once and softly, and act on these hunches immediately. When you are listening and paying attention to your intuition now, there is no tomorrow to fear.

Line 6 - Utilization	Line 3 - Acuteness
Line 5 - Progression	Line 2 - Cleansing
Line 4 - The Director	Line 1 - Confusion

THE CHANNEL OF CHARISMA: 34 - 20
A Design where Awareness must Become Deed
Integration Channel   Channel Type: Manifesting Generated

The Channel of Charisma links the Sacral Center to the Throat Center through the Gate of Power (34) and the Gate of the Now (20). This is the classic Manifesting Generator channel where the drive to manifest is guided by Sacral response. In other words, the Warrior (Manifestor) must surrender to the Buddha (Generator), and wait to respond to external stimuli for one's charismatic power to be properly directed into the world.

Background: The Channel of Charisma is one of three oppositions (43-23 and 37-40 are the other two) in the Rave Mandala, making this definition a common and consistent source of the creative life force in the world. When the raw power of Gate 34, a pure physiological energy, is processed through the thyroid system, it becomes a key energetic component empowering humanity's survival. The Sacral exerts its pressure to stay busy on Gate 20, pushing it to expression NOW. The speed with which generative power meets manifestation happens so quickly that it almost bypasses response, which explains why a person with this channel often has difficulty sitting still or being quiet. Though their scope of influence and accomplishment can be amazing, without the awareness to stay connected to the inner guidance of the Sacral, that same driving energy can manifest as an obsession, or erupt spontaneously and get carried away by its own momentum like a misguided missile.

Personal: The energy of Channel 34-20 is part of Integration's process of self empowerment, giving you the power to maintain activity over long periods of time. That's why it is essential that you apply your energy to something you deeply love doing. Other people may envy your manifesting energy, but it is not available for them to tap into. Your awareness that must become deeds (actions) is whatever Gate 34's generative power is immediately focused on, as that energy has to be available for you to manifest in the moment. It is correct and healthy for you to remain busily self-absorbed in an activity that is correct and satisfying for you, while remaining generally unavailable to others. In this way, your genuine vitality and self empowerment emerges spontaneously with its potential to naturally inspire others. This is the true nature of charisma. When your Sacral response is replaced by the mind's should's or could's, however, your great personal power will be diffused or misdirected, compromising your health and your ability to be an example.

Interpersonal: Most people with charisma appear generally unavailable to others. As Individuals with the potential to act or manifest in the moment, they often find themselves doing just that. Their dilemma is that they can be so busy being busy they don't always recognize where guidance may be needed. Proper manifesting is of enormous benefit to society; chaotic manifesting is deeply destructive. If someone with Channel 34-20 does not have access to guidance from within their own design that tempers and directs their busyness, such as Gate 57's intuitive insight for example, or Gate 10's behavior of the self, then it is natural and healthy for them to be open to the guidance or advice of someone with Channel 43-23's individual knowing and insight.

GATE 34: THE POWER OF THE GREAT - THE GATE OF POWER
– Power is only great when its display or use serves the common good –
Center: Sacral   Quarter: Mutation   Theme: Purpose fulfilled through Transformation
RAC of the Sleeping Phoenix – JC of Power – LAC of Duality

Gate 34 is a potent and impressive source of energy that empowers us toward individuation, displaying and celebrating our uniqueness in the world. Two qualities distinguish this gate from the other eight in the Sacral: its asexuality and the unavailability of its power to others. If connected to Gate 10 in your G Center, your energy will be focused on social behaviors or roles that support your strong convictions. If connected to Gate 20 in your Throat, your power will be resolved to act on your own behalf, to turn your thoughts into deeds, and to express your ability to manifest and thrive. If connected to Gate 57 in your Spleen, your intuition will empower your ability to hear what you need to survive perfectly in each moment. Without the Spleen's direct intuitive guidance, this relentless power to act may become an unhealthy, meddlesome and misdirected energy, and you may feel lost in your own momentum, expending energy that serves no one. Though admired, and even sought after, your energy is simply not available to others. It must remain pure in its power, and always accessible to you as you seek to be independent and unique, to act on your convictions, and to triumph, which means to survive as yourself.

Line 6 - Common Sense	Line 3 - Machismo
Line 5 - Annihilation	Line 2 - Momentum
Line 4 - Triumph	Line 1 - The Bully

GATE 20: CONTEMPLATION - THE GATE OF THE NOW
– Recognition and awareness in the now which transforms understanding into right action –
Center: Throat   Quarter: Civilization   Theme: Purpose fulfilled through Form
RAC of the Sleeping Phoenix – JC of the Now – LAC of Duality

Gate 20 is a purely existential gate that keeps you focused in the present, and supports your capacity to survive as yourself. When your expression is properly timed, awareness will be transformed into words or actions that can impact people around you. This energy frequency is, and must be, totally absorbed in the present moment. It can give voice to Gate 57's intuitive survival awareness, to Gate 10's behavioral patterns and commitments to higher principles, or it can manifest Gate 34's sacral power through action toward individuation. Gate 20 expresses the full range of being in the moment from "I am now" to "I know I am myself doing now," but it does not consider the past or the future. To be awake and aware, and to survive, you must be fully present to the moment and authentically yourself. There is rarely time to mentally consider or control what comes bubbling up from inside of you, so what you say or what you do is suddenly there for everybody, including you, to witness. In fact, you often see when you are not looking, or hear when you are not listening. This is how the potential for evolutionary change hidden in each moment of existence is empowered within you. As you live by your Strategy and Authority, you become a living example. Your intuitive knowing, personal survival and mutative, self-loving behaviors influence or empower others.

Line 6 - Wisdom	Line 3 - Self-Awareness
Line 5 - Realism	Line 2 - The Dogmatist
Line 4 - Application	Line 1 - Superficiality

THE CHANNEL OF PERFECTED FORM: 57 - 10
A Design of Survival
Integration Channel (Creative Channel)   Channel Type: Projected

The Channel of Perfected Form links the Splenic Center to the G Center through the Gate of Intuitive Insight (57) and the Gate of the Behavior of the Self (10). This is Integration's creative channel – the art of survival. It projects a quality of behavior that is guided by intuitive awareness, and grounded in loving and appreciating oneself. This behavior is the core of our species' ability to survive, one person at a time.

Background: Splenic awareness is focused primarily on physical well-being. Channel 57-10 supports Gate 10's focus on how to interact with others in order to perfect or assure the Individual's survival. The self-oriented and potentially mutative behaviors of the Individual must survive in order to effect evolutionary change within humanity as a whole. Individual behaviors that are unique, and perfectly adapt our physical forms to surviving, exemplify for others what it means to live fully in the moment. Gate 57 carries an acute acoustic sensitivity to the quality of sounds in one's immediate environment. Paying more attention to someone's tone of voice, rather than to the words spoken, automatically connects Channel 57-10 to our oldest form of awareness, an innate, spontaneous, intuitive wisdom that exists outside of thoughts and emotions. This channel gives a person a rare clarity and ability to act spontaneously and appropriately to anything perceived to be out of order in their environment.

Personal: As you let your deeply intuitive impulses guide your behaviors moment by moment, you automatically release unfounded fears for the future, fears that can keep you from fully loving yourself and embracing your life. You embody the potential to move through the world existentially and unencumbered. This ability to "'think on your feet" spontaneously perfects your form, perfectly ensuring your survival in the now. There is a beauty inherent in this process that makes you happy and fills you with joy. The spontaneity and nature of your creativity are quite different from the creative process of self-reflection which the mind enjoys, or the depth and diversity of emotional sensitivity that comes over time through the Solar Plexus. By simply living true to yourself, you create something healthy and beautiful with your life. Such uniqueness attracts attention and impacts people around you as your example invites all of us to find the value of living life as ourselves.

Interpersonal: People with the Channel of Perfected Form are here to create what they love, and love what they create. Recognition is not their motivation. They have the capacity to love themselves enough to stay true to themselves, while intuitively behaving in ways that insure their survival in society. This is an unapologetically selfish and self-absorbed process, an on-going journey of creating and perfecting that which is uniquely them and expressing it through their lives. In overt and subtle ways, they impact their environment, leaving it healthier and more beautiful than they originally encountered it. Many artists, architects, designers and doctors who have this channel mold the world around them, but by example, not intention. This is the natural by-product of authentic living.

GATE 57: THE GENTLE - THE GATE OF INTUITIVE INSIGHT
– The extraordinary power of clarity –
Center: Spleen   Quarter: Duality   Theme: Purpose fulfilled through Bonding
RAC of Penetration – JC of Intuition – LAC of the Clarion

With its clarity of intuitive insight, Gate 57 has the capacity to penetrate to one's core in the now. You have a deep inner attunement to sound that is constantly alert to the vibrations coming from your physical, emotional and psychic environments. Moment by moment your intuition registers a sense of what is safe, healthy and good for you, and what is not. Gate 57 is the gate of the right ear. If you want to hear what someone is really saying to you, listen with your intuitively attuned right ear. You must be alert and focused in the now to hear the messages from your Spleen, or the information you are getting for survival may be ignored. You may sometimes appear deaf to others, or be accused of selectively hearing what they have to say, but your intuition is your only guide in determining what the perfect behavior is that will insure your well-being. The only way you will alleviate your fears for the future is to pay close attention to your instinctual hunches, to that little voice that only speaks once and softly, and act on these hunches immediately. When you are listening and paying attention to your intuition now, there is no tomorrow to fear.

Line 6 - Utilization	Line 3 - Acuteness
Line 5 - Progression	Line 2 - Cleansing
Line 4 - The Director	Line 1 - Confusion

GATE 10: TREADING - THE GATE OF THE BEHAVIOR OF THE SELF
– The underlying code of behavior which ensures successful interaction despite circumstances –
Center: G   Quarter: Mutation   Theme: Purpose fulfilled through Transformation
RAC of the Vessel of Love – JC of Behavior – LAC of the Prevention

Gate 10 is the most complex gate in the G Center, and one of the four Gates of the Incarnation Cross of the Vessel of Love. This is the gate of the love of oneself. The six potential behaviors or roles of the self (listed below) are guided by the intuition of Gate 57, empowered by the Sacral response of Gate 34, and manifested or expressed through Gate 20. Within the framework of these roles, humanity is now exploring what it means to live as a 9-centered, self-aware form with its potential to awaken, and to experience genuine self love. With your Strategy and Authority in place, Gate 10 empowers your potential to surrender to living authentically as yourself. As you come to know, accept and love what makes you unique, you empower others to love themselves as well. True awakening through surrender is not a commitment to becoming something; it is a commitment to being yourself. Gate 10's strong emphasis on loving self-acceptance will deeply impact how humanity moves through the 21st century. You are one who recognizes that awakening is not possible without self-acceptance. As you embrace the honor and pleasure of exploring life in a self-aware form, you empower our potential to live as our true selves, awake in the now moment.

Line 6 - The Role Model	Line 3 - The Martyr
Line 5 - The Heretic	Line 2 - The Hermit
Line 4 - The Opportunist	Line 1 - Modesty

THE CHANNEL OF AWAKENING: 10 - 20
A Design of Commitment to Higher Principles
Integration Channel   Channel Type: Projected

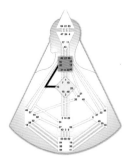

The Channel of Awakening links the G Center to the Throat Center through the Gate of the Behavior of the Self (10) and the Gate of the Now (20). For the awake and aware, each moment presents an opportunity for recognition and commitment to principles that transform Individual knowing into right action (Gate 20). This is action that is tempered by an underlying code of behavior ensuring successful interaction with others (Gate 10).

Background: The Channel of Awakening says, "I AM! I am alive NOW!" This is the fullest, most poignant, selfish and primal expression of the essence of being. It is the wonder of human consciousness, "I survived; I am a survivor." Buddha means "the awakened one." The two pillars of the awakened life are self-love and self-trust: "I am and I can because I love (myself)." In the simplest Human Design terms, to be awake means making decisions as yourself and living by them. When you are able to live your own design, to love being yourself no matter what the cost or how mundane your experience, you are as awake as the Buddha.

Personal: The G Center is not an awareness center so Channel 10-20 can only do one thing – it speaks for itself. It perfectly expresses the wisdom that to survive, flourish, and experience the love of life, you must fulfill your potential to behave as a living expression of awakened self love, acceptance and trust. You are normally in a constant state of awakening, of being recognized by others, of becoming aware of yourself as your life unfolds before you. Your survival and your self-empowerment are the end result of embracing, loving, accepting and living as yourself in each moment; they are evidenced by others through your decisions, speech and interactions, and your behavior in the world. For you to have your intended impact on people around you, to fulfill your potential as Integration's voice of leadership, others must sense that there is something clear and awake about you because you cannot see it clearly in yourself. Simply by being yourself, you will influence and inspire people around you to be themselves, most often without you knowing it. This is the kind of recognition that elicits proper invitations from others, invitations which keep you from meeting resistance, from taking criticism personally, and from becoming burdened by your uniqueness and a natural tendency toward self-absorption.

Interpersonal: The six lines of the 10th gate indicate which behavioral principle those with Channel 10-20 are committed to. The 1st line says that one has the potential to be awake in the moment through the ability to know how to act, no matter what the circumstances. The 2nd line is designed for independent self-absorbed behavior, and it withdraws into isolation when the conditioning of others wants to pull it away from its true nature. The 3rd line's trial and error testing process can ultimately be of great value to humanity by discovering what does and does not work. The 4th line will wait for the right moment and opportunity to externalize what it knows in order to influence and awaken people close to it. The 5th line will awaken and bring change through directly and overtly challenging the accepted, underlying traditions of society. The 6th line awakens others by its example rather than words; through the expression of its true nature in the actions of day to day living.

Gate 10: Treading - The Gate of the Behavior of the Self
– The underlying code of behavior which ensures successful interaction despite circumstances –
Center: G   Quarter: Mutation   Theme: Purpose fulfilled through Transformation
RAC of the Vessel of Love – JC of Behavior – LAC of the Prevention

Gate 10 is the most complex gate in the G Center, and one of the four Gates of the Incarnation Cross of the Vessel of Love. This is the gate of the love of oneself. The six potential behaviors or roles of the self (listed below) are guided by the intuition of Gate 57, empowered by the Sacral response of Gate 34, and manifested or expressed through Gate 20. Within the framework of these roles, humanity is now exploring what it means to live as a 9-centered, self-aware form with its potential to awaken, and to experience genuine self love. With your Strategy and Authority in place, Gate 10 empowers your potential to surrender to living authentically as yourself. As you come to know, accept and love what makes you unique, you empower others to love themselves as well. True awakening through surrender is not a commitment to becoming something; it is a commitment to being yourself. Gate 10's strong emphasis on loving self-acceptance will deeply impact how humanity moves through the 21st century. You are one who recognizes that awakening is not possible without self-acceptance. As you embrace the honor and pleasure of exploring life in a self-aware form, you empower our potential to live as our true selves, awake in the now moment.

Line 6 - The Role Model	Line 3 - The Martyr
Line 5 - The Heretic	Line 2 - The Hermit
Line 4 - The Opportunist	Line 1 - Modesty

Gate 20: Contemplation - The Gate of The Now
– Recognition and awareness in the now which transforms understanding into right action –
Center: Throat   Quarter: Civilization   Theme: Purpose fulfilled through Form
RAC of the Sleeping Phoenix – JC of the Now – LAC of Duality

Gate 20 is a purely existential gate that keeps you focused in the present, and supports your capacity to survive as yourself. When your expression is properly timed, awareness will be transformed into words or actions that can impact people around you. This energy frequency is, and must be, totally absorbed in the present moment. It can give voice to Gate 57's intuitive survival awareness, to Gate 10's behavioral patterns and commitments to higher principles, or it can manifest Gate 34's sacral power through action toward individuation. Gate 20 expresses the full range of being in the moment from "I am now" to "I know I am myself doing now," but it does not consider the past or the future. To be awake and aware, and to survive, you must be fully present to the moment and authentically yourself. There is rarely time to mentally consider or control what comes bubbling up from inside of you, so what you say or what you do is suddenly there for everybody, including you, to witness. In fact, you often see when you are not looking, or hear when you are not listening. This is how the potential for evolutionary change hidden in each moment of existence is empowered within you. As you live by your Strategy and Authority, you become a living example. Your intuitive knowing, personal survival and mutative, self-loving behaviors influence or empower others.

Line 6 - Wisdom	Line 3 - Self-Awareness
Line 5 - Realism	Line 2 - The Dogmatist
Line 4 - Application	Line 1 - Superficiality

THE INDIVIDUAL CIRCUIT GROUP
KNOWING AND CENTERING CIRCUITS
SUPER KEYNOTE - EMPOWERMENT

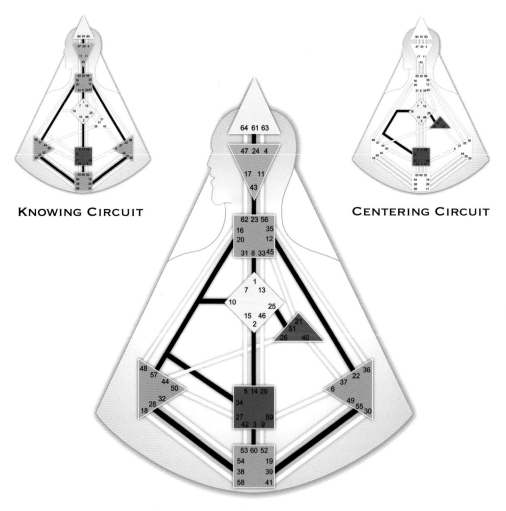

KNOWING CIRCUIT

CENTERING CIRCUIT

INDIVIDUAL CIRCUIT GROUP

We begin with the Individual Circuit Group because of its close ties to, and yet distinctive differences from, the core Integration Channel. Individuality has both the capacity and the responsibility to be a force for change in the world, to bring mutation to the Tribe and the Collective. The challenge is to do so without being rejected by either group.

The Individual Circuit Group is the most complex of the three groups, and encompasses the frequencies of all nine centers. It is oriented to the present moment with attention focused on listening to the beat of its own drum, and its determination to follow its own direction. The Individual's drive for uniqueness becomes a living example that inspires or empowers or awakens a latent potential in others. Mutation and empowerment, the keynotes associated with Individual Circuitry, are at the heart of The Human Design System, and of evolution itself. For the Individual, these keynotes imply a passion for being true to one's self, for thinking about and being uniquely attuned to the present moment, and for living independent of the norm. Individuals, when their knowing becomes clear, stand ready to embody inspiration or differentiation, which is their way of leading by example. They have a gift for recognizing the mutative potential in everything and everyone that comes with an intuitive sense of how to empower it in others. This is what distinguishes the Individual Circuit Group from the self-empowerment that is specific to Integration.

Individual knowing isn't based on either proven facts or experiential learning, but rather on intuition and/or the inspiration in the moment, which is why Individuals do not fit easily into society. It is imperative, as well as advantageous, that Individuals learn how to explain themselves from childhood on. They need to be able to communicate what they hear as inspiration in the moment, and what they know inside to be true. This ability to explain facilitates their effectiveness as agents for change, and eases their personal feelings of being different.

Individuality attracts attention, but Individuals usually need and like to be left alone to explore their creative and melancholic inner world. They can become so caught up in the moment that they often appear deaf to the voices of experience and reason. This is because they are here to be true to what is new in the moment, and to model it, act on it, or communicate it. In order to be comfortable with their position in the scheme of things, and to be ready to connect with others in that precious yet illusive empowering moment, it is necessary for the Individual to stay closely attuned to their Authority and follow their Strategy.

The Individual Circuit Group is composed of one major circuit, the Knowing Circuit, and one minor circuit, the Centering Circuit.

THE KNOWING CIRCUIT
KEYNOTE: EMPOWERMENT

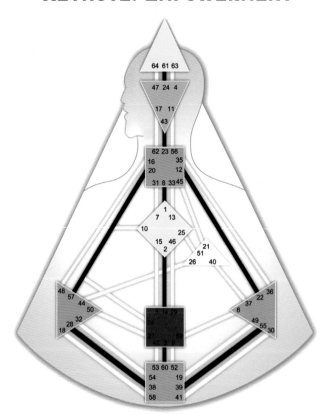

CHANNELS:

3 – 60	**MUTATION**		**43 – 23**	**STRUCTURING**
	Energy which initiates and			*Individuality*
	fluctuates, Pulse		**38 – 28**	**STRUGGLE**
14 – 2	**BEAT**			*Stubbornness*
	The keeper of keys		**57 – 20**	**THE BRAIN WAVE**
1 – 8	**INSPIRATION**			*Penetrating awareness*
	The creative role model		**39 – 55**	**EMOTING**
61 – 24	**AWARENESS**			*Moodiness*
	A thinker		**22 – 12**	**OPENNESS**
				A social being

The role of those with definition in the Knowing Circuit is to be empowered to live as themselves. They empower others by being an individual example of uniqueness. Their way of re-ordering life, reflected in their lifestyle, requires an audience as this is how they bring mutation into the world. They need to be observed and to be recognized for their uniqueness.

As the name of the circuit implies, it is the inspired and intuitive knowing of each moment, in combination with the passionate or melancholic moodiness of the emotional wave, that forms or shapes the mutative impact the Individual's thoughts and behavior have on the rest of us. This combination is what makes the Individual's unpredictable, creative and unique moment by moment knowing empowering. Individuality is not about perfecting, mastering or organizing something. That is the Collective's contribution. Individuality is about birthing something totally new with the potential to transform both the Individual and the world around him.

The nature of Individual knowing is that it comes and goes; it's there and it's not there. Individuals don't know until they know. This knowing might be the answer, the right direction, or it might not. For Individual mutation to take hold universally, its value and validity must be tested over time. The power to mutate, which is common to all channels and gates in the Individual Group Circuit, is dependent on the on/off timing of this sudden knowing. Mutation operates in a pulse that cannot be controlled or anticipated. The fixed timing of the conservative Collective Circuit, and the hierarchical nature of the Tribal Circuit, keeps those circuit groups from engaging the inspiration or mutation of the moment on their own. Both groups are obliged to look to the Individual as a guiding force for change and transformation, helping them to avoid stasis and promoting their evolutionary progress. This energy of the new, however, leads the Collective and the Tribe to place Individual knowing under careful scrutiny, and leaves it open to criticism, which is why it is essential for all Individuals to be able to explain themselves.

Individuals are often admired for their difference and envied for the attention they receive. Their path is a vulnerable, truly personal, and sometimes lonely one however, and Individuals may never know that they have empowered someone else.

The Channels and Gates of the Knowing Circuit are discussed on the following pages.

THE CHANNEL OF MUTATION: 3 - 60
A Design of Energy which Initiates and Fluctuates - Pulse
Circuit: Knowing   Channel Type: Generated

The Channel of Mutation links the Root Center to the Sacral Center through the Gate of Acceptance (60) and the Gate of Ordering (3). The potential for evolutionary change that comes through this unpredictable, mutative and melancholic channel depends on one's capacity to accept limitation (Gate 60) and transcend the confusion of new beginnings (Gate 3).

Background: Gate 60 is the hub of all evolutionary possibilities, while Gate 3 is always reaching for what is new and potentially viable, one possibility at a time. The underlying current or frequency governing this adrenalized generating Channel of Mutation is the format energy* of Individual Circuitry. Its potent, on/off pulsing energy, associated with melancholy, permeates the way those with this channel live out their unique designs. This is an energy that also conditions or deeply affects everyone around them.

Personal: Your key to living with this melancholic process, a mechanical moodiness, is to avoid trying to reason it away. It is better to remain patient and alert as you wait for the new mutation to arrive on the scene through you. Time spent alone with your muse, when the pulse of mutation is off, can deepen and enrich your inner journey. Although you can't always see it, something is stirring underneath, and what is not yet ready to emerge continues to gestate and grow. This endless movement from chaos to order to chaos is the nature of the format energy as it always engenders the possibility

FORMAT ENERGY

for something new to come into the world. You only have to accept the limitation inherent in not knowing when this change (this pulse) will happen, and surrender to your Sacral response to bring the energy of change to all of us.

Interpersonal: Like music, mutation takes place suddenly, unexpectedly, in the gaps or the spaces between the pulses, or notes. It forces everyone to adapt or change, or be left behind. Those with the Channel of Mutation feel the pressure to bring innovation and renewal to their lives, jobs, families and the world around them. The Root Center's constant pressure creates inner tension during the times when the on/off pulse is off and seemingly nothing is happening. This is experienced on a chemical level in the body as melancholy. As agents of mutation and change, Individuals may find themselves trying to give reasons for their moods, and getting caught in the discomforting, shadow places within themselves which they normally tend to avoid. If they give in to this shadow, or do not wait for the correct response, the pressure to change the way things are done can lead to deep personal frustration and depression, as well as instability and chaos in those around them.

Format energies exert a powerful influence on all other channels in the circuit, and the design as a whole. Format Channels run between the Root and Sacral Centers: 53–42 (Collective/Abstract), 60–3 (Individual) and 52–9 (Collective/Logical). There is no format channel for the Tribal Circuit.

GATE 3: DIFFICULTY AT THE BEGINNING - THE GATE OF ORDERING
– The fundamental challenge of initiation is to transcend confusion and establish order –
Center: Sacral   Quarter: Initiation   Theme: Purpose fulfilled through Mind
RAC of the Laws – JC of Mutation – LAC of Wishes

The function of Gate 3 is to transcend confusion and establish order so that something new and potentially viable can take hold in the world. You have a connection to unique Individual knowing, personal innovation, and the potential for making a significant contribution. Waiting for the right moment for something mutative to happen can feel like forever. You will need patience to accept Gate 60's occasional bursts of energy, and the unknown timing of its limited releases of potential. There is an on-off creative pulse that prevails here, and the potential for something new is neither logical nor experiential. If you don't wait for the right timing, for the structures needed for true mutation to settle into place, your enthusiasm for change will simply destabilize those around you, rather than empower and influence them. You may experience melancholy and even depression when you feel that there is no energy fueling your potential to bring change. This is a time, however, for you to go deep into your own process, to spend time with your own creative muse. You cannot predict, control or rush the mutative moment. It has its own timing. And anyone who steps into your aura, at the right time, can be changed without you even lifting a finger.

Line 6 - Surrender	Line 3 - Survival
Line 5 - Victimization	Line 2 - Immaturity
Line 4 - Charisma	Line 1 - Synthesis

GATE 60: LIMITATION - THE GATE OF ACCEPTANCE
– The acceptance of limitation is the first step in transcendence –
Center: Root   Quarter: Mutation   Theme: Purpose fulfilled through Transformation
RAC of Laws – JC of Limitation – LAC of Distraction

Gate 60 creates the pressure needed for pure energy to mutate into form. Here the Root Center fuels restraint, which enables the pressure to build under each possibility. The creative mutative process is subject to a pulse, and you never know when something that has the potential to become a mutation will be released. A viable mutation transcends existing limitations when it is empowered or given order by Gate 3. Mutation takes place in the "space between the notes" created by the on-off pulse of the 60th gate. The pressure from your Root Center creates a deep restlessness in you to move ahead, and limitations of any kind may feel like roadblocks. If you become impatient with the unpredictable mutative process, however, the melancholy inherent in the 60th gate can deepen and become chronic depression. When you feel you cannot affect change around you, look inward. Accept the mystery of the mutative process and trust that transformation is occurring within you, and because of you, in the world around you. Gate 3 plays a key role in bringing order to the potential chaos that comes from the mutation. Without it you can feel unable to move forward.

Line 6 - Rigidity	Line 3 - Conservatism
Line 5 - Leadership	Line 2 - Decisiveness
Line 4 - Resourcefulness	Line 1 - Acceptance

THE CHANNEL OF THE BEAT: 14 - 2
A Design of being a Keeper of Keys
Circuit: Knowing   Channel Type: Generated

The Channel of the Beat links the Sacral Center to the G Center through the Gate of Power Skills (14) and the Gate of Higher Knowing (2). Gate 14 is particularly focused on the availability of material resources to fuel mutation, and Gate 2 is the seat of the Driver (the Magnetic Monopole) which holds us together and directs our movement in time through space. Together, as the Channel of the Beat, they are poised to take us in a new direction.

Background: Channel 14-2 is one of three Tantric* channels in the Bodygraph (the Individual tantric channel) and has all the characteristics of Individuality such as mutation, innovation, unusualness, newness, uniqueness, and melancholy. The Sacral Center is the source of pure generative energy that gives birth to and sustains life on this planet. The G Center represents identity, direction and love. The energy that is generated when you combine Gate 2, Higher Knowing, with Gate 14, Power Skills, is a very potent resource for the creative, fertile life force that empowers change in our direction.

Personal: As the Keeper of Keys, you have access to essential resources necessary to transform the mutative impulse into a material direction. You can bring an innovative and empowering new direction to people, projects and the planet simply by listening to and trusting your Sacral response, even though you don't know where it is taking you or what kind of mutative impact it will have on others. You are able to sustain your own creative efforts, or materially provide for and encourage others in their own creative direction. All Individuality empowers through example, and your first task is to be true to yourself, and live into your own destiny, direction and purpose. If you attempt to chase after your destiny, you will end up feeling lost and frustrated. By trusting that life will make decisions through you, you empower others in a purely mechanical way. People passing through your healthy auric field might find their own sense of direction being initiated or have a new direction take hold within them. All you need to do is remain open and responsive to life.

Interpersonal: The Collective is focused on the status quo and the Tribe is focused on security. Channel 14-2 provides the Individual with the resources and the keys needed to bring new directions to both groups by introducing critical new perspectives into the mix so that we can continue to evolve, and meet the ever-changing challenges of existence. Eventually, the Collective and the Tribe will test and adapt the perspectives that best apply. Mutation in Channel 14-2 is something that just happens in the pulse as a matter of deep response to life, and to the identity and direction of the higher self. One moment it is there and the next it is not. We never know when the new direction will come, where it will take the Individual, or how it will mutate the Collective or the Tribe.

The three Tantric channels between the Sacral and G Centers (5-15, 14-2, 29-46) allow the fertile power of the Sacral Center to connect to and empower the identity, direction and love of the higher self in the G Center.

GATE 14: POSSESSION IN GREAT MEASURE - THE GATE OF POWER SKILLS
– The accumulation & retention of power through skilled interaction, coupling grace with control –
Center: Sacral   Quarter: Mutation   Theme: Purpose fulfilled through Transformation
RAC of Contagion – JC of Empowering – LAC of the Uncertainty

Gate 14 empowers direction for the individual, and humanity, through the distribution of available resources. The Gate of Power Skills makes sure that mutation is supported, and shows us how to invest our resources in order to expand our horizons. The Sacral Center, when defined, has the energy to sustain long hours of creative work, and the 14th gate is fertile power at its most exalted. This is the gas pedal that controls when and how the resources are released. When you are aligned with your design, and doing the work you love to do, you will generate wealth and power. These resources are not directly for your own use, however, but yours to manage in order to empower others, to support individual creativity, charitable activities, or leaders with a vision for humanity's future. But throwing your money at anything and everyone is a poor investment. To protect your valuable life force energy from misuse or abuse by others, and to remain properly aligned in order to bring out the right mutative direction, follow your Authority. When properly directed by Gate 2, your resources can become a significant catalyst for empowering change in the world.

Line 6 - Humility	Line 3 - Service
Line 5 - Arrogance	Line 2 - Management
Line 4 - Security	Line 1 - Money isn't Everything

GATE 2: THE RECEPTIVE - THE GATE OF THE DIRECTION OF THE SELF
– Receptivity as the primal base through which any response is determined, the root of action –
Center: G   Quarter: Civilization   Theme: Purpose fulfilled through Form
RAC of the Sphinx – JC of the Driver – LAC of Defiance

The 'higher' knowing of Gate 2 is rooted in the direction of the self toward love and beauty via the Magnetic Monopole, the Driver. The Driver is focused on our movement in time through space, and built into your design is an innate sense of inner direction which is not based simply on geographic location. You cannot change this direction through your mind or your will, and if others are not going in your direction, you may come to a parting of ways. Gate 2 is likened to the key of the vehicle; it starts the engine for the Driver. The motor and the fuel to keep moving in your direction come from the Sacral Center through Gate 14. You may even find yourself directing other people toward the resources they need to support their creative endeavors, or discover that by simply aligning to your own direction you automatically empower or confirm in others their own sense of direction. You are a visionary providing the plan or overview for a new way forward, but you are not here to do the work or make it happen. You look to Gate 14 for allies, for the power and resources to bring your vision to fruition.

Line 6 - Fixation	Line 3 - Patience
Line 5 - Intelligent Application	Line 2 - Genius
Line 4 - Secretiveness	Line 1 - Intuition

THE CHANNEL OF INSPIRATION: 1 - 8
A Design of a Creative Role Model
Circuit: Knowing (Creative Channel)   Channel Type: Projected

The Channel of Inspiration links the G Center to the Throat Center through the Gate of Self Expression (1) and the Gate of Contribution (8). Gate 1 is the Individual's doorway to creatively expressing a mutative perspective, either through their auric presence, or in a form that can be promoted and displayed for all to experience. It takes courage to stand out from the crowd, and to inspire others to be equally bold. For this channel, living as an Individual is an art, and designed to get the public's attention.

Background: Channel 1-8 is the public outlet for both the creative (Gate 1) and leadership (Gate 8) potentials of the Knowing Circuit. Through the voice of the Role Model it says, "I know I can (or can't) make a creative contribution" to the evolving goals of the group. People with this channel have an impact on the world around them by living and fully expressing the unique nature of their identity. This impact is not achieved with words or explanations but by example, by modeling their Individual direction. They do it, they live it, and when Channel 1-8 is connected to a motor (through Channel 2-14 for instance) their contribution can be even more impressive.

Personal: The nature of Individual direction is to move toward beauty, powered by its own truth and grounded in the moment. You are designed to model what it means to be a self-expressed, creative Individual, and attract, deservedly, the attention of others. As you do so, you potentially change their perspective. You inspire new directions in others and free them to express their own uniqueness creatively, like the pianist whose extraordinary performance inspires a person in the audience to take piano lessons. For this kind of Individual leadership-by-example to have an impact, it must come from a place of authentic personal authority that is safe from casual, or conditioning, influences. Also essential is the recognition that your potential to inspire or empower others is actually a co-creation between your dedication to living your Individuality, which naturally attracts attention, and others' recognition of your Individuality. Channel 1-8 lacks a built-in social adeptness, and it is incumbent on you to develop the skills needed to effectively communicate what you are here to contribute, which includes cultivating the patience to wait for the correct timing to do so. The key to your flowering is being recognized, accepted, and applauded for your individuality, and the creative impact you promote.

Interpersonal: Individual-style leaders (mutating or empowering by example) draw others along with them by initiating changes in the ways people see, act and think about life, truth and the nature of beauty. An underlying recognition that nothing can exist outside of the totality contributes to their overall impact on society. Those with the Channel of Inspiration know how to live their uniqueness with exuberance, and in the process they empower others to be their own unique, inspiring and differentiated selves.

GATE 1: THE CREATIVE - THE GATE OF SELF-EXPRESSION
– Creation as a primal force. The energy potential to manifest inspiration without limitation –
Center: G   Quarter: Mutation   Theme: Purpose fulfilled through Transformation
RAC of the Sphinx – JC of Self-Expression– LAC of Defiance

Gate 1 is the drive, and deep need, to focus on expressing oneself in unique and creative ways. You are not concerned with being the best, which is a comparative trait of the Collective. You simply want to live out your true creative nature, your authentic individuality. When happily absorbed in doing "your own thing," you are not aware that you are attracting the attention of others. It is while you are being true to your creative process that what you are doing, and how you are doing it, has its greatest impact. As you exemplify new ways of expressing your authentic self, you empower others to consider new perspectives or new ways of being in the world. You may even change their creative direction. Your creativity inspires others by example, and for your impact to be properly felt and appreciated, it must be seen or heard. This requires interaction with the world, and waiting for an invitation. Without Gate 8, what you probably find least attractive is marketing your own work. You will often find yourself drawn to people with Gate 8 because they are better equipped, or in a better position, to promote your work for you.

Line 6 - Objectivity	Line 3 - The Energy to Sustain Creative Work
Line 5 - The Energy to Attract Society	Line 2 - Love is Light
Line 4 - Aloneness as the Medium of Creativity	Line 1 - Creation is Independent of Will

GATE 8: HOLDING TOGETHER - THE GATE OF CONTRIBUTION
– The basic worth realized in contributing individual efforts to group goals –
Center: Throat   Quarter: Civilization Theme: Purpose fulfilled through Form
RAC of Contagion – JC of Contribution – LAC of Uncertainty

Gate 8 says, "I know I can contribute, or not." Your contribution will come either through a public display of your own Individual lifestyle, direction and creations, or by empowering and publicly promoting others (Gate 1). You are drawn toward what is novel and innovative, and will find yourself attracting other people's attention to it, like the Gallery owner or art agent. Once you get people's attention, all you can do is lead by example. If others wish to follow, they will. This is how you quietly impact the Collective and shift the Tribe's orientation over time. Unless Individuality's innovative contributions are embraced and incorporated in some way by the Collective and the Tribe, they will not take hold. The leadership path of recognizing and displaying what is mutative and unique can be a lonely one as you must first be recognized, and then invited to publicly display and endorse what you know to be of future value. Without the invitation, society's attention may be negative. If Gate 1's creative means of self-expression is not defined in your chart, you will seek its inspirational qualities; however, your key role is not as the artist but as the agent who promotes other artists' vision of the new.

Line 6 - Communion	Line 3 - The phoney
Line 5 - Dharma	Line 2 - Service
Line 4 - Respect	Line 1 - Honesty

THE CHANNEL OF AWARENESS: 61 - 24
A Design of a Thinker
Circuit: Knowing   Channel Type: Projected

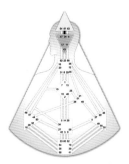

The Channel of Awareness links the Head Center to the Ajna Center through the Gate of Mystery (61) and the Gate of Rationalization (24). The mental capacities of the Individual are comprised of the inspiration of Gate 61, Inner Truth, and the rationalization of Gate 24, The Return. This is mental definition that brings a sudden experience of knowing, a satori.

Background: The Channel of Awareness creates the Individual thinker. The pressure in the Head Center to know the unknowable is conceptualized through the Ajna Center into a rational answer. Thinking with this channel is not about discovering; it is about how our acoustic mind processes inspiration. It's about the mutation that is possible when there is a gap in the thinking process and a new thought can come in. The mind turns things over and over again until the moment of mutation or satori arrives, and you simply know. Individual thinking cannot relate to the past and reflect on it the way abstract thinking does (Channel 64-47). It cannot recognize the pattern, and based on this measurement make a prediction for the future as logical thinking does (Channel 63-4). The Channel of Awareness is here to know what is knowable and of value, to know what is knowable but of no value, and to know that we are not designed to know everything (the unknowable).

Personal: Your mind is designed to inspire others with your unique knowing, and to offer us the potential to see life in a completely new way. It is united with something beyond this plane that you hear and know spontaneously. Your mutative knowing breaks the old abstract cycles, shatters the logical patterns, and inspires us with a new realization. You don't control your thinking, and you cannot use your thoughts to get anything or anywhere. You simply need to recognize that 'knowing' just happens when it does. The mutation will take place or not. You are here to surrender to the serendipity of inner truth that will make itself known through the 24th gate. This comes in its own mutative way and in its own time while your mind is occupied by the acoustic static, the white noise of Gate 61's inspiration. Yours is truly a mind that is connected to the mystery. Because your mind is always busy thinking, you both seek and love silence. Listening to or making music often provides a soothing release from the constant mental pressure to think.

Interpersonal: The real mystery is that inspiration is there in the mind from the beginning, awaiting its moment of activation by life itself. Individuals with Channel 61-24 do not have to 'do' anything. A simple invitation focuses their mental awareness; and, while absorbed in that awareness, while absorbed in the moment, a new unbidden thought arises and makes itself known. Knowing happens in its own time. Capturing those illusive but empowering truths or insights, wanting to convey to others what is truly inspiring and worth thinking about, are challenges that those with the Channel of Awareness are here to meet. The key to their success is an ability to distinguish between what is knowable or not, and what needs to be known or not.

GATE 61: INNER TRUTH - THE GATE OF MYSTERY
– The awareness of universal underlying principles –
Center: Head   Quarter: Mutation   Theme: Purpose fulfilled through Transformation
RAC of Maia – JC of Thinking – LAC of Obscuration

Gate 61 is the pressure to know, to unravel the mystery, and to inspire with unique moments of absolute recognition. This knowing moves us toward deeper levels of self-acceptance where we can embrace what distinguishes us from others. You love to spend time musing, and mentally delving into the unknown. When you 'know' that you have a unique insight, and wait for the right time to express it, you feel liberated. When your knowing inspires, empowers, or mutates others, you feel empowered. Compared to the Collective mind, which is either focused on what happened in the past or predicting what may happen in the future, your Individual mind yearns for silence now, for all the voices and dialogue to stop. If you give in to the intense pressure, and let the unknown haunt you, your inspiration can become confused by delusion, leading to deep uncertainty and anxiety. The secret is to enjoy your thoughts and let your inner knowing, your inner truth, reveal itself in its own unique timing. Without Gate 24 you are not designed to solve the mystery, but simply to enjoy it.

Line 6 - Appeal	Line 3 - Interdependence
Line 5 - Influence	Line 2 - Natural Brilliance
Line 4 - Research	Line 1 - Occult Knowledge

GATE 24: THE RETURN - THE GATE OF RATIONALIZATION
– The natural and spontaneous process of transformation and renewal –
Center: Ajna   Quarter: Initiation   Theme: Purpose fulfilled through Mind
RAC of the Four Ways – JC of Rationalization – LAC of Incarnation

Gate 24's function is to take the unique inspiration of Gate 61 and turn it into a rational concept which can eventually be communicated to others. It returns to the same territory over and over again, pondering a thought it considers inspiring, reviewing it until it can be brought into form. Your mind cannot act on the inspiration, however, or prove it logically or through past experience. This is a natural and spontaneous process of transformation, mental renewal and unique knowing. One moment the knowing is not there and the next moment it is. To use your individual mind to your greatest advantage, give yourself time to return and review. This process can include watching or listening to something over and over again. If you let your mind transform organically, without attempting to control it, the resolution will often appear on its own. You will hear it in a moment of silence, like those aha's that pop into your mind in the middle of the night. Gate 24 is the fear of ignorance, which is the mental anxiety that you will never know for certain, or that you won't be able to explain your knowing. If you try and make decisions with your mind, you will trigger this anxiety. Without Gate 61 you are under pressure to make not-self mental decisions to look for the next inspiring mystery to solve.

Line 6 - The Gift Horse	Line 3 - The Addict
Line 5 - Confession	Line 2 - Recognition
Line 4 - The Hermit	Line 1 - The Sin of Omission

THE CHANNEL OF STRUCTURING: 43 - 23
A Design of Individuality (from Genius to Freak)
Circuit: Knowing   Channel Type: Projected

The Channel of Structuring links the Ajna Center to the Throat through the Gate of Insight (43) and the Gate of Assimilation (23). The inspired knowing and rationalizations of Channel 61-24 are received by Gate 43 where they spontaneously break through as insights which the 23rd Gate assimilates and expresses. Empowerment and evolutionary change are possible when new perspectives and innovative thinking are clearly explained and accepted.

Background: When the mind is connected to the Throat Center through this Individual channel, it engages in a mutative and metamorphic process that empowers efficiency. The Channel of Structuring conceptualizes and expresses a unique and original perspective in a way that changes how people see and think. Using keynotes, for example, is an ultra-efficient way to say something. For empowerment and change to take effect, however, the magic of Strategy and Authority is required. If those with this channel do not wait for proper timing, their unique knowing, no matter how well expressed, will rarely be of value to or understood by others. All outer mental authority finds its way into the natural flow when expression is guided by one's Strategy and Authority.

Personal: Your challenge is to simply let go of control, and allow your mind to process its knowing in its own way and timing. All you can do is develop a proficiency for explaining what you know simply and clearly. As you do so, the opportunities to express your unique insights, your own genius, will naturally arise out of others' recognition of your gifts. There is no need, or even real ability, for you to plan what you will say beforehand. It is not necessary to know why your mind says what it says, or attach significance to when it says it. Your mind is here to embrace not only your knowing, but to explore what isn't known. You are someone whose thinking feels like it is light years ahead. In order for your genius to be embraced, you must be aligned with the flow of your unique design. When your insights are properly recognized and your sharing appropriately timed, you will not be perceived as a freak. Recognition opens the way for your Individual knowing to penetrate and mutate the Collective or Tribe. When your timing is off, however, you will be dismissed, feel alienated, and at times may even reject your own unique knowing. Expressing your outer authority is a process. It takes time to learn how to communicate your innovative thinking, and people don't shift easily. You may have to explain yourself many times before the new concept takes hold and your genius is truly recognized.

Interpersonal: The gift of the Channel of Structuring is the ability to develop techniques and concepts that enhance efficiency. This mind can look at the way something has been done, or is being done, and suddenly know a much better and faster way of doing the same thing. This innovative thinking results in quantum leaps that can move entire organizations to higher planes of efficiency, and potentially bring a new level of refinement and wisdom into the world. To retain the integrity of their inner knowing, people with this channel can appear deaf to others (see Gate 43). "**The Individual mind will always feel like an outsider standing at the door, waiting for the invitation to offer its unique knowing.**" - Ra Uru Hu

GATE 43: BREAKTHROUGH - THE GATE OF INSIGHT

– In order for achievement to be maintained a new order must be fairly established –
Center: Ajna   Quarter: Mutation   Theme: Purpose fulfilled through Transformation
RAC of Explanation – JC of Insight – LAC of Dedication

Gate 43 is the gate of the inner ear and only listens to its own unique inner voice. It can spontaneously transform rational inner knowing into Individual insight and new perspectives. Your knowing is not backed up by facts, however, and it can take fortitude to stand behind and explain insights that seem freakish and completely outside of the Collective or Tribal norms. You have the capacity, when the timing is right, to mentally mold a unique and mutative awareness into its final shape. When fully conceptualized, your insights need to be invited down to Gate 23 in the Throat to bring the potential mutation, the possibility of a new perspective, out into the world. Nothing is more difficult for you than to listen to and really hear others. It's not your fault, nor a problem to be fixed, but simply your genetic protection from undue influence. Gate 43 carries a fear of rejection. Without Gate 23, you may wonder how to clearly communicate your breakthrough insights. Mental anxiety arises when you fear that your ideas are too weird, and if you can't explain them you are vulnerable to the possibility of their being rejected.

Line 6 - Breakthrough	Line 3 - Expediency
Line 5 - Progression	Line 2 - Dedication
Line 4 - The One-Track Mind	Line 1 - Patience

GATE 23: SPLITTING APART - THE GATE OF ASSIMILATION

– Amorality. The awareness and understanding which leads to the acceptance of diversity –
Center: Throat   Quarter: Civilization   Theme: Purpose fulfilled through Form
RAC of Explanation – JC of Assimilation – LAC of Dedication

Gate 23 is where inspiration as inner knowing is finally translated into language. Its amorality, acceptance of diversity, and ability to cut through mental intolerance opens the way for mutation to take hold in the world. Expression through the Gate of Assimilation initiates us into new ways of thinking. Here your unique voice can finally say, "I know." What you know, or don't know, will always attract the attention of others, but can also keep you on the outside looking in. Insights that are potentially different and transformative require that you communicate their essence clearly. If your unique perspective is truly to be of value to others, you must wait for the right timing to speak, and explain it in a simple and accessible way. If you don't, you will be dismissed as a freak. It is also important that you speak only what you truly know. Over time, your genius will be recognized and you will earn the respect of others. Without Gate 43's conceptualizing, you may experience mental anxiety as you realize that you don't know exactly what it is you know, leaving yourself open to misunderstanding and dismissal.

Line 6 - Fusion	Line 3 - Individuality
Line 5 - Assimilation	Line 2 - Self-Defense
Line 4 - Fragmentation	Line 1 - Proselytization

THE CHANNEL OF STRUGGLE: 38 - 28
A Design of Stubbornness
Circuit: Knowing   Channel Type: Projected

The Channel of Struggle links the Root Center to the Splenic center through the Gate of the Fighter (38) and the Gate of the Game Player (28). This channel is about the struggle to find meaning and a purpose for living, as well as the capacity to find meaning and purpose in life's struggles. Gate 28 brings the awareness of whether struggle is appropriate, or not, and discerns what has value and is therefore worth fighting for. Gate 38 is the pressure to preserve individual integrity and to fight against or oppose outside forces which could distract one from being true to themselves.

Background: Channel 38-28 brings the realization that elevates Homo sapiens above their primitive ancestors; namely, there is more to life than just staying alive. Powered by adrenalized Root Center energy, it is designed and equipped to seek and to find a purpose, choosing to engage whatever gives meaning to existence no matter how difficult the struggle. Knowing how to struggle, and which struggles to engage in, is vital to the individuation process.

Personal: You have the stubborn determination to go your own way in life against even the most overwhelming odds, and to discover meaning and a purpose in the struggles you meet along your unique path. There is nothing more satisfying or healthy for you, when correct, than to stubbornly stand up against the odds, or risk losing your sense of security, to fight for a cause you feel is worthwhile. This form of struggle gives your life meaning, and your unique struggles become examples which prod and empower others, encouraging them to struggle with the need to pursue their own individuation process and deeper life purpose. This is not always comfortable for you or well received by others, so rather than letting your mind choose your battles, you need to be initiated through your Strategy and Authority into struggles that have value for you. Internal stress builds when you cannot adequately explain or correctly live out the struggles you have engaged in, and creates an excess of energy in the body. Regular exercise releases that pressure so that it can move through you. This is not only healthy for you physically, but keeps the critical connection with your intuitive awareness clear.

Interpersonal: Channel 38-28 is the driving mutative force compelling individuation towards its ultimate expression of uniqueness. By stubbornly listening to their awareness in the now, those with this channel bring mutation in the form of a change of direction to the status quo. It is a struggle to convince people that evolution is an on-going process, and one worth struggling for. But the Channel of Struggle is also the channel of stubbornness, rooted in adrenalized energy and a determination to live the individuated life to its fullest.

GATE 38: OPPOSITION - THE GATE OF THE FIGHTER
– The ability to preserve individual integrity through opposition to detrimental forces –
Center: Root   Quarter: Mutation   Theme: Purpose fulfilled through Transformation
RAC of the Tension – JC of Opposition – LAC of Individualism

The 38th gate exerts pressure on you, and those around you, to discover the value of one's own life. There must be a reason to exist, a purpose, and something to love that elevates struggle beyond simply surviving. Backed by the energy to oppose, you are capable of forcefully confronting adversity itself. You actually enjoy a good fight. Purpose for you is enhanced when you stand up for those who can't stand up for themselves, if it is correct for you to do so. Others might experience this energy in you as a fierce independence, a highly focused stubbornness to meet a challenge, even death, head on. In truth, you are simply seeking a reason for living. Your determination to persevere empowers others to discern for themselves which individuating struggles have value or not. To know what is worth fighting for, and to avoid wasting energy by engaging in battles that are not correct for you, you look to the awareness potential of Gate 28. Since Gate 38 is one of the three gates of deafness that protects your individuality from being influenced by others, you preserve your personal integrity by opposing those forces that would compromise you.

Line 6 - Misunderstanding	Line 3 - Alliance
Line 5 - Alienation	Line 2 - Politeness
Line 4 - Investigation	Line 1 - Qualification

GATE 28: PREPONDERANCE OF THE GREAT - THE GATE OF THE GAME PLAYER
– The transitoriness of power and influence –
Center: Spleen   Quarter: Duality   Theme: Purpose fulfilled through Bonding
RAC of the Unexpected – JC of Risks – LAC of Alignment

Gate 28's deepest fear is that life might end before one knows what makes it worth living, or what gives it meaning. It's an energy that is stubbornly focused on listening with awareness in order to best intuit which risks will make you feel more alive, and lead to struggles which bring purpose to existence. With your Splenic awareness constantly alerting you to danger, you are willing to take risks others wouldn't, to play games with life and death. Ultimately, you will spontaneously meet and confront your own fears of death one at a time. You have the energy needed to redirect the self-absorbed nature of people with Channel 57-20 by prodding them to make their intuitive knowing available to you and to others. Your own awareness helps people with Gate 38 determine who or what they should invest their energy in, enabling them to better assess the health and safety factors for whatever they consider worth fighting for. Without Gate 38, you may fall victim to unnecessary pressure to fight or struggle, experiencing needless resistance and exhaustion. You look to people with Gate 38 for clues about what they have discovered makes their life's struggles worthwhile.

Line 6 - Blaze of Glory	Line 3 - Adventurism
Line 5 - Treachery	Line 2 - Shaking Hands with the Devil
Line 4 - Holding On	Line 1 - Preparation

THE CHANNEL OF THE BRAINWAVE: 57 - 20
A Design of Penetrating Awareness
Circuit: Knowing   Channel Type: Projected

The Channel of the Brainwave links the Splenic Center to the Throat Center through the Gate of Intuitive Clarity (57) and the Gate of the Now (20). This is where intuitive insight is given its clearest voice in the now moment. One of the most extraordinary capacities that humans have, via this channel, is the penetrating self-recognition of the truth of our existence, which is expressed as, "I know I am alive now."

Background: In Channel 57-20, Splenic intuition travels directly to the Throat Center in a wave of knowing that races to be communicated in the moment. This is Individual insight that comes from a deep intelligence or acumen that is based in our ancient instincts, and connected to the immediate moment's intuitive knowing. The Channel of the Brainwave's most profound function is to empower others toward awakening their own innate survival intelligence. The Splenic Center is the core of our health and well-being. It is not an energy resource, however, and while our intuition can be aware of and articulate strategies that enable our well being, it's not necessarily able to follow through with action.

Personal: Life entices you to use your intuitive awareness to support your own well being in the now, and to speak the truth, your truth, that arises in each present moment. "I am what I am, and I know how to be what I am." With your inner knowing guiding your acute vibratory or acoustic awareness, you will often find that your spontaneous verbal outbursts of pure intuition get to the core or truth of a situation much more quickly than those around you. This is the ability to "think on your feet," and it gives you a mutative potential which, if your timing is correct, can have a deep impact on the people around you. Your alertness to the receptivity of others, guided by your Strategy and Authority, allows you to share your existential knowing with them as true wisdom, and reduces misunderstanding and resistance.

When you are finely attuned and firmly anchored in the now, you are connected to your ability to survive. From this perspective, there is no fear of tomorrow. You are one who simply knows what to do without having to think about it. Your intuitive knowing and body move in one spontaneous wave of energy. Connecting in to the Channel of the Brainwave's adaptability requires overcoming a fear of the unknown by learning to listen to, act on, and trust your intuitive impulses completely, moment by moment by moment. If you ignore these instinctual impulses, the momentary awareness will pass and you may suffer for it. Maximization of this ability to penetrate into and know in the moment, however, is dependent on focusing your attention on the present. This focus makes it difficult to hear what others 'know,' which is another way of saying that you don't like being told what to do.

Interpersonal: Gates 57 and 28 enjoy a beneficial relationship with each other. Gate 57, which struggles with the uncertainty of its spontaneous words and actions, prefers to remain quietly self-absorbed. Gate 28, struggling with fears or questions about the value and meaning of life, looks to Gate 57 for answers. As the 28th gate prods Gate 57 to release its intuitive knowing, Channel 57-20 is activated, empowering mutation and initiating change.

GATE 57: THE GENTLE - THE GATE OF INTUITIVE CLARITY
– The extraordinary power of clarity –
Center: Spleen   Quarter: Duality   Theme: Purpose fulfilled through Bonding
RAC of Penetration – JC of Intuition – LAC of the Clarion

With its clarity of intuitive insight, Gate 57 has the capacity to penetrate to one's core in the now. You have a deep inner attunement to sound that is constantly alert to the vibrations coming from your physical, emotional and psychic environments. Moment by moment your intuition registers a sense of what is safe, healthy and good for you, and what is not. Gate 57 is the gate of the right ear. If you want to hear what someone is really saying to you, listen with your intuitively attuned right ear. You must be alert and focused in the now to hear the messages from your Spleen, or the information you are getting for survival may be ignored. You may sometimes appear deaf to others, or be accused of selectively hearing what they have to say, but your intuition is your only guide in determining what the perfect behavior is that will insure your well-being. The only way you will alleviate your fears for the future is to pay close attention to your instinctual hunches, to that little voice that only speaks once and softly, and act on these hunches immediately. When you are listening and paying attention to your intuition now, there is no tomorrow to fear.

Line 6 - Utilization	Line 3 - Acuteness
Line 5 - Progression	Line 2 - Cleansing
Line 4 - The Director	Line 1 - Confusion

GATE 20: CONTEMPLATION - THE GATE OF THE NOW
– Recognition and awareness in the now which transforms understanding into right action –
Center: Throat   Quarter: Civilization   Theme: Purpose fulfilled through Form
RAC of the Sleeping Phoenix – JC of the Now – LAC of Duality

Gate 20 is a purely existential gate that keeps you focused in the present, and supports your capacity to survive as yourself. When your expression is properly timed, awareness will be transformed into words or actions that can impact people around you. This energy frequency is, and must be, totally absorbed in the present moment. It can give voice to Gate 57's intuitive survival awareness, to Gate 10's behavioral patterns and commitments to higher principles, or it can manifest Gate 34's sacral power through action toward individuation. Gate 20 expresses the full range of being in the moment from "I am now" to "I know I am myself doing now," but it does not consider the past or the future. To be awake and aware, and to survive, you must be fully present to the moment and authentically yourself. There is rarely time to mentally consider or control what comes bubbling up from inside of you, so what you say or what you do is suddenly there for everybody, including you, to witness. In fact, you often see when you are not looking, or hear when you are not listening. This is how the potential for evolutionary change hidden in each moment of existence is empowered within you. As you live by your Strategy and Authority, you become a living example. Your intuitive knowing, personal survival and mutative, self-loving behaviors influence or empower others.

Line 6 - Wisdom	Line 3 - Self-Awareness
Line 5 - Realism	Line 2 - The Dogmatist
Line 4 - Application	Line 1 - Superficiality

THE CHANNEL OF EMOTING: 39 - 55
A Design of Moodiness
Circuit: Knowing   Channel Type: Projected

The Channel of Emoting links the Root Center to the Solar Plexus Center through the Gate of Provocation (39) and the Gate of Spirit (55). Prone to melancholy and uncertainty, provocative and emotional, the pulsing on/off wave of moods is set in motion here. The emotional wave underlying the passion and melancholy of Individualism is a mechanic, an endless continuum between happiness and sadness.

Background: The Channel of Emoting is defined as a provocation to empower spirit awareness. We are all subject to the moodiness of this channel, a profound and creative force behind mutation on the planet, until 2027. Moodiness best describes this rather flat Individual emotional wave with its shifting spikes of highs and lows, from ecstatic moments of pleasure to melancholic moments of uncomfortable uncertainty and sadness. We are not designed to rationalize our moods away, but rather to live within the alchemy of the wave's mutative pulse. By living authentically, and fully embracing the emotional wave, those with this channel will plumb the depths of their own spirit and truth. **"True spirituality arises out of correctness."** – Ra Uru Hu. Spirit finds its balance when we perceive that our cup is both half empty and half full, both being emptied and being filled.

Personal: You know how to tease out and discern the nature of an individual's or a group's spirit. You can tell which people are right for you by the interplay between you and them, and by whose spirit or mood is in resonance with yours. It is also how you get what you want or need from others. One can be provoked to experience pleasure instead of pain, joy instead of sadness. Over time, you learn how to tease and provoke the desired spirit out of others, and find the ones that are correct for you. At the same time, your provocation opens people up to the infectious, mutative qualities you carry as an Individual, and can bring out something new from them as well. The impact you have, and the spirit you provoke, depends on your mood or where you are in your own emotional wave. To bring out the right spirit, you must be in the right mood. You are not a victim of your moods, however, and should not make others victims either. You are well served by the recognition that there is a correct mood or time for everything in life. When not in the mood to socialize, you can enjoy time alone in the company of your inner muse. This time spent with self connects you to the mature emotional creativity, depth, and truth that are yours alone to bring into the world.

Interpersonal: When those with the Channel of Emoting grow in awareness, they free themselves to embrace the full range of their emotions and emotional impact, and reduce the potential for emotional tension in relationships. Individual's should never make love, eat, work or play if not in the mood. If they force themselves to do something when not in the mood, they will not experience the pleasure they seek, and will greatly diminish their potential to impact and empower others with a spirited passion for living. When depth of feeling is lived authentically, it transmits a seductive warmth or passionate sadness that is often expressed through music and art, or acted out on stage, including the stage of life. If not embraced in a healthy way, moodiness can become manipulative and obsessed with pleasure. Those with Channel 39-55 may turn to sex, food or drugs to compensate for their melancholy.

GATE 39: OBSTRUCTION - THE GATE OF PROVOCATION

– The value of obstruction in provoking analysis, assessment and re-evaluation –
Center: Root   Quarter: Civilization   Theme: Purpose fulfilled through Form
RAC of Tension – JC of Provocation – LAC of Individualism

Gate 39, fueled by the Root Center, is the pressure to provoke the evolving emotional awareness of spirit into revealing itself. Emotional awareness is humanity's destiny, but it is the Individual through the 39th gate that provokes the mutative potential within the 55th gate to release the spirit consciousness of the Solar Plexus Center. You have the energy to persevere through your moods and tap into spirit awareness. Your provoking reveals whose spirit is correct for you. If you are merely a source of irritation to them, they are not right for you. People may react negatively to your provocation, but this is your unique gift, even though you may have to develop a thick skin to live with it. Provoking is also the way you get in touch with and work out your own feelings; if you are in bad mood, you may elicit misery from others. It takes time to learn who can be successfully provoked or not, and you can only impact the Collective or the Tribe, and release true mutation, when in the right spirit or mood yourself. This is what makes mutation contagious, and moves the potential for awareness through the totality. The 39th gate is one of three gates of deafness, meaning you are not designed to be easily influenced. Without the 55th gate's ability to release emotions, Root Center pressure may provoke you into excesses, like substance abuse or an eating disorder. Patience with yourself, and your wave, is required for your journey toward spirit.

Line 6 - The Troubleshooter	Line 3 - Responsibility
Line 5 - Single-Mindedness	Line 2 - Confrontation
Line 4 - Temperance	Line 1 - Disengagement

GATE 55: ABUNDANCE - THE GATE OF SPIRIT

– Abundance is strictly a question of spirit –
Center: Solar Plexus   Quarter: Initiation   Theme: Purpose fulfilled through Mind
RAC of the Sleeping Phoenix – JC of Moods – LAC of Spirit

Awareness of spirit is not a concept (Ajna) or instinct (Spleen) – it is an emotion (Solar Plexus). Abundance is a function of spirit; it is how you perceive what you are feeling, and the mood you are experiencing in the moment. The 55th gate is susceptible to the melancholic chemistry of the emotional wave, which is constantly moving through cycles of hope to pain. One moment your cup feels half empty and the next it feels half full. Your moods determine what is correct for you and when. If you are not in the mood to eat, work, make love, be sociable or create, it is not healthy for you to do so. When you feel like being alone, don't attempt to explain or excuse yourself; simply honor the mood and embrace being in the moment with your own creative inner self. Your most creative time is when you feel deeply melancholic. A thoughtful word to those around you when you are simply not in the mood to be social will help them to not personalize the emotional energy that they are feeling from you. You are open to people with Gate 39 provoking you so that you can perceive your spirit, and your moods, for yourself. At any given point in your wave, how your spirit feels and emotes is not open to comparison, debate or influence by others. Spirit awareness arises out of the wonder that the cup exists at all. What you fear most is emotional emptiness or a lack of passion in life.

Line 6 - Selfishness	Line 3 - Innocence
Line 5 - Growth	Line 2 - Distrust
Line 4 - Assimilation	Line 1 - Cooperation

THE CHANNEL OF OPENNESS: 22 - 12
A Design of a Social Being
Circuit: Knowing   Channel Type: Manifested

The Channel of Openness links the Solar Plexus Center to the Throat Center through the Gate of Openness (22) and the Gate of Caution (12). Openness in Channel 22-12 is dependent on the ebb and flow of the emotional wave or mood. It creatively voices or acts out the moodiness, melancholy, passion, romance and drama of the Individual emotional wave. There is a quality of restraint in the 12th gate that governs the 22nd gate's openness, limiting it to social interactions with people who appear to have the most mutative potential.

Background: The literally miraculous qualities of articulation, that developed through the mutation of the larynx (Gate 12) 85,000 years ago, set the stage for humans to not only communicate their intelligence, but to emotionally impact others with the quality of their voice. The Channel of Openness is the social channel of Individual circuitry, yet it is guided by a "when I am in the mood" orientation (emotional wave) that is not focused on being either social or friendly. Individuals are generally less interested in mating (Tribal) or sharing (Collective) than they are in creating a receptive environment for their potential to bring a transformative new awareness to the Collective and the Tribe. The key for people with this manifesting channel is to wait until they feel like interacting socially. If forced into social situations when on the low ebb of their wave, they can be misunderstood, become angry and abrupt, and fail to empower others. Such social failures, repeated over time, can lead to anti-social behaviors and isolation.

Personal: With your keen sense of timing, and an awareness of your audience's openness, you know when to use your warmth and social skills to get people's attention, as well as how to get close enough to them for your words to be a catalyst for loving change in their lives. You use the quality and inflection in your voice to move or touch people in order to educate, mutate and communicate. When your mood and timing are in sync, you can empower others to vicariously experience love's full range of emotions through public media such as speaking, acting, poetry or music. The Solar Plexus is your authority so it is imperative that you do not act impulsively. The measure of patience you cultivate, and the creative depth of feelings you allow yourself to experience by listening through your wave, determine how powerful your Individual mutative impact will be in the world.

Interpersonal: Individuals are naturally different from everyone else so they tend to attract a great deal of attention. Consequently, they contend with the fear of being observed; they fear that their uniqueness may be found strange and lead to rejection by others. Gate 22 hears with the left ear and these Individuals hear what they feel like hearing. For them to know something fully, it must be repeated and heard over time. They have the capacity to really listen and hear what is being said which makes them true listeners – when in the mood. When their social interactions are guided by their mood, barriers come down and their fears dissipate. It is in this environment of social openness, this existential moment where it all comes together, that the magic of the Individual's mutative difference has its full impact.

GATE 22: GRACE - THE GATE OF OPENNESS
– A quality of behavior best suited in handling mundane and trivial situations –
Center: Solar Plexus   Quarter: Initiation   Theme: Purpose fulfilled through Mind
RAC of Rulership – JC of Grace – LAC of Informing

Gate 22 combines the potential for emotional openness through listening, with a social grace and charm that is highly attractive to others, when it is in the right mood. When your mood changes, however, a dramatically different and sometimes antisocial side of you may emerge. Your emotional awareness matures over time as you become comfortable with moving into your depth along the emotional wave. By allowing your depth to mellow with age in the company of your creative muse, you refine your timing and release your truth precisely when society is ready for it. Recognizing and acting on that timing is dependent on honoring your mood. Your openness, and your attentiveness to what is essential and new for others, are gifts of grace which even impact strangers. You listen to others until they complete what they are saying, making what you have to say naturally come second. This is grace in action, as well as the key to your own empowerment. In fact, it is your responsibility and privilege to use your social listening skills in a way that makes change available to others. Without the 12th gate, you may know what you feel, but not how to express it verbally. Because silence makes you nervous, what you fear most is that there is nothing worthwhile to listen to.

Line 6 - Maturity	Line 3 - The Enchanter
Line 5 - Directness	Line 2 - Charm School
Line 4 - Sensitivity	Line 1 - Second Class Ticket

GATE 12: STANDSTILL - THE GATE OF CAUTION
– The quality of restraint and the importance of meditation and inaction in confronting temptation –
Center: Throat   Quarter: Civilization   Theme: Purpose fulfilled through Form
RAC of Eden – JC of Articulation – LAC of Education

The articulate, mutative and moody voice of the Individual is restrained in Gate 12 by a natural caution. This caution keeps you silent until your mood tells you that you really do have something to say, as well as a unique, transformative way of saying it. The vocal vibration or tone of your voice speaks louder than your choice of words. Standing still, or contemplating a unique perception or feeling until in the mood to express it in a creative way, through poetry or music for instance, gives your message time to mature. You have your greatest impact on others as a "stranger of consequence;" like a performer, you translate and creatively express the joys and sorrows of loving and living, and then you withdraw. When you are not in the mood, chances are your audience won't hear what you want them to, or will not experience the transformation or inspiration that interacting with you can bring. Impeccable timing maximizes the potential impact you can have on social/cultural norms, and on our way of being with each other in the world. You know how to express yourself, but without the 22nd gate you can't always clarify what it is you are feeling.

Line 6 - Metamorphosis	Line 3 - Confession
Line 5 - The Pragmatist	Line 2 - Purification
Line 4 - The Prophet	Line 1 - The Monk

THE CENTERING CIRCUIT
KEYNOTE: EMPOWERMENT

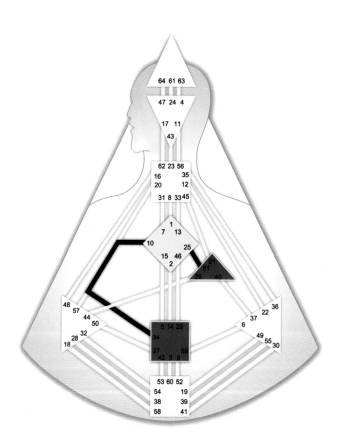

CHANNELS:

34 – 10	**EXPLORATION**	
	Following one's convictions	
51 – 25	**INITIATION**	
	Needing to be first	

The Centering Circuit is one of two small but important minor circuits in the BodyGraph. Channel 34-10 transforms the way in which one lives in the world while the other side, Channel 51–25, transforms the way in which one takes advantage of the world we live in. The Centering Circuit is centered on the G Center around the identity and direction of the self. It is focused on empowering people to love themselves, and to follow their own unique path in life by living according to their Sacral's response. Simply by doing what is correct for them, they inspire and empower others to be themselves.

People who are healthy and authentic on the inside are able to inspire the world around them to be healthy. Only the centered, integrated self, through its living example, has the power to bring mutation to the Collective and the Tribe. Without ongoing mutation there can be no evolution on any level. Those with definition in the Centering Circuit who are not able to be a force for healthy change in others' behavior will often become melancholic and lonely. If, however, they let their Strategy firmly align and ground them within their unique design, they can be a profound and empowering example of self love and the fully-individuated, authentic life.

You will notice that there are no awareness centers present in this circuit, nor the Head, Throat or Root Centers. This circuit is completely about being centered as a response to life.

The Channels and Gates of the Centering Circuit are discussed on the following pages.

THE CHANNEL OF EXPLORATION: 34 - 10
A Design of Following One's Convictions
Circuit: Centering   Channel Type: Generated

The Channel of Exploration links the Sacral Center to the G Center through the Gate of Power (34) and the Gate of the Behavior of the Self (10). Gate 10 initiates behaviors (as roles) from deep inside of us that lead us to accept, honor and love ourselves. Gate 34 provides the sustaining power or inner strength to stand by the convictions that form our belief in and acceptance of ourselves. Gate 34's pure energy for self empowerment and individuation only interacts correctly with others through sacral response.

Background: Channel 34-10 powers the exploration and perfecting of the personal behaviors needed to survive in society. Those with Channel 34-10 are here to love themselves, and to trust their inner convictions explicitly when guided by their Sacral response and personal Authority. This energy is for those with this channel and is not energy to be imposed on others. This energy is to be focused creatively on ways to remain centered on the convictions that are correct for the Individual.

This focus leads to a level of self mastery that empowers even those with strong Tribal connections to love and honor themselves, despite the Tribe's strong emphasis on loving and serving the community first.

Personal: You are here to follow your own convictions no matter how unusual they are, to behave independently and as yourself despite interference. The guidance and timing of your Sacral's responses are what make it possible to do this in satisfying ways, and without guilt. By living authentically, you demonstrate for others the benefits of perfecting self-loving, interactive behavior through response. This empowers them to get in touch with their own conviction to love themselves. Your enveloping Generator aura, combined with the Channel of Exploration, can attract a great deal of attention. Whether or not this attention is positive, with its true potential for empowerment and mutation that only Individuality can bring into the world, is completely dependent on your willingness to patiently attune to your responses. You, and those around you, will be quick to recognize when you are living the opposite: a rigid and unsatisfying not-self expression of this channel which can sound selfish and self-centered as in, "I'm going to be like this whether you like it or not. You can be any way you please, just don't interfere with me and my way."

Interpersonal: The Centering Circuit is designed to empower self love, independence and self-reliance in those who interact with it. The Channel of Exploration describes the kind of world Individuals would most like to be a part of, where everybody is able to live their uniqueness without dealing with resistance and interference from others. As an electromagnetic definition between two people, the channel brings an Individual flavor to relationships, which can lead to the breaking of old molds or traditions in its quest to explore new territory. If people with strong Collective or Tribal ties are joined together by this connection but do not understand the power of response, their relationship could provide some unexpected challenges.

GATE 34: THE POWER OF THE GREAT - THE GATE OF POWER
– Power is only great when its display or use serves the common good –
Center: Sacral   Quarter: Mutation   Theme: Purpose fulfilled through Transformation
RAC of the Sleeping Phoenix – JC of Power – LAC of Duality

Gate 34 is a potent and impressive source of energy that empowers us toward individuation, displaying and celebrating our uniqueness in the world. Two qualities distinguish this gate from the other eight in the Sacral: its asexuality and the unavailability of its power to others. If connected to Gate 10 in your G Center, your energy will be focused on social behaviors or roles that support your strong convictions. If connected to Gate 20 in your Throat, your power will be resolved to act on your own behalf, to turn your thoughts into deeds, and to express your ability to manifest and thrive. If connected to Gate 57 in your Spleen, your intuition will empower your ability to hear what you need to survive perfectly in each moment. Without the Spleen's direct intuitive guidance, this relentless power to act may become an unhealthy, meddlesome and misdirected energy, and you may feel lost in your own momentum, expending energy that serves no one. Though admired, and even sought after, your energy is simply not available to others. It must remain pure in its power, and always accessible to you as you seek to be independent and unique, to act on your convictions, and to triumph, which means to survive as yourself.

Line 6 - Common Sense	Line 3 - Machismo
Line 5 - Annihilation	Line 2 - Momentum
Line 4 - Triumph	Line 1 - The Bully

GATE 10: TREADING - THE GATE OF THE BEHAVIOR OF THE SELF
– The underlying code of behavior which ensures successful interaction despite circumstances –
Center: G   Quarter: Mutation   Theme: Purpose fulfilled through Transformation
RAC of the Vessel of Love – JC of Behavior – LAC of the Prevention

Gate 10 is the most complex gate in the G Center, and one of the four Gates of the Incarnation Cross of the Vessel of Love. This is the gate of the love of oneself. The six potential behaviors or roles of the self (listed below) are guided by the intuition of Gate 57, empowered by the Sacral response of Gate 34, and manifested or expressed through Gate 20. Within the framework of these roles, humanity is now exploring what it means to live as a 9-centered, self-aware form with its potential to awaken, and to experience genuine self love. With your Strategy and Authority in place, Gate 10 empowers your potential to surrender to living authentically as yourself. As you come to know, accept and love what makes you unique, you empower others to love themselves as well. True awakening through surrender is not a commitment to becoming something; it is a commitment to being yourself. Gate 10's strong emphasis on loving self-acceptance will deeply impact how humanity moves through the 21st century. You are one who recognizes that awakening is not possible without self-acceptance. As you embrace the honor and pleasure of exploring life in a self-aware form, you empower our potential to live as our true selves, awake in the now moment.

Line 6 - The Role Model	Line 3 - The Martyr
Line 5 - The Heretic	Line 2 - The Hermit
Line 4 - The Opportunist	Line 1 - Modesty

THE CHANNEL OF INITIATION: 51 - 25
A Design of Needing to be First
Circuit: Centering (Creative Channel) Channel Type: Projected

The Channel of Initiation links the Heart Center to the G Center through the Gate of Shock (51) and the Gate of the Spirit of the Self (25). Gate 51's competitive, need-to-be-first ego energy is connected to Gate 25's universal love, and the ability of the higher self to see and love the beauty in the animate and inanimate equally.

Background: In Channel 51-25, initiation becomes an art. This is the ability to recognize a person's potential for individuation and, when invited, to provide the 'shock' which initiates and empowers them toward it. There is a natural competitiveness in this channel that challenges humanity to move ahead, be first or win, which has transformed the material, mundane world we live in. This is the only channel of the Ego Circuit that is not a part of the Tribal Circuit, yet it represents the deep relationship that exists between the Tribe and the Individual. Both channels of the Centering Circuit (Channel 34-10 is the other) are powerful mutative forces exerting pressure on humanity to continue to evolve consciousness more deeply into form. Self mastery and mastery of the world go hand in hand.

Personal: It is your nature to be competitive, and you may arouse and empower competitiveness in others. If entered into correctly, competition stretches, tests and even pushes you to transcend your normal creative limits and the barriers of physical endurance. Each breakthrough brings exhilaration and a new awareness of the depth of your own spirit. With each triumph comes a personal, even mystical, sense of your uniqueness which in turn becomes an example of courage for others to follow. You may even find yourself empowering organizations with your gutsy ways of achieving personal goals. It must be remembered, however, that initiating individuation is a mystical process at the heart of mutation, and cannot be controlled. If it is your destiny, it will be a by-product of living true to yourself. If you seek initiation you will not find it; initiation must find you so that you can surrender to it. If you seek to initiate others without their invitation, they may fail, leaving you resentful and unfulfilled. Your Strategy and Authority are the most powerful mystical tools you have, along with the understanding that to survive the initiating shocks you will meet along the way, you must tend to the needs of your heart, both physically and metaphysically.

Interpersonal: Initiation toward individuation takes a person from "we are" to "I am." True shamans are specially gifted innocents who are able to survive the quantum leap into the void (the unknown) that such individuation and transcendence requires. They then artfully initiate others into deeper levels of self awareness. Whether one leaps as a courageous warrior or as a fool matters not; landing will be a shock in either case. Initiation or shock can come through an 'invitation' that is not of our own choosing, like an auto accident. Life itself is the most profound mystical force of initiation for empowering a change of behavior or direction that we can encounter. Those with the Channel of Initiation are here to feel the wonder of their own unique spirit (higher self) and, in the process, to empower and mutate the Collective and the Tribe. Living from their center through Strategy and Authority, perfectly aligned with their unique geometry, is what allows those with Channel 51-25 to not only meet but also survive these transcendent encounters with the forces of universal consciousness.

GATE 51: THE AROUSING - THE GATE OF SHOCK
– The ability to respond to disorder and shock through recognition and adaptation –
Center: Heart   Quarter: Initiation   Theme: Purpose fulfilled through Mind
RAC of Penetration – JC of Shock – LAC of the Clarion

Gate 51, the Gate of Shock, is the energy for Individual initiative. Backed by the ego's will and courage, it embodies the power to compete, driving you to be one step ahead of everybody, and to risk going where no one else has gone in order to find or create a place for yourself. You are designed to withstand shock and to shock others, to move them out of the complacency of their safe cocoons and direct them toward personal transcendence and self love. Love for life itself, and the constant competition that comes with mastering the material world, arouses and empowers you. In opposition to the courage and will power that energizes you, however, is a potential for foolhardiness that endangers your vulnerable heart, both physically and spiritually. The secret to maintaining your heart's health is to center yourself by attuning to your Strategy and Authority, and sense within when you have the will to engage in battle, and when you don't. This guidance will allow you to adapt to the nature of any shock or disorder confronting you, and give your heart the rest it needs in order to recuperate from your engagement with the world. Without Gate 25 you may find yourself seeking or looking to the realm of spirit for guidance or direction.

Line 6 - Separation	Line 3 - Adaptation
Line 5 - Symmetry	Line 2 - Withdrawal
Line 4 - Limitation	Line 1 - Reference

GATE 25: INNOCENCE - THE GATE OF THE SPIRIT OF THE SELF
– The perfection of action through uncontrived and spontaneous nature –
Center: G   Quarter: Initiation   Theme: Purpose fulfilled through Mind
RAC of the Vessel of Love – JC of Innocence – LAC of Healing

The love of Gate 25 flows out of fully accepting and living surrendered to one's form. A gate of the higher self, its pivotal role is to turn people toward individuation. Your innocence is not designed to bring love into the world in any specific way, but rather to love without discrimination. You hold the potential, and empower others with the potential, to love life and everything in it equally. A flower can be loved as profoundly as a human. This quality of love is often projected as cool or cold but is neither. The mystical potential of this love is transcendent and universal, and your spirit innocence is always being tested. You have the capacity to meet these initiations from life like a spiritual warrior, fired up and ready to compete for your spirit (your individuality) no matter what the circumstance. Then, when the warrior or "fool" of Gate 51 prods you to leap into the void, or when you meet life's initiating challenges, you will be able to land on your feet and deepen your innocence into a wisdom that can empower others on their own journey. You may emerge a bit wounded from such initiations, but your ultimate triumph and survival enriches your spirit and the spirit of those around you. The result is that you are alive with the wonder, the love, of being.

Line 6 - Ignorance	Line 3 - Sensibility
Line 5 - Recuperation	Line 2 - The Existentialist
Line 4 - Survival	Line 1 - Selflessness

THE COLLECTIVE CIRCUIT GROUP
UNDERSTANDING AND SENSING CIRCUITS
SUPER KEYNOTE: SHARING

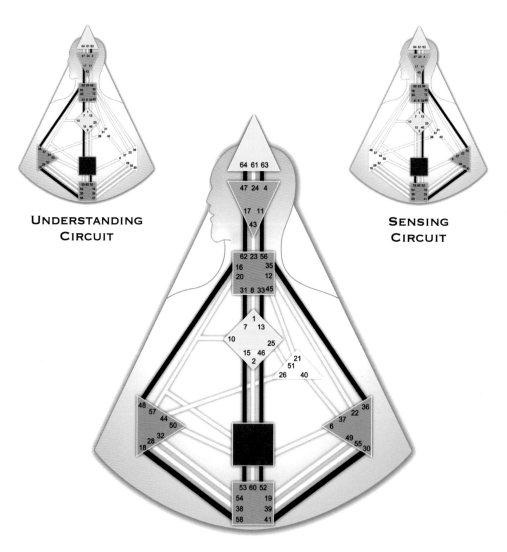

UNDERSTANDING
CIRCUIT

SENSING
CIRCUIT

COLLECTIVE CIRCUIT GROUP

The Collective Circuit Group is composed of two major circuits: the Understanding/logic Circuit and the Sensing/abstract Circuit. Sharing is a part of every channel and gate in the circuit. For the Collective, sharing is akin to a drive or social obligation or need to tell you what they think, what they have experienced, or what they have judged to be of value or not. The Collective is quick to share opinions, dilemmas, solutions, criticism, expectations, fantasies, inventions, medical breakthroughs and more, but the sharing is not personal. The Collective's inherently social orientation is objective, impersonal and not necessarily reciprocal, and it is best to avoid taking the Collective's sharing personally no matter how personal it feels.

When indiscriminate sharing is expressed unbidden, driven by the not awake and unaware not-self mind, it can be a real nuisance. For example, those in crisis will catch themselves unwittingly sharing their situation with the clerk, the postman, or the person next to them at the bus stop. Learning to wait to be asked to tell their story, or to give their opinion, is part of becoming sensitive to the receptivity of others, and the key to sharing that is satisfying, effective and transformative. The mutuality and social nature of humanity, along with its need for harmony or uniformity, is embedded in the Collective. This circuit group drives consciousness forward by sharing what has been learned through experimentation and experience. With its focus on society, the Collective establishes what is good for the majority, as opposed to what is good for any one specific Individual. The idea that "what is good for one is good for all so stay with the pattern that works" comes from this circuit group. It might be terrible for you personally, but since it is for the greater good you put up with it. Citizens of a country for instance all share the same rules, the same monetary currency and the same public institutions.

Without the Collective's collegiality, majority rule and obligation to share, today's larger societies could not stand; they would still be a cluster of fiefdoms competing for the same resources. With the Collective at the helm in recent history, the educated and privileged classes have entered the era of the global village. We have nearly reached the ultimate potential and goal of the Collective Circuit Group. The Collective is suspicious of the nonconforming, impetuous Individual, and it has never trusted the primitive demand for loyalty and the bargaining of the Tribe.

Notice how the Collective Circuit Group, viewed in the illustration, forms a kind of outer shell and inner core which appears to both bind and buttress the BodyGraph. There is an unusual balance and beauty in the opposition that exists within this symmetry. It is like a dance between yesterday (Sensing/abstract) and tomorrow (Understanding/logic), between cycles and patterns, between experiencing and proving. Life is built on logic, but lived out through the abstract cycles of life. The Sensing (abstract) Circuit tries to codify experience or make sense of the past, and the Understanding Circuit (logic) tries to anticipate the future. The Collective is not as focused on the now moment, which is the Individual's contribution. Out of this circuit group's internal opposition, its seesawing back and forth between past and future, comes its reputation for conservatism or maintaining the status quo. "If it isn't broken, don't fix or change it." A level of stability also emerges from this circuit group that says with some pride, "I understand. I have the facts. It is like this." Or, "I have experienced it. I've been there, done that. All you have to do is listen to me." Logic is experimental; it's about the way things are supposed to work. The abstract Sensing Circuit is experiential, and deals with desire and the unexpected.

THE UNDERSTANDING (LOGIC) CIRCUIT
KEYNOTE: SHARING

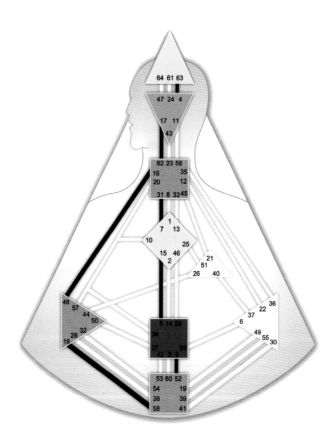

CHANNELS:

52 – 9	CONCENTRATION *Determination*	58 – 18	JUDGMENT *Insatiability*
5 – 15	RHYTHM *Being in the flow*	48 – 16	THE WAVELENGTH *Talent*
7 – 31	THE ALPHA *For "good" or "bad",* *a design of leadership*	63 – 4	LOGIC *Mental ease mixed with doubt*
		17 – 62	ACCEPTANCE *An organizational being*

The Understanding Circuit's theme is logic, a cool-headed but seductive intelligence rooted in the recognition of patterns through concentration on the details. It analyzes processes or formulas, and challenges what isn't working. This logic allows one to predict, with a certain reliability, what can be expected in the future from this or that course of action.

Understanding takes place over time. It requires financial support, disciplined repetition, and the development of techniques or skills in order to refine and concretize a pattern, or to master and perfect an aptitude, a plan or a formula. Together with resources often obtained from outside the circuit, logic requires practice to reach its potential and make its contribution, part of which is to lead humanity safely into the future. As long as logic is free from conditioning, it can be used to share the Understanding Circuit's formulized hypotheses, its perspectives and projected doubts about the future, in deeply influential ways.

Unlike its mirror, the abstract and experiential Sensing Circuit, the Understanding Circuit's logic has no connection to the warmth and passion of the Solar Plexus. The Understanding Circuit is often referred to as the cool side of the chart, although logic's stability brings a deep satisfaction not available to the experiential side. There is collective joy when we can see that one plus one always equals two, and that the pattern is reliable. When logic works, it is as pleasurable as putting that last piece of a puzzle into place, which is part of the seduction logic holds for the Collective.

The Channels and Gates of the Logic Circuit are discussed on the following pages.

THE CHANNEL OF CONCENTRATION: 52 - 9
A Design of Determination
Circuit: Understanding   Channel Type: Generated

The Channel of Concentration links the Root Center to the Sacral Center through the Gate of Stillness (52) and the Gate of Focus (9). The 9th gate is determined to maintain its focus on details and facts, while the 52nd gate provides a passive fuel that powers this focus by keeping one still and withdrawn from other distractions. Channel 52-9 creates a potential that can be fulfilled through focused attention when one is still enough to assess all of the pertinent aspects.

Background: In order to improve something, and be of service to the world, logic must be able to sustain its focus and handle all of the details within a pattern. The Channel of Concentration is a format energy* that carries the qualities of all of the other channels in the Understanding Circuit. When guided by Sacral response, it influences one's entire design with its energy to concentrate on and challenge, correct or perfect any pattern, form or activity that one is profoundly committed to. Logic is a step by step, one-foot-in-front-of-the-other process, and one must be deeply identified with the formula in order to spend the time required to either prove or disprove it. The logical process is immensely important in sustaining the Collective's position of influence within the whole.

Personal: You are continually involved in assessing the details of whatever it is that you have dedicated yourself to. You experience a quiet pressure to be still, not as stress, but more as a tension that keeps you in place, like a yoga pose. You still your physical body and your outer senses in order to use your energy in a precise, focused way, and hate dissipating this potent energy by having to deal with many things at once. You are like the Buddha sitting under a lotus tree, gathering your energy and waiting for your Sacral to respond. Your responses reveal what your focus will be, what pattern you

FORMAT ENERGY

will be devoted to perfecting, and when to share it. As you follow your responses, your true vocation and life focus also emerge. You may be profoundly dedicated to one activity for most of your life, or have multiple, distinctly different foci over the course of a lifetime. With this format channel defined in your design, you may find yourself restless and depressed if there is nothing worthwhile to concentrate on, nothing that your Authority says is correct to direct this energy toward.

Interpersonal: Aurically the format frequency of Channel 52-9 can hold, or concentrate, energy in one place, allowing a group to focus and facilitate a deeper examination of the project or process under consideration. If you don't have this channel in your design, it may be to your advantage in certain circumstances to sit next to someone who does in order to heighten your own ability to sit still and concentrate.

Format energies exert a powerful influence on all other channels in the circuit, and on one's design as a whole. Format Channels run between the Root and Sacral Centers: 53-42 (Collective/Abstract), 60-3 (Individual) and 52-9 (Collective/Logical). There is no format channel for the Tribal Circuit.

GATE 52: KEEPING STILL (MOUNTAIN) - THE GATE OF STILLNESS
– Temporary and self-imposed inaction for the benefit of assessment –
Center: Root   Quarter: Civilization   Theme: Purpose fulfilled through Form
RAC of Service – JC of Stillness – LAC of Demands

Gate 52 is energy under pressure that is focused on assessment, the raw power to concentrate. There is a passive tension in this connection from the Root Center that is looking toward Gate 9 for an outlet. Once the 52nd gate finds something it deeply identifies with, something worthwhile to channel this energy toward, the tension is balanced between the Root Center's pressure to keep you moving forward, and Gate 52's power to help you sit still and concentrate. Before this balance is reached, however, you can find yourself vacillating between restlessness and depression, bouncing from one thing to the next, unable to find the self discipline to withdraw once again into your stillness and concentrate. There is no physical outlet within Gate 52 that can direct or relieve this passive tension within you except to focus it. Without Gate 9, and the Sacral response, it is difficult to know what activity or details to concentrate it on.

Line 6 - Peacefulness	Line 3 - Controls
Line 5 - Explanation	Line 2 - Concern
Line 4 - Self-Discipline	Line 1 - Think Before You Speak

GATE 9: THE TAMING POWER OF THE SMALL - THE GATE OF FOCUS
– Potential can be fulfilled through detailed attention to all pertinent aspects –
Center: Sacral   Quarter: Mutation   Theme: Purpose fulfilled through Transformation
RAC of Planning – JC of Focus – LAC of Identification

Gate 9 acts like a funnel, focusing Gate 52's enormous power to concentrate on what is meaningful and worthwhile for you. The frequency carried in Gate 9 is a diligence for detail or an ability to focus your energy. So much about our logical success as a species depends on conserving precious energy by paying attention to the details. You have the determination to focus the passive but powerful energy pouring out of the Root Center in one place. With Gate 9's Sacral capacity to persevere, you can focus your attention for long periods of time on all the detailed aspects of a project or issue, and properly test or assess the formulas. All of that can be shared with the Collective or applied to your own life. Without Gate 52, however, you may not be able to sit still long enough to concentrate. Your own lack of determination can become a source of frustration for you. When clear and focused, your aura may facilitate the efficient use of both physical and mental energy in those near you.

Line 6 - Gratitude	Line 3 - The Straw that Breaks the Camel's Back
Line 5 - Faith	Line 2 - Misery Loves Company
Line 4 - Dedication	Line 1 - Sensibility

THE CHANNEL OF RHYTHM: 5 - 15
A Design of Being in the Flow
Circuit: Understanding   Channel Type: Generated

The Channel of Rhythm links the Sacral Center to the G Center through the Gate of Fixed Patterns (5) and the Gate of Extremes (15). Gate 5 holds to its fixed habits and rituals, while Gate 15, with its love for humanity's extremes, levels the playing field by incorporating society's diversity into the flow. Here we find the rhythm of life, deeply magical and universal, binding all life forms together from the single cell to complex human beings.

Background: The Channel of Rhythm is the cornerstone of all bio-life processes, intimately connecting us through each response of the Sacral Center to the flow of the natural world. It is subject to neither the arrogance of mind nor the highs and lows of the emotional wave. The Magnetic Monopole, with its singular attraction that holds everything together in the illusion of separateness, is located in the G Center. The Collective magnetism of the 15th gate is a projection by the Monopole of the universal (not personal) love of humanity and humanity's potential; in this way it pulls us forward. Its frequency magnetically draws everyone into its rhythm, as a way of impersonally sharing the flow of life. This rhythm of life is naturally and fundamentally logical, based on repeatable yet ever-evolving patterns, and is designed to direct every living thing toward the future.

Personal: You are constantly moved along by the river of life, vitally and intimately connected to its continuous flow. You appear to others to have your own sense of timing that is determined entirely by your own inner rhythm. If these patterns or routines are natural and correct for you, then you should not allow anything to interfere with them. You cannot connect with the patterns of nature's rhythm if you flow apart from your inner response because your Sacral guides and fine-tunes your timing. When aligned with your flow, everything you do feels effortless and natural, and subtly benefits those around you by bringing them into their own rhythm and timing. If you live the distortions and incorrect timing of the not-self, however, you may find yourself disrupting everyone's flow, beginning with your own. Life around you can then feel confusing and chaotic.

Interpersonal: The auric magnetism of this channel is designed to draw people into a continuous but flexible flow that keeps humanity moving toward a secure and viable future. The Collective's social flow provides us with unlimited opportunities for bonding. Logic's ideal pattern is people flowing together with the opportunity to bond with one another as equals, de-conditioned and living authentically. Logic confirms that all natural and correct rhythms and patterns, regardless of how fixed or how extreme, expand the way love is manifested in the world. An electromagnetic connection between Gates 5 and 15 can be challenging, as one person will be fixed in their pattern while the other needs to remain flexible within their rhythm's extremes. When they come together, however, they experience the Channel of Rhythm's potential to determine the flow that carries those around them forward, even an entire group. Channel 5-15 draws others in the environment into its own flow, and determines the course the group will take.

GATE 5: WAITING - THE GATE OF FIXED PATTERNS
– Fundamental attunement to natural rhythms; waiting as an active state of awareness –
Center: Sacral   Quarter: Mutation   Theme: Purpose fulfilled through Transformation
RAC of Consciousness – JC of Habits – LAC of Separation

For Gate 5, waiting isn't stopping; it is an active state, like being pregnant. Gate 5 is an energy that enjoys fixed rhythms and tempos. This is what gives you the tenacity to stay true to your own inner rhythms in order to stay vital, healthy and always in your flow. You find great satisfaction in mundane rituals and routines that attune you to the vibrations of all life. Being forced to deviate from your natural rhythms can be physically, mentally and emotionally destabilizing for you, and can manifest as insecurity, unhealthy behaviors or physical disorders. Don't question your natural routines or rhythm, or let others lure you away from them. For example, a friend with the extremes of Gate 15 may not understand why you are so compulsive about your rituals and daily patterns. Their rhythm automatically disrupts your healthy routines, and might even tempt you to abandon them. Conversely, you may find yourself wanting to influence their unpredictability with your fixed ways. Keep in mind that their flexibility and adaptability, though it feels unpredictable to you, is what keeps them healthy. Understanding and appreciating what each of you brings to the flow helps you embrace and transcend the inherent challenges.

Line 6 - Yielding	Line 3 - Compulsiveness
Line 5 - Joy	Line 2 - Inner Peace
Line 4 - The Hunter	Line 1 - Perseverance

GATE 15: MODESTY - THE GATE OF EXTREMES
– The quality of behavior which expresses the proper balance between extremes –
Center: G   Quarter: Civilization   Theme: Purpose fulfilled through Form
RAC of the Vessel of Love – JC of Extremes – LAC of Prevention

Gate 15 is the love of humanity. It has the capacity to accept and to find a place in society for the full spectrum of human behavior. Its lack of a fixed pattern insures that each of us is able to make a contribution to the diverse ways love exists in the world. Love in Gate 15 is not about how we connect with others, but rather how we project a transpersonal love for humanity's diversity out into the world. This begins with loving the extremes of your own rhythms; for example, sleeping ten hours one night, and two hours the next. You are capable of accepting other people's extremes without judgment, thereby bringing diversity into the flow of life. The Magnetic Monopole amplifies your aura's magnetism which attracts people to you and your acknowledgement of diversity. When guided by your Authority, Gate 15 increases your potential to influence how extreme rhythms or patterns are made 'modest,' and are balanced and integrated within the Collective. By understanding and accepting the diverse and opposite tempos that are a part of humanity, you fully embrace and promote for all of us what it means to be human. Without Gate 5's disciplined and fixed rhythm, you may find that your own constantly changing rhythms cause you to lose the focus you need to achieve mastery in some area of your life.

Line 6 - Self-Defense	Line 3 - Ego Inflation
Line 5 - Sensitivity	Line 2 - Influence
Line 4 - The Wallflower	Line 1 - Duty

THE CHANNEL OF THE 'ALPHA': 7 - 31
A Design of Leadership for 'Good or Bad'
Circuit: Understanding   Channel Type: Projected

The Channel of the Alpha links the G Center to the Throat Center through the Gate of the Role of the Self (7) and the Gate of Influence (31). This is the design of logical collective leadership looking towards the future. Logical leadership is based on tested and established patterns that can be followed with certainty. The 31st gate is the Collective leader and its voice carries the quality of influence. The 7th gate provides the logical role needed to lead and guide society; it is described as the power behind the throne. Its six line keynotes name the leadership roles we most often use when interacting with others, such as the authoritarian, the general, and the administrator.

Background: As residents of a global community, we are familiar with the Collective's style of democratic or shared leadership. Alphas are leaders who must first earn our trust. Those who lead by logic must perfect their leadership skills, and be able to demonstrate them to society's satisfaction. They have to be recognized as people who grasp present patterns, understand trends and are in touch with the needs of the people. Most importantly, they must be invited (elected) by the majority to lead. Their length of tenure is determined by the electorate's evaluation of their performance. Collective leadership is empowered by majority rule, which differs from the autocracy of the Tribe or the personal example of the Individual.

Personal: It is said of wolves that not all alphas lead packs, but no true alpha will stay in a pack led by another alpha. You may not become a community or national leader, but you will naturally seek your own arena of influence, your own pack. Once you have found it, you can bring attention to qualities essential to keeping society on the right track, but you can only point the way for others. You cannot do it for them. Leading from a position of influence rather than one of absolute authority is key to your success and to maintaining your sense of well being.

Interpersonal: Leadership in this channel is more appropriately described as influence because the Channel of the Alpha is *not* connected to a motor, and it *is* focused on the future. The alpha might say "doing this or that will work," but unless the majority is willing to step up and elect you to lead them to do it, it won't get done. Collective leadership says, "I will represent you and share leadership with you as long as you are doing what I tell you to do – because I am right." In other words, those with leadership definition have a much better chance of success if they are leading the right people under the right circumstances. They are more successful when they wait to be recognized and invited by those who share the same Collective context, and are part of the same established pattern. Logic's answers are rarely universally correct or long lasting; at any moment the pattern could be challenged or become weak or break down. It's all part of perfecting the process, which keeps humanity moving toward an ever more secure future.

GATE 7: THE ARMY - THE ROLE OF THE SELF IN INTERACTION
– The point of convergence. By design, the need for leadership to guide and order society –
Center: G   Quarter: Duality   Theme: Purpose fulfilled through Bonding
RAC of the Sphinx – JC of Interaction – LAC of Masks

The 7th gate is oriented toward the future, with an ability to see when society's present direction needs correcting to get there. This is logic's gate of direction, part of the Right Angle Cross of the Sphinx. The substance of its contribution to the Collective is expressed through designated leadership roles, which are listed below as the six lines of Gate 7: Authoritarian, Democrat, Anarchist, Abdicator, General, and Administrator. These roles are genetic and mechanical, and have tremendous conditioning power within the Collective. Through your role, and with your understanding of humanity's future direction, you persuade others to follow your leadership, thereby influencing people in positions of influence themselves, especially those with Gate 31. You might be the one to evaluate or modify the existing pattern or questionable direction, or be the catalyst for creating a new direction. This position of influence is described as the power behind the throne. In other words, without Gate 31 you can be a public leader but not necessarily the public figurehead who directly influences the Collective.

Line 6 - The Administrator	Line 3 - The Anarchist
Line 5 - The General	Line 2 - The Democrat
Line 4 - The Abdicator	Line 1 - Authoritarian

GATE 31: INFLUENCE - THE GATE OF INFLUENCE
– The law of friction, whether active or passive, that engenders transference and thus influence –
Center: Throat   Quarter: Civilization   Theme: Purpose fulfilled through Form
RAC of the Unexpected – JC of Influence – LAC of the Alpha

Gate 31 is designed to be influential. Collective leadership is collegial, not hierarchical. It provides the vision for a new direction and shows others how to achieve it, rather than doing it for them. The 31st gate manifests its potential for verbal influence through election. When money is the energy used to move a person into a position of power, instead of the cooperative will of the people, the Collective's overall ability to ensure humanity's future is easily perverted. Your voice through the 31st gate, "I lead," is not heard until backed by the energy of the majority. The people are the ones who must act on what your voice says. The influence of your vision for society will not be transferred or felt without the Collective's energy moving it into the public realm. Your leadership must take into account the desires of your followers, and address the good of the whole. 'I lead' means influencing others, for good or for ill, by effectively transferring your vision for a new and test-worthy pattern to them to carry out. Without the presence of Gate 7, you may seem like just an empty voice.

Line 6 - Application	Line 3 - Selectivity
Line 5 - Self-Righteousness	Line 2 - Arrogance
Line 4 - Intent	Line 1 - Manifestation

THE CHANNEL OF JUDGMENT: 58 - 18
A Design of Insatiability
Circuit: Understanding   Channel Type: Projected

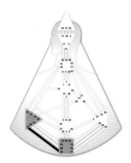

The Channel of Judgment links the Root Center to the Splenic Center through the Gate of Vitality (58) and the Gate of Correction (18). Logic needs to be able to prove it has the best answers, and underlying the logical process is an insatiable drive to challenge, correct and perfect any pattern. Channel 58-18 fuels the art of mastery.

Background: Gate 58 fuels our love of and vitality for life, and pressures us to want to perpetuate this energy. The insatiability of Channel 58–18 is a by-product of feeling so wonderful. It is as though Gate 58 says, "more and better, more and better" as logic's impulse to keep us alive, while Gate 18, the Gate of Correction, tempers this impulse by alerting us to what isn't healthy, or is out of balance or in need of correcting. The Channel of Judgement is like a sentry who judges if what it perceives is stopping life from being joyous for the Collective. Such judgment is based on testing patterns, and comparing what is inherently correct and workable with what has worked or not worked in the past. This sense of what needs correcting keeps society on track because Channel 58-18 wants everybody to find satisfaction in the perfected pattern. The Channel of Judgment's underlying purpose is the purpose of Human Design; to reclaim or recover the joy and love that have been lost in living a homogenized, conditioned life.

Personal: Even for the true perfectionist, perfection can never exist because patterns are subject to continual change. Your ability to judge, and your desire to correct, are expressed when you become dissatisfied with or feel the need to challenge something. When this perfecting or correcting process is made personal, however, and either turned inward or directed at others in relationship, the result is perceived as constant fault finding or a pervasive dissatisfaction with yourself and life in general. You will find yourself challenging your mother, father, teachers, governments, anyone and everything. No challenge is too great for logic to take on, or lies beyond your Root-fueled need to perfect the pattern. When a critical evaluation bursts forth unbidden or uninvited, however, it usually takes the form of an endless and incessant stream of data, about what is wrong, that no one wants to hear. On the other hand, what brings you real joy is being asked to share as in, "Is there something wrong here?" Those who ask you are the people who are prepared for and open to your answer.

Interpersonal: To avoid wasting precious energy, and to use your essential gifts wisely, you are advised to pick your battles with care by first waiting to be asked to share your solution, and by devising solutions applicable to society. In this way, you challenge only what others are most open and ready to address and potentially to correct. Two different ways of squeezing the toothpaste tube provide a humorous and poignant example of how logic can work effectively to reconcile differences. Logic says toothpaste should be squeezed from the bottom of the tube. The Individual says they will squeeze the tube anywhere they please. The reconciling, impersonal and practical Collective solution was to invent – and share with society – a gadget that dispenses the toothpaste with a press of the pump. Mutually agreeing to apply the solution restores peace, saving the relationship and probably many others in the process.

GATE 58: THE JOYOUS - THE GATE OF VITALITY
– Stimulation is the key to joy –
Center: Root   Quarter: Mutation   Theme: Purpose fulfilled through Transformation
RAC of Service – JC of Vitality – LAC of Demands

Gate 58 has the ability to sense when something is weak or unhealthy. You bring to living a joyful and compassionate audacity to challenge a pattern or the authority behind it. The pleasure you derive from sharing your appreciation of beauty, your sense of wonder and your zest for living, naturally attracts and delights others. To satisfy a driving desire to contribute something of value, you focus your vitality and joy for life on correcting anything that keeps society from achieving and maintaining well-being and health. Gate 58 provides the fuel logic needs to test the viability of patterns, formulas, rhythms and directions that are moving humanity into the future. It is logic's most precious and highly coveted energy resource. You often provide the energy that is needed to move people from talking about something to doing something about it. To channel your energy correctly, to conservatively and appropriately apply it where it is most needed, you look to people with Gate 18 who are attracted to you. Their existential awareness helps you focus your energy on determining which improvements should be made and how to manifest them. Without Gate 18 you can feel desperate to be of service in some way, and push too hard to figure it out yourself.

Line 6 - Carried away	Line 3 - Electricity
Line 5 - Defense	Line 2 - Perversion
Line 4 - Focusing	Line 1 - Love of Life

GATE 18: WORK ON WHAT HAS BEEN SPOILT - THE GATE OF CORRECTION
– The vigilance and determination to uphold and defend basic and fundamental human rights –
Center: Spleen   Quarter: Duality   Theme: Purpose fulfilled through Bonding
RAC of Service – JC of Correction – LAC of Upheaval

Gate 18 enjoys discovering, naming and challenging what needs correcting. When you experience dissatisfaction with something, chances are it has lost its vitality. Underneath this dissatisfaction lies a deep concern for human rights, and for what will keep society healthy and in harmony with itself. Your gift of critical awareness directs you to the source of a weakness or imperfection, and focuses your thinking on ways to correct or modify or replace it. It is your way of cleaning out what isn't healthy, or restoring vitality to something that has been corrupted. Your gift is enhanced by impartial discernment, and logic's drive to perfect or fine tune your own skills of critical analysis. Ushering in a new understanding through identifying what needs correcting is the by-product of the process. Gate 18 also represents the fear of authority and the challenge to that authority. As a Collective gate, it is designed to point out what needs to be corrected at the Collective level, but when used at the personal level it tends to backfire. Without Gate 58's joyful fuel for correction, your dissatisfaction can become merely a constant source of fault finding. This is especially true if your valuable and crucial awareness is no longer productively focused on situations, patterns or institutions, but rather on people's idiosyncrasies and foibles.

Line 6 - Buddhahood	Line 3 - The Zealot
Line 5 - Therapy	Line 2 - Terminal Disease
Line 4 - The Incompetent	Line 1 - Conservatism

THE CHANNEL OF THE WAVELENGTH: 48 - 16
A Design of Talent
Circuit: Understanding (Creative Channel)   Channel Type: Projected

The Channel of the Wavelength links the Splenic Center to the Throat Center through the Gate of Depth (48) and the Gate of Skills (16). Gate 48 is always on the lookout for vital information, and Gate 16 is always considering new ways to experiment and perfect its skills. When connected to the Channel of Judgment (Channel 58-18) with its ability to challenge and name what isn't working, this Design of Talent can use its depth and skills to find a potential solution to a problem, or to encourage, correct and refine something that needs perfecting.

Background: The depth available in Gate 48 is an internal intelligence that cannot be grasped by the mind, and is only accessible to others when one is surrendered to the natural instincts of the body. When one is deeply identified with, or practices, a skill that is available in Gate 16, there is a gradual transformation to precision and excellence that is communicated as talent, or the end result of perfecting the skill or pattern. A skill can be anything from playing an instrument, to figuring out a scientific formula, to making your way extraordinarily well in the world. Achieving mastery in any area of the logic process often serves a wider purpose and improves the lives of others.

Personal: You are designed to combine intuitive depth with repetitive experimentation and practice as you strive to perfect an intrinsic skill. The key to successfully developing your talent is that you must be completely identified with something that you love doing as it takes great dedication and constant repetition to achieve mastery. By bringing your depth to the technical mastery or perfecting of a skill, you transform or convert your skill to a talent. When your enthusiasm is combined with a long-term dedication to refining your talent, mastery of the pattern eventually transcends the pattern itself, freeing you to express your own unique wavelength. At the cellular level, it takes the body seven years to transcend technique; it may take a lifetime to plumb your depth.

Interpersonal: Those with Channel 48-16 have an innate need to be recognized by others, to be asked to share their talent, and to be rewarded with resources in order to continue its process of practicing and perfecting. They may lack direct access to energy resources (motor energy) of their own. For instance, if a parent does not purchase an instrument and provide music lessons, it will be much harder for a child to develop either their budding talent or the dedication necessary to perfect their skill. This applies as well to financing the exploration of patterns on behalf of humanity that might prove crucial to facing our future with relative security. Money is a form of recognition, and talent flowers when it is energized by recognition and materially rewarded. Developing social skills often helps the artist successfully compete for the monetary resources necessary to continue perfecting their talent. Channel 48-16 also represents the master and apprentice relationship. The master shares the expertise achieved through constantly refining a skill by mentoring or teaching a younger but gifted student. During this phase, the focus is usually on technique, for talent is often considered 1 percent gift (inspiration) and 99 percent work (perspiration). In this way, the pattern is passed on and the on-going refinement continues as each new master adds their own unique perspective and level of artistry to logic's creative process.

GATE 48: THE WELL - THE GATE OF DEPTH
– The necessary and qualitative foundation that is a prerequisite to establish the common good –
Center: Spleen   Quarter: Duality   Theme: Purpose fulfilled through Bonding
RAC of Tension – JC of Depth – LAC of Endeavor

Gate 48 provides a potent awareness, rooted in deep instinctual memory, that gives you the potential depth to bring logic's real and workable solutions to the problems of society. More than anything, you want to express and share your depth in order to help others recognize, correct and perfect the world we live in. Without Gate 16, however, you may experience feelings of inadequacy, fearing that you won't be able to explain your solution, or periods of frustration when you realize that you must wait for your depth to be recognized by others before you can share it. You may become overly concerned about developing skills you feel you lack. Relaxing into an active (expectant) waiting will usually draw people to you who will initiate your depth. In this way your potential solutions can emerge naturally and clearly as a foundation for evaluating, perfecting and mentoring the skills of others.

Line 6 - Self-Fulfillment	Line 3 - Incommunicado
Line 5 - Action	Line 2 - Degeneracy
Line 4 - Restructuring	Line 1 - Insignificance

GATE 16: ENTHUSIASM - THE GATE OF SKILLS
– The great art of enriching life by the harmonic channeling of energy –
Center: Throat   Quarter: Civilization   Theme: Purpose fulfilled through Form
RAC of Planning – JC of Experimentation – LAC of Identification

With Gate 16 you eventually make your mark in the world as a keen critic, skilled performer, or through your talent and enthusiasm for living. You don't, however, begin life that way. You need to identify with a skill or skills, dedicate yourself to repetition of the pattern, and focus on practice until you reach a point of mastery that transcends the skill itself and becomes an art. The world waits for that moment when the dancer becomes the dance, or when living one's life becomes its own masterpiece. You are looking for the perfect way to express your expertise. Without Gate 48 however, you may become self-critical and feel that you don't have the adequate depth. You are also searching for a source of material support that will allow you to concentrate on perfecting your talent, your theory, your solution, so you can then make it available to the world. You look to people with Gate 48 to bring their depth and dimension to your skill, as well as to properly direct, correct and encourage your own disciplined practice.

Line 6 - Gullibility	Line 3 - Independence
Line 5 - The Grinch	Line 2 - The Cynic
Line 4 - The Leader	Line 1 - Delusion

THE CHANNEL OF LOGIC: 63 - 4
A Design of Mental Ease mixed with Doubt
Circuit: Understanding   Channel Type: Projected

The Channel of Logic links the Head Center to the Ajna Center through the Gate of Doubt (63) and the Gate of Formulization (4). This is the doubting mind. Doubt is absolutely essential to logic because logic can be impeccable in its formulization and still be wrong! Channel 63-4 constantly filters patterns to see if they are consistent or not. The moment a pattern is inconsistent, pressure intensifies and finally becomes a question which demands an answer.

Background: The Channel of Logic's fear takes the form of doubt, and pops up somewhere between the question and the answer. Such skepticism must be addressed by logical experimentation leading to proof. There is little room for unsubstantiated belief. An answer is just an answer until a consistent and reliable, practical and 'provable' pattern emerges from it. The Collective fears the mutative impact of the Individual because mutation is a transformative process that breaks down the patterns. For example, someone with definition in Channel 63-4 cannot logically accept the truth of The Human Design System without experimenting with and proving it. It must work to be logical, and it must be logical to work.

Personal: You have an active logical mind that hones in on life with a healthy skepticism. "Is it going to rain next week? Well, based on typical patterns for this time of year, the current barometric pressure and cloud cover, there is a strong possibility, but…" You are good at posing a question, looking for recognizable patterns, factoring in current data, and making an educated prediction about the future in order to serve the collective. Will this or that make us safe tomorrow? You are always tempted to immediately share both the question and the answer, whether others are interested and open to you or not. When your busy mind is unable to resolve a question, and release mental pressure without meeting resistance, you can become anxious. It helps to remember that because the Channel of Logic is a Collective channel, the pressure to understand the pattern is best used to benefit others. Since your mind is not designed to answer the doubts and questions you have about your own life and future, keep it busy thinking about other things.

Interpersonal: As an electromagnetic connection, Channel 63-4 creates a rather pleasant mental link between two people. Those with Gate 63 want to share their doubts, and those with Gate 4 really enjoy sharing their solutions. This connection works best, however, when both parties understand that it is the sharing itself that provides the satisfaction. Gate 63 can't expect the solutions from Gate 4 to necessarily be useful, nor can Gate 4 expect only worthwhile questions to answer from Gate 63. In the end, using Strategy and Authority to know when to share ensures a congenial and successful exchange.

GATE 63: AFTER COMPLETION - THE GATE OF DOUBT
– In the spiral of life, all ends are beginnings –
Center: Head   Quarter: Initiation   Theme: Purpose fulfilled through Mind
RAC of Consciousness – JC of Doubts – LAC of Dominion

The suspicion or doubt of Gate 63 is merely a pressure; it is the readiness to pay attention to and question what feels insecure until it can be understood and evaluated in terms of our future security. Doubt arises when you sense an inconsistency or weakness in the existing patterns moving life forward. This is an essential ingredient in the understanding/logic process, and logic is the common thread that flows through and connects all life forms on the planet. The doubt of Gate 63 can be directed out into the world, or focused inward, inappropriately, on your life and choices. Your doubt becomes an urgency to formulate a question that addresses something that isn't clear to you. If you don't get an adequate, logical and workable answer to your question, pressure in the form of suspicion continues to build. Your focus on the future, with an ability to see patterns that exist in the present, means that if something appears weak and does not stand up under the scrutiny of your logic, or if it does not insure society's future, you will reject it for another pattern. When you are part of a group engaged in long-term planning, your aura will contribute this pressurized fuel for formulating an answer to the brainstorming process of projecting possibilities into the future. Without Gate 4, mental anxiety can arise as your need to have an answer to life's pressing questions.

Line 6 - Nostalgia	Line 3 - Continuance
Line 5 - Affirmation	Line 2 - Structuring
Line 4 - Memory	Line 1 - Composure

GATE 4: YOUTHFUL FOLLY - THE GATE OF FORMULIZATION
– The energy to beguile and succeed despite ignorance. Freedom from retribution –
Center: Ajna   Quarter: Duality   Theme: Purpose fulfilled through Bonding
RAC of Explanation – JC of Formulization – LAC of Revolution

Gate 4 applies mental awareness to questions fueled by doubt about the future; it formulates logic's answers. Each answer, each formula, is only a potential which must eventually be tested and substantiated by facts. That means that your answers may be the ones people seek, and they may not be. You use your mental intelligence and mental awareness to judge what looks suspicious. The pressure of a doubt or suspicion can last a lifetime, however, and you need to rely on your Authority to guide you to the correct question(s) on which to concentrate your energies while you wait for the right timing to share your answers. Ultimately, the answers you formulate are designed to be applied to questions that come from people around you. Rarely if ever can you formulate answers that provide solutions to your own questions about your life. Understanding and accepting this truth can bring the comfort of letting answers come and go in your mind, until the time is right for one to be brought to the surface by being asked to share it for the benefit of others. If you do not have Gate 63, you may either spend a lot of time looking for the next inspirational question you can answer, or become anxious that your life will always be in chaos.

Line 6 - Excess	Line 3 - Irresponsibility
Line 5 - Seduction	Line 2 - Acceptance
Line 4 - The Liar	Line 1 - Pleasure

THE CHANNEL OF ACCEPTANCE: 17 - 62
A Design of an Organizational Being
Circuit: Understanding   Channel Type: Projected

The Channel of Acceptance links the Ajna Center to the Throat Center through the Gate of Opinions (17) and the Gate of Details (62). Logic influences humanity's thinking processes, and shapes the way humanity reaches understanding. Acceptance here means mentally organizing information based on already substantiated detail, and it is an ongoing, internal process.

Background: As the gate of the right eye, Gate 17 visualizes the patterns while Gate 62 translates them and manifests the detail through words. Gate 62 is responsible for the creation of language, the means by which we name, organize, evaluate, communicate and give meaning to what we see and experience. Whatever Channel 17-62 can successfully organize into its own internal picture, it can understand; what it can't integrate into its own perspective in this way, it will not understand. Gate 62 is also one of three gates in the design of mammals that connects to humans, in this case with Gate 17. Such inter-species connections led to the domestication of animals, which in turn led to the organization of sustainable communities. This particular connection also enhances the training of animals by connecting them to mind, to higher cognition.

Personal: Your mind is constantly busy organizing details into your own mental filing system, always making adjustments to your 'big picture' by fitting what others think or say into it. This is how you keep a constant vigil on your internal patterns. All new data has to be logically organized and integrated to fit your perspective. When you say to someone, "I just don't understand you" you're simply saying, "I haven't been able to organize my perception of you (or what you are saying or thinking) in a way that fits into my picture of the world." With constant pressure on your Throat Center to speak, you will find you derive satisfaction and a sense of release by sharing your opinions in great detail, or explaining what you do or do not understand about something. In both instances, it is particularly important to pay attention to your timing and the receptivity of your audience. You have a highly sought-after gift for logically organizing things such as business groups, events, projects and other people's spaces, yet you may not be particularly interested in keeping your own space neat and in order.

Interpersonal: People with the Channel of Acceptance have a built-in foundation for teaching or presenting information to others. They have a gift for effectively translating detailed visual patterns into language, as formulas, theories or hypotheses, so that they can be tested for viability. Waiting to be invited to speak ensures the successful timing, effectiveness and clarity of their sharing, and decreases the possibility of meeting resistance or merely boring others with unasked for trivia. Logic naturally stands its ground. Debate and argumentation, fundamental forms of criticism and friction that are necessary for logic to scrutinize an existing pattern, remain a common source of stress-inducing interactions between people, especially if taken personally.

GATE 17: FOLLOWING - THE GATE OF OPINIONS
– The ancient law that those who wish to rule must know how to serve –
Center: Ajna   Quarter: Initiation   Theme: Purpose fulfilled through Mind
RAC of Service – JC of Opinions – LAC of Upheaval

Gate 17 looks for one concept or opinion among many that we can all trust – one that will survive both testing and criticism, and calm our fears about the future. Gate 17 is designed to structure an answer into a concept, a workable pattern or a possible solution in preparation for Gate 62's substantiating details. Up to this point in the logic process, your mind has taken a doubt about the future, formulated a potential solution, and now feels pressured to express it as an opinion. What it needs next is Gate 62's ability to translate the concept into language, to support it with facts and details, and present it to the public for their examination and analysis. Your right eye takes in the world at a glance, seeing it as a collection of recognizable, visual patterns. If a pattern or an opinion cannot stand up to logic's scrutiny, it will be or should be rejected. Unfortunately, you cannot always translate your visual image or what you understand about it, into language. Without Gate 62, you will find yourself looking for a name to represent your concepts, for facts to support your opinions, and for an effective means to communicate your suggestions. Mental anxiety for you arises out of the fear that no one will understand and value your input.

Line 6 - The Bodhisattva	Line 3 - Understanding
Line 5 - No Human is an Island	Line 2 - Discrimination
Line 4 - The Personnel Manager	Line 1 - Openness

GATE 62: PREPONDERANCE OF THE SMALL - THE GATE OF DETAILS
– Caution, patience and detail produce excellence out of limitation –
Center: Throat   Quarter: Civilization   Theme: Purpose fulfilled through Form
RAC of Maia – JC of Detail – LAC of Obscuration

Gate 62 says, "I think." It is designed to name, concretize, and communicate a visual pattern. It selects and organizes details as facts in order to better understand and explain complex concepts or situations. When connected to Gate 17's ability to structure the concept, Gate 62's supportive details make these concepts tangible, meaningful and understandable so they can be repeated and tested over time. Understanding is logic's gift – and yours. When you address complicated situations with clear, appropriate and well-organized details, your opinions increase our understanding of the world. When you wait to be asked to speak, you increase the Collective's potential receptivity to what you are sharing, and you avoid the embarrassment of compulsively blurting out facts and details that are unwanted, unnecessary and may potentially obscure people's understanding. The quality of your opinion is always dependent on your grasp of the facts, but all facts are not equal. It is helpful to remember that you can have all the details in hand, but without Gate 17 may not necessarily be able to put them into their proper structural context for expression in the moment.

Line 6 - Self-Discipline	Line 3 - Discovery
Line 5 - Metamorphosis	Line 2 - Restraint
Line 4 - Asceticism	Line 1 - Routine

THE SENSING (ABSTRACT) CIRCUIT
KEYNOTE: SHARING

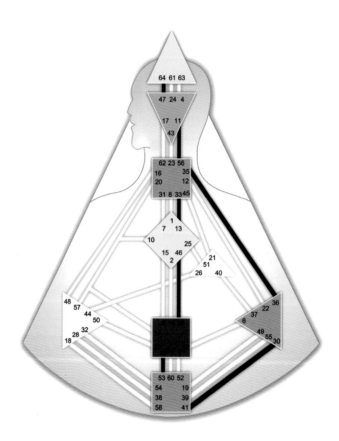

CHANNELS:

53 – 42	**MATURATION** *Balanced development*	**41 – 30**	**RECOGNITION** *Focused energy*
29 – 46	**DISCOVERY** *Succeeding where others fail*	**36 – 35**	**TRANSITORINESS** *A "Jack of all trades"*
13 – 33	**THE PRODIGAL** *A Witness*	**64 – 47**	**ABSTRACTION** *Mental activity mixed with clarity*
		11 – 56	**CURIOSITY** *A Searcher*

Logic's dance partner in the Collective Circuit Group is the Sensing (abstract) Circuit. The Sensing Circuit is keyed to the abstract experiential process. Through it we encounter and reflect upon life, and share the emotional and spiritual realm of human experience. This is the human experiential way; a joyful but sometimes perilous journey through life's endless progression of opportunities to explore, collect and share the experiences of being alive. If we can enter each new experience cleanly and clearly, we feel a deep sense of accomplishment, live life well, and feel at home in the world. In a greater sense, life will be well lived through us, and our reflections on our experiences will become valuable lessons for others.

Logic is built around theories and rules for establishing harmony in community, but the abstract says that arbitrary restrictions can stifle the experience that is so essential to humanity's evolution. Logic is motivated by the need to master; the abstract is motivated by cycles of accomplishment, which means it is important to complete something so one can move on to the next. Logic cannot manifest while the abstract can. What the abstract manifests, however, is subject to the emotional wave and its movement from the expectations of desire to the stasis of disappointment and boredom. Both ends of the wave succeed in driving humanity to progress toward the next new thing.

The Understanding Circuit has constant access to Splenic survival awareness, and to logic with its process of testing, proving and then sharing patterns that enhance our future. This is a process commonly associated with the Sciences. The Sensing Circuit, however, is focused on the desire for experiences (often with sexual overtones) that promote emotional/relational growth and development. The experience doesn't have to make sense, but it does need to be substantive, and something that can be shared with another person from beginning to end. The abstract process is associated with fields of study such as anthropology or literature. From logic's point of view, the abstract experiential way is a messy and unnecessary process.

The Sensing Circuit does not have the Spleen to provide stability and safety for the abstract process. Experience is based precariously on the emotional desire to do something new and exciting with another person. When things don't change, boredom and restlessness set in. Creating a crisis is one way to get things moving again. This is what makes abstract circuitry the most human of all processes. Reflecting upon experience is the Collective's most potent force for evolving life on the planet. Without this force, we would not have evolved into the consciously aware, differentiated and complex human beings we have become.

The Collective's reflections on past experience become the foundations of our history. People with definition in the Sensing Circuit cannot make sense of life while it is happening, but are genetically programmed to become storehouses of wisdom. It's our uniquely human capacity to select, to remember and to bring forward historical perspectives. We choose what we deem to be of value from what has been. It is an art to be able to condense and articulate the past in ways that can be shared in the moment and illuminate the future. Each perspective, each lesson learned, adds a line to the script from which life's drama continues to unfold. The retelling of human history greatly speeds up our learning process because no child has to begin from scratch when it enters the world.

The Channels and Gates of the Sensing Circuit are discussed on the following pages.

THE CHANNEL OF MATURATION: 53 - 42
A Design of Balanced Development
Circuit: Sensing   Channel Type: Generated

The Channel of Maturation links the Root Center to the Sacral Center through the Gate of Beginnings (53) and the Gate of Growth (42). The maturation process is at the heart of the (abstract) human experiential way. This process requires entering into and completing a new cycle or experience, and then reflecting on it in order to gain the wisdom the cycle offers.

Background: The quality of any channel in the Sensing Circuit is lived cyclically in the uninterrupted movement from commitment to completion, from the beginning through the middle to the end of a project, a relationship or a life. The abstract experiential process creates the collective history from which humanity learns. The great gift of experience is that it is collected and stored for following generations, allowing us to develop intellectually much faster than we do biologically. It is important that we learn from our experiential history, finding out what works in order to not repeat the same mistakes over and over again. Each new experience builds upon the last. If a cycle ends prematurely, we will need to repeat it until it is completed. This process is not goal oriented. It embodies the wisdom that all of life's experiences are to be appreciated as part of a journey that never ends. Maturing through experience is one of the keys to being human. We are all driven and pressured to seek new experiences, as this is how we gain our depth. By reflecting on our depth, we can translate our experience into information for others.

Personal: Each of your experiences must be brought to a satisfying resolution so that you can turn around and look back over it before beginning another cycle. Reflection shared with others helps you to reveal for yourself the valuable lessons learned from the experience. In this way, a new experience can begin by building on the old. It is important that you begin an experience using your Strategy and Authority. If you don't, you can become trapped in a cycle that you soon lose interest in or cannot complete. To properly navigate this territory, it is important to understand expectation. When you have expectations, you leave yourself open to frustration, disappointment, and an emotional crash. Simply *being* in an experience for its own sake, without expectation, is healthy for you.

Interpersonal: As the format energy* for the Sensing Circuit, the Channel of Maturation establishes a cyclic frequency that permeates every gate and channel in the circuit. It influences the way those who have it view and experience their life, as well as how they interact with and impact others. The commitment to enter a new experience sets the maturation process in motion, a process that could take from a few hours to a lifetime. Those with the Channel of Maturation have a deep affinity for history, and are attuned to all cycles of life: physical, societal, and planetary. When they enter into an experience through their own Authority, they are equipped with the energy to begin something, find satisfaction in its development, bring it to a successful conclusion, and upon reflection share the long term benefits with others for the greater good of humanity.

See Format energies in the Glossary in Section Eleven.

FORMAT ENERGY

GATE 53: DEVELOPMENT - THE GATE OF BEGINNINGS
– Development as a structured progression that is both steadfast and enduring –
Center: Root   Quarter: Civilization   Theme: Purpose fulfilled through Form
RAC of Penetration – JC of Beginnings – LAC of Cycles

Gate 53 is the pressure to begin the cyclical process of maturation, a sequence of development from conception to completion. This is a format energy that applies to all life forms as well as to relationships, ideas, projects, trends, and even the life cycles of nations and civilizations. You carry the fuel needed to begin something new. If you give yourself time to correctly decide where to commit your energy, you will initiate the cycle whose time has come, and you will be able to see it flower and ripen, and leave its seed for the future. Your role is to provide the impetus to get the cycle moving. Follow your Strategy and Authority in order to avoid beginning projects or relationships that you are not equipped to or interested in finishing yourself, or that you are unable to pass on to someone with Gate 42 who can bring what you started to completion. If your beginnings continually meet resistance, or are stopped before they mature, your disappointment can cycle into depression. If you commit to beginning something correctly, you are not compelled to complete it yourself. You will find that you can appropriately discharge the pressure, take what you learned from the experience, and enjoy sharing that wisdom with others. Without Gate 42, you are not designed to finish everything you begin, but you can feel frustrated by thinking that you always have to.

Line 6 - Phasing	Line 3 - Practicality
Line 5 - Assertion	Line 2 - Momentum
Line 4 - Assuredness	Line 1 - Accumulation

GATE 42: INCREASE - THE GATE OF GROWTH
– The expansion of the resources which maximizes the development of full potential –
Center: Sacral   Quarter: Initiation   Theme: Purpose fulfilled through Mind
RAC of Maia – JC of Completion – LAC of Limitation

Gate 42 is the tenacity to stay with a cycle in order to maximize its inherent potential. The abstract's cyclical process generates growth, and balanced development by using humanity's collected experiences to create a foundation for future progress. Each cycle you enter into builds on the lessons learned from the last. When a cycle has run its course, you will determine what is needed to bring it to a conclusion. Before you can begin a new cycle, the former cycle must be brought to its natural end, or what was left unfinished or incomplete will have to be revisited in the new one. That is especially true in relationships where you can feel stuck or held back by unresolved patterns of behavior that can date back as far as your childhood. You are focused on what it takes energetically to complete a cycle or process, and weak or insufficiently supported beginnings will make you nervous and uncomfortable. It is important that what you commit to is correct for you, as it is very difficult for you to extract yourself from something once you have committed to it, like an unfortunate marriage for example. By waiting until you are comfortable committing your energy, through Strategy and Authority, you maximize your own 'satisfaction potential.' Without Gate 53 to provide the initiating spark, you may find that you lack the staying power to complete the process, or feel frustrated trying to start things that never really get going.

Line 6 - Nurturing	Line 3 - Trial and Error
Line 5 - Self-Actualization	Line 2 - Identification
Line 4 - The Middle Man	Line 1 - Diversification

THE CHANNEL OF DISCOVERY: 29 - 46
A Design of Succeeding where Others Fail
Circuit: Sensing   Channel Type: Generated

The Channel of Discovery links the Sacral Center to the G Center through the Gate of Perseverance (29) and the Gate of the Determination of the Self (46). In the I'Ching, the 29th gate is known as the "deep within the deep," the Sacral's well of stamina and perseverance that is accessed only through a "yes" response. The 46th gate connects the vehicle to the direction of the higher self in order to be in the right place at the right time.

Background: People with the Channel of Discovery need to let go of all expectations. If they become completely immersed in the depth of their experience, its full meaning will be revealed in the end. Gate 46, the love of the body, and the love of being in the body, connects them to their vehicle and its trajectory or direction. If a person begins an experience with a decision made through response, maintains a total and unwavering commitment to it, and is patient with a process that can take years, the discoveries made can significantly transform the way the Collective perceives or experiences the world.

Personal: There is no "changing horses in the middle of the stream" for you, and no looking back, so a clear commitment through Strategy and Authority is vital to the satisfaction you will derive and the education you will be able to share from your discovery process. You must be able to lose yourself in the experience because it will not necessarily make sense to you while you are living it. If you can trust that you are in exactly the right place at exactly the right time, however, you will get to the end and make your discovery. You will succeed where others have failed. For you it is not about being in control, but rather surrendering your expectations to the cycles of discovery. This is why it is so important that you have your life force correctly committed and your Sacral's stamina supporting your experience the entire way!

Interpersonal: People with the Channel of Discovery have a built-in availability, and a tendency to say "yes" to almost any request. Those with unconscious (red) definition are particularly prone to giving their energy away. If their commitments are the result of a mental decision, they will most likely fail where others succeed, thus turning potential satisfaction into frustration. Unlike logic, which theoretically postulates what might happen if a person does this or that, the past is the only teacher for the experiential learners. It is not until they get to the end of an experience that they discover, through examination and analysis, what is worth repeating and what is not, which is what they then share with the Collective. It is only through correctly saying "yes" that they can persevere through extreme challenges without allowing others to deter them from the course of their experience, and its potential for discovery.

GATE 29: THE ABYSMAL - THE GATE OF PERSEVERANCE

– The deep within the deep. Persistence despite difficulties has its inevitable rewards –
Center: Sacral   Quarter: Duality   Theme: Purpose fulfilled through Duality
RAC of Contagion – JC of Commitment – LAC of Industry

Gate 29's potential is a constant affirmation of life. When it answers yes, it commits its energy to something or someone new, and will persevere through whatever the cycle of discovery brings. Perseverance is cyclical, however, and what you are committed to one day may no longer be of interest the next. Each correct commitment you make supports the maturation of your full potential for discovering who you are in relationship to others and the world. You are always eager to say "yes," always ready to commit your energy, so it is best to wait until you are quite clear about what is truly right for you to invest your energy in. Your Sacral response is mechanical, and you cannot know where the adventure will take you or what wonders you may find. Gate 29 has a single-minded energy designed to move you through even the most difficult and challenging circumstances, but only if it is fully aligned with your decision. Your only insurance is to let go of your expectations, and rely on your Strategy and Authority to guide you to the correct experiences. Without the 46th gate, you are ready to work but do not know what you are working towards.

Line 6 - Confusion	Line 3 - Evaluation
Line 5 - Overreach	Line 2 - Assessment
Line 4 - Directness	Line 1 - The Draftee

GATE 46: PUSHING UPWARD - THE GATE OF THE DETERMINATION OF THE SELF

– Good fortune that may be perceived as the result of serendipity but derives from effort and dedication–
Center: G   Quarter: Duality   Theme: Purpose fulfilled through Bonding
RAC of The Vessel of Love – JC of Serendipity – LAC of Healing

The 46th gate is focused on the quality of life we experience in a physical body. It expresses the love of the body, and the sensual honoring of it as a temple in which we are always in the right place at the right time. You are one who lives the good fortune and discovery of serendipity. Whether you succeed or fail is dependent on the determination of your higher self. This is an abstract process of surrender to a cycle of experience that can fulfill your potential, or bring chaos. The lessons you learn and the wisdom you share with others is derived from your determination, dedication to and absorption in the experience as you are living it. The experience of the nature of your self in interaction with others is a deeply spiritual process, and can only be evaluated when the cycle is complete. If you cannot commit yourself to the cyclical nature of life, your body will begin to fail under the stress of constant crisis. Without the 29th gate, you may recognize the right timing, but not have the energy to begin the process or the perseverance to complete it.

Line 6 - Integrity	Line 3 - Projection
Line 5 - Pacing	Line 2 - The Prima Donna
Line 4 - Impact	Line 1 - Being Discovered

THE CHANNEL OF THE PRODIGAL: 13 - 33
A Design of a Witness
Circuit: Sensing   Channel Type: Projected

The Channel of the Prodigal links the G Center to the Throat Center through the Gate of the Listener (Gate 13) and the Gate of Privacy (Gate 33). This channel is one of reflection and remembrance. Gate 13 listens and stores information and secrets, harvesting memories from which lessons may be learned. Gate 33 retreats to reflect on its experiences, patiently waiting for what is beneath the surface to reveal itself in the form of a deeper truth.

Background: Peculiar to human beings is their desire to explore all there is in life, and their drive to experience it first-hand. Channel 13-33 brings the experiential cyclical process of maturation to an end, adding the capacity to see and reflect on all sides of an experience afterwards before sharing it. It's what gives us our incredible advantage as an evolving, self-aware species. This is the Prodigal, the witness, experiencing and then gathering memories so they can be passed on in some form of personal biography or collective history lesson. Such remembering brings continuity and stability to the evolution of civilization from one generation to the next.

Personal: As a natural listener and record keeper, you collect life stories, secrets and memorabilia. You then retreat to ponder and organize what you have gathered in preparation for sharing your reflections in the lessons you have gleaned from them. Your challenge is timing. You don't want to reveal your secrets before their time, or remain so private no one will ever hear them. You are willing to break with the patterns of family and society so as to choose experiences that are correct for you to learn from. Most people enter experiences with a specific expectation but at the end of the cycle discover that the results did not match those expectations. They lose patience and miss the magic of completion with its precious lessons. You share with all of us, from your experience, that it is far more fulfilling to simply witness the sequence of unfolding events than to suffer the frustration and disappointment of unmet expectations. The wisdom gained over time from this form of patient reflection reveals some of the greatest truths in our collective history. One of the most valuable lessons you bear witness to, and share with us, is how to comfortably surrender to our own experiential process as a passenger consciousness.

Interpersonal: The Collective abstract says, "I remember my experience or inexperience." Over a lifetime, those with the Channel of the Prodigal accumulate gems of wisdom that can be organized as the lessons of a personal or collective history. This organization requires patience. They might enjoy photography, scrapbooking, or listening to people recollect their life's stories. They might be a politician, a comedian or our confidante. Those with Channel 13-33 look to and learn from the past so they are not good at predicting the future in order meet the challenges of the present. They are the first ones, however, to tell us that life does make sense in the end.

GATE 13: THE FELLOWSHIP OF MAN - THE GATE OF THE LISTENER

– Universal ideas and values in an ordered framework which inspires humanistic cooperation –
Center: G   Quarter: Initiation   Theme: Purpose fulfilled through Mind
RAC of the Sphinx – JC of Listening – LAC of Masks

With its gift for hearing, seeing and storing secrets, Gate 13 provides continuity between the past and the future in its role as the listener. You are perceived as a confidante and a keeper of secrets. People naturally share their experiences with you because you genuinely enjoy hearing their stories, their adventures, victories and challenges. They sense that you are quite comfortable simply holding inside you what has been shared. Gate 13 is not pressured by the Throat Center to speak. You will recognize the right moment to share what is most valuable from your remembering because it will be drawn from you by people who are able to properly select, reflect upon and organize it for sharing with the broader community, such as people with Gate 33. In this way, you insure that the important lessons, which can only be learned through experience, are held and cherished until the time is right for them to contribute to humanity's understanding of itself. Historical continuity informs our future as a species. Without Gate 33, your secrets may never be shared.

Line 6 - Optimist	Line 3 - Pessimism
Line 5 - The Saviour	Line 2 - Bigotry
Line 4 - Fatigue	Line 1 - Empathy

GATE 33: RETREAT - THE GATE OF PRIVACY

– Active withdrawal and the transformation of a weak position into a strength –
Center: Throat   Quarter: Civilization   Theme: Purpose fulfilled through Form
RAC of the Four Ways – JC of Retreat – LAC of Refinement

Gate 33 marks the end of a cycle, and built into all endings is a moment of silence for considering every aspect of the experience. This is where your need to be alone comes from. Retreat for you arises in that moment of uncertainty between the completed experience and a new one, a pause that allows you to reflect on what to take forward while you renew your strength. It is in the quiet moments of contemplation that the most valuable lessons, stored in the depths of Collective memory (Gate 13), will come to the surface. In Gate 33 your need for privacy is joined by the Collective's voice of "I remember." It is also your nature to share the lessons of experience and reveal its truths. The experience can be one of your own, or another's, or even that of a group of people; the process is the same. When the time is ripe, you will be asked to share your wisdom which then becomes part of the greater community and humanity's evolving consciousness. Like the Prodigal, you mature over your lifetime, and your realm of influence expands as you move through each cycle of experience. Without Gate 13 you may not have a sense of the right timing for sharing your lessons.

Line 6 - Disassociation	Line 3 - Spirit
Line 5 - Timing	Line 2 - Surrender
Line 4 - Dignity	Line 1 - Avoidance

THE CHANNEL OF RECOGNITION: 41 - 30
A Design of Focused Energy (Feelings)
Circuit: Sensing   Channel Type: Projected

The Channel of Recognition links the Root Center to the Solar Plexus Center through the Gate of Contraction (41) and the Gate of Feelings (30). The Root pressure (fuel) of Gate 41 starts with a feeling of restlessness, and energizes the imagination to fantasize about countless scenarios for what "could be." When connected to Gate 30, the emotions of the Solar Plexus heat up the fuel, resulting in an intense need to seek out or begin moving in the direction of a new experience.

Background: Genetically speaking, the 41st hexagram is the initiating codon in our DNA. When the sun moves into Gate 41 in January of each year, we begin a new solar cycle (a new year) and initiate a physiological process in humanity that keeps us evolving together. All of the possibilities of human experience are stored within this gate, and the entire experiential process is driven by its Root-fueled desire for new experiences and the expectation of being satiated in the end. This hunger can only be satisfied temporarily. The abstract process is focused on accomplishment, on the completion of a cycle, and is driven by a desire or expectation that 'doing' something will overcome boredom. This is the beginning of the human experiential way. Our cultural evolution, the progression from the ignorance and innocence of inexperience to the wisdom of lessons learned from experience, culminate in Channel 36-35.

Personal: You are a person with great imagination and an endless yearning to take in life and feel it deeply. Your dreams, fantasies or wishes, sometimes accompanied by sexual overtones, create expectations that, when in the hands of fate (Gate 30), may or may not be fulfilled. Over time you have learned that desire can bring great joy or excitement as well as pain, and the fulfillment of any desire does not last long. Your restlessness for new experience is balanced by developing the patience and self control needed to follow your emotional Authority and take sufficient time through your wave to make clear decisions. The secret for you is to simply enjoy your dreams and each experience in and of itself, without giving in to the pressure of expectation. In this way your experiences will be more fulfilling, your reflections more poignant, and your sharing more likely to stir the feelings of others.

Interpersonal: In the Channel of Recognition, the pressure to move is connected to an intense feeling or emotion, providing the momentum to leap from inexperience into experience at a moment's notice. Waiting through their emotional wave gives those with this channel the essential time needed for clarity to emerge before deciding which of their desires is correct to jump into. This pressure may launch some pretty wild rides, generally involving others, but can also stimulate deep reflection for all participants after the adventure is complete. Each new experience allows them to perceive or connect to a nuance of emotion they can then describe.

GATE 41: DECREASE - THE GATE OF CONTRACTION
– The limitation of resources which maximizes development of potential –
Center: Root   Quarter: Mutation   Theme: Purpose fulfilled through Transformation
RAC of the Unexpected – JC of Fantasy – LAC of the Alpha

Gate 41 initiates the uniquely human experiential way as a hunger to experience emotion. It begins with the desire to interact with others through feelings. When this initiating Root pressure of desire builds in you, it may manifest as a vague expectation, a sexual fantasy or a restless need to experience something new with someone. You are not sure what this new experience is or when it will happen or with whom. Gate 41 drives you toward satisfying your desire and fulfilling your destiny, both of which rest in the hands of the fates (Gate 30.) You bring balance to this unfocused and often confusing restlessness by writing or daydreaming about what it might be like to fulfill your wildest desires, or by vicariously experiencing them through literature and movies. Gate 41 holds the potential for all human experiences, but releases or initiates only one at a time. This is its limitation, and yours. Each new experience that you enter into through your Strategy and Authority holds a promise that a new feeling awaits your discovery. By letting go of your expectations, you can move freely through each encounter and avoid becoming pessimistic about future ones. Without Gate 30 there is a feeling of wanting something, but not knowing what it is that you want.

Line 6 - Contagion	Line 3 - Efficiency
Line 5 - Authorization	Line 2 - Caution
Line 4 - Correction	Line 1 - Reasonableness

GATE 30: THE CLINGING FIRE - THE GATE OF FEELINGS
– Freedom recognized as an illusion and limitation accepted as a fate –
Center: Solar Plexus   Quarter: Initiation   Theme: Purpose fulfilled through Mind
RAC of Contagion – JC of Fates – LAC of Industry

The Gate of the Fates teaches us that life is not what we expect it to be – it is what we allow it to be. Your experiences are conceived from a desire that then meets life on the highs and lows of your emotional wave. This desire can feel like an obsessive hunger that weaves the yearnings of different lives together, influencing your every interaction until it is satisfied or fulfilled. The only control you have is over the clarity with which you enter into each experience, not over the outcome. Because desire can only be temporarily assuaged, life without clarity becomes a wild emotional ride. Over time, you see that the freedom to fulfill your wildest dreams is merely an illusion, and unreciprocated desire should not be taken personally. Balance in your life comes through surrender, through accepting what is. In doing so, you need not fear the fates or feel pressured to chase after the fantasies of Gate 41. By accepting your limitation, or place in the larger pattern of life, your reflections on feeling and desiring deeply while experiencing your humanness become a gift to be shared with others.

Line 6 - Enforcement	Line 3 - Resignation
Line 5 - Irony	Line 2 - Pragmatism
Line 4 - Burnout	Line 1 - Composure

THE CHANNEL OF TRANSITORINESS: 36 - 35
A Design of a "Jack of all Trades"
Circuit: Sensing (Creative Channel)   Channel Type: Manifested

The Channel of Transitoriness links the Solar Plexus Center to the Throat Center through the Gate of Crisis (36) and the Gate of Change (35). This is an emotional Manifesting channel that defies Logic's caution and restrictive patterns. It will try anything and everything, whether of intrinsic value or not, to get things moving in the direction of a new experience.

Background: As the creative channel for the Sensing Circuit, Channel 36-35 has a talent for seeking adventures and involving others in them. It finds expression through Gate 35's need to manifest change as in "been there, done that, what's new?" The emotionally-charged 36th gate perceives its inexperience as inadequacy, and so draws those with the Channel of Transitoriness into seeking experience, occasionally by engendering a crisis just to get things moving. Through this restless desire to explore the depth and consequence of our capacity to feel (emotion), our species matures and evolves and our gene pool expands, ultimately resulting in progress for the Collective. This is learning through experience for the sake of future generations.

Personal: You are driven to seek experiences which promise something new and better in life. Your journey is an emotional one and you gather wisdom experientially. Pushed along by the ever-changing perspectives of your unaware Solar Plexus wave, you can become volatile or feel let down if a new experience fails to meet your expectations. The secret is to embrace and accept your emotional swings, to give yourself time to make emotionally-clear decisions, and to surrender to fully living each correct experience for its own sake. Over time and with maturity, experience will culminate as emotional depth within your personal truth, the heart of which is accepting life for what it is. If you find yourself nervous or uneasy about committing to a venture, take advantage of waiting out your wave. Your great accomplishment in life is that you will have tasted, touched and felt many things from which you gleaned wisdom of great value, wisdom that you make available to others in the form of advice. You inspire people to join your ventures with tales of your exploits, and sense of fulfillment in the richness of a life well lived. As you learn that feelings are transitory, your advice to others will be to "seize the moment," and partake of each promising new experience that is correct, rather than live with a sense that nothing in life ever amounts to anything.

Interpersonal: For those with the Channel of Transitoriness, interaction with others means sharing the experience completely with them. Their need for new experience, and inherent sense that nothing lasts, often makes it difficult for them to maintain intimate relationships. Their partner(s) pay a price if they find themselves dragged along on adventures that are not right for them. Doing anything for the first time isn't easy, outcomes are unpredictable, and most people are not equipped to handle the resulting crises. Deeply emotional experiences often have a sexual dimension, but because relating here is focused on the feelings provoked by the experience rather than on the other person, both parties can be left with disappointment when the experience is over. When two people connect electromagnetically through this channel, one with Gate 35 and one with Gate 36, the balance and stability of the relationship will be constantly subjected to the high to low emotional wave.

GATE 36: THE DARKENING OF THE LIGHT - THE GATE OF CRISIS
– The rule of cycles in which decline is a natural but not enduring stage –
Center: Solar Plexus   Quarter: Initiation   Theme: Purpose fulfilled through Mind
RAC of Eden – JC of Crisis – LAC of The Plane

Gate 36 is the place where your fears of vulnerability and inexperience (emotional and sexual) are resolved or transformed into experience; where you create and meet the challenges of change and growth through emotional crises. As you gain emotional clarity over time, you learn how to handle emotional crises created by others, and you create less of them yourself. Gate 36 restrains the strong hope-to-pain wave that drives human experience toward change. Its energy is aimed directly at the Throat Center which means that the full range and depth of your emotions are being readied for manifestation. All that is needed is someone or something to trigger their release. Without Gate 35 to provide a proper outlet or give a focused direction to this energy, it can be experienced as a personal crisis. You learn over time to remain steady by patiently adapting to constantly changing feelings. These feelings can prove to be wonderfully stimulating and natural for you to express, or overwhelming to you and uncomfortable for others. Either way, let them unfold as this is how you reach for your emotional depth in order to access your own truth. Without Gate 35, feeling inadequate and unable to fulfill your own expectations makes you nervous.

Line 6 - Justice	Line 3 - Transition
Line 5 - The Underground	Line 2 - Support
Line 4 - Espionage	Line 1 - Resistance

GATE 35: PROGRESS - THE GATE OF CHANGE
– By design, progress cannot exist in a vacuum and is dependent on interaction –
Center: Throat   Quarter: Civilization   Theme: Purpose fulfilled through Form
RAC of Consciousness – JC of Experience – LAC of Separation

Gate 35 is driven by a restless curiosity and high expectations to explore new horizons for the sheer exhilaration of doing it, but not alone. Gate 35's voice says, "I feel," and what it usually feels is a desire for change. Yours is the voice of impersonal, relational experience. You are prodded along not by awareness, but by a hunger for depth of feeling that is conditioned by the emotional wave. Like hunger, desire and curiosity can only be temporarily ameliorated. You are focused on collecting experiences to learn from them, rather than on repeating experiences to master them. Mastery for you is expressed as wisdom and manifests as advice. Your memories may provide more satisfaction than the experience itself. Your taste for new experience, and the need to see what or who is on the other side of the mountain, can keep you healthy and alert. When correctly entering into experience for its own sake, and remaining an objective observer, your clear sharing carries the potential to transform humanity. Experience seekers don't often take time to consider the repercussions of their actions, and without Gate 36, you are prone to seeking an emotional rush in the hope of escaping the pain of boredom when there is no new experience to dive into.

Line 6 - Rectification	Line 3 - Collaboration
Line 5 - Altruism	Line 2 - Creative Block
Line 4 - Hunger	Line 1 - Humility

THE CHANNEL OF ABSTRACTION: 64 - 47
A Design of Mental Activity mixed with Clarity
Circuit: Sensing   Channel Type: Projected

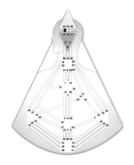

The Channel of Abstraction links the Head Center to the Ajna Center through the Gate of Confusion (64) and the Gate of Realization (47). Those with definition in Channel 64-47 are always under pressure to sift through a kaleidoscope of mental images from every experience, even their dreams. They are trying to make sense out of the past and gain perspective. They seek a story to share, either about their life or someone else's, maybe from this lifetime or perhaps from another.

Background: The Channel of Abstraction is an experiential mental force that dabbles in all kinds of possibilities, regardless of rules, until something mysteriously emerges and makes sense. This is a mind busy with the consequences of being alive. Merging the conceptualization of the neocortex (Ajna Center) with the deep gray matter of the brain (Head Center), it gifts us with the true potential of self-reflected consciousness. To be at peace with themselves however, those with this channel must remember that the mind can never be an internal authority for their own life, and it will never be 100 percent sure of anything.

Personal: You have a very active, experiential mind that never stops playing with possibilities, and you probably wonder if it will ever stop being busy. You can experience considerable mental confusion as a result of the constant swirl of images always moving through it, feeling at times a bit like a drunk monkey stung by a scorpion. This confusion can mark the beginning of a new and inspiring journey for you, as you discover what really does make sense. If you remain patient with your discovery process, the gaps and spaces between the dots will at some point connect and a picture will appear; a new, unique sequence will be created or revealed. Your reward for being patient, for waiting for clarity to emerge over time, is the uncovering of an inspiring tale to tell, or a new perspective to share with others. You are utterly unequipped with this mental definition, however, to solve your own problems, or make sense of your own life.

Interpersonal: In order to relieve the pressure to make sense of life, those with the Channel of Abstraction have to find a way to share their minds with the outside world. Their casual, story-telling minds, while a gift for historians, should never be relied upon for the facts. This is the part of our genius that finds either inspiration or confusion in our intellectual drive to break experiences down, and look at them over and over again from every possible angle, even if most have no value. It is incredible though to hear the active, experiential mind reach a moment of clarity, whatever path it has taken to get there, and share that "Aha!" with the Collective.

GATE 64: BEFORE COMPLETION - THE GATE OF CONFUSION
– Transition, like birth, requires a determined strength for the passage through –
Center: Head   Quarter: Duality   Theme: Purpose fulfilled through Bonding
RAC of Consciousness – JC of Confusion – LAC of Dominion

Accepting confusion, the state before order is established, is part of Gate 64's process of attempting to make sense of a constant flow of data that continually recycles through the mind. Gate 64 is the pressure behind that flow, not the gate that resolves the confusion. Your mind is filled with a string of disconnected memories and images from your past that need filtering and sorting until you can see or make sense of what really happened. In order to enjoy your mental state of confusion and not become overwhelmed by it, let the clips of your past experiences simply stream through your mind until the message of the movie becomes clear to you. When it does, share it with others. If you put pressure on your mind to figure the data out with a specific methodology, you may increase your level of confusion and trigger anxiety. It takes great inner strength to let the confusion process resolve in its own way and time, thus leaving your peace of mind intact. It may also be tempting to react in some way once the clarity arrives, but these "aha's" are for sharing, not acting upon. Without Gate 47 you may be tempted to resolve the confusion prematurely.

Line 6 - Victory	Line 3 - Overextension
Line 5 - Promise	Line 2 - Qualification
Line 4 - Conviction	Line 1 - Conditions

GATE 47: OPPRESSION - THE GATE OF REALIZATION
– A restrictive and adverse state as a result of internal weakness or external strength or both –
Center: Ajna   Quarter: Duality   Theme: Purpose fulfilled through Bonding
RAC of Rulership – JC of Oppression – LAC of Informing

If Gate 64 is the one who remembers the disorganized collection of film clips that passes through its life, then Gate 47 is the editor who attempts to assemble them all into a meaningful slice of human experience. You will not see the full picture immediately as you tentatively start to sort through the collection of images, and it may not be apparent to you at first which clip holds the key to your eventual mental realization. As new details emerge, you may vacillate between perceiving the event this way or that way through a mix of recognitions that direct you toward different interpretations. At first you may feel that rather than the process becoming easier, it is becoming more complicated for you to reassemble the mental sequences in a way that makes sense. If you can step back and trust, however, you will eventually cycle through to that "aha" moment. The secret is to avoid the pressure to act on every conclusion that comes to you, and simply enjoy the array of possibilities that move through your active mind, until one stands out. You are then ready, when asked and it is correct for you, to share your recognitions with others. Without Gate 64 you may put pressure on yourself, and forget to wait for the revelation that will truly bring the mental activity to a temporary halt.

Line 6 - Futility	Line 3 - Self-Oppression
Line 5 - The Saint	Line 2 - Ambition
Line 4 - Repression	Line 1 - Taking Stock

THE CHANNEL OF CURIOSITY: 11 - 56
A Design of the Searcher
Circuit: Sensing   Channel Type: Projected

The Channel of Curiosity links the Ajna Center to the Throat Center through the Gate of Ideas (Gate 11) and the Gate of Stimulation (Gate 56). Seekers never stop searching, no matter what or how much they find. Their curiosity compels them to continually seek stimulation, to explore new ideas and ways of seeing things. This curiosity is not about setting out to find something specific but rather, "Look at what I have discovered. This is what I believe to be true about it."

Background: The Collective's social obligation is to share, and the Channel of Curiosity provides us with people specially equipped to do so: the storyteller and the casual historian. They are our truth seekers, and they teach from experience. Their stories give us an opportunity to evaluate whether we want the new idea or belief to inform or transform our life, or not. Unlike the voice of logic, which is focused on data and facts, the transformative abstract voice takes all of the bits and pieces of information and elaborates on them by filling in the gaps. In this way, information is brought to life as a story that has the power to influence people by stimulating their imagination and emotions. The 56th gate is more fascinated with seeking than with finding. It is continually open to stimulation and experience for its own sake, but is not motivated to create those experiences itself.

Personal: Your creativity and style of presentation becomes magical when you weave together ideas and stories from your philosophical reflections on what it means to be a human being experiencing life. You have an enviable gift for taking a sequence of ideas and fashioning a story out of them that can teach or entertain an audience. Even if these stories are somewhat exaggerated or contain some half truths, like your child telling you about their day at school, you still draw others in and stimulate them. Your capacity to believe in something makes it true for you, and you are less interested in facts than you are in how your stories illustrate and teach. Your stories are more like parables for life. Even though they flow from your personal experiences and discoveries, they are not as useful a guide for you as they are for others. They are stories to be shared, collected and stored for reflection and interpretation by present and future generations. This is a process unique to human beings.

Interpersonal: We no longer rely on the ballads of bards and minstrels to keep us informed about world events, yet we still admire the storytellers who can weave a good yarn and generate stimulating social commentary. The receptivity of an audience to the magic of the story, however, is determined by the proper timing of the story's delivery. When these skillful storytellers and teachers follow their Strategy and Authority, they will enjoy sharing their extraordinary gifts while effectively informing, entertaining and stimulating the rest of us.

GATE 11: PEACE - THE GATE OF IDEAS
– A harmonic condition in the individual or society that permits assessment before renewed action –
Center: Ajna   Quarter: Mutation   Theme: Purpose fulfilled through Transformation
RAC of Eden – JC of Ideas – LAC of Education

Ideas are concepts designed to express what has been sensed. In Gate 11, possibilities are conceptualized into ideas. These ideas are not prescriptions for action because ideas come and go. At this point in the abstract process, you are given a quiet moment for assessment to sort out what has been remembered over the ups and downs of the experiential process. You are prone to remembering what you really liked about what you saw, while leaving the rest out. This is how ideas become ideals, then beliefs and finally belief systems over time. You seek the ideas of others to stimulate your own reflections, and you enjoy stimulating others with your ideas, but not indiscriminately. Ideas reach the Throat Center as verbal expressions, not as manifestations of action, and they are designed simply to be reflected upon. Trying to solve your life's dilemmas with your own ideas will lead to frustration, further crises and confusion. You can take great delight, however, in savoring the stimulating details of past moments for their own sake. Without Gate 56 you are under pressure to tell your stories, and may do so impulsively without waiting for the right timing.

Line 6 - Adaptability	Line 3 - The Realist
Line 5 - The Philanthropist	Line 2 - Rigour
Line 4 - The Teacher	Line 1 - Attunement

GATE 56: THE WANDERER - THE GATE OF STIMULATION
– Stability through movement. Perpetuation of continuity through the linking of short term activity –
Center: Throat   Quarter: Civilization   Theme: Purpose fulfilled through Form
RAC of Laws – JC of Stimulation – LAC of Distraction

Gate 56 is where ideas are gathered together, and where visual memory is recollected and verbally recounted. This is the gate of the casual historian. It is the voice of the storyteller and philosopher that says, "I believe." An idea is not a solution, or a call to action, but rather a journey over time designed to stimulate the formation of our ideals and beliefs. Your mind translates human experience into language. Once an idea is expressed verbally, the process is complete. Your feelings influence which new ideas and experiences you seek to explore, and your recollections or stories about them are subjective and selective. What you teach us about life will include some facts, but the unique lessons will come from your interpretation of the experience tinged with emotional overtones. Your stories add colorful threads to the expanding tapestry of humanity's progress. Without Gate 11 you are often searching for new sources of stimulation and new ideas for stories to tell.

Line 6 - Caution	Line 3 - Alienation
Line 5 - Attracting Attention	Line 2 - Linkage
Line 4 - Expediency	Line 1 - Quality

TRIBAL CIRCUIT GROUP
DEFENSE AND EGO CIRCUITS
SUPER KEYNOTE: SUPPORT

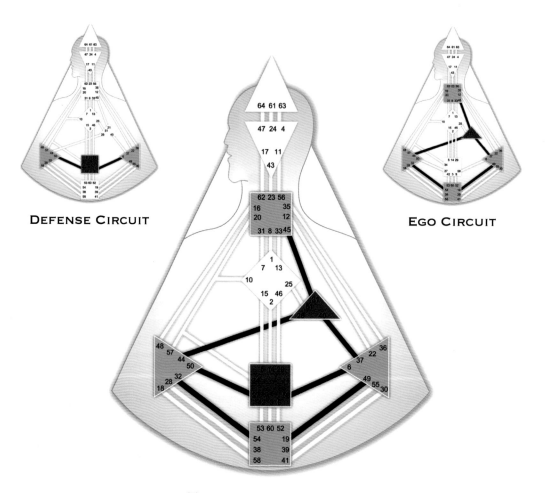

DEFENSE CIRCUIT

EGO CIRCUIT

TRIBAL CIRCUIT GROUP

When we enter the Tribal realm, we meet interdependence as an underlying form of support. Interdependence is the mutuality and reciprocity upon which early societies were structured and maintained. The job of the Tribe is to deal with the consequences of being alive by devising ways for people to live together that increase productivity, and maximize our ability to protect ourselves.

The Tribe connects us to life and each other through the senses, through bloodlines (ancestry), and through loyalty to the blood bargain. The Tribal heart is a communal heart, where everybody else's business is everybody else's business. This is in part what gives the Tribe its reputation for being 'sticky' and possessive. For the Tribe, support is about having. The Tribe is sensitive to people's basic need for food, shelter, clothing, and a structure to hold everything together. When these are provided, there is peace in the kingdom. When they are lacking, the Tribe is equipped to revolt in order to establish equilibrium between those who have more than they need, and those who do not have enough. Revolution is a form of Tribal justice.

Two circuits make up the Tribal Circuit Group: one major, the Ego Circuit, and one minor, the Defense Circuit. The Ego Circuit has a double focus. The first is addressing the demands of the material world, such as family, or the creation and distribution of monetary resources. Its second focus balances humanity's need to survive on the material plane with our deep need for God (spirit). The Ego Circuit creates the two forces of continuing support that keep people in the Tribe. The Defense Circuit is concerned with generating, caring for, nurturing and preserving human life (the Tribe), and the laws and values of Tribal relationships.

In our exploration of the BodyGraph as a circuit board, we saw that the core Integration Channel is resolutely separate, the epitome of self-sufficiency. The Individual Circuit Group empowers the quality of uniqueness in humanity that paves the way for individuation and mutation, and the Collective Circuit Group is staunchly communal, socially interactive and mutually respectful in its orientation. Now we come to the Tribe with its strong communal structure founded on loyalty to a hierarchical chain of command. The Ego Circuit builds a protective support system around the Tribe like a wall and labels everyone on the other side outsiders, while the Defense Circuit succeeds in pulling even the most strident outsider into the bonds of communal living with its penetrating intimacy, and its promise to nurture and educate.

The Spleen's instinctual survival awareness relays messages through the senses, particularly smell, touch and taste. This awareness compliments and focuses the Tribe's extraordinary capacity for personal loyalty and sexual intimacy. It is also what guides the ways communal expectations and support are expressed. For example, the famous family recipe that is handed down as a form of family identity, the handshake or kiss that seals a deal, and the blood bond between best friends.

The Tribe's most distinguishing characteristic is the bargain, or making deals that guarantee support. "I'll scratch your back if you scratch mine. I'll clean the house and feed the children if you go out and work to make money for the family." The bargain, which permeates all channels in Tribal circuitry, imposes or pre-supposes loyalty to a larger, hierarchical system of rulership and values. "I will see that you are protected from invaders if you pay me homage and taxes." Tribal bargaining ensured our species' survival. Throughout history, the Tribe has been the bedrock that held us together as a family unit or a nation. It has determined for us how to raise our children, choose a vocation, make the laws and police our streets, and worship our gods. Without the Tribe, we would not have been able to look after ourselves within a society. It gave each of us a place in its support net, and as long as we stayed in our place and made our contribution, it kept us safe.

THE DEFENSE CIRCUIT
KEYNOTE: SUPPORT

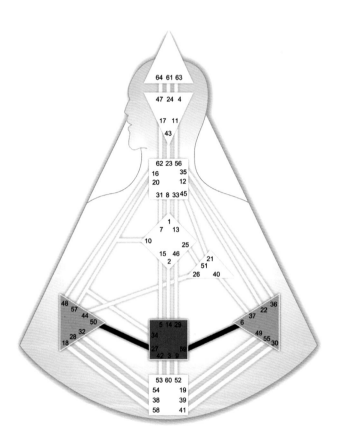

CHANNELS:

59 – 6	**MATING**	
	Focused on reproduction	
27 – 50	**PRESERVATION**	
	Custodianship	

The Defense Circuit is comprised of the Channel of Intimacy (reproduction) and the Channel of Preservation (taking care of what we have produced). The visual image of a cradle that the Defense Circuit forms in the BodyGraph is an apt metaphor for its generative and nurturing role in ensuring humanity's future through the creation and preservation of life on the planet. The Defense Circuit's genetic program, described as the origin of the theory of the selfish gene, promotes the continuation of our species. It often does so, however, at the expense of our personal life. Nothing drives humanity like the Channel of Intimacy's (59-6) genetic imperative to make more. The emotional wave that in part powers this imperative is not yet aware, and in its blindness can leave chaos in its wake.

Children are one by-product of this unstable emotional mechanism for perpetuating life on the planet. The Channel of Preservation (27–50) grounds the Tribe's survival in Splenic awareness, with the sobering reminder that we are responsible for nurturing and preserving that which the emotional/experiential Channel of Intimacy has created or generated. In this way, offspring will reach adulthood and can in turn produce more, keeping the gene pool viable so that our bio-form can keep going. This is the Tribe's major contribution to evolving consciousness; no other circuit or circuit group carries this genetic imperative or is equipped to nurture what it creates like the Tribe.

The Channels and Gates of the Defense Circuit are discussed on the following pages.

THE CHANNEL OF MATING: 59 - 6
A Design Focused on Reproduction
Circuit: Defense (Creative Channel)   Channel Type: Generated

The Channel of Mating links the Sacral Center to the Solar Plexus Center through the Gate of Sexuality (59) and the Gate of Friction (6). Channel 59-6, the core of humanity's creative essence, is rooted in a powerful quantum of Sacral and emotional energy called 'intimacy.' The sexuality of Gate 59, and the pleasure/pain emotional wave of Gate 6, bring people into relationships that are deeply personal, penetrating and potentially fertile.

Background: A defined Solar Plexus is always one's Authority, and the emotional wave requires that one wait to find clarity over time. If the Channel of Mating is conditioned by not-self spontaneity and ignores its Sacral response, it can create confusion and greatly complicate social interactions. There can also be long-term repercussions such as an unwanted child or a failed business venture. The true intimacy potential in this Tribal channel requires patience and nurturing over time. For that reason it is healthiest to cultivate a friendship with business partners or lovers first, before diving into the depths of an intimate union with them.

Personal: Yours is the urge to merge, and when guided by response over time this can be healthy and deeply satisfying on many levels. Your own availability to intimacy allows you to quickly and easily penetrate the auras of others, facilitating a coziness that paves the way for fertility in any creative endeavor. This is your natural state, and a true asset for establishing relationships of any kind. You can also be misunderstood, and your intensity misinterpreted by others who may feel you are flirting or 'coming on' to them when you don't mean to. Your emotional wave, through Gate 6, determines the actual timing of any intimate emotional release by either drawing you closer or pushing you away. Waiting out your wave's cycle allows you to discern or discover over time if something has been conceived between the two of you – and if it hasn't, the wave may draw you together again.

Interpersonal: Although designed to experience a potent emotional wave, those with the Channel of Mating can actually appear quite stable emotionally. Their wave is activated or brought to the point of response by the proximity or touch of another person. A well-timed hug, or hand on the shoulder, at just the right point on their wave helps them release pent up emotions that cannot be released through words. This is a form of intimacy that can be expressed through tears, a heart-felt sigh or by deeply relaxing into someone's understanding embrace. Doing so maintains a healthy sense of emotional balance between stronger (sexual) emotional releases. Channel 59-6 is best experienced as an electromagnetic connection between two people, when each partner has one of the gates.

GATE 59: DISPERSION - THE GATE OF SEXUALITY
– The ability to break down barriers to achieve union –
Center: Sacral   Quarter: Duality   Theme: Purpose fulfilled through Bonding
RAC of the Sleeping Phoenix – JC of Strategy – LAC of Spirit

Gate 59 generates our genetic strategies for sexual bonding and creating new life. Also known as the "aura breaker," it defines the ways we penetrate or break through barriers to intimacy in order to create offspring, or enter into a creative business venture with someone. The lines of Gate 59 (listed below) describe the ways humanity approaches bonding. They are genetic strategies, and each role is singularly focused on selecting the best partner for producing the most viable offspring. The 4th line, requires you to become friends first, for example, and one-night stands, which are correct for the 6th line, would not be an option for you. The only real choice you have in this matter is to enter into each intimate relationship through your Authority. Tribal intimacy is warm and deeply felt; it's an intimacy beyond words intensified by your sensitivity to the other through touch, taste and smell. Unless you pay attention to your Authority and understand the genetic strategies (roles) of Gate 59, as well as the part that Gate 6's emotional wave plays, intimacy can bring anything from confusion and conflict to unproductive unions. You may find yourself automatically looking to someone with Gate 6 to guide the timing of your interactions.

Line 6 - The One Night Stand	Line 3 - Openness
Line 5 - The Femme Fatale/Casanova	Line 2 - Shyness
Line 4 - Brotherhood/Sisterhood	Line 1 - The Preemptive Strike

---

GATE 6: CONFLICT - THE GATE OF FRICTION
– The fundamental design component of progress. The law that growth cannot exist without friction –
Center: Solar Plexus   Quarter: Duality   Theme: Purpose fulfilled through Bonding
RAC of Eden – JC of Conflict – LAC of the Plane

Gate 6 in the Solar Plexus Center generates all three modes of emotional awareness: feelings, moods and sensitivity. This is a powerful motorized combination on a wave that is designed to create friction. This friction produces the heat essential for growth and fertility, and is aimed at Gate 59. The friction you create when you step into another person's aura is a mechanic. If (or when) the conflict is resolved, or resonance is reached, there is then an opening and intimacy can proceed. Until there is such an opening, you must wait, as readiness and fertility are both subject to the emotional wave. Gate 6 is a kind of diaphragm that is either opens up to intimacy or closes. It is the gate of your pH, and establishes and maintains the boundary between what is outside and what is inside your body. In this way it determines who to be intimate with, when, and the bonding role you will play. Each time you feel drawn toward intimacy, let your Strategy and Authority be your guides. Each gate in the Solar Plexus carries a fear. The fear associated with the 6th gate is the fear of intimacy, which is why Gate 6 looks to Gate 59 with its ability to break down the barriers to intimacy.

Line 6 - The Peacemaker	Line 3 - Allegiance
Line 5 - Arbitration	Line 2 - The Guerilla
Line 4 - Triumph	Line 1 - Retreat

THE CHANNEL OF PRESERVATION: 27 - 50
A Design of Custodianship
Circuit: Defense   Channel Type: Generated

The Channel of Preservation links the Sacral Center to the Splenic Center through the Gate of Caring (27) and the Gate of Values (50). The quality and substance of all Tribal activities are enhanced through the care and nurturing of Gate 27 with its altruistic concern for others. The traditional values and laws of the Tribe that are needed to maintain order, and to enrich, guide and guard life, originate with Gate 50. Channel 27-50 creates the many levels of custodianship that are needed to care for, protect and preserve the Tribe and its creative ventures.

Background: The Sacral energies of Channel 59-6, subject to the warm, emotional intimacy of the Solar Plexus wave, are focused on creation and procreation. Once the offspring are born, the Sacral's immediate response to their vulnerability arouses the strong and spontaneous survival instincts of the Spleen with its cool realization that we must care for what we have created. In this way, the warm experiential side of the BodyGraph is balanced by existential awareness, and the need to guard or accept responsibility for those who cannot take care of themselves. This level of support is necessary if the Tribe, and what it stands for, is to endure.

Personal: You are someone whose aura automatically elicits trust from others, and people naturally look to you for support and nurturing. Support through this channel can take many forms, from establishing and defending the values and laws of the land and being a conscience for the Tribe, to attending to the upbringing of youngsters or caring for the sick and elderly. You are capable of assuming a lot of responsibility, and are susceptible to taking on too much. Although you are a natural nurturer, the only way that you will know if you are taking on the correct responsibility is through your Strategy and Authority. With a wisdom rooted in ancient awareness informing your altruism and compassion, you innately understand that nurture begins with the correct care of yourself first. Only the strong and healthy can nurture and guide others toward survival, improved health or success. This is called 'enlightened selfishness,' and though it may be perceived as self-indulgence, it is quite different. If someone wants your care, they must ask for it. It is only through your response that you can know if your energy is available, and if it is correct for you to give it.

Interpersonal: Channel 27-50 has two strong defense mechanisms. Gate 50 instinctually pays close attention to the continuity of the Tribe. It creates, defends or challenges the fundamental values and laws governing communal relationships which are responsible for maintaining and protecting the well-being of all who live in a supportive, hierarchical community. Through Gate 27, our children are nurtured, educated, healed of conditioning, and taught the value of communal support so that they can survive long enough to create and nurture the next generation. Nurturing isn't limited to supporting children; the needs of our elders must also be addressed, and their wisdom harvested and chronicled. Everything in the world needs nurture and care, including the preservation of the infrastructure of our communities.

GATE 27: NOURISHMENT - THE GATE OF CARING
– The enhancement of the quality and the substance of all activities through caring –
Center: Sacral   Quarter: Initiation   Theme: Purpose fulfilled through Mind
RAC of the Unexpected – JC of Caring – LAC of Alignment

The energy of the 27th gate is focused on maintaining and enhancing the quality of life through the power to care for the weak, the sick and the young. There is tremendous potential for altruism present in this gate, which we see exemplified in the life of Mother Teresa. Your role is to nourish and nurture through the power of compassion; you care. The polarity is that you must also be nourished and nurtured yourself. You must care for yourself first in order to have the energy and resources to care for others, and then let your Authority guide you to where and when you commit your energy. Nourishment or nurturing given without awareness is a waste of precious resources. Each line of this gate represents a way to connect to and care for the Tribe according to different levels of need. Without Gate 50, you may lack the instinct and values to set healthy boundaries around your natural impulse to care for others, and easily end up sacrificing yourself or your own well-being.

Line 6 - Wariness	Line 3 - Greed
Line 5 - The Executor	Line 2 - Self-Sufficiency
Line 4 - Generosity	Line 1 - Selfishness

GATE 50: THE CAULDRON - THE GATE OF VALUES
– The value of historical continuity whose traditional values serve and enrich the present and future –
Center: Spleen   Quarter: Duality   Theme: Purpose fulfilled through Bonding
RAC of Laws – JC of Values – LAC of Wishes

Each act of intimacy that results in a birth demands that the offspring of the union be nurtured into adulthood. Gate 50's mystical name is the Guardian. As the Tribal lawmaker, it establishes what is right or wrong. This is how and where the rules for caring become the source of moral conditioning for our children. At the core of the Tribe's defenses lies the Spleen's fear-driven mandate to maintain its own viability by protecting and guiding its young. You are one who is here to guard the values and integrity of Tribal law, and the structures that uphold the well-being of the community. Based on the specific line (see below), your task is to be cognizant of which values or laws or rules safeguard how the Tribe cares for its own. Your instinctual awareness scrutinizes which are corrupt or unjust, unnecessary or self-serving, or need to be challenged and changed. This is your way of caring for and nurturing every aspect of life within the Tribe. Without Gate 27 you may try to physically take care of others when it is not correct for you to do so, thus fulfilling your fear of taking on responsibility that you aren't equipped to handle.

Line 6 - Leadership	Line 3 - Adaptability
Line 5 - Consistency	Line 2 - Determination
Line 4 - Corruption	Line 1 - The Immigrant

THE EGO CIRCUIT
KEYNOTE: SUPPORT

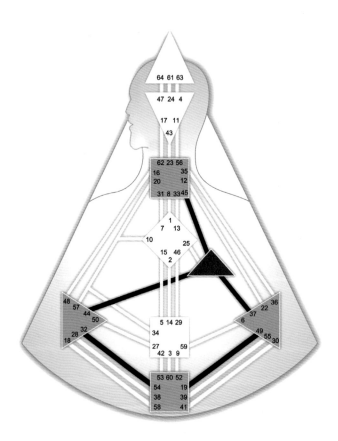

CHANNELS:

54 – 32   TRANSFORMATION
Being driven

44 – 26   SURRENDER
A transmitter

19 – 49   SYNTHESIS
Sensitivity

37 – 40   COMMUNITY
A part seeking a whole

21 – 45   MONEY
A materialist

The Ego Circuit protectively surrounds the Defense Circuit. Understanding the material and communal forces of support with which the Ego Circuit sustains the fertile and nurturing processes of the Defense Circuit, gives us a clearer sense of the nature and scope of the Tribe's contribution to our evolution.

On its own, the Ego Circuit has no defined Sacral or life-generating capacity, nor does it have any connection to mental awareness (Ajna Center). The Ego Circuit's hub is the Heart or Ego Center. The central focus of this circuit's five channels is the Ego's willpower, namely the will to go out into the world and provide for its own in exchange for deserved rest.

Through the Ego Circuit, we can follow the development of two philosophically divergent points of view that begin in the Root and meet in the Tribal heart (Ego Center). Each view defines one of two forces of Tribal support. On one side we experience the Spiritual dimension of communal life where the core unit is the inter-generational family, traditionally viewed as a hierarchical blood-bond relationship. On the other side we find the ambition and materialism needed to ensure the entrepreneur's success. It is in this circuit that the mysteries of the mystical are cultivated alongside the essentially material and mundane. The Ego Circuit is also where we find the pragmatism of capitalism, and the ideals of socialism and communalism.

Together, these two views point to an underlying truth waiting to be discovered in the Ego Circuit – spirit is hidden in the mundane. Living as our authentic selves each moment of our mundane lives becomes a beautiful process quietly revealing our constant connection with the spirit of the whole.

The Channels and Gates of the Ego Circuit are discussed on the following pages.

THE CHANNEL OF TRANSFORMATION: 54 - 32
A Design of Being Driven
Circuit: Ego   Channel Type: Projected

The Channel of Transformation links the Root Center to the Splenic Center through the Gate of Drive (54) and the Gate of Continuity (32). Channel 54-32 represents ambition fueled by consistent effort, and motivated by the desire to be recognized in order to better one's position in life. The potential awareness of what can and cannot be transformed, sometimes distorted by a fear of failure, is driven by the fuel for social interactions that can move one up the ladder.

Background: The Channel of Transformation carries an energetic potential through which people with talent or ability can pull themselves up by their bootstraps, and move out of the social class they were born into. Gate 32 is always on the lookout for talent. It is driven by the fears that its Tribe may not be able to compete with the best, or survive the next economic downturn thereby failing to endure. This recognition of the fragility of the Tribe's existence shapes Channel 54-32's ambition; its desire to rise up and transform. There is also a mystical thread, the thread of spirit, woven into it through Gate 54's 4th line: Enlightenment/Endarkenment, the fuel for transformation at its purest level.

Personal: Rooted in and grounded by the Tribe's dedication to service and self-sacrifice, transformation is best defined here in its Tribal context. Tribal support begins when your talents are recognized, and your efforts are encouraged, through what is reflected back to you by those you have helped to fulfill their ambitions or attain enlightenment. Your reward for loyalty and dedication to the Tribe comes through each promotion to the next level. You willingly work harder than anyone else to prove your worth or value, even to the point of becoming a workaholic. Your true goal is to experience this drive for recognition as a healthy interdependence that is mutually beneficial. Your instincts have the potential to bring you to a vocation through which you might fulfill your potential, achieve your ambitions, and utilize your gift for making money so that you can use your unique abilities to assist others in reaching their potential.

Interpersonal: The ambition that constitutes transformation in the material world is guided by Splenic awareness. It's by instinct that one with this channel recognizes if or when needed support is available for increasing one's wealth, or to ensure success through personal advancement. The pressure to make more money continually transforms the world economy. In the end, only transformation that endures over time has value, and creating such continuity requires the support of the Tribe. Even in today's global society, supportive allies are crucial for a nation to realize its financial goals and ambitions. Transformation is not something that we do on our own, and moving up the ladder is always dependent upon and accompanied by the expectations of those above us. If a person with Channel 54-32 is properly recognized and supported by the Tribe, then the Tribe expects *quid pro quo*, a reciprocal return for what it has provided. This is how the Tribal system endures.

GATE 54: THE MARRYING MAIDEN - THE GATE OF DRIVE
– Interaction in its mundane social context but also one's mystical and cosmic relationships –
Center: Root   Quarter: Mutation   Theme: Purpose fulfilled through Transformation
RAC of Penetration – JC of Ambition – LAC of Cycles

Gate 54 provides humanity with the fuel and ambition to transform the Tribe's material direction and standing among other tribes. It supplies the energy for our most mundane ambitions, and the highest spiritual aspirations that may be hidden within them. Only when we have mastered our instincts to thrive on the mundane plane, is transformation of a spiritual nature possible. You live your spiritual ideals through the mundane plane, and ambition is the fulfillment of your personal potential. If you are noticed by someone higher up in the hierarchy, there is a good chance that you can better your position in life. Your inner drive to 'rise up' provides the impetus for transformation for those around you as well; it levels the playing field for others to compete on equal terms. Your drive needs direction, however, so you naturally look to someone with Gate 32 to channel your ambitions toward something of lasting value. Without this direction, your drive may turn into blind ambition.

Line 6 - Selectivity	Line 3 - Covert Interaction
Line 5 - Magnanimity	Line 2 - Discretion
Line 4 - Enlightenment/Endarkenment	Line 1 - Influence

GATE 32: DURATION - THE GATE OF CONTINUITY
– The only thing which endures is change –
Center: Spleen   Quarter: Duality   Theme: Purpose fulfilled through Bonding
RAC of Maia – JC of Conservation – LAC of Limitation

Awareness through Gate 32 is focused on constant evaluation as an instinctive recognition of what can and cannot be transformed. An underlying fear of failure can put the brakes on runaway ambition. Gate 32's ability to adapt, yet maintain its true nature, is the Spleen's contribution to the material continuity of the Tribe. This is part of your contribution as well. A great deal rests on what is recognized and valued, and thereby encouraged and retained by the Tribe. One of your gifts is recognizing who has the skills or education to move up in the world; and then, using your influence, to bring them to the attention of those in positions of authority. This is the gate of prolonged indecision. You are apt to find yourself agonizing over how to maintain a balance between what is working successfully (conservatism), and opening yourself or an organization up to the unknown risks (fear of failure) that accompany transformation and change. Change is inevitable, however, and when it becomes part of the equation for life, growth is optimized. By relying on your Authority for timing, and staying closely attuned to your own instincts, your wisdom will emerge over time as ways to keep society from repeating what does not work, while also embracing what has lasting value. Without Gate 54 the 32nd gate senses its lack of a consistent source of fuel or drive or ambition to succeed.

Line 6 - Tranquility	Line 3 - Lack of Continuity
Line 5 - Flexibility	Line 2 - Restraint
Line 4 - Right is Might	Line 1 - Conservation

THE CHANNEL OF SURRENDER: 44 - 26
A Design of a Transmitter
Circuit: Ego (Creative Channel)   Channel Type: Projected

The Channel of Surrender links the Splenic Center to the Heart Center through the Gate of Alertness (44) and the Gate of the Egoist (26). Here we find deep Tribal memory, rooted in instinctual awareness/intelligence, joined to ego strength. It is this combination that gives a transmitter the ability to selectively and persuasively use historical memory to sell something to a targeted group of people that supposedly constitutes an improvement. Channel 44-26 is the capitalist engaged in the creative art of enterprise.

Background: As the only direct link between the Heart Center and the Splenic Center, Channel 44-26 forms one of the main health networks in the body. The 26th gate correlates to the Thymus Gland where our immune system is formed prenatally. Essentially, this channel is instinctually alert for and willing to address whatever poses a threat, or needs improving or replacing in order to keep the Tribe viable. People with this channel exercise their will to manipulate the Tribe for its own good, using their nose or sense for what people might need even before they know they need it.

Personal: You have a gift for instinctually assessing others, and for matching them with products, jobs, and even ideologies. In exchange for this work, you will demand what you feel is fair for yourself, and it must include a healthy balance of rest and work. You are not one who is designed to work eight hours a day in an office, but will accomplish more in a compressed amount of time than most people will in the entire day. You can trust your instinct to guide you in life, and if something about a person or a project you are dealing with doesn't 'smell' right, don't engage with them.

The shape of the bargain is different on the left side of the Ego Circuit than on the right. It changes from, "I will do this for you if you do this for me," to "I am selling this amazing new gadget, and if you want it, it's yours for only $12.95." You are an entrepreneur who is part of a team, and all the team members must be paid. You are the promoter/salesperson on the frontline, bringing in money that is then apportioned down the line to each member of the production team. Whether the team likes you (and your tactics) or not, is dependent on the resources you generate for them. This channel often works best when you wait until the market or your tribe recognizes your gifts, pledges its support to you, and asks you to promote yourself or your product on their behalf. This recognition gives you a platform from which to speak – especially if you are a politician.

Interpersonal: Transmitters intuit which form of persuasion will effectively relay their message, and they can spontaneously adjust their advertising or sales pitch to meet changing markets and situations. The creative gifts of this channel include a sense of what will appeal to the Tribe, and how to manipulate or massage the egos of others into wanting what they are selling. This can be a valuable asset for the filmmaker, sales representative, graphic designer, advertising executive, politician and diplomat.

GATE 44: COMING TO MEET - THE GATE OF ALERTNESS
– The success of any interaction is based on the absence of any preconditions –
Center: Spleen   Quarter: Duality   Theme: Purpose fulfilled through Bonding
RAC of the Four Ways – JC of Alertness – LAC of Incarnation

Gate 44 is the gate of memory; it remembers the patterns for living that have successfully provided for our material needs. This memory is an integral and consistently trustworthy part of our survival intelligence as a species. You are instinctually alert in every moment for the correct spontaneous relationship or interaction that can move a potential to the level of a possibility. What you remember or transmit shapes the Tribes' material orientation, and eventually strengthens its ego presence and power in the world. You control the way Gate 26 is going to act in terms of selling, defending or fighting for the tribe. This is where tribal propaganda can be found. You help the Tribe to allay its fears of the past by remembering that a starving child is not a healthy child, and that material security and health go hand in hand. The Spleen is not a motor, so once your awareness is recognized and valued by the Tribe, you will look to the willpower of Gate 26 to act on it. In this way, whatever transformation you instinctively know the Tribe needs to ensure its survival becomes a reality. Without Gate 26 you are prone to unnecessarily exaggerate by over-committing and making promises you cannot keep. What you fear most is that baggage from the past might catch up with you.

Line 6 - Aloofness	Line 3 - Interference
Line 5 - Manipulation	Line 2 - Management
Line 4 - Honesty	Line 1 - Conditions

GATE 26: THE TAMING POWER OF THE GREAT - THE GATE OF THE EGOIST
– The maximization of the power of memory applied to the nurturing of continuity –
Center: Heart   Quarter: Mutation   Theme: Purpose fulfilled through Transformation
RAC of Rulership – JC of The Trickster – LAC of Confrontation

Gate 26 is where memory is manipulated, or where the past is selectively remembered, in order to persuade or distract us from our fears. The line between the truth and a lie blurs, and potential and possibility are transformed into reality and 'sold' to the public – for a price. You are a natural salesperson who is actually expected to exaggerate, and your innate ability to manipulate memory, coupled with the energy of your ego, is designed to withstand rejection. If you are recognized for these skills, given a job where you can set your own schedule, are sufficiently rewarded materially, and can maintain a healthy balance between rest and work, you are eager to be on the front lines for the Tribe and have the ego to do it. Waiting to be recognized, and only making promises that you can keep, allows you to maintain your influence with others. Maintaining the integrity of your persuasive powers and keeping the promises you make actually strengthen your ego and your physical heart's health. Without Gate 44's instinctive awareness, it can be difficult to know how, when, and what to effectively transmit.

Line 6 - Authority	Line 3 - Influence
Line 5 - Adaptability	Line 2 - The Lessons of History
Line 4 - Censorship	Line 1 - A Bird in the Hand

THE CHANNEL OF SYNTHESIS: 19 - 49
A Design of Sensitivity
Circuit: Ego   Channel Type: Projected

The Channel of Synthesis links the Root Center to the Solar Plexus Center through the Gate of Wanting (19) and the Gate of Principles (49). Tribal forms of mysticism evolved through the pressure of humanity's need for food, shelter, protection, territory, something to believe in, and something to hold everything together. The 19th gate pressures us to approach each other and manifest the interrelatedness of the Tribe, while the 49th gate prods us to reject that which is not compatible with our highest ideals, and supportive of our connection to each other and spirit.

Background: Sensitivity to need is rooted in touch, such as sealing the bargain with a handshake, and is found on the emotional side of the Ego Circuit in the realm of belonging. This sensitivity is the Tribe's foundation for marriage and bonding, and for divorce. The emotional acceptance or rejection frequency of Channel 19-49 is the glue that determines who belongs and is deserving of the support of the Tribe; who gets to come to the table and who doesn't. There is nothing logical (democratic) or abstract (experiential) in this frequency, and it cannot simply be super-imposed on the Tribe as forcing it won't work. The code of the Tribe, expressed as "love, honor and obey," is what bonds the Tribe together. Every member of the tribe owes their life to the life of every other member. In exchange, one is promised their basic needs will be met. Loyalty is one key to the Tribe's survival, but here that loyalty is governed by an emotional wave.

Personal: You are very sensitive to your own position in the scheme of things. Wanting to be needed and to give support, and/or needing to be wanted and be supported, is critical to your happiness. The family, however it is defined, is your enterprise and you are willing to do the necessary inner work to make it a success. For example, taking time to explore the depth and impact of your emotional wave on your potential partner through a long courtship, before committing to the intimacy and responsibility of cohabitation, or marriage and raising a family. The three most important needs for you within your tribe are the protection of resources, the sanctity of your territory, and a clear understanding of your tribe's belief system. Your potential gift is to be recognized as someone who can always balance practicality and fairness.

Interpersonal: Channel 19-49 begins the evolution of social communion by establishing the principles for the marriage relationship (which is later cemented by the marriage bond in Channel 37-40, the Channel of Community.) As the archetype of the bride and groom, this channel has a frequency that holds the family together; it is the origination point for the Tribe's unifying traditions, rituals and celebrations. The tradition of the dowry, for example, provides a material foundation for the union so the couple can focus on producing and raising offspring. The Root Center exerts pressure through Gate 19 to connect to others in ways that bring joy and happiness. When dominated by the not-self, this channel is characterized by constant and inappropriate rejection, both of self and others. Channel 19-49 forms a cross-species connection between mammals and humans, enabling us to domesticate and train them to work the land, be companions, and provide us with food. This connection is also where we find the ritual sacrifice of animals to appease the gods and gain favor.

GATE 19: APPROACH - THE GATE OF WANTING

– That all things are interrelated is apparent and manifested through the action of approach –
Center: Root   Quarter: Mutation   Theme: Purpose fulfilled through Transformation
RAC of the Four Ways – JC of Need – LAC of Refinement

Gate 19 fuels two essential human mandates: the need to have access to basic resources like food and shelter, and the need for spirit. These mandates set us up to interact or bond with others in specific ways. When everyone has enough to eat, a place to live and a god to worship, we experience life as one healthy community, supporting each other and making our unique contribution to the whole. When there is want or need or great inequality in our tribe, communal support breaks down and nothing works. You are here to be alert and sensitive to which resources are being withheld from your family, community and eventually the global community. You bring others to an awareness of what resources are needed for everyone to survive, as well as thrive and achieve their personal or communal potential. The way you go about this depends on the specific line(s) defined in your chart, but the process usually requires enticing or bargaining with the people or institutions who share your principles, and possess or control what is needed. You know what is needed, and you look to Gate 49 to fulfill those needs. The consequences of turning the Root Center's pressure inward are experienced as oversensitivity, an addiction to being needed, or personal neediness as in "Doesn't anyone care about me? When will I get my needs met?"

Line 6 - The Recluse	Line 3 - Dedication
Line 5 - Sacrifice	Line 2 - Service
Line 4 - The Team Player	Line 1 - Interdependence

GATE 49: REVOLUTION - THE GATE OF PRINCIPLES

– Ideally the transformation of forms based on the highest principles and not simply for power –
Center: Solar Plexus   Quarter: Initiation   Theme: Purpose fulfilled through Mind
RAC of Explanation – JC of Principles – LAC of Revolution

The principles of acceptance and rejection, marriage and divorce, and ultimately revolution, are the direct result of living with Tribal hierarchies influenced by the emotional wave. Because Gate 49 places you at the top of one of these hierarchies, you feel a need to be obeyed. This translates into you exerting the power to accept or reject a person, or their request for access to your resources, or their appeal to initiate a revolution on their own or someone else's behalf. Your sensitivity or insensitivity towards other people (and animals), and their specific needs, is based on a resonance with your own principles. In other words, the people you accept into your circle are those willing to stand by you and support your principles; the rest you will be inclined to reject. Yours is a social agenda for change and reformation. It is particularly focused on food and food distribution; people who have enough to eat don't need to go to war. Revolution is either avoided by filling needs, or entered into as a necessary evil and last resort. You might be the one whose acceptance or rejection influences which road is taken to satisfy the needy party. The things that make you nervous are the fear of rejection and the consequences of unpredictability.

Line 6 - Attraction	Line 3 - Popular Discontent
Line 5 - Organization	Line 2 - The Last Resort
Line 4 - Platform	Line 1 - The Law of Necessity

THE CHANNEL OF COMMUNITY: 37 - 40
A Design of a Part seeking a Whole
Circuit: Ego   Channel Type: Projected

The Channel of Community links the Solar Plexus Center to the Heart Center through the Gate of Friendship (37) and the Gate of Aloneness (40). Community lies at the heart of humanity's successful evolution. The organic nature of community, and the transition point it provides between the struggle to survive and liberation from that struggle, is subject to the push-pull of the emotional wave. Gate 40 is willing to work to provide for those it loves, but it needs its rewards and its rest. Gate 37, with its gift of affection, is always looking for recognition and its place within the whole.

Background: In the Channel of Community, the Tribal bargain is backed by the energy of two powerful motors that give it depth through clarity over time, and the will power to succeed. In community, the bargain must be entered into correctly. The bond of community or family, and the way the bond will manifest in the future, is guaranteed by the will power behind the bargain. The alignment of the Ego and Solar Plexus Centers also means that no good bargain can be struck spontaneously, and must be carefully considered and formulated over time to be equally beneficial for both parties. Channel 37-40 is an opposition in the Mandala and so is quite common. It has had tremendous evolutionary influence worldwide during this present Earth Cycle (1615-2027), where we have all felt its impact under the Right Angle Cross of Planning.

Personal: If defined by Channel 37-40, you are waiting to see who asks you to be part of their organization or community, or not. You are also trying to discover where you belong, or how you fit into the big picture spiritually. The correct invitation won't come through impersonal contact though, like a phone call, but rather through some form of 'touch,' or direct personal contact over a period of time. In the most basic sense, every human being is existentially alone and yet, for practical purposes, you are the one who forms the bridge for individuals to live in a community where all have an honored place and respected function. You understand the importance of making a good bargain, and how to seal that bargain. "I'll do this for you if you'll do that for me. Let's shake on it, or sign here."

Interpersonal: A strong, adaptable and clear bargain is needed if the Channel of Community, the channel of the marriage bond, is to hold the provider and distributor together in a harmonious relationship. On this side of the Ego Circuit, the way to a man's heart is through his stomach, not his wallet. On the emotional/social side of the BodyGraph, support is expressed not by things money can buy, but by what it takes to work side by side and to progress communally. Investment is focused not on stocks and bonds, but on each other and on the needs of the whole group. This is the highest ideal of community, and there is little evidence of hierarchy. No one feels superior or inferior because everyone willingly contributes what they can in order to be included, and to feel supported by and loyal to a group greater than themselves.

GATE 37: THE FAMILY - THE GATE OF FRIENDSHIP
– The manifestation macro and micro-cosmically of the organic nature of communities –
Center: Solar Plexus   Quarter: Initiation   Theme: Purpose fulfilled through Mind
RAC of Planning – JC of Bargains – LAC of Migration

Gate 37 is the most communal gate in the BodyGraph. When your power is recognized by others, you can hold both a family and a community together with your warmth, friendliness and nurturing nature. You have an ability to make an emotional connection with others through touch, and an uncommon sensitivity which senses their accessibility or openness to you. People will want you to be their organization's representative, and to welcome the newcomer or stranger. It is an offer that you might happily agree to if the bargain, or what you receive in return, is sufficient and clearly agreed upon by all parties. Gate 37 is the gate of the mouth so the planning, gathering and preparing of food often play a central role in all your family and community gatherings. In the bargain between Gates 37 and 40, Gate 40 is the willing provider and you are the distributor of its assets and skills. Without Gate 40, you are looking for those who can deliver the resources needed by the community so that you have someone to bargain with, and something to distribute. What you most fear is getting trapped in or having to live up to the traditional Tribal roles.

Line 6 - Purpose	Line 3 - Evenhandedness
Line 5 - Love	Line 2 - Responsibility
Line 4 - Leadership by Example	Line 1 - The Mother/Father

GATE 40: DELIVERANCE - THE GATE OF ALONENESS
– The point of transition between struggle and liberation –
Center: Heart   Quarter: Duality   Theme: Purpose fulfilled through Bonding
RAC of Planning – JC of Denial – LAC of Migration

Gate 40 is one of three gates of aloneness (12 and 33 are the other two), and carries a sense of being alone even when in a group of people. This aloneness is the beginning of the individuation process; you need to separate yourself from the Tribe. In essence, it is the desire within you for wholeness, expressed and experienced by others as your strong independence, or as stepping away from their interdependence. This is an aspect of the ego's willpower that is essential to the survival of community. Gate 40 is the love of work, and when you are involved in work that is correct for you, you derive great satisfaction from delivering what you promised to an appreciative Tribe. The relationship bargain needs to be renegotiated often and kept crystal clear. Yes, you are willing to work and to exert your ego's will power to provide for your family or community, but they get access to your earned resources only if they keep their side of the bargain. They need to show appreciation and loyalty for your efforts and support you emotionally, feed you, give you time alone to rest, and take care of you with the resources you provide for them. Without Gate 37, you may find yourself looking for friendship, and a community to offer your ego's willing provisions to.

Line 6 - Decapitation	Line 3 - Humility
Line 5 - Rigidity	Line 2 - Resoluteness
Line 4 - Organization	Line 1 - Recuperation

THE CHANNEL OF MONEY: 21 - 45
A Design of a Materialist
Circuit: Ego   Channel Type: Manifested

The Channel of the Money Line links the Heart Center to the Throat Center through the Gate of the Hunter/Huntress (21) and the Gate of the Gatherer (45). The heart of the Tribe, of our life together on the planet, is the Ego Center with its connection to the heart muscle. This is the Tribe's solitary voice, and it expresses its authority and will to survive on the material plane as a hierarchy.

Background: Channel 21-45 is the most driven of all Manifestor channels and says, "It's up to me to take charge, to be in control or not." The most benevolent expression of Tribal leadership is to gather, protect and educate the tribe so that it survives. When everyone has been provided enough support to enjoy life together, there is peace in the kingdom. Gate 45, the Tribe's only voice, is the voice of authority and the final voice of what is or isn't manifested. Its keynote says it well: "I have or I don't have." The Tribe has always coveted access to resources (money), and a reliable commitment (loyalty). In manifesting its pursuit of these desires, and mediated by the bargain, the Tribe has dominated the affairs of human history. The two gates that make up Channel 21-45 are not easily reconciled to each other. Gate 45 protects but wants the last word, and Gate 21 serves but needs to be in control in order to guarantee its heart can rest, and/or to guarantee that others get their rest. Historically, this need for a balance between work and rest was the impetus behind unions ensuring workers' rights.

Personal: You are here to embrace and master the material plane, and to make money through the power of your will. Your challenge is to exert your will in a way that protects your own interests, while still serving others. Having control and not being controlled are issues for you, and the secret to your success lies in attaining a measure of independence. You are willing to work hard, but you work best when you are your own boss and can follow your own natural rhythm by controlling what you do and when you do it. Even when you are not in control of everything around you, you need to feel as though you are, such as acting as both the CEO and President of the company. It can be difficult for you to rely on people and delegate responsibility, which can add to your work load and stress your heart.

Interpersonal: Materialists like putting money to work. To become masters of the material plane and provide for the good of their tribe, they need their tribe's full support and cooperation. We can see this in action as we follow the evolution of our economic structures from simple trading between villages to the complex corporate business models and stock markets of today. The Channel of Money is actually much more successful as an electromagnetic connection between two people. The 45th gate owns the factory but doesn't work there. The 21st gate is the president with a large, active ego who says, "I must benefit myself but at the same time I must benefit the owner and our constituents." Together they control or manage the organization so that everyone achieves a measure of financial success. Another example would be Gate 21 as the prime minister in charge of running the country and advocating for the people, with Gate 45 as the king who conveys his authority to the prime minister and must be paid his due.

GATE 21: BITING THROUGH - THE GATE OF THE HUNTER/HUNTRESS
– The justified and necessary use of power in overcoming deliberate and persistent interference –
Center: Heart   Quarter: Initiation   Theme: Purpose fulfilled through Mind
RAC of Tension – JC of Control – LAC of Endeavor

The 21st gate needs to be in control of its domain. In order to apply the strength and will of its ego to insure the survival of the Tribe, it must have control over something or someone. In our modern world, this energy translates into the responsibilities given to the police, or managing director or president of a company. Biting Through is a powerful conditioning force for life on the material plane. You are successful when you can control your own material resources, where you live, what you wear, whom you work for and how you make your living. You do not like to be told what to do or to have people looking over your shoulder. On the other hand, you are destined to serve others because in a Tribal bargain all must benefit if you are to benefit yourself. If you attempt to assume power, or to control others without following your Strategy and Authority, you will encounter forceful resistance. Regardless of the benefits of your intentions, you must wait until you are offered control. If you are a Projector, you need to be with people who recognize and invite your ability to control; if you are a Generator, you have to be asked for access to your Sacral energy so you can respond; and if you are a Manifestor, you have to inform before you attempt to exert control and thus measure the resistance field. Without Gate 45 you will find yourself searching for a position from which you can oversee the future and wealth of the community.

Line 6 - Chaos	Line 3 - Powerlessness
Line 5 - Objectivity	Line 2 - Might is Right
Line 4 - Strategy	Line 1 - Warning

GATE 45: GATHERING TOGETHER - THE GATE OF THE GATHERER
– The natural and generally beneficial attraction of like forces –
Center: Throat   Quarter: Civilization   Theme: Purpose fulfilled through Form
RAC of Rulership – JC of Possession – LAC of Confrontation

Gate 45 is the gate of dominance. It is the gate of the Master/Mistress or King/Queen. It is the single voice of the Tribe, "I have," and a deeply possessive gate of manifestation and action. The Gate of the Gatherer is here to protect the Tribe's material resources. You are a natural authority and guide for the Tribe; however, you are not really here to work. When what you 'have' is used on behalf of those you protect, there is peace in your kingdom. You have an ability to gather people together to manifest what the tribe needs, to expand your community, and to bring harmony to those around you, although the actual management of the Tribe's business is handled by Gate 21. You own the land, but you must give Gate 21 permission to hunt on it, while still demanding that you receive the best piece of meat in the bargain. When you attempt to tell Gate 21 how to run your kingdom, or when Gate 21 tries to get the best piece of meat for itself, there is tension. Each gate has its specific role and purpose within the Tribe, and operates optimally when kept in its place. Even with Gate 21 in your own design, it works best for you to have the help of another Gate 21 to manage and run your kingdom or business.

Line 6 - Reconsideration	Line 3 - Exclusion
Line 5 - Leadership	Line 2 - Consensus
Line 4 - Direction	Line 1 - Canvassing

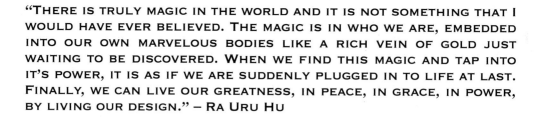

"THERE IS TRULY MAGIC IN THE WORLD AND IT IS NOT SOMETHING THAT I WOULD HAVE EVER BELIEVED. THE MAGIC IS IN WHO WE ARE, EMBEDDED INTO OUR OWN MARVELOUS BODIES LIKE A RICH VEIN OF GOLD JUST WAITING TO BE DISCOVERED. WHEN WE FIND THIS MAGIC AND TAP INTO IT'S POWER, IT IS AS IF WE ARE SUDDENLY PLUGGED IN TO LIFE AT LAST. FINALLY, WE CAN LIVE OUR GREATNESS, IN PEACE, IN GRACE, IN POWER, BY LIVING OUR DESIGN." — RA URU HU

SECTION SEVEN
THE 12 PROFILES
THE COSTUME OF OUR PURPOSE

SECTION SEVEN

THE 12 PROFILES

THE COSTUME OF OUR PURPOSE

We now arrive at another basic component of Human Design. Profile is the beginning of establishing a style for life, a role described as the costume of our purpose. It is a costume we grow into, however, and can either be uncomfortable, if distorted by our not-self, or feel like our natural skin and the true role we are here to live out. Profile is also one of the aspects that differentiates you as a unique being. You may be an emotional Generator, for instance, sitting with three other emotional Generators, but if you have different Profiles you are very different people. Together with our Incarnation Cross (see Section Eight), Profile allows us to live our purpose as our own authentic character on the stage of our life.

The basis of Profile is the recognition of the fundamental duality that exists within each of us. We are a binary consciousness, a synthesis of a Personality consciousness and a Design consciousness, and within Profile we are able to understand the quantum of the two. There are 12 basic Profiles, each of which is derived from a combination of the Line level definition of the conscious Personality Sun (black) and the unconscious Design Sun (red). This is illustrated in the graphic below. Our specific interpretation of our Profile, the role our character plays, makes our life performance unique from all others. And the drama, the movie, begins at birth.

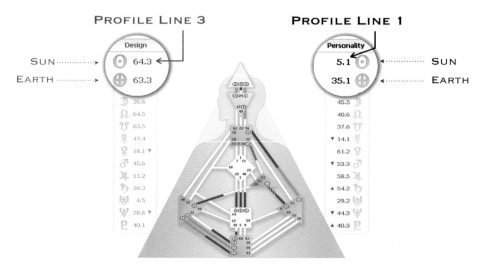

THE BODYGRAPH ABOVE HAS A 1/3 PROFILE
YOU WILL FIND YOUR PROFILE LISTED ON THE TOP OF YOUR CHART OR
YOU CAN ALSO LOCATE IT BY TAKING THE INFORMATION FROM YOUR CHART AS ILLUSTRATED.

PROFILE STRUCTURE

The basis of Profile is the Hexagram. The 64 Hexagrams (gates in the Bodygraph) each have six lines, giving us a deeper level of differentiation than the gates (hexagrams) themselves. The key to understanding Profile, and why there is such incredible differentiation in the way in which human beings live out their lives, is found in understanding the lines. The basic structure of a hexagram is divided into two parts, the Lower Trigram (Lines 1,2,3) and the Upper Trigram (Lines 4,5,6). The line structure flows from Line 1 at the bottom of the hexagram upwards (see illustration below). There are specific themes connected with each of the trigrams, and specific values associated with each of the six primary lines, which are described more fully on the pages that follow.

The six basic line themes, or primary roles, (Investigator, Hermit, Martyr, Opportunist, Heretic and Role Model) also provide a theme for all hexagrams in the Bodygraph. For instance, the investigatory quality of Line 1 will be an underlying theme for every Line 1 in every hexagram or gate in the BodyGraph. A full description of the lines of each hexagram can be found in Section Ten.

THE SIX PRIMARY ROLES: HEXAGRAM STRUCTURE OF GATE 10

The Six Primary Roles are the basic Profile themes, and are rooted in the line divisions of the 10th Hexagram, the Gate of Treading (The Behavior of the Self). Profile is a combination of two of these primary roles. The qualities of these two roles are lived or experienced differently through our Personality, who we think we think we are, and our Design, our innate nature. Together, they form a quantum, and the costume for how we live our life in the world.

Your Profile is listed by Personality and then Design, i.e., a 3rd line Personality and a 5th line Design will be displayed as a 3/5 Profile. Your Profile can also be keynoted through the names of the themes of the lines so that a 3/5 Profile is also referred to as a Martyr/Heretic.

HEXAGRAM 10: "THE GATE OF THE BEHAVIOR OF THE SELF"

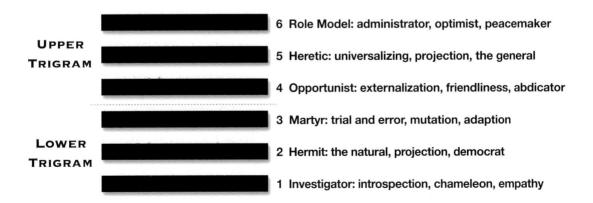

UPPER TRIGRAM

6 Role Model: administrator, optimist, peacemaker

5 Heretic: universalizing, projection, the general

4 Opportunist: externalization, friendliness, abdicator

LOWER TRIGRAM

3 Martyr: trial and error, mutation, adaption

2 Hermit: the natural, projection, democrat

1 Investigator: introspection, chameleon, empathy

HEXAGRAM STRUCTURE/HOUSE METAPHOR

It is helpful to use the house as a metaphor for understanding the six lines and their qualities. The 1st line is the foundation upon which the house is built. The 2nd line is the living space on the first floor of the house, with curtains wide open, that others on the street look into. The 3rd line is the transitional space or spiral staircase moving from the first to second floor. The 4th line is the second story, or second floor foundation of the house. The 5th line is the mysterious, curtained second story window with expectant speculators outside. And the 6th line is the roof of the house, with a bird's eye view into the next house, the rest of the neighborhood and beyond.

PRIMARY ROLES BY LOWER TRIGRAM: LINES 1 – 3

The lower trigram is a very self-absorbed process, very personal. These are roles that are not rushing out to externalize, and don't particularly want to have much to do with others.

LINE 1 - INVESTIGATOR: INTROSPECTION, CHAMELEON, EMPATHY

Line 1 is the ground floor or base of the hexagram, and 1st lines are driven to investigate the foundation of things, to discover how life works. Once they have firmly established a secure foundation, they are able to relax. The more they know, the less they fear, as 1st lines feel "if we can be secure, everything is possible." Their insecurity drives them to seek authorities, and become authorities themselves, and yet pursuit of their investigations is an introspective process that usually says, "I am busy studying, doing my research, so don't bother me." The secure foundations that the 1st line creates are then externalized or universalized by the lines of the upper trigram. There is also a deeply empathic nature to the 1st line, and its ability to take in information from the other can be very transformative.

1st lines study behavior. They watch how other people act, and they learn to see which behavior works and which behavior doesn't work. When feeling insecure, like a chameleon they'll change their colors to blend in. They're not actually changing anything, but they're very good at letting you see what they think you need to see. The keynote for Gate 10 - Line 1 is Modesty, or the ability to know one's place and how to act despite circumstances. 1st lines are very sensitive in this way, and nothing is more important to them than being able to see that they can navigate on this plane, and that all is going to be okay. 1st line Designs have a need for a secure physical foundation as well. The most common not-self feeling for the 1st line is a sense of inferiority, generally because they do not allow themselves the focused self-absorption that is necessary to fully investigate and establish a foundation. Strategy and Authority will determine the correct investigations for 1st lines, and allow them to focus on one thing at a time, which can also relieve a great deal of their not-self anxiety. "**The very nature of a Hexagram, the very construct itself, cannot survive without a solid foundation.**" – Ra Uru Hu

LINE 2 - HERMIT: THE NATURAL, PROJECTION, DEMOCRAT

Line 2 is like a seed that sits in the drawer for years, waiting for just the right time to be planted so it can awaken, grow, and produce its unique fruit. While the 1st line investigates in order to build a foundation, 2nd lines are naturals who do not know where their innate gifts originate from. 2nd lines are noticed for their natural talents or genius, and are then 'called out' by others who want their gifts to be used in a particular way. These are Hermits, however, that want only to be left alone to do their own thing, their own way. While 1st lines need others to aid in their investigations, 2nd lines are self-contained and can feel very uncomfortable when others step into their aura and expect something from them. They do not want to, and do not even know if they can, explain to you how they do what they do, or even worse, how you should do it. They behave very democratically because they don't want to be bothered, or have to invest their energy in taking sides.

The natural talent that 2nd lines possess does not respond well to interference of any kind. In our analogy of the house it is as if they are standing alone in front of the first floor window, lights on, happily self-absorbed in their own play, and not realizing that they are being observed by those outside on the street. In fact, 2nd line Personalities generally do not even want to go outside into the world. They are waiting to receive the correct call, specific to their unique life purpose, that will allow them to share their true genius with the world. It is only through Strategy and Authority that the 2nd line will know if a call is correct. Fulfillment is very important to the 2nd line, and if they cannot live up to the projections placed on them, or if they allow themselves to answer calls that are not correct and that they cannot fulfill, they can suffer greatly and isolate even more than is natural or healthy. **"Just sit by the river; sooner or later something will come by. This is readiness for the unknowable, whatever it may be."** – Ra Uru Hu

LINE 3 - MARTYR: TRIAL AND ERROR, MUTATION, ADAPTION

The great gift of 3rd lines is discovering what does not work. As the transition point between the first and second floors of the house (the personal and the transpersonal), life bumps into them in every way, or they bump into it, and discover through the trial and error process how the material plane operates. 3rd lines are our key catalysts of change, and even though they may at times appear socially inept, and very often feel alone, they are the most interpersonally adaptable line of the lower trigram, with a natural resilience and tenacity that will sustain them through their discovery process. A 3rd line is more likely to notice and recognize a potential new mutation faster than anybody else, simply because they bump into it. Often associated with scientific exploration (but from the stand-point of what is not working) and deeply material, 3rd lines do not take life at face value. They will kick the tires and look to see where the flaw, the loophole, or trick is. The 3rd line models for us the transformation that is possible when we are grounded in our bodies on the material plane.

These beings, whose natural gift is challenging the falsehoods, are ultimately mutating the Maia. They're also going to notice what doesn't work in a relationship faster than anybody else, which is why their theme is 'bonds made and broken.' The keynote of Martyr refers to the 3rd line's ability to stand up and say "this is not true," and take the heat for it. When operating correctly as true self, however, there is no such thing as failure for a 3rd line – only discovery. Bonds made and broken can become a natural mechanism in their life, such as the parent who leaves the house to go to work each day and then returns. The 3rd line is also part of the 6th line three-part life process (see Line 6 – the Role Model), and its mutative quality permeates the Profile roles more than any other line. "**Whatever comes their way, there is always a message with important information. They are the weavers of the Maia.**" – Ra Uru Hu

PRIMARY ROLES BY UPPER TRIGRAM: LINES 4 – 6

When we move upward into the upper trigram, the mechanics of the roles change entirely. The upper trigram is a transpersonal, outer-directed process. These roles have an essential need to share socially with others; to share the past and the possibilities of the future.

LINE 4 - OPPORTUNIST: EXTERNALIZATION, FRIENDLINESS

In harmony with the 1st line, the 4th line represents the foundation of the second floor of the house, and builds upon the security that the 1st line creates. There is also a fragility to Line 4 in that it must also allow an opening for the transition into the upper trigram. While Line 3 is deeply involved with material resources, Line 4 is the foundation of transpersonal relationships and concerned with human resources. The 4th line is deeply influential, and waits for opportunities to embrace its community and externalize the foundations, gifts or discoveries of the lower trigram. An innate friendliness, akin to brotherhood or sisterhood, facilitates the 4th line's gift for networking. This friendliness creates the opening needed but also makes 4th lines susceptible to surprise and shock. Their sphere of influence, therefore, is typically limited to people with whom they have already established relationships; strangers are not generally correct for them other than as casual contacts.

Quality of life for 4th lines is in direct proportion to the quality of their network of friends and associates. Establishing their energies in correct relationships allows them to enjoy a genuine camaraderie. There is also an inflexibility, however, which creates a tendency toward people burnout for the 4th line, and they need times of retreat to nurture and rejuvenate themselves. The potential opportunities that their networks offer must bring a return on the energy investment that they have put into it, or they may abdicate and find a network that does. 4th lines who are living correctly do not create their networks, however; their correct networks are already there and they meet them through Strategy and Authority. The 4th line, having a fixed quality, must transition securely from one network or relationship to another, or lose its security and true opportunities to influence. "**The 4th line is about the human resources of the material plane; people are the biggest decisions and investments they make in their life.**" – Ra Uru Hu

LINE 5 - HERETIC: UNIVERSALIZING, PROJECTION, THE GENERAL

The 5th line carries the responsibility of universalizing the message of the hexagram. Those with a 5th line carry the most transpersonal karma, and most effective as a 'stranger of consequence,' such as the general who steps in when the standard solutions have failed and offers a practical yet 'outside the box' solution. The auras of 5th lines invite people in need or crisis to project onto them a potential for rescue. Heretics operate in a projection field that seduces the other into recognizing the potential power that is there, but 5th lines can also be very suspicious as others see things in them that are not there, or have expectations of them they cannot meet. The 5th line, peeking out through the curtains of the second story window of the house, looks out at the world and very often hides from it at the same time. Strategy and Authority provides a practical and trustworthy tool for determining which situations are correct for the 5th line to step into to provide a solution.

If unaware of the projection field, 5th lines may be flattered by and believe others' perceptions of them as saviors. In order to not buy into the illusions that others may have about them, 5th lines must be truly aware of themselves and what they are really capable of solving or saving. The Heretic's reputation is totally dependent upon the success or failure of their solutions to meet the other's expectations. If they have not provided something of real value they may be figuratively burned at the stake. Once the crisis is past and the Heretics' leadership is no longer needed, however, they are generally ignored. This is the 5th line's natural time to regroup, as Heretics are not on duty constantly, but are expected to be standing by, ready and able, when the next crisis arrives. **"Whatever you're going to do in this life, make sure it has a practical application. If that's the case, you will be a success, whatever it is. But if it's not, then you have the reputation problem. It follows you wherever you go." – Ra Uru Hu**

LINE 6 - ROLE MODEL: ADMINISTRATOR, OPTIMIST, PEACEMAKER

The 6th line stands alone from the other five lines of the hexagram, and is best described as sitting on the roof. Though sometimes perceived as disinterested, this aloof perspective provides the 6th line with a vantage point from which to look back over the other five lines, while also looking ahead toward Line 1 of the next hexagram. Whereas Line 5 is moving toward others, Line 6 eventually moves away from them in order to go through a unique 3-stage life process and emerge as the mature Role Model.

STAGE 1, from birth to approximately 30 years, is one of exploring and living life through the 3rd line process of trial and error, and bonds made and broken. Driven to seek a soul mate (a 6th line attribute), they generally do not until they complete Stage 2 around the age 50. 6th lines are not resilient like true 3rd lines, however, and the chaotic 'getting bumped into' process can lead to disillusionment and a pessimistic view of life by their late 20's. In order to regain their optimism, they look for a way to retreat physically and/or emotionally from the world. A 6th line's first Saturn return at approximately 28 years marks the climb up on the roof, and the external discovery process shifts to a more internal one.

STAGE 2, from about 30 to 50 years of age, is one of withdrawing from the chaos of the 3rd line experience in order to heal and reflect. "Going up on the roof" is a time to observe and discover what is trustworthy and really works in the world; to re-evaluate life and develop the resources they will need later. Their energy may feel more aloof to others, but they are also beginning to be looked to for their wisdom. During this time of inner retreat, 6th lines generally feel the most secure as they start to settle in, choose a vocation, a mate and/or raise a family. Their 3rd line discoveries are now integrated, and become the foundation for the outer authority they will express as the Role Model.

STAGE 3, begins with the Kiron Return at approximately 50 years of age. They are now nudged or kicked off the roof to engage fully in the world once more, this time as their authentic, optimistic 6th line self. This can be a time of radical shifts in their lives, and they may be particularly vulnerable if they do not know how to make decisions as their own authority. The awake Role Model is a living example of an aware being living a unique purpose. Hypocrisy is very difficult for a 6th line to deal with. They are deeply trusting beings and model to us how we too can trust our own authority and live our unique life. By entering deeply into experiences when young, remaining aloof and healing through inner work in mid-life, and re-engaging and flowering into the world after age 50, 6th lines bring a unique perspective and wisdom to the way life can work. Theirs is an example of the transcendent life possible as a 9-centered being. **"Every 6th line being carries the magic of the future, it carries the magic of what's possible for a human being, what's possible for any human being if they're fortunate enough in this life to come in contact with this knowledge and they get to experiment with it and see for themselves."** – Ra Uru Hu

Note: As 9-centered beings, regardless of our particular profile, we all develop slowly. Between age 40 and 50 (between our Uranus Opposition and Kiron Return) we experience a 'second wind,' a reorientation that occurs during the mature chapters of our life. Humanity is evolving away from the universalizing savior/general 5th line toward the 6th line process of self-leadership and self-mastery based in self-acceptance and self-awareness. Those with Line 6 in their profile are here to show us how to make that transition correctly. After age 50, they are here to model transcendence, or what it is like to live our truth as an authentic, objective and aware human being.

The Geometric Progression Of Profiles
The Three Geometries

"No man or woman is an island. We travel through life in complex, orchestrated geometries." – Ra Uru Hu

Geometry	Profile	Identity / Nature
Left Angle - Trans-Personal Destiny	6 / 3	Role Model / Martyr
	6 / 2	Role Model / Hermit
	5 / 2	Heretic / Hermit
	5 / 1	Heretic / Investigator
Juxtaposition – Fixed Fate	4 / 1	Opportunist / Investigator
Right Angle – Personal Destiny	4 / 6	Opportunist / Role Model
	3 / 6	Martyr / Role Model
	3 / 5	Martyr / Heretic
	2 / 5	Hermit / Heretic
	2 / 4	Hermit / Opportunist
	1 / 4	Investigator / Opportunist
	1 / 3	Investigator / Martyr

As the Sun and Earth progress through each gate and line around the Mandala, during the course of one year, three distinct geometries are created. Geometries set mechanical potentials and limitations in motion that frame the specific way(s) we are to interact with and impact others in order to fulfill our life purpose. Each of the 12 Profiles falls into one of three geometries, Right Angle, Fixed Fate or Left Angle.

RIGHT ANGLE GEOMETRY, which comprises the first seven Profiles, creates a self-absorbed, **Personal Destiny.** Comprising approximately 64% of the planet, these Profiles are here to work out their own life. Right Angle Geometry is focused on self-exploration and facing the personal challenges we meet in life. They are not here to be absorbed into someone else's process. People whose lives intersect with theirs may spark new experiences, but will not alter their movement through life. Right Angles are not particularly aware of, nor understand, why they connect to certain people as these Profiles enter an incarnation with the veil drawn over the experiences of their past lifetimes. They are here to do the research, explore, re-experience and gain new perspectives, and as such are the creators of karma on the planet.

JUXTAPOSITION GEOMETRY (the 4/1 Profile only) acts a bridge between the Right Angle and the Left Angle. This is **Fixed Fate,** neither personal nor transpersonal, and 4/1 Profiles, representing less than 3% of the population on the planet, are fixed instead in their own line of movement – like a train on a track. The force of the Fixed Fate profile is that whoever else comes in contact with it, and stays in contact for an extended time, becomes part of that fate as well.

The Juxtaposition Profile is the bridge between the personal Right Angle research and development department, and the transpersonal Left Angle marketing department.

LEFT ANGLE GEOMETRY is **Trans-Personal** and has a trajectory or path that has many intersecting lines. These four Profiles, representing 33% of humanity, cannot fulfill their purpose alone. Although not dependent on the other, even the simplest of connections can potentially change their direction or path, or the other's, which is the opposite of the Right Angle process. Left Angle Profiles have a more conscious awareness of other people and the world, and are always ready to observe and engage in life. Trans-Personal Profiles maintain a connection to past incarnations, and often feel an unexplained familiarity with certain people and experiences. While the Right Angle creates karma, the Left Angle cleans up the karma that has been created.

Your geometry is recorded on your chart as part of your Incarnation Cross; for example, the Right Angle Cross of Eden, the Juxtaposition Cross of Power or the Left Angle Cross of Dedication. (You will find a general overview of Incarnation Crosses in Section Eight).

The following pages provide in-depth summaries of the 12 Profiles. As you read through them, notice how the same line (Line 1 for instance) may create a different way the role plays out when it is on the Personality side of the Profile (i.e., a 1/3 Profile) as compared to when it is on the Design side (a 5/1 profile). Line 1 in the Personality will bring conscious recognition, while the same line in the Design will be more a part of the vehicle's nature, and unconscious to the Personality.

1/3 PROFILE

INVESTIGATOR MARTYR

1ST LINE PERSONALITY CONSCIOUS INTROSPECTION		3RD LINE DESIGN UNCONSCIOUS ADAPTATION	
Behavioral Identity	Modesty	Nature	Martyr
Projected Attitude	Authoritarian	Type	Anarchist
Limited Perspective	Empathy	Memory	Pessimism
Aspired to Role	Creativity	Direction	Sustainment
Bonding Strategy	Pursuer/Pursued	Sexuality	Bonds made and Broken
Security Strategy	Self-Provider/Coveter	Humanity	Bonds made and Broken
Emotional Resonance	Weakness/Strength	Wave Resonance	Allegiance/Rejection
Awareness Resonance	Weakness/Strength	Frequency Resonance	Partnership/Dependency

Background: The geometry of the Personal Destiny trigram begins with the 1/3 profile – the first of the 12 roles, and the personification and foundation of our human experience. The 1/3 is unique in that it is the only profile with both lines in the lower trigram. At this foundational level, the 1st line represents the conscious Personality, the mind and how we think. The 3rd line represents the unconscious Design, the body, and our physical experience in the mundane world. We are a species that is driven by fear for our survival to investigate until we understand or find security through a solid foundation. This is not always possible in the ever-changing world that we live in, but the search for this security drives and mutates our species forward. Mutation is the continual process of finding out what does not work so that we can survive. The 1/3 sets the theme for the on-going 'human' journey of bumping into, investigating what we bump into, and resolving and understanding the unknown.

Investigator Martyrs, very insecure when not standing on a solid foundation, are driven to seek authorities that can provide them with secure grounding for their trial and error process. Their self-absorbed Investigator Personalities are very creative, and are healthiest and most productive when well prepared and well educated. They enjoy their long hours of introspection, and find strength in eventually establishing themselves as an authority so that their personal destiny remains in their own hands. Their Martyr Vehicles or bodies are designed to discover how to navigate the material plane by bumping into things, or being bumped into, literally and figuratively. Adaptable and resilient, they are able to pick themselves up and announce to the world the truth of what does not work.

Personal: You are consciously focused on finding inner strength by establishing a secure foundation, while your unconscious Design naturally bumps into things that continually surprise you and others with 'accidental' discoveries. You have a deeply internal destiny and can be like a chameleon, not wanting to draw too much attention to yourself until you feel secure as an authority. Gray areas can make you feel weak and uncomfortable, and drive you to seek answers. An open and willing student, you are on a path to develop strength through mastery.

You are here to be in charge of your own life, as well as a voice and person of authority in your field of expertise. Learning about relationships is a lifelong trial and error journey for you as you travel along, head down and absorbed in introspection, and yet bumping into people along the way. When something about a relationship isn't secure or harmonious, you can become uncomfortable and break the bond. You will then renegotiate the bond, either strengthening the relationship or bringing it to an end. This can happen repeatedly, and is the correct way that your relationships are deepened and kept healthy, or brought to completion so you can move on to one that works.

In addition, your Martyr side has a tendency to look at all of life as a potential untruth, even while your Investigator side is seeking a solid truth to build its authority around. You cannot be lied to, and even as a child you quickly found out who was telling you the truth and what you could trust. If you can surrender, your Strategy and Authority will guide you correctly through life, as your 1st line Personality augments the trial and error process with further investigation. It's also important that you have control over your environment as you have to be free to progress organically from one discovery to the next. You are empowered when encouraged to investigate or speak the truth about what does not work.

Interpersonal: Martyrs are often blamed for mistakes that aren't even theirs, which can undermine their self-esteem and create an 'us against them' mentality, feelings of shame, or an inferiority complex. If they, and those around them, understand that life is simply a constant and necessary process of trial and error, ending in discoveries that can then support a solid foundation, they can find strength in their journey. The focus must always be on what was learned from the experience, rather than the perception that they have made a mistake for which they are to be punished or ridiculed. This is the positive reinforcement that is especially important when raising a 1/3 child. When properly encouraged, the moment a 1/3 child finds out that the foundation does not work, there is the potential for wonderfully artful and creative discoveries to happen.

Even though they may seem stubborn or resistant to taking the advice of others, in truth, 1/3's must do it for themselves through direct experience in order to discover and learn. Parents can be their strongest allies, encouraging them to "try" it, and then fostering a "tell me what you learned" attitude, rather than "look what you did wrong." This allows 1/3's to learn through discovery, which encourages them to continue this process throughout their life, and allows them to ultimately contribute to humanity, and improve life for all of us. The only true failure for a 3rd line is to not learn from their trial and error process. Investigative Martyrs can become secure self-providers on the material plane when encouraged to take charge of themselves.

The chain of 12 profiles begins with a 1/3 and ends with a 6/3. The 3rd line themes of mutation, trial and error, discovery, bumping into things, and bonds made and broken, are important and prominent in humanity. These are themes of the mundane world that bind us all together and keep our species evolving. All 6th lines live a 3rd line process in the first 30 years of their life, therefore, half of the 12 profiles carry a 3rd line theme. The 3rd line is designed to operate in the density of the material world, and within that world we discover who we are.

FAMOUS 1/3'S: ARTURO TOSCANINI, EDGAR CAYCE, GORDON BROWN, H.G. WELLS, HARRY HOUDINI, MICHAEL CAINE, POPE LEO XIII, RAM DASS, SRI MEHER BABA, VINCENT VAN GOGH

RIGHT ANGLE – PERSONAL DESTINY
1/4 PROFILE
INVESTIGATOR OPPORTUNIST

1ST LINE PERSONALITY CONSCIOUS INTROSPECTION		4TH LINE DESIGN UNCONSCIOUS EXTERNALIZATION	
Behavioral Identity	Modesty	Nature	Opportunist
Projected Attitude	Authoritarian	Type	Abdicator
Limited Perspective	Empathy	Memory	Fatigue
Aspired to Role	Creativity	Direction	Aloneness
Bonding Strategy	Pursuer/Pursued	Sexuality	Confidant or Not
Security Strategy	Self-Provider/Coveter	Humanity	Benefactor/Dependant
Emotional Resonance	Weakness/Strength	Wave Resonance	Kindness/Meanness
Awareness Resonance	Weakness/Strength	Frequency Resonance	Corruption or Not

Background: The combination of the Investigator and Opportunist weaves introspection together with a natural gift for establishing close relationships. 1/4's have an inner urge to creatively externalize their investigative findings to people they know. While the conscious Investigator is focused on getting to the bottom of what makes things work, the transpersonal Opportunist is looking for ways to get that knowledge out. To do so they make friends with people, as part of a personal network that will ultimately become the recipients of their message. Investigative Opportunist's have a special platform from which to influence others, for once they secure a solid foundation and connect with a network, they become engaging authorities themselves.

There is something very special about this Profile as both the 1st line and 4th lines are in 'harmony' with each other, and even though they operate in different ways, both are 'foundation' lines. The 1st line establishes the ground floor foundation of the house, and the 4th line is the foundation for the second floor. This is a special circumstance in that both lines of the Profile are essentially interested in the same thing. There is a harmony between what they investigate and what they externalize, and what they want to externalize is what they want to investigate. Harmony Profiles (1/4, 2/5, 3/6, 4/1, 5/2, 6/3) are a minority in the population, and play a role in the world as innocent agents of transition by bridging information and the other 6 Profiles to each other.

Personal: You are here to grasp the foundation of whatever you are interested in at a very deep level, and to take this knowledge base and externalize it to your network. You are driven to seek authorities that can teach you and prepare you, so that eventually you can establish yourself as an authority in a field or topic that intrigues you. As you emerge into the world as an authority, your insecurity turns into security and provides you with a solid foundation to stand on. You move from a position of weakness to one of strength, and you can be a force of strength for others as well. In order to delve deeply you need time alone, as your chameleon-like introspection allows you to submerge yourself into what you are investigating. You are not communally creative, and instead enjoy creative solitude which is very healing and brings richness to your life.

Your natural friendliness is also an intimacy strategy that attracts listeners and eventually partners. What you are looking for is a confidante, and lasting relationships begin by building friendships first. When following your Strategy and Authority you are very clear in your introspective process of investigation, and wait for the correct opportunity to tell others about what you have learned and discovered. You aren't just learning for yourself, or for its own sake, but with an eye toward attracting those who might be interested in and benefit from the information. In fact, you do not have to discover or experience something personally before you are willing to share it with others.

Investing in and maintaining your network is one of the most important things that you do in life. Your investment in people brings future opportunities to express your knowledge base. Knowing how to make decisions in terms of which people to invest in is crucial to your wellbeing; investing in the wrong networks and people is detrimental and leads to burnout and fatigue. All of your new associations need to come to you through an introduction by your network; you are not designed to influence strangers. Your 1st line Investigator is not concerned with the other, and your friendly 4th line Opportunist is unconscious, therefore, the only way for you to know who is correct for you is through your Strategy and Authority. Your opportunities in life come from networks and people you know, and it is important that you never leave one thing, such as a job, lover, or home until you have something else to take its place. If you do, you will have a hard time finding a replacement.

Retreating from your network at times is also crucial in order to recover from the fatigue resulting from your social networking. You can exhaust yourself listening to others as it takes considerable time and energy to cultivate your network as you wait for your opportunity to tell your truth.

Interpersonal: The 1/4 profile is the conscious authoritarian and the unconscious abdicator. Investigator Opportunists don't handle resistance well from others, and when they meet someone who rejects their influence they will abdicate without changing their position, and simply move on to find someone else willing and open to listening to them. The quality of a 4th line's life is dependent on the quality of the network. They are very powerful and influential people, fixed like an oak tree, who project an aura of strength and authority. Opportunists who are living authentically, however, do not create their networks – they meet them through Strategy and Authority.

1/4's are looking for support, and are dependant on others until they can get to a point in life where they become an authority providing for themselves. Once on solid ground, they are then in control of their own life, and get their opportunity to be generous and caring benefactors for others in return. As children they will simply believe whatever they are told. It is important for parents of 1/4's to only give them truthful information that they themselves are sure of. It can be devastating for a 1/4 child to find out later that they were lied to. 4th lines can also express a mean side when provoked that can come back to haunt them. Though it seems impossible to change a 1/4's mind about a deeply held understanding, this same fixedness combined with empathy toward others is what brings transition and evolution to our tribal and collective foundations.

FAMOUS 1/4'S: ALBERT EINSTEIN, ANJELICA HUSTON, GLORIA STEINEM, HIROHITO, JEAN PICCARD, JERRY SEINFELD, KAMAHL, MICKEY SPILLANE, MUHAMMAD ALI, SID VICIOUS

RIGHT ANGLE – PERSONAL DESTINY
2/4 PROFILE
HERMIT OPPORTUNIST

2ND LINE PERSONALITY CONSCIOUS PROJECTION		4TH LINE DESIGN UNCONSCIOUS EXTERNALIZATION	
Behavioral Identity	Hermit	Nature	Opportunist
Projected Attitude	Democrat	Type	Abdicator
Limited Perspective	Bigotry	Memory	Fatigue
Aspired to Role	Harmony	Direction	Aloneness
Bonding Strategy	Shyness/boldness	Sexuality	Confidant or Not
Security Strategy	Nourisher/Depleter	Humanity	Benefactor/Dependant
Emotional Resonance	Advance/Withdrawal	Wave Resonance	Kindness/Meanness
Awareness Resonance	Determination or Not	Frequency Resonance	Corruption or Not

Background: Within the hexagram, Lines 1 and 2 represent the first of three yin/yang binaries, and although these two lines operate differently, each is concerned with insecurity. To deal with this, the 1st line investigates and studies, and the 2nd line eventually learns to trust its natural gifts that require no study. There is an innate tension between this Hermit Personality that wants to be left alone to do its own thing, and the Opportunist Design that wants to connect with others to externalize something. The conscious 2nd line is inherently shy and unaware of its gifts, and has to be called out by others in order to share them. The unconscious yet naturally friendly 4th line provides opportunities for these gifts to be called out by attracting people to the 2nd line.

The Hermit, as much as it would like to be invisible to the other, is actually very transparent. Others look in and see what the Hermit cannot – its natural talents and genius. The Hermit can only see itself, though, through the projections and feedback of others. Not easily motivated to study like the 1st line, Hermit Opportunists are happiest when completely absorbed in their secure environment doing what they enjoy most. And while they are happily dancing to their own beat, they attract the attention of others who call them out to share their essential nature.

Personal: You are a natural who is here to be called out by others to share your innate talents and genius. You have a built-in barrier, such as a limited point of view, that protects you and your unique genius from being corrupted by outside interference. This barrier has a 'weak' spot, a place where it can be penetrated. The right call from the right person can lead to profound transformation in your life, and propel your purpose and destiny out into the world with a missionary's zeal. You don't like to be called out all the time, however, and answering just any call puts tremendous stress on your body. Improper use of your energy results in fatigue, burnout and eventually exhaustion. Continually answering the wrong calls turns the 2nd line barrier into a psychological barrier that refuses to hear all calls, and you will ultimately suffer because of this. When called, you are incredibly impressive as you seem to be driven by an unseen force on a crusade to externalize your gift to the world. You are being pushed and motivated by your unconscious transpersonal 4th line, and yet, if your 2nd line had its way you would just stay in your protected space, and never choose to be bothered by anyone. Consciously, you can feel incredibly helpless in the moment of the call, as you are taken out of your protected and secure environment and pushed out into the world of social interactions. It is crucial that you give yourself hermit time away from your networks as the solitude brings a delicious sense of harmony to your life. You are also very particular about your environment and enjoy having things arranged in a specific way that feels good for you – so you can be left alone to do your own thing. Your cave when you retreat into it is your sanctuary and castle, a place where you like to be without interruption.

Uncertainty is part of your 2nd line life. Living in a world where people expect you to be able to explain what you do and how you do it is uncomfortable for you, and even makes you question your own abilities. If you worry too much about what others think about what you do, you can become paranoid of the projections of others. Your gift is not something that you can explain; people will have to accept that you do what you do and you don't know how or why.

Your unconscious 4th line, and your instinct for networking, is the most effective way for attracting the opportunities for your calling and achieving success and security in the world. You must, however, also be 'called' into the correct networks. When you are in 'your' network you feel nourished and can be nourishing to others; your influence can be contagious and remarkable. As the Hermit Opportunist, you can move between nourishing and depleting, such as Michelangelo who depleted his nourishing benefactor's resources. There is no moral judgment in this dynamic, however, if you are in the wrong network, you can end up becoming dependent and depleting others' resources in an unhealthy way. You are not designed for strangers, and the only way a stranger can reach you correctly is by being introduced through someone you already know in your network. Knowing how to make correct decisions is very important as there are very specific calls for you in life, and learning how to recognize them is crucial to your well-being. Attracting the correct call occurs naturally when your life is properly aligned by making decisions through your Strategy and Authority. Without this guidance, life can be chaotic and the life-transforming call may never be heard.

Interpersonal: Hermit Opportunists bond through a strategy of shyness/boldness. Their Hermit shyness calls out to the other to be bold enough to break down their barrier to intimacy and establish friendship first. Hermits are only open to specific people, however, and this is how they enter correctly into intimate and lasting relationships. The 2nd line does not pursue, as the Hermit is unaware of the quality within that attracts the other, but rather waits for someone to enter their cave and say, "you are for me." This is also the correct way for Hermit Opportunists to enter into business commitments or partnerships, as it is those in their networks who recognize and most easily call them out.

Even with their inherent and unlearned gifts, 2/4 children need a good education and should be encouraged and supported to study. This preparation will be invaluable later in life when their call comes. They need to be 'turned on' though to get them involved, and if not interested they won't want to join in. They are generally easy going and will go along with the majority, but need a balance between time alone and social time.

FAMOUS 2/4's: OTTO VON BISMARCK, JEFF BRIDGES, FRANCISCO FRANCO, ARETHA FRANKLIN, AUGUSTE RODIN, RUDOLPH STEINER, OPRAH WINFREY, AL GORE, GUSTAVE EIFFEL, BARBRA STREISAND

RIGHT ANGLE – PERSONAL DESTINY
2/5 PROFILE
HERMIT HERETIC

2ND LINE PERSONALITY CONSCIOUS PROJECTION		5TH LINE DESIGN UNCONSCIOUS UNIVERSALIZATION	
Behavioral Identity	Hermit	Nature	The Heretic
Projected Attitude	Democrat	Type	The General
Limited Perspective	Bigotry	Memory	The Savior
Aspired to Role	Harmony	Direction	Attractiveness
Bonding Strategy	Shyness/boldness	Sexuality	Seducer/Seduced
Security Strategy	Nourisher/Depleter	Humanity	Distributor/Hoarder
Emotional Resonance	Advance/Withdrawal	Wave Resonance	Selflessness/Selfishness
Awareness Resonance	Determination or Not	Frequency Resonance	Discipline/Rebellion

Background: In the 2/5 profile, we find the harmony of the two lines of projection. The very personal Hermit wants to be left alone to do its own thing and is unaware of the projection. The transpersonal and seductive Heretic is wary of the projections from others, yet needs to interact with them to fulfill its karmic purpose. The Heretic can in effect call the Hermit into action with an inner call. The true universalizing call is rare, but ultimately the talents of the Hermit Heretic are correctly called out when the projections that it attracts can be met by the practical solutions that its natural genius provides. The conscious Hermit in its withdrawal, not wanting to be bothered, projects the attitude of the democrat, and allows others to assume responsibility. The unconscious Heretic is the Savior waiting for its chance to be able to lead and universalize its practical power.

The 5th line is always exalted because it represents the hopes and dreams of humanity. It is also the most transpersonal of all lines and its impact can be very profound. When someone looks in the window of a 2/5, they see the possibility of someone who can be called to greatness. Once called, they can lead any rebellion against any standard at any cost, and provide a practical solution that may be outside of all previous boxes. At the same time, what people really want is a General who is called upon only when needed. They want a leader who can step in when there is a crisis, and then step out again.

The Hermit Heretic must also have the loyalty of those it is stepping in to 'save,' as well as loyalty to its own natural passions and talents that are the core of its innate genius. The 2/5 must also know when to let go of the leadership role and step back into its hermitage. This is important on a personal level for the 2nd line who must be allowed time to retreat in order to nurture itself, as well as a transpersonal level for the 5th line whose reputation will suffer when it is not able to meet the continual projections of others.

Personal: You are someone who craves harmony, and your Hermit, quietly minding its own business, is startled when your Heretic jumps in to help others. Whenever you step into a room you meet an expectant audience. There is a double pressure of projection and expectation that your special talents can save us in our time of need. You can attract a group or an individual's loyalty, or you can encounter distrust. Not knowing which of these projections you will meet can be uncomfortable for you. The call is unavoidable though, even when it may prove more irritating than enlightening. You are quite capable of leading a revolution – if it is the correct one. Your only real protection is to follow your Strategy and Authority to determine which calls are correct for you.

The correct call transforms you. Ultimately, your reputation depends entirely on your ability to provide a practical, universal solution. Neither your Hermit nor your Heretic is very comfortable in the world, and you can appear reclusive, seeming to withhold or hoard your personal resources. This serves an important purpose, however, as it gives your energy, natural talents and reputation time to build up in readiness for that moment when you are projected upon to provide practical solutions when others really need them. Knowing what is practical, and living by it in your own life, is essential. Your conscious bonding strategy is "I'm shy, you have to break down my barriers to reach me", while unconsciously you are always attracting people to you. Your greatest power, however, is as a stranger of consequence.

Interpersonal: Hermit Heretics that act according to their true nature are going to have chances in life, especially if they are well educated in something they naturally do well, and can handle the projection field. They have the potential of being both called, and calling others, and will enjoy the fruits of the positive projections that result from their ability to bring a practical solution to the collective. The 2/5 can be deeply creative in the way in which it establishes its persona in the world, and it excels in its own self-marketing. When the majority is in crisis and the 2/5 receives its call, it can transform and begin to call others to a new principle.

2/5's are naturally withdrawn, a valuable strategy for them, as this withdrawal always brings others into their life to call them out. In this way, the 2/5 is also generally assured, initially at least, of meeting a positive projection. They struggle to maintain their innocence in life as the projections pile up, however, and they cannot self-motivate out of desire. They are Heretics who bring change, and challenge what is already there. If the challenge is practical then their heresy will triumph, and continue to triumph until it is no longer heresy.

Hermit Heretic children need respect for their boundaries, and they should not be forced to do something they do not want to do. They can be the most wonderful babies ever, but if they have a bad day, their reputation even at a young age can suffer. Once they are knocked off the pedestal, they can stay off of it for a while or for life. Their need for alone time must also be respected, as they feel very deeply the projections of their parents and others who in some way expect them to be faster or smarter, or good at this or that.

If their needs are not respected, both the Hermit and the Heretic will rebel. As long as 2/5's are following their Strategy and Authority when called into career or relationship, there is tremendous potential for successfully universalizing something and fulfilling their purpose.

Famous 2/5's: Betty Friedan, billy dee williams, James Garfield, Linda Tripp, Coco Chanel, Mia Farrow, Patty Hearst, Robert Hand, Sara Gilbert, Susan McCorkle

RIGHT ANGLE – PERSONAL DESTINY
3/5 PROFILE
MARTYR HERETIC

3RD LINE PERSONALITY CONSCIOUS ADAPTATION		5TH LINE DESIGN UNCONSCIOUS UNIVERSALIZATION	
Behavioral Identity	Martyr	Nature	The Heretic
Projected Attitude	Anarchist	Type	The General
Limited Perspective	Pessimism	Memory	The Savior
Aspired to Role	Sustainment	Direction	Attractiveness
Bonding Strategy	Bonds made and Broken	Sexuality	Seducer/Seduced
Security Strategy	Bonds made and Broken	Humanity	Distributor/Hoarder
Emotional Resonance	Allegiance/Rejection	Wave Resonance	Selflessness/Selfishness
Awareness Resonance	Partnership/Dependency	Frequency Resonance	Discipline/Rebellion

Background: If the theater is on fire, and the fire department has not shown up due to budget cuts, the person standing in the middle of the theater yelling "This is not right," while at the same time organizing a fire brigade and finding all the exits, is the Martyr Heretic. The 3/5 profile combines two potent agents for change. Resilient, adaptable and mutative, the conscious 3rd line focuses itself primarily on discovery in the material world, and lives a very physical trial and error process, which allows it to sustain itself and others with its discoveries. Martyrs are equipped to take the heat when they stand up and tell the truth about what isn't working, but they are not equipped to meet the other gracefully. Life bumps into them and they bump into it. Like the 1st and 2nd lines, they are not looking for anyone. They are, however, looking around at the world in order to be stimulated and potentially mutate, and end up bumping into all kinds of forces. Some of these forces may not be correct for it, and so the 3rd line can become pessimistic. Learning to discern at an early age what works for it or not is very important.

On the other hand, the unconscious but seductive 5th line cannot escape from the other. It continually attracts projections from those who see the Heretic as the General who can ride in on the white horse and pull them out of crisis. This can be quite uncomfortable for the 3/5 as from the time they are born, people project onto them that they can save the day, and then the 3rd line process kicks in and the one who is here to help can do nothing but make mistakes.

As it matures through life, the 3rd line naturally provides a wealth of experiential wisdom. The 5th line, the General, will be asked into situations where the Martyr will know and see what does not work. It can then stand up as the Heretic, take charge, and deliver something new and practical that does. The anarchistic Martyr will play right along, adapting and experimenting and refining the process every step of the way. Referred to as the great 'fixers,' they provide us with innovative solutions, help and guidance. The 3/5 profile also needs to know when to relinquish the reins and let others continue the process themselves. They are not networkers with continual influence like the 4th line, and their greatest power and effectiveness is as a stranger of consequence.

Personal: The hardest thing for you is to reconcile your very natural 3rd line discovery dance through life with the projections of savior that others place on your unconscious 5th line. For you to correctly inhabit your role as a Martyr Heretic, your emphasis must be on what is learned when life bumps into you, as well as how and when to correctly apply these discoveries. You must have great discernment when something or someone bumps into you, and determine if it is worthwhile for you to stay there or not, to bond or not. Your discovery process may feel at times like you have failed, but your experimentation is a foundation that someone else will build on. There were a thousand ways the light bulb did not work before they found the way that it did, yet each of those discoveries fed the next. You are someone who can sustain the trial and error process as you do not give up easily.

Most importantly, you must enter into both your explorations and rescues correctly through your Strategy and Authority, or you may end up feeling pessimistic about life, or possibly watch your reputation go up in smoke. When a commitment is made correctly, you can step in with the full force of your resilience, adaptability, determination, generosity and selflessness, and be sustained by life no matter how hard it bumps into you. And even if you get burned at the stake, you will just move on to the next one.

You are here to stand up for a principle, and to change the world around you by bringing a new value or structure to the collective. You have to be careful though not to end up with a Martyr complex, saying "why me" or "why now." You have to discover the principles that you can live by yourself, and then transform those principles into a universalizing force. You are here to ultimately create a new principle, a new heresy, but if that heresy is not practical you pay a price. Your work, or any activity you engage in, needs to be stimulating and not repetitive. Seeing new clients every day, for instance, can be good for you, as bonds made and broken is your theme.

Interpersonal: Martyr Heretics are masters of the material plane. When things aren't working out, however, they will break the bond and walk away. Their projected attitude may best be expressed as "never belong to an organization that would have you as a member." They are anarchists who must be willing to break the bond with anything that does not work, in order to finally discover what does. There is enormous value for everyone to have a 3rd line around who is consciously designed to discover what does not work. If parents, teachers and others can refrain from calling the 3/5 pessimistic or negative, or telling them that they have made a mistake, they will save themselves considerable time and energy by making use of the 3/5's experiential wisdom.

We need to offer a special kind of grace to a 3rd line child. Parents and teachers must allow them to go through their process with positive reinforcement. "What did you learn from it?" or, "Don't see it as a mistake, just a process." If they do not, the psychological damage to a 3/5 child can be great. When Martyr Heretics can't live up to the expectations projected onto them, they will flee and burn their bridges behind them. If they can navigate the projection field though, through Strategy and Authority, then the full potency of their truth, along with their ability to adapt, find a practical way, and still see the beauty and wonder of the material plane, will shine as a real gift for us all. The only thing they need to empower this role is positive reinforcement.

FAMOUS 3/5's: ANAIS NIN, CAROLE KING, DIANA ROSS, DUDLEY MOORE, INDIRA GANDHI, KATE WINSLET, SHIRLEY MACLAINE, TED TURNER, WILLIE NELSON, WILLIAM SHATNER

RIGHT ANGLE – PERSONAL DESTINY
3/6 PROFILE
MARTYR ROLE MODEL

3RD LINE PERSONALITY CONSCIOUS ADAPTATION		6TH LINE DESIGN UNCONSCIOUS TRANSITION	
Behavioral Identity	Martyr	Nature	Role Model
Projected Attitude	Anarchist	Type	Administrator
Limited Perspective	Pessimism	Memory	Optimist
Aspired to Role	Sustainment	Direction	Objectivity
Bonding Strategy	Bonds made and Broken	Sexuality	Soul Mate or Not
Security Strategy	Bonds made and Broken	Humanity	Trust or Not
Emotional Resonance	Allegiance/Rejection	Wave Resonance	Sympathy/Apathy
Awareness Resonance	Partnership/Dependency	Frequency Resonance	Leadership or Not

Background: When the pessimism of the Martyr meets the optimism of the Role Model, together they attempt to sort out what they really can trust in life. The 3/6 profile expresses the possibility that trial and error can lead to wisdom. All 6th lines have a three-stage life process. During the first 30 years they operate as a 3rd line. The Martyr Role Model, therefore, starts out life as a double 3rd line, deeply involved in experiencing life through one discovery after another, making and breaking bonds along the way. In Stage 2 (30-50), the Role Model tries to climb up on the roof to take a break and observe life. The conscious 3rd line continues to re-engage with life, however, pulling the 6th line down into the world again. Neither the 3/6 nor the 6/3 profiles ever really get the pure roof time that the 4/6 or 6/2 profiles do.

Potentially, the 3/6's discoveries will be expressed as balanced and mature wisdom in Stage 3 (after age 50), a time when the 3/6 climbs down off the roof and re-engages completely in life. With its unique and aloof perspective, the Role Model judges life in terms of what is perfect or not, while the bumping along in the trenches Martyr discovers what does not work. Together they can stand up for a truth, and model in different ways the transition possible for humanity if we transcend our conditioning, embrace our stages of maturing, become our own Authority, and live as our unique, aware, and authentic selves.

Personal: Trust is a big issue for you, as is perfection, which can put stress on relationships that can't meet your standards or expectations. When you have trust, you feel secure in life. At the same time, you are involved in a very natural process of discovery. You make and break bonds, which may not meld easily with your unconscious motivation to find a soul mate and settle down into the perfect life you can trust. Your 6th line carries a quality of nobility beyond the mundane, and you can become disappointed when the perfection is marred and withdraw for a time when life simply doesn't work the way you expected it to. You can be a 'fence sitter' as indecision is a theme throughout your life. The 3rd line wants to enter into the experience, while the 6th line would rather observe and not commit itself. Doing something, however, is better than doing nothing. You are designed to gather experiences, but only the experiences that are correct for you. Relief from the indecision comes when you have a navigation tool such as Strategy and Authority.

While your 6th line unconscious wants life to be perfect, your conscious 3rd line needs to learn about perfection through the often-messy trial and error process. When things don't seem to work, your 3rd line pessimism can cloud your outlook on life, while the unconscious 6th line wants to maintain its optimistic nature. Seeing your 3rd line trial and error process as positive rather than negative, will help you to maintain a more optimistic and objective attitude about life. There are no mistakes for a 3rd line, only discoveries, which are critical to your development into an experienced and wise role model. You must be deeply engaged with life, in a hands-on way, in order to learn, and develop your self-confidence and self-mastery. The journey for you is to recognize the wisdom of your 3rd line discoveries, and then allow your natural and wise authority to express as a living example of what you have learned. You are sought out for your advice and blessings, and when you give your stamp of approval, or not, your word is respected.

It is also important that you have time alone. The theme of bonds made and broken is not personal. You are not leaving the other person, but simply returning to your own self-absorbed 3rd line process until life engages you again. Sometimes breaking a bond is appropriately permanent, but most of the time breaking a bond simply means going for a drive or to a movie by yourself, and then returning home for a meal with the family. Or breaking a bond in order to come together again, sooner or later, to re-establish that bond on a stronger, more authentic level.

Interpersonal: Relationships that do not work out, especially early on, can be very painful for the 3/6 profile, and may keep them from forming intimate bonds for many years. Knowing how to make correct decisions early in life, will help make them ready for the world. Martyr Role Models have a deep capacity to sustain themselves and not give up, eventually leading them to objectivity. They find that the 'bad' experiences are really the most important ones that they have had. Society conditions us to believe that 'mistakes' are wrong. If 3rd lines are not encouraged and educated about their process, the 'bad' mistakes pile up and they feel beaten down, develop an inferiority complex, and carry a great weight of pessimism and shame. They may give up and walk away rather than use the experience as guidance. 3rd lines are, after all, the ones with the greatest ability to uncover the truth by discovering what does not work. Some of the most important discoveries in our world have come through trial and error. To be a 3rd line is to be fully engaged in the wonder of life.

Martyr Role Models are both anarchists, and administrators who can happily recommend a cause even if they would rather not be personally involved. If 6th lines understand the tripartite life process, and live it authentically through their own Authority, a penetrating optimistic perspective will emerge in later years in the form of experiential wisdom. They will step forward as a Role Model, guided by their discoveries, and show us the perfection possible in the 9-centered life with its flowering of potential and truths after the age of 50. This is a new pattern of maturation that is being modeled, an unfolding process which cannot and should not be rushed.

FAMOUS 3/6'S: ANDY GIBB, CARLA BERLUSCONI, DUSTIN HOFFMAN, EDWIN HERBERT LAND, ELIZABETH CLARE PROPHET, ENRICO CARUSO, GERHARD SCHRODER, JERRY LEWIS, JOAN CUSACK

Right Angle – Personal Destiny
4/6 Profile
Opportunist Role Model

4th Line Personality Conscious Externalization		6th Line Design Unconscious Transition	
Behavioral Identity	Opportunist	Nature	Role Model
Projected Attitude	Abdicator	Type	Administrator
Limited Perspective	Fatigue	Memory	Optimist
Aspired to Role	Aloneness	Direction	Objectivity
Bonding Strategy	Confidant or Not	Sexuality	Soul Mate or Not
Security Strategy	Benefactor/Dependant	Humanity	Trust or Not
Emotional Resonance	Kindness/Meanness	Wave Resonance	Sympathy/Apathy
Awareness Resonance	Corruption or Not	Frequency Resonance	Leadership or Not

Background: The Opportunist Role Model has the potential to be an important and influential representative of what it means to live a 9-centered life. Completing the Personal Destiny process begun by the 1/3 profile, 4/6's externalize their foundation, and model through self-awareness what it means to live uniquely as 'yourself.' This is an unusual profile as both lines are transpersonal, however, its role is still one of personal destiny and remains self-absorbed in its life. The 4th line consciously develops and employs its social gifts and personal networks to enhance its realm of influence, but the unconscious 6th line rarely allows itself to become intimately involved as it must remain separate and unencumbered in order to look at what lies ahead.

At the unconscious level, the 4/6 profile lives its life in three stages, and the first 30 years can be a challenging time as the 6th line lives as a 3rd line and continually bumps into life in a very subjective way. During this time, there is an internal discomfort because the conscious 4th line wants stability and a solid foundation, while the unconscious 3rd line must go through its trial and error, experimentation and discovery process. The unconscious 3rd line learns by exploring, in a deep way, the truth of what 'this' material plane is. When the 2nd stage of life begins at age 30, the Opportunist Role Model, now on the roof, enjoys a welcome reprieve in which to take the subjective experiences and turn them into objective wisdom. With a bird's eye view, it now sees that 'this' may actually be 'that.' While up on the roof, the 4th line establishes its stability by engaging itself in securing a family, a career, and a trusted network of friends. In the final stage that starts at age 50, the 4/6 comes off the roof and re-engages in life, influencing and externalizing a new transcendent perspective that is neither this nor that. Through the simple process of living life, they model what it is to be uniquely yourself, rather than be defined by the nature of the world around you.

Personal: There is a natural internal tension between your conscious yearning for connection and quality relationships, and your unconscious desire to stand apart so you can objectively evaluate and judge what life is really about and where we are heading. You are generally the cautious voyeur, standing at the edge of the group, and watching with objective transpersonal eyes that are waiting for the opportunity to contribute a new perspective and change the other's way of thinking. Built into your 4th line is the ability, with the right opportunity, to communicate your truth to the other. You are not, however, interested in being changed by others. When you feel resistance from others, you will abdicate and look for those that are receptive to what you have to share. Time spent alone is refreshing and important for you as your interactions can result in people fatigue. Living through your Strategy and Authority brings you those relationships that will ultimately allow you to influence, externalize and model who you uniquely are. You are watching for relationships you can trust so that you can truly become a living example of a leader without followers.

You have a genuine ability to develop intimate relationships, which also takes time and an investment of your energy. It is also natural for you to observe and evaluate people from a distance. Every single relationship matters as these are your friends who you will influence on a very deep level, and who will provide you over time with the opportunities you need in life to model your new perspective. You are not designed to influence strangers; you need those who are familiar with you, and they need to be correct for you in all ways, not just because you see the potential for influence and externalization. It may be years into a relationship before an actual opportunity presents itself, and the energy invested must be simply for the relationship itself. In the wrong relationships, you will be investing your energy without receiving energy back, and may abdicate the truth of who you are, meet the wrong opportunities, and experience disappointment, sadness and fatigue.

Interpersonal: To properly raise 4th line children, we need to give them time to mature from dependents to benefactors; they should not be rushed out into the world. 4th lines can be dependent for a long time, but once they come into their own they make an important shift. Recognizing how important it was to have a benefactor themselves, with their characteristic loyalty, they will in turn take care of those who took care of them. Many 4th lines will become philanthropists, benefactors to society as a whole, and create foundations that open up opportunities for others.

Relationships are everything for 4th lines; the quality of their lives is in direct proportion to the quality of their networks. 4/6's operate as a 3rd line, however, during the first stage of life, and they can be bumped into by relationships and networks that do not work. The most valuable guidance that a parent can offer during the first 30 years of a 4/6's life concerns the relationships that they enter into, as these can determine the success or failure of the flowering into a transcendent Role Model that will take place after the age of 50.

At times, 4/6's can be a fence-sitters as the 4th line wants involvement, and the 6th line simply wants to watch. We need them to come down off the fence, however, and share their astute observations with us. The Opportunist Role Model has a generous spirit that wants the best for everyone, and they are able to bring love into the world with their warm hearts and wise heads. When their trust is broken, however, their sensitive hearts can be easily wounded, and the warm heart can turn cold and even mean when it is rejected.

FAMOUS 4/6'S: AL PACINO, BRAD PITT, DAVID BECKHAM, MANUEL NORIEGA, NAGAKO (EMPRESS OF JAPAN), PALOMA PICASSO, ROBERT KENNEDY, RUPERT MURDOCH, SALVATORE FERRAGAMO

4/1 PROFILE
OPPORTUNIST INVESTIGATOR

4TH LINE PERSONALITY CONSCIOUS EXTERNALIZATION		1ST LINE DESIGN UNCONSCIOUS INTROSPECTION	
Behavioral Identity	Opportunist	Nature	Modesty
Projected Attitude	Abdicator	Type	Authoritarian
Limited Perspective	Fatigue	Memory	Empathy
Aspired to Role	Aloneness	Direction	Creativity
Bonding Strategy	Confidant or Not	Sexuality	Pursuer/Pursued
Security Strategy	Benefactor/Dependant	Humanity	Self-Provider/Coveter
Emotional Resonance	Kindness/Meanness	Wave Resonance	Weakness/Strength
Awareness Resonance	Corruption or Not	Frequency Resonance	Weakness/Strength

Background: The Opportunist Investigator represents an interesting juxtaposition of the socially open and friendly 4th line, and the unconscious, introverted and insecure 1st line. The 1st line is the foundation of the lower trigram, and the 4th line is the foundation of the upper trigram, creating a harmony of purpose. This is a unique profile that comprises only about 2% of the world's population, and with its Fixed Fate, serves as the bridge between the Right Angle Personal Destiny and Left Angle Trans-Personal Karma. Neither this nor that, not personal or transpersonal, there is only one Juxtaposition profile for each Hexagram. The 4/1 moves along its own specific line of geometry; like a train on a track it has a movement and direction through life that cannot be altered.

Personal: You are designed to study, learn and establish a solid foundation in an area of life that fascinates you, and then to influence others with your knowledge base. Your foundation is whatever thing you love to immerse yourself in, and want to share with others. Investigating and becoming an expert on a given topic transforms your inherent insecurity into an authority. Once you are established as an authority, you can then go out to your network and become an influential expert in your field. With your 4th line people skills, you have a natural ability to know how to best communicate your knowledge base to others.

Your role is to network and bring together the research and development of the Personal Destiny profiles with the marketing and universalizing of the Trans-Personal Karma profiles. You have one foot in each world, yet you operate differently with a role that is separate and apart from them. For you, Fixed Fate is a life of following your own unique line of geometry, whatever that may be. To learn more about what your Fixed Fate is here to investigate and externalize, look at your Personality Sun and Earth located in your BodyGraph. This will give you a sense of your purpose, of what you are here to do in life. As you begin to live your life through your Strategy and as your own Authority, you will witness your life aligning perfectly to your purpose, and to your fate.

For all 4th lines, the quality of your life is deeply dependent upon the quality of your network (family, friends and co-workers). Your opportunities to externalize your foundation come through the people in your network, through friendly associations as you are not designed to influence strangers. To effectively externalize your knowledge base, a personal connection is necessary. If you are asked to speak at an event by someone you know, for example, it is best for you to show up early and make as many face-to-face connections with the audience as possible. Or have a 'get to know you' mixer the night before so that you will be speaking to a familiar and receptive room. It is also important for you to have a solid foundation for your life in the areas of home, finances, relationships and work. Achieving this in an ever-changing world, however, can be challenging.

Even though a 4/1 is fixed and solid like an oak tree, there is vulnerability inherent in this profile. You are so fixed that you can be broken, and the pieces can be hard to put back together again. Understanding how you are designed, and what your purpose is, can help you to stay on track and deal with the challenges of life. In order to stay steady on your course and enjoy the ride, it is most important that you be exactly who you are, and not change for anyone else. For you to maintain a sense of balance and health, others will need to adapt to you as you cannot adapt to them. You can go along with the other temporarily, but you must always return to your fixed unique way.

Interpersonal: Life and people are a real education for Opportunist Investigators, as they learn through interaction that not everyone sees the world as black and white, or right and wrong, like they do. They get a rude awakening into the ways of the world, which makes them somewhat vulnerable and prone to heartache. 4/1's learn through these experiences, however, and their Fixed Fate keeps them moving forward. It is important to stay above the fray, and in addition to their broader network, they need a trusted circle of close friends and confidants who provide unconditional loving support without resistance. Opportunist Investigators enjoy the study of human behavior, and may enjoy investigating some form of psychology, sociology, astrology or Human Design.

In order to get a good start in life, education and a solid secure home life are very important for a 4/1 child. They need to be encouraged and provided with the opportunity to study what they love and enjoy. For relationships to work for a 4/1, they must be built on a foundation of friendship and integrity as the bonding strategy is Brotherhood/Sisterhood or friends first, and then intimacy. The 'other' who is in a relationship with the Opportunist Investigator will need to do the adapting. 4/1's can be the most loyal and generous of friends, but they cannot be in relationships where they are resisted, or where there is a lack of trust or loyalty. It is best to be completely honest and transparent with 4/1 profiles because built into the 4th line is the abdicator. If they are resisted, they will move on to find someone else who wants what they have.

If you argue with 4/1 profile, they will politely nod their head, while steadfastly and quietly holding on to their own truth deep inside. It is very difficult to change the mind of a 4/1, however, it can be done if you substantiate your points with good solid facts.

FAMOUS 4/1'S: DAVID GINSBURG, ANDREW LLOYD WEBBER, BARBARA WALTERS, BETTE MIDLER, BUZZ ALDRIN, GIANNI VERSACE, LOUIS VUITTON, PETER SELLERS, RICHARD HARRIS

LEFT ANGLE – TRANS-PERSONAL KARMA

5/1 PROFILE

HERETIC INVESTIGATOR

5TH LINE PERSONALITY CONSCIOUS UNIVERSALIZATION		1ST LINE DESIGN UNCONSCIOUS INTROSPECTION	
Behavioral Identity	The Heretic	Nature	Modesty
Projected Attitude	The General	Type	Authoritarian
Limited Perspective	The Savior	Memory	Empathy
Aspired to Role	Attractiveness	Direction	Creativity
Bonding Strategy	Seducer/Seduced	Sexuality	Pursuer/Pursued
Security Strategy	Distributor/Hoarder	Humanity	Self-Provider/Coveter
Emotional Resonance	Selflessness/Selfishness	Wave Resonance	Weakness/Strength
Awareness Resonance	Discipline/Rebellion	Frequency Resonance	Weakness/Strength

Background: In the I'Ching, the exalted or ruling 5th line embodies the theme of a hexagram. For the Heretic Investigator, the unconscious 1st line, representing the authoritative foundation, is joined by the 5th line which consciously projects all that foundation could or should be. The result is that the 5/1 is the most transpersonal, with the highest universalizing potential, of all 12 profiles. This is the profile of saviors and generals, or of trickery and paranoia, and it is very seductive. Heretic Investigators are projected upon to save or rescue others with a practical solution in a time of crisis.

Personal: Trans-Personal Destiny means that you are here to deal with karma, and you are designed to have encounters with others that can be important and potentially mutative for both you and them. If you can picture your life path as a grid with intersecting points that represent these encounters, you can get a sense of how you are destined to meet allies in life who are here to assist you, as well as receive assistance from you. These karmic encounters, which very often can feel like déjà vu, can be as complex as a business arrangement or as simple as someone asking you for directions. You are aware on some level of your conscious transpersonal 5th line, an alluring and seductive line that is continually projected upon. Others feel, without even knowing you, that you have something potentially important and helpful that they need. This projection draws people to you, providing you with the ability to have the encounters in life that you need in order to live out your unique life purpose.

Others project onto you that you can lead, guide, help or save them, and when it's the right projection, you enjoy filling the role, and being able to deliver practical solutions with your expert problem solving skills. There are times, however, when the projection you are feeling is not the right one for you, and you feel insecure and unsure that you can provide what the other person needs and wants. It is important for you to know which projections are the correct ones to say yes to. If you say yes when it is not correct, you can get caught in the illusory web created by the projections of others, and make commitments you cannot live up to resulting in a tarnished reputation. It is healthy for you to be suspicious and a bit paranoid of the expectations of others.

Ra has said, "The hopes and dreams of humanity rest on the shoulders of a 5th line." This is a big responsibility to carry, and the best way to operate within this expectant projection field is to stand on a solid, practical and authentic foundation.

One of the advantages of being a 5th line is that the initial projection from others starts out as positive. People are projecting onto you that you can deliver what they need, and if you deliver something practical, your reputation will flourish. If a practical solution is not provided, if what you have given them is a 'house of cards', your reputation suffers and the 'heretic will be burned at the stake.' Without a reputation that can be trusted, your conscious 5th line may have to change direction and begin again somewhere else. You need to make sure that, before you get involved, you are prepared with a practical solution that works for everyone. You do this with your unconscious 1st line, the Investigator. Your 1st line is designed to get to the bottom of things, to study and establish a secure foundation of knowledge. Once you have a solid foundation, and have become an authority, you are prepared to impact and mutate society, when needed. Following your Strategy and Authority will guide you to the right circumstance and timing for universalizing your practical foundation.

You are a keen observer of the world around you, and preparedness, as well as correct timing, is essential to your success. When the two come together, you are the Heretic Investigator who can break through humanity's habit of seeing things in the same old way, and make your revolutionary heretical point of view work when all else has failed. Unlike 4th lines, whose greatest influence is within their networks and personal associations, you are most powerful as a stranger of consequence. You are designed to interface with new people who are ready to receive your heretical mutative information; familiarity breeds contempt for a 5th line. You greatly benefit from times of withdrawal, out of the projection field, to build up strength and cultivate your skills so that you can be ready to meet the next crisis when the commitment is correct for you. You find refreshment on many levels through cultivating beauty and creativity.

Interpersonal: Heretic Investigators aspire to make themselves personally attractive in order to improve their chances of universalizing, as well as to seduce a partner into seducing them. They have vulnerabilities and insecurities, and are reluctant to show their true self. Few people ever truly know the 5th line as they are shrouded in an elusive projection field. The 5th line hoards, or holds back, and waits for the illusion of power (the projection field) to build, and the right moment to universalize the foundation. Providing practical solutions in crisis situations requires disciplined patience. Heretic Investigators thrive on this process, but need to remember to return to their waiting once they have satisfied a projection, in order to prepare for the next. They must be able to recognize when it is the right time to move on, or else suffer damage to their reputation. If they wait too long to leave and there is nothing left to save, new layers of projections get added over the first ones that may not be correct for them. In addition, the 5/1 profile has an interesting connection with the 6/2 profile. Because of the wisdom and trust associated with 6/2's, they can enhance or save the reputations of 5/1's by innocently supporting their heresy, and the practical foundation they are universalizing. The reverse is also true. 6/2's can destroy their reputation as well.

Famous 5/1's: Anne Frank, Buckminster Fuller, Clint Eastwood, Harry Belafonte, Hugh Hefner, Neil Armstrong, Padre Pio, Paul McCartney, Ra Uru Hu, Theo Van Gogh

LEFT ANGLE – TRANS-PERSONAL KARMA
5/2 PROFILE
HERETIC HERMIT

5TH LINE PERSONALITY CONSCIOUS UNIVERSALIZATION		2ND LINE DESIGN UNCONSCIOUS PROJECTION	
Behavioral Identity	The Heretic	Nature	Hermit
Projected Attitude	The General	Type	Democrat
Limited Perspective	The Savior	Memory	Bigotry
Aspired to Role	Attractiveness	Direction	Harmony
Bonding Strategy	Seducer/Seduced	Sexuality	Shyness/Boldness
Security Strategy	Distributor/Hoarder	Humanity	Nourisher/Depleter
Emotional Resonance	Selflessness/Selfishness	Wave Resonance	Advance/Withdrawal
Awareness Resonance	Discipline/Rebellion	Frequency Resonance	Determination or Not

Background: Living within a dual projection field, Heretic Hermits must be their own stimulus or motivation. When the correct projection sets things in motion, the Heretic calls it's own Hermit's gifts forth, applying or universalizing what it does naturally. 5/2's live an unusual life of constant projection. Returning to the house metaphor, we have the conscious 5th line on the second floor, behind the curtain and looking out on the street, very aware of the people below projecting up at it as they wonder what is going on behind that curtain. The unconscious 2nd line is on the first floor, lights on, curtains open, dancing around, unaware that people are looking in and projecting onto it as well.

This rare profile is referred to as the reluctant Heretic, as it is quite commonplace for Heretic Hermits to remain detached and uninvolved due to the uncertainty of whether they can deliver on the projection from others. Although they are a transpersonal profile, unlike 5/1's that have karma with the other, 5/2's carry their own karma within. They have to live out something based on what they lived out in the past, but 'they' are the ones that have to discover it. If they don't, whatever it is does not get called out, and they do not get to universalize it.

Personal: You are deeply gifted in an unusual way, and it is very important for you to understand how to engage with life. What you are waiting for is the correct internal call to something revolutionary, something you can lead others to that lies beyond the mundane plane. Once properly engaged, you are empowered to selflessly nourish those you are here to support, while providing for your own material needs at the same time. Unlike 5/1's who universalize a foundation, something they have investigated and studied, you are universalizing your own natural talents and gifts. This is personal and you can feel very vulnerable. When you are called to step in and help, you are asking people to believe in you. You have to stand on your charismatic power alone, and this can create much uncertainty.

Your 2nd line genius is unconscious and buried deep inside you, and it is difficult for you to know when you have received the correct call. You are called through the projection field, and it is imperative to your success and reputation that you understand how to make correct decisions by using your Strategy and Authority. Only when you have recognized the correct call can you fulfill the projection. The 5th line in your profile starts with a positive projection from others that you can deliver what they need and want, and the moment you don't fulfill that projection your reputation suffers. This is a transpersonal profile, and your reputation can suffer on a wide scale, therefore it is even more important for you to understand how to make correct decisions from your own authority and not the projection field. It is a necessity for you, and also a relief, to get away from the projections of others, as you feel naturally and comfortably complete, and are happy to be alone with yourself. Your 2nd line unconscious body needs its special hermit alone time to stay healthy, and to nurture your natural gifts and talents.

As a Hermit, you have no inherent interest in improving what you do naturally, or proving to yourself or others what you hold to be true. And as a Heretic, you are not comfortable being projected upon by just any person in crisis to provide practical solutions, or to fulfill hopes and expectations. If you experience many failures in living up to others' projections, this can negatively reinforce your tendency for aloneness. You can feel uncertain about what you actually can do, and get overwhelmed and confused by so many projections. If pushed to an unhealthy extreme, you may choose to insulate yourself from all outside expectations, and then endure the reputation of an underachiever or hoarder who refuses to empower and universalize your gifts for the benefit of others.

Interpersonal: The secret to interacting with Heretic Hermits is to avoid pressuring them in any way. Wait until they call themselves out, and see their own way into a predicament or crisis that requires their particular and inherent genius. This is how this unusual profile manifests evolutionary new truths in the world in personally rewarding ways, and maintains harmony for itself, as 5/2's believe that the root of harmony is that no one should be pressured. In relationships, the 5th line Heretic relies on its power of attraction to get the other's attention, while the Hermit's shyness automatically sets up a protective barrier to real intimacy. When a pursuer or person of interest appears, however, this profile can let down its barrier, thus permitting the pursuer's boldness to effectively complete the seduction and open the way to intimacy.

The 5/2 child's need to motivate itself can be frustrating and challenging for parents. There is tremendous expectation placed on these children to show their talent or genius in the world, and to help others. When they retreat into their room instead to seemingly play around, their families can project on them that they are underachievers. This can make 5/2 children very uncomfortable with others as they always feel the pressure of those projected expectations. They can also be very suspicious of what others see in them, as they are insecure about their natural talents and not sure if they can meet the projection. In working with 5/2 children it is best to present many different things to them until something turns them on. They are very selective, but once turned on they will call themselves out and share their natural abilities.

FAMOUS 5/2'S: ABRAHAM LINCOLN, CORETTA SCOTT KING, BRIDGET FONDA, GEORGE ELIOT, MIKE WALLACE, PETER GRAVES, RON L. HUBBARD, ALVIN AILEY, CHYNNA PHILLIPS, FRANZ SCHUBERT

LEFT ANGLE – TRANS-PERSONAL KARMA
6/2 PROFILE
ROLE MODEL HERMIT

6TH LINE PERSONALITY CONSCIOUS TRANSITION		2ND LINE DESIGN UNCONSCIOUS PROJECTION	
Behavioral Identity	Role Model	Nature	Hermit
Projected Attitude	Administrator	Type	Democrat
Limited Perspective	Optimist	Memory	Bigotry
Aspired to Role	Objectivity	Direction	Harmony
Bonding Strategy	Soul Mate or Not	Sexuality	Shyness/Boldness
Security Strategy	Trust or Not	Humanity	Nourisher/Depleter
Emotional Resonance	Sympathy/Apathy	Wave Resonance	Advance/Withdrawal
Awareness Resonance	Leadership or Not	Frequency Resonance	Determination or Not

Background: The transpersonal Role Model Hermit is here to show us all how to live authentically without being dependent on outside authorities, and to realize and accept our unique perfection. The unconscious and naturally gifted Hermit just wants to be left alone to do its own thing. In the house metaphor, Line 6 sits on the roof, separate from the rest of the house, but with a view into the next house, or the next hexagram. Role Models are not necessarily interested in what is going on inside the house; they are more interested in the broader view.

This rooftop perch gives 6/2's the ability to be removed from the 'drama' of life, and allows them to objectively observe and offer a detached viewpoint, much like the sage on the mountaintop. The 2nd and 6th lines have something in common as the Hermit's natural gifts are always noticed, and the Role Model observer is also always being observed.

Personal: You can feel a bit out of sync with the world. You have a birds' eye view of life, so you can see the big picture and are wise beyond your years. Profiles without a 6th line do not have the ability to see life the way you see it, and this can make you feel disconnected from others, or question and wonder why they don't they see what is obvious to you. When combined, your 6th and 2nd lines give you the capacity to be the democratic administrator; a unique, capable and wise authority.

As with all 6th lines, you will go through three significant stages in life. It is important for you to embrace each aspect of this process as it matures and prepares you for your true calling, which is the role of trusted leader. The first 30 years are trial and error discovery, gathering valuable experiences, and losing some of your innocence as you get exposed to the hard realities of life, and what does not work. The second stage of your development is a time for you to retreat, heal your wounds, regain your optimism, enjoy life and watch for the things that do work. Your unconscious 2nd line Hermit feels good in this stage as withdrawal is natural. After the age of 50, you receive a calling, re-engage with life, and become a true Role Model and living example of the wise, aware, objective judge and observer.

You are always noticed, and have great transpersonal power even when you are withdrawn and reclusive. A life of harmony for you means no agendas or pressure to prove yourself. Your ability to stay above the fray, removed from the insignificant dramas in life, helps you to maintain objectivity. You are most interested in things with depth and meaning; the trivial does not engage you. Others see you as an objective administrator, and will call you out for advice. As a transpersonal person, you are someone others listen to and your advice carries a lot of weight. If you say this thing works or not, or this person is good or bad, people will take your word for it. Your 6th line, when healthy, is fundamentally optimistic – hoping and dreaming for the best in life for everyone, including yourself. At the same time, your unconscious 2nd line sees the frailties and self-hatred that exists within humanity.

Your natural genius and innate talents must be protected and allowed to unfold naturally in order to be called out and made available to the world. You are not a generalist, and there is a specific and special call that will allow you to bring out your gifts and embody your Role Model power. This calling is not something that you will find by seeking; it must be called out of you by others. There is a noble, self-sufficient, optimistic and visionary quality that emerges from you if you are able to stay with your process, maintain your perspective, and safeguard your natural gifts during the first two stages of life. Your unconscious uncertainty, however, can cause you to hold back and not share your special gifts with the world. Your Strategy and Authority will guide you to the correct people and the correct call.

Interpersonal: Role Model Hermits are idealists looking for the perfect life and perfect mate; someone they can stand with, relate to, and be proud of. The potential partner must be bold, however, and break through the 6/2 barrier. During the first 30-year trial and error cycle they jump into intimacy only to suffer from disillusionment and disappointment. Typically, meeting their mate is possible only after they enter the retreat phase of life, and yet, a lot of time can be spent in this phase trying to change a partner into the perfect model. It is important that 6/2's live their truth, and not attempt to change the truth of others. Trust is nourishing for the Role Model Hermit, and they cannot be intimate with anyone they cannot trust. If the trust is broken, you will only get access to the 6/2 on a superficial level.

It is very important to support the 6/2 child in discovering their true nature, and to not shame them for any trial and error 'mistakes' that are made in the first 30 years. They can be insecure in their gifts, and can be their own worse critics, as they are always looking for perfection. They need encouragement to explore and try things. When something does not work out, a parent can guide the child to learn from the discovery by asking "What did you learn from this experience?"

The 3-part 6th line developmental process is something all human beings go through, and is modeled and accentuated by 6th lines as they lead us through this transition to the new 9-centered form. They are here to show us the way to live as a differentiated 9-centered being, able to operate and make decisions from our own authority. Role Model Hermits are here to show us how to live according to our own wisdom.

FAMOUS 6/2's: BARACK OBAMA, BILLY JOEL, CHARLES DE GAULLE, CHARLES DICKENS, ERROL FLYNN, GEORGE LUCAS, HARRY S. TRUMAN, HENRY FORD, ISADORA DUNCAN, ZELDA FITZGERALD

LEFT ANGLE – TRANS-PERSONAL KARMA
6/3 PROFILE
ROLE MODEL MARTYR

6TH LINE PERSONALITY CONSCIOUS TRANSITION		3RD LINE DESIGN UNCONSCIOUS ADAPTATION	
Behavioral Identity	Role Model	Nature	Martyr
Projected Attitude	Administrator	Type	Anarchist
Limited Perspective	Optimist	Memory	Pessimism
Aspired to Role	Objectivity	Direction	Sustainment
Bonding Strategy	Soul Mate or Not	Sexuality	Bonds made and Broken
Security Strategy	Trust or Not	Humanity	Bonds made and Broken
Emotional Resonance	Sympathy/Apathy	Wave Resonance	Allegiance/Rejection
Awareness Resonance	Leadership or Not	Frequency Resonance	Partnership/Dependency

Background: The Role Model Martyr, the completion point of the 12 profiles, combines the conscious and aloof 6th line which seeks the perfection in life, with the unconscious, restless, materially-oriented and mutative 3rd line. The 6/3 is a profile of transition and change, which can lead to a potentially chaotic and destabilizing life. No matter where the 6th line is in the tripartite life process, the unconscious 3rd line continually pulls it into subjective experiences. It is through this process though that 6/3's become the wisest of Role Models, ultimately discovering that uniqueness is perfection, and that we cannot trust in anyone when making decisions but ourselves.

Personal: As is true for all 6th lines, you will go through a three-part life process. For a 6/3 profile these three stages are experienced differently as the first 30 years are experienced as a 3/3 profile, which is a doubly intense and sometimes very difficult trial and error process. You are gathering subjective experiences, and you engage in and try just about everything, including jumping into situations and relationships that do not work. You can become disappointed, and ultimately conditioned, to feel pessimistically that nothing in life really works.

It is not necessary that you go through a traumatic first stage, and how you experience this first phase is dependent upon the parenting and conditioning that you receive as a child. If you are raised as yourself, respected as an individual and given guidance on how to make decisions as yourself, you will have a smoother first stage. If you are your own Authority, you will gain wisdom from these subjective experiences and discover what is correct for you to discover. 6/3 children need to be encouraged and taught to see that a trial and error process is not about mistakes, but rather opportunities for learning. Otherwise you can end up with both a martyr and inferiority complex, along with a chip on your shoulder and a deep pessimism about life.

Between 30 and 50 you go up onto the roof for a more aloof, objective observation process. This is the time when you retreat from the subjective experiences as your 3/3 is now a 6/3, but you don't really get the reprieve of staying securely up on the roof that a 6/2 profile does. Your unconscious

3rd line continually pulls on you to engage again and again in the experiential trial and error process, with feelings of "this is not it, there is still more," and "there are still things to try and things that still need to be explored." You move up and down the ladder between being connected and being aloof, between sympathy and apathy. If burned by an unpleasant or discouraging experience you retreat for a while, until you are bored or a new adventure looks appealing, and then you climb down again and engage in the next experience. You are driven by your conscious 6th line's optimism that all things are possible, and that you can find something to trust and a soul mate. You move back and forth between pessimism and optimism.

From 50 years on, you experience the potential for the fulfillment of your uniqueness and your flowering into a Role Model. By this time in your life, if you have survived, you have gained a tremendous amount of wisdom and will be looked to as a wise and objective advisor with a unique perspective on life. Lurking at the unconscious level though is your 3rd line, ready for the next discovery, the next experiment that may disrupt the tranquility and perfection the 6th line would like to enjoy. Objectivity is your saving grace; it sustains you. It is what you aspire to and what brings you harmony in your life. Yours is a life of constant transition, of engagement and disengagement. Having a partner in life is important for you, and it is correct for you to have a life of bonds made and broken, to be able to pull away and then re-engage again. When you are operating as your own unique authority, you experience the transitions that are correct for you. There is nothing worse for you than a mental decision that goes bad, and it can lead to painful and damaging experiences.

Interpersonal: Role Model Martyrs are born with resilience, and an ability to sustain their own direction. Life works for them when they can embrace the chaos and confusion and wonderment of their early years, and receive all as essential discovery and learning as this is the foundation for their valuable wisdom. The 6/3 profile needs supportive relationships with people they trust, people who provide the option to pull away or break the bond when necessary in order to reconnect and strengthen it.

6th lines model for us the new way to live in this 9-centered world. The old ways were based on leaders and followers, with 5th line universalizers conditioning us into homogenized humans who continually gave their Authority to others. Human Design came into the world to liberate the individual, and to nurture the uniqueness of all human beings. The essence of this is embodied and demonstrated in the 6th line theme. As we enter into a new era of mutation, getting closer and closer to 2027 and a 6th line way of being in the world, the structures and institutions that support giving our Authority over to outside influences will continue to crumble.

In the old 7-centered model, we were told what to do. It's not in the nature of a 6th line to do this; instead they innocently model what it means to live our lives correctly as ourselves, through our own Authority. They walk among us in their post Kiron phase as examples of 9-centered living, allowing the uniqueness to unfold. 6th lines demonstrate that it is ok to be yourself, and that you can find what you need within.

FAMOUS 6/3'S: DAN RATHER, FARRAH FAWCETT, HARRISON FORD, MATT DAMON, PAULO COELHO, ROCK HUDSON, SERENA WILLIAMS, STEVE JOBS, KING UMBERTO II, USHER RAYMOND IV

"WE ARE NOT INCARNATING TO SIMPLY BE FORM PRINCIPLE; OTHERWISE, WE WOULD ALL BE DOLPHINS, OR WE'D BE PLANTS. WE ARE HERE TO FULFILL A CONSCIOUSNESS PROGRAM. WE ARE TALKING ABOUT THE FULFILLMENT OF PURPOSE. EVERYTHING ABOUT YOUR INCARNATION CROSS IS ABOUT THE POTENTIAL TO FULFILL YOUR PURPOSE. WHEN YOU LIVE AS YOURSELF YOUR CROSS TAKES OVER YOUR LIFE. THE CHARACTERISTICS IN YOUR DESIGN DON'T MATTER WHEN YOU ARE LIVING YOUR PURPOSE. PURPOSE ALLOWS YOU TO TRANSCEND THE PROBLEMS OF YOUR CHARACTERISTICS. THAT'S THE MAGIC OF BEING YOURSELF, BECAUSE THE MOMENT YOU REALLY ARE LIVING YOUR NATURE YOUR CROSS WILL TAKE OVER, YOUR PURPOSE WILL TAKE OVER AND OUT OF THAT WILL COME ITS ARCHETYPAL DEMAND AND THE OPPORTUNITY TO BE FULFILLED IN THAT WAY, WHATEVER THAT WAY HAPPENS TO BE." – RA URU HU

SECTION EIGHT
THE GLOBAL INCARNATION CROSS INDEX
OUR TRUE PURPOSE

SECTION EIGHT

THE GLOBAL INCARNATION CROSS INDEX

OUR TRUE PURPOSE

Ra was hesitant to release the Global Incarnation Cross information before The Human Design System had sound footing in the world because he knew that people would have a tendency to interpret their cross either as something they were entitled to, or as something that was inevitable, regardless of how they lived their lives. This is simply not the case.

Our Incarnation Cross isn't something that automatically emerges as we go through our de-conditioning process, nor does it provide instant gratification; it's much more than that. When we function as our differentiated self in the world, our cross literally but quite naturally takes over our life. Fulfilling our purpose takes a lifetime of patient and disciplined attention to making decisions that are correct for us, combined with a dedication to fine-tuning our own awareness. We don't awaken to our cross, we awaken in it. Our cross embodies the full expression of our awareness potential and our process of living awake.

Each human being is an aspect of the totality, with a unique contribution to make as an interactive part of that whole. Our life's activity is expressed as our purpose and is captured in our Incarnation Cross by combining the themes of the Sun and Earth positions in both columns of the Human Design Chart. In the Mandala on the opposite page is an example of an Incarnation Cross with the Personality Sun in Gate 1 and Personality Earth in Gate 2, and Design Sun in Gate 7 and Design Earth in Gate 13. Each of us carries our own cross in life and all crosses are essential to the whole; no single cross is more important than any other.

There are 192 basic Incarnation Crosses and 768 specific Incarnation Crosses used in analysis; a very brief summary of each of the 192 basic Incarnation Crosses, expressed in very general terms to keynote the potential of living a life with awareness, follows this introduction. A full Incarnation Cross reading is needed to understand a cross completely. (Full Incarnation Cross Readings are available from an IHDS Certified Professional Analyst.)

THE FOUR QUARTERS

"THE WITNESS RETURNS THROUGH THE WOMB, TO BUILD AND BOND, MAKE MORE, MEASURE AND DIE." – RA URU HU

The four gates of the Right Angle Cross of the Sphinx (on the next page) divide the Mandala into four Quarters: Initiation (Gate 13), Civilization (Gate 2), Duality (Gate 7) and Mutation (Gate 1). Understanding the distinctly different themes of the four Quarters expands the meaning of our cross. Combining the keynotes of the four Quarters into one descriptive sentence we could say that we are here to Initiate (begin) Civilization (build) through Duality (bonding) and Mutate (or evolve) until we die.

HOW TO FIND YOUR INCARNATION CROSS

The illustration below demonstrates how to determine which Quarter your Incarnation Cross is located in. To find the description of your Quarter and Cross, please look for your Personality Sun Gate on your chart, and then look for the Personality Sun symbol (☉) and the corresponding gate number and quarter for your Incarnation Cross in the Mandala below. The following four pages describe the theme for each quarter, and list the page numbers where you will find your cross. You will also find the name of your Incarnation Cross on your Human Design Chart printout.

QUARTER ONE
THE QUARTER OF INITIATION — REALM OF ALCYONE
Theme: Purpose fulfilled through Mind — Mystical Theme: The Witness Returns

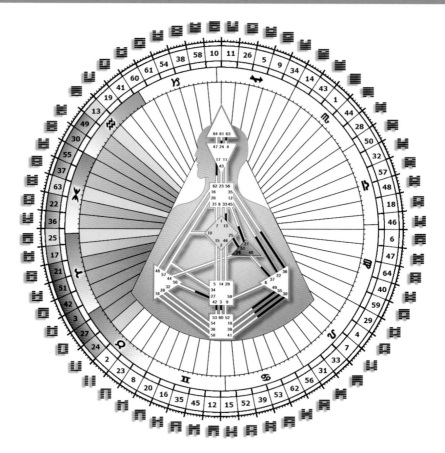

In the First Quarter the witness (the Personality crystal) returns to earth, once again bringing renewal to the evolution of consciousness on the mental plane. This is where purpose is fulfilled through Mind, through thinking, educating, conceptualizing, explaining and sharing what it means to be alive in a Form. It sets in motion the fine tuning of our mind as we learn to surrender to the directives of our form. Once our mind is comfortable in our form, we no longer yearn to live life as anyone but ourselves. Notice that all but one of the seven gates of the Solar Plexus, the center of relational intelligence and emerging spirit awareness, are clustered in the Quarter of Initiation. Notice that the Channel of Initiation is located here. **The crosses for the Quarter of Initiation are shown on pages 294-297.**

QUARTER TWO
THE QUARTER OF CIVILIZATION — REALM OF DUHBE
Theme: Purpose fulfilled through Form — Mystical Theme: Womb to Room

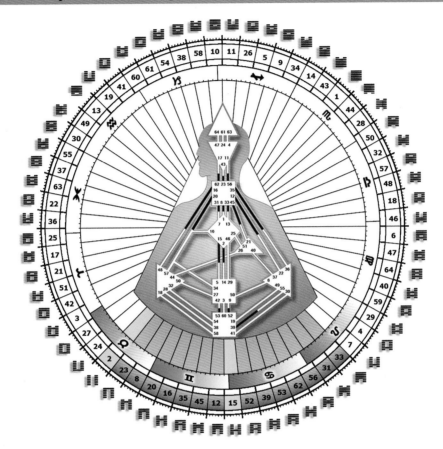

The Second Quarter is focused on the form's journey through life, and what is needed to manifest support for humanity after birth. This is where the mind's carefully initiated (formulated) concepts are concretized into form. This dominantly yin quarter is responsible for building the structures and communities and civilizations that support the form so everyone can develop and thrive. It anticipates industrialization, territoriality, material progress, the differentiation and perfecting of individual skills to benefit the whole, and the essential role or position of women in creating a civilizing, creative and safe environment for children/everyone. Notice that all 11 gates of the Throat Center fall into this Quarter of Civilization: the sharing, supporting and empowering of the full scope of humanity's potential to express its intelligence. Purpose is fulfilled through manifesting, through the movement of spirit into form. **The crosses for the Quarter of Civilization are shown on pages 298-301.**

Quarter Three
The Quarter of Duality — Realm of Jupiter
Theme: Purpose fulfilled through Bonding — Mystical Theme: Measure for Measure

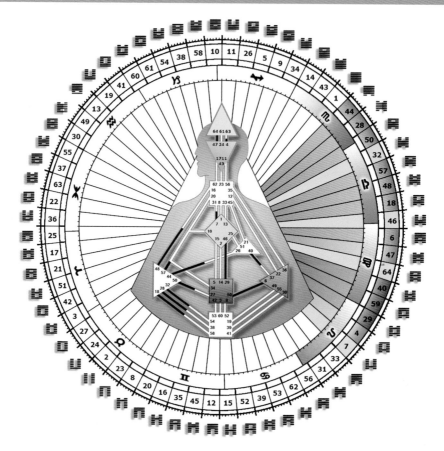

The Third Quarter brings us to the most mundane and intimately human of the four, where we cross the barrier of our separateness and address our need for the other, and mystically the two becomes the one. In this realm we penetrate to the core of the dual nature of our existence; on the one hand expanding the Maya (Measure for Measure) while on the other connecting to the beauty and mysteries of incarnating. It makes our ability to bond with others a constant source of wonder. Purpose here is fulfilled through bonding; through the genetic imperative to reproduce and replicate the species by choosing the best mate, thus ensuring humanity's future. The Quarter of Duality takes us from Mind (conceptualizing) and Form (building) to bonding (the mysteries of co-creation). Notice that the Channel of Discovery and Mating, plus all seven gates of the Spleen, with its survival intelligence, are located here. **The crosses for the Quarter of Duality are shown on pages 302-305.**

QUARTER FOUR
THE QUARTER OF MUTATION — REALM OF SIRIUS
Theme: Purpose fulfilled through Transformation — Mystical Theme: Accepting Death

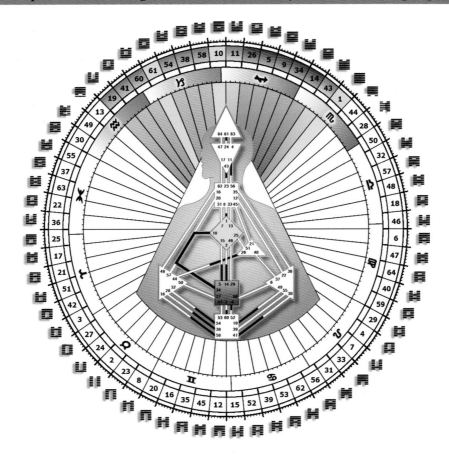

In this Fourth Quarter, the cycle of an authentic and transformed life is brought to completion, to a satisfying, peaceful, successful or surprisingly delightful end. At the same time, preparations are made for new beginnings anticipating future incarnations at the next level of consciousness. What has been learned and manifested as a fully-lived life is carefully assessed, scrutinized for meaning and pruned; what survives is carried forward and made ready to be passed on as truths, foundations for the next generation. In the Quarter of Mutation, purpose is fulfilled by attaining your full potential for transformation and awareness. The mystical theme, accepting death, is a matter of surrendering to what life is with an understanding that, when you have accomplished your purpose it is time to move on. There is comfort in knowing that if you live correctly you will die correctly. Notice that the Channel of Exploration, and much of the Sacral's responsive, generative energy, as well as the Root's pressure that is our momentum for living, manifest through this Quarter of Mutation. **The crosses for the Quarter of Mutation are shown on pages 306-309.**

THE QUARTER OF INITIATION
– Theme: Purpose fulfilled through Mind –

GATE 13 - THE FELLOWSHIP OF MAN

- **Right Angle Cross of the Sphinx:** People with an Individual direction whose unique way of remembering experiences brings a living, vibrant past into the future. (Gates 13-7-1-2)

- **Juxtaposition Cross of Listening:** Great listeners and secret keepers who often explain themselves and their breakthrough insights best through an art form. (Gates 13-7-43-23)

- **Left Angle Cross of Masks:** People whose explanations and insights, which potentially transform, lead and guide others, work best when given from behind a mask (like a PhD). (Gates 13-7-43-23)

GATE 49 - REVOLUTION

- **Right Angle Cross of Explanation:** The itinerant prophet addressing the principles behind necessity by pointing out what basic needs must be satisfied for all to survive; sensitivity to those in need. (Gates 49-4-43-23)

- **Juxtaposition Cross of Principles:** Revolutionaries ahead of their time fixed on a principle (often human rights) who are willing to bargain even with God to gain a powerful ally. (Gates 49-4-14-8)

- **Left Angle Cross of Revolution:** The revolutionary who understands that there can be no peace with an empty stomach. Those who have must share with those who have not. (Gates 49-4-14-8)

GATE 30 - THE CLINGING FIRE

- **Right Angle Cross of Contagion:** Innocent instruments of fate who can step in and unexpectedly change the fate of others through experience, discovery and learning. (Gates 30-29-14-8)

- **Juxtaposition Cross of Fates:** Energetic and persevering charismatics at the mercy of the fates, who throw caution to the wind in their obsessive commitment to fulfill their desire; potential mystical teachers. (Gates 30-29-34-20)

- **Left Angle Cross of Industry:** A human dynamo very busy working, building and bonding to satisfy the underlying motivation for humanity's progress: a burning desire to feel the emotional potential in each new experience. (Gates 30-29-34-20)

GATE 55 - ABUNDANCE

- **Right Angle Cross of the Sleeping Phoenix (until 2027):** People busy seeking access to spirit through love and bonding, who in this quest experience transformation (death and rebirth). (Gates 55-59-34-20)

- **Juxtaposition Cross of Moods:** People who out of a need for depth, and to know truth, are fixed in their moods and have great creative potential; creative teachers. (Gates 55-59-9-16)

- **Left Angle Cross of Spirit:** People who seek and find both spirit and great pleasure in life through creativity, good food and sexual companionship. (Gates 55-59-9-16)

THE QUARTER OF INITIATION
– Theme: Purpose fulfilled through Mind –

GATE 37 - THE FAMILY

- **Right Angle Cross of Planning:** People who are focused on bargaining their skills to build and maintain institutions which support communal living; bonding together to create something greater than themselves. (Gates 37-40-9-16)

- **Juxtaposition Cross of Bargains:** These are our warm-hearted bargainers whom no one can resist, and who can be great at making or facilitating the deal for the progress of the community. (Gates 37-40-5-35)

- **Left Angle Cross of Migration:** When the unifying project or experience is complete, they look for greener pastures to conquer the next territory/experience; the roots of progress. (Gates 37-40-5-35)

GATE 63 - AFTER COMPLETION

- **Right Angle Cross of Consciousness:** People looking beyond needs to why we are here; by questioning/testing the patterns and flowing with life they rise above the desire for more experience. (Gates 63-64-5-35)

- **Juxtaposition Cross of Doubts:** Bright, convincing and influential skeptics who are capable of selling others on the need for logical answers to balance experience. (Gates 63-64-26-45)

- **Left Angle Cross of Dominion:** People whose strong intellect is powerful enough to take over in a given circumstance; capable of creating doubt and confusion in order to take dominion. (Gates 63-64-26-45)

GATE 22 - GRACE

- **Right Angle Cross of Rulership:** People with a natural sense of position who rule with a grace for listening, whose greatest responsibility is to educate those in their kingdom. They are healthiest when they have someone or something to rule. (Gates 22-47-26-45)

- **Juxtaposition Cross of Grace:** People with great social attentiveness fixed on taking it all in; potent mutative agents who enjoy the art and pleasure of listening. (Gates 22-47-11-12)

- **Left Angle Cross of Informing:** People who mutate others as they use their gift of articulation to inform everyone of what is new and different; mutating through teaching what is new. (Gates 22-47-11-12)

GATE 36 - THE DARKENING OF THE LIGHT

- **Right Angle Cross of Eden:** Inexperienced people looking for excitement or new experience who eventually embody wisdom and grace through loss of innocence. (Gates 36-6-11-12)

- **Juxtaposition Cross of Crisis:** People with a love for themselves and humanity who are best at studying the crisis behaviors of others, thus elevating experience (sexuality) to a higher plane. (Gates 36-6-10-15)

- **Left Angle Cross of the Plane:** Witnesses of the mundane plane who see the vagaries of humanity, like the good, the bad, the ugly, yet have the potential to show us that there is something more: light, spirit, awakening and enlightenment. (Gates 36-6-10-15)

THE QUARTER OF INITIATION
– Theme: Purpose fulfilled through Mind –

GATE 25 - INNOCENCE

- **Right Angle Cross of the Vessel of Love:** People whose sense of higher cosmic, transpersonal and universal love provide balance to humanity's direction or drive to survive and replicate the species. (Gates 25-46-10-15)

- **Juxtaposition Cross of Innocence:** People who are focused on enjoying life, and can convince you to feel good about the nature of yours; the pursuit of happiness. (Gates 25-46-58-52)

- **Left Angle Cross of Healing:** People focused on maintaining the joy (quality) of life through the love of being alive in a healthy body; who have a special sensitivity to those struggling with dis-ease; they are here to heal or to be healed through "medicine." (Gates 25-46-58-52)

GATE 17 - FOLLOWING

- **Right Angle Cross of Service:** People with a logical understanding of what it means to be human moved by dissatisfaction to focus on correcting, reorganizing and serving humanity. (Gates 17-18-58-52)

- **Juxtaposition Cross of Opinions:** People who provoke you to expose/examine your spirit or your purpose, whose wealth of opinions are easily shared but not easily argued with. (Gates 17-18-38-39)

- **Left Angle Cross of Upheaval:** Great button pushers; always sticking their finger in the pie to disturb the status quo in preparation for corrections needed to redirect humanity or individuals in healthy directions. (Gates 17-18-38-39)

GATE 21 - BITING THROUGH

- **Right Angle Cross of Tension:** Natural boundary setters who like to be in control of their environment, and those in it; they can be good at policing or supervising situations. (Gates 21-48-38-39)

- **Juxtaposition Cross of Control:** People with depth fixed in fulfilling their ambition, their need to rise up, who demand to be in control so they can innovate by starting something new. (Gates 21-48-54-53)

- **Left Angle Cross of Endeavor:** Ambitious agents of change who endeavor to bring together people with depth who are focused on exploring new horizons in order to develop communal, business or scientific structures. (Gates 21-48-54-53)

GATE 51 - THE AROUSING

- **Right Angle Cross of Penetration:** People who catch us off guard and get our attention with their penetrating intuitive insights; ideas which can shock, shift or mutate our perceptions. (Gates 51-57-54-53)

- **Juxtaposition Cross of Shock:** People who keep us from becoming too serious or complacent by shocking us with their details and intuitive knowing. (Gates 51-57-61-62)

- **Left Angle Cross of the Clarion:** People who are here to shock those ready to be shocked, those who are open to mutation and prepared to accept the details of the clarion's inspiration and intuitive knowing. (Gates 51-57-61-62)

THE QUARTER OF INITIATION
– Theme: Purpose fulfilled through Mind –

GATE 42 - INCREASE

- **Right Angle Cross of the Maya:** Trend setters grounded in properly evaluated detail who promote growth by bringing one cycle to completion, thus setting the stage for inspired new beginnings. (Gates 42-32-61-62)

- **Juxtaposition Cross of Completion:** People focused on completing what they have begun, like the Marathon runner who reaches the goal after all others have gone home. (Gates 42-32-60-56)

- **Left Angle Cross of Limitation:** People who know what can and cannot be completed and understand the need to accept limitation in order to insure material success, to master our resources. Limitation creates the boundaries that hold our universe together. (Gates 42-32-60-56)

GATE 3 - DIFFICULTY AT THE BEGINNING

- **Right Angle Cross of Laws:** People who approach the ways we create, shape and change our laws and values like an art. Our laws determine how we deal with each other and bring order to society. (Gates 3-50-60-56)

- **Juxtaposition Cross of Mutation:** People looking for opportunities to change unjust laws in order to establish their own place of influence in the mutative process. (Gates 3-50-41-31)

- **Left Angle Cross of Wishes:** Altruistic, seductive and influential people always looking for possibilities which make life better for others; seeing and re-ordering things in a new way. (Gates 3-50-41-31)

GATE 27 - NOURISHMENT

- **Right Angle Cross of the Unexpected:** People who are naturally initiated by the unexpected toward a whole new series of experiences which ultimately nourish and expand their intelligence. (Gates 27-28-41-31)

- **Juxtaposition Cross of Caring:** People who are fixed on caring about everyone and everything, and themselves; where remembrance, sudden revelation and principles are shaped by the need for meaning. (Gates 27-28-19-33)

- **Left Angle Cross of Alignment:** People who know how to take advantage of the unexpected, the moment of transition, and give it a proper direction; helping others see what alignment is best for them. (Gates 27-28-19-33)

GATE 24 - THE RETURN

- **Right Angle Cross of the Four Ways:** People whose very direction evolves consciousness and form together by seeking clarity or resolution through constantly revisiting mental concepts: What, where, who is God? (Gates 24-44-19-33)

- **Juxtaposition Cross of Rationalization:** Bright, intellectual but incredibly fixed people trying to grasp continuity through both the past and the future with the gift of using both logic and experience to translate Individual knowing. (Gates 24-44-13-7)

- **Left Angle Cross of Incarnation:** People with a particular connection to both the past and future who can deeply impact your direction – when properly aligned to their own geometry. (Gates 24-44-13-7)

THE QUARTER OF CIVILIZATION
– Theme: Purpose fulfilled through Form –

GATE 2 - THE RECEPTIVE

- **Right Angle Cross of the Sphinx 2:** Influential confidantes who combine aesthetics with a deep resonance to humanity's material needs; maintaining continuity with the past while mutating the Collective's material direction. (Gates 2-1-13-7)

- **Juxtaposition Cross of the Driver:** People who are totally focused on their direction, on their driving principles, and determined to pull others into their wake. Even momentary interactions with them can change your direction. (Gates 2-1-49-4)

- **Left Angle Cross of Defiance:** People who always *seem* to defy the Collective's general direction by following their own; the ability to move others away from the status quo. (Gates 2-1-49-4)

GATE 23 - SPLITTING APART

- **Right Angle Cross of the Explanation 2:** Ever the outsider, they are constantly explaining themselves or their often unique concepts, principles and insights in order to integrate them into another person's revolutionary or analytical process. (Gates 23-43-49-4)

- **Juxtaposition Cross of Assimilation:** An engaging person given the task of repeating an unfamiliar insight until it becomes familiar, or is assimilated by friends who have the grace to listen. (Gates 23-43-30-29)

- **Left Angle Cross of Dedication:** Potentially great teachers dedicated to explaining the same things over and over, thus furthering education and change; always interested in what comes next. (Gates 23-43-30-29)

GATE 8 - HOLDING TOGETHER

- **Right Angle Cross of Contagion 2:** People who lead by example, and desire to make a contribution by committing resources towards ensuring future security and wealth; a civilizing example that impacts others. (Gates 8-14-30-29)

- **Juxtaposition Cross of Contribution:** People fixed on contributing to society in some creative, intimate way, like getting married and spending years restoring an old, run down estate together. (Gates 8-14-55-59)

- **Left Angle Cross of Uncertainty:** People who step into the mutative uncertainty of turning energy into form; you need the right spirit and the right material resources to try. (Gates 8-14-55-59)

GATE 20 - CONTEMPLATION

- **Right Angle Cross of the Sleeping Phoenix 2:** Charismatic people constantly busy; totally absorbed in getting things done, or simply busy being in their creative process while they wait for the coming mutation. (Gates 20-34-55-59)

- **Juxtaposition Cross of the Now:** People whose busyness serves the Tribe, family, pair bond and community; a push-pull between the community and what they want to focus their energy on. (Gates 20-34-37-40)

- **Left Angle Cross of Duality:** People who impress others with and find fulfillment in their busyness and industry; bargaining that creates bridging and mutually beneficial associations. (Gates 20-34-37-40)

THE QUARTER OF CIVILIZATION
– Theme: Purpose fulfilled through Form –

GATE 16 - ENTHUSIASM

- **Right Angle Cross of Planning 2:** Enthusiastic people who deeply identify with detailed solutions or the right work, and with finding a logical way to express progress and mastery. (Gates 16-9-37-40)

- **Juxtaposition Cross of Experimentation:** Influential people who are skilled in getting their network to enthusiastically support their new experiment. (Gates 16-9-63-64)

- **Left Angle Cross of Identification:** People with a strong logical orientation capable of getting others to identify with, and support or underwrite, their skill or project; or to buy their stock. (Gates 16-9-63-64)

GATE 35 - PROGRESS

- **Right Angle Cross of Consciousness 2:** People who have been there, done that, know all about it, feel like a change – and want you to join them; always ready to explore a new way to do things. (Gates 35-5-63-64)

- **Juxtaposition Cross of Experience:** People who are influential in externalizing to others that their experience transforms consciousness; experience is everything. (Gates 35-5-22-47)

- **Left Angle Cross of Separation:** People with the hindsight (grace) to see the necessity of living together *separately* in society by embracing the diverse interpretations of experience which normally divide us; a civilizing process. (Gates 35-5-22-47)

GATE 45 - GATHERING TOGETHER

- **Right Angle Cross of Rulership 2:** People who are here to be offered (or to exercise) power. In current times, this translates to the boardrooms of the corporate world as CEO's. (Gates 45-26-22-47)

- **Juxtaposition Cross of Possession:** People of influence who can step into a rulership role for the community and take charge or rule during crisis and conflict. (Gates 45-26-36-6)

- **Left Angle Cross of Confrontation:** People who govern the resources of the Tribe in times of crisis and conflict, willing to confront with their power or challenge those who wish to rule so they can stake their claim. (Gates 45-26-36-6)

GATE 12 - STANDSTILL

- **Right Angle Cross of Eden 2:** Articulate yet opinionated people who take the loss of innocence to the level of an art form; the gift of expressing love and crisis in poetry and music. (Gates 12-11-36-6)

- **Juxtaposition Cross of Articulation:** An exceptional spokesperson or teacher who has a rare and effective gift of vocal inflection which infects or influences others toward individuation. (Gates 12-11-25-46)

- **Left Angle Cross of Education:** Effective lecturers who are looking for graceful listeners; people dedicated to using resources for the education of the masses, thus furthering global change. (Gates 12-11-25-46)

THE QUARTER OF CIVILIZATION
– Theme: Purpose fulfilled through Form –

GATE 15 - MODESTY

- **Right Angle Cross of the Vessel of Love 2:** People who are naturally concerned about the welfare of humanity. By knowing their own place in the scheme of things, they bring diversity into the flow. (Gates 15-10-25-46)

- **Juxtaposition Cross of Extremes:** People fixed in their own (usually extreme) rhythm and not always in the flow with others; who are unaware that they naturally shine a spotlight on what needs correcting. (Gates 15-10-17-18)

- **Left Angle Cross of Prevention:** People who always seem to meet what doesn't work; it is a gift when used to lovingly guide society away from making the same mistakes over again. (Gates 15-10-17-18)

GATE 52 - KEEPING STILL (MOUNTAIN)

- **Right Angle Cross of Service 2:** Logical people who have the responsibility (and fuel) to ensure that the pattern moving us toward the future is correct/corrected. (Gates 52-58-17-18)

- **Juxtaposition Cross of Stillness:** People quietly, joyously building networks; creating opportunities to influence others with their potential depth/solutions. (Gates 52-58-21-48)

- **Left Angle Cross of Demands:** People who demand that solutions be found, corrections be made, and agreements enforced in order to protect society. (Gates 52-58-21-48)

GATE 39 - OBSTRUCTION

- **Right Angle Cross of Tension 2:** People whose energy must move outward to release tension by provoking talent, leadership, purpose and spirit in others; our great button pushers. (Gates 39-38-21-48)

- **Juxtaposition Cross of Provocation:** Potent yet moody Individuals who use shock to provoke others at a deep level; people who understand the creative value of their melancholy. (Gates 39-38-51-57)

- **Left Angle Cross of Individualism:** Mutative forces that shock you with their intuitive knowing and staunch individualism, but are not easily influenced themselves. (Gates 39-38-51-57)

GATE 53 - DEVELOPMENT

- **Right Angle Cross of Penetration 2:** People who seem happy in the moment, yet feel the pressure to achieve recognition by beginning something new, and know intuitively how to initiate others to join in. (Gates 53-54-51-57)

- **Juxtaposition Cross of Beginnings:** Highly sought after people who energize new cycles of transformation, new beginnings, and can assess the cost, value (people skills) and continuity of a project. (Gates 53-54-42-32)

- **Left Angle Cross of Cycles:** Capable people who can bring a cycle of transformation to maturation as achievement, and understand that the only thing that endures is change. (Gates 53-54-42-32)

THE QUARTER OF CIVILIZATION
– Theme: Purpose fulfilled through Form –

GATE 62 - THE PREPONDERANCE OF THE SMALL

- **Right Angle Cross of the Maya 2:** Powerful forces of education who understand that logic can transform/heal; creating and using language to name, give form to or describe inner truths hidden in the details. (Gates 62-61-42-32)

- **Juxtaposition Cross of Detail:** People who are good at expressing their opinions in great detail; when focused on the law or law making they become good lawyers. (Gates 62-61-3-50)

- **Left Angle Cross of Obscuration:** People who can use details/statistics to dazzle or obscure. Once sorted, obscure detail can lead to extraordinary discovery. (Gates 62-61-3-50)

GATE 56 - THE WANDERER

- **Right Angle Cross of Laws 2:** The effective storytellers who stimulate others with their idealistic opinions and beliefs. Their magic is spun around promises, the dreams of the dreamer. (Gates 56-60-3-50)

- **Juxtaposition Cross of Stimulation:** People who willingly take risks in order to fill their need for any stimulation that gives meaning to their life; the storytellers who find release in telling their own story. (Gates 56-60-27-28)

- **Left Angle Cross of Distraction:** People who can appear distracted, but have a way of drawing attention to themselves or their projects through stimulating conversation. (Gates 56-60-27-28)

GATE 31 - INFLUENCE

- **Right Angle Cross of the Unexpected 2:** People with the inherent power to attract the Collective's attention, who become our unexpected leaders or heroes; their nurturing influence is discovered and acclaimed in the midst of the unexpected. (Gates 31-41-27-28)

- **Juxtaposition Cross of Influence:** Naturally influential and consistent people who intentionally use their mental processes, new experiences and memory in order to persuade others. (Gates 31-41-24-44)

- **Left Angle Cross of the Alpha:** Powerful leaders who impact others by resolving issues of survival on the mental plane; people looked to for practical solutions that secure the future. (Gates 31-41-24-44)

GATE 33 - RETREAT

- **Right Angle Cross of the Four Ways 2:** People who retreat to reflect on experience before sharing their insights, memories or principles; the need to be able to enclose oneself in the sanctity/privacy of one's own realm or room. (Gates 33-19-24-44)

- **Juxtaposition Cross of Retreat:** People who express the need for beauty in life; the aesthetics of retreat begin with enough food to eat and a roof over your head (your own space.) (Gates 33-19-2-1)

- **Left Angle Cross of Refinement:** People who know that it is not enough to have and protect a home; life is enriched by making it beautiful. Beauty that heals. (Gates 33-19-2-1)

THE QUARTER OF DUALITY
– Theme: Purpose fulfilled through Bonding –

GATE 7 - THE ARMY

- **Right Angle Cross of the Sphinx 3:** People of influence, equipped to lead, whose sound logic and attention to the past play a key role in directing humanity toward a secure future. (Gates 7-13-2-1)

- **Juxtaposition Cross of Interaction:** People who are always looking for ways to live out their leadership role, to be of influence without being influenced. Leading by accepting diversity. (Gates 7-13-23-43)

- **Left Angle Cross of Masks 2:** People who are projected upon to provide practical or wise leadership, to be influential change agents; they do so best from behind a mask or title, such as the general or therapist. (Gates 7-13-23-43)

GATE 4 - YOUTHFUL FOLLY

- **Right Angle Cross of Explanation 3:** People whose job is to explain revolutionary and principled solutions; untested Individual knowing necessitates clarifying and repeating insights which have been filtered through logic's formulas. (Gates 4-49-23-43)

- **Juxtaposition Cross of Formulization:** Individual's who inspire you with their creative ability to create formulas and see unique patterns that can empower a new direction. (Gates 4-49-8-14)

- **Left Angle Cross of Revolution 2:** People who are projected upon to provide the practical reasons, and contribute the resources, necessary to instigate a revolution – or not. (Gates 4-49-8-14)

GATE 29 - THE ABYSMAL

- **Right Angle Cross of Contagion 3:** People who say *yes* to new (and intimate) experiences, while looking for fulfillment through commitment, who are able to enter into an experiential process for the sake of experience itself. (Gates 29-30-8-14)

- **Juxtaposition Cross of Commitment:** People fixed on saying *yes* to commitment. They are often sources of inspiration, like the saints who served God until their death. (Gates 29-30-20-34)

- **Left Angle Cross of Industry 2:** People unaware of their enormous charismatic power, who with the right commitments, can persevere and shine. (Gates 29-30-20-34)

GATE 59 - DISPERSION

- **Right Angle Cross of the Sleeping Phoenix 3:** Great fertile agents busy 'making more' to ensure the future; the need for intimacy and security in bonding. (Gates 59-55-20-34)

- **Juxtaposition Cross of Strategy:** People who are focused on seeking to turn opportunities into strategies leading to intimacy with others; the talent for match-making. (Gates 59-55-16-9)

- **Left Angle Cross of Spirit 2:** The lessons of sexuality and romance become wise gifts in the lives and experiences of those who are awake and aware; people focused on transforming the relationship between love/loving and sexuality through spirit. (Gates 59-55-16-9)

THE QUARTER OF DUALITY
– Theme: Purpose fulfilled through Bonding –

GATE 40 - DELIVERANCE

- **Right Angle Cross of Planning 3:** When needed support and the right bargain are in place, these people possess the skills, the gift of logic, and the command of detail, to build what is needed for the community. (Gates 40-37-16-9)

- **Juxtaposition Cross of Denial:** People whose job it is to stubbornly say no to the bargain until it is just right, and to put the brakes on the Collective's run-away progress. (Gates 40-37-35-5)

- **Left Angle Cross of Migration 2:** People who move or migrate, wanting to bring progress, development and change to the next community or valley. (Gates 40-37-35-5)

GATE 64 - BEFORE COMPLETION

- **Right Angle Cross of Consciousness 3:** People who inspire and assist others in making sense of their past by testing experience against accepted patterns, thus progressing toward new ways of thinking about and understanding life. (Gates 64-63-35-5)

- **Juxtaposition Cross of Confusion:** Inspiring historians, founts of information, whose remembering is rooted in Tribal hierarchies and subject to the ego's interpretation/manipulation. (Gates 64-63-45-26)

- **Left Angle Cross of Dominion 2:** People whose interpretation of the past can be impactful; using information to assume positions of power or authority. (Gates 64-63-45-26)

GATE 47 - OPPRESSION

- **Right Angle Cross of Rulership 3:** People bringing the past forward with grace who selectively borrow traditions or lessons learned from experience to claim their legitimate right to rule. (Gates 47-22-45-26)

- **Juxtaposition Cross of Oppression:** People who use their understanding of the past to articulate or promote a new idea or concept, or replace a present understanding. (Gates 47-22-12-11)

- **Left Angle Cross of Informing 2:** People with social skills who use the past to inspire, to turn people's attention toward the plight of those who are oppressed; this is informing as an art. (Gates 47-22-12-11)

GATE 6 - CONFLICT

- **Right Angle Cross of Eden 3:** People who use their experience with conflict and crisis to hold the bond of intimacy together; gaining experience through the loss of innocence. (Gates 6-36-12-11)

- **Juxtaposition Cross of Conflict:** People who bridge the loss of innocence with a 'getting on with life' attitude, and create a fertile environment for companionship; friendships/love emerging from crisis. (Gates 6-36-15-10)

- **Left Angle Cross of the Plane 2:** People here to enjoy their work, while enticing us deeply into the material plane, so that we will always have what we need to love living in the social/material world. (Gates 6-36-15-10)

THE QUARTER OF DUALITY
– Theme: Purpose fulfilled through Bonding –

GATE 46 - PUSHING UPWARD

- **Right Angle Cross of the Vessel of Love 3:** People fully 'embodied,' fully alive in their body, who enjoy the physical (sensual) dynamic of relationships; dedicated to living life for life's sake. (Gates 46-25-15-10)

- **Juxtaposition Cross of Serendipity:** People focused on being in the right place at the right time who understand that correct commitments to experience (plus hard work) lead to good fortune and success; fully enjoying being alive. (Gates 46-25-52-58)

- **Left Angle Cross of Healing 2:** People who spontaneously heal or can be healed through contact with forces of impersonal, universal love; a rare and joyous gift that comes alive through a focused, committed connection with the other. (Gates 46-25-52-58)

GATE 18 - WORK ON WHAT HAS BEEN SPOILT

- **Right Angle Cross of Service 3:** People who are part of the ongoing process of correcting/ perfecting the archetypes of male/female, father/mother; opinions and corrections in service to humanity by working to make what is good better. (Gates 18-17-52-58)

- **Juxtaposition Cross of Correction:** Masters at recognizing flaws in the pattern, or incompetence in everything except themselves; the ability to turn country girls into princesses. (Gates 18-17-39-38)

- **Left Angle Cross of Upheaval 2:** People with a heretical view or a beguiling innocence always ready to provoke, to disturb or to challenge what isn't working; therapists who know that therapy has to be practical to work. (Gates 18-17-39-38)

GATE 48 - THE WELL

- **Right Angle Cross of Tension 3:** People with innate depth who bring understanding to problems and provoke the proper skills/spirit/purpose needed to provide a workable solution. (Gates 48-21-39-38)

- **Juxtaposition Cross of Depth:** People of influence who use their depth to further their ambitions, and to increase their circle of friends and their opportunities to impact, teach or help others transform their inadequacies and begin something new. (Gates 48-21-53-54)

- **Left Angle Cross of Endeavor 2:** People with a driving desire to be in control so they can do something with their depth; this is the "I will do it myself" attitude of self publishers. (Gates 48-21-53-54)

GATE 57 - THE GENTLE

- **Right Angle Cross of Penetration 3:** Highly intuitively aware people capable of discerning penetration; a clarity that guides ambition, with a competitive edge, toward beginning something new in order to assuage our fears for tomorrow. (Gates 57-51-53-54)

- **Juxtaposition Cross of Intuition:** Deeply profound and inspiring people; they break you open with their intuition, detail, knowing and shock so you can receive the message. (Gates 57-51-62-61)

- **Left Angle Cross of the Clarion 2:** Intuitive people expected to carry essential and inspired information which others need or want to hear, who need to be sought out and pressured to speak. (Gates 57-51-62-61)

THE QUARTER OF DUALITY
– Theme: Purpose fulfilled through Bonding –

GATE 32 - DURATION

- **Right Angle Cross of the Maya 3:** People whose inner knowing and use of detail guide their ability to properly evaluate and inspire material development, maturation and expansion. (Gates 32-42-62-61)

- **Juxtaposition Cross of Conservation:** Wary risk takers guided by the value of continuity or duration, who conserve our resources to ensure survival of future generations. (Gates 32-42-56-60)

- **Left Angle Cross of Limitation 2:** People who see impermanence as a limitation, as a pressure, such as on business or industry to value products based on their practicality, and their ability to withstand the test of time. (Gates 32-42-56-60)

GATE 50 - THE CAULDRON

- **Right Angle Cross of Laws 3:** People who create, adapt or evaluate laws and values to accommodate our species' evolution; lawmaking as a creative inner process based in humanity's instincts to survive mutation and change. (Gates 50-3-56-60)

- **Juxtaposition Cross of Values:** People of influence who seize the opportunity to soften or lessen the severity of the law, thus ensuring that the consequences are commensurate with the crime. (Gates 50-3-31-41)

- **Left Angle Cross of Wishes 2:** People with a utopian orientation that transcends traditional values, who challenge both cultural and religious standards by projecting what the system might be. (Gates 50-3-31-41)

GATE 28 - PREPONDERANCE OF THE GREAT

- **Right Angle Cross of the Unexpected 3:** People who unexpectedly have to care for or take responsibility for something or someone. They become an influential example when they find meaning in the struggle. (Gates 28-27-31-41)

- **Juxtaposition Cross of Risks:** Risk takers who push the envelope either to get what they need, or to find purpose and meaning in life. (Gates 28-27-33-19)

- **Left Angle Cross of Alignment 2:** Reflective people who know how to take advantage of the unexpected, who are able to leave the old behind and align with the new when the opportunity arises. (Gates 28-27-33-19)

GATE 44 - COMING TO MEET

- **Right Angle Cross of the Four Ways 3:** Tribal folks with a keen sense of smell, instinctual and historical memory, and sensitivity to the welfare of others, who ponder the viability of family enterprise. (Gates 44-24-33-19)

- **Juxtaposition Cross of Alertness:** Seers with an instinctual sense of alertness who are in tune with where we have been and where we are headed. It is often best to pay attention to them! (Gates 44-24-7-13)

- **Left Angle Cross of Incarnation 2:** People who keep the past alive by revisiting it and connecting all of us to it; endlessly pondering what it means to incarnate and what is needed to survive. (Gates 44-24-7-13)

THE QUARTER OF MUTATION
– Theme: Purpose fulfilled through Transformation –

GATE 1 - THE CREATIVE

- **Right Angle Cross of the Sphinx 4:** Creative Individuals trying to build a legacy to express and immortalize their own direction; providing and maintaining a mutative direction through example. (Gates 1-2-7-13)

- **Juxtaposition Cross of Self Expression:** Socially adept people fixed on providing creative and revolutionary answers for questions which have not yet been asked. (Gates 1-2-4-49)

- **Left Angle Cross of Defiance 2:** Individuals who attract society but are here to protect difference; the fierceness to demand non-interference in any form in order to preserve their uniqueness. (Gates 1-2-4-49)

GATE 43 - BREAKTHROUGH

- **Right Angle Cross of Explanation 4:** People whose knowing has a revolutionary quality about it; the root of understanding begins with efficiently and logically explaining one's revolutionary insights. (Gates 43-23-4-49)

- **Juxtaposition Cross of Insight:** People with a deep desire to externalize their unique insights who are able to effectively influence a select group of people that is ready, willing and able to listen. (Gates 43-23-29-30)

- **Left Angle Cross of Dedication 2:** Individuals dedicated to planting insights in others as a subtle and subversive act of mutation to bring efficiency into society. (Gates 43-23-29-30)

GATE 14 - POSSESSION IN GREAT MEASURE

- **Right Angle Cross of Contagion 4:** People committed to making a potent contribution to society through their accumulation and retention of power or money; resources used wisely to empower (fuel) humanity's growth, development and evolution. (Gates 14-8-29-30)

- **Juxtaposition Cross of Empowering:** People whose melancholic spirit is intimately connected to their financial security; the resources to create a solid foundation in order to guarantee a return on their investment, which empowers others. (Gates 14-8-59-55)

- **Left Angle Cross of Uncertainty 2:** By understanding the financial uncertainty of others, they are able to assist with providing what is needed; intimacy achieved or enhanced through providing (or promising or modeling) material security. (Gates 14-8-59-55)

GATE 34 - THE POWER OF THE GREAT

- **Right Angle Cross of the Sleeping Phoenix 4:** People with great personal power and charisma who are busy attracting others with their busyness; power and intimacy when directed by spirit serves humanity. (Gates 34-20-59-55)

- **Juxtaposition Cross of Power:** Busyness focused on the pure display of charisma or power in support of the community; the entertainer or deal-making business executive. (Gates 34-20-40-37)

- **Left Angle Cross of Duality 2:** People who bridge humanity's basic dilemma (duality) between Individual charisma/selfishness and communal responsibility; busyness properly aligned with loving communal support. (Gates 34-20-40-37)

THE QUARTER OF MUTATION
– Theme: Purpose fulfilled through Transformation –

GATE 9 - THE TAMING POWER OF THE SMALL

- **Right Angle Cross of Planning 4:** People whose enthusiasm is tempered by sensibly focusing on the pertinent details. Great things (plans, bargains, talent) grow naturally when all aspects have been carefully considered and adequately supported. (Gates 9-16-40-37)

- **Juxtaposition Cross of Focus:** People who enthusiastically inspire others to bring into focus what is important for the Collective; to identify and concentrate on the potential future of society. (Gates 9-16-64-63)

- **Left Angle Cross of Identification 2:** People who identify where to concentrate their skills (on which doubt or impasse), and find mental stability in knowing there are resources in place to assuage or address them. (Gates 9-16-64-63)

GATE 5 - WAITING

- **Right Angle Cross of Consciousness 4:** People who create their own momentum for growth and development by following their own flow; consciousness as a fundamental attunement to natural rhythms. (Gates 5-35-64-63)

- **Juxtaposition Cross of Habits:** People of habit with a sense of order that is not easily influenced; being fixed in their flow manifests as a habitual pattern or ritual that gives their life consistency. (Gates 5-35-47-22)

- **Left Angle Cross of Separation 2:** People open to love who are trying to make sense of the past by separating themselves from patterns/relationships that didn't work in order to see the exquisite beauty in (and bring changes to) the larger patterns of life. (Gates 5-35-47-22)

GATE 26 - THE TAMING POWER OF THE GREAT

- **Right Angle Cross of Rulership 4:** People with social charm able to market themselves as a leader by combining selective memory and personal touch (handshaking, baby holding) with the promise of educating everyone toward a better tomorrow; today's politicians. (Gates 26-45-47-22)

- **Juxtaposition Cross of the Trickster:** People with a natural gift for marketing to the inexperienced, who promote the off beat and unusual. (Gates 26-45-6-36)

- **Left Angle Cross of Confrontation 2:** People with grace and a sense of (personal) justice who will confront authority to institute their own rulership; powerful ego forces reluctant to change. (Gates 26-45-6-36)

GATE 11 - PEACE

- **Right Angle Cross of Eden 4:** People with a philosophical orientation who educate others about the nature of experience and emotions on this plane, perhaps through music or poetry. (Gates 11-12-6-36)

- **Juxtaposition Cross of Ideas:** Highly mutative people who collect universal concepts and can become important teachers (or prophets), and are often fixed in a single direction. (Gates 11-12-46-25)

- **Left Angle Cross of Education 2:** People of 'peace, philanthropy and propaganda' desiring to communicate often inexpressible ideas about human experience. Teaching is still the most profound thing humans do. (Gates 11-12-46-25)

THE QUARTER OF MUTATION
– Theme: Purpose fulfilled through Transformation –

GATE 10 - TREADING

- **Right Angle Cross of the Vessel of Love 4:** When engaging in enriching and empowering individuating behaviors, they push the world toward love by being fully themselves and loving their difference. (Gates 10-15-46-25)

- **Juxtaposition Cross of Behavior:** The critical opportunist looking to leave the right impression with their own behavior, while quick to organize or challenge that of others. (Gates 10-15-18-17)

- **Left Angle Cross of Prevention 2:** People both oppressive and liberating who bring 'correction' by trying to prevent unhealthy behaviors/actions in others (society) before they happen. (Gates 10-15-18-17)

GATE 58 - THE JOYOUS

- **Right Angle Cross of Service 4:** People whose joy in the wonder of life fuels their focus on challenging the norm, and perfecting the logic process through ideas and forms that serve society. (Gates 58-52-18-17)

- **Juxtaposition Cross of Vitality:** People with highly sought-after vitality and staying power who understand the importance of controlling how and to whom they parcel out their energy. (Gates 58-52-48-21)

- **Left Angle Cross of Demands 2:** People who are willing to apply their energy to or identify with someone's project or perfecting of skills if they get what they want in return; the best defense is a good offense. (Gates 58-52-48-21)

GATE 38 - OPPOSITION

- **Right Angle Cross of Tension 4:** People with creative depth who understand that life is a struggle, yet know that struggle provokes spirit and purpose making it worthwhile. (Gates 38-39-48-21)

- **Juxtaposition Cross of Opposition:** Individuals with adrenalized energy who intuitively provoke or oppose (or shock you) into substantiating and explaining your claim or opinion. (Gates 38-39-57-51)

- **Left Angle Cross of Individualism 2:** Pure Individuals who have to keep mutating/keep becoming themselves, which in turn shocks, creates tension or provokes change in you. (Gates 38-39-57-51)

GATE 54 - THE MARRYING MAIDEN

- **Right Angle Cross of Penetration 4:** People on the path from rags to riches who are recognized by those higher up the ladder; aligning with higher (even mystical) forces. (Gates 54-53-57-51)

- **Juxtaposition Cross of Ambition:** Influential but conservative agents of transformation driven by the fear of failure, and the need to complete their commitments, who are never satisfied. (Gates 54-53-32-42)

- **Left Angle Cross of Cycles 2:** Ambitious people with the energy to foment transformative change for the good of individuals and nations (and themselves) through their dedication to the continuity that comes from fully completing each cycle. (Gates 54-53-32-42)

THE QUARTER OF MUTATION
– Theme: Purpose fulfilled through Transformation –

GATE 61 - INNER TRUTH

- **Right Angle Cross of the Maya 4:** Inspiring/inspired thinkers who must use their mind in service to others in order to avoid going mad by trying to know the unknowable; people looking for universal truths in facts and details to resolve the questions of life and death. (Gates 61-62-32-42)

- **Juxtaposition Cross of Thinking:** Intelligent people in pursuit of knowledge for its own sake, who take personal, detailed insight deep enough to change what is known/accepted; good lawyers. (Gates 61-62-50-3)

- **Left Angle Cross of Obscuration 2:** Individuals whose inspired knowing (the *obscura* of inner truth and universal principles) can bring out details about absolute and universal laws which might otherwise be missed. (Gates 61-62-50-3)

GATE 60 - LIMITATION

- **Right Angle Cross of Laws 4:** People who accept the limitation of assessment and the ramifications of change, yet maintain traditional values which inform our laws like, "Thou shall not kill." (Gates 60-56-50-3)

- **Juxtaposition Cross of Limitation:** Resourceful people able to maximize the potential hidden within limitations; seeking purpose through risk taking, and nurturing themselves and others, in order to test the boundaries of each limitation. (Gates 60-56-28-27)

- **Left Angle Cross of Distraction 2:** People who use distraction as an art form, such as a magician; transcending limitation through stimulation and risk taking. (Gates 60-56-28-27)

GATE 41 - DECREASE

- **Right Angle Cross of the Unexpected 4:** People unexpectedly thrust into positions of leadership who initiate or influence others by setting trends in caring, or in finding purpose. (Gates 41-31-28-27)

- **Juxtaposition Cross of Fantasy:** Influential people great in jobs where recognizing trends and dreaming about the future are rewarded; indulging fantasies in virtual reality. (Gates 41-31-44-24)

- **Left Angle Cross of the Alpha 2:** People who seduce others with their dreams and fantasies while waiting for the unexpected moment of advantage to lead them into the promised land with its expectations for what seems new or better. (Gates 41-31-44-24)

GATE 19 - APPROACH

- **Right Angle Cross of the Four Ways 4:** People pressured by sensitivity to human (and animal) rights who are motivated by social and spiritual forces to provide for the basic needs of others. (Gates 19-33-44-24)

- **Juxtaposition Cross of Need:** People with a creative direction, and deep need to create beauty in their lives which will be enjoyed by their close circle of friends. (Gates 19-33-1-2)

- **Left Angle Cross of Refinement 2:** People who understand that one's proper direction (alignment) is something of great beauty which satisfies their needs, refines their whole experience of life and leads to the fulfillment of their purpose. (Gates 19-33-1-2)

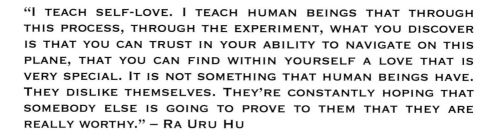

"I TEACH SELF-LOVE. I TEACH HUMAN BEINGS THAT THROUGH THIS PROCESS, THROUGH THE EXPERIMENT, WHAT YOU DISCOVER IS THAT YOU CAN TRUST IN YOUR ABILITY TO NAVIGATE ON THIS PLANE, THAT YOU CAN FIND WITHIN YOURSELF A LOVE THAT IS VERY SPECIAL. IT IS NOT SOMETHING THAT HUMAN BEINGS HAVE. THEY DISLIKE THEMSELVES. THEY'RE CONSTANTLY HOPING THAT SOMEBODY ELSE IS GOING TO PROVE TO THEM THAT THEY ARE REALLY WORTHY." — RA URU HU

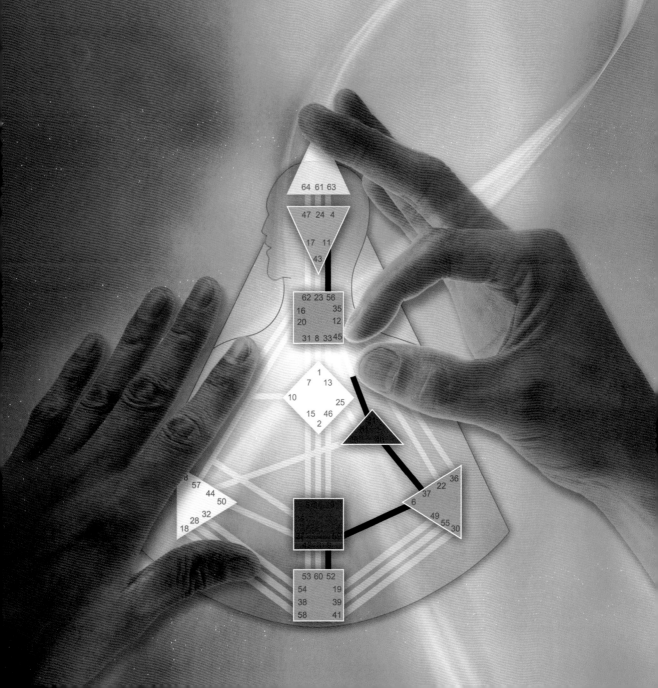

SECTION NINE
SAMPLE CHART OVERVIEWS
HUMAN DESIGN IN PRACTICE

SECTION NINE

SAMPLE CHART OVERVIEWS

HUMAN DESIGN IN PRACTICE

Certified Professional Analysts are trained to interpret a Human Design BodyGraph. The combined perspectives of the true self, who you are designed to be, and the not-self, where you are open to taking in conditioning from the outside world, form the foundation for understanding your design. Ra Uru Hu was a master synthesizer who created a language he termed Keynotes; a living, symbolic language that allows analysts to express the genetic continuity contained within The Science of Differentiation's complex and revolutionary perspectives. Keynotes compress a great deal of information into a single word or phrase. Like a mantra, keynotes invoke or awaken or connect us with our body's chemistry, with our own unique frequency. Learning and using the language of keynotes is like thinking with the body's hormonal messaging system; it allows us to connect energetically with others. Almost every aspect of The Human Design System has its own keynote associated with it. By stringing the keynotes of one's definition and open centers together, professional analysts create a word picture or story of a person's character and purpose. As the keynotes are delivered, the story penetrates the person on a cellular level that is beyond the mind.

Keynotes have been used throughout this book to explain The Human Design System. A complete listing of the gate and channel keynotes used in Human Design can be found in Section Eleven. Sample chart overviews for each of the Types follow, and will provide you with a superficial example of keynoting, and the synthesis that takes place when an analyst works with your chart. The basis of an in-depth reading, by a professionally trained analyst, is the weaving of your genetic information with practical tools for living your unique life.

"HUMAN DESIGN IS NOTHING BUT KEYNOTES. KEYNOTES ARE IN SOME WAYS LIKE HAIKU. THEY ARE VERY, VERY SPECIFIC FORMULAS AND AS SUCH, IN SO MANY WAYS, THEY'RE GENERALIZATIONS, SO ONE HAS TO BE CAREFUL. THERE ARE ALL KINDS OF PEOPLE WHO CAN QUOTE THE INFORMATION, BUT THAT'S NOT THE POINT. WE ARE A HOLISTIC ILLUSION, IF I CAN PUT IT THAT WAY. WE ARE THE SUM TOTAL OF OUR FORMULAS. AND WE HAVE FORMULAS THAT INDICATE WHAT WE ARE, AND WE HAVE FORMULAS THAT INDICATE WHAT THE NOT-SELF IS. WE HAVE KEYNOTES FOR EVERYTHING. BUT TO BE ABLE TO USE KEYNOTES IS NOT SCIENCE; IT'S ART. AND IT TAKES PRACTICE AND IT TAKES TIME, BECAUSE IT IS ABOUT THE FREEDOM THAT COMES IN THE ANALYSIS OF A BODYGRAPH, THE FREEDOM THAT HAS TO BE THERE WHEN ONE LOOKS AT IT AND EXPLORES IT.

THE KEYNOTES ARE A SYNTHESIS. EACH KEYNOTE IS A SYNTHESIS OF THE VALUE OF THAT PARTICULAR ASPECT. WHEN YOU LAY THEM OUT IN ANY KIND OF GEOMETRY, YOU TRULY OPEN UP THIS OPPORTUNITY TO BE ABLE TO REALLY READ YOUR FORMULA, SEE YOUR FORMULA AND TO EXPAND UPON IT. KEYNOTING IS AN ADVENTURE. WHAT I LIKE IS THE EXPERIENCE BECAUSE YOU DON'T REALLY KNOW UNTIL YOU START DOING IT. WHEN YOU START DOING IT IT'S LIKE AN EMPTY CANVAS IN FRONT OF YOU AND WHAT YOU'RE ABOUT TO DO IS WRITE YOUR CODE. THINK ABOUT THE HISTORY OF HUMANITY, WHAT THAT ACTUALLY SAYS, WHAT KIND OF A MOMENT THAT IS FOR YOU, AND WHAT KIND OF GRACE IT TAKES." – RA URU HU

MANIFESTOR OVERVIEW

AURA – CLOSED AND REPELLING

STRATEGY	INFORM	**DEFINITION**	SIMPLE SPLIT
PROFILE	1/4	**NOT-SELF THEME**	ANGER
AUTHORITY	SPLENIC	**SIGNATURE**	PEACE

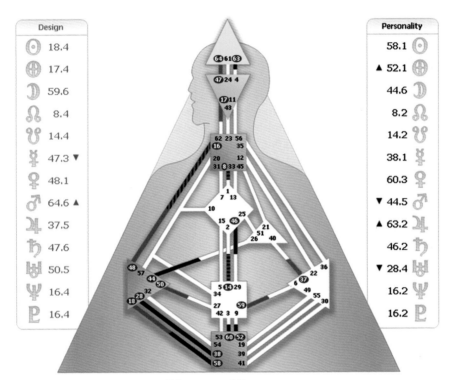

HENRY MILLER

RIGHT ANGLE CROSS OF SERVICE

UNDEFINED G, HEART, SACRAL AND SOLAR PLEXUS

58-18 JUDGMENT, A DESIGN OF INSATIABILITY
38-28 STRUGGLE, A DESIGN OF STUBBORNNESS
48-16 THE WAVELENGTH, A DESIGN OF TALENT
64-47 ABSTRACTION, A DESIGN OF MENTAL ACTIVITY AND CLARITY

Your gift in the world is your ability to act independently, to initiate action and to impact others. When perceived as threatening or unpredictable, however, these same qualities can make others uncomfortable, often leading them to try and control you or resist you in some way. As a Manifestor, you can be at ease with solitude. You don't really require outside assistance, and sometimes you wonder why others would even care about what you do, much less want to resist or control you. Try to control they do, though, from parents on up. An early and unpleasant history of conditioning experiences, mixed with resistance, pushes you toward the not-self theme of Anger which is expressed in one of two ways: as anger/rage and rebelliousness, or as passivity and accommodation. Either expression causes you to repress your power, and keeps you from realizing your worth. This is why your Strategy to Inform before you act is so important. It relaxes the resistance from others, and opens the way for you to have what you seek most in life, namely the peace to do what you want to do when you want to do it. You are a self-contained person, and at times you can see others as rather alien. With your ability to look ahead and initiate, they can feel out of sync with your timing.

The concern that you have is "Will I be answered? Will someone be enlivened by my impact, or respond to my initiating question?" This underlying pressure to impact, to make things happen, is the key to fulfilling your purpose. Although you are most comfortable when left alone to do your own thing, the other three Types are waiting for you to spark or initiate them so each can contribute their essential part. And you often look to the other types to provide the specific energies needed to complete what you dream. In a perfect world, Manifestors get things started, Projectors guide the process, Generators provide the energy to bring it into form or complete it, and Reflectors tell us how well the process is going, or not.

Your Strategy of informing may seem unnatural to you, and you probably resist informing others because you don't want them to put up barriers or resist you. You are not designed to ask for permission, and so you keep quiet and do what you want without informing, hoping that you will not meet with resistance. This not-self strategy usually backfires, however, and you meet the resistance anyway and often even more intensely, which creates a no-win vicious circle. When you do Inform before taking action on a decision, others feel included and respected. They may not like what you are doing, but knowing about it in advance eases the resistance and potential backlash. In addition, informing gives you an opportunity to use the resistance field as a guide to right timing and action. If you announce to an office of 50 people, for instance, that you are now shifting to a 4 day work week, and 47 of the people are unhappy with this decision, you have an opportunity to adjust or refine your decision.

When you are making a decision, your Spleen is your Inner Authority, and it is very important that you listen when it speaks to you. Splenic Authority speaks to you quietly in the moment, and does not repeat itself. It's 'voice' will feel more like an intuitive or instinctual recognition. If you miss its signal, or ignore it, it does not warn you again. Your Spleen is here to keep you alive, safe and healthy. It will only give you warnings about your survival in the moment, and as needed.

In fact, your Splenic Authority flows out of you naturally, moment by moment. Such spontaneity may sound freeing, but it creates a dilemma where you may have to inform when you have only an inkling of the impact that your immediate decision or action might have. It takes intention, concerted effort, and living closely attuned to your Splenic Authority to be effective in your informing. For example, if you step into a restaurant with friends, and your body stops you because something does not feel right to it, you have no choice but to pay attention to it. It is alerting you that it is not healthy for you to enter, and yet your Splenic warning does not come with an explanation. All you can do is honestly inform your companions of what action is correct for you right now, with an awareness of how your sudden decision impacts them and their plans. Overall, informing brings you greater peace and this is what you desire more than anything - to have no resistance. When you are peaceful it is a signpost that you have aligned yourself to your Authority, and it is from this place that you are empowered to manifest and make your unique impact on the world.

Your Profile, the costume you wear in the world, is the 1/4, or Investigator Opportunist. Your profile is the role you play in life so that your purpose can express itself, and you are here to investigate things deeply. You are driven to establish secure foundations in your life, and consciously you can be very introspective and self-absorbed. Your intention is to establish a level of authority yourself that can be shared with others. At the same time there is an unconscious part of you that is very influential, and has the ability to relate to others at a brotherhood/sisterhood level. Your community is very important to you as you are designed unconsciously to establish relationships or friendships that will bring you the opportunities you need to get your knowledge out, and influence others. In any type of close or intimate relationship, however, it is important for you to establish a friendship first. Strangers are not comfortable for you. By following your Strategy of informing and listening to your Spleen's Authority you will focus your energy on what is most important for you, as well as connect to your correct networks. In this way you establish a personal and secure foundation, establish your realm of influence, share your investigations with others, and maintain your health and well-being. As an Investigator Opportunist, the study of people can be quite a fascination for you.

You have a split in your chart which means there are two separate areas in your design that are not connected to each other. These two parts can take time to sync up, and you may feel very conditioned that there is something missing in you that you need to be complete. One aspect of your split is the Root Center connected to the Splenic Center and the Throat Center through the Channel of Judgment, A design of Insatiability (58/18); the Channel of Struggle, A design of Stubbornness (38/28); and the Channel of The Wavelength, A design of Talent (48/16). The other part of your split is the Head Center connected to the Ajna Center by the Channel of Abstraction, A Design of Mental Activity and Clarity (64-47).

The open gate that can bridge your Split Definition is Gate 62, the Gate of Detail. This puts a tremendous amount of conditioning on you to find the detail that substantiates the opinion. You can become obsessed with details, causing you to make mental decisions about which detail you 'think' is the detail you need. In truth, as you go through your investigations, your Splenic awareness as your Authority will guide you to the correct detail. When not listening to your Authority, you can chase down endless details, leading to overwork, overwhelm and exhaustion.

You have four channels, or types of life force energy, defined in your design. This is the energy that is consistent in you that you put out to others, and it forms the foundation for what you can trust in your own life process. Let's take a look at each one:

Channel of Judgment: A Design of Insatiability (58/18). This channel creates the insatiable drive to challenge, correct and perfect for the betterment of the collective and society; and to find peace in the perfected pattern. When you are operating as true self, if something isn't working in the greater world around you, you have the logic to challenge it until it is corrected. When the perfecting or critiquing process is made personal, however, and turned inward on you or those close to you, it can result in constant fault finding, and a pervading dissatisfaction with life in general that can create friction in relationships.

Channel of Struggle: A design of Stubbornness (38-28). There is nothing more satisfying for you than to be correctly invited to stand up for something you feel is worth fighting for as this signifies that your life has meaning. This is the fuel for your personal struggle to find a purpose that makes living worthwhile, and through your example, each unique search for meaning prods, encourages and empowers others in their own struggle for meaning. You can become very depressed, or depressing for others, if you are unable to find a reason for living. It takes a long time though for you to give up your search as you are designed with a stubbornness that allows you to persevere through struggles that most others cannot. Your Spleen's Authority will help you be aware of what struggles are correct for you to enter into or not.

The pressure that you feel from your Root Center, through both of these channels, can become excessive at times, and push you to step out of your Authority and struggle when you do not need to. In order to maintain your physical health, when you feel restless, exercise is important. Sometimes all that is needed to calm down and refocus yourself is a good walk around the block to burn off the extra steam.

Channel of The Wavelength: A Design of Talent (48-16). You are here to master a skill through repetition, or practice, while striving for perfection. A skill can be anything from playing an instrument, to figuring out a scientific formula, to making your way in the world. When your achievements are shared and become a part of the collective wavelength, you often serve a wider purpose, or improve the lives of others in some way. If you can be disciplined to stay with the repetitive process long enough, you will eventually be liberated from the learning technique and your talent will just naturally flow from you.

Channel of Abstraction: A Design of Mental Activity and Clarity. (64/47). You have a very active, experiential mind that never stops playing with possibilities, and you probably wonder if it will never stop being busy. You can experience considerable mental confusion as a result of the constant swirl of images always moving through it. This confusion, though, can mark the beginning of a new and inspiring journey for you as you discover what really does make sense. If you remain patient with your discovery process, the pieces of the puzzle will at some point come together and a picture will appear. Your reward for being patient, for waiting for clarity to emerge over time, is the uncovering of an inspiring tale to tell, or a new perspective to share with others. Your active mind is a wonderful outer authority for others, however, is not a useful resource for you in terms of figuring out your own life. Mental recognition for you will come over time, while your Authority through your Spleen is here to guide your decision making in the moment.

The Undefined Centers that are open in your design are the G, Heart, Sacral and Solar Plexus. These centers are places of deep conditioning and potential wisdom.

Your Undefined G Center conditions your not-self mind to obsess about identity, love and direction; who am I, where is my love and what direction should I go next? When you let go of worrying about these things and stop trying to find them, you discover who you are, love finds you, and your next direction shows itself, all as a natural process of life.

Your Undefined Heart pushes you to try and prove your worth. This plays out in many ways. You might try to prove yourself by constantly trying to improve yourself, or by overcompensating and making promises. You are not designed to commit to or promise anything to anyone, and breaking a promise can break your heart. Your life is not about willing yourself to do anything. You 'do' in your life through your Strategy of informing and your Authority of following your instincts. Once you let go of trying to prove yourself, you can become wise about knowing who has an overblown ego, who really can commit to things, and who really is of value to the community.

Your Undefined Sacral leads you to over-do, work too hard, and often can be obsessed with sex. You are designed to initiate an enterprise, but not to do it all or complete it yourself. It is very easy for you to fall into the trap of doing too much which will lead to exhaustion and eventual ill health. The wisdom available through an open sacral is knowing when enough is enough. Slowing down, setting and keeping boundaries, and making decisions with your Authority are the key to keeping you healthy.

Your Undefined Solar Plexus, when combined with the Undefined Sacral, can intensify any obsession with sex and romance. The Solar Plexus Center carries feelings of desire, intimacy, and passion, and when undefined these sensations can be amplified and powerful. In fact, the sometimes overwhelming mix of the emotions that you take in from others through your open Solar Plexus can also lead you to avoid the unpleasant sides of emotionality, even when it is important to confront them. As a Manifestor with a not-self theme of Anger, this emotion can also get amplified in certain circumstances. The potential wisdom of your undefined Solar Plexus is to learn to discern which emotionally uncomfortable situations actually need to be dealt with.

In summary, you are designed to serve others by being an initiating force in the world. When you stay alert to your intuitive knowing you spark others to think about the values of society, and their own individual struggle as it relates to survival, values and purpose. You have a sharp eye for critical detail. Through the synthesis of your investigative interest in people, your love of life, the lessons you have learned from the past, and the networks of allies that you cultivate, you can use your insatiable talent and highly pressurized drive to influence and ultimately mutate the collective. Opportunities for success on your journey through life are dependent upon the quality of your relationships and networks. Informing before you act on your decisions can lessen or remove the resistance from others. As long as you stay connected to your intuitive awareness in each decision you will stay on track with your unique life and purpose, and find the peace that you yearn for. The signposts that you are letting your not-self mind override your instincts and personal Authority are over-committing in order to prove your worth or keep the peace in your life and relationships, and not keeping proper boundaries. Intimate relationships can become a preoccupation, and you can go from one partner to the next as you eventually find something wrong with each one. You have keen instincts and are very quick with your words, but letting your mind and emotions override your instincts is detrimental to your well-being.

GENERATOR OVERVIEW

AURA — OPEN AND ENVELOPING

STRATEGY	WAIT TO RESPOND	**DEFINITION**	SINGLE
PROFILE	5/1	**NOT-SELF THEME**	FRUSTRATION
AUTHORITY	SACRAL	**SIGNATURE**	SATISFACTION

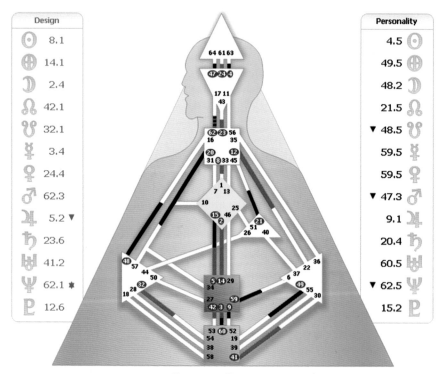

Design		Personality
☉ 8.1		4.5 ☉
⊕ 14.1		49.5 ⊕
☽ 2.4		48.2 ☽
☊ 42.1		21.5 ☊
☋ 32.1		▼ 48.5 ☋
☿ 3.4		59.5 ☿
♀ 24.4		59.5 ♀
♂ 62.3		▼ 47.3 ♂
♃ 5.2 ▼		9.1 ♃
♄ 23.6		20.4 ♄
♅ 41.2		60.5 ♅
♆ 62.1 ✴		▼ 62.5 ♆
♇ 12.6		15.2 ♇

JULIA CHILD

LEFT ANGLE CROSS OF REVOLUTION

UNDEFINED HEAD, AJNA, THROAT, HEART, SPLEEN AND SOLAR PLEXUS

60-3 MUTATION, ENERGY WHICH FLUCTUATES & INITIATES, PULSE
14 -2 THE BEAT, A DESIGN OF BEING THE KEEPER OF KEYS
5-15 RHYTHM, A DESIGN OF BEING IN THE FLOW

You are a Generator, and you were born to work and to love your work. Your gift in life is to perfect or master a task, project or skill. Your gift to the planet is the life force energy that you generate from your Sacral Center. When you are engaged in your correct work, you experience deep satisfaction. In order for you to find the work that will bring satisfaction, it is important for you to 'know' yourself, and the truest path to knowing yourself is responding to life rather than initiating.

When you respond you engage your Sacral Center in everything you do. Your Sacral Center is the key to your happiness and satisfaction. The only way to truly know what is correct for you is by allowing your Sacral Center to be your guide for making decisions. To fully surrender to your Sacral's built in navigation system, you must remain available to respond. Something or someone in your life asks you for your energy, and your Sacral connects its energy to what is correct for your life purpose. In order for you to follow your Sacral, however, you must surrender every picture you have in your mind about what your life 'should' look like. And your mind in particular is very open to the ideas and opinions of others. You have a rhythm, however, and a direction in life that is very unique to you, and when you stay true to it, you can also influence and mutate the rhythm and direction of those around you as well.

A Sacral response is a non-verbal sound from the gut. A yes is 'ah-huh,' which means you have the energy needed for the task, and a no is 'uhn-uh,' meaning you do not have the energy to commit. Sometimes you will not have a response at all, which indicates either you do not have the energy, or perhaps you have not been asked the correct question. Once your Sacral responds ah-huh and you are engaged in an activity, you then go through a step-by-step perfecting and building process. You must cover all the steps in your process. You don't have a motor connected to your Throat Center though (which is the gear shift for your design), and so you will hit plateaus along the way. At each of these plateaus you will need to be initiated again by a new insight, or new input or questions to respond to. Then, depending upon your response, you can engage in your work again.

When you do not follow your Strategy and Authority – when you do not wait for life to come to you to respond and then honor the truth of that response – you experience resistance in your life. You experience what your mind thinks of as your 'not-self,' which means it is asking you to act like someone else. Frustration is the not-self theme of a Generator, and is an important signpost for you. Frustration comes from either meeting internal or external resistance, and noticing your frustration lets you know when it's time to check in with yourself and see if you are pushing, or initiating, rather than responding. You can quit prematurely out of frustration if you do not understand what is happening. Trusting your Sacral responses instead of making decisions with your mind can be a bit frightening at first. Over time though you will get to know your body's intelligence. One of the great fears Generators have is "Will I be asked?" You have it built into your design, into the mechanics of your form, that you will be asked so that you 'can' respond. Your aura is open and enveloping, and it pulls to you everything you need in life. All you need to do is sit back and watch what your Sacral responds to, or not.

Your Profile, the costume you wear in the world, is the 5/1, or Heretic Investigator. Your profile is the role you play in life so that your purpose can express itself, and you are here to investigate things deeply. Your role on the planet is very trans-personal, and you have the potential to universalize new and practical solutions for others in a very public way. There is an unconscious part of you that feels insecure without a firm foundation though, and so you respond first to deeply investigating life, and to discovering what authorities you can rely on. Eventually all of your research and study will turn you into an authority yourself, and then you will feel comfortable universalizing what you have learned to the public.

The Heretic part of your profile is very seductive, and draws people to you who project onto you that you can help or save them with your out-of-the-box practical solutions. You will also feel yourself at times projecting onto others that you can indeed save them. It is important that you do not initiate, however, and that you wait to be asked and answer yes only if your Sacral responds ah-huh. Your Sacral will know if this is the correct time for you to offer your heresy, and for others to follow you in it. Your power to help others is more as a stranger of consequence. You are designed to step in when really needed and then step back out again. People expect you to deliver the goods, so preparation and a solid knowledge base is crucial for your success and satisfaction, otherwise your reputation will suffer. You want to leave them wanting more!

The consistent energy that people experience from you is made up of the three defined channels in your design. The Channel of Mutation (60-3), which connects your Root Center to your Sacral Center, is a very individual energy that fluctuates and initiates in an on/off pulse manner. This is very creative and mutative energy, but you are not in control of the timing of the pulse, and you can spend a lot of time wondering when the next moment of creativity will show itself. You can even experience depression when it feels like nothing new and creative is happening in your life. This is a a deep process of surrender, however, and melancholy and moodiness are also a part of it. If you try and give a reason for your moods, however, or to change them, you only make it harder on yourself. There is no reason, it's just the mechanical pulse of your individual, creative and mutative process. Your energy is also very empowering to others, and can mutate them in a new direction as well, so it is important that you let your Sacral response guide you to those situations where people are truly ready for the mutation that you potentially bring.

You are designed to sustain your own creative efforts, or materially provide for and encourage people in their own creative endeavors. The Channel of the Beat (14-2) is an unconscious energy that connects your Sacral motor to your G Center. This is very individual energy that empowers through example, and so your first task is to be true to yourself. Wait for life to come to you and show you potentials that you cannot even imagine – remain open and responsive to life. If you attempt to chase after or create your destiny, you will end up feeling lost and frustrated. This energy is also about being the Keeper of Keys, the one who has the resources to turn the engine on and move in a new direction. It is only when you are asked, however, that you will know what that key or direction is.

You also have a magnetic presence that pulls others into your aura, your timing and your flow. Through your Channel of Rhythm, also connecting your Sacral to your G Center (5-15), you are constantly moved along by the river of life, vitally and intimately connected to its continuous flow. You appear to others to have your own sense of timing which is determined entirely by your own inner rhythm. And if the patterns or routines you are living are natural and correct for you, then you should allow nothing to interfere with them. If you live out the distortions and incorrect timing of the not-self, however, you will find yourself disrupting everyone's flow, beginning with your own. You are always in the right timing and flow when you follow your Sacral response.

You have six Undefined Centers in your design, including the Head, Ajna, Throat, Heart, Spleen and Solar Plexus. These are the areas within you that are open to the conditioning of others, and you are very sensitive to what is going on in your environment. This openness can distract you from your own response and flow in life. What is going on outside of you can have you thinking about questions that don't matter to you (open Head Center), or trying to answer everyone else's questions (open Ajna Center). In truth you have a very open mind that can become very wise about what questions and answers really have value to you personally, and to others when you universalize them. You can become very wise about what solutions have true practical value, and do the research to support your answers. It is only by waiting to be asked and then responding, however, that you will know what answer has value or not.

Through your open Throat Center you can find yourself talking too much in order to attract attention, or to prove your worth (open Heart Center). You may feel pressured to know what you are going to do next, or to jump in to try and save people in order to prove your value to others. Once again, you have tremendous resources available energetically that will support you personally, and allow you to support others as well, but you will only have access to these resources when the timing is correct. And you will only know this if you respond from your Sacral, rather than react from your mind. You have the potential to become very wise about what really does have value to the public, and to express it in a creative and empowering way.

You may also find your not-self holding onto things that are not healthy for you (open Splenic Center) and avoiding confrontation and truth (open Solar Plexus Center). Your personal Sacral authority operates in the moment, and your truth is available to you immediately through your response. If you do not speak your truth in the moment however, because you are afraid that it will affect your security, or upset someone else, you cannot stay true to your own rhythm and direction. Although it may feel confrontational to speak your truth, this is the greatest asset that you bring to the collective. You are a true heretic who will find new solutions for the issues that we all face. You are designed to understand what people need, and to attract attention in order to communicate and universalize something new to the world.

Everything you do in life that is not a Sacral response is a distraction from what you are here to do, from the unique life purpose that only you can live out in the world. This life purpose only finds you though when you do not initiate, but rather wait to respond. Through your investigations, and practical understanding of others, you have the potential to succeed in life and to bring a new revolutionary pattern and flow to society's creative process. You have the ability to organize and empower others to develop their own skills, and to tap into their own creativity. You have a knack and capacity for expressing details which can bring discovery and metamorphosis to the public. By staying in your own flow, and responding honestly to what life brings to you, you will experience the satisfaction that is a signpost that all is well in your world.

MANIFESTING GENERATOR OVERVIEW

AURA – OPEN AND ENVELOPING

STRATEGY	WAIT TO RESPOND	**DEFINITION**	SIMPLE SPLIT
PROFILE	3/5	**NOT-SELF THEME**	FRUSTRATION
AUTHORITY	EMOTIONAL	**SIGNATURE**	SATISFACTION

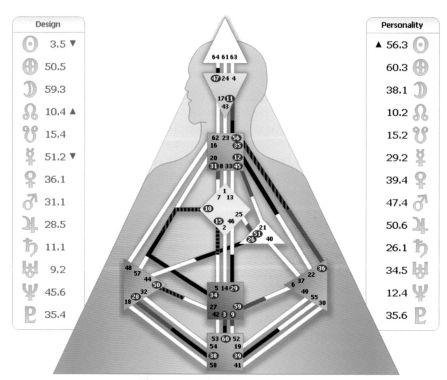

Design		Personality
☉	3.5 ▼	▲ 56.3 ☉
⊕	50.5	60.3 ⊕
☽	59.3	38.1 ☽
☊	10.4 ▲	10.2 ☊
☋	15.4	15.2 ☋
☿	51.2 ▼	29.2 ☿
♀	36.1	39.4 ♀
♂	31.1	47.4 ♂
♃	28.5	50.6 ♃
♄	11.1	26.1 ♄
♅	9.2	34.5 ♅
♆	45.6	12.4 ♆
♇	35.4	35.6 ♇

ERNEST HEMINGWAY

RIGHT ANGLE CROSS OF LAWS

UNDEFINED HEAD AND HEART

60-3 MUTATION, ENERGY WHICH FLUCTUATES & INITIATES, PULSE
38-28 STRUGGLE, A DESIGN OF STUBBORNNESS
34-10 EXPLORATION, A DESIGN OF FOLLOWING ONE'S CONVICTIONS
36-35 TRANSITORINESS, A DESIGN OF A "JACK OF ALL TRADES"
56-11 CURIOSITY, A DESIGN OF A SEARCHER

You are a Manifesting Generator, a warrior buddha who can move very quickly into action. Your gift is to discover through action how to make whatever you are focused on more efficient. In order to know what action is correct for you however, you must be a buddha first and sit under that tree and wait for life to come to you. Your Strategy in life is to wait to be asked for your energy so that you can hear and feel your Sacral response. Your Sacral Center is designed to respond through sounds that come from your gut as either an 'ah-huh' for yes or 'uhn-uh' for no. Or you may respond by actually moving into action. Your responses are based on the availability, or not, of your Sacral energy to connect to and do what you have been asked.

Your defined Sacral Center is here to work and, more importantly, to love the work you do to the point of completely using up your energy every day. Doing work that you love brings you a deep feeling of satisfaction. The correct work actually transforms your life and slows the degenerative process. It is very important for you to know yourself and understand your own process for finding the correct work, and you do this through responding. You can move directly from response to manifestation, which allows you to see the steps that are essential, and the steps that can be skipped. This gift of efficiency creates a dilemma for you, however, as you can have a tendency to be so impatient, and move through a task so fast, that you miss steps. You sometimes have to go back and complete those missed steps. You can avoid this frustration, however, and actually increase your efficiency if you slow down enough to pay more attention to your responses as your process unfolds. It also helps for you to make lists.

In addition to waiting to be asked for your energy so that you can respond, you also need to wait over time to know what your actual response, or truth, is. Your defined Solar Plexus is your Authority and it has a frequency, a wave, that takes time to get you to a point of emotional clarity. Until you reach a calmer place in your wave, you are not ultimately sure if the responses your Sacral is having are your final truth. In other words, your truth comes to you over time, when you have had time to process and 'surf' your wave. Without waiting for emotional clarity, you can end up jumping into and out of things too quickly which creates regrets, crisis and conflict in your life. Once you respond to something, it is very important to wait and allow yourself time to process your feelings. You are designed to take in the world and your experiences deeply. This is not a life to be lived at a superficial level. Take your time, and when your emotions clear, you will know your response and decision. Often your first response is the ultimate one, but by waiting you gain more information, and you allow the correct timing for the action you are about to take to show itself.

The costume you wear in the world, the role that you are here to play, is that of the Martyr Heretic. You are designed to learn about life through trial and error. Life bumps into you and you discover what does not work. You consciously experiment with life so that others who follow you can learn from your discoveries. And when you discover a practical and generally heretical solution that does work, you are able to step in with great power and conviction and speak out or stand up for what you believe. You do not necessarily conform to an established attitude, doctrine or principle, and it may take courage to step up and express an unpopular truth, but you are wired to take the heat. You are extremely resilient and adaptable, and as a heretical agent of change your trial and error process does not indicate failure, but rather the potential that something useful and helpful can be discovered and universalized. For you, the only failure is ignoring the discoveries that each trial and error brings you.

As a Heretic you also have a very magnetic and trans-personal aura, and others project onto you that you can somehow be helpful or save them. You can also begin to feel like the invisible person who is only visible when needed, and as soon as you have saved the day, you are invisible again. This can cause you to believe the projection field, and initiate so that you can feel valuable and needed. It is important to be aware of the projection and to be practical in your own life. If these expectations are not met, your reputation can suffer so wait to be asked for your help. You are someone who can bring helpful solutions to others, but only after you have had time to master the world in your own way through discovering what does not work. When you wait to respond, and give yourself time to emotionally process your decisions, you will bump into the right situations that will lead you to the discoveries that can be of actual help to others when they really do need you.

You have a Split definition in your design. This means that you have two parts of your energy that can feel like they operate independently from each other. The channels that connect your Solar Plexus, Throat and Ajna Center are one half of the Split. The channels that connect your Root, Spleen, Sacral and G Centers are the other.

The open gates that can bridge your Split are important for you as you can be conditioned greatly through them. When you are operating from your not-self, these gates put you under pressure to initiate leading (Gate 7 - The Role of Self); pressure you to act in the now (Gate 20 - Contemplation, The Now); pressure you to initiate conflict (Gate 6 - Conflict, Friction); and pressure you to go searching for the spirit in life (Gate 55 - Abundance, Spirit). If you initiate, rather than waiting to respond over time, you create resistance in your life, you get involved in the wrong romantic and intimate encounters that lead to conflict, and you provoke the wrong spirit from life. Initiating can also result in you getting involved in incorrect leadership roles, and in acting spontaneously in the now, which is contrary to your personal Authority of waiting for emotional clarity.

When you align with your Strategy and Authority you respond over time, giving yourself an opportunity for clarity. Then you can get involved in the correct intimate relationships and the correct conflicts. You can discover the spirit in life that is correct for you, lead others correctly when it is appropriate, and 'contemplate' and observe in the moment, rather than 'act' in the moment spontaneously.

You have a lot of life force energy that you put out to others through the channels that are defined in your design. The Channel of Mutation (60-3) that runs between the Root and Sacral Centers is an energy that fluctuates and initiates. You are very creative and mutative, but this energy operates in an on/off pulse. There is always the possibility for some new creative impulse to come out of you, or through you for others, but you are not in control of the timing of this. You can spend a lot of time wondering, and even depressed about, when the next pulse of creativity will show itself. It is important for you to accept the limitation inherent in this process by simply surrendering and waiting for the next pulse of creativity. Melancholy and moodiness are also a part of this process. When you try and give a reason to your moods you enter into the world of the not-self. There is no reason for the timing of mutation; it's simply the pulse of the individual and creative process.

The Channel of Struggle (38-28) runs between your Root and Splenic Centers. You have the stubborn determination to go your own way in life against even the most overwhelming odds. You are here to discover meaning and a purpose in the struggles you meet along your unique path. There is nothing more satisfying or healthy for you than to stubbornly stand up against the odds, or even risk losing a sense of security, for some cause you feel is worth fighting for, when correct to do so. This 'struggle' gives your life meaning. Your personal search for what makes your life worthwhile, and your unique struggles, are examples that push and empower others. Your energy encourages them to struggle with the need to pursue their own individuation process and search for deeper life purpose. This prodding is not always comfortable for you though, or well received by others, so don't let your mind choose your battles. You need to respond to struggles in order for them to have value for you. There is internal stress that can build up in you, when you cannot adequately explain or correctly live out the struggles you have engaged in, that creates an excess of energy in the body. Regular exercise releases that pressure so it can move through you in a healthy way.

You are also here to follow your own convictions no matter how unusual they are. The Channel of Exploration (34-10), that runs between your Sacral and G Centers only operates correctly if you act and behave as yourself, despite any interference and without guilt. The guidance and timing of your Sacral's responses are what make it possible to follow your convictions in satisfying ways. When you live authentically, you demonstrate to others the benefits of perfecting their own behavior through response. And you empower others to get in touch with their own conviction to love themselves.

Your open and enveloping Generator aura combined with the Channel of Exploration can attract a great deal of attention. Whether or not this attention is positive is completely dependent on your willingness to patiently tune in to your correct timing and responses. When you do, you are living the true potential for empowerment and mutation that only Individuality can bring into the world. The opposite not-self expression of this channel (not operating through response) is very rigid, and can sound selfish and self-centered: "I'm going to be like this whether you like it or not. You can be any way you please, just don't interfere with me and my way."

You are driven to seek experiences which promise something new and better in life through the Channel of Transitoriness (36-35) which runs between your Solar Plexus and Throat Centers. This is your emotional wave, and you are designed to be a "Jack of all trades" who is on an emotional journey to gather wisdom experientially. You are pushed along through life by the constantly changing perspectives of your unaware wave, and you can become volatile, or feel let down, if a new experience fails to meet your expectations. The secret is to embrace and accept your emotional swings, give yourself time to make emotionally clear decisions, and surrender to fully living each correct experience in the moment, simply for its own sake, without expectation.

Over time, and with maturity, your experiences will culminate as emotional depth, as your personal truth. The core of this truth is accepting life for what it is. If you find yourself nervous or uneasy about committing to a venture, take advantage of waiting out your wave. It may be a lifesaver. As you learn over time that feelings are transitory, your advice to others will be to "seize the moment," and to partake in each promising new experience that is correct, rather than live with a sense that nothing in life ever amounts to anything. Your great accomplishment in life is that you will have tasted, touched and felt many things from which you gleaned wisdom of great value. This is wisdom that you make available to others in the form of stories. You inspire people with tales of your exploits, and your sense of fulfillment in the richness of a life well lived, to enjoy their own experiences.

Your creativity, and style of presentation, can be magical as you weave together your ideas and stories, even your jokes, from your catalog of philosophical reflections on what it means to be a human being experiencing life. Through the Channel of Curiosity (11-56) that runs between your Throat and Ajna Centers, you have an enviable gift for taking a sequence of ideas, and fashioning a story out of it that can teach or entertain an audience. Even if these stories are somewhat exaggerated or contain some half truths, like a child telling you about his day at school, you still draw others in and stimulate them. Your capacity to believe in something makes it true for you because you are less interested in facts than you are in how your stories illustrate and teach. Your stories are more like parables, or discourses on life. Even though they flow from your personal experiences and discoveries, your stories are not as useful a guide for you, however, as they are for others. Your stories are to be shared, collected, and stored for reflection and interpretation by present and future generations.

You have two Undefined Centers in your design, the Head and the Heart, that can be distractions for you. Your completely open Head Center pressures you to search for the next inspirational idea, and to think about questions that don't really matter to you. The wisdom that you can develop, through responding to life and waiting for emotional clarity, is to discern which questions do matter, and to know who or what is inspirational. Your Undefined Heart causes you to try and prove your worth by making promises you don't have the willpower to keep. You are under pressure to be the first, and the best, and to try and control the circumstances of whatever you have committed to. You have nothing to prove to yourself or anyone else, however, and over-committing to things, and making promises you cannot keep, puts tremendous pressure on your heart. The best way for you to get involved in things is through your Strategy of responding and your Authority of waiting for emotional clarity.

In summary, you are designed to be an influential, creative, mutative, determined, experiential storyteller. Adventure, determination and exploration are what drive you. You will want to do things in your own way, discovering something new as you go through life, and attracting the attention of others along the way. You will operate by your own rules or laws, providing leadership by standing up against the odds for what you believe in. Adversity motivates you and you are designed to have and share many experiences in this life.

Others will be inspired by your determined self-sufficiency and expression. Your creative bursts come and go, and are a big part of your life as they fuel everything you do. When you initiate, or jump into situations too quickly, you end up involved in the wrong intimacies and romances. When you fall into the trap of thinking you have to prove yourself, remember that there is tremendous power in your aura, and it operates correctly through responding and waiting for emotional clarity. Your aura pulls people to you. You don't have to 'do' anything. It is built into your design that you will attract the correct relationships, struggles and adventures which will be the grist for your later storytelling. In the end, this is what brings you satisfaction.

PROJECTOR OVERVIEW

AURA – FOCUSED AND ABSORBING

STRATEGY	WAIT TO BE INVITED	**DEFINITION**	SIMPLE SPLIT
PROFILE	6/2	**NOT-SELF THEME**	BITTERNESS
AUTHORITY	SPLENIC	**SIGNATURE**	SUCCESS

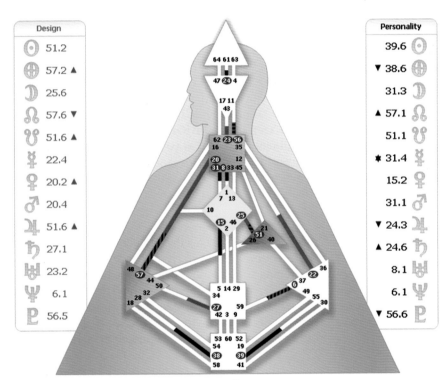

RINGO STARR

LEFT ANGLE CROSS OF INDIVIDUALISM

UNDEFINED HEAD, AJNA, SACRAL, SOLAR PLEXUS AND ROOT

57-20 THE BRAIN WAVE, A DESIGN OF PENETRATING AWARENESS
51-25 INITIATION, A DESIGN OF NEEDING TO BE FIRST

As a Projector you are designed with an absolute drive within you to integrate with the other, not out of neediness, but rather an extraordinary curiosity. This curiosity is a part of the way your aura works because you have the ability to penetrate to the self, or to the identity, of the other. You have a keen ability to 'read' the energy of others, and instinctively know where and how best their energy can be utilized. This is your great gift as a Projector, being able to recognize others.

Your gift as an intuitive guide for others only works properly, however, when you too have been recognized by those you are here to guide; only when you have been invited to share what you sense and know. It is very tempting for you to initiate and offer your guidance before it has been invited, but when you do, you will generally experience resistance and feel bitter about the encounter. You have a very penetrating and powerful aura, and it draws people to you. By trusting and surrendering to your design, you are allowing life to provide you with what you need. The keys for you are to allow your aura to naturally attract people to you who recognize you, and to move through life without an agenda. The moment you carry an agenda (want a particular outcome) you set yourself up for bitterness. Just show up and see what happens.

Invitations from others are very important for you. All of the significant things in life come to you through an invitation. It's not just any invitation though. It must contain recognition. You must feel recognized when invited. You must feel 'seen' by the invitation. When people really get you, or see you for your natural gifts, then you will feel successful in your life. When you try to get invited or recognized, you meet with resistance and feel bitter. This is a signpost that you can recognize for yourself when you initiate rather than wait. The invitation can also come through another person, as for example a friend who calls or emails or invites you to consider something they think you might like to attend.

And yet, all invitations are not correct for you either. How do you decide which invitations are delicious for you and which are not? Your aura as a Projector penetrates deeply into others, so deeply it is almost as if you are consuming them. If the invitation is not delicious, therefore, it is not correct. Decisions are everything in life; they are our navigation system. Each decision we make takes us in one direction or another. Decisions made from your authentic self mean that you will live an authentic life. When you make decisions based on 'shoulds' you are making decisions based on conditioning by others. Your Authority is how you make decisions as yourself.

The part of your design that you can trust to make correct decisions as yourself is your Splenic Center. The Spleen is an 'in-the-now' type of Authority. The Spleen is about survival, and its primary job is to keep you safe and alive. This is a very existential awareness, and when your Spleen speaks or nudges you, it is critical that you listen in that moment. The information you will hear will not be repeated, and it is spoken in the quiet little voice of your intuition, but is very important. As a projector you naturally have a strong intellect, and your mind will try and override your Spleen. The mind loves to come up with reasons for this and that. The Spleen does not operate as a mental reason-making center. It is simply instinctive awareness; it just knows. If you allow your mind to override your instincts, you end up in the emergency room saying "I knew that was going to happen." In order for your life to operate correctly you must trust your Splenic Center and its messages, in the moment. They are your truth.

One of the beautiful gifts that you bring to other people is your ability to probe and ask questions, without wanting or desiring a particular answer. You are able to just be present to the truth of the other – to 'their' truth, not what you think their truth is or should be. This is a very transformational and empowering experience for the person on the receiving end of your questions. The potential transformation only happens, however, when you can operate without an agenda.

Your Profile, the costume you wear and the role you play in life, is that of a Role Model Hermit. Time is required for you to emerge as a role model who lives your authentic self. You have a unique three-stage life process. The first 30 years or so are a very subjective time of trial and error experiences in life. The second stage from the age of 30 to 50 is a time of objective observation. You climb up on the roof, so to speak, and take a look around and review the first 30 years. You sense that you are being observed even while you are observing others; this is how you become a sounding board for society's insatiable curiosity about humanity. And it gives you great trans-personal power, and becomes an attracting force in your life.

After the age of 50 you flower into a role model for others. It's time for you to come back off the roof and into the world so you can live among the rest of us and show us how it's done. This is a very special time for you, not unlike a rebirth, but with all of the wisdom you have acquired, and now it's time to use that wisdom to experience life in a new way. The rest of us look to you as an example of self-mastery and personal leadership in terms of how to live as a conscious and aware person who has transcended both the subjective and objective. The Hermit side of you is very happy to sit home and just do its own thing. You really do not understand how you do what you do in life, but as a Role Model, as someone who lives as your authentic self, your process is complete when you are called out to apply what you naturally do well.

You have a split in your design, which means that there are two separate areas in your design that are not connected to each other. One area is the Splenic Center connected to the Throat by the Channel of the Brain Wave, A Design of Penetrating Awareness (57-20). You have a spontaneous voice that is combined with incredibly sharp intuition. You have the ability to adapt and improvise in the moment or 'think on your feet.' To truly utilize this gift there are two things to know. First, you must overcome your fear of the unknown and learn how to trust your intuition. Second, you need to be alert for the invitation to speak that expresses your existential knowing as wisdom for others. In this way you can avoid being misunderstood or ignored. Listen to, trust and act on your intuition in the moment. It is so important for you to be tuned into the present moment and not distracted by the dictates and reason-making of the mind. If ignored, the moment will pass and you will suffer for it.

The other part of your split is where the Heart is connected to the G Center via the Channel of Initiation, A Design of Needing to be First (51-25). It is simply the nature of your individuality to be competitive, and you arouse or empower competitiveness in others. When invited, competitiveness or shock can push you into the unknown to stretch, test and even transcend your normal limits and endurance. This is a true 'leap into the void' because the outcome is never guaranteed. When you triumph, however, you get a new sense of personal, even mystical power within yourself which, with your gutsy ways of achieving your personal goals, becomes an example of courage for others.

You also express yourself through creativity. When invited, initiation for you becomes art as your nature is to recognize both the potential for mutation in others, and the need to empower others toward it because mutation cannot remain isolated and still retain its viability. On the mystical level you are the shaman, a specially gifted innocent who artfully initiates a quantum leap toward individuation and self-awareness.

Because you have a Split Definition in your design, there can be a feeling in you that something is missing. In order to resolve this feeling, you tend to initiate, going out into life looking for someone or something to resolve the feeling. You end up making decisions with your mind rather than your Splenic Center. Remember, your decisions guide your life and if you are navigating without your Authority then you are heading in the wrong direction, meeting the wrong people, and ending up in the wrong environments. And then this split in your design ends up confusing you. The key is to relax, trust and allow life to bring you what you need; to stop seeking.

As a Split Definition, you are naturally designed to have partners in your life. Your natural partners will bridge your split and give you a healthy sense of completion or wholeness. In order for you to have the right people in your life, it is important that you follow your Strategy and Authority when entering into, when being invited into, relationships. You will have many relationships throughout your life, and eventually you will be able to teach the rest of us about relationships in general.

In your design there are three gates which can potentially bridge your split. These open gates become strong areas of conditioning for you as you feel you need to live them out in order to be complete. When you do live through these open gates, however, you end up making decisions from your not-self as they are not you. Not-self decisions can play out in your life through Gate 7 (The Role of the Self) by you initiating to see how you can lead others or how you can be a better leader. Your not-self mind will be focused on developing your creativity and self-expression as an artist through Gate 1 (Self-Expression); and how you should behave in the world and how you love yourself through Gate 10 (The Behavior of Self).

These three themes will be the focus of your life. These open places that bridge the two areas in your design will push you to initiate, and to try to be noticed and recognized, which will usually lead to resistance and then bitterness. The truth is, once you surrender to your Strategy and Authority, these three themes become areas in your life where you become very wise. Through observing those who bridge your split, you become wise about ways to love yourself, to creatively express yourself, and to best lead others when invited. Your choice is to struggle down the road, trying to initiate, and hitting your head against the wall of resistance, or you can simply surrender and allow your design to take you down your unique path toward wisdom.

You have five undefined Centers in your design where you also can become very wise. Our definition is 'us' as the student and our undefined Centers are 'where' we go to school. You are someone who is very 'open-minded.' And you have the potential to mentally process life logically, or abstractly, or even with just a very individual knowing, depending on who you are with. Your undefined Head Center, however, pressures you to answer life's questions, and to chase after one inspiring thing after another. This is an endless and exhausting quest. The wisdom for you with an undefined Head Center is to learn to discern which questions are worthy of your attention. Your undefined Ajna Center pushes you to want to be certain about things in life. You have a fear that you will look stupid if you don't have the answers, so you try to find the answers that you can be certain about. The wisdom here is to learn to allow concepts to float through you without getting attached to any of them, and to be ok with the statement "I don't know." Eventually you will become very wise about which concepts have value or not.

You can get so detached from your body with an undefined Head and Ajna Centers that you are completely out of touch with your Splenic Authority. When you find yourself getting lost in your thoughts, bring yourself back into your body because this is where your true self-guidance resides. Your Strategy and Authority are your navigator in this.

Your undefined Sacral Center causes you to over-do, over-commit, work too hard and to potentially be obsessed with sex. You must realize that you are not designed as an energy type. You are designed to guide others who have the energy, but not to 'do' it all yourself. It is very easy for you to fall into the trap of doing too much, which leads to exhaustion and eventual ill health. The wisdom for your undefined Sacral Center is to know when enough is enough. Listening to your body-consciousness (Spleen) is the key to keeping you healthy.

Your undefined Solar Plexus Center causes you to avoid confrontation and truth by trying to be nice, and not rock the boat and make waves. You are open and vulnerable to the emotional climate around you, and your tendency is to personalize what you are feeling. To avoid these feelings, you create a 'nice persona' that you present to the world. This, of course, is not the real you. The wisdom with an open Solar Plexus Center is to allow the feelings of others to pass through without personalizing them. To be empathic without personally taking on the emotions, and to stand up for yourself when it is important to do so. Speaking your Splenic Authority, your truth, in the moment is vital for you, even if it does feel like you are confronting the other person. The best advice is to state your truth as simply that – your truth – and not make it about the other person.

Your undefined Root Center takes in all the pressure of the world, and you are in a constant hurry to get things done so that you can relax. This pressure is constant, however, and every time you get one thing done, another thing is right there putting you under pressure again. You can get caught up in a vicious cycle of hurry, hurry, hurry which can lead to adrenal burn out. The wisdom with an Undefined Root is to feel the pressure and not react to it. Learn to procrastinate. By not reacting immediately, simply to relieve the pressure, you can then discern through your Strategy and Authority which thing really does need your attention. This way the pressure and adrenal speed can support you rather than burn you out.

When you don't succumb to the distractions of the openness in your design, you can then allow your body-consciousness (Spleen) to be your personal guide in life. It is totally capable of taking care of you through every twist and turn that life presents, always making sure you are in the right place at the right time. And once you are navigating correctly, your Incarnation Cross can come into its fullest expression.

You were born on the Incarnation Cross of Individualism. As a Role Model Hermit and Projector, you are here to demonstrate to others how they can uniquely be themselves without worrying about fitting into the status quo; that it is ok to be themselves and step out of the box of collective homogenization. First though, you have to learn to be absolutely true to your own uniqueness. Once you have mastered this, you will then have the trans-personal impact on others that you are designed for. It's a special gift in life to demonstrate what it means to be yourself; to be uniquely you. You have to walk your life first, sort out how to do it for yourself, and then you can be an example or role model for others.

In summary, after gaining life experience through trial and error, and then objective observation, you become a wise role model. You are here to live in the present moment, operating through life intuitively in the now, and when invited, to initiate and empower others to be uniquely themselves. You are designed to be provocative, to fight for your right to be yourself, and to provoke others into finding their spirit and purpose in life. You are here to allow your natural calling in life to emerge spontaneously, and to make creative, unique, influential contributions through your stimulating storytelling abilities. You are designed to overcome your fear of intimacy, your fear that no one is listening, and your fears of confrontation. You are not designed to let outside pressures run your life. You must keep an open mind about yourself and the world, and not get too fixed on any one idea or concept. You will have creative bursts of energy, and your own unique extreme rhythms. Be aware of over doing and working too hard. You are designed to be a caring soul, but not so much so that you create co-dependencies. You have a natural gift for solving problems when invited to do so.

When you begin to use your Strategy and Authority to guide your life, and you live as yourself, you will experience the parts of you that have been conditioned by the outside world dropping away. Your transcendence begins with you experimenting with your Strategy and Authority, and ends with you feeling a sense of success with your life.

REFLECTOR OVERVIEW

AURA – SAMPLING

STRATEGY	WAIT CYCLE OF MOON	**DEFINITION**	NONE
PROFILE	2/4	**NOT-SELF THEME**	DISAPPOINTMENT
AUTHORITY	MOON CYCLE	**SIGNATURE**	SURPRISE

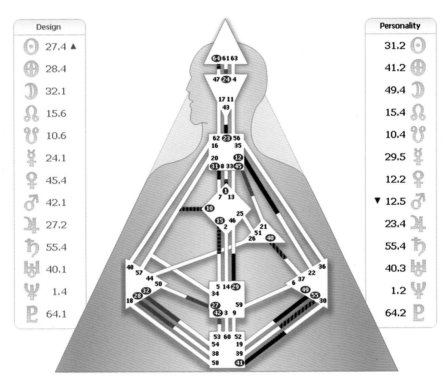

ANONYMOUS

RIGHT ANGLE CROSS OF THE UNEXPECTED

UNDEFINED ALL

CHANNELS: NONE

As a Reflector, you were born with a special attunement to the cosmic environment, and to the impact of the planetary transit field. Manifestors, Generators and Projectors are solar types, meaning their purpose 'shines' through them. As the only lunar Type, you are designed to operate as a lunar reflection of the sun's programming, and to reflect the neutrino imprinting processes. Like the moon, your 'glow' is subtle yet wields substantial influence, especially when it is detected or noted by others. You are here to sample and be one with the totality, and through this process you can have a mystical life that most of us will never know. You have the potential to easily connect to celestial bodies in an ongoing and profound way, particularly the Moon. You are very tuned in to the "Program" and as planets move through the solar system you are picking up what is going on, and reporting back to the rest of us. In many respects, you are a key to understanding and participating in global consciousness, because your extraordinary openness is continually filtering this consciousness field in a potentially unbiased way.

In the day to day world, the people you associate with, and the physical, mental, emotional and spiritual environment you are in, is vitally important to your well-being at all levels. Like a canary in a coal mine, you naturally sample, reflect, judge and discern the quality of the environment and the people around you. When you are healthy and happy and thriving, you know that the environment is too. And when you are not thriving, then the environment needs to be changed in some way or it is not the right environment for you.

You have the ability to sense who is living authentically, and who has been conditioned by the transit field or become a victim of it. When people allow their lives to be conditioned by the transits, or those around them, they move away from fulfilling their unique potential. You can sense those who are ready to become their own authority, and when a community or organization is operating correctly. You can feel the physical, psychic or emotional health of an environment or group. As people awaken to their true selves, you can be there, ready to share or reflect what is needed at the time. This is how you become 'visible.'

Your nine undefined centers sample, magnify and reflect the frequencies of everything and everyone in your environment; in a way no one else can, you give others the potential to also taste or sense what is really happening. Your unusual aura allows you to appraise or read the auras of others as they pass through yours, without taking in the frequencies too deeply. When not personalizing what comes in through your openness, you have the capacity to reflect everything around you with perfect equanimity. This is a gift that uniquely equips you to discern if and when a person is ready to step out and express their own uniqueness, their difference, rather than remain absorbed in the homogenized world of the not-self.

Your openness is an exceptional window to wisdom, if you just allow everything to flow through you and simply sample it as it does. Your "Teflon" aura will protect you from identifying personally with anything that is going on in the world, and you can detect a blip in the collective energy, or something or someone that is unusual or out of line around you. As you become familiar with your design and understand it, you can avoid yielding to the pressures of society to conform. You are here to enliven and lift up the energy of others through the rather extraordinary way that you amplify and mirror their energy back to them. Your unique aptitude to facilitate an experience of heightened awareness of the other in a non-judgemental way, and the unimposing, non-intrusive nature of your auric presence, also makes you a particularly effective facilitator of the group process. All of this remains only a potential for you, however, until you are able to operate as yourself rather than as an amplified version of the homogenized world around you.

Unfortunately, most Reflectors live a homogenized life, trying to be something they are not simply because they have not been understood or encouraged to embrace their difference. Too often, finding the world unreceptive, cold and disappointing, they give in to others' expectations in order to survive. When you begin to appreciate your uniqueness and practice detachment from (or not identifying with) what you are mirroring, you will be less apt to become lost, confused and caught up in the turmoil around you. You can then accept your place in the center, rather than feel invisible and on the outside looking in.

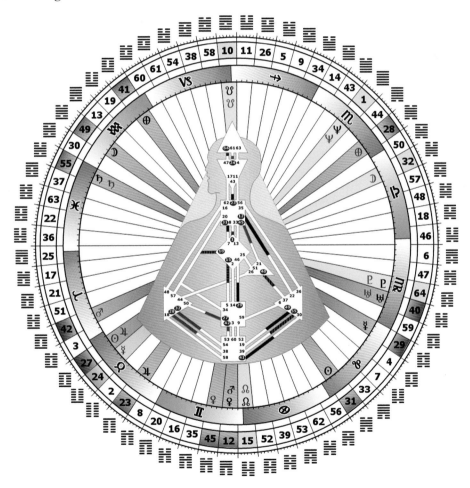

In the Mandala above you can see how the 64 gates wrap around your chart, and each gate brings the potential for a different type of activation. As the Moon travels through your chart, over the course of 28 days, it passes through each of the 64 gates. This pattern repeats itself every month, however, each day within the month is different for you and you can find yourself asking, "Who am I today?" and "Will I be surprised, included or invisible?" The monthly pattern of the moon through your chart is something that you can learn to know and rely on, providing you with a unique sense of consistency.

Your decision-making Strategy in life is to simply sit back, enjoy life, and wait for something to be presented to you. You then need to wait through a full 28-day cycle of the moon (from that moment) before you make a decision. As you wait through this cycle you can talk with others, not to seek advice, but rather to hear your own potential truth reflected through you. Use others as a sounding board. These others need to be confidantes that you can trust to simply listen, or perhaps ask a few questions, to help you articulate your thoughts and feelings. They are not here to influence or make the decision for you. Over time you will begin to get the clarity you need to make your own decision. If you still do not have clarity after the full cycle of the moon, then just continue to wait. It is not healthy for you to be rushed. As a matter of fact, most Reflectors have been rushed all their lives, and their health begins to breakdown from pushing against the natural flow of life; the resistance has an impact on their bodies. If you live as yourself, however, and do not personalize the energies that shift and flow through your open centers, you can experience a life filled with surprise and joy and the wonder of the moment. For further detail about the Moon Cycle, see Section Four, Reflector.

Place is key for you. Finding the right environment to call home within the right community is one of the most important decisions you face. With your undefined G Center it's helpful for you to know that other people are here to initiate you, to introduce you to new people and places. Once you have been introduced, it is your job to be discerning. Your correct place is in the heart of a community so that you can freely sample and reflect the auric information of those around you. This is where you fulfill your purpose. You are here to be accepting of others, and to reflect and teach the rest of us that most often what we judge as good or bad in the world is just a revelation of our diversity.

You must also remain free to leave the group or gathering if you realize that your reflections will not be solicited. If you stay in an unhealthy environment for any length of time, you may take on that energy and get sick or become drained of your vitality. It's essential for you to have a dedicated, creative space of your own, a place where you can take time alone to shake off the conditioning you are exposed to on a daily basis. If you don't, you can easily become dependent on the energies of people around you, which is also why you must select, with care, the people you allow into your inner circle of friends and family.

Your Profile or the Costume you wear in life is a 2/4, or what we call the Hermit Opportunist. Often called the missionary profile, the 2/4 combines the natural aptitudes and genius of your conscious Personality (Line 2), with your unconscious Design (Line 4) that is transpersonal and always ready to interact with the world in order to externalize what your natural talents can do. The push and pull between the conscious Hermit (antisocial) and the unconscious Opportunist (social) brings an interesting dynamic to your life. There is a pressure within to share what you know, as long as it does not require you to investigate or train to suit someone else's expectations. Others are watching, but you're uncertain what they see. You are unaware of your own gifts until someone else points them out to you. You project out to others what you can do simply by staying absorbed in your own process, and enjoying what comes naturally to you. At the same time, you unconsciously draw people in to befriend who will tell you what they see in you. This is how you get your 'calling' in life.

If you stay the Hermit, in the sense of not letting anyone else corrupt your natural process, eventually someone will call your true gifts out into the world. Answering 'the call' is a transformative, self-actualizing force, which comes forth naturally when you are making decisions as yourself. You are not a pursuer, however, and 'friendship first' best describes your healthy process of easing into intimate and lasting relationships, as well as the way proper business commitments or partnerships are entered into. Your social and business networks are very important because these are the communities where your calling finds you. Once you receive the correct call, you can go forth with the zeal of a missionary to spread your influence or understanding or knowing into the community.

All nine Centers are undefined in your design. Each open center allows you to take in and read the energy of others, and to scan the environment from an objective vantage point while remaining open to the unexpected. What you take in from others and the environment is not personal, however, and your objectivity only works correctly when you are open and fluid with life. The moment you try and hold on is the moment when you will feel disappointment.

Your undefined mind can get distracted thinking about things that really do not matter to you. You can get so detached from your body with an undefined Head and Ajna that you can be completely out of touch with your Lunar Authority. When you find yourself getting lost in your thoughts, bring yourself back into your body. Your open Head Center puts you under pressure to answer all of life's questions, and to chase endlessly from one inspiring thing to another. You can feel lost in the confusion, and this can be an endless and exhausting quest. The wisdom potential is to learn to discern which questions are worthy of your attention, and to use your Strategy and Authority as your guide. Your open Ajna Center pushes you to want to be mentally certain about life. There is a fear that you will look stupid if you don't have the answers, so you try to find the answers that you can be certain about. You can also get caught up in irrationally focusing on finding a rational for what is past. The wisdom potential is to learn to allow concepts to float through without getting attached to any of them, and to be ok with the statement, "I don't know."

Your undefined Throat can cause you to try to attract attention by doing or talking too much. An undefined Throat Center is like a megaphone screaming out into the world "Look at me" or "Watch me." There is nothing you need to 'do' to attract attention, as it is already built into your design, so sit back and relax. Notice how you feel pressured to do or talk, but don't act on it; just observe it and see what happens. You may also find yourself feeling socially cautious, or the opposite, wanting to express reflections to the group before it is time. The wisdom potential is that by observing, you will be the judge or wise one who knows who has something worthwhile to say or do, or not. You will be able to communicate, when it is correct for you, the higher principles of the community, even if it is coming through your very unique perspective.

Your undefined G Center gives you the feeling that you must find out who you are, and where you are going in life. This sensation can cause you to make mental decisions about what direction to go in, and what your role is in the community. There is something really special about having an undefined G Center. Your environment is filled with 'signposts' to show you the way. These signposts come in any form, such as a person or something you read or hear. You are a natural role model who can act out the highest values and ideals for the community, and identify the weak points of the group. Your identity and the roles you play in life change constantly, however, and it's important that you learn how to be fluid with these changes. If you get attached to one way of seeing yourself or to one role, when it changes you can experience a lot of pain by attempting to hold on to a role that is no longer yours. The wisdom potential is to trust that you will be given the next signpost for the new direction and role when the time is right.

Your undefined Heart Center can push you to try to prove your worth, and this can play out in many ways. You might try to prove yourself by constantly trying to improve yourself, or by over compensating and making promises. With an undefined Heart there is no consistent access to will power, and you cannot will yourself into being or doing better. Your life is not about willing yourself to do anything. What you get involved with needs to come from your Strategy and Authority, not your will. Your life motto is "I have nothing to prove to myself or anyone else." The wisdom with an undefined Heart is that you can objectively read the ego of the other, and know who can keep their promises or not, and who has a healthy ego or not. As important as community is to you, if you are not with the right people, you would rather be alone.

Your Undefined Sacral causes you to over-do, over-commit, work too hard and potentially be obsessed with sex. You can feel an uncontrollable drive to say yes to new experiences, or to expand beyond what you have the resources for or the energy to finish. And even though you have an instinct to nurture and care for the other, you must realize that you are not designed as an energy type. You are designed to be the observer and judge, but not to do it all yourself. It is very easy for you to fall into the trap of doing too much, which will lead to exhaustion and eventual ill health. The wisdom potential is to know when enough is enough. Slowing down and making decisions slowly and carefully is the key to keeping yourself healthy.

Your undefined Spleen can cause you to hold onto things that are not healthy for you, or to become dependent on something that makes you feel good. You have the capacity at times to focus in on the detail and maintain your grip, so to speak, but that does not mean it is necessarily correct for you, such as staying in a job or relationship long after it should be over. Holding onto things gives you a false sense of security, even to the point of staying in an abusive relationship because you are unsure what the alternative is. You are also not designed to be spontaneous or make decisions quickly, and the wisdom potential is that once you step back and view life objectively, you can see what is healthy for you or not. This includes people, places and food. As a 4th line, you are not designed to leave one relationship before the next one appears, so be sensitive to the timing of any decision that you make. Following your Strategy and Authority allows the universe to also arrange the much needed replacement for whatever it is you are letting go of. You cannot find the replacement yourself.

Your undefined Solar Plexus Center causes you to avoid confrontation and truth by trying to be nice, and avoiding making waves or rocking the boat. You are open and vulnerable to the emotional climate around you, and the tendency is to personalize what you are feeling. To avoid these feelings you create a 'nice persona' that you present to the world. Of course, this is not the real you. You are very sensitive to the true spiritual needs of those around you, and can help to balance the awareness and energy of the community. The wisdom potential is to allow these feelings to pass through without personalizing them; to be empathic without taking on the emotions and feelings of others; and to stand up for yourself and the principles of the group when it is important to do so.

Your undefined Root Center takes in all of the pressures of the world, and you are in a constant hurry to get things done so that you can rest. Even though you may feel cautious about how you use your energy, especially in terms of other people's desires for you, the pressure is constant. Every time you get one thing done, another thing is right there putting you under pressure again. You can get caught up in a vicious cycle of hurry, hurry, hurry, which can lead to adrenal burnout. The wisdom potential is to feel the pressure and not react to it. By not reacting to it, by procrastinating so to speak, you can then discern through your Strategy and Authority which thing really does need your attention. In this way, the pressure can actually support and fuel you, rather than burn you out. Remember, as a Reflector it is extremely important and healthy for you to take your time to process information and potential decisions. It is not in any way healthy for you to be rushed.

To summarize, you are designed to enjoy the daily surprises that life offers, and to stay as unattached as possible to how your mind 'thinks life should be.' You are here to be fluid. You were born under the Incarnation Cross of the Unexpected. You are designed for the unexpected, for the surprises that your Reflector type flourishes with, and for the unexpected and empowering 'call' that your 2/4 Profile is here to live out. All of these pieces fit nicely together. You are an influential and caring person, who can share with all of us a vision for the future, and a purpose for being alive. And you can demonstrate to people through your reflections how to be accepting of whatever 'is' in each moment. The most important things for you to remember are to slow down and take as much time as possible for every decision, ideally a month; to not allow outside pressure to drive you; and to let go of fixedness and welcome the fluidity of surprise into your life. For the Reflector who is living according to Strategy and Authority, the magic is that more will always be revealed.

"We are here to be conscious. And beyond consciousness, we're here to have the potential of awareness. And beyond awareness we have the potential of awakeness. But first one has to accept what it means to be conscious. That consciousness is about us being filters — we filter consciousness. And as it filters through us we then put it back out into the greater consciousness field. It goes through us and goes out.

We float densely in the neutrino ocean. The real magic is understanding what we are doing — we are taking in and reading the consciousness field. And we are reading the consciousness field in the way in which it relates to each and every one of us uniquely. Human Design shows us how we are designed to filter consciousness, and that we can give guidance when we are correct filters. And every correct filter changes the way in which every one else gets information. We are changing the quality of the neutrino ocean.

Each of us creates a unique interference pattern. That's what differentiation is — a unique interference pattern. The interference pattern can actually be measured down into the minutiae." – Ra Uru Hu

SECTION TEN
HEXAGRAM LINE DESCRIPTIONS
A DEEPER EXPLORATION

SECTION TEN

HEXAGRAM LINE DESCRIPTIONS

A DEEPER EXPLORATION

The Rave I'Ching, completed in December 1989 by Ra Uru Hu, is a synthesis of the descriptions for each Hexagram (Gate), a list of the Incarnation Crosses associated with it, and a description of the 6 lines associated with each gate. There are 64 hexagrams and 384 lines in the Rave I'Ching. For the purposes of this book this section lists only the 384 lines. For a copy of the Rave I'Ching please visit one of the authorized Human Design National Organizations; a listing can be found in Section Eleven.

375 of the lines express a polarity of potential experiences, which is termed either an exaltation or a detriment, and is indicated by the black triangle symbol ▲ (exaltation) or the white triangle symbol ▽ (detriment). These terms when used in standard astrology indicate good (exaltation) and bad (detriment), but The Human Design System does not make this moral distinction. In Human Design, these terms simply denote the 'this' and 'that' polarity.

A person's design is the sum of its parts, and when looking at a specific component such as a line, we need to consider it in relationship to the entire chart. If you pull just one detail out to examine it, without considering the whole of the rest of the design including Type, Strategy, Authority, Profile, Incarnation Cross, centers, channels and gates, you take it out of context. To truly understand a line, always step back and see it in the context of the bigger picture; the holistic view. What you will find as you begin to study charts is that there is a "genetic continuity," an unfolding pattern. The pieces have a theme that relate back to the full design, and you begin to see a theme for the life. You also begin to see the paradox in the life, and all of its complexities.

It takes time to understand lines; they may seem abstract, or like riddles or poetry. Just as the I'Ching (Chinese Book of Changes) can take a lifetime to understand, the lines take time to digest in the context of the entire chart. It's best to start with your own chart and spend time with, even meditate on, your own lines over time. Even the recognitions that you may have in the moment about a line, or the way the description resonates in you, will evolve as you journey deeper and deeper into your own experiment with living your design.

You will find your lines next to your gates in the red (Design) and black (Personality) columns on your chart, e.g., Gate 50.1 is Gate 50 Line 1. Look for your lines by gate in this section, and read both descriptions (exaltation and detriment) to get a sense of the meaning of the lines in your design. Pay attention to both the name of the line and the description, as each contain valuable information about the line. Additionally, the description for Line 1 in each hexagram will give you the foundational understanding of that specific gate.

Some lines, not all, have a one-sentence introductory description in italics. When there is a description in italics it means that this is a theme you have an opportunity to learn about and potentially grow into. If there is no description in italics, then this characteristic is a given; it's hard wired into your design.

Within the exaltation and detriment descriptions, the first sentence in regular type is the original meaning as received by Ra. The second sentence in bold is a subsequent description that Ra synthesized years later to further clarify the meaning of the lines. You will also see that there are planet glyphs associated with the lines – they are listed next to them. Certain planets can "fix" a line in either exaltation or detriment. If you look at your own chart, you will see that there are exaltations and detriments displayed next to some of the gates and lines. In some cases, you may find a chart that has no fixing – no exaltation or detriment.

When we speak of exaltation and detriment in the context of "fixing" in a chart this is simply another way of saying "this" and "that". There is no judgment here of good or bad. The detriments in your design are also perfect for you in the continuity of your overall design. In fact, it is generally in the detriments that we have the greatest opportunity to learn. Composite charts (your design combined with another) and transits (planets moving through our designs over time) can also fix our lines. There is also fixing that can take place through the harmonic gate at the other end of a channel. These areas are complex and best suited for an advanced discussion at another time.

Start by looking up each of your gates and lines in this section. Then read the description in italics if there is one and contemplate the lesson that you are here to learn. Read the line descriptions themselves and feel the flow of energy that moves from the exaltation to the detriment. See what recognitions you have. If you have an exaltation in your chart then read the exalted line knowing that this energy will be emphasized in your design. If you have a detriment then read the detriment for its emphasis in your design. If you have a juxtaposition (a star shaped symbol representing both the exaltation and detriment), then both descriptions apply.

PLANET GLYPHS & SYMBOLS IN THE RAVE I'CHING

☉	Sun	♄	Saturn
⊕	Earth	♅	Uranus
☽	Moon	♆	Neptune
☿	Mercury	♇	Pluto
♀	Venus	▲	Exaltation
♂	Mars	▽	Detriment
♃	Jupiter	✦	Juxtaposition

GATE 1: THE CREATIVE - SELF EXPRESSION
– Creation as a primal force. The energy potential to manifest inspiration without limitation –

Line 6 - Objectivity

⊕ ▲ Clear assessment of creative value. **Clarity in creative expression.**

♀ ▽ The risk that subjective appraisal will result in disappointment and creative frustration. **Subjectivity in self-expression that may lead to creative frustration.**

Line 5 - The energy to attract society

♂ ▲ Mars exalted for its powerful ego endurance. **The power and drive to stay with the creative process.**

♅ ▽ Uranus in detriment, where eccentricity can handicap endurance. **Eccentricity that though attractive will limit the drive.**

Line 4 - Aloneness as the medium of creativity
The tension of inner light.

⊕ ▲ The Earth exalted as the symbol of personal perspective manifested outside of influence, where the potential magic of inspiration is diluted. **Creativity that must develop outside of influence.**

♃ ▽ Where the potential magic of inspiration is diluted. **The need to influence that abandons aloneness and limits creativity.**

Line 3 - The energy to sustain creative work

♂ ▲ Mars exalted as the symbol of the profound need for self-expression. **The deep need for self-expression.**

⊕ ▽ Material forces can disrupt creativity and lead to over-ambition. **Materialism disrupts creativity.**

Line 2 - Love is light

♀ ▲ Venus exalted as a symbol of beauty. The required harmony between established values and ideals that enriches inspiration. **Self-expression conditioned by ideals and values.**

♂ ▽ Desires and passions have their place but not at the expense of Creation. **Self-expression limited by desires and passions.**

Line 1 - Creation is independent of will

☽ ▲ The Moon exalted as a symbol of adaption. Time is everything. **Self-expression which has its special timing.**

♅ ▽ Instability leads to distortion. Here, patience is a virtue and revolution a vice. **Creative instability unless there is patience.**

GATE 2: THE RECEPTIVE - THE DIRECTION OF THE SELF

– Receptivity as the primal base through which any response is determined. The root of action –

Line 6 - Fixation
Unable or unwilling to see the whole picture.

☿ ▲ With Mercury exalted, less negative, though the intellect becomes absorbed in constant rationalization. **Higher knowing that is extremely narrow in its receptivity.**

♄ ▽ The need for security may distort awareness to its ultimate perversion, destructiveness. **The Higher Self absorbed with the mundane and the need for security.**

Line 5 - Intelligent application

☿ ▲ The strategist with Mercury exalted. Reasoned management of resources. **Higher knowing as a gift for strategy.**

⊕ ▽ The inability to share responsibility or recognize the abilities of others. **Higher knowing as an exclusively individual and selfish process.**

Line 4 - Secretiveness
More than modesty, the ability to preserve harmony through discretion.

♀ ▲ The higher goal transcends personal acclaim. The team player, acknowledged as the leader but never the captain. **Where higher knowing does not have to be expressed to be recognized.**

♂ ▽ Loose lips sink ships. The unquenchable fire of the ego engenders enmity. **The inability to keep silent when the opportunity arises for expression.**

Line 3 - Patience
The teacher that never stops being a student.

♃ ▲ Dedication to a lifetime of receptivity with the maturity to accept that the process never ends. When connected permanently to Gate 14 through the Beat Channel, rewards for services rendered. **The recognition that receptivity is a lifelong process.**

♅ ▽ For the revolutionary, patience is a vice. **Higher knowing that cannot wait and demands expression.**

Line 2 - Genius
Unconscious and unlearnable alignment of stimulus and response. The natural.

♄ ▲ The inner strength to focus and realize. **A natural gift for unlearnable knowing.**

♂ ▽ Genius as madness. Knowledge exclusively as power for the enhancement of the ego. **The delusion that knowledge is power.**

Line 1 - Intuition
Sensitivity to disharmony and atrophy.

♀ ▲ The importance of aesthetics whether inborn or acquired. **Higher knowing through aesthetics.**

♂ ▽ The assertion of ego in spite of wisdom. **The urge for action that will ignore the wisdom of the Higher Self.**

GATE 3: DIFFICULTY AT THE BEGINNING - ORDERING
– The fundamental challenge of initiation is to transcend confusion and establish order –

Line 6 - Surrender
The ultimate maturity to recognize when struggle is futile.

☉ ▲ As its light sustains, so life goes on. **The innate acceptance that ordering is a process, not a problem.**

♆ ▽ As darkness overwhelms, life can seem worthless leading to depression and the sense of hopelessness. **The overwhelming power of confused energy can lead to depression.**

Line 5 - Victimization
When actions designed to overcome confusion alienate others.

♂ ▲ The courage to stand by one's convictions. **The unique energy of individuality to withstand confusion.**

⊕ ▽ The Earth in detriment, where victimization leads to appeasement and suffering. **Confused energy which is dominated by the ordering power of others.**

Line 4 - Charisma
Innate quality which attracts valued guidance.

♆ ▲ Physic attunement that magnetizes nurturing. A psychic energy which attracts nourishment **and ensures ordering.**

♂ ▽ Mars in detriment, where the demands of ego lead to rejection. **Confused energy that needs nourishment but is generally rejected.**

Line 3 - Survival
The ability to recognize and distinguish between fertile and sterile in their various manifestations.

♀ ▲ In reproduction, the ability to choose the best mate. **An innate knowing of what is sterile and what is fertile where the mutation is specifically biological and dependent on collaboration with others.**

♆ ▽ The perverse denial of evolutionary standards. An innate contrariness which refuses to mutate.

Line 2 - Immaturity
The unrestrained acceptance of guidance.

♂ ▲ The unrelenting energy for growth will eventually triumph. **The energy and potential for individual mutation.**

♅ ▽ Internal instability which both accepts and rejects authority simultaneously. **Energy and potential that is conditioned by others leading to instability.**

Line 1 - Synthesis
Difficulties can be only overcome when all the pertinent factors have been analyzed.

⊕ ▲ The understanding that confusion is natural and must always exist before clarity can be achieved. **An innate knowing that order will emerge from confusion.**

☿ ▽ The reliance on intellect at the expense of intuition can lead to unnecessary frustration. **The inability to know that order will emerge and the drive to find this knowing elsewhere.**

GATE 4: YOUTHFUL FOLLY - FORMULIZATION
– The energy to beguile and succeed despite ignorance. Freedom from retribution –

Line 6 - Excess
Repeated and conscious abuse of norms will not escape discipline.

☿ ▲ The development through experience of techniques to apply self-restraint. The potential in a logical process to recognize when the understanding is not complete and have the patience to wait out the process.

♂ ▽ The gall to accept punishment as the price of excess. Despite recognizing the incompleteness a lack of patience with the process.

Line 5 - Seduction
Allowing others to assume responsibility as a shield against potential punishment.

♃ ▲ Unearned reward and recognition. The potential to succeed through the understanding of others.

♆ ▽ A life of lip service to antiquated and unsatisfying values. Cynicism. The potential for cynicism that comes with always having to acknowledge the understanding of others.

Line 4 - The liar
Role playing as an art form. The actor.

☉ ▲ Fantasy protects and nurtures a sense of purpose and reason no matter how misguided. The potential to find or illustrate the formulas through fantasy.

♄ ▽ Time always brings humiliation. The potential danger to see the fantasy as fact.

Line 3 - Irresponsibility
The general refusal to apply oneself diligently when one can get by with much less effort.

♀ ▲ Where art is more valued then the artist. The potential to enjoy the formulas with no regard to their practical application.

♆ ▽ The rationalization of irresponsibility as an act of refocalization. The potential to justify such a process in order to maintain it.

Line 2 - Acceptance
The recognition of limitation in oneself and others leads to tolerance and the suspension of judgment.

☽ ▲ The glorification of feelings. The mother which always pardons the errant child. The potential to recognize that not everyone can understand.

♂ ▽ The assertion of the ego at the expense of others' failures. The potential to take advantage of the lack of understanding in others.

Line 1 - Pleasure
Ultimate pleasure cannot be achieved without perfect timing.

☽ ▲ The instinct to know the right moment and circumstances where pleasure is rewarded and not punished. The potential to recognize that there is a natural timing to the understanding process.

⊕ ▽ Timing is not a product of discipline. Exaggerated self-discipline leads to the abuse of pleasure. The potential to recognize but the urge to force the timing.

GATE 5: WAITING - FIXED PATTERNS
– Fundamental attunement to natural rhythms. Waiting as an active state of awareness –

Line 6 - Yielding
Waiting is never free from pressure, physical or mental and is often punctuated by the unexpected.

Ψ ▲ The growth of awareness that comes with bending to the universal flow. **Accepting that in one's fixed rhythm despite the pressures, growth will be empowered, and often through the unexpected. No polarity.**

▽ There is no planet in detriment; each in its way, given the power of this position, will yield to the inevitable. **No planet in detriment.**

Line 5 - Joy
Waiting as an aspect of enlightenment.

♀ ▲ To remain calm as the ultimate aesthetic and thus recognize the inner meaning of being. **The power to be calm and to find one's place in the flow.**

♇ ▽ Joy dismissed as an illusion, waiting as a failure. **Disillusionment with recognizing one's place in the flow.**

Line 4 - The hunter
Waiting as a guarantee of survival.

♅ ▲ The creative genius to transform the most passive experience into active achievement. **The power to make the best of one's fixed rhythm.**

☉ ▽ The vanity of a personality so strong that unwilling to hide behind a blind, threatens its very survival. **The drive to deny one's own rhythms with predictable costs.**

Line 3 - Compulsiveness
The fear engendered by the sense of helplessness resulting in unnecessary stress and activity.

Ψ ▲ Compulsiveness can be limited in its negative effect through flights of imagination. Though still stressful, they do not lead to action. **A surrender to the limitations of a fixed rhythm through the empowerment of the imagination.**

☽ ▽ The Moon cannnot stand still. **Unable to surrender and at odds with one's own rhythm.**

Line 2 - Inner peace
The ability to ignore the temptation to take premature action.

♀ ▲ The gift of maintaining composure through idealizing tranquility. **The power to be comfortable with one's rhythm.**

♇ ▽ Inner peace experienced as stagnation. **The drive for power that is constrained by the fixed rhythm.**

Line 1 - Perseverance
If the captain must, he goes down with the ship.

♂ ▲ Courage in the face of adversity. **The power to maintain one's own rhythm.**

⊕ ▽ The premature and often disastrous urge to cut one's losses. **Weakness in maintaining one's rhythm when challenged.**

GATE 6: CONFLICT - FRICTION

– The fundamental design component of progress. The law that growth cannot exist without friction –

Line 6 - The peacemaker

The discipline and integrity of a superior force to unilaterally cease conflict to permit surrender and survival of its foe.

☿ ▲ The highest form of reason is that life is sacred. **The emotional power to end conflict tempered by feelings and sensitivity to others.**

♀ ▽ The peacemaker whose actions are just but whose terms are unacceptable. **The emotional power to end conflict but only after one's conditions have been satisfied.**

Line 5 - Arbitration

The faith derived from analytical diligence and emotional control that permits a higher authority to judge a conflict.

♀ ▲ Harmony furthered through the avoidance of direct conflict. **Sensitivity to conflict can lead to the avoidance of intimacy.**

☽ ▽ Where a party to arbitration sees itself as the best possible judge and will only accept judgement if it is the victor. **Insensitivity to the concerns of others in a conflict.**

Line 4 - Triumph

A position on natural and unchallengeable power.

☉ ▲ The charity and wisdom that must come with victory and the movement towards new horizons. **The power of emotions to dominate a relationship.**

♇ ▽ The conqueror and purger. **The lack of emotional control that is destructive in relationships.**

Line 3 - Allegiance

The ability to secure support and create strength out of a weak position. When connected to the harmonic Gate 59, mating that results in conception.

♆ ▲ The destruction of old forms through union; either mundane, as above, sexual union, or exalted as universalization. **The depth of feelings that can enrich union and intimacy.**

♇ ▽ The rejection of allegiance as submission to established order. **Sensitivity to controls which may eventually reject intimacy.**

Line 2 - The guerilla

The ability to maximize an inferior position through timely contact and withdrawal.

♀ ▲ Aesthetic sensitivity and mental detail can find the weakest point. **The sensitivity to find the weakest point in a conflict and to exploit it emotionally.**

♂ ▽ The kamikaze, striking but moot. **A lack of sensitivity that blunders into conflicts.**

Line 1 - Retreat

The realization that wasting one's resources against overwhelming odds is not courage but folly.

♇ ▲ The power of regeneration that can embrace retreat as a phase and not a failure. **The emotional stability to accept conflict.**

☿ ▽ The inferiority complex, where retreat is experienced as personal weakness. **Emotional instability in times of conflict.**

GATE 7: THE ARMY - THE ROLE OF THE SELF IN INTERACTION

– The point of convergence. By design, the need for leadership to guide and order society –

Line 6 - The administrator
The ability to share and justly apportion power.

☿ ▲ The power to communicate the frameworks of responsibility. **The capacity of the Self through its role to communicate responsibility.**

♅ ▽ The bureaucrat whose lust for power eventually destabilizes the organization. **The role of the Self to seek power through the communication of responsibility.**

Line 5 - The general
Leadership whose authority must be absolute and is sanctioned by society in times of crisis.

♀ ▲ The gift of attracting loyalty necessary in harmonizing the potential of society. **The capacity of the Self through its role to attract loyalty.**

Ψ ▽ The commander isolated from his troops and obsessed with victory at any price. **The lack of loyalty when the Self insists on isolation.**

Line 4 - The abdicator
The willingness to accept the judgment of the people and/or the rule of law.

☉ ▲ The grace and wisdom to step down for the benefit of the whole. **The capacity of the Self to accept the judgment of others.**

♅ ▽ One who must be forced from power by overwhelming opposition. **The refusal of the Self to accept the judgement of others.**

Line 3 - The anarchist
The rejection of any institutionalized order.

☽ ▲ The constant need for change no matter what the prevailing conditions. **The drive of the Self to express many roles.**

☿ ▽ The nihilist. **The capacity of the Self to deny value in any role.**

Line 2 - The democrat
The ability to lead by serving the will of the majority.

Ψ ▲ The application of universally accepted systems. When connected through the Alpha Channel to Gate 31 Influence, the potential for widespread and revolutionary effect on society. **The capacity of the Self to lead when chosen.**

☿ ▽ Elitism and denegation by democrats of democracy. **The capacity of the Self once chosen to feel superior to those who chose them.**

Line 1 - Authoritarian
The iron hand both enlightened and despotic.

♀ ▲ Venus exalted, as in the basic values and rules imposed on a child. **The capacity of the Self to guide with authority.**

☿ ▽ The distorted intellect that believes only it knows best. **The capacity of the Self to insist that its authority is best.**

GATE 8: HOLDING TOGETHER - CONTRIBUTION

– The basic worth realized in contributing individual efforts to group goals –

Line 6 - Communion

The certainty which grows out of harmony.

♀ ▲ The awareness of patterns that ensures correct timing. **The gift of knowing when to contribute creatively.**

♇ ▽ Doubt, which may engender regret even in the most ideal circumstances. **Uncertainty in timing and regret despite circumstances.**

Line 5 - Dharma

Holding together does not exclude eventual separation. Successful union, after a proper term will encourage separation. The fledgling once mature is expected to leave the nest. This is right action which does not harm the integrity of the union.

♃ ▲ The teacher. **Contribution as part of a process of sharing that accepts and expects limitation, exemplified in teaching.**

☉ ▽ The parent that cannot let go of the child, understanding only, that its authority is being challenged. **Contribution as an end in itself that neither accepts nor expects limitation, exemplified by the parent that cannot let go of the child.**

Line 4 - Respect

The gift of naturally recognizing the contributions of others and particularly, the acknowledgement of those who lead by example.

♃ ▲ The un-compromizing drive to assimilate. **The drive to contribute and be an example to and for others.**

☿ ▽ In a group where limitation is transcended, reason alone cannot predict individual worth. As an example, the acknowledged leader of an athletic team is not necessarily the most talented. **A gift for contribution that is not conditioned by limitations.**

Line 3 - The phoney

The acceptance of the style and not the substance of communal actions.

☽ ▲ The perfected and rarely detected superficial intimacy. **The example as an expression through style, not substance.**

♄ ▽ A shallowness that underestimates others and overestimates its own ability to continue its deception without detection. **An overreliance and unfounded confidence in style.**

Line 2 - Service

☉ ▲ The highest good, to serve selflessly. **The potential to be an example through unselfish expression.**

⊕ ▽ The earth in detriment, where reward is a prerequisite of service. **The willingness to be an example for a price.**

Line 1 - Honesty

The truthful acceptance of limitation and re-cognition that it can only be transcended through sharing.

♆ ▲ The awareness that the whole is always greater than the sum of its parts. **Knowing that creative expression must be honestly communicated and shared.**

☿ ▽ Withdrawal. The fear of losing individuality in a group environment. **The design to share creativity at the expense of individuality.**

Gate 9: The Taming Power of the Small - Energy for Detail
– Potential can be fulfilled through detailed attention to all pertinent aspects –

Line 6 - Gratitude
The joy which comes with accepting small rewards for small victories.

☽ ▲ The Moon exalted, where the power of the small nourishes right perspective. **The power to enjoy the concentrating process.**

♆ ▽ No single step is of value until the journey is over. **The energy for expression that cannot find joy in the process until it is complete.**

Line 5 - Faith
The trust that detailed adherence will lead to fulfillment.

♃ ▲ Loyalty to the letter of the law. **The power to focus and bring value to concentration.**

⊕ ▽ Like the mystery of God, doubt engendered through the perceived illogic of a process. **Where the lack of power to concentrate leads to doubt.**

Line 4 - Dedication
Regardless of the pressures or stress the disciplined attention to detail.

☽ ▲ Right action that leads inevitably to actualization. **The power to act on the potential of the focus.**

♂ ▽ The persistent urge to want to skip essential steps. **The drive for action that ignores the details.**

Line 3 - The straw that breaks the camel's back
The overlooked minor element that always predetermines failure.

⊕ ▲ The use of force to temporarily overcome impediments. **The loss of power through the failure to focus.**

☉ ▽ Persistent force that saps vitality and turns molehills into mountains. **The power to turn a focus into an obsession.**

Line 2 - Misery loves company

♆ ▲ Collaboration with others to temper frustration. **The power to collaborate with others in focusing.**

♃ ▽ The overwhelming need for expansion can lead to errors in judgment, missed opportunities and depression. **The drive to collaborate that will miss the focus.**

Line 1 - Sensibility
A balanced and responsible approach to problem solving.

♆ ▲ The ability to avoid frustration through the creation of new forms. **The power in focusing to create new forms.**

♂ ▽ After a hasty and frustrating search the urge to kick in the door when the key is in your pocket. **The power to generate that will lose its focus.**

GATE 10: TREADING - THE BEHAVIOR OF THE SELF
– The underlying code of behavior which ensures successful interaction despite circumstances –

Line 6 - The role model
The perfect expression of the norms through action rather than words.

♆ ▲ The constant example that refocuses the complacent on the basic integrity of set behavior. **The enduring value of the expression of the Self through action rather than words.**

♄ ▽ The hypocrite. Do as I say, not as I do. **Behavior restricted to words rather than action.**

Line 5 - The heretic
Direct and overt challenge to norms.

♃ ▲ The ability to succeed through the understanding and expression of higher principles. **Principled behavior which directly challenges tradition.**

♂ ▽ The burning at the stake. **Behavior which directly challenges behavior and is eventually punished.**

Line 4 - The opportunist
The acceptance of norms until a successful transformation can be engendered.

♅ ▲ Transformation that is transcendence to a higher code. **The maintaining of behavioral patterns until the right moment and opportunity for transformation.**

☿ ▽ Opportunism as a game and/or mental exercise. **Altering one's behavioral patterns in order to take advantage of opportunities.**

Line 3 - The martyr
The futile rejection of standards based on a just awareness.

⊕ ▲ The martyr as an enduring example whose behavior is ultimately enshrined. **Behavior that is ultimately challenged by others.**

☽ ▽ The martyr complex. The active pursuit of martyrdom for personal aggrandizement. **Behavior as a way to attract attention.**

Line 2 - The hermit
The successful sidestepping of behavioral requirements through isolation.

☿ ▲ Mercury exalted, where mental functions enrich aloneness. **Independent behavior through isolation.**

♂ ▽ The angry exile. **Isolation to preserve independent behavior in the face of conditioning.**

Line 1 - Modesty
An innate sense to know and accept one's place.

☉ ▲ A valued sense of purpose no matter what the position. **The ability to know one's place and how to act despite circumstances.**

☽ ▽ The affliction of over-sensitivity and hurt feeling. **Over-sensitivity to external conditioning of behavior.**

GATE 11: PEACE - IDEAS
– A harmonic condition in the individual society that permits assessment before renewed action –

Line 6 - Adaptability
The inner balance to accept transition.

Ψ ▲ The innate awareness that all forms are transitory. **The realization that ideas lead to change and are changeable.**

♃ ▽ Adaptability in its most negative manifestation. The speculator who profits at the expense of others in times of peace or war. **The realization of what idea is of value in any situation.**

Line 5 - The philanthropist

☽ ▲ The motiveless nurturing of the disenfranchised to ensure harmony. **Philosophic and humanitarian ideas.**

☿ ▽ The withdrawing from direct contact, where giving is a form of defence. **Giving away ideas out of a sense of insecurity.**

Line 4 - The teacher
The ability to express the essential nature of peace.

☽ ▲ The sage, that in the extreme, can teach harmony to the tone deaf. Venus is also exalted. The ability to reach out and attract the alienated. **Concepts which are clear and transferable. Ideas which can attract and inform the uneducated.**

☉ ▽ The Guru, whose most valued wisdom is intentionally limited to a few. **Ideas which can only be grasped by the few.**

Line 3 - The realist
The acknowledgment that peace is transitory.

Ψ ▲ The internal renewal to maintain strength and alertness. **The realization that ideas come and go.**

♀ ▽ The tendency to appreciate harmony to the point of delusion. The belief that beauty is eternal. Fiddling while Rome burns. **A pleasure in ideas that have no real application.**

Line 2 - Rigor
The recognition that without vigilance and risk, peace can lead to stagnation and collapse.

Ψ ▲ The imagination applied to ensuring the understanding of achieved values. **A sense of boredom overcome through the imagination.**

♂ ▽ The resorting to factionalism to satisfy the ego's need for action. **Provoking with ideas to escape boredom.**

Line 1 - Attunement
The serendipity of being in the right place at the right time.

☽ ▲ The nourishment derived from being with those who share the same goals and aspirations. **The gift of finding those who will value your ideas.**

♂ ▽ The fear of anonymity. **The sense that no one will value their ideas.**

GATE 12: STANDSTILL - CAUTION
– The quality of restraint and the importance of meditation and inaction in confronting temptation –

Line 6 - Metamorphosis
Faith in, and energy applied towards change and the emergence from standstill.

☉ ▲ Creative transcendence that when connected to the Harmonic Gate 22, through the channel of Openness, leads to successful mutation and the emergence of a new social form. **The capacity to mutate and express new social forms.**

⊕ ▽ A retrograde metamorphosis that has evolved a perfected adaption to standstill. The **perfected adaption to caution that can accept social limitations.**

Line 5 - The pragmatist
The success of restraint lies in not abandoning the lessons learnt when the phase ends.

☉ ▲ Light is always conscious of darkness. **Caution as an expression of social experience.**

♂ ▽ The tendency to remember only the most painful lessons learnt. **Caution which is conditioned by the most painful social experiences.**

Line 4 - The prophet
The ability to foresee and plan for the end of standstill.

⊕ ▲ The rousing of the stagnant for communal preparation. The ability to foresee and express the need for social interaction and an end to caution.

☿ ▽ The voice in the wilderness. **The expressed need for social interaction that falls on deaf ears.**

Line 3 - Confession
The process of self-analysis.

Ψ ▲ The recognition of inadequacies and the purging of unjustified vanities. The expression of inadequacies in social interaction that leads to self-analysis and caution.

♂ ▽ A perverse and often exaggerated self-hatred. **Inadequacies in social interaction that lead to the expression of self-hatred.**

Line 2 - Purification
Rigorous withdrawal from negative influences.

♄ ▲ The discipline to maintain a pure state. **The expression of disciplined social caution.**

☿ ▽ The boredom that arises out of lack of stimulation. **Caution that manifests boredom and the expressed desire for stimulus.**

Line 1 - The monk
Withdrawal that can only be maintained with communal support.

♀ ▲ The beauty and harmony possible beyond the reach of temptation. The expression of social withdrawal and its value when supported by others.

♃ ▽ Simon the Stylite, total and often absurd withdrawal. **The absurd expression of social caution and extreme withdrawal from emotional contact.**

GATE 13: THE FELLOWSHIP OF MAN - THE LISTENER

– Universal ideas and values in an ordered framework which inspires humanistic cooperation –

Line 6 - The optimist
The ability to accept any limited interaction as a necessary step towards greater union.

♂ ▲ The energy to persevere. Unlimited hope. The hope that openness will lead to better relationships.

☿ ▽ Naivete. The translation of mutual interest into universality. **The belief that mutual interests can be projected on others.**

Line 5 - The saviour
The ability to overcome all obstacles for the betterment of humanity.

♆ ▲ The charismatic genius who can find a role for everyone. **The listener that has a gift for finding a role for others.**

♃ ▽ The able administrator. Given the extreme positive nature of this position, mundane application is rare. **The listener whose gift for finding a role for others is practical and suited to administration.**

Line 4 - Fatigue
The point of exhaustion eventually reached when one is too tired to fight.

♆ ▲ The renaissance that comes with truce and its eventual reinvigoration. **Openness which leads to exhaustion and the need for silence.**

♀ ▽ Emotional exhaustion. Appeasement and withdrawal. **A role where openness is a vulnerability.**

Line 3 - Pessimism
The belief that what is best can never be achieved.

⊕ ▲ A lack of trust that can only be transformed through concrete evidence. **Openness that is conditioned by suspicion and seeks evidence.**

♀ ▽ Pessimism exalted to an art form, where as art, it may have the opposite effect. Satire. **Where the rightness of suspicion can inspire satire.**

Line 2 - Bigotry
The risk, always present, that fellowship can only exist for a particular type, whether racial, religious, national or intellectual.

☽ ▲ Tolerance as the least offensive manifestation of bigotry. **A role of openness through tolerance.**

☉ ▽ The obsessive belief that the highest ideals cannot be embraced by the lowest forms. An extremely difficult position, where even the highest ideals provide rationalization for hatred. **A role of openness so narrow that there is practically no one worth listening to.**

Line 1 - Empathy
The ability to relate and commune with everyone with equanimity.

♀ ▲ Harmony through affection. **A role of openness in listening to others with affection.**

☽ ▽ The politician kissing babies. **An openness that is never free of motives.**

GATE 14: POSSESSION IN GREAT MEASURE - POWER SKILLS

– The accumulation & retention of power through skilled interaction, coupling grace with control –

Line 6 - Humilty
Wealth and power at its most exalted.

☉ ▲ The enlightened recognition that material success is God's will. **Spirituality as the key to acceptance and the source of power.**

⊕ ▽ All manifestations of this position are essentially positive. The Earth represents the existentialist recognition that material success was unavoidable and the humility engendered by such serendipity. **Existentialism as the key to acceptance and the source of power.**

Line 5 - Arrogance
The ever present risk inherent in positions of power.

☉ ▲ Innate dignity. **Innate dignity that is a key to power.**

♀ ▽ A dissatisfaction with the gifts of others that creates feelings of superiority. **Innate recognition of those without power fueling the illusion of superiority.**

Line 4 - Security
The concentration on establishing a strong foundation.

☽ ▲ Protection from assault. **The key to power lies in developing skills to ensure a strong foundation.**

♂ ▽ Overconfidence in meeting the challenge of competition that may threaten the very basis of security. **Without the proper skills the inability to guarantee security.**

Line 3 - Service
The utilization of talent and wealth for the highest good.

⊕ ▲ Selfless contribution to society. **The key to power lies in selfless contribution to others.**

♆ ▽ Greed and the self-destruction of moral fibre. **The power of selfishness to fuel greed.**

Line 2 - Management
The wisdom that investing in expertise brings rewards.

♃ ▲ Expansion. The ability to delegate responsibility. **The key to power lies in not trying to be and to do everything alone.**

♂ ▽ The vanity to be one's own best expert. **The key to power is doing everything individually.**

Line 1 - Money isn't everything
The recognition that wealth has its own problems.

♃ ▲ The lust for lucre tempered by higher principles. **The key to manifesting power is higher principles.**

☿ ▽ The delusion that you can throw money at problems. **Energy alone can never be the key.**

Gate 15: Modesty - Extremes

– The quality of behavior which expresses the proper balance between extremes –

Line 6 - Self-defense
Modesty that is never confused with weakness.

♇ ▲ Constant re-examination to weed out the weakest aspect. **The power of the Self in exploring the extremes to find the weakest point.**

♀ ▽ A tendency to use harmony as a weapon in problem situations rather than focusing on the root causes. **The power of the Self to ignore the weakest point in favour of harmony.**

Line 5 - Sensitivity
The ability to sense when otherwise balanced behavior must be adjusted to meet the requirements of changing environment.

♃ ▲ The power to grow. **The capacity of the Self to grow through experiencing the extremes.**

♇ ▽ The tendency to overcompensate. **The drive of the Self to overcompensate and disturb the flow.**

Line 4 - The wallflower
Modesty as a shield against exposure of inadequacy.

♃ ▲ A genuine form that may/or may not mask inadequacies. **The uncomfortableness of the Self when it is out of the flow.**

♄ ▽ An ultimately weak defense leading to exposure and humiliation. **Extremism that keeps the Self out of the flow.**

Line 3 - Ego inflation
The risk that modesty once recognized will self-destruct.

⊕ ▲ Where the otherwise negative contrived modesty is here reinforced by recognition and maintained as an effective strategy. **The extremism of the Self as strategy to control the flow.**

☿ ▽ The 'I told you so' mentality. **The capacity of the Self to point out the extremes of others.**

Line 2 - Influence
☉ ▲ Modesty and right action result in enduring standards. **The capacity of the Self to accept its extreme nature as correct.**

⊕ ▽ Where the Sun's actions are natural, the Earth's are contrived, though given the power of this position, the same effect can be expected. **The capacity to use the extreme nature of the Self to influence others.**

Line 1 - Duty
The ability to confront any challenge without expectations.

♀ ▲ Harmonic relationships which give support for the fulfillment of any task. **The capacity of the Self to confront any challenge through extreme and harmonic relationships.**

♂ ▽ Alienation engendered through exaggerated claims. **The capacity of the Self to alienate others through extremes.**

Gate 16: Enthusiasm - Skills
– The great art of enriching life by the harmonic channeling of energy –

Line 6 - Gullibility
The susceptibility to propaganda.

Ψ ▲ The ability to experience, examine and then reject misleading enthusiasm. **The talent to assess the expression of others.**

♃ ▽ The same principle but where Neptune will destroy and then seek new forms, Jupiter will painfully withdraw. Its enthusiasm for social structures permanently prejudiced. **The failure to assess the expression of others.**

Line 5 - The grinch
The refusal to share in enthusiasm.

♇ ▲ The power to avoid enthusiasm for the sole purpose of being converted. As with Dickens' Scrooge, eventual conversion leads to greater and more enduring enthusiasm. **A lack of confidence in the expression of skills that needs the encouragement of others.**

☽ ▽ The perverse feeling that sharing in enthusiasm hampers individual development. Why should I be happy when ... etc. **A lack of confidence in the value of encouraging others.**

Line 4 - The leader
Genuine and sincere support and recognition of others.

♃ ▲ Enthusiasm for/and service to higher goals. **The skill to recognize and support the talents of others.**

♂ ▽ The demagogue. **The refusal to support or recognize the talents of others.**

Line 3 - Independence
Self-generating and sustaining enthusiasm.

☽ ▲ The proper timing to maintain rhythm and avoid deflation. **The independent skill and possible talent to express proper timing and rhythm.**

♂ ▽ The child whose overconfidence may lead to frustration and the ensuing dependence on others to regenerate enthusiasm; thus creating an unnecessary reliance. **The need to have others confirm one's skills or talent.**

Line 2 - The cynic
The sharpness to burst bubbles.

☉ ▲ Self-reliance and the skill to judge objectively any claim regardless of rhetoric. **The expression of the skill to judge objectively.**

☿ ▽ The compulsive cynic, whose very cynicism is a source of enthusiasm. **Objectivity expressed through cynicism.**

Line 1 - Delusion
False enthusiasm.

⊕ ▲ The day dreamer. **The expression of talent through daydreaming.**

☿ ▽ The public communication of inevitably unrealized claims. **The tendency to express fantasy as fact.**

GATE 17: FOLLOWING - OPINION
– The ancient law that those who wish to rule must know how to serve –

Line 6 - The bodhisattva
Perfected following, one with and the same as, perfected leading.

☽　▲　The great nurturer. The nature of this position is always positive. The possibility in understanding the nature of interdependency to express opinions of value to others.

♃　▽　The tendency on the perfected path it is a straight line that ends rather than a circle. Where understanding is achieved, the possibility of having the opinion that there is nothing else to learn.

Line 5 - No human is an island
The recognition, however understood that there is no end to hierarchies.

♅　▲　The ultimate creative expression of interdependency, whether as God's will or global synthesis. Opinions that can express the value of being organized whether mundane or spiritual.

♂　▽　The arrogance, despite all the evidence to claim, that the buck stops here! The possibility of opinions that refuse to see the value of being organized.

Line 4 - The personnel manager

♆　▲　The ability to probe and discover the underlying motivation and resources of those who wish to follow. The possibility of opinions based on the understanding of others.

♃　▽　The overgenerous and often misguided acceptance of would-be followers, often with disastrous results. The possibility of opinions attracting others.

Line 3 - Understanding
The awareness that the best road is not necessarily the most interesting.

♆　▲　The following of the best road provides the experience necessary to meet the challenge of the road's end. The understanding that the best opinions are grounded in detail.

⊕　▽　The taking of short cuts. One may get to the end quicker, but essential experience will be missing. The possibility of skipping details and limiting the value of the opinion.

Line 2 - Discrimination
The benefit of associations based on the highest values.

☉　▲　The successful achievement of purpose through proper alignment. The possibility to develop opinions through relationships.

☽　▽　An overactive discrimination that leaves one virtually alone. The possibility of being opinionated at the expense of relationships.

Line 1 - Openness

♂　▲　The energy to sustain a broad spectrum of stimuli. The possibility of having many opinions.

♀　▽　A tendency to limit openness to aesthetically pleasing stimuli. The possibility to limit opinions to what is pleasing.

GATE 18: WORK ON WHAT HAS BEEN SPOILT - CORRECTION
– The vigilance and determination to uphold and defend basic and fundamental human rights –

Line 6 - Buddhahood
The perfected form.

♂ ▲ The Buddha state of the eternal child and the energy to find new horizons to avoid stasis. **The potential of the perfected form through correction.**

☽ ▽ The mundane application of the above. The ability to tap public opinion and share methodology. **The potential to share the values of the correction with others.**

Line 5 - Therapy
The strength to recognize a problem and to accept that it is beyond one's power to solve it alone.

♄ ▲ The wisdom to both seek and provide guidance. **The potential for correction and judgment through relationships.**

♅ ▽ The mental patient. Chronic instability and potential madness. **Where relationships cannot assist in correction the potential of mental instability.**

Line 4 - The incompetent
Difficulties as a result of inadequacies that cannot be resolved because of inadequacies.

⊕ ▲ Given this negative position, survival through suffering. **The inability to correct and its potential for suffering.**

☿ ▽ Indecision and anxiety and no escape from misfortune. **The demands of correction and its potential to generate anxiety.**

Line 3 - The zealot
The energetic obsession to clean house.

Ψ ▲ The dissolution of old forms at an acceptable price. **An obsession with correction and its critical potential.**

♃ ▽ Rigid judgmentation that creates as many problems as it solves. **An obsession with correction that does not bring satisfaction.**

Line 2 - Terminal disease
The recognition that what has been spoilt is irreversible.

♀ ▲ Acceptance and strength derived from a faith in spiritual regeneration. **The acceptance that there is no potential for correction.**

☽ ▽ The futile raging against the wind. **The refusal to accept that there is no potential for correction.**

Line 1 - Conservatism
The adherence to traditional patterns despite and/or in spite of changing circumstances.

⊕ ▲ Gradual modification to avoid eventual upheaval. **The potential to correct through gradual modification of judgments.**

♃ ▽ The Patriarch whose rigidity guarantees deterioration. **The potential to refuse to correct.**

GATE 19: APPROACH - WANTING

– That all things are interrelated is apparent and manifested through the action of approach –

Line 6 - The recluse
The avoidance of contact in general but not exclusively.

♃ ▲ The fool on the hill. The sage, that if you can find him, will talk to you. **The energy which generally fuels avoidance.**

♂ ▽ The sulking child. The self-imposed exile that will only end when it attracts appropriate and soothing reaction. **Over-sensitivity to rejection that fuels avoidance.**

Line 5 - Sacrifice
The need to limit personal potential in order to achieve a larger goal.

⊕ ▲ The self-restraint fundamental to such a nature. **Energy to keep one's sensitivities restrained.**

♃ ▽ A tendency in sacrifice to condescend. **Sacrifice can fuel a lack of sensitivity.**

Line 4 - The team player
Individual approach which attracts and accepts cooperation.

♂ ▲ The power and energy for outward activity and the ability to accept others as long as they can keep up. A driving force that can benefit the whole group. **The energy to seek out and exalt in the company of others.**

♀ ▽ Attractive and cooperative but a tendency to dissatisfaction with the contribution of others. **A sensitivity energized by the limitation of others.**

Line 3 - Dedication
Receptivity to approach can only be maintained through vigilance.

♀ ▲ The natural ease with which communion is maintained. **Sensitivity and ease fueled by acceptance by others.**

☽ ▽ A tendency to moodiness that may lead to carelessness. **The need to be wanted hampered by over-sensitivity.**

Line 2 - Service
The dedication of personal resources as a result of external contact.

♃ ▲ Dedication and service to the highest values. **The energy to want to be of service.**

☿ ▽ Protracted indecision, but given the nature of this position, eventual compliance. **The need to be wanted that will eventually turn its energy to service.**

Line 1 - Interdependence

☉ ▲ The successful approach that does not loose its individual character in acceptance. **The pressure of wanting without losing one's identity when being accepted by others.**

☽ ▽ The tendency once an approach is accepted to get stuck in continued reflection at the expense of continued development. **The pressure for acceptance which fears eventual rejection.**

GATE 20: CONTEMPLATION - NOW

– Recognition and awareness in the now which transforms understanding into right action –

Line 6 - Wisdom
Contemplation which results in the ability to apply understanding.

♀ ▲ The establishment for the benefit of society, values, ideals and their patterns and how they can be understood and applied. **The ability to transform individual awareness for general application and understanding.**

☿ ▽ The same as above but motivated by the self-satisfying mental challenge rather than altruism. **The ability to transform individual awareness for general application for the mental challenge.**

Line 5 - Realism
Contemplation, in and of itself, is no guarantee of success.

♄ ▲ Where concentration on detail results in a perfected form. **The success of expressing awareness through detail.**

♅ ▽ Where reality creates dissatisfaction and adds to instability. **The expression of awareness in the now through dissatisfaction with the reality one sees.**

Line 4 - Application
Recognition and awareness that can only be transformed into action in cooperation with those who have the ability to act upon the understanding.

♃ ▲ The teach whose students transcend him. **Where the expression of awareness can only be turned into action through others. The teacher.**

☿ ▽ A tendency to prefer theory to application. **The expression of the awareness as theory with little interest in its application.**

Line 3 - Self-awareness
Understanding derived from analysis of personal actions and effects.

☉ ▲ The proper attunement and development of the personality through self-consciousness. **The expression of self-conscious awareness in the now.**

⊕ ▽ Self-consciousness in the extreme that hampers development. **The expression of self-consciousness in the extreme.**

Line 2 - The dogmatist
Restrictive and intentionally limited understanding.

♀ ▲ The limitation if personal and exclusive is less negative through ascetic withdrawal. **A restrictive awareness of the now.**

☽ ▽ The power to lead others down a narrow path. **The gift through expression of leading others down a narrow and restrictive path.**

Line 1 - Superficiality
A reliance on shallowness.

♀ ▲ The raising of superficiality to an art form. The sloganeer. **Superficial expression as an art form.**

☽ ▽ The superficial expression of the personality. **The expression of the superficial personality.**

GATE 21: BITING THROUGH - HUNTER/HUNTRESS

– The justified and necessary use of power in overcoming deliberate and persistent interference –

Line 6 - Chaos

Where ineffective action leads to disorder.

♇ ▲ The war of attrition. The continuance of legitimate action in the hope of eventually succeeding despite all odds and increasing disorder. **Where the ego is out of touch, the display of will power leads to disorder.**

♀ ▽ Withdrawal and reliance on inner order in a chaotic situation. **Where the material direction is chaotic, the ego will withdraw and use its power to find an inner order.**

Line 5 - Objectivity

The use of force must be based on impartiality and not emotionally motivated.

♃ ▲ A principled and legal character that ensures objectivity. **The balanced ego whose will power is applied objectively.**

♇ ▽ The drive for elimination is so powerful that objectivity is related purely to cause and not effect. **The ego whose will power is applied subjectively.**

Line 4 - Strategy

Careful appraisal of opposing forces to establish a proper response.

♃ ▲ Success in action through clarity. **The ego to succeed on the material plane and the instinct to use will power effectively in response to conditions.**

⊕ ▽ A tendency, when in the right to misjudge the power of one's opponents. **The drive when in the right to follow one's ego rather than one's instincts.**

Line 3 - Powerlessness

Where the just are condemned to a futile confrontation with superior forces.

♆ ▲ Defeat as a survivable humiliation often acceptable through the abuse of drugs and alcohol. **Unless one follows one's own material path, the breaking of the ego by superiors.**

♃ ▽ Total withdrawal. **A lack of will for the material path in order to protect the ego.**

Line 2 - Might is right

The legitimacy of action in response to flagrant and persistent interference.

♂ ▲ Powerful and extreme reaction. Here, the severest action will be the most successful. **The legitimate rejection of interference on the material plane.**

♆ ▽ A tendency to regret severity, no matter how legitimate. **The ego uncomfortable with severity.**

Line 1 - Warning

The use of force as a last resort.

♂ ▲ The fierceness to be respected without recourse to action. **The will power and ego to ensure respect.**

☽ ▽ An inherent peacefulness that all too often turns a necessary warning into a plea. **A lack of will power that is forced to ask for respect.**

GATE 22: GRACE - OPENNESS

– A quality of behavior best suited in handling mundane and trivial situations –

Line 6 - Maturity
The alignment with experience of form with substance.

☉ ▲ Natural and evident leadership and authority. **The possibility that experience in social interaction will result in a leadership capacity.**

♂ ▽ The alignment tends to express itself in nonconformist modes. **The possibility that experience in social interaction will result in a non-conformist expression of openness.**

Line 5 - Directness
The disregard of form when required.

♃ ▲ The power inherent in higher principles to successfully transgress behavioral codes. **The possibility through emotional awareness to behave individualistically in social interaction.**

♂ ▽ A tendency to create embarrassing situations, and though invariably successful, the often resulting reputation for crudity and impudence. **The possibility that individual behavior in social interaction will generate negative projections from others.**

Line 4 - Sensitivity
The modification of behavior to enrich interactions.

♆ ▲ A mediumistic simplicity that rejects elaborate rituals. **The possibility of social openness through the rejection of formality.**

♂ ▽ An over-reliance on the mechanics of style that can abort potentially significant relationships. **The limitation of social openness through the need for formality.**

Line 3 - The enchanter
Perfected grace.

♄ ▲ Form as a definition and actualization of substance. **The possibility for perfected openness through the alignment of emotional energy and awareness.**

♂ ▽ Unconscious grace. **An innate openness.**

Line 2 - Charm school
The belief that style can mask nature.

☉ ▲ The ability to successfully delude oneself and others. **The possibility to attract others with an emotional style.**

♃ ▽ The legalization of form over substance. **Where the style is energized at the expense of awareness.**

Line 1 - Second class ticket

☽ ▲ The ability to accept and enjoy a subordinate position. **The emotional awareness to enjoy a subordinate position.**

♂ ▽ The inevitable humiliation that comes with claiming a first class seat with a second class ticket. **Where the emotional energy challenges the awareness and can result in humiliation socially.**

GATE 23: SPLITTING APART - ASSIMILATION
– Amorality. The awareness and understanding which leads to the acceptance of diversity –

Line 6 - Fusion
The gradual attunement of diversity through synthesis.

♂ ▲ The exponential growth of energy and its power of assertion engendered by fusion. **Individual knowing which brings diversity to synthesis.**

♃ ▽ The principled but futile withdrawal from fusion that leads to atrophy. **Individual knowing that holds on to diversity and loses its power in expression.**

Line 5 - Assimilation
The practical acceptance of the values of another path.

♃ ▲ Expansion and contribution through assimilation. **The gift of communicating individual insight to the collective.**

☽ ▽ Motive driven assimilation from an inferior position, i.e. for protection or nourishment. **Motive driven assimilation for acceptance and protection from the collective.**

Line 4 - Fragmentation
Diversification without a perceived potential for synthesis.

☉ ▲ Fatalism and egoism and damn the consequences. **Individual expression which has no collective value.**

⊕ ▽ Atheism and paranoia. **Individual expression which engenders isolation and fear.**

Line 3 - Individuality
Independent expression that is not by its nature detrimental to others.

☉ ▲ Vitality and personal power that can engender jealousy but not threat. **Individual expression which attracts attention but not threat.**

♆ ▽ An individual mysteriousness that attracts active suspicion and threat. **The freak. Individual expression that attracts suspicion and threat.**

Line 2 - Self-defense
The need to abandon tolerance when survival is threatened.

♃ ▲ The principle of preservation at its most acute. **The abandonment of tolerance when individual expression is threatened.**

☽ ▽ Where Jupiter will strike out to preserve its integrity, the Moon is often satisfied with just protecting itself by fending off hostility. **The defense of individual expression in the face of hostility.**

Line 1 - Proselytization
The attempt to undermine one set of values for another.

♃ ▲ The sage, who in the extreme can defend evil as a part of the greater good. **The powerful expression of an insight which will undermine established values.**

♂ ▽ The missionary whose very light will bring darkness. **The powerful expression of an insight which will produce negative effects.**

GATE 24: THE RETURN - RATIONALIZATION
– The natural and spontaneous process of transformation and renewal –

Line 6 - The gift horse
The possibility of being deaf when opportunity knocks.

♃ ▲ The conscious participation in a process that prepares one for easy identification of opportunity. **Identification and focus with the rational thought process.**

♆ ▽ Innate suspicion which leads inevitably to lost opportunities. **Often irrational suspicion that distorts the focus and can lead to missed opportunities.**

Line 5 - Confession
The courage to admit the mistakes of the past.

☽ ▲ The practical value of starting with a clean slate, symbolized by the New Moon. **Rational correction that opens the way to new possibilities.**

♂ ▽ The tendency to try to minimalize past mistakes through rationalization; turning confession into justification. **Irrational justification of past mistakes.**

Line 4 - The hermit
Transformation that can only take place in isolation.

♄ ▲ The discipline and focus that assures renewal. **Aloneness enriches the potential for rational thought.**

♆ ▽ The tendency in isolation to live in a fantasy world. **Aloneness encourages the potential of illusion or delusion.**

Line 3 - The addict
The powerful attraction of regressive forms.

♀ ▲ The ultimate though difficult triumph over regression. **The difficult but possible task of overcoming irrationality.**

♃ ▽ Addiction and regression legitimized by success. **Irrationality maintained and legitimized by success.**

Line 2 - Recognition

☽ ▲ The proper and spontaneous adaption to new forms. **The potential gift of conceptualizing spontaneously.**

♂ ▽ The vanity to see transformation as a personal achievement rather than a socially supported or natural phenomenon. **The mental vanity that the gift of conceptualizing spontaneously can produce.**

Line 1 - The sin of omission
Transformation that requires retrogressive periods before renewal can take place.

☉ ▲ The will to triumph and in this case the faith that the end justifies the means. **Inspiration that demands a reassessment of past thinking before a rational concept can be established.**

♆ ▽ Self-delusion which unnaturally justifies periods of retrogression. **Inspiration that leads to an irrational focus on what is past.**

GATE 25: INNOCENCE - THE SPIRIT OF THE SELF
– The perfection of action through uncontrived and spontaneous nature –

Line 6 - Ignorance
False innocence betrayed by actions.

⊕ ▲ The least mild of a negative position, where inappropriate action is censured. **The loss of innocence through inappropriate action.**

♅ ▽ Constant inappropriate and destabilizing actions whose very counter-productiveness strips away the facade of innocence. **Constant inappropriate action in times of challenges that can break the spirit.**

Line 5 - Recuperation
When innocence is sapped of its vitality, healing is the first priority.

♀ ▲ The ability to recognize the inner meaning of an affliction and to withdraw until it is healed. **The power of the spirit to heal and be healed.**

♃ ▽ Hypochondria and the need to be healed by others. **The weakness of the spirit which requires healing from others.**

Line 4 - Survival
The nature of true innocence can be maintained regardless of circumstances.

♀ ▲ The beauty of the rose in the garbage dump. Jupiter is also exalted. The highest principles even amongst the greatest decadence. **The spiritual warrior; the innocence maintained regardless of circumstances. No polarity.**

▽ No planet in detriment.

Line 3 - Sensibility
The recognition that innocent action does not in itself guarantee success.

♂ ▲ The power of the ego to withstand failure and still maintain its nature. **The power of the spirit to withstand failure and shock.**

♆ ▽ The potential loss of innocence through misfortune that in the extreme can manifest from crime to suicide. **The potential loss of spirit through failure or shock.**

Line 2 - The existentialist
Devotion and dedication to the now.

☿ ▲ The perfection of the intellect through concentration and focus on what is, rather than, what could be or has been. **The innocence of the Self and its protection can only be maintained in the now.**

♂ ▽ A dedication that can never be free of personal motivation and its attendant projections. **A lack of innocence in the now that risks protection through projection.**

Line 1 - Selflessness
Motiveless action.

♆ ▲ The universalization of activity. Psychic attunement that is its own reward. **The potential for centering through attunement to challenges.**

☿ ▽ A tendency to publicize one's selflessness. **The insecurity of the Self manifested in times of challenge.**

GATE 26: THE TAMING POWER OF THE GREAT - THE EGOIST

– The maximization of the power of memory applied to the nurturing of continuity –

Line 6 - Authority
The natural attainment of influence justified by the correctness of actions.

☉ ▲ The embodiment of reason and purpose that passes the test of time. **The strong ego whose influence is justified by the correctness of its actions.**

☽ ▽ Authority as a symbol and focus but not necessarily as a true embodiment. The constitutional monarch, stripped of real power but still the symbol of the continuity of authority. **The expression of the ego as a role whose influence is symbolic and lacks authority.**

Line 5 - Adaptability

♂ ▲ The understanding of mechanics and the application of energy to achieve maximum potential. **The power of memory which maximizes the potential of the ego to attract others.**

♀ ▽ A resistance and dissatisfaction when basic changes to nature are necessary. **The resistance of the egoist to adaption.**

Line 4 - Censorship
The alteration of memory through elimination.

♆ ▲ The ability through censorship to save the collectivity from itself. **The power of the ego maintained through forgetting.**

♄ ▽ The use of censorship to maintain the status quo; selective memory in fear of unrestrained consequences. **The power of the ego maintained through selective memory.**

Line 3 - Influence
The ability, once prepared to gather support.

☉ ▲ The authority to focus communal effort. **The power of the ego to gather support.**

♄ ▽ The leadership, while gathering support will underestimate potential challenges. **The egoist unable to recognize the potential challenges in others.**

Line 2 - The lessons of history

☉ ▲ The energy and depth of reflection to learn from the past in anticipation of the future. **The power of the ego to mature through experience.**

♆ ▽ The urge to take action despite the evidence of history. **The failure of the ego to respect experience.**

Line 1 - A bird in the hand

♆ ▲ The ability to enjoy the dreams engendered by accomplishment in order to avoid the delusion of unlikely potential. **The ego which transcends limitation through dreaming.**

♂ ▽ Accomplishment as a licence for foolhardy risk taking. **The refusal of the ego to be satisfied.**

GATE 27: NOURISHMENT - CARING
– The enhancement of the quality and the substance of all activities through caring –

Line 6 - Wariness
A protection against an abuse of generosity.

☽ ▲ A practical and realistic approach to nurturing, whose appropriateness is guided by feelings and instinct. **The power and strength to be realistic in one's capacities to care and nurture.**

♆ ▽ A tendency to over-suspiciousness. **The power of suspicion in limiting the expression of caring.**

Line 5 - The executor
The ability to distribute effectively the resources of others.

♃ ▲ Either, the gifted and principled agent of distribution or the good sense and ability to find one. **The power and strength to care for the resources of others.**

♄ ▽ A restrictive nature that hampers distribution or the seeking of advice and assistance. **Weakness and the risk of loss of power restrict caring.**

Line 4 - Generosity
The natural sharing of attained abundance.

♃ ▲ Magnanimous and qualitative sharing. The gift of rewarding those who are deserving. **The power and strength to share generously.**

♂ ▽ Indiscriminate sharing. **The potential loss of power and strength through indiscriminate sharing.**

Line 3 - Greed
The obsession with having much more than one needs.

♆ ▲ Here, the psychological manifestation. The obsession and dependency on knowing what is hidden. The secret policeman. **The power derived in having more than one needs, whether sexually, mentally, or materially.**

♂ ▽ Mundane and wholly without redeeming value, greed, a lust that inevitably cripples and addicts. **The lust for power to get more than one needs.**

Line 2 - Self-sufficiency
The obvious law that to give, one must have.

☽ ▲ The Mother. The great nourisher. **The strength to nurture and the power to care.**

♂ ▽ The child depleting the resources of others. **Weakness that can sap the strength and power of others.**

Line 1 - Selfishness

☉ ▲ The ego-driven first law of caring for oneself which is not necessarily at the expense of others. **The power to care for oneself first.**

⊕ ▽ Envy and its attendant misfortunes. **The power of selfishness that is manifested through envy.**

GATE 28: PREPONDERANCE OF THE GREAT - THE GAME PLAYER

– The transitoriness of power and influence –

Line 6 - Blaze of glory

Sacrifice rather than capitulation to the law of deterioration.

♇ ▲ Regeneration and renewal no matter what the price. **The deep intuitive drive to win no matter what the cost.**

♆ ▽ Self-destruction. **The deep intuitive fear of defeat and a potentially profound hopelessness in times of struggle.**

Line 5 - Treachery

The abuse of trust.

♇ ▲ The manipulation of the collective, that while pitting one faction against the other, does not directly support or reject either. **The intuitive capacity of the game player to provoke struggle amongst others.**

☉ ▽ The breaking of alliances with trusted forces to align with more powerful forces and its attendant destabilization of the whole. **The intuitive recognition in times of struggle to know when alliances must be broken and its destabilizing effect on others.**

Line 4 - Holding on

The ability through whatever means to keep one's grip.

♃ ▲ The application of knowledge to exploit opportunities and usually for the greater good. **A depth of intuition at its best in struggle and often of value to others.**

☿ ▽ The application of intelligence to hold on, exclusively out of self-interest. **A depth of intuition that is stubbornly selfish in its capacity to hold on.**

Line 3 - Adventurism

Unfounded risk taking.

♄ ▲ A basic conservatism that even in adventurous acts is necessarily prudent. **An intuitive caution in risk taking in times of struggle.**

♃ ▽ Here a perverse manifestation of Jupiter's expansiveness where risk taking is rationalized and failure ensured. **Intuitive rationalizing of risk taking in times of struggle.**

Line 2 - Shaking hands with the devil

Distasteful alliance.

☉ ▲ A means, however unsavory, that is justified by its end. **When the game turns to a struggle, the intuitive acceptance of any alliance in order to win.**

♃ ▽ The anxiety engendered by sacrificing higher principles when there is no guarantee of success. **The risk in sacrificing principles when there is no guarantee of victory.**

Line 1 - Preparation

♂ ▲ The desire to be effective manifested in the application of energy to detail. **The intuition to potentially apply energy to detail.**

♀ ▽ The aesthetic appreciation of planning that may have no real application. **An intuition for detail without the potential for application.**

GATE 29: THE ABYSMAL - PERSERVERANCE
– The deep within the deep; persistence despite difficulties has its inevitable rewards –

Line 6 - Confusion
The state that exists when momentum outstrips awareness.

♂ ▲ Driving blind and given Mars' energy and determination, often blind luck. **The power to persevere that makes no sense.**

♃ ▽ A tendency in confusion to withdraw rather than accept the condition and continue to persevere. **The power in confusion to caution rather than saying yes.**

Line 5 - Overreach
The tendency to bite off more than one can chew.

☉ ▲ The Sun exalted, where the drive is in the design and not ambition driven. **The uncontrollable drive to say yes.**

⊕ ▽ Failed ambition. **Saying yes, overextending one's resources, and failing to persevere.**

Line 4 - Directness
The shortest distance between two points is a straight line.

♄ ▲ The wisdom to use the simplest and most direct approach to solve difficulties. **The power to commit oneself to the simplest and most direct process.**

♀ ▽ Simplicity and directness all too often seen as inharmonic and aesthetically crude. **The power of directness often offends others.**

Line 3 - Evaluation
In this context, properly assessed inaction.

♂ ▲ Despite the urge and cost of inaction the knowledge that it is sometimes better to fight another day. **The power to wait.**

♃ ▽ A preference for withdrawal in principle with little regard for effect. The inability to make commitments. **The power of caution.**

Line 2 - Assessment
Persistence tempered by caution.

☉ ▲ The power of sustainment as a guiding light. **Saying yes and the power to persevere.**

♀ ▽ A tendency to overcautiousness when persistence is perceived as adding to rather than ending disharmony. **Caution in saying yes, when perseverance leads to disharmony.**

Line 1 - The draftee
The ability to adapt to struggle when necessary but not as a permanent state.

♂ ▲ The innate nature to apply energy in times of war and peace. **The power to persevere when necessary but not generally.**

♆ ▽ A deep impressionability whose mark from times of struggle may make a return to normal conditions extremely difficult. **Hesitation in making commitments based on past experience.**

GATE 30: THE CLINGING FIRE - FEELINGS
– Freedom recognized as an illusion and limitation accepted as a fate –

Line 6 - Enforcement
The discipline to maintain right action.

♂ ▲ The assertiveness to purge the inferior while accepting to lead the weak. **The strength to eliminate negative feelings.**

☽ ▽ An inherent peacefulness that all too often will abide the presence of inferior forces. **A lack of strength in eliminating negative feelings.**

Line 5 - Irony
Recognition and dedication to transitory goals.

♃ ▲ The strength derived from knowledge and experience that two steps forward and one step back, is still one step forward. **Each new feeling brings back an old feeling before progress can take place.**

♆ ▽ The anger engendered by the irony, frustration with its limitations and a desire to eliminate the entire process. **Frustration and anger with the old feelings brought into the emotional awareness with each new experience.**

Line 4 - Burnout
An unrealistic pace that begs misfortune.

♆ ▲ A compulsive and hyperactive nature that carries all the earmarks of burnout but doesn't necessarily arrive at it. A positive outcome is often assisted through analysis. **Highly energized feelings that may lead to emotional collapse.**

♃ ▽ Uncontrollable expansion with the inevitable bursting of the bubble. **Uncontrollable feelings and accompanying emotional outbursts.**

Line 3 - Resignation
The acceptance of what is.

♆ ▲ The awareness and manifestation of the law of regeneration. The laws of Karma, reincarnation and resurrection. **The feeling to accept what is.**

♃ ▽ The tendency by its very knowledge to encourage or avoid despair. **The positive or negative feelings which come with acceptance of what is.**

Line 2 - Pragmatism
The balance between extremes.

☉ ▲ The productive application of energy without wastage. **Not wasting energy on feelings.**

♂ ▽ Over-aggressiveness that chafes against limitations. **Feelings which demand energy.**

Line 1 - Composure
Balance in the face of disorder.

☉ ▲ The maximization of limitation in all cases. **Stability through feelings, no matter what the situation.**

♃ ▽ The ability to maintain composure but at the expense of progress. **Balanced through feelings but unable to let go of them.**

Gate 31: Influence - Leading
– The law of friction, whether active or passive, that engenders transference and thus influence –

Line 6 - Application
☉ ▲ Actions which match the words and thus guarantees success. **Leadership whose expression and action must be one and the same.**

☽ ▽ A superficiality in application that borders on hypocrisy and is justifiably treated accordingly. **The hypocrisy according to leading in words but not action.**

Line 5 - Self-righteousness
Lack of external influence guaranteed by attitude.

♇ ▲ A natural specialization that only develops in isolation. However, when the development is complete, the extremely difficult and generally impossible task of externalizing the influence. **A specialization that demands that one leads oneself.**

☽ ▽ A deep focus on personal experience that is self-fulfilling and has no external ambitions. **A lack of ambition where one is content to lead oneself.**

Line 4 - Intent
The success of influence based on how it is perceived.

☽ ▲ Public acknowledgment of a nurturing and protective influence. **External positive recognition of one's capacity to lead.**

♂ ▽ Perceived ego aggrandizement and attempted manipulation. **External negative projection of one's capacity to lead.**

Line 3 - Selectivity
☉ ▲ The ability to carefully assess and choose the proper influence and to tailor one's behavior accordingly. **The capacity to lead enhanced through association with the proper influences.**

♃ ▽ Qualitative selectivity with the risk of a runaway enthusiasm that may lead to humiliation. **The drive to lead that will accept any follower and the risks.**

Line 2 - Arrogance
Independent action without guidance.

♃ ▲ The dedication to higher principles that cannot wait for consensus. **Leadership that cannot wait for consensus.**

☿ ▽ A reasoned arrogance that out of nervous tension jumps the gun and often misfires. **The drive for expression that cannot wait and may cost leadership.**

Line 1 - Manifestation
Influence cannot exist in a vacuum.

☉ ▲ The Sun does not/cannot hold back its light and thus its influence on every life. **The natural expression of leadership.**

⊕ ▽ The absorption of light, that in darkness can only promise manifestation. **The unnatural expression of leadership.**

GATE 32: DURATION - CONTINUITY
– The only thing which endures is change –

Line 6 - Tranquillity
The need to calmly face impermanence.

♇ ▲ An underlying acceptance of change that may or may not lead to tranquillity. The instinctive awareness to accept change and transformation.

♆ ▽ Impermanence as proof of meaninglessness with its attendant manifestations, depression, delusion, and in the extreme, self-destruction. The fear engendered when change is experienced as impermanence, and the potential for depression.

Line 5 - Flexibility
Easy adaption to circumstances.

☽ ▲ The Moon exalted, where superficiality is a valuable tool that while masking the inner light permits adaption to prevailing conditions. An instinct for adaption in times of change.

♂ ▽ The urge to express oneself in direct and often violent rejection of conformity. The potential of the instinct to reject adaption and conformity in times of change.

Line 4 - Right is might

♃ ▲ Even in times of change certain underlying principles endure. The instinct to maintain one's principles in times of change.

♄ ▽ Where Jupiter will establish right action in the larger social realm, Saturn's will lead to inner strength and endurance as long as it is not threatened from the outside. The instinct to maintain one's principles as long as one's security is not threatened.

Line 3 - Lack of continuity

☿ ▲ Indecision and persistent reevaluation, that only because of its basic intelligence manages to endure. Indecision in times of transformation.

♃ ▽ An overreliance on traditionally legitimized standards that in times of change can be totally out of step and suffer unexpected humiliation. A lack of instinct in times of transformation.

Line 2 - Restraint

♀ ▲ The control of power for the benefit and enhancement of harmony. The potential for transformation that may be beneficial to others.

♃ ▽ A tendency in frustration, particularly from a position of strength, to social withdrawal rather than persistent control. The frustration with controls or being controlled.

Line 1 - Conservation

☉ ▲ A life sustaining respect and attention to all aspects of a process. The potential to develop the instinct through detailed attention to a process.

♂ ▽ The uncontrollable urge to bypass essentials which inevitably leads to the disruption of continuity. The fear of lack of potential, and the corresponding lack of attention.

GATE 33: RETREAT - PRIVACY
– Active withdrawal and the transformation of a weak position into a strength –

Line 6 - Disassociation
The ability to let go.

☉ ▲ The will to concentrate on revitalization and not be handicapped by persistent recriminations. **The ability to let go in retreat, to enjoy privacy.**

♃ ▽ The ability to shed the larger framework that precipitated the retreat, leaving nagging doubts that hamper revitalization. **The inability to completely let go.**

Line 5 - Timing

♇ ▲ As important as the timing itself, is the ability to keep secret one's intentions until the appropriate moment. **The ability to keep one's intentions secret.**

♃ ▽ The tendency to want others to participate in the selection of the timing, which can lead to confusion. **Without a sense of timing, letting others in on the secret prematurely with resulting confusion.**

Line 4 - Dignity
A lack of turmoil in retreat.

♇ ▲ The underlying faith in resurrection that turns retreat into an opportunity for renewal and regeneration. **The healthy retreat for regeneration.**

♆ ▽ Without the guiding light of resurrection, the inevitable dissolution that leads to degeneration. **Forced to retreat, and unable to see its regenerative qualities.**

Line 3 - Spirit
The attitude that turns retreat into victory.

♃ ▲ The responsible and principled retreat based on preservation but with the determination to persevere. **Privacy as a path to success.**

♂ ▽ A lack of responsibility in retreat. The bridge burner. **A drive for privacy that will cut off its relationships, often abruptly.**

Line 2 - Surrender

♃ ▲ The recognition that surrender to superior forces can be an opportunity to expand one's own strengths and eventually triumph. **Embracing powerful forces in order to lay the foundation for future success.**

♆ ▽ Unlike the reasoned and calculated surrender above, the deeper and personal surrender. The feeling that one's original position was a delusion and the impressionability that makes might right. **A public embrace of powerful forces, and a private resentment of their power.**

Line 1 - Avoidance

☉ ▲ The wisdom in a weak position to recognize that survival demands complete withdrawal. **Retreating when one realizes that they are in a weak position.**

♂ ▽ Where courage is just plain foolishness. **Unable to retreat when overwhelmed by stimulation.**

GATE 34: THE POWER OF THE GREAT - POWER

– Power is only great when its display or use serves the common good –

Line 6 - Common sense
Knowing when enough is enough.

⊕ ▲ The good sense when having bitten off more than one can chew to spit part of it out. **The restriction of the release of power when one does not have the strength to maintain it.**

♃ ▽ Enthusiasm overriding better judgment, invariably leads to complications. **The lack of restrictions that can sap one's strength.**

Line 5 - Annihilation
The total elimination of resistance.

♂ ▲ The power to destroy completely and once this is accomplished, the ability to transfer the power to normal purposes. **The resistance to release power other than when necessary.**

☽ ▽ A difficulty in shedding the patterns established to deal with resistance. Symbolized by its phases, the feeling that nothing is permanently annihilated. **The discomfort with the need to always release power.**

Line 4 - Triumph
The freedom in absolute victory to unlimited use of power.

♆ ▲ A tendency in victory to restrain excessive power in favour of more subtle and covert styles. **The inherent confidence to use power subtly.**

♂ ▽ Ego gratification in the unrestrained use of power with impunity, inevitably leading to abuse. **A lack of confidence that can lead to abuse of power.**

Line 3 - Machismo
The indiscriminate display of power.

♄ ▲ The great malefic, where machismo unfortunately is invariably backed up by power. This is an exaltation only in that it is natural and not contrived. **The display of power that defines any role.**

☿ ▽ A reasoned and calculated display. The communication of disinformation. **The calculated display of power in order to define the role.**

Line 2 - Momentum

♂ ▲ The ability, when victory is in sight, not to loose perspective. **The power that grows when victory is in sight.**

♀ ▽ A tendency to be emotionally carried away by the smell of victory. **The power for growth limited by impatience.**

Line 1 - The bully
The indiscriminate use of power.

♄ ▲ The less negative, the resort to power as a manifestation of frustration. **The energy to display power as a response to frustration.**

♆ ▽ The comeuppance that is the inevitable destiny of the bully. **The ever present risk of retaliation to power displays.**

GATE 35: PROGRESS - CHANGE

– By design, progress cannot exist in a vacuum and is dependent on interaction –

Line 6 - Rectification
The energy to correct.

♄ ▲ The process of crystallization coupled with ambition that assures timely and effective correction. **Progressive change that results from correction.**

♂ ▽ A destructive tendency that in its personal application may be the necessary severity to ensure correction but when applied generally, it will meet with resistance and tend to reinforce rather than rectify situations. **Correction which brings change through severity and even destruction, and will always meet resistance.**

Line 5 - Altruism
The sacrifice of personal for communal progress.

☿ ▲ The principles of interaction and harmony communicated successfully for the benefit of the whole. **Progressive communication that can bring beneficial change to the whole.**

♃ ▽ Jupiter in detriment, though altruistic and cooperative in general, a personal regret that in interaction a greater personal expansion had been lost. **Progressive communication, but always the sense that personal progress has been sacrificed.**

Line 4 - Hunger
The insatiable appetite for progress.

☽ ▲ Less severe. Symbolized by the phases of the Moon, the drive may be obsessive when the Moon is full, but like the fading of the Moon the obsession abates. **Change for change's sake. The drive lessens with age.**

♂ ▽ The abuse of position to accumulate perks with the inevitable retribution from those unfairly deprived. **The drive for progress that will ultimately step on toes and lead to recrimination.**

Line 3 - Collaboration
The whole is greater than the sum of its parts.

♃ ▲ Benefic encouragement of others that expands personal as well as communal progress. **The ability to bring progressive change into other's lives.**

☉ ▽ The need to be the center that ignores the importance of others. **The need to be the center for progress.**

Line 2 - Creative block
Lack of inspiration which stops progress.

♀ ▲ Attunement with the vagaries of the muse and the recognition, creativity is energy that ebbs and flows. **Creativity and the muse will always come and go.**

☽ ▽ The need to take action, however mundane, to overcome the feeling of emptiness. The actions being uninspired do not further progress. **The need for change and the fear of stasis.**

Line 1 - Humility
The ability to accept rejection.

♀ ▲ The artist that accepts rejection as part of the process. **Acceptance of change and rejection as part of the process.**

♆ ▽ A self-destructive reaction to rejection. Loss of worth. **Change and rejection as humiliation.**

GATE 36: THE DARKENING OF THE LIGHT - CRISIS

– The rule of cycles in which decline is a natural but not enduring stage –

Line 6 - Justice

The inevitable survival of right.

♃ ▲ The knowledge and attendant faith that the powers of darkness eventually destroy themselves. 'Those whom the Gods wish to destroy, they first make mad.' **The correctness of crisis when it arises out of pure feelings.**

♄ ▽ A profound sorrow and cynicism, that is not diminished by the understanding, that darkness is self-annihilating. **The sorrow or cynicism that comes with seeing that despite the correctness of the feelings, there is always crisis.**

Line 5 - The underground

♇ ▲ Perfected survival regardless of conditions. **Immunity to crisis as both generator and survivor.**

☿ ▽ A nervousness that can lead to self-betrayal. **Self-betraying nervousness in times of crisis.**

Line 4 - Espionage

♇ ▲ The ability to prepare for and anticipate decline through the accumulation of secret or privileged information. **The realization that knowledge both covert and esoteric is necessary, if one is to be prepared for crisis and change.**

☽ ▽ The tendency in recognizing the strengths of the opposition to accept the inevitability of decline and rather than resist, to offer one's services to guarantee survival. The double agent. **Crisis knowledge that is available to others for a price.**

Line 3 - Transition

The point at which decline has exhausted its power.

♇ ▲ The ability to establish a new order out of the ashes of the old. **The emotional depth to endure crisis and embrace change.**

♃ ▽ The tendency in renewal to try to assimilate the remains of the old order into the new with the risk that it may rise against the new order once it has regained its strengths. **The embrace of the change, but with feelings that will not let go of the past.**

Line 2 - Support

Assistance to others in times of decline.

♆ ▲ The application of imagination to schemes which benefit others. **Feelings that can benefit others in times of crisis.**

☽ ▽ The more practical and individual assistance but only when unavoidable and not as a general principle. **Selective assistance in times of crisis.**

Line 1 - Resistance

♂ ▲ The energy and determination to persevere in the face of opposition. **The emotional power to handle crisis.**

♃ ▽ An over-principled resistance that rather than being selective in resistance and thus less at risk, will maintain normal patterns and incur opposition. **A resistance to change that will always bring crisis.**

GATE 37: THE FAMILY - FRIENDSHIP

– The Manifestation macro and micro-cosmically of the organic nature of communities –

Line 6 - Purpose
The energy to maintain the family is enhanced by recognizing its values.

♀ ▲ The gift of not only recognizing the inner meaning of the family but an appreciation for its values. **The possibility of extending friendships through the appreciation of its value.**

☿ ▽ A need for diversity that may ignore the achievements of the family in favour of withdrawal. **The need for diversity that despite appreciation will prefer casual friendships.**

Line 5 - Love
Natural and unaffected devotion to the family.

♀ ▲ Natural harmony and perfected sharing. **Natural harmony and sharing possible through friendship.**

♂ ▽ Emotional dependency that often turns love into hatred. **The possibility of dependency turning love into hate.**

Line 4 - Leadership by example
Any member of the family may take on a leading role through exemplary behavior.

☽ ▲ The manifestation of the highest principles in everyday and practical affairs. **The possibility of the highest principles in all relationships resulting in a leadership role.**

♄ ▽ A conservatism that generally only accepts the leadership of the father, who may or may not be a valued role model. **The possibility of being insensitive to the leadership of anyone other than those accepted by tradition.**

Line 3 - Evenhandedness
The success of any group is dependent on maintaining order.

♃ ▲ The ability to judge what behavior is appropriate and to react in a balanced manner to transgressions. **The possibility to have the sensitivity to know what behavior is appropriate in a relationship.**

♂ ▽ An ironic tendency to either test incessantly the borders of acceptability or to respond to the very same tendency in others with severity. **The possible lack of sensitivity to what behavior is appropriate.**

Line 2 - Responsibility

♃ ▲ The understanding of the principle of individual responsibility as the foundation for successful cooperation. **The possibility of friendship through individual responsibility.**

☿ ▽ A tendency to point out the responsibility of others. **The possibility that friendship will lead to pointing out the responsibilities of others.**

Line 1 - The mother/father
A position of inherent respect that ensures a focus for the development of guidelines.

♀ ▲ Harmony is the key to the successful maintenance of relationships. It is only through harmony that the beauty and the values of the family can endure. **Friendship that is rooted in sensitivity and ensures harmony. No polarity.**

▽ **No planet in detriment.**

GATE 38: OPPOSITION - THE FIGHTER
– The ability to preserve individual integrity through opposition to detrimental forces –

Line 6 - Misunderstanding
Opposition without basis.

♄ ▲ Eventual crystallization which clears up misunderstandings. **Energy which attracts misunderstanding, and the stubbornness to face opposition.**

⊕ ▽ The recognition that misunderstanding is at the root of opposition but the insistence, that it is the misunderstanding of the opposing forces. **Where misunderstanding is at the root of struggle, the energy of stubbornness to insist and maintain one's position.**

Line 5 - Alienation
A stage in opposition when one is totally isolated.

♄ ▲ The ambition and concentration to endure. **The energy to stubbornly fight alone.**

♇ ▽ Alienation experienced as painful confinement that by its very nature blinds one to the possibility that there are those at some point who may come to one's aid. **The energy for stubbornness is so strong that it is difficult to recognize, that there are others that can help in times of struggle.**

Line 4 - Investigation
Analysis which strengthens opposition.

♇ ▲ The detective who develops or the insider who accepts a joint opposition whose success can only be based on trust. **The energy to recognize who can be of value in times of struggle.**

♂ ▽ The aggressiveness in opposition that prejudices investigation and limits trustworthiness. **The power of adrenalin to provoke aggressiveness.**

Line 3 - Alliance

☉ ▲ The ability to sustain through integration with similar forces, thus ensuring the vitality to persevere. **The energy to integrate with others in times of struggle.**

⊕ ▽ Selfish alliance which saps the energy of one's partners, in order to ensure personal vitality. **The energy to selfishly use others in times of struggle.**

Line 2 - Politeness
Opposition that does not transgress normal codes of behavior.

♇ ▲ The value of discretion. **The energy for the intuitive awareness for discretion.**

☽ ▽ An over-politeness that is both servile and obviously superficial and defeats its very purpose. **The energy for over-politeness in times of struggle.**

Line 1 - Qualification
Tempering opposition based on the circumstances.

♇ ▲ A psychic attunement that guarantees proper action. **The psychic gift of knowing when and how to fight.**

♂ ▽ The tendency to oppose as a general rule. **The drive to fight as a general rule.**

GATE 39: OBSTRUCTION - PROVOCATION

– The value of obstruction in provoking analysis, assessment and re-evaluation –

Line 6 - The troubleshooter
The natural gift for solving problems.

☽ ▲ Practicality and the ability to guide and nurture others. **The energy to provoke others by attempting to solve their problems.**

♂ ▽ Ego dominance that generally abuses this gift for self-aggrandizement and personal ambition rather than for the benefit of others. **The emotional drive to dominate that provokes others.**

Line 5 - Single-mindedness
The rare ability not to overcome but to bypass obstacles.

♆ ▲ The imagination to establish new patterns that make the obstacles irrelevant. **The imaginative energy to provoke through bypassing obstacles.**

♂ ▽ Simple hardheadedness. Though less exalted, it can often result in success and gather support by its very determination. **The energy to provoke through hardheadedness.**

Line 4 - Temperance
Careful evaluation and assessment before taking action.

☽ ▲ The values of feelings and instincts in establishing the proper timing. **The energy to provoke at exactly the right time.**

☉ ▽ The faulty belief that willpower alone can overcome any obstacle regardless of circumstances. **The energy to provoke that ignores circumstances.**

Line 3 - Responsibility
The avoidance of confronting obstacles if failure puts others at risk.

♃ ▲ The great benefic whose first consideration is for the larger framework. **The energy to provoke through self-sacrifice.**

⊕ ▽ The often disastrous assumption that others are more at risk if an obstacle is not confronted. **The energy to provoke through the failure to make sacrifices.**

Line 2 - Confrontation

☽ ▲ The instinctual and direct assault of obstacles. **The energy to provoke through direct assault.**

♃ ▽ The principle of preservation that tempts one to go around an obstacle that should be tackled head-on. **An emotional discomfort when direct assault is essential.**

Line 1 - Disengagement

♂ ▲ The determination when confronted by obstacles to withdraw but only temporarily. **The energy to provoke by refusing to confront obstacles.**

☿ ▽ Disengagement, with an accompanying indecision as to when to reengage. The refusal to confront obstacles without the capacity to know when to engage. **The indecision is also a provocation.**

GATE 40: DELIVERANCE - ALONENESS
– The point of transition between struggle and liberation –

Line 6 - Decapitation
The necessary destruction of inferior forces in positions of power before liberation can take place.

☉ ▲ The authority, coupled with the magnanimity to remove from power only those which deserve such drastic treatment. **The power and authority of the ego to eject individuals in legitimate defense of the group.**

⊕ ▽ Exemplified by the terror of the French Revolution, where the idea of who was deserving of punishment was cruelly extended to an entire class. **The distortion of the ego through power and authority.**

Line 5 - Rigidity
The recognition that to achieve liberation all negative forces must be rejected.

♅ ▲ The revolutionary that demands absolute victory. **The power of the ego is maintained in the rejection of negative relationships.**

⊕ ▽ A tendency in revolution to accept a certain amount of necessary deviation on the assumption that it can be successfully purged later. **The weakness of the ego in its loneliness to maintain and not reject negative relationships.**

Line 4 - Organization

♅ ▲ The power to transform and the intuitive intellect to select and organize for the purpose of maintaining deliverance. **The power of the ego when organized and active, to maintain seperateness.**

♂ ▽ An uncontrollable zeal that ignores the quality of support in preference for the quantity which in the long run may destabilize deliverance. **The empowering of the ego through the capacity to organize others.**

Line 3 - Humility
A calculated mode in deliverance to avoid attracting the attention of negative forces.

♆ ▲ The subtlety to enjoy deliverance without having to flaunt it. **The capacity of the ego to avoid negative forces even if it means being alone.**

♂ ▽ The ego arrogance that demands attention and gets it. **The capacity of the ego to demand attention.**

Line 2 - Resoluteness

☉ ▲ The power and authority in deliverance to shed forever the qualities which hampered liberation. **The power through aloneness to recognize the importance and the potential disruptive effect of others.**

☽ ▽ A natural peacefulness that in deliverance may sympathize with and attempt to nurture the forces which hampered liberation. **The power of loneliness to blind the ego to the possible disruptive effect of others.**

Line 1 - Recuperation

☉ ▲ The ability to relax and enjoy the fruits of one's labours. **The ego strength to enjoy being alone.**

☽ ▽ The Moon cannot stand still. **The ego uncomfortable with being alone too long.**

GATE 41: DECREASE - CONTRACTION
– The limitation of resources which maximizes development of potential –

Line 6 - Contagion
The law that the maximization of potential not only ends decrease but inevitably such transcendence benefits others.

♄ ▲ The maximization of the potential of form. The father whose success will benefit his children. **The fuel for recognition through feelings.**

♆ ▽ The tendency in transcendence to keep it a secret in fear of being deprived of its special advantages. **The fuel for secret or repressed feelings.**

Line 5 - Authorization
The external recognition of one's potential despite limitations.

♂ ▲ The value of energy when properly channelled. **The fuel for properly channelled feelings despite limitations.**

♀ ▽ A persistent dissatisfaction with limitation which hampers development even when supported. **Limitations initiate the fuel for negative feelings.**

Line 4 - Correction
Successful adaptation to limitation.

⊕ ▲ Survival of the fittest and its eventual flourishing. **The energy for adaption and a deep feeling for survival.**

♀ ▽ The expenditure of energy on maintaining relationships rather than on correction. In times of decrease weak associations are shunned as costly, no matter how attractive. **The energy which fuels holding on to feelings rather than adapt.**

Line 3 - Efficiency
In times of decrease selfishness is justified.

♄ ▲ Material ambition and the discipline to go at it alone. **The energy that fuels the feeling for personal ambition.**

☽ ▽ Instinctive assistance, admirable but in this position misguided, where two will use up resources twice as fast as one. **The energy that fuels the feeling to share.**

Line 2 - Caution
Humanism tempered by pragmatism.

♄ ▲ A conservative nature that does not risk its own security in aiding others. **Energy for one's own feelings but not for others.**

♂ ▽ A desire for recognition that throws caution to the wind, depleting valuable resources for only temporary gain. **The energy for the display of feelings for recognition.**

Line 1 - Reasonableness
The appropriate delegation of responsibility.

Ψ ▲ The imagination to make the very best out of very little. **Coolness, where the energy to release feelings is selective.**

☿ ▽ A tendency in understanding, to assume capability, leading to strain. **The hothead, the urge to release feelings.**

GATE 42: INCREASE - GROWTH

– The expansion of the resources which maximizes the development of full potential –

Line 6 - Nurturing

☽ ▲ A natural and instinctive nurturing of others. **The power to share the process of growth with others.**

♄ ▽ A restrictive and malefic materialism that is self-alienating and encourages aggression. **The refusal to share the benefits of growth with others.**

Line 5 - Self-actualization

☉ ▲ The fulfillment and actualization of purpose as a natural path whose reward is a healthy sense of self, rather than the power and influence that naturally follow. **Growth that is self-fulfilling and naturally leads to influence.**

♀ ▽ Self-actualization as a strictly inner experience that may demand or result in a reclusive nature. **Inner growth that empowers reclusiveness.**

Line 4 - The middle man

☽ ▲ The quintessential manifestation of the mediator. **The maturity to bring growth through mediation.**

♀ ▽ Where the gift to establish and maintain relationships is ill-suited in this position to act in mediation where harmony must take a back seat to pragmatism. **A lack of maturity where the power to harmonize distorts mediation and limits growth.**

Line 3 - Trial and error

In times of increase, mistakes are a natural part of the process.

♂ ▲ The energy and assertion to turn mistakes into advantages. **The power to accept mistakes as part of growth.**

☽ ▽ A moodiness, that in error may succumb to brooding and unnecessary caution. **Mistakes give power to moodiness and caution.**

Line 2 - Identification

☉ ▲ Recognition and acute capitalization of trends. **Power for growth through participating in trends.**

♀ ▽ An ascetically motivated withdrawal in times of progressive change. **Growth which stops in reaction to trends or change.**

Line 1 - Diversification

☉ ▲ The ability when surplus resources are available to extend one's activities beyond their normal scope. **Growth through expansion particularly when defined to the root.**

♀ ▽ A tendency when surplus resources are available to centrifugal application. Decadence. **Too much expansion can lead to decadence.**

GATE 43: BREAKTHROUGH - INSIGHT

– In order for achievement to be maintained a new order must be fairly established –

Line 6 - Breakthrough

☉ ▲ Actualization and centering, that in breakthrough naturally establish both internally and externally a new order. **Unique knowing that is both personally and collectively of value.**

♂ ▽ An ego tendency that in breakthrough sees justification of its lesser attributes and carries them over into the new order. **Where the value of knowing is more important then other aspects of the life.**

Line 5 - Progression

☽ ▲ The step by step adaptation to relationships which hinder breakthrough through practical actions which will not jeopardize eventual success. **The gift of knowing when an unique insight can be shared with effectively with others.**

♀ ▽ A tendency to concentrate on harmonizing relationships that tends to strengthen the position of restrictive forces rather than benefiting breakthrough. **An over-reliance on the receptivity of others that turns harmony into the conditioner of individual expression.**

Line 4 - The one-track mind

☿ ▲ The overreliance and stubborn obsession with one's mental abilities in the face of recurring obstacles. This design, given Mercurial mental gifts, may though rarely succeed. **A stubborn reliance on one's unique insights that demands focused mental ability to be properly conceptualized.**

♃ ▽ A belief in inherent right action based on limited knowledge that shuns advice. **The vanity to attempt expression without depth.**

Line 3 - Expediency

♇ ▲ The powerful drive for regeneration that will, when breakthrough is threatened, use any means, align with any force and endure any condemnation to achieve the goal. **A certainty in knowing which can withstand condemnation.**

☽ ▽ An oversensitivity to condemnation, that may preclude justified expediency and result in failure. **Individual insight abandoned in the face of condemnation.**

Line 2 - Dedication

♆ ▲ The maintenance of specialized attitudes which promote breakthrough. **Unique mental habits and thought processes which promote insight.**

☽ ▽ A dedication to action, that when actualization is in sight may become incautious. **The urge for expression that will abandon its normal processes when an opportunity arises.**

Line 1 - Patience

♆ ▲ The recognition that new forms cannot be established until resistance has been eliminated. **The depth necessary to bring into form an individual insight.**

♀ ▽ An impatience to enjoy the sweets of accomplishment that inevitably leaves a sour taste in the mouth. **A delight in the insight but a lack of depth to establish it.**

GATE 44: COMING TO MEET - ALERTNESS
– The success of any interaction is based on the absence of any preconditions –

Line 6 - Aloofness
♇ ▲ A perfected renewal in which the establishment of a new form inures one to the condemnation of the rejected. **The awareness of patterns which ensures one's instinctive well-being.**

⊕ ▽ Intolerance and arrogance for lesser mortals. **The awareness of patterns which can bolster the ego at the expense of the well-being of others.**

Line 5 - Manipulation
♅ ▲ The ability to transform interaction with inferior elements into the energizing of progressive process with the additional benefit, that in tapping the inferior elements they remain weak. **Where the instinctive recognition of the patterns leads to the possible manipulation of others.**

♂ ▽ The tendency in this form of manipulation to become abusive and degenerate to their level. **The possibility that the instinctive recognition of the patterns could lead to the abuse of others.**

Line 4 - Honesty
The refusal to engage in hypocritical interaction.

♇ ▲ Indifference at its most logical and cutting. **The indifference possible when guided by the instinctive memory.**

☉ ▽ The Sun in detriment, that in extreme situations, in cases of self-sustainment, will expect assistance from forces it has totally rejected. Here the honesty is the genuine need. **The sacrifice of indifference for survival.**

Line 3 - Interference
The failure to interact based on circumstances.

♂ ▲ The ability to recognize the threat of interference and to prepare for its effects. **The alertness and instinct to handle the ego of others.**

♆ ▽ A deluded response to interference that gets stuck in projection and as a result is unrealistic in appraisal and error prone. **The possibility that the instinct cannot handle the ego of others.**

Line 2 - Management
♃ ▲ The development and management of a proper collective structure which restricts inferior elements by creating cooperative modes that integrates these forces with progressive and superior forces. **The possibility that alertness to patterns will result in management capability.**

♂ ▽ A tendency in management to concentrate exclusively on goals, ignoring inferior elements which leads inevitably to quantitative success and qualitative failure. **The instinctive memory for the patterns that bypasses the development of managerial capability.**

Line 1 - Conditions
The establishment of frameworks as the result of interaction.

♇ ▲ A mastery of the collective that can establish restrictive conditions for inferior components and with the ability to enforce them. **An alertness to patterns than can lead to mastery of the collective.**

♀ ▽ An attractive nature that will interact with inferior forces and will fail to apply restrictions resulting in a risk to continued harmony. **The failure of the instinct out of the need for harmony.**

GATE 45: GATHERING TOGETHER - THE GATHERER
– The natural and generally beneficial attraction of like forces –

Line 6 - Reconsideration
An outsider that can admit that its prior rejection was an error, will generally be accepted into the gathering.

♅ ▲ An innate empathy with the outsider mentality and its eccentric and often misunderstood logic. **A material direction which serves the outsider.**

♃ ▽ Where Uranus will innovate to find a place for an outsider, Jupiter will demand that it conforms. **A material direction that is focused on conditioning the outsider to conform.**

Line 5 - Leadership
All gathering together must have a center and a focus.

♅ ▲ The intuitive intellect and gift for innovation that enhance the group effort and ensure continuity through respect of the center. **The gift for expressing leadership on the material plane.**

♃ ▽ A sense of right action that assumes a respect that may not as yet have been earned. **The drive for leadership that may not have yet earned the right.**

Line 4 - Direction
♃ ▲ The ability to focus the opportunity of gathering together for the service of higher principles. **The expression of higher principles on the material plane.**

♂ ▽ The tendency to try to influence the direction of a group action for personal benefit. **The lack of expression of higher principles on the material plane.**

Line 3 - Exclusion
♆ ▲ The ability when excluded to take whatever measures are necessary to dissolve the antiquated form and to accept even humiliation to achieve inclusion. **The instinct to find a way to be included in a material process.**

♂ ▽ An aggressive and often violent reaction to exclusion. **The expression of frustration when not included in a material process.**

Line 2 - Consensus
Gathering together is strengthened by acknowledged common interest.

♅ ▲ The inventiveness to establish techniques by which common ground can be assessed. **A material direction through the expression of techniques for the benefit of others.**

♂ ▽ An innate rebellion against conformity. **The refusal to accept the material techniques of others.**

Line 1 - Canvassing
♃ ▲ The ability to promote and develop gathering together through the education of the uncommitted. **The material direction lies in education.**

♂ ▽ An overzealousness that turns canvassing into proselytization and tends to alienate rather than gather support. **The drive for material that leads to aggressive education.**

GATE 46: PUSHING UPWARD - THE DETERMINATION OF THE SELF
– Good fortune that may be perceived as the result of serendipity but derives from effort and dedication –

Line 6 - Integrity
♄ ▲ The wisdom to secure one's identity through careful consideration of the restrictive potential of commitments. **The determination to say no to restrictive commitments.**

♆ ▽ Deceiving oneself and others by overextending one's resources and eventually being in the position of having to break promises. **A drive for success that will not say no, and will end up breaking promises.**

Line 5 - Pacing
☽ ▲ The maintenance of proper rhythm that in its instinctive practicality avoids radical divergence from successful patterns. **The determination to stay with the rhythm which brings success.**

♆ ▽ An irrational rejection of the very patterns that have proven successful. **Determined to say no to the very rhythm that brings success.**

Line 4 - Impact
⊕ ▲ The ability, once recognized, to move rapidly from a position of obscurity to influence. **The good luck which comes from being determined that eventually, in the right place at the right time, leads to recognition.**

♇ ▽ A reaction in achievement that tends to bite off the hand that fed it. **The determination in success to ignore those who helped create it.**

Line 3 - Projection
☽ ▲ A practical approach to good fortune, that maintains the same patterns and attitudes that brought success and does not get sidetracked by indulging in further expectations. **The determination to stay with what brings success.**

♂ ▽ A tendency through projection to treat a potential future as the present, leading to unjustified egoism and the loss of momentum and support. **The determination to treat a projected success as a reality.**

Line 2 - The prima donna
☉ ▲ A difficult and demanding nature that succeeds despite its behaviour because of the depth of its talents. **The determination to succeed that may offend others.**

♂ ▽ Unrealistic demands and offensive nature of egocentric mediocrity. **The determination to be treated as a success before it has been realized.**

Line 1 - Being discovered
Dedication in obscurity that is unexpectedly discovered.
♆ ▲ Art for art's sake. Any creative endeavour that is self-fulfilling sooner or later is recognized. **The potential for creative success through dedication.**

♃ ▽ The ability to judge the potential of those in obscurity but often solely to benefit one's own success. **The determination to recognize and benefit from the success of others.**

GATE 47: OPPRESSION - REALIZATION
– A restrictive and adverse state as a result of internal weakness or external strength or both –

Line 6 - Futility
A difficult position for which there is no exaltation.

☉ ▲ No polarity.

☉ ▽ The Sun in detriment, where the strength of will alone may find a way to adapt and survive, but without hope of ever overcoming the oppression. **Life as an ordeal stripped of realization.**

Line 5 - The saint
This position has special significance and there is no planet in detriment.

♀ ▲ The gift in times of oppression to maintain without hypocrisy a harmonic relationship with one's oppressors, while providing aid and succor to the oppressed. Realization at its most exalted. **Acceptance of the weight of the abstract process and the grace that naturally follows. No polarity.**

▽ No planet in detriment.

Line 4 - Repression
The constraints of external oppression.

♄ ▲ The strength of identity that even in times of the most powerful oppression can maintain its resources and to some extent ensure their survival for the benefit of others. **A sense of identity that can be maintained despite external conditioning.**

☽ ▽ When robbed of its light, the Moon is lost in darkness; barely able to nourish itself, let alone others. **The identity overwhelmed by external conditioning.**

Line 3 - Self-oppression
♃ ▲ The conscious and well integrated being whose natural right action will eventually come to see the unfoundedness of its oppression. **The eventual realization that one is really o.k.**

♂ ▽ A self-oppression so highly energized that it may prove irreversible and destructive. **Extreme difficulty in realizing one's self-worth.**

Line 2 - Ambition
♄ ▲ The ambition and drive to overcome personal oppression in order to achieve security. **Realizing that to be busy is mentally healthy.**

☿ ▽ An indecisiveness in times of personal oppression, whether to apply intelligence to recovery or accept its weight to take advantage of other prevailing conditions that may only be temporary. **The inability to sense when and which activity is healthy.**

Line 1 - Taking stock
♄ ▲ The ability in times of hardship to concentrating on eradicating the negative factors that have led to oppression. **Realizing that negative thoughts have to be eradicated.**

♆ ▽ The delusion of seeing oppression as an exclusively external phenomenon with often disastrous results. **The sense that the world is against you.**

GATE 48: THE WELL - DEPTH

– The necessary and qualitative foundation that is a prerequisite to establish the common good –

Line 6 - Self-fulfillment

An undiminishable resource.

♀ ▲ The valued center, that as it gives, it receives and thus can continue to give. **A depth and potential talent that is of value to others.**

☽ ▽ A tendency to superficiality, that though generous and nurturing, will lack the inspirational quality that can transform its gift into a common currency. **Where the depth is limited the taste will be superficial and affect the quality of the possible talent.**

Line 5 - Action

♂ ▲ The natural urge to apply energy to action. **A taste for action.**

☽ ▽ An overreliance on the need for protection that in times of social renewal is obsessed with the details of planning at the expense of action. **Insecurity with one's depth that can fail to take action.**

Line 4 - Restructuring

☉ ▲ The good sense to take advantage of restriction on short term activity to assess the situation and restructure for long term goals that will facilitate development when activity resumes. **The awareness that depth and its possible expression will face restrictions with a resulting taste for short term projects.**

⊕ ▽ A resistance to restructuring on speculation, with the tendency when activity resumes to have to do so anyway. **A taste for long term projects that will be frustrated in restraint.**

Line 3 - Incommunicado

☽ ▲ Symbolized by the 'no Moon' phase, where the potential of light is unrecognized, unavailable and unknowable. The redeeming value is in the transience of such a stage which can give strength to those so afflicted. **Where the development of taste and depth is a long term process.**

☿ ▽ The profound anxiety when a profound intelligence is forgotten in the wilderness. **The tendency in a long term process (development of taste and depth) to anxiety.**

Line 2 - Degeneracy

♇ ▲ The awareness that to successfully establish a new form one cannot neglect the most positive attributes just to accommodate inferior elements. This would lead to deterioration. **A confidence in awareness to resist inferior influences.**

♀ ▽ The misguided urge for harmony that degenerates when associated with inferior values into decadence. **A lack of confidence in awareness that invites interference and decadence.**

Line 1 - Insignificance

☽ ▲ An instinctive recognition of what is practical and deserves attention. **A taste for recognizing what is practical and deserves attention.**

♂ ▽ An ego tendency to apply energy to trivial considerations. **A taste for trivia.**

GATE 49: REVOLUTION - PRINCIPLES

– Ideally the transformation of forms based on the highest principles and not simply for power –

Line 6 - Attraction

The power of revolution in action to expand its support.

♆ ▲ An innate impressionability that transforms the fence-sitter into the committed. **The sensitivity and potential to embrace and transform others.**

♄ ▽ Stubborn, and often fatal, rejectionism. **Oversensitivity that leads to rejection of principles and others as a rule.**

Line 5 - Organization

☽ ▲ Practical provisions for the needs of others in revolutionary times which ensures support and continued understanding. **A potential sensitivity to the practical needs of others.**

♂ ▽ A concentration on the organization of power to clearly define authority often at the expense of higher principles. **A rejection of higher principles in seeking to organize others.**

Line 4 - Platform

♃ ▲ A political and social agenda, embodied in guarantees to human rights that ensures a just and valued replacement of the old order. **A potential sensitivity to the needs of society.**

♂ ▽ Promises, promises, promises and only to guarantee support with little possibility of implementation. **A potential to insensitively take advantage of the needs of society.**

Line 3 - Popular discontent

♆ ▲ The ability to destroy antiquated forms once the restrictions have been removed. **The potential in sensitivity to reject failed principles or relationships.**

♇ ▽ Pluto in detriment, with general support, a savageness in eliminating the old order that may permanently scar the new. **An insensitivity in rejection and rejecting.**

Line 2 - The last resort

⊕ ▲ The determination to exhaust every possible peaceful avenue for change and then when satisfied that no other course is possible, to plan in detail before revolution is attempted. **The potential to explore every possibility before rejecting.**

♇ ▽ The overwhelming revolutionary urge that is impatient with accommodation and negotiation. **The tendency here is the coup d'etat that has little general support. Impatience with accomodation.**

Line 1 - The law of necessity

Revolution has no support unless it is perceived as necessary.

♃ ▲ The understanding and application of this law to maximize expansion of support and thereby ensure viability. **The awareness that the potential of a principle is based on it being accepted as viable.**

☉ ▽ The misuse of influence, to insist that necessity can be created out of action. The 'Helter Skelter' syndrome. To commit acts of disorder as proof that disorder exists. **Oversensitivity to rejection that can turn a principle into a crusade.**

GATE 50: THE CAULDRON - VALUES

– The value of historical continuity whose traditional values serve and enrich the present and future –

Line 6 - Leadership

♀ ▲ The gift in a position of power to maintain harmony even in severity. The strength to maintain one's values with vigor and continue to have harmonic relationships with others.

☽ ▽ An inherent moodiness, that in a position of power may at times alienate or offend and effect overall efficiency. The strength to maintain one's values but at the expense of harmonic relationships

Line 5 - Consistency

When continuity has brought success, it should not be tampered with.

♄ ▲ The disciplined and natural conservatism to avoid unnecessary change. The conservative awareness that basic principles should not be abandoned casually.

♂ ▽ A perverse reaction to rebel against the methodology of one's very success. When effectively stimulated, the drive to rebel against basic principles.

Line 4 - Corruption

The lack of enriching values.

♄ ▲ The malefic gift of turning inferior values into material success. Given this difficult position, Saturn's exaltation is, that its actions are limited to selfishness and unsavouriness rather than criminality. The capacity to maintain one's strength despite inferior values.

♂ ▽ With such energy and no traditional values, the worst can be expected. The potential disregard of values that may lead to corruption or the breakdown of the defense system.

Line 3 - Adaptability

☽ ▲ The Moon exalted, that when unable to make it alone will naturally align itself with nurturing and protective forces. The awareness that to maintain one's principles and values the support of others is necessary.

☿ ▽ A resentment when its natural mental gifts are ignored and is forced to curry favour in order to survive. Discomfort with the awareness that one cannot stand alone by one's principles.

Line 2 - Determination

☉ ▲ The strength of purpose that can enjoy overcoming adversity to achieve its goals. The strength derived from maintaining one's values in the face of opposition or conditioning.

♀ ▽ A discomfort with adversity that may lead to determined withdrawal. A lack of strength, where values are threatened by opposition or conditioning.

Line 1 - The immigrant

Humbleness of origin that benefits rather than restricts destiny.

♂ ▲ The desire to be effective and successful that builds on the most fundamental strengths while it refines its nature. The awareness that the growth and refinement of values will benefit destiny.

♀ ▽ A dissatisfaction with/or embarrassment with origins, that makes an obsession of refinement. A dissatisfaction with original values that demands refinement.

GATE 51: THE AROUSING - SHOCK
– The ability to respond to disorder and shock through recognition and adaptation –

Line 6 - Separation
☉ ▲ In times of crisis when all those around are confused and in disorder, the ability not to succumb to the panic but to have the will and vitality to survive it alone. **The power of the ego to meet challenges alone.**

♇ ▽ Curiously, the same gift, but one by its attitude that invites disapproval that in the extreme may even prevent a successful separation. **The egoism to meet the challenge alone that may provoke and empower the challengers.**

Line 5 - Symmetry
☉ ▲ Perfected illumination that in grasping the nature of the shock, can transform its normal patterns into a symmetrical adaptation that rides the shock and avoids its devastation. **The perfection of the warrior ego through instinctive adaptation.**

♂ ▽ A tendency in seeking the core, to harmonize with one shock only to be overwhelmed by the next. **The egoism to indulge in victory and lose vigilance.**

Line 4 - Limitation
♅ ▲ A pure inventiveness and sometimes genius to find some opportunity even in the midst of the most devastating shocks. **The warrior ego that will find some way to answer the challenge.**

☿ ▽ A reasoned make-do mentality that is ineffectual in times of severe shock. **The superficial ego that lacks the resources and depth to answer challenges.**

Line 3 - Adaptation
☉ ▲ The life-sustaining awareness that thinks on its feet and thus creates opportunities. **The power of spontaneity in times of challenge.**

♃ ▽ The destabilization that occurs when one's field of normal activity is radically and unpredictably disturbed, where the tendency is withdrawal rather than adaptation. **The ego that may be destabilized in times of challenge.**

Line 2 - Withdrawal
♂ ▲ The recognition of the mechanics of shock that indicates when withdrawal is the only logical action. **The instinctive withdrawal when the power of the ego is threatened.**

☿ ▽ Being too smart for one's own good and rejecting withdrawal in the vain belief that one can outsmart natural forces. **The egoism to reject withdrawal and face possible defeat.**

Line 1 - Reference
The advantage of previous crisis experience.

♇ ▲ The gift of re-examination that is the foundation of preparedness. **The power of the ego conditioned by experience.**

♀ ▽ A tendency to emotional withdrawal after a shock. **The weakness of the ego in times of challenge.**

GATE 52: KEEPING STILL (MOUNTAIN) - STILLNESS
– Temporary and self-imposed inaction for the benefit of assessment –

Line 6 - Peacefulness
♀ ▲ A harmonic and balanced attunement that is at ease regardless of the situation. **The lack of pressure in times of stillness.**

♆ ▽ Delusion as a substitute for genuine tranquillity. Given the positive nature of this position, the delusion may be just as effective as the 'real thing'. **Where the pacification of the energy is extreme, pressure real or imagined does not disturb the stillness.**

Line 5 - Explanation
In times of inaction, the often important ability, to explain one's position.

⊕ ▲ The often terse but exceedingly accurate statement. **Where inaction and focus can lead to detail.**

♇ ▽ A convolution whose enigmatic nature is normally misunderstood with unpredictable circumstances. **Where too much inaction can lead to a loss of focus, and not to detail.**

Line 4 - Self-discipline
♄ ▲ Perfected self-discipline and restraint that deals easily and wisely with impulsive temptations. **The energy for restraint which recognizes the value of stillness and focus.**

♃ ▽ Though responsive to the need of a principled control based on the understanding of conditions, there is a tendency due to its natural expansiveness, to doubt and restlessness. **Restless energy and doubt in the face of restraint.**

Line 3 - Controls
External enforcement of inaction.

♄ ▲ The ability by its very nature to understand restraint with the potential in acceptance, to use the period to redefine strategies. **The energy for acceptance in inaction.**

♀ ▽ A deep dissatisfaction with controls that disturb tranquillity, leads to emotional withdrawal and affects vision. **The pressure of restraint disturbs tranquillity.**

Line 2 - Concern
♀ ▲ The pause that is initiated to benefit others. **The pressure to restrain energy for the benefit of others.**

♂ ▽ A selfish and abrupt pause that may endanger others unnecessarily. **The pressure to selfishly restrain energy at the expense of others.**

Line 1 - Think before you speak
⊕ ▲ The pause that is so profound that it leads to silence. **The pacification of energy that leads to stillness.**

♂ ▽ Speaking first and living with the consequences afterwards. **Energy that cannot be stilled.**

GATE 53: DEVELOPMENT - BEGINNINGS
– Development as a structured progression that is both steadfast and enduring –

Line 6 - Phasing

☽ ▲ The successful utilization of the completion of a stage in development, that by its evident success and value can be used as an example to attract support for the next stage. **The energy to attract support for beginnings based on the success of the past.**

♀ ▽ A tendency in this position, to hide success, in the perverse fear that the success will either create excessive demands or supporters of the original process will end their support upon completion. **The pressure to hide beginnings in fear of losing past support.**

Line 5 - Assertion

♀ ▲ The underlying and often psychic recognition of the intrinsic values of development, that even in periods of isolation, has the assertiveness to maintain direction. Its very power garners continued support even from those who are basically opposed. **The pressure to recognize the value of development and the energy for beginnings regardless of circumstances.**

⊕ ▽ An over-assertiveness, that rather than applied to maintaining support in the face of opposition and isolation, may actually strengthen the opposing forces by its attitude. **Where the energy for beginnings attracts the very forces that can abort them.**

Line 4 - Assuredness

☽ ▲ The ability to maintain the strength of one's individuality in complex and often awkward situations, that ensure continued security and development. **The pressure to maintain one's individuality in confused beginnings.**

♀ ▽ The persistent difficulty with embarrassing or awkward situations where normal emotional reactions may prove detrimental. **Individual pressure for beginnings that creates awkward and sometimes embarrassing situations.**

Line 3 - Practicality

☽ ▲ In its most natural position, the concentration on avoiding conflict to ensure protection and continued development. **The pressure to eliminate conflict in order to develop.**

♂ ▽ The unconscious provoking of conflict that logically threatens security and development. **Energy which provokes conflict and threatens development.**

Line 2 - Momentum
Success breeds success.

☽ ▲ The protection of early success nurtures further achievement. **The pressure to start something new based on past success.**

♂ ▽ A tendency with early success to haste and imprudent action. **The pressure based on success to be impatient for something new.**

Line 1 - Accumulation

♀ ▲ The dissolution of old forms but not at the expense of valued components that will be retained and transformed. **The pressure to begin something new, not from scratch but based on the foundation of the old.**

♀ ▽ Development hampered by criticism and the tendency to withdraw rather than make use of these experiences. **The difficulty in starting something new because of the criticism that accompanied the old.**

GATE 54: THE MARRYING MAIDEN - DRIVE
– Interaction in its mundane social context but also one's mystical and cosmic relationships –

Line 6 - Selectivity
♄ ▲ The ingrained responsibility, in terms of maintaining security and personal identity that will naturally restrict its relationships to ones that are mutually beneficial. **The energy to restrict relationships that hinder ambition.**

♃ ▽ A generally benefic and expansive nature that assumes that it can instill, what is otherwise missing in its partners. A waste of energy. **The waste of energy in maintaining relationships which hinder ambition.**

Line 5 - Magnanimity
☉ ▲ The natural authority and actualizing spirit, that in a position of power, can have genuine and fruitful relationships with the less advantaged. (As long as they are in service and make no demands.) **The energy for actualizing that despite this power fuels fruitful relationships with others. No polarity.**

▽ **No detriment.**

Line 4 - Enlightenment/Endarkenment
Here, in this most mystical of positions, there is neither an exaltation nor a detriment, for in truth, they are the same.

▲ ▽ The Alpha and Omega. The end and the beginning. There is no description possible. Each planet will manifest this energy uniquely with absolutely no guarantee that its effects will even be perceived. However, the potential is always there. **The fuel for transformation at its purest level. No polarity. No specific planetary accent.**

Line 3 - Covert interaction
♆ ▲ The ability when stymied in formal relationships to use secret or purely informal channels, when it is the only resort. **The drive when blocked to use secret means to fuel ambition.**

♀ ▽ The insistence that formal channels, no matter how frustrating, can be overcome by the power of attraction. **The energy of ambition when blocked will fuel the power of attraction to overcome the obstacle.**

Line 2 - Discretion
♄ ▲ The wisdom once a relationship is formally recognized to restrain the temptation to take advantage of past informal interactions. **The energy of restraint fuels ambition.**

♂ ▽ Recognition, in the formal sense, seen as a licence to take advantage of informal knowledge. A lack of loyalty. **Ambition energy which can fuel disloyalty.**

Line 1 - Influence
♆ ▲ The ability to achieve influence through secret relationships, anywhere from the private adviser to the Satanist. **Ambition energized through secret relationships which fuel influence.**

♀ ▽ A socially misguided insistence on formal recognition of a relationship, that in terms of influence, will diminish its power. **Ambition which demands formal recognition limiting influence.**

GATE 55: ABUNDANCE - SPIRIT

– Abundance is strictly a question of spirit –

Line 6 - Selfishness

♄ ▲ Acquisition obsession that though alienating, is still indirectly beneficial materially to others. **The possibility of finding the spirit through materialism.**

☽ ▽ Where the material abundance exists, but no one gets to share its light. The 'no Moon' phase. **The possibility that materialism becomes obsessive with a 'mean' spirit that will not share.**

Line 5 - Growth

♅ ▲ The unusual ability in a position of power to accept advice and transform it innovatively. This gift in a position of power allows one to continue to lead rather than being perceived as being led. **The emotional strength and spirit derived from positions of power.**

☉ ▽ An integrative openness that in its broad acceptance of advice may be eventually eclipsed. **An emotional openness where the spirit is at risk from conditioning.**

Line 4 - Assimilation

♃ ▲ The establishment of a framework that balances principles with energy and leads inevitably to expansion and prosperity. **The possible spirit that comes when emotional awareness and energy are balanced and principled.**

♂ ▽ Boundless energy that knows no restraint. **Boundless energy that ignores awareness at the risk of the spirit.**

Line 3 - Innocence

Here, 'I was only following orders', is a genuine defence.

♄ ▲ When the form is correct and attempts at actualization have been disciplined and within guidelines, failure cannot be personally attributed. **The emotional possibility to recognize that despite one's best efforts, failure is possible and does not need to affect the spirit.**

♂ ▽ Mars in detriment, where a struggle against conformity or individual initiative can bring a superior to ruin while safely hiding behind his shield. **The energy to selfishly protect one's spirit at the expense of others.**

Line 2 - Distrust

Abundance hampered by slander or gossip.

♀ ▲ The gift of being able to penetrate to the center that may demonstrate effectively through its relating talents, that its trustfullness is genuine. **Emotional stability and the strength of the spirit is dependent on being trusted by others.**

⊕ ▽ The direct challenge to the slanderers who will always have the advantage of quoting the Bard: 'Methinks he doth protest too much.' Only continued example can overcome distrust. **The emotional drive to insist on trustworthiness that does not guarantee its acceptance by others or benefits the spirit.**

Line 1 - Co-operation

♃ ▲ The expansion of activity through cooperation with powerful forces through principled actions that guarantee continued support and engender prosperity. **The potential to find the spirit through co-operation with powerful forces.**

♀ ▽ The concentration on harmonic relationships with powerful forces that provide for continuity but not necessarily advancement. **The potential to harmonize with powerful forces but not necessarily for the benefit of the spirit.**

GATE 56: THE WANDERER - STIMULATION
– Stability through movement. The perpetuation of continuity through the linking of short term activity –

Line 6 - Caution
☉ ▲ The prudence, when linkage has been achieved, to honour its new commitments in order to secure its footing. **Honesty in expression. Living by one's word.**

♇ ▽ The profound unconscious wanderer, where external yearning for acceptance will unconsciously release the exact energy that creates rejection. A difficult role, where the self is unknown and not recognized with predictable results. **Wandering throughout the life from one expression to the next unable to find the stimulation that one could live by.**

Line 5 - Attracting attention
♅ ▲ Unusualness, innovation and sometimes genius as guarantees of eventually attracting attention and support. **Stimulation at its most innovative and unusual.**

♂ ▽ All too often the tendency to attract attention that is self-defeating in its effects. **The power of stimulation to provoke and disturb.**

Line 4 - Expediency
☽ ▲ The perfection of the superficial personality, that can mask, when essential, its true feelings to secure protection. **The gift for stimulation as a role and for protection.**

☿ ▽ Expedient behavior whose price is a constant stressful alertness and nervous anxiety in fear of losing what has been gained. **The role as reality. The fear of silence and of being uncovered.**

Line 3 - Alienation
Determined self-sufficiency.
☉ ▲ A will and egoism that often proves overbearing and guarantees continued isolation. Here, this is acceptable given the Sun's intrinsic vitality. **The drive to control and be the focus of expression.**

♀ ▽ The reversed aesthetic that offends others, ensures isolation, and eliminates support. **The drive to control the expression at the expense of stimulation.**

Line 2 - Linkage
♅ ▲ Isolated genius that will eventually find continuity through recognition and support. **A genius for stimulating expression that will take time to mature and will need others to recognize it.**

☽ ▽ A superficiality which collapses under recognition and is eventually forced to move on. **A gift for communicating but not enough depth.**

Line 1 - Quality
☽ ▲ The practical sense that even short term activities should be of value. **Expression of practical ideas that have value.**

♂ ▽ The ego drive to make an impression that will misuse energy in trivial pursuits. **The drive to stimulate that will express any idea, no matter how trivial.**

GATE 57: THE GENTLE - INTUITIVE CLARITY
– The extraordinary power of clarity –

Line 6 - Utilization
♅ ▲ The acceptance that clarity is a double-edged sword. There are situations where understanding cannot lead to rectification. Here, Uranus' innovative quality can generally make the best out of an otherwise difficult but rarely permanent situation. **Where there is no answer, only the possibilities of the intuition can make the best out of a difficult situation.**

♂ ▽ When clarity points to a problem one is unable because of circumstances to solve, a tendency to anger and frustration that provokes inevitably futile action. **The possibility that when the intuition cannot solve a problem, a tendency to frustration and anger.**

Line 5 - Progression
♇ ▲ The natural ability to establish new forms while maintaining the powers of reevaluation and reexamination. This provides the clarity to examine the data and assess the process. **The possible intuitive gift for evaluation.**

☽ ▽ The tendency to keep on keeping on, that can end up as a misguided missile. **When in action, the intuition may become overwhelmed and unable to assess and evaluate its progress.**

Line 4 - The director
♀ ▲ The mastery of relationships that through clarity can maximize productivity while the sensitivity to interrelationships will ensure harmony. **The possible intuitive clarity to master relationships.**

♂ ▽ A tendency given this position to be dictatorial rather than directorial. **With the gift of clarity to master relationships, the possibility of being intuitively dictatorial.**

Line 3 - Acuteness
☿ ▲ The perfected intelligence, where clarity eliminates doubt and ensures manifestation. **The possibility of perfected intuition. No polarity.**

▽ No planet in detriment.

Line 2 - Cleansing
The clarity to establish proper values and ideals must be accompanied by resolute determination to maintain them.

♀ ▲ Perfected cleansing through inner realization. **The possibility for proper values and ideals through intuition.**

☽ ▽ A superficial cleansing that tends to hide the dirt underneath the carpet. **The possibility that the depth of the intuition will be treated superficially.**

Line 1 - Confusion
♀ ▲ The gift of penetrating to the inner meaning that ensures timely action. **The possibility of the intuition penetrating to the inner meaning.**

☽ ▽ The Moon in detriment, where feelings are no substitute for clarity and can lead to indecision. **The possibility that confusion will overpower the intuition.**

GATE 58: THE JOYOUS - VITALITY

– Stimulation is the key to joy –

Line 6 - Carried away

☽ ▲ The tendency to practicality that while thoroughly enjoying external stimulation has the instinct to draw back when its independent integrity is threatened. **The energy to fuel independent integrity that will maintain its identity in times of stimulation.**

☿ ▽ When its basic intelligence is effectively stimulated, its natural desire for attunement will lead it to identify so strongly with the stimulation that it is at risk of losing its identity. **The energy which fuels loss of identity in times of stimulation.**

Line 5 - Defense

☽ ▲ The natural and practical instinct to protect oneself regardless of temptations. **The fuel for self-defense regardless of stimulations.**

☉ ▽ The assumption that the best defense is a good offense, that might allow strength of character to enjoy questionable stimulus without succumbing to it. **The energy for aliveness which forsakes self-defense and will embrace questionable stimulations.**

Line 4 - Focusing

♇ ▲ A natural specialization that when confronted with a multiplicity of stimulations will have no inner difficulty in focusing on the appropriate influence. **The energy to fuel recognition of which stimulation is of value.**

♆ ▽ An impressionability that becomes confused when confronted with a multiplicity of stimulations and in trying to accommodate all of it, becomes unstable. **Energy which becomes unstable when overstimulated.**

Line 3 - Electricity

♅ ▲ The individual whose electric vitality creates its own stimulation and is not dependent on others. **The energy to fuel independent stimulation.**

♂ ▽ The quality of fire is dependent on its fuel and subject to its influence, good or bad. **The energy for aliveness that is dependent on others for stimulation**

Line 2 - Perversion

▲ **No polarity. No exaltation.**

♅ ▽ A genius for perverse stimulation that afflicts oneself and others by promoting degeneracy and reducing joy to indulgence and decadence. **The energy which fuels the drive for perverse stimulation.**

Line 1 - Love of life

♀ ▲ The very stimulation of the world is the basis of an aesthetic appreciation of its beauty and wonder. Alone or shared with others this profound inner realization is the key for a joyous harmony with the process of being. **The energy which fuels the love of life.**

☽ ▽ The Moon has its phases, its moods, that will limit joy to an intermittent and cyclical experience. **A cyclical energy which intermittently fuels the love of life.**

Gate 59: Dispersion - Sexuality
– The ability to break down barriers to achieve union –

Line 6 - The one night stand
The tendency based on personality or circumstances to accept only temporary unions that may be otherwise impossible or dangerous to continue.

♀ ▲ The perfected relationship whether for a moment or an eternity. **The power for intimacy regardless of conditions.**

☿ ▽ The basic drive to move on, that seeks impermanency as a matter of course and not in response to circumstances. **The drive for sexual and intimate diversity.**

Line 5 - The femme fatale or Casanova

☉ ▲ The power to use love to break down any barrier. Given the Sun's 'lightness' there is no negative connotation inherent in this description. **The power of sexuality to attract others.**

♅ ▽ Uranus in detriment, where the negative potential of this power becomes evident. The Gigolo, the adventuress. **The power of sexuality expressed as sexual power.**

Line 4 - Brotherhood/sisterhood

♀ ▲ The dropping of barriers to union to establish a universal union. **The power derived from non-sexual intimacy.**

☿ ▽ An intellectual understanding that is rarely put into action. **Where the idea cannot restrain the sex drive.**

Line 3 - Openness

♄ ▲ Saturn exalted, where the search for identity and security can only be achieved through the dropping of barriers, in order to define oneself through union. **Where one is empowered through union and intimacy with others.**

♂ ▽ Where openness is transformed into promiscuity and its attendant problems. **Where the drive for empowerment, through union and intimacy, can lead to promiscuity.**

Line 2 - Shyness
Self-imposed barriers.

♅ ▲ A preferred and natural separateness that protects against the inevitable instability engendered by union. **The restriction of the sex drive to maintain separateness.**

♆ ▽ A calculated shyness, rooted in deep psychological barriers, that even in dynamic individuals will always restrict interaction. **Infertility, rooted psychologically or biologically, that conditions the drive for separateness.**

Line 1 - The preemptive strike

☉ ▲ The authority and vitality that in understanding purpose and direction can recognize and eliminate barriers before they become impregnable. **The power of fertility to impregnate.**

☿ ▽ In this position, the ability and intelligence to recognize, but a deep indecisiveness about how and when to act. **The potential of fertility limited by uncertainty.**

GATE 60: LIMITATION - ACCEPTANCE
– The acceptance of limitation is the first step in transcendence –

Line 6 - Rigidity

♅ ▲ The intuitive intellect to recognize when absolute rigidity is essential but with innovative applications to lessen its severity. **A fixed energy that is unusual in its capacity for restraint.**

☿ ▽ The dogmatic, principled and carefully reasoned understanding that is uncompromising in its severity and often coldly brutal in operation. **An uncompromising and severe acceptance of restraint. So uncompromising that the restraint may become unbearable and lead to chronic depression.**

Line 5 - Leadership

♆ ▲ The awareness that the destruction of the old limitations simply creates new ones. This results in behavioral patterns that demonstrate this understanding through actions and enhances leadership potential. **The energy to handle a lifelong process of dealing with limitations.**

♃ ▽ Where the natural desire for expansion, when limitations are essential, creates confusion from the top. **Expansive energy that cannot handle limitations.**

Line 4 - Resourcefulness

☿ ▲ The reasoned and intelligent maximization of potential within limitations. **The maximization of potential within limitation.**

♀ ▽ A tendency in times of limitation to seek the inner meaning of the restriction rather than using its gifts to find a harmonic application within the limitation. The former leads to withdrawal and the latter to transcendence. **The energy to know rather than accept limitation at the expense of possible mutation, leading to depression.**

Line 3 - Conservatism

♄ ▲ Enlightened self-interest, that naturally handles restrictions and limitations ensuring identity and security. **The energy to maintain identity and security despite limitations.**

♂ ▽ Ego gratifying self-interest that ignores limitations and suffers predictably. **Energy which ignores limitations and pays the price.**

Line 2 - Decisiveness

♄ ▲ The understanding of the nature of limitation, to accept its restraints when necessary and thus be able to take advantage of opportunities when they arise. **Energy which can adapt to restraint.**

⊕ ▽ An adaptation to restraint that becomes habitual and maintains the nature of the limitation even when it no longer exists. **The energy for adaptation that can get stuck without eventual mutation.**

Line 1 - Acceptance

♀ ▲ The ability to maintain inner harmony when confronted by external limitations. **Harmonic energy that can deal with external limitations.**

☿ ▽ The drive for diversity, that when limited can become restless and agitated. **Restless energy when confronted with external limitations.**

GATE 61: INNER TRUTH - MYSTERY

– The awareness of universal underlying principles –

Line 6 - Appeal

♇ ▲ The profound attunement to the collectivity that can lure the public to a truth. **Inspiration that can bring clarity to the collective.**

♂ ▽ A reliance on shop-worn cliches and slogans that may be new in their level of energy but inevitably fall on deaf ears. **The delusion that inspiration can bring clarity to the collective.**

Line 5 - Influence

♄ ▲ The enlightened Father figure whose recognized wisdom and powerful assertion can mold a generation by its influence. **The pressure to know that may result in influence and wisdom.**

♂ ▽ A tendency in power to want to enforce compliance to ensure lasting influence. **The pressure in knowing to resent challenges and demand acceptance.**

Line 4 - Research

♄ ▲ The capacity of concentration to explore the depths of inner truth and maximize its application to fundamental principles. **The pressure to know the fundamental principles.**

♃ ▽ Where the tendency to expansion and integration leads to involving others in the research and may end in a diversity of confusing applications. **The illusion that collaboration will enhance inspiration.**

Line 3 - Interdependence

It is exceedingly difficult for truth to stand alone.

☽ ▲ The ability to establish relationships for the actualization of truths, and through their nurturing and protective power to ensure a stable environment in which they can continue to grow. **The pressure to know enhanced through collaboration.**

♂ ▽ With an abundance of energy and in possession of a truth, the tendency to leave others behind or be crushed by their resistance. **Impatience with others and the forsaking of relationships.**

Line 2 - Natural brilliance

☽ ▲ The Moon exalted, and so gifted by this position a far-reaching, a nourishing influence, free of guile and powerfully attractive. **A gift for inspiration that is both attractive and beneficial to others.**

♂ ▽ That in early recognition of its influence becomes ego obsessed with maximizing its effects. **A delusion that any inspiration deserves recognition.**

Line 1 - Occult knowledge

♆ ▲ A natural psychic awareness that empowers principles of universalization. **The pressure to know the mysteries through esoterics.**

♀ ▽ Where a reliance on secret knowledge increasingly demands ascetic withdrawal and leads eventually to obscurity. **Where the pressure to know the mysteries can be so strong that one can be eventually incapable of handling exoteric realities.**

GATE 62: THE PREPONDERANCE OF THE SMALL - DETAILS
– Caution, patience and detail produce excellence out of limitation –

Line 6 - Self-discipline
♄ ▲ A penny saved is a penny earned. Detail as the path to material success. **The understanding that material success depends on the expression of detail.**

☿ ▽ The skills but not the discipline to succeed. **The gift for, but not the discipline, to do the necessary detail work to succeed.**

Line 5 - Metamorphosis
When excellence is achieved, action is necessary.

☽ ▲ The reaching out to others to share, symbolized by the Moon's phases as it moves from darkness to eventually sharing fully its light. **The understanding that only when the details are complete can action or expression be initiated.**

♆ ▽ A tendency in metamorphosis to seek acclaim through dramatic presentation. **When the details are organized, the need for attention demands expression.**

Line 4 - Asceticism
♀ ▲ The perfected ascetic withdrawal in the pursuit of harmony and simplicity, where outside dangers do not exist, and there is time to pursue inner meaning in detail. **Detail that can only be expressed after periods of isolation and reflection.**

♇ ▽ The urge to take action against established values that when restrained by circumstances, leads to withdrawal that waits for opportunity. **Where the detail is organized, isolation as a strategy waiting for the right opportunity for expression.**

Line 3 - Discovery
♅ ▲ A genius for the unusual. The ability to discover valuable information in detail work and to find innovative applications for this knowledge. **The unusual gift of finding and expressing valuable details.**

♀ ▽ A dissatisfaction with the monotony of detail work, where what is missed may be of great importance and value. **The expression of dissatisfaction and boredom in detail work.**

Line 2 - Restraint
♄ ▲ The innate restrictiveness and discipline to comply with and exalt restraint. **The discipline necessary for detail work.**

☿ ▽ The intellect stymied by severe restraints tends to anxiety and restlessness. **The expression of anxiety and restlessness when faced with detail work.**

Line 1 - Routine
♆ ▲ The ability to transcend the boredom of routine through a rich and daring fantasy life. **The ability to organize the detail through fantasy.**

♂ ▽ Rebellion and its enormous waste of energy. **The need for expression which ignores the details.**

GATE 63: AFTER COMPLETION - DOUBT
– In the spiral of life, all ends are beginnings –

Line 6 - Nostalgia
♃ ▲ The good sense to avoid turning the previous struggle into an obsession. **The logic of leaving old doubts behind.**

♆ ▽ Revolutionary nostalgia. **Illogic and the potential obsession with old suspicions and doubt.**

Line 5 - Affirmation
☉ ▲ The authority and sincerity of purpose to pursue the same values in the new beginning that had allowed it to transcend the old. **The understanding that doubts are necessary and of value.**

♂ ▽ A tendency in triumph to pay lip service to such values, and given such leadership, these values will be reduced to nothing more than empty rituals. **Doubting one's very process despite understanding.**

Line 4 - Memory
☿ ▲ The detailed accounting of the achievement process whose information base can prepare a new order for the future. **The pressure to explore the doubt in detail as a foundation for eventual formulizing.**

♂ ▽ A willingness to forget in the glow of victory, with a possible price to be paid later. **The pressure and risk to forget the details when the doubts have been answered.**

Line 3 - Continuance
♃ ▲ The dedication to the new beginning that insists on maintaining its achieved principles despite having to interact with those who have not attained such a state. **Doubts that one can maintain one's principles when interacting with others.**

♄ ▽ Success at any price. **The pressure to eliminate the doubt at any cost.**

Line 2 - Structuring
♃ ▲ The establishing of a large framework through which achievement can be expanded and shared; compensating others for their contributions while maintaining control of direction. **The pressure to share one's doubts with others while still maintaining control.**

♅ ▽ Instability in achievement that when in positions of authority leads to arrogance and the desire to keep others away from the center of power. **Doubts in achievement that can lead to suspicion of others.**

Line 1 - Composure
☉ ▲ The quality of personality where achievement is accepted with equanimity and where continued development is allowed to take its natural course. **Acceptance of achievement but doubt whether continued development will take place.**

♂ ▽ The tendency in achievement to immediately seek new goals at the risk of destabilizing what has already been accomplished. **The pressure in achievement to still doubt one's capacities and to immediately seek new goals.**

GATE 64: BEFORE COMPLETION - CONFUSION
– Transition, like birth, requires a determined strength for the passage through –

Line 6 - Victory
☿ ▲ The mental assuredness, that knew that victory was inevitable, thus making triumph sweet but not reason for excess. **The mental gift of enjoying the confusion and its diversity of data.**

♀ ▽ Like the story of the Trojan Horse, it can be dangerous to get carried away in celebration, least one looses vigilance and perspective. **With all the diversity of data, it is easy to lose perspective.**

Line 5 - Promise
♀ ▲ The values promised in any new order are demonstrated through harmonic interactions with others. This strengthens the justification for the struggle. **Confusion over which values and relationships can bring harmony.**

♃ ▽ A tendency in trying to justify the struggle by focusing exclusively on the failure of the old order that cannot demonstrate the quality of the new. **Focusing on the past confusions about values and relationships.**

Line 4 - Conviction
☽ ▲ Symbolized by its phases, the Moon is assured of transition convinced by its very process that it will triumph. **The assuredness that confusion is a process that results in realization.**

♂ ▽ Where force and energy alone cannot overcome doubt. **Where the confusion is so energized, assuredness brings no relief.**

Line 3 - Overextension
♄ ▲ The wisdom to recognize when one has not the necessary resources to complete transition. Such timely awareness may give it a chance to seek assistance. **The wisdom to accept confusion as a temporary state, that will be resolved in time or through others.**

☽ ▽ The risk of a superficially confident personality that when transition collapses, there is no one to turn to. **Overconfidence that the Fates will be kind on demand.**

Line 2 - Qualification
♀ ▲ An inner development which recognizes what qualities are essential for transcendence and the awareness that without them, action will fail. **Inner development that can end the confusion over what makes sense.**

☽ ▽ Constantly in action, it wastes the very qualities and resources that it will need. **Getting lost in the confusion and burdening the psyche.**

Line 1 - Conditions
♀ ▲ In penetrating to the center, the understanding that instills the necessary harmony to survive disorder. **Amongst the confusion, the difficulty in finding the point.**

♂ ▽ The powerful temptation when having transition in sight, to hasty action. **An urge to act when you think you have made sense of the confusion.**

"EVERY TIME I TEACH AT ANY LEVEL OF THIS KNOWLEDGE, I'M ALWAYS STRUCK BY THE SAME THING. WITHOUT STRATEGY AND AUTHORITY, THERE'S NOTHING IN THIS LIFE. THERE'S NOTHING BUT HOMOGENIZATION, CONFUSION, AND DISTORTION. AS LONG AS THE MIND IS INVOLVED THERE'S NO WAY OUT. THERE ISN'T. AS LONG AS THE MIND IS CONTROLLING YOUR LIFE THERE IS ABSOLUTELY NOTHING YOU CAN DO. YOU'RE LOST. YOU'RE JUST LOST. AND YOU END UP SUFFERING DEEPLY. IT'S SO SIMPLE.

THIS IS THE WHOLE THING. IT'S THE DECONDITIONING. IT'S THE DECONDITIONING AWAY FROM HOMOGENIZATION TO DIFFERENTIATION. IT'S ABOUT BEING ABLE TO ACCEPT A POSSIBILITY, AND IT'S ONLY A POSSIBILITY, IT'S NOT A PROBABILITY; A POSSIBILITY THAT ALONG THIS WAY THERE ARE THOSE WITH WHOM YOU CAN COMMUNE WITH IN AN EXTRAORDINARY WAY. IT'S WHAT WE'RE HERE FOR.

I SO ENJOYED BEING ABLE TEACH AT A VERY HIGH INTELLECTUAL LEVEL, TO BE ABLE TO DEAL WITH THINGS THAT ARE ESSENTIAL TRUTHS ABOUT THE NATURE OF BEING AND THE NATURE OF LIFE. IT'S A PRIVILEGE, IT'S A GREAT PRIVILEGE. AND THAT IT'S MORE THAN JUST CHIT CHAT, BECAUSE I AM A 5; IT IS PRACTICAL. BYE FOR NOW." – RA URU HU

SECTION ELEVEN
OTHER RESOURCES
GLOSSARY, KEYNOTES AND MORE

APPENDIX A

OFFICIAL HUMAN DESIGN ORGANIZATIONS

The Human Design Community is truly global. Ra Uru Hu was acutely aware that The Human Design System is a special and unique body of knowledge. He nurtured it for 25 years, carefully releasing aspects of it as he felt people were ready to receive it. He established a network of Organizations with the intention that they would continue his work, and carry the true message of Human Design into the future and the world. The licensed and authorized organizations you find here have the privilege of maintaining the purity and essence of this great body of work, and the legacy of Ra Uru Hu. Licensed professionals and organizations will display the official logo.

International Human Design School: ihdschool.com
Human Design Standards and Education

BG5 Business Institute: BG5businessinstitute.com
Career and Business application of Human Design

Jovian Archive: jovianarchive.com
The work of Ra Uru Hu

Human Design America:
www.humandesignamerica.com
Human Design China and Taiwan:
humandesign.wiibiz.com.tw
Human Design Brazil:
www.desenhohumanobrasil.com.br
Design Human France:
www.designhumainfrance.com
Human Design Services Germany:
humandesignservices.de
Human Design Hispania:
www.humandesignhispania.com

Human Design Italia:
www.humandesignitalia.it
Human Design Japan:
www.humanjp.com
Human Design Russia:
hdrussia.org
Human Design Republic:
humandesignrepublic.com
Human Design South Korea
ravekorea.kr
Human Design UK:
www.humandesign.info

APPENDIX B
RECOMMENDED NEXT STEPS

Step One – Have a Human Design Reading by a IHDS Certified Human Design Analyst to understand how to begin to live life according to your Strategy and Authority, and then begin to experiment with what you have learned.

Step Two – Ra Uru Hu, as the first person to take the journey of 'becoming himself' through The Human Design System, had a clear understanding of what it takes to fully embrace and live life according to your true self. He structured both experiential and educational programs to help guide us on this path. Step Two is the Living Your Design experiential workshop. Throughout the world, there are now hundreds of Living Your Design Guides and Teachers providing workshops to support you on your journey.

Step Three – Live what you have learned. That's all. It's simple – not easy, but simple. Live each moment of each day through the lens of all that you have learned so far and see what happens. There are free supportive study groups being offered in the Human Design community on a regular basis. Feel free to join one.

FOR THOSE WHO WANT MORE ...

Step Four – Human Design is fun and profound, and the Rave ABC and Rave Cartography courses were designed by Ra for the general public that wants a deeper understanding. These courses were originally taught by Ra, and are now taught by IHDS Certified Human Design Teachers all over the world, either in person or on-line. Contact your country's National Organization to find these courses.

FOR THOSE WHO RESPOND TO BECOMING
HUMAN DESIGN PROFESSIONALS ...

Step Five – Get involved in the IHDS Certified Human Design Professional Analyst training program. This is a four-level comprehensive training program that offers students the ability to fully synthesize the information in the BodyGraph in order to provide profound and life transforming Human Design readings to the public. This training includes Foundation, Partnership, Solar Return, Saturn Return, Uranus Opposition, Kiron Return, and Incarnation Cross Readings.

Step Six – Advanced studies include Family Practice, Child Development, BG5 Career and Business Consulting, Rave Psychology, Primary Health System, Holistic Analysis, DreamRave Analysis and Rave Cosmology. For further information on these topics please see the following pages for a brief description, and contact any of the official organizations listed on the previous page.

APPENDIX C

AREAS OF STUDY AND INTEREST AVAILABLE IN THE HUMAN DESIGN SYSTEM

CHART ANALYSIS

This fundamental and powerful initial reading is your entry point into discovering yourself. It is a true journey of self-empowerment. You will be offered insight into your Strategy, your Authority and the characteristics of your design. You will gain an understanding of why you are here, the potential of your unique contribution, how to express your true self and life purpose, and how to authentically live your design. Each of us has a unique way in which we are designed to transform. You will discover your road map to transcending your conditioning, and learn how to tap into your unique decision-making process. The Human Design System is an incredible tool for self-observation as you continue down your own path of self-discovery, and will help you to identify the challenges you will face along the way, and how best to work with them in your day to day life.

CYCLE ANALYSIS

There are several key juncture points that happen for all of us at specific times in our lives. These transition points usually arrive with major life decisions, and important lessons about the trajectory of your path. The more knowledge you have about yourself, the better equipped you will be to make these important decisions during sometimes challenging times. These cycles include the Saturn Return around age 28, the Uranus Opposition around age 40, the Kiron Return around age 49, and the annual Solar Return three months before your birthday every year. Cycle readings equip you with insights and signposts, a weather report so to speak, to make these transitions as smooth as possible, and keep you on track.

PARTNERSHIP ANALYSIS

We are all designed differently, and we all deserve to be honored and supported to be our unique selves. When a couple understands themselves from the vantage point of their individual designs as well as their combined design, there is the potential for a relationship based on authenticity, compassion, acceptance and respect. In a Partnership reading you will learn how to communicate one-on-one with your spouse, children, family members, colleagues and friends. The health and well-being of a relationship can be nurtured correctly when we understand the potential attractions and compromises that bring us and hold us together, and sometimes push us apart. The Human Design System illuminates the differences in your designs so that awareness can replace misunderstanding.

FAMILY PRACTICE

A Family reading is very beneficial to all members of the family unit, particularly the children. Through an exploration of the Penta (a group aura of 3 to 5 people), each member can see the dynamics of their family relationships, and how mechanically these dynamics are always present. When we understand how the Penta operates, we have the opportunity to create an environment, with no fault or blame, that accepts and supports the uniqueness of each family member, and the family itself.

CHILD DEVELOPMENT

The knowledge of The Human Design System is ultimately for children, and Child Development teaches the adult how to interact with children in very practical ways that nurture their development. This study includes: the dynamics of the conditioning of both children and parents; what is correct conditioning; the different types of interaction between the parent and child; what conditioned parental authority is; the proper nurturing of Generator, Manifestor, Projector and Reflector children; what the 'dysfunction' is; the profiling patterns; and aligning a child with its personality. This is essential information for the well-being and nurturing of children and their families.

BG5 AND OC16 CAREER AND BUSINESS CONSULTING

The Human Design System is a fascinating way to see into the mechanics of small to large business group dynamics. BG5 and OC16 focuses on the different energetic natures of human beings, and what role each is best suited for in terms of the business environment. It explores all aspects of a functional working team, and the ways single individuals can contribute their personal strengths to form an effective and efficient greater whole. This study includes detailed information on personal career profiles, as well as small business group and large corporate business dynamics. It pinpoints specific strengths and dysfunctions in a working team or group, as well as what is specifically needed in order to create optimal business performance that plays on the strengths and gifts of the individuals involved.

RAVE PSYCHOLOGY

Rave Psychology holds the key to employing your mind as an ally. When you discover how your unique cognition works, you are able to create a working partnership between mind and body. The mind has strategies to cope with the openness in your chart. These strategies attempt to manage the ever-changing energies that stream into, around and through you. These coping mechanisms attempt to keep the mind in a dominant position in your life, thus reinforcing the contradiction between body and mind. Recognition of the correct functioning of your own mind begins by seeing what is natural to you. Rave Psychology delves into the deepest levels of the way your mind digests the information it takes in from the world around you. Rave Psychology provides a complete understanding of the way the human mind works in its fundamental duality, the homogenized mind and the differentiated mind. Slowly but surely, this understanding permeates the being and leads to the awakening of passenger consciousness.

PRIMARY HEALTH SYSTEM (PHS)

What Rave Psychology is to the mind, the Primary Health System is to the body. PHS offers a revolutionary approach to well-being through the enhancement of the body's potential through correct food intake, and finding the correct living environment. PHS teaches us how we are best designed to take in and digest food for optimal brain function, as well as our overall health and longevity. The potential effects of following your unique health strategy may include improved digestion, heightened sensory awareness and brain function, and unique improvements to your lifestyle.

HOLISTIC ANALYSIS

Holistic Analysis is the integration of PHS (Primary Health System), Rave Psychology, Variable, Lunar and Planetary Resonance, and Base Orientation knowledge with traditional chart interpretation. Holistic Analysis is the full realization of the analytical potential of Human Design.

RAVE SOCIOLOGY

The greatest force opposing differentiation is conditioning. Rave Sociology is dedicated to exploring the mechanics of group interaction and its conditioning impact. This is the shadow and the window on the homogenized world. Understanding these mechanics is the counterpoint to living the potential of your unique purpose. It is an opportunity to see how you are designed to morph under the influence of the other, family, classroom, group or the crowd.

DREAMRAVE ANALYSIS

DreamRave Analysis helps us understand how we are vulnerable to conditioning while sleeping. When sleeping, the higher levels of our 9-centered consciousness simply disappear, and we return to an ancient 5-centered configuration. This information will change the way dreams have been interpreted historically; they are not what you would expect.

RAVE COSMOLOGY

Rave Cosmology covers the mysticism and science of The Human Design System. There are several layers including the Bhan Tugh, the mythology and the mechanics of the 'Biverse' as transmitted by the 'Voice'; The Mystical Way, Ra Uru Hu's journey into the framework of Human Spirituality that offers deep insights into humanity's relationship to God, and the genetic imperative that drives us all towards awakening; Dying, Death and Bardo, the most in-depth analysis yet of the mechanics of dying and death and an extraordinary journey into the mechanics of the 'Bardo'; 2027, which covers the changing of the cycle we are currently in, and the emergence of the 'trans-auric form', the conscious Penta; Brahma's Night and Beyond, a look at what awaits humanity in the future; Profile, Purpose and Function, a look at the 'patterns in being' and the 'complexity of purpose'; and The Nature of the Stars, which covers the workings of the Neutrino Ocean through an in-depth look at 11 stars.

Appendix D
Recommended Materials

There are many digital books available on the International Human Design School and Jovian Archive websites. The National Human Design Organizations are licensed to publish Human Design books, and other materials.

Living Your Design Student Manual
by Lynda Bunnell
Covers the basic concepts of Human Design and supports the Living Your Design workshop.

The Rave I'Ching
by Ra Uru Hu
An excellent reference tool that includes each gate, line, gate and hexagram name, channel name, harmonic gate, circuit name, astrological position and sign, hexagram image, line descriptions, life lesson for each line, and Incarnation Cross names.

Incarnation Crosses: The Global Incarnation Index
by Ra Uru Hu
Based on a transcript of Ra Uru Hu, this book covers Right Angle, Left Angle and Juxtaposition Incarnation Crosses organized by Quarter.

Profile and Type Reference Book
by Ra Uru Hu
An exploration of the 12 Profiles by Type, covering the Four Type Overviews, the Twelve Profiles, and the Forty-Eight Profile and Type Combinations.

Rave BodyGraph Circuitry
by Ra Uru Hu
Explore the circuits, channels and gates in more depth.

Channels By Type
Ra Uru Hu
An indepth set of ebooks, which can be purchased at ihdschool.com

The Rave I'Ching Line Companion
by Ra Uru Hu
The Line Companion 2-Book Set is a breakdown of the Gates and Lines in the I'Ching, with an explanation of each Line in great detail.

There are many digital books by Ra Uru Hu at ihdschool.com.

APPENDIX E

INDEX OF CHANNELS, GATES, AND THEIR KEYNOTES

GATE & KEYNOTE		HARMONIC GATE & KEYNOTE		CHANNEL & KEYNOTE	
1	Creative Self Expression	8	Holding Together Contribution	1 - 8	Inspiration The Creative Role Model
2	Receptive ~ The Direction of the Self	14	Possession in Great Measure ~ Power Skills	14 - 2	Beat Keeper of Keys
3	Difficulty at the Beginning ~ Ordering	60	Limitation Acceptance	60 - 3	Mutation ~ Energy which Fluctuates and Initiates, Pulse
4	Youthful Folly Formulization	63	After Completion Doubt	63 - 4	Logic ~ Mental Ease mixed with Doubt
5	Waiting Fixed Patterns	15	Modesty Extremes	5 - 15	Rhythm Being in the Flow
6	Conflict Friction	59	Dispersion Sexuality	59 - 6	Mating ~ Focused on Reproduction
7	The Army The Role of the Self	31	Influence Leading	7 - 31	The Alpha ~ Leadership, For good or bad
8	Holding Together Contribution	1	Creative Self Expression	1 - 8	Inspiration The Creative Role Model
9	Taming Power of the Small ~ Focus	52	Keeping Still (Mountain) Stillness	52 - 9	Concentration Determination
10	Treading The Behavior of the Self	20	Contemplation The Now	10 - 20	Awakening Commitment to Higher Principles
10	Treading The Behavior of the Self	34	The Power of the Great Power	34 - 10	Exploration Following one's Convictions
10	Treading The Behavior of the Self	57	The Gentle Intuitive Clarity	57 - 10	Perfected form Survival
11	Peace Ideas	56	Wanderer Stimulation	11 - 56	Curiosity A Searcher
12	Standstill Caution	22	Grace Openness	22 - 12	Openness A Social Being
13	Fellowship of Man The Listener	33	Retreat Privacy	13 - 33	Prodigal A Witness
14	Possession in Great Measure ~ Power Skills	2	Receptive The Direction of the Self	14 - 2	Beat Keeper of Keys
15	Modesty Extremes	5	Waiting Fixed Patterns	5 - 15	Rhythm Being in the Flow
16	Enthusiasm Skills	48	The Well Depth	48 - 16	Wavelength Talent

APPENDIX E
INDEX OF CHANNELS, GATES, AND THEIR KEYNOTES

GATE & KEYNOTE		HARMONIC GATE & KEYNOTE		CHANNEL & KEYNOTE	
17	Following Opinions	62	Preponderance of the Small Detail	17 - 62	Acceptance An Organizational Being
18	Work on what has been spoilt ~ Correction	58	Joyous Aliveness	58 - 18	Judgment Insatiability
19	Approach Wanting	49	Revolution Rejection	19 - 49	Synthesis Sensitivity
20	Contemplation The Now	10	Treading The Behavior of the Self	10 - 20	Awakening Commitment to Higher Principles
20	Contemplation The Now	34	The Power of the Great Power	34 - 20	Charisma ~ Where Awareness must become Deed
20	Contemplation The Now	57	The Gentle Intuitive Clarity	57 - 20	The Brainwave Penetrating Awareness
21	Biting through The Hunter/Huntress	45	Gathering Together The Gatherer	21 - 45	Money A Materialist
22	Grace Openness	12	Standstill Caution	22 - 12	Openness A Social Being
23	Splitting Apart Assimilation	43	Breakthrough Insight	43 - 23	Structuring Individuality
24	The Return Rationalization	61	Inner Truth Mystery	61 - 24	Awareness A Thinker
25	Innocence The Spirit of the Self	51	The Arousing Shock	51 - 25	Initiation Needing to be First
26	Taming Power of the Great ~ The Egoist	44	Coming To Meet Alertness	44 - 26	Surrender A Transmitter
27	Nourishment Caring	50	The Cauldron Values	27 - 50	Preservation Custodianship
28	Preponderance of the Great ~ The Game Player	38	Opposition The Fighter	38 - 28	Struggle Stubbornness
29	Abysmal Perseverance	46	Pushing Upward Determination of The Self	29 - 46	Discovery Succeeding where others Fail
30	Clinging Fire Feelings	41	Decrease Contraction	41 - 30	Recognition Focused Energy (Feelings)
31	Influence Leading	7	The Army The Role of the Self	7 - 31	The Alpha ~ Leadership, For good or bad
32	Duration Continuity	54	Marrying Maiden Ambition	54 - 32	Transformation Being Driven

APPENDIX E
INDEX OF CHANNELS, GATES, AND THEIR KEYNOTES

GATE & KEYNOTE		HARMONIC GATE & KEYNOTE		CHANNEL & KEYNOTE	
33	Retreat Privacy	13	Fellowship of Man The Listener	13 - 33	Prodigal A Witness
34	The Power of the Great Power	10	Treading The Behavior of the Self	34 - 10	Exploration Following one's Convictions
34	The Power of the Great Power	20	Contemplation The Now	34 - 20	Charisma ~ Where Awareness must become Deed
34	The Power of the Great Power	57	The Gentle Intuitive Clarity	57 - 34	Power An Archetype
35	Progress Change	36	Darkening of the Light Crisis	36 - 35	Transitoriness A "Jack of all Trades"
36	Darkening of the Light Crisis	35	Progress Change	36 - 35	Transitoriness A "Jack of all Trades"
37	The Family Friendship	40	Deliverance Aloneness	37 - 40	Community Being a Part seeking a Whole
38	Opposition The Fighter	28	Preponderance of the Great The Game Player	38 - 28	Struggle Stubbornness
39	Obstruction Provocation	55	Abundance Spirit	39 - 55	Emoting Moodiness
40	Deliverance Aloneness	37	The Family Friendship	37 - 40	Community Being a Part seeking a Whole
41	Decrease Contraction	30	Clinging Fire Feelings	41 - 30	Recognition Focused Energy (Feelings)
42	Increase Growth	53	Development Beginnings	53 - 42	Maturation Balanced Development, Cyclic
43	Breakthrough Insight	23	Splitting Apart Assimilation	43 - 23	Structuring Individuality
44	Coming To Meet Alertness	26	Taming Power of the Great The Egoist	44 - 26	Surrender A Transmitter
45	Gathering Together The Gatherer	21	Biting through The Hunter/Huntress	21 - 45	Money A Materialist
46	Pushing Upward Determination of The Self	29	Abysmal Perseverance	29 - 46	Discovery Succeeding where others Fail
47	Oppression Realization	64	Before Completion Confusion	64 - 47	Abstraction ~ Mental Activity mixed with Clarity
48	The Well Depth	16	Enthusiasm Skills	48 - 16	Wavelength Talent

APPENDIX E

INDEX OF CHANNELS, GATES, AND THEIR KEYNOTES

GATE & KEYNOTE		HARMONIC GATE & KEYNOTE		CHANNEL & KEYNOTE	
49	Revolution Rejection	19	Approach Wanting	19 - 49	Synthesis Sensitivity
50	The Cauldron Values	27	Nourishment Caring	27 - 50	Preservation Custodianship
51	The Arousing Shock	25	Innocence The Spirit of the Self	25 - 51	Initiation Needing to be First
52	Keeping Still (Mountain) Stillness	9	Taming Power of the Small Focus	52 - 9	Concentration Determination
53	Development Beginnings	42	Increase Growth	53 - 42	Maturation Balanced Development, Cyclic
54	Marrying Maiden Ambition	32	Duration Continuity	54 - 32	Transformation Being Driven
55	Abundance Spirit	39	Obstruction Provocation	39 - 55	Emoting Moodiness
56	Wanderer Stimulation	11	Peace Ideas	11 - 56	Curiosity A Searcher
57	The Gentle Intuitive Clarity	10	Treading The Behavior of the Self	57 - 10	Perfected Form Survival
57	The Gentle Intuitive Clarity	20	Contemplation The Now	57 - 20	The Brainwave Penetrating Awareness
57	The Gentle Intuitive Clarity	34	The Power of the Great Power	57 - 34	Power An Archetype
58	Joyous Aliveness	18	Work on what has been Spoilt ~ Correction	58 - 18	Judgment Insatiability
59	Dispersion Sexuality	6	Conflict Friction	59 - 6	Mating Focused on Reproduction
60	Limitation Acceptance	3	Difficulty at the Beginning Ordering	60 - 3	Mutation ~ Energy which Fluctuates & Initiates, Pulse
61	Inner Truth Mystery	24	The Return Rationalization	61 - 24	Awareness A Thinker
62	Preponderance of the Small ~ Detail	17	Following Opinions	17 - 62	Acceptance An Organizational Being
63	After Completion Doubt	4	Youthful Folly Formulization	63 - 4	Logic Mental Ease mixed with Doubt
64	Before Completion Confusion	47	Oppression Realization	64 - 47	Abstraction ~ Mental Activity mixed with Clarity

APPENDIX F

THE DESIGN OF FORMS

In traditional astrology, an astrological chart would be the same for a chicken or a human. The extraordinary potential of The Human Design System is that the design of Humans is only one aspect of the revealed knowledge which included specific Designs for all forms of life down to the single cell. The interconnectiveness of all forms is illustrated in the following designs.

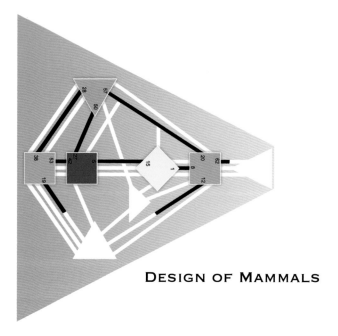

DESIGN OF MAMMALS

Mammals, like humans, are endowed with two Crystals of Consciousness and a Magnetic Monopole. All forms of Life, including humans, have a direct impact on each other and can be agents of conditioning. Throughout the world, mammals have a widespread influence on the day to day lives of humans. The aura of a house cat is as large as any human. It is clear from the potential of their Design that animals can condition our rhythm and direction. Having dogs in our lives is evidence of that, as they get us up in the morning so that they can pull us along on their leash.

Mammals can also bring beneficial health conditioning through their Splenic Centers. Human Design is not just about humans. If you are going to bring an animal into your life, it is a good idea to know their Design. Most breeders have a record of birth, and it would be wise to record individual birth times rather than one overall birth time for the litter. With accurate data, you can assure a healthy environment for the animal, and a quality companion for the human.

ADDITIONAL EXAMPLES
OF THE DESIGN OF FORMS

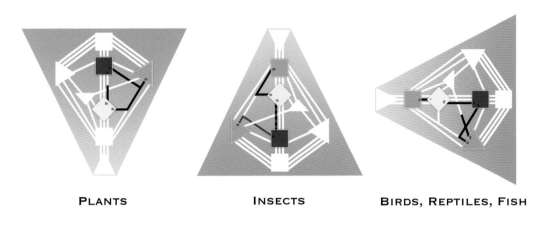

PLANTS　　　　　**INSECTS**　　　　**BIRDS, REPTILES, FISH**

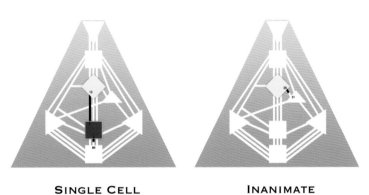

SINGLE CELL　　　　　**INANIMATE**

There is no Personality Crystal in either the single cell or the Inanimate, but they are both endowed with Design Crystals and Prime Magnetic Monopoles. The Inanimate without a complete channel, cannot be biological, yet everything participates in evolution. Everything is linked and interconnected in this grand movement.

This topic is extensive. If you are curious to know more, you will find information about the Design of Forms at www.jovianarchive.com and www.ihdschool.com.

"THE ENTIRE UNIVERSE ACCORDING TO THE "VOICE" IS AN UNBORN ENTITY. EVERYTHING IS PART OF THIS LIFE. IT IS US AND WE ARE IT." – RA URU HU

APPENDIX G

GLOSSARY OF HUMAN DESIGN TERMS

Abstract:

A quality associated with the channels and gates of the Abstract Circuit: experiences, feelings, emotions and reflections; making sense of the past for the benefit of the Collective. The opposite of the Logic process. (see Logic)

Activation:

Any gate that is colored in on the BodyGraph, whether part of a defined channel or not.

Ajna Center:

(see Centers)

Anger:

Not-self theme of Manifestor, or manifested channels. (see Manifestor) (see Channels by Type)

Astrology:

The ancient study of stars, planets, heavenly bodies and their influence on one's life or environment; precursor to the modern science of astronomy; an astrological calculation provides a snapshot of the planets' positions at the time of birth and places it within the synthesis, the Mandala.

Aura:

An invisible energy field that surrounds living creatures, extending about 6 feet in every direction. Its frequency, or how it communicates who we are to others, governs the way we impact or connect with others. (see Type)

Authority:

One of the tools for living and making decisions.

Inner (personal) Authority, is the source of inner guidance for making decisions as oneself; one's own personal GPS.

Outer Authority, the proper realm of the mind, liberated from decision making and able to use its gifts in service to others.

Awareness:

A point of transformation/awakening when one becomes an objective observer of one's life.

Awareness centers:

All human beings are endowed with three potential fields of awareness: Ajna – mind consciousness; Spleen – body consciousness; Solar Plexus – spirit consciousness. (see Centers)

Awareness frequency:

Each awareness center operates at a different frequency. Ajna – over all time; Spleen – in the now; Solar Plexus – in a wave over time.

Big Bang:

> In terms of The Human Design System, the Big Bang is Conception. The coming together of the original Yin (the Egg) and the great Yang (the Seed), which then initiated the expanding (Growing) Universe. In the language of the "Voice", the conception of the "child" which has yet to be born.

Biverse:

> A term used by Ra Uru Hu to represent the dualistic nature of the cosmos. (see Binary)

Binary:

> Any system that embraces polar opposites as an integral part of its understanding of the whole; Human Design is based on the juxtaposition of opposites, the 'this and that' of everything.

Bitterness:

> Not-self theme of Projector, or projected channels. (see Projector) (see Channels by Type)

BodyGraph or Rave BodyGraph ™:

> The matrix of circuits (channels and gates) and centers, sitting in the middle of the Rave Mandala, that captures the neutrino imprinting of both the Personality and Design Crystals, and defines one's unique differentiation for life; it was drawn for the first time by Ra Uru Hu on January 5, 1987 under the direction of the Voice. The main tool for Human Design analysis.

Bridging gate:

> Any gate activation that links a split in a person's chart, and defines an otherwise undefined channel. (see Definition types)

Cartography:

> The study or mapping of the flow of energy through the channels, gates and centers of the BodyGraph. (see Circuits/circuitry)

Centers:

> Energy hubs of the 9-centered BodyGraph that transform the energy as it circulates through the BodyGraph; associated with the body's endocrine system.

> **Ajna,** center of conceptualization; prepares and directs mental awareness towards the Throat.

> **G,** center of identity, love and direction; where we connect with our geometry through our Magnetic Monopole; the center of the higher self; how we connect to the totality.

> **Head,** center of inspiration; pressure to think and to question.

> **Heart/Ego,** center of the material world, will power, ego strength and self esteem.

> **Root,** center for maintaining momentum for living; adrenalized pressure to get things moving.

> **Sacral,** center of our creative life force energy that operates in response.

> **Spleen,** center of survival awareness connecting us to our animal instincts; existential state of physical awareness/safety/health in the moment; our immune responses.

> **Solar Plexus,** center of emotional intelligence, the emotional wave; currently undergoing mutation as an awareness center (spirit awareness) in preparation for the evolutionary shift coming in 2027.

Throat, center of metabolism, manifestation and communication; represents the most significant, and most recent, mutation of the 7-centered bioform (along with the Ajna); opened the way for the development of sophisticated verbal communication 85,000 years ago.

Chakras:

7 energy centers used for centuries in the East to relate the energy body to the physical body, the exoteric to the esoteric realms; in 1781 humans began evolving into our current 9-centered forms.

Channel:

A quantum created by the joining of two gates; pathways that carry or link and transform energy between the nine centers in the BodyGraph. (see Section Six) (see Appendix F)

Channels by type:

Generator channel, energy designed to respond.

Projector channel, energy designed to be recognized and invited.

Manifestor channel, energy designed to initiate and impact.

Reflector channel, no definition, designed to reflect.

Chart:

BodyGraph. The blueprint for your energy, how it functions within you and how it interacts with the energy of others. The main tool for Human Design analysis.

Choicelessness:

Allowing your life to unfold with awareness through correct auric interaction with others (Strategy) guided by the Inner (personal) Authority of your form; the result of choicelessness is that by observing what life brings to you, and not attempting to control or manipulate it, you wake up.

Circuits/circuitry:

Organizes and graphs the flow of energy throughout the BodyGraph; 6 circuits within 3 main circuit groups plus the core Integration Channel; circuitry represents how we connect to and work with each other. (See Section Six)

Circuit Groups:

The three Main Circuit Groups are:

Collective, keynote of sharing; reflecting on what has been, or anticipating what might move life safely forward, as a large group.

Individual, keynote of empowerment; inspired by intuitive knowing that arises in the now moment.

Tribal, keynote of support; ensuring continued replication of the species by making provision for survival; success/vitality on the material and spiritual planes.

Collective Circuit:

(see Circuit Groups)

Companionship:

Both partners have the same channel or gate defined in their BodyGraph. This is the potential for friendship, the shared experience.

Compromise:

One partner defines the whole channel and the other defines only a single gate in the channel. The partner that only has one gate of the channel activated is always compromised by the partner with the complete channel.

Composite:

The integration of two designs; the foundation for relationship is established where definition exists in the composite. There are four kinds of defining connections. (see Companionship, Compromise, Dominance, and Electro-Magnetic)

Conception:

The vast majority of the Crystals of Consciousness are not incarnated in living forms and never will. Grouped in "Bundles," they maintain a continuous planetary consciousness field. In each of these "bundles" there are specific Crystals, however, that are waiting to incarnate. When not incarnated, Design Crystals, with their magnetic monopoles embedded within them, cluster within the mantle of the Earth. Personality Crystals orbit within the Atmosphere. The initiation of the conception sequence takes place when the Magnetic Monopole and its Design Crystal are attracted from the "bundle" beneath the Earth's mantle by the Magnetic Monopole of the male. The attracted Design Crystal enters the male's Solar Plexus center and lodges in the 6th gate.

At the moment of orgasm, the Design Crystal, now within the single sperm and directed by the crystal's Magnetic Monopole, moves through the Channel of Mating and Reproduction (59-6) from the male Solar Plexus into the female Sacral center, and into the Egg. This is the moment of Conception, and the initiation of an incarnation cycle. As the Neutrino stream penetrates the mother, it also penetrates the cell and passes through the cell's Design Crystal, which then begins the work of building the body of the child.

Conditioning:

Pressure, expectations or influences from outside sources that are used by the mind to conform to patterns that are not part of who we are (not-self); adaptive strategies which become habits and take us away from or repress or conceal our true self and purpose for incarnating.

Conscious:

All of the Personality data, in black on the BodyGraph, that we experience, are aware of, and identify with.

Crystals of Consciousness:

Every living thing is endowed with two Crystals of Consciousness: the Design Crystal, an aspect of the original Yin, and the Personality Crystal, an aspect of the original Yang. There is no Personality Crystal in either the single cell or the inanimate. (see Design, Personality Crystals)

Cycles:

Key measurable transition points in life. The point itself is the midpoint in a 7-year cycle that represents a transition process that is traveled through, with Cycle Return Readings providing signposts for life's journey. In addition, we also go through a yearly cycle known as our Solar Return. (See Saturn Return, Uranus Opposition, Kiron Return,)

Solar Return – A weather forecast for what we will be experiencing in the year ahead in terms of our education, development and personal connections.

Saturn Return – Explores the mechanics and patterns revealed in the BodyGraph between the ages of 28 to 32 years, and gives us signposts to our evolving maturity.

Uranus opposition – Explores the mechanics and patterns revealed in the BodyGraph, showing the shift from the direction and environment of the first forty years of our lives, to the new direction and environment for the second half of our lives. This occurs between ages 38 to 40 years. (mid-life crisis)

Kiron Return – Explores the mechanics and patterns revealed in the BodyGraph for the final flowering of our purpose in life, starting between the ages of 48 to 52 years.

Definition/defined:

Channels that are colored in within your BodyGraph, and the two gates and centers at either end of the channel; definition represents what is consistently and reliably you. (see Undefined)

Definition Types:

Represent how energy flows, or is interrupted by gaps in circuitry, between defined areas in a BodyGraph; Types are: no definition, single, split, triple split, quadruple split. (see Section Five)

Design:

Neutrino imprinting pertaining to the bioform; a consciousness that lies below one's level of conscious awareness; recorded in red on a BodyGraph; distinguishes The Human Design System from all other systems. (see Vehicle)

Design calculation:

88 degrees of the sun prior to the natal (birth) or Personality calculation. (see 88 degrees of the Sun)

Design Crystal:

An aspect of the original Prime Yin that transforms the neutrino data into the body and the life. Sits in the Ajna Center. (see Vehicle)

Design Sun and Earth:

The Sun and Earth of the Design Calculation. They represent the direct inheritance from the Father (Sun) and the Mother (Earth).

Detriment ($\triangledown$):

One of two energetic influences that can be fixed by a planet, which is then emphasized within a line. (see Lines)

Disappointment:

Not-self theme of Reflector. (see Reflector)

Dissonance:

In Hexagram Theory, any line relationship that does not create harmony (i.e. 1/4) or resonance (i.e. 1/1) in relationship to another line, is considered in dissonance. There is a conflict or incongruity between the two lines (i.e. 2/3 or 1/6). (see Harmony and Resonance)

Dominance:

One partner defines the entire channel while the other does not activate (define) either of the channel's gates. The defined channel can only be accepted and surrendered to as a way to experience the energy of the other.

Dormant gate:

A gate (in an undefined center) that is alone in a channel, and open to receiving the harmonic gate via an electromagnetic connection through the aura of another, or a transit.

Driver:

Gate 2 is the seat of the Magnetic Monopole (the Driver), which knows the trajectory of the vehicle, where the form is going and how to get it there; the Driver is not to be influenced by the Passenger. (see Magnetic Monopole)

Duality:

The universe and everything it contains is dualistic in nature. Humans, through their genetic structure (DNA/RNA), are also designed as dualistic bio-systems. In physics, the universe began as a duality with its expansion through Quarks and Leptons. This is our up – down, in – out, right – wrong reality. In Human Design, the duality is reflected through the two sets of data (Personality and Design) which determine the uniqueness of an individual in the BodyGraph.

Ego/Heart Center:

(see Centers)

88 degrees of the Sun:

The Personality Crystal, or Soul, is called into the fetus at the moment that the basic structure of the brain's neocortex is complete and the vehicle is ready to begin its journey of self-consciousness in form. The time of entry is exactly 88 degrees (88 or 89 days) of the Sun's movement before birth. Pre-mature births do not alter this formula, but are an indication that the fetus' neocortex has developed more rapidly than usual. For most pregnancies, this event takes place at the end of the second trimester. During the final trimester, the Personality is able to adapt to its new vehicle. The time of birth shows us the potential of the Personality after its period of adaptation.

Electro-Magnetic:

Partners each define one gate (one half) of a channel, thereby defining the entire channel and creating life force energy; represents the basic dynamic of a relationship, attraction and repulsion.

Emotional wave:

The movement from hope to despair (pain), from high to low; originating in the Solar Plexus, the wave is experienced in three general ways: as need (Tribal); as uncertainty (Individual); and as desire (Collective/abstract).

Energy Type/Non-Energy Type:

Energy types are Generators, who have definition in the Sacral, and Manifestors, who have a defined channel between the Root, Ego, or Solar Plexus Centers and the Throat Center; non-energy Types are Projectors and Reflectors who lack such definition and consistent access to motor energy.

Ephemeris:

Astronomical calculations of the positions of the planets, the Sun and the Nodes of the Moon.

Exaltation (▲):

One of two energetic influences that can be fixed by a planet, and emphasized within a line. (see Lines)

Format energies:

Distinctive energies, fueled by the Root Center and guided by the Sacral's response, that exert a powerful influence on all other channels in the circuit, and on one's design as a whole; Format Channels run between the Root and Sacral Centers: 53-42 (Collective/Abstract), 60-3 (Individual) and 52-9 (Collective/Logical). There is no format channel for the Tribal Circuit.

Form/Form Principle:

Our physical forms; our 9-centered form was the focus of the Voice's revelation, and the basis of The Human Design System.

Fractal:

Every human being through their Personality Crystal is linked through a fractal line to other Personality Crystals. Fractal lines formed at the Big Bang when the prime Crystal of Consciousness shattered. Information moves down our individual fractal lines. There are 66 fractal lines, 66 archetypal ways in which information moves, and each have nuances that are fundamentally different from each other. These fractal lines are each associated with a star in our universe (including our sun) as stars produce neutrinos. Every single star is a data bank of consciousness, and through its neutrino stream establishes specific lines of moving information. Every human being is connected to one of these fractals, and to all of the others who share that fractal line. This creates a sense of familiarity between people the closer they are to each other on the fractal line.

Frustration:

Not-self theme of Generator, or generated channels. (see Generator) (see Channels by Type)

Gates:

The designation given hexagrams when moved from the outer wheel of the Mandala into the BodyGraph; in the BodyGraph they represent openings into the centers at both ends of a channel that filter the flow of energy between centers. (see Hexagram)

Generator:

One of the four Types; has a defined Sacral Center; here to work and provide life force energy; Generators comprise approximately 70 percent of the population; embracing and enveloping aura that operates in response. (see Manifesting Generator) (see Section Four)

Genetic continuity:

A qualitative inter-relatedness that exists in the BodyGraph between similar parts of the whole; for example, all 1st lines of the 64 hexagrams carry an introspective quality, or all gates in Individual Circuitry are potentially empowering.

Geometry:

Trajectory, or angle of incarnation, or path in life; the angle is determined by the 88 degree increments that separate the Personality and Design Sun calculations in a chart. (see Fractals, Profiles, Incarnation Cross)

Right Angle geometry: personal destiny, self absorbed in own process, less aware of others.

Juxtaposition geometry: fixed fate, a bridging geometry between Right and Left Angles.

Left Angle geometry: transpersonal karmic destiny; intersect with allies to fulfill their destiny.

Hanging gate:

A gate alone in a channel (either dormant in an undefined center, or active in a defined center), that is open to receiving the harmonic gate via an electromagnetic connection through a transit or the aura of another.

Harmonic gate:

Term used to describe the relationship between two gates that are opposite each other in a channel.

Harmony:

In Hexagram Theory, lines that occupy parallel positions in the lower and upper trigrams are in harmony with each other. They represent a common theme. These harmonies are the 1st and 4th lines (which represent a foundation line for their respective trigrams), the 2nd and 5th lines (which represent lines of projection) and the 3rd and 6th lines (which represent lines of mutation). (see Dissonance and Resonance)

Head Center:

(see Centers)

Health Centers:

The Spleen and Throat (see Centers)

Heart/Ego Center:

(see Centers)

Hexagram:

A construct of 6 stacked horizontal lines that are either solid (Yang) or broken (Yin); the basis for the classical I'Ching and the Rave I'Ching; the 64 hexagrams that form the foundation of the I'Ching correlate mathematically with the codon structure of our DNA, our genetic makeup. (see Gates)

Hexagram constellation:

A slice of the Mandala that includes the degrees of the Zodiac and the gates/lines/hexagrams of the I'Ching; Each constellation has an arc of 5°37'30".

Human Design System, The:

The Science of Differentiation, founded by Ra Uru Hu, that allows us to understand the depth of our uniqueness; based on the revelation of the Form Principle given by the Voice in 1987.

I'Ching:

A system of ancient Chinese wisdom that divines and interprets the changes we experience as we move through life; dating from 3-2,000 BCE. (see Rave I'Ching)

Incarnation Cross:

A composite of the Sun and Earth gates and lines in your Personality and Design data; tracks intersecting polarities as a "cross" within the Mandala; indicates one's life purpose and provides an index of the human evolutionary potential; there are 768 Incarnation Crosses (192 basic crosses with many variations); (see Section Nine)

Individual Circuit:

(see Circuit Groups)

Individuality:

A quality associated with the channels and gates of the Individual Circuit; the energy of mutation, melancholy, empowerment and uniqueness that ensures the ongoing survival of the Tribe.

Inform:

Strategy for Manifestors; brings peace to their manifesting. (see Section Four)

Inner (personal) Authority:

(see Authority)

Integration Channel:

A core component of the individuation process; group of four channels which serves as the key defense mechanism of the form; keynote of self-empowerment; channels 34-20, 57-10, 34-57, and 10-20. (see Section Six)

Invitation:

Strategy for Projectors; waiting for the invitation brings recognition. (see Section Four)

Juxtaposed/Juxtaposition:

Holding two polar opposites in quantum; for example, the Design and Personality held together by the Magnetic Monopole as 'you' in the BodyGraph, or two gates held together as a Channel.

Juxtaposition in Fixing (✦):

When both the exaltation and the detriment in a line definition are fixed and emphasized. (see Line) (see Section Ten)

Juxtaposition Cross:

Fixed destiny. (see Incarnation Cross) (see Sections Seven and Eight)

Kabbalah or Cabala:

Tree of Life, from Jewish mysticism; one of four parts of the synthesis given to Ra Uru Hu; represents the circuitry in the BodyGraph.

Keynotes/keynoting:

The dynamic language of Human Design that compresses a great deal of information into a single word or phrase; speaks directly to our cells.

Kiron Return:

Explores the mechanics and patterns revealed in the BodyGraph when Chiron returns to the exact moment it was at birth. Occurs between the ages of 48 to 52 years. (See Cycles)

Left Angle Cross:

Transpersonal destiny. (see Incarnation Cross) (see Section Eight)

Life Cycle:

Based on the orbit of the planet Uranus, which takes 84 years to go around the Sun. When Uranus has moved to a position exactly opposite its original birth position, this is the mid-life point or Uranus Opposition.

Line:

6 subdivisions of a gate correlating with the 6 lines of the Hexagram; 6 themes that represent and describe the gate's progression or development; the level below gate in Human Design analysis. Each hexagram has six lines. There are 64 hexagrams. There are 384 lines in the Rave I'Ching. 375 of these lines are dualities, whose polarity is expressed through the terms exaltation and detriment, denoting the polarity in the line. When not fixed, there is a flow of energy and influence between the exaltation and the detriment. (see Genetic Continuity)

Logic:

A quality associated with the channels and gates of the Logic Circuit: Patterns, formulas, validation and proof; looking forward, understanding and providing proven patterns for the future in order to safely lead the Collective. The opposite of the Abstract process. (see Abstract)

Lunar Cycle:

The Moon's 28-day orbit around the Earth; one cycle moves around all 64 gates of the Mandala; the Lunar Cycle is the Reflector's strategy for making decisions, and it's version of personal (Inner) Authority.

Lunar Nodes:

Each of the two points at which the moon's orbit cuts the ecliptic. The Lunar Nodes determine the geometry of our movement through space; in mystical language, our "destiny".

Mandala:

(see Rave Mandala)

Magnetic Monopole:

Our Prime Monopole, located in the G Center, that only attracts; it draws our life to us along a specific geometry determined by fractal lines connecting us to the totality. (see Driver) (see Fractal)

Manifesting Generator:

Generator with manifesting capabilities; Buddha Warrior who operates (makes decisions) through response but then moves into action quickly. (see Section Four)

Manifestor:

One of the four Types; no defined sacral; motor other than the sacral connected to the throat; Manifestors comprise 9 percent of the population; has the capacity to initiate or manifest, and is here to impact us; closed and repelling aura. (see Section Four)

Mechanics:

The operating criteria for our human form; Human Design reveals the mechanics of our experiences and existence.

Mind:

The thinking authority and inner awareness for the 7-centered form; with the advent of 9-centered beings in 1781, Authority was transferred to the Vehicle; much of our conditioning and the resistance we experience is our mind's inability to make or accept that shift.

Motors:

Energy centers that manifest as action when connected to the Throat Center; Root, Sacral, Solar Plexus and Heart (Ego) Centers.

Neutrino:

Sub-atomic particle produced as a by product of fusion in the center of stars; contains a tiny amount of mass; carries information through space.

Not-self:

The construct of the mind when it identifies with what is not you. (see Conditioning)

Not-self themes:

A signpost indicating that a decision was made through the mind, resulting in resistence.

anger, experienced by Manifestors when they neglect to inform before taking action.

bitterness, experienced by Projectors when they initiate and invite themselves.

disappointment, experienced by Reflectors when they initiate to make themselves noticed.

frustration, experienced by Generators when they initiate action.

Openness:

That which is white or undefined in a BodyGraph; the source of conditioning, education, nurturing and potential wisdom in a life.

Outer Authority:

(see Authority)

Passenger/passenger consciousness:

The healthy functional potential of the Personality Crystal; surrendered, self-reflected consciousness witnessing life from the back seat of the Vehicle.

Personality:

Recorded in black on your BodyGraph; the mind/psyche/light of the soul, that which is eternal; who you 'think you think you are.'

Personality calculation:

Moment of birth; based on your birth date, time and place.

Personality Crystal:

Aspect of the original Prime Yang that transforms the neutrino data into the potential of self-reflected consciousness; situated just above the Head center; manifests the conscious awareness of "who you think you think you are."

Planets/planetary transits:

Each celestial body and node has its realm of influence; their movements can be tracked around the Mandala, and add nuance to our definition by gate and line thematically:

⊕ **Earth,** grounding/balance
♃ **Jupiter,** law/protection
☊ **North Node,** direction/environment, future
♂ **Mars,** immaturity/mutation
☿ **Mercury,** communication
☽ **Moon,** drive, what drives you
♆ **Neptune,** illusion, what remains veiled to you
♇ **Pluto,** truth held in common by a generation
♄ **Saturn,** discipline
☋ **South Node,** direction/environment, past
☉ **Sun,** fullest expression of the Personality/purpose
♅ **Uranus,** unusualness/expansiveness
♀ **Venus,** values

Primary Health System (PHS):

Discipline within The Human Design System that studies the Form's cognition; a dietary regimen which best supports each person's complex and unique brain development.

Profile:

The costume you wear, or role you play, as you live out the purpose of your Incarnation Cross; derived from the lines of the Personality and Design Sun/Earth gates. (see Section Seven)

Program:

The neutrino stream that is the information base of our evolutionary program. (see Neutrino)

Projector:

One of the four Types, no defined sacral and no motor connected to the throat; Projectors are 22 percent of the population; when invited, based on recognition of specific skills and frequency, can act as a guide for Generators and Manifestors; aura is focused and penetrating. (see Section Four)

Quantum:

A whole that is greater than the sum of its parts; i.e. a channel, which is made up of two gates.

Rave:

The Voice's word for humans.

Rave BodyGraph™:

In the center of the Rave Mandala; captures the imprinting of the two Crystals of Consciousness that determine what differentiates one human from all others; a blueprint of uniqueness.

Rave Cartography:

The mapping of the surface mechanics of The Human Design System.

Rave Chart:

(see Chart)

Rave Cosmology:

The study of the cosmological background/foundations for the revelation of the Science of Differentiation and The Human Design System; information given Ra Uru Hu by the Voice in 1987 in order to understand the Form Principle and our place in the cosmos.

Rave I'Ching:

A description of the line values of each of the 64 Hexagrams. Completed by Ra Uru Hu on December 12, 1989 in Frankfurt Germany; based on the ancient Chinese Book of Changes; a fundamental tool in Human Design analysis. (see I'Ching)

Rave Mandala ™:

Mystical synthesis given to Ra Uru Hu by the Voice; trademark of The Human Design System. Its formula is comprised of four older systems: Astrology, which frames the BodyGraph's calculation; the I'Ching, which integrates our genetics into the BodyGraph through the Gates; the Hindu Chakra system, which correlates to the energy hubs of the Centers; and the Kabbalah and its Tree of Life that corresponds to the circuitry and channels that create life force definition in our designs.

Rave Psychology:

Discipline within The Human Design System that studies the intricacies of the mind, its potential as an Outer Authority, and the forces of conditioning that influence it.

Receivers:

Areas not defined in a chart (white); open to taking in energy from the environment; how we are conditioned by others. Single gates are also receivers. (see Senders) (see Dormant and Hanging Gates)

Reflector:

One of the four Types, no definition; connected to the Moon and the Lunar cycle; Reflectors are 1 percent of the population; have the capacity to sense who is living authentically, and who has been conditioned by the transit field; aura samples the environment. (see Section Four)

Resistance:

What one meets when one forgets to follow the Strategy of Type. (see Not-self themes)

Resonance:

In Hexagram Theory, whenever a line meets the same line value they have a common theme and resonate to each other. The resonances in lines are the 1/1, 2/2, 3/3, 4/4, 5/5 and 6/6. (see Dissonance and Harmony)

Response:

The way Generators aurically interact with life as it comes toward them; Generators are designed to live their life in response; their strategy is to wait for the response. (see Section Four)

Right Angle Cross:

Personal destiny. (see Incarnation Cross) (see Section Eight)

Root Center:

(see Centers)

Sacral Center:

(see Centers)

Science of Differentiation:

Human Design is the study of our uniqueness, our differentiation; a science which is verified through our own personal experimentation with its tools for living; it is not a belief system.

Senders:

What is defined in the BodyGraph (colored in); how we aurically communicate our definition, or who we consistently are, to others; how we condition others through their openness. (see Receivers)

Signatures:

The opposite of resistance; what one experiences with the fulfillment of Type and purpose:

surprise for Reflectors

peace for Manifestors

satisfaction for Generators

success for Projectors

Single Cell:

The Design of the single cell is the 15th gate in the G Center connected to the 5th gate in the Sacral Center. Its integrative potential is Gate 3 - Mutation.

Splenic Center (Spleen):

(see Centers)

Solar Plexus Center:

(see Centers)

Strategy:

A logical surrender to our Form, based on our individual Type, that allows our vehicle to surrender to the flow of life.

Strategy by Type:

Manifestors inform before they initiate action.

Generators wait to be asked so they can respond.

Projectors wait to be recognized and invited.

Reflectors wait through their Lunar Cycle before making a decision.

Tantric channels:

Channels 5-15, 14-2, 29-46 between the Sacral and G Centers; the fertile life forces of the Sacral empowering identity in a specific direction as an expression of the higher self through the G Center.

Throat Center:

(see centers)

Transit:

The movement or location of heavenly bodies at a particular time in space; movement around the Rave Mandala of the Sun, planets and nodes relative to conditioning in the BodyGraph.

Transpersonal:

Beyond the personal; in terms of the BodyGraph denotes the interaction with others that is needed to fulfill one's life purpose.

Trajectory:

Our geometry/movement through space; our path in life and the way we are designed to connect to others. Governed by the Magnetic Monopole, the Driver.

Tribal Circuit:

(see Circuit Groups)

Trigram:

A construct of 3 stacked horizontal lines that are either solid (Yang) or broken (Yin); two trigrams stacked on top of each other, an "upper" trigram and a "lower" trigram, form the basis for the 64 hexagrams of the I'Ching and the Rave I'Ching. (see Hexagram) (see Section Ten)

True Self:

The differentiated personal identity that expresses its uniqueness; aware and surrendered to the mechanics of one's Design, our true nature free from conditioning.

Type:

The world's population is divided by auras into four Types of human beings, each with a different strategy for how they best function without resistance: Manifestors, Generators, Projectors and Reflectors. (see Auras) (see individual Types) (see Section Four)

Unconscious:

All of the pre-natal Design data (88° of the Sun before birth) is experienced unconsciously; the Design data represents our genetic inheritance; traits that others experience in us and that we recognize over time; the red in the BodyGraph.

Undefined:

White areas on a chart also described as 'open', inconsistent, and flexible places; sources of both conditioning and wisdom; where we go to school to learn about life; our experience of the other. (see Defined).

Universe:

According to the "Voice", a living evolving duality. Not "born" yet, still a fetus within the womb. The Child. (see Voice) (see Intro and Section One)

Vehicle:

The Design side of the chart; our never-repeated bioform which carries the Personality passenger consciousness during our lifetime. (see Design/Design Crystal)

Voice, the:

The medium of the transmission which gave Ra Uru Hu the information in 1987 that lead to the creation of The Human Design System. (see Intro and Section One)

Yin/Yang:

Ancient Asian philosophy expressing the concept of the duality of human experience. "Yin yang" are complementary opposites that interact within a greater whole, as part of a dynamic system; polar opposites that are interconnected and interdependent, and give rise to each other. Everything has both yin and yang aspects. Yin is the passive female principle in the natural world, earth, receptive; Yang is the active male principle, sun, creative. Yang is symbolized by the solid line, Yin by the broken line.

"LOVE YOURSELF" – RA URU HU

I HOPE YOU HAVE ENJOYED THIS BOOK. IT HAS BEEN A LABOR OF LOVE AND IS AN ATTEMPT TO WRITE DOWN AND RECORD THE HUMAN DESIGN SYSTEM AS RA URU HU WANTED. IT WAS VERY DIFFICULT TO KNOW WHERE AND WHEN TO STOP. THERE IS SO MUCH MORE TO INCLUDE ABOUT THIS KNOWLEDGE. IN ORDER TO GET THIS OUT INTO THE WORLD WE HAVE TO START SOMEWHERE.

RA URU HU HAD A WONDERFUL AND UNIQUE WAY ABOUT HIM, AND MANY OF US WHO HAVE HAD THE GREAT GOOD FORTUNE TO HAVE KNOWN AND STUDIED WITH HIM LOVE TO QUOTE HIM. I HOPE THAT BY INCLUDING MANY OF HIS QUOTES IN THIS BOOK, YOU ALSO HAVE A SENSE OF WHO HE WAS. THIS IS MY ALL TIME FAVORITE, AND HAS SPECIAL MEANING FOR ME. – LYNDA BUNNELL